Encyclopedia of Race and Racism

Encyclopedia of Race and Racism

VOLUME 3

S–Z

primary sources, index

John Hartwell Moore

EDITOR IN CHIEF

MACMILLAN REFERENCE USA

A part of Gale, Cengage Learning

GALE
CENGAGE Learning™

Detroit • New York • San Francisco • New Haven, Conn • Waterville, Maine • London

GALE
CENGAGE Learning

Encyclopedia of Race and Racism
John Hartwell Moore, Editor in Chief

For more information, contact
Macmillan Reference USA
A part of Gale, Cengage Learning
27500 Drake Rd.
Farmington Hills, MI 48331-3535
Or you can visit our Internet site at
gale.cengage.com

LIBRARY OF CONGRESS CATALOGING-IN-PUBLICATION DATA

Encyclopedia of race and racism / John H. Moore, editor in chief.
p. cm.
Includes bibliographical references and index.
ISBN 978-0-02-866020-2 (set : alk. paper) — ISBN 978-0-02-866021-9 (vol 1 : alk. paper) — ISBN 978-0-02-866022-6 (vol 2 : alk. paper) — ISBN 978-0-02-866023-3 (vol 3 : alk. paper) — ISBN 978-0-02-866116-2 (ebook)
1. Racism—United States—Encyclopedias. 2. United States—Race relations—Encyclopedias. 3. United States—Ethnic relations—Encyclopedias. 4. Minorities—United States—Social conditions—Encyclopedias. 5. Race relations—Encyclopedias. 6. Racism—Encyclopedias. I. Moore, John H., 1939- II. Title.

E184.A1E584 2008
305.800973—dc22

2007024359

ISBN-13: 978-0-02-866020-2 (set);
ISBN-10: 0-02-866020-X (set);
0-02-866021-8 (vol. 1);
0-02-866022-6 (vol. 2);
0-02-866023-4 (vol. 3)

This title is also available as an e-book.
ISBN-13: 978-0-02-866116-2; ISBN-10: 0-02-866116-8
Contact your Gale representative for ordering information.

Printed in the United States of America
2 3 4 5 6 7 14 13 12 11 10 09 08

Editorial Board

Editorial and Production Staff

PROJECT EDITORS

Rachel Kain
Mark Mikula
Nicole Watkins

CONTRIBUTING EDITORS

Deirdre Blanchfield
Jason M. Everett
Dawn M. Sobraski
Andrew Specht

EDITORIAL TECHNICAL SUPPORT

Mark Drouillard
Mike Weaver

MANUSCRIPT EDITORS

Judith Clinebell
Jessica Hornik Evans
Peter Jaskowiak
Christine Kelley
John Krol
Michael J. O'Neal
Dave Salamie

PROOFREADERS

Stacey Chamberlin
Pamela S. Dear
Melodie Monahan
Kathy Wilson

INDEXER

Laurie Andriot

PRODUCT DESIGN

Pamela A. E. Galbreath

IMAGING

Leitha Etheridge-Sims
Lezlie Light

GRAPHIC ART

Pre-PressPMG

RIGHTS ACQUISITION MANAGEMENT

Sue Rudolph

Mardell Glinski-Schultz

Tracie Richardson

COMPOSITION

Evi Abou-El-Seoud

MANUFACTURING

Wendy Blurton

DIRECTOR, NEW PRODUCT DEVELOPMENT

Hélène Potter

PUBLISHER

Jay Flynn

Contents

S

SAINT MARTIN DE PORRES

SEE *Porres, Martin de, St.*

SANTA BARBARA PLAN

SEE *El Plan de Santa Barbara.*

SCIENTIFIC RACISM, HISTORY OF

Scientific racism is the act of justifying inequalities between natural groups of people by recourse to science. It is the result of a conjunction of two cultural values or ideologies: (1) that natural categories of the human species exist and are of different overall worth; and (2) that science provides a source of authoritative knowledge. These ideas arose separately, but at about the same time in the late seventeenth century.

The rise of science in the seventeenth century challenged the authority of other forms of knowledge—such as revelation and meditation. In particular, two new forms of knowledge came to assume privileged positions: mathematical generalization (most famously embodied in the work of Sir Isaac Newton [1642–1727]), and empirical demonstration or experiment (in the works of early scientists such as Galileo, William Harvey, and Robert Hooke). Along with newly emerging standards of truth and validity came public authority, and with this public authority came the usurpation of that authority in the gray zone of "pseudoscience," usually only distinguishable as such in retrospect.

The term *pseudoscience* refers to any work that appeals to the authority of science despite being methodologically flawed or incompetently reasoned, even if carried out by credentialed scientists. Such misrepresentations are usually caused by a conflict of interest, whether it be personal ambition, class or financial interests, or ideological commitment.

Racism, the attribution of inferiority to large natural groups of people, is a relatively recent idea. To the extent that ancient peoples held various groups in different degrees of regard, this was predicated on nonracial features—such as the ability to speak Greek, dignified behavior, or valor—and to the extent that they recognized differences of physical appearance, these carried no codes of social rank (Isaac 2004; Snowden 1948) and each was considered to be a local variation, not a continental quintessence. The concept of race was a product of the rise of scientific biological taxonomy, which is the formal clustering of animals analytically into groups, along with a parallel dissolution of large groups of animals into their constituent smaller groups. Scientific racism, then, being predicated on newly emerging concepts of science and of race, must be regarded as a Euro-American product of the last three centuries. This obviously does not mean that group hatreds have not existed elsewhere and at other times, but only that they have usually not been based upon a theory of race and were not considered to be validated by science; they thus fall outside the scope of scientific racism.

Subspecies of Homo sapiens, rearranged from Linnaeus

	American	European	Asian	African
Color	Red	White	Yellow	Black
Temperament	Irascible, impassive	Hearty, muscular	Melancholy, stern	Sluggish, lazy
Face	Thick, straight, black hair; broad nose; harsh appearance; chin beardless	Long blond hair, blue eyes	Black hair, dark eyes	Black kinky hair, silky skin, short nose, thick lips, females with genital flap, elongated breasts
Personality	Stubborn, happy, free	Sensitive, very smart, creative	Strict, contemptuous, greedy	Sly, slow, careless
Covered by	Fine red lines	Tight clothing	Loose garments	Grease
Ruled by	Custom	Law	Opinion	Caprice

SOURCE: Reprinted from systema *Naturae*, 10th ed., 1758.

Table 1.

Early taxonomic practice relied on an intellectual framework that was largely intact since the time of the ancient Greeks. Real, existing creatures, human or otherwise, were considered to be deviants or degenerates from an ideal form, whose true nature was perfect, transcendent, and otherworldly. As applied to people, this involved specifying features that were not necessarily accurate descriptors, but rather represented the underlying form or essence of which real people were simply imperfect embodiments. Thus, the Swedish botanist-physician Carl (Carolus) Linnaeus (1707–1778) could formally define the European subspecies as having long, flowing blond hair and blue eyes, regardless of the fact that most of them did not actually possess these characteristics. His purpose was to describe the idealized form that underlay the observable variation. Likewise, his descriptions of Africans as lazy or Asians as greedy was intended to be a statement of their basic natures, not necessarily an empirically based generalization.

Clearly Linnaeus was inscribing popular or folk prejudices upon the continental groups he was formally defining. To some extent he recognized this, as he grouped the Lapps, or Saami, (Scandinavian reindeer-herders) within the European subspecies; he consciously strove to romanticize the Saami, even as they were commonly "othered" in both popular and scholarly minds. Human taxonomy thus served to formalize social ideologies about sameness and difference.

By the end of the eighteenth century, German zoologist and anthropologist Johann Friedrich Blumenbach had jettisoned the personality and cultural traits used by Linnaeus in favor of only physical traits. However, he also modified the Linnaean system by ranking, rather than simply listing, the races (Gould 1998). Moreover, scholars at this time began to apply the previously informal term "race" (which had been used by the French naturalist Count de Buffon to refer to a local strain of people) to the formal Linnaean subspecies. The result was a parallel usage of the term, in which groups of people, diversely constituted, could be called "races," and their essences could be defined in accordance with whatever they were taken to be. Concurrently, the natures of large continental "races" could stand as formal taxonomic entities. Thus, races could exist within races, or they could crosscut other races. Because the attributes of the Irish, Italians, or Jews were Platonic essences taken to be inscribed in the very cores of the people in question—by virtue of simply being born into the group—it did not much matter what an individual representative looked like or acted like. These were not so much group-level generalizations, which have always existed as folk taxonomies, but group-level scientific definitions, which were something new.

THE ORIGINS OF RACES

A French scholar named Isaac de la Peyrère published a controversial hypothesis in 1655. He suggested that certain biblical passages were consistent with multiple divine creations of people, of which the story related in Genesis was only one. These "Pre-Adamites" were the progenitors of the most divergent forms of people, who might thereby be considered to be different in both nature and origin, as they were the product of different creative acts by God. La Peyrère was subsequently invoked as the founder of a school called *polygenism,* which gained popularity in the nineteenth century as American scholars increasingly sought to justify the practice of slavery by recourse to science (although that had not been La Peyrère's intent).

As the slavery debate crystallized in America and Europe, the scientific issues centered on whether races had a single origin (monogenism) or separate origins (polygenism). Monogenists tended to invoke a literal reading of the Book of Genesis in support of abolitionist politics, which also necessitated the development of explanations for the emergence of human physical diversity since the time of Adam and Eve. They thus tended to be biblical literalists, social liberals, and early evolutionists, a fusion of ideologies that may seem incongruous from a modern standpoint. Polygenists rejected biblical literalism in favor of textual interpretation, yet they held to a strictly creationist view of human origins in which people are as they always have been. This view was used to support the oppression of presumably inferior peoples.

The linkage of these ideas can be seen in the writings of the Count de Buffon, whose *Histoire Naturelle* was one of the most widely owned and read works of the French Enlightenment. A monogenist, Buffon surveyed human diversity in 1749 and included a stinging digression on the treatment of Africans:

> They are therefore endowed, as can be seen, with excellent hearts, and possess the seeds of every human virtue. I cannot write their history without addressing their state. Is it not wretched enough to be reduced to servitude and to be obliged to labor perpetually, without being allowed to acquire anything? Is it necessary to degrade them, beat them, and to abuse them worse than beasts? Humanity revolts against these odious oppressions which have been put into practice because of greed, and which would have been reinforced virtually every day, had our laws not curbed the brutality of masters, and fixed limits to the sufferings of their slaves. They are forced to labor, and yet commonly are not even adequately nourished. It is said that they tolerate hunger easily, that they can live for three days on a portion of a European meal; that however little they eat or sleep, they are always equally tough, equally strong, and equally fit for labor. How can men in whom there rests any feeling of humanity adopt such views? How do they presume to attempt to legitimize by such reasoning those oppressions that spring solely from their thirst for gold? But let us abandon those callous men, and return to our subject.

In 1766, speculating on the origins of animal diversity, Buffon used the diversity and interfertility of the human species as a key argument both for monogenism and microevolution:

> The Asian, European, and Negro all reproduce with equal ease with the American. There can be no greater proof that they are the issue of a single and identical stock than the facility with which they consolidate to the common stock. The blood is different, but the germ is the same.

The polygenist position underwent a revival in the mid-nineteenth century, however, as the American Civil War loomed. In England, the Ethnological Society of London, founded in 1842, was torn apart as polygenists left to form the Anthropological Society of London in 1862. A similar schism took place in France, with the formation of Paul Broca's *Société d'Anthropologie de Paris.* Ultimately, the Darwinian naturalists would side with the monogenist "ethnologists" against the polygenist "anthropologists," whose societies and cause would become obsolete before the end of the century (Stocking 1987).

CRANIAL SIZE AND SHAPE

There is a crudely materialist proposition that identifies the qualities of one's mind by the features of one's brain. While this affords a theoretical basis for modern neurophysiology, it also has proved very easy to overvalue. In practice, this overvaluation has ranged from the estimation of intelligence based on the size of the brain to inferences of personality from the bulges on particular parts of the skull (phrenology). Indeed, the most prominent nineteenth-century craniologist, Dr. Samuel George Morton (1799–1851) of Philadelphia, was also an avid phrenologist.

Morton amassed a large collection of skulls from Native Americans, and subsequently from other peoples as well. While his analytical tools were primitive, he nevertheless was able to establish a scientific, anatomical basis for the fundamental difference and alleged relative inferiority of the nonwhite races by the 1830s. That difference, he said, lay in the inferior quality (due to the inferior size) of their brains.

One key question addressed at this time was whether the prehistoric architectural and cultural features of the Midwest could reasonably be ascribed to the ancestors of the local Indians, or whether they could be attributed instead to a mysterious, cranially distinct and intellectually superior people. It was not until the latter half of the century that careful archaeological excavations would settle the question of "who built the mounds" with clear evidence of cultural continuity: They were built by Native Americans, not by Vikings, Egyptian emigrants, or anyone else.

Other anatomists discovered other features of the heads of non-Europeans that seemed to explain or reinforce their inferiority. The cranial or cephalic index, devised by the Swedish anatomist Anders Retzius, measured the shape of the head. When applied to the peoples of the world, the Europeans appeared more brachycephalic (broad-headed) than the Africans, who were dolichocephalic (long-headed).

Josiah Nott, who had studied anatomy with Morton and went on to become one of the leading physicians in Mobile, Alabama, developed the theory of the fundamental craniological difference and inferiority of the African, and explicitly tied it to the slavery question. His principal work, *Types of Mankind* (1854), written with the diplomat George C. Gliddon, found considerable popularity in the South.

Dr. Samuel George Morton. *A prominent nineteenth-century craniologist, Morton studied the skulls of Native Americans and determined that their brains were smaller than those of whites.* EMMET COLLECTION, MIRIAM AND IRA D. WALLACH DIVISION OF ART, PRINTS AND PHOTOGRAPHS, THE NEW YORK PUBLIC LIBRARY, ASTOR, LENOX AND TILDEN FOUNDATIONS.

Certainly the most prestigious American involved on the scientific polygenist side was the Harvard naturalist and Swiss émigré Louis Agassiz (1807–1873). Agassiz wrote a preface to Nott and Gliddon's volume and lent scientific credibility to the entire enterprise through his advocacy of their work and politics. In France as well, the leading anatomist, Paul Broca (1824–1880), was also the leading craniologist and polygenist.

Darwinism should have put the lie to the polygenism-monogenism question once and for all, because interbreeding made all people one species, and taxonomic entities at any level were now seen to be related by common descent. Thus, all humans had to have a common origin. Nevertheless, versions of polygenism invoking parallel evolution were revived in the twentieth century by the German anatomist Hermann Klaatsch (who held that the races were particularly related to different species of great apes), the Canadian botanical geneticist R. R. Ruggles Gates (who considered the question of interbreeding irrelevant), and the American anthropologist Carleton Coon (who held that different races evolved into *Homo sapiens* separately from different races of *Homo erectus*).

THE RADICAL CRITIQUE OF EGALITARIANISM (I)

The same year that Nott and Gliddon published *Types of Mankind*, a disaffected French nobleman published an original and brilliant synthesis of contemporary conservative politics and racist scientific thought. His name was Count Arthur de Gobineau (1816–1882), and his *Essai sur l'inégalité des races humaines* (Essay on the inequality of the human race) (1854) would serve as a model for the leading racist writers of the next two generations.

Gobineau's goal was to justify the existence, and to emphasize the necessity, of the declining ancient social order by producing a unified theory of race and civilization. Observing that civilizations had risen and fallen, he asked why. His answer was that civilizations rise as a function of the intellects of their individual members, or, more specifically, of their leaders, and that civilizations fall as that elite blood is dissipated through interbreeding with the masses. Steering a course between the monogenists and polygenists, he argued that, irrespective of Adam and Eve, races since biblical times have been stable strains. Citing the craniometric work, Gobineau argued that the white intellect is higher than the black or yellow, and that, within the white race, the Aryans are the intellectually superior subrace. Of his ten identifiable civilizations, Gobineau attributed at least seven to Aryan blood, and found no civilization at all in sub-Saharan Africa. An American edition of Gobineau was supervised and prefaced by Josiah Nott.

There was, of course, no alternative theory of civilization, and as curious as Gobineau's thesis was, it was tightly argued. Past civilizations, and by implication, the fate of the present one, were governed by the purity of blood of the aristocracy, whose position in the social order was ordained by nature. Social change and mobility, as well as social equality, were contrary to nature. The future of civilization lay in the recognition of the unequal abilities of races, and in the preservation of the social hierarchy from which it sprang. It is worth noting that Gobineau was nearly an exact contemporary of Karl Marx (1818–1883), whose considerably more erudite writings lay on the other end of the political spectrum, promoting human equality regardless of biology, real or imaginary. Gobineau's argument would be reiterated and adapted in the writings of Houston Stewart Chamberlain (1855–1927) in Europe (*Foundations of the Nineteenth Century*, 1899) and Madison Grant (1865–1937) in America (*The Passing of the Great Race*, 1916).

SOCIAL DARWINISM

In his own lifetime, Gobineau's racial theory of civilization was eclipsed by the arrival of Darwinism, which seemed to imply a much more unstable biological nature

Herbert Spencer, c. 1900. *English philosopher Herbert Spencer is credited with coining the phrase "survival of the fittest."* ERNEST H. MILLS/GETTY IMAGES

than Gobineau supposed. And yet there was an attraction inherent in Gobineau's scientific rationalization for the aristocracy. As the social and economic power of the ancient aristocracy was replaced in the nineteenth century by a newer aristocracy—that of capitalist entrepreneurs—Gobineau's ideas were blended with Darwin's to construct a powerful rationalization for the emergence of the new elite. This was embodied in English philosopher Herbert Spencer's phrase "survival of the fittest" and came to be known as "social Darwinism."

The argument of social Darwinism was rooted in Victorian ideas of progress. Because civilization was an obvious improvement over savagery and barbarism, just as science was an obvious improvement over superstition and religion, it was reasonable to ask (as Gobineau did) what the engine of progress was. To Spencer, it was not "race" *per se,* but unfettered competition. Competition led to differentiation and specialization, which led to overall complexity and improvement, not only in the natural world, but also in the social and political worlds. If the old aristocracy was in decline, it was not a threat to civilization, but a consequence of it. The aristocrats were losing out to the emergent class of tycoons, moguls, and robber barons, who had taken over the leadership of civilization. The masses still had little, and deserved little, in this theory, but competition replaced race as the impetus for progress.

Within the class structure of Anglo-American society, social Darwinism was only tangentially a racial theory, for it had little formal recognition of race. It retained the goal of justifying the social hierarchy by recourse to nature, but the hierarchy it justified was differently composed. The *nouveau riche* were now the vanguards of progress and civilization, and it was neither clear nor relevant whether their endowments were innate, lucky, or simply the product of hard work. The ultimate goal of social Darwinism was simply to get government off the backs of the people—or at least of the rich people—by removing or resisting limits on their power and control, as reflected in social reforms like child labor laws and collective bargaining.

The principal American exponent of social Darwinism was the Yale political scientist William Graham Sumner (1840–1910). Sumner aggressively taught and wrote on behalf of the survival of the fittest, and he maintained that "if we do not like the survival of the fittest, we have only one possible alternative, and that is the survival of the unfittest. The former is the law of civilization; the latter is the law of anti-civilization. We have our choice between the two, or we can go on, as in the past, vacillating between the two, but a third plan—the socialist desideratum—a plan for nourishing the unfittest and yet advancing in civilization, no man will ever find."

Unsurprisingly, some of the most well-known tycoons of the era—most notably, John D. Rockefeller and Andrew Carnegie—were attracted to the theory. It encoded a Puritan ethic of advancement through hard work, justified their own social position, and supported their business practices. That it was also a shamelessly self-serving appeal to nature in support of avarice was not lost on its critics.

There was a darker racial side to social Darwinism, however. While the theory was constructed to justify the newly emerging class structure in Europe and America, it could also be applied to the relative ranking of the colonized nations, who had apparently not yet risen above a state of savagery or barbarism. A militaristic version of progress-via-competition, easily understood as a justification for genocide, could be found in diverse social Darwinian writings, such as those of the German Ernst Haeckel and the Frenchman Georges Vacher de Lapouge. The pre-Darwinian evolutionist Robert Chambers had written in 1844: "Look at the progress even now making over the barbaric parts of the earth by the best examples of the Caucasian type, promising not only to fill up the waste places, but to supersede the imperfect nations already existing." According to this theory, if the people over there were less perfect, if they had not progressed as far in the struggle that is life's history, then they were simply standing in the way of the glorious future of the species, which was emanating from Europe. The English paleontologist William J. Sollas put it this way in his 1911 book, *Ancient Hunters*: "Justice belongs to the strong, and has been meted out to each race according to its strength; each has received as much justice as it deserved. ... It is not priority of occupation, but the power to utilize, which establishes a claim to the land. Hence it is a duty which every race owes to itself, and to the human family as well, to cultivate by every possible means its own strength ... [lest it incur] a penalty which Natural Selection, the stern but beneficent tyrant of the organic world, will assuredly exact, and that speedily, to the full" (Bowler 1995; Sommer 2005). It was precisely this kind of bio-political rhetoric that set the American politician William Jennings Bryan, a staunch pacificist and isolationist, against Darwinism.

CIVILIZATION AS CULTURE

Darwinism had actually already been rescued from social Darwinism through the conceptual innovation of a Quaker scholar, Edward B. Tylor. In his *Primitive Culture* (1871), Tylor set out a program for a "reformer's science," based on the conceptual divorce of a people's biological or racial features from their learned or behavioral features. He called these latter aspects "culture, or civilization" and the science he called "anthropology."

Culture/civilization was, to Tylor, "that complex whole which includes knowledge, belief, art, morals, law, custom, and any other capabilities and habits acquired by man as a member of society." Since all peoples had roughly the same mental powers (a doctrine known as "the psychic unity of mankind"), but some simply had not come as far as others in the trajectory of civilization, and had thus not acquired its maximum benefits, one could reasonably conclude that a rational and humane approach to other peoples was not to dispossess them and kill them, as the militaristic social Darwinians would have it, but to civilize them. Tylor thus substituted ethnocentrism for the racist genocidal ideas of the militarist social Darwinians, which was certainly an improvement.

Somewhat later, a young German-born anthropologist named Franz Boas would spearhead a move to reconceptualize culture as something that all peoples had, not to greater or lesser degrees, but equally. All cultures provided a particular way of seeing the world, of thinking and communicating about it, with rules governing the interaction of its members and a means for extracting the necessities of life. While "culture" was still put forward as a contrast to "race," representing learned knowledge, there was no longer a forward march to culture (*qua* civilization); there were only different individual cultures, each successfully permitting its members to cope, understand, and reproduce.

Anthropology thus became reinvigorated as the field that studied cultures, some of which were modern or "civilized," but whose properties were located externally to the bodies of the people, the biological organisms. Thus, as Franz Boas forcefully articulated in his 1911 classic, *The Mind of Primitive Man,* race was not a determinant of civilization; rather, social processes and events—the vagaries of history—were.

INTELLIGENCE

Anthropology had little to offer in the way of marketable skills or products, however. Psychology, on the other hand, grew rapidly in size and prestige with the development of standardized mental tests, or psychometrics. Initially developed by the Frenchman Alfred Binet as a way of identifying schoolchildren who might require special attention, the intelligence test was imported into America in the early part of the twentieth century, principally by Lewis Terman of Stanford and Robert Yerkes of Yale. They modified the original interpretation of the results, however, by believing that the number they generated (an "intelligence quotient," or IQ) was a measure of overall mental output, minimally affected by the conditions of life and set by heredity.

Giving a large battery of such tests to American soldiers in World War I, psychologists concluded that Americans were "feeble-minded"—that is to say, stupid—and in imminent danger of becoming more so. In addition, tests given to immigrants showed that feeble-minded people were arriving on American shores in large numbers. In fact, the only people who seemed to do consistently well on these tests were urban, acculturated, wealthy English speakers. Cultural biases in the tests were widely acknowledged, such as a question asking which path was best to take to get from here to there. Samoans picked the prettiest path, while the "correct" answer was actually the shortest path. Privileging American efficiency is reasonable but arbitrary, and thus hardly a valid way to estimate anyone's raw intellectual powers.

The inheritance of intelligence—or more precisely of its opposite, feeble-mindedness—was shown "scientifically" to be due to a single major recessive allele by Charles Davenport, the most prominent human geneticist in America. Feeble-mindedness seemed to be most prominently associated with poor people and especially with poor people from outside of northern Europe. It was to be found especially commonly in nonwhites, poor whites of the South, and in the poor immigrants arriving in America in large numbers from southern and eastern Europe early in the twentieth century. Feeble-mindedness was diagnosable from several key behavioral features, Davenport explained in his 1911 textbook on human genetics: "the acts of taking and keeping loose articles, of tearing away obstructions to get at something desired, of picking valuables out of holes and pockets, of assaulting a neighbor who has something desirable or who has caused pain or who is in the way, of deserting family and other relatives, and of promiscuous sexual relations."

With such a loose set of phenotypes as a guide, the feeble-mindedness allele could obviously be identified very widely. Family studies seemed to show that it was indeed inherited simply. The most famous of these was a study of the pseudonymous Kallikak family, published by the psychologist Henry H. Goddard in 1912. Tracing back two sides of a family to a single eighteenth-century progenitor, Martin Kallikak, Goddard purported to show that the hundreds of modern descendants through his dalliance with a "nameless feeble-minded tavern girl" were mainly feeble-minded burdens on society; while those modern descendants through Martin's Quaker wife, Rachel, were solid citizens. The clear implications were that feeble-mindedness is everywhere, is transmitted genetically, and if only the tavern girl had never bred, the social problems caused by her descendants would never have come to exist.

In fact, most of the fieldwork of the Kallikak study was carried out by Goddard's assistants, who gave intelligence tests to some of the people they interviewed, but used surrogate estimators of intelligence in other cases. Goddard's book candidly noted that these surrogates ranged from interpreting the way dead ancestors were talked about to just looking at people:

> The father, a strong, healthy, broad-shouldered man, was sitting helplessly in a corner. The mother, a pretty woman still, with remnants of ragged garments drawn about her, sat in a chair, the picture of despondency. Three children, scantily clad and with shoes that would barely hold together, stood about with drooping jaws and the unmistakable look of the feeble-minded. Another child, neither more intelligent nor better clad, was attempting to wash a few greasy dishes in cold water. The deaf boy was nowhere to be seen. On being urgently requested, the mother went out of the room to get him, for he was not yet out of bed. … A glance sufficed to establish his mentality, which was low. … The father himself, though strong and vigorous, showed by his face that he had only a child's mentality.

The shoddiness of the research upon which the strong conclusions were founded did not prevent the results from being widely disseminated in the genetics and psychology literature for decades. In fact, when challenged on the question of how he could know that the tavern girl was feeble-minded when he didn't even know her name, Goddard consulted his field worker and then publicly responded with a barefaced lie to the effect that her name was indeed known, but had been deliberately concealed.

THE EUGENICS MOVEMENT

The take-home message of the Kallikaks was that an ounce of genetic prevention was worth the proverbial pound of cure—if only something had been done about the tavern girl, society would have been spared the burden of her feeble-minded degenerate descendants. Both sides of the Kallikak family were white (indeed, they were Anglo-Saxon) so racism was not an overt issue, but if feeble-mindedness was a unitary phenomenon with a single cause, then the Kallikak conclusions would have significant implications for global feeble-mindedness.

An Englishman named Francis Galton had been working on mathematical approaches to heredity, particularly to the heredity of intelligence, since the mid-nineteenth century. Thomas Malthus had famously founded the science of demography at the turn of the century with the argument that the human population was increasing in size faster than its resource base, which entailed a gloomy forecast for the distant future. But fertility rates were not equal across all economic strata, and the poor were outbreeding the rich. While this might seem to necessitate the development of social programs for the poor, Galton saw things in a more pessimistic light. If the poor were outbreeding the rich, and if one believed the poor were genetically inferior to the rich, then the future could only hold catastrophe for the entire species. Indeed, the very existence of the prolific poor seemed to be a subversion of the natural order, if it were believed they were genetically inferior to the rich. Galton's cousin, Charles Darwin, had devised a theory to account for the diversity of life on earth that was premised on "the fittest" surviving and breeding disproportionately. If the human species were being led by the prolific poor, that would seem to go against the history of life on earth.

Clearly something needed to be done. People, Galton argued, must take control of their own genetic future. The poor must be discouraged from breeding, and the rich must be encouraged to breed. Galton called for the scientific control of human breeding, a plan he called "eugenics." It is the first of many ironies of the eugenics movement that Galton died without issue.

The eugenics movement gained scientific credibility, and international popularity, after the rise of Mendelian genetics at the beginning of the twentieth century. Across diverse political systems, eugenics implied a utopian, scientific approach to impending social problems. Eugenics was adopted and integrated into diverse national traditions: In England, it involved biometry and class; in America, it involved genes and race; in Germany, the metaphor of national illness and health prescribed a movement of "race hygiene;" while in Latin America the focus was more on public sanitation.

The eugenics movement inherited from the social Darwinists the idea that natural hierarchies were at the root of social hierarchies in human societies. However, the eugenicists tied their ideas to the emerging science of genetics, and they sought active government intervention in the problems they perceived, which was quite antithetical to the social Darwinists' *laissez-faire* political goals. But the social landscape had changed. The first decade of the twentieth century had seen an enormous rise in the number of poor immigrants into the United States from Italy and eastern Europe. In an era without federal assistance for the poor, they lived in crime-ridden urban slums.

An International Congress in 1912 stimulated much interest in the eugenics movement. In America, its leading exponent was Charles Davenport, whose 1911 book, *Heredity in Relation to Eugenics*, was the first major text of human genetics in America. Davenport tackled many of the same problems as Franz Boas, whose book *The Mind of Primitive Man* was published the same year. But where Boas saw biology as largely irrelevant to the past or future of civilization, Davenport saw things quite differently. Civilizations rose and fell on account of their genes, and one's lot in life was determined by one's genes. Phrenologists and craniologists had justified their inferences on the grounds that the brain was the seat of thought and was contained within the skull, whose features could therefore stand as surrogate measures for the quality of one's thoughts. Davenport's eugenics took this one step further, for it was the genes that determined the structure of the brain and skull, and thus of the quality of the thoughts they contained. Like phrenology, then, there was a seductively materialist, if stunningly crude, logic to it.

Davenport's friend, a Yale-educated lawyer and amateur naturalist named Madison Grant, syncretized Davenport's genetics with Gobineau's racism and articulated a political platform for social change based on modern science. For Grant the problem was genetics; in particular, racial genetics. What concerned him most was the relative quality of the impoverished Italians and Jews immigrating in large numbers and living in crime and squalor. Grant contrasted the "Nordic" northern European to the "Mediterranean" southern European (a distinction drawn by the anthropologist William Z. Ripley in his 1899 *The Races of Europe*), and found the Nordic to be superior in body and mind; indeed (as per Gobineau), he found the Nordic "race" to be the fountain of all civilization. This interpretation of the past led to a nightmarish projection for the future, when one considered the flood of dirty, swarthy, unfit, and prolific poor people now entering America—worse even than the poor Irish immigrants of the previous generation.

In his 1916 bestseller, *The Passing of the Great Race*, Madison Grant articulated a solution that would empty the jails, balance the budget, and send America on the path to world leadership. It involved the scientific control of reproduction, with the main goal being the widespread application of surgical sterilization for men and women. In chilling terms, he explained:

> A rigid system of selection through the elimination of those who are weak or unfit—in other words, social failures—would ... enable us to get rid of the undesirables who crowd our jails, hospitals, and insane asylums. ... [Sterilization] can be applied to an ever widening circle of social discards, beginning always with the criminal, the diseased, and the insane, and extending gradually to types which may be called weaklings rather than defectives, and perhaps ultimately to worthless race types.

Grant's book was criticized by a few scholars, such as Franz Boas, but was well received in the scientific community generally. When the American Eugenics Society was formally incorporated in the 1920s, Madison Grant was one of its directors, and most of America's leading biologists served on its advisory board under him. Grant and the eugenicists had two principal political goals for the short term: a program for sterilizing the poor, and one for restricting the immigration of "alien scum," as they liked to call the non-northern European immigrants.

In addition to the scientific community, Grant's 1916 book was well received across a diverse political spectrum. Theodore Roosevelt, with whom Grant had worked in founding the New York Zoological Society, wrote him a letter of effusive praise. (After reading the 1925 German translation, so did Adolf Hitler.)

By the late 1920s, the eugenicists had had considerable success in the United States. In 1924, Congress enacted a major restriction of the immigration of Italians and eastern European Jews. Two years later, the Supreme Court decided that the state of Virginia had the right to sterilize Carrie Buck, a poor white woman, against her will. Basing their ruling on the latest science, which had convinced them that America was destined to be "swamped with incompetence" unless action was taken, the Court ruled 8 to 1 that "three generations of imbeciles are enough."

American sterilization laws were enacted at the state level, though often half-heartedly. Thirty states actually sterilized people over the next few decades, with California leading the way (sterilizing more than 20,000 citizens), and eleven other states each sterilizing more than 1,000 citizens. Europe provided more fertile ground for a state that wanted to subsume reproduction to its perceived scientific needs, and the emergence of a racist totalitarian government in Germany gave German eugenicists a chance to take the movement to its logical conclusion.

THE DECLINE OF EUGENICS IN AMERICA, AND ITS RISE IN GERMANY

American biologists, particularly geneticists, were reluctant to criticize the eugenics movement. In the first place, two of the most powerful biologists in America were among its leaders: Charles Davenport of the Cold Spring Harbor Laboratory, and Henry Fairfield Osborn of the American Museum of Natural History. In the second place, the biologists were themselves products of their own era and class, and they thus often shared the values and prejudices of the eugenics movement. And finally, even if one did feel that Madison Grant overstated the case for genetics, he was nevertheless an advocate for the field.

The fruit fly geneticist (and later, Nobel laureate) Thomas Hunt Morgan, who worked in the same building as Franz Boas at Columbia University, was the only major figure in his field who played no part in the American Eugenics Society. But even Morgan refrained from using his scientific stature to criticize the eugenics program. The bacterial geneticist Herbert Spencer Jennings of Johns Hopkins University found that the statistics presented by the eugenicists to Congress in the early 1920s, ostensibly showing that American immigrants from southern Europe were more prone to crime than those from northern Europe, had been improperly analyzed. He alerted the American Eugenics Society's president, the Yale economist Irving Fisher, but was dissatisfied with the Society's lack of interest in the scientific mistakes it had presented to Congress, and he quietly resigned and dissociated himself from the Society. In 1927, his colleague Raymond Pearl published the first critique of eugenics program by an American biologist.

Prior to the publication of Pearl's 1927 article, the only critiques of eugenics had been published by people outside the mainstream of modern biological science. The journalist Walter Lippman had taken on the IQ testers in an angry series of articles in the *New Republic* in 1922–1923. Conservative Christians, especially Catholics, objected to governmental intervention in reproduction, which they took to be the affairs of God. Social scientists objected to the eugenicists' naïve genetic theory of history and civilization, while civil libertarians objected to their insistence on the perceived needs of the state taking precedence over the individual's civil rights, especially the right to privacy. The famed lawyer Clarence Darrow, who had defended modern biology in the 1925 trial of John T. Scopes for teaching evolution, savaged modern biology the following year for its devotion to eugenics. In the literary magazine *The American Mercury,* Darrow argued that "amongst the schemes for remolding society this is the most senseless and impudent that has ever been put forward by irresponsible fanatics to plague a long-suffering race."

The American Mercury was edited by the Baltimore-based journalist and critic H. L. Mencken, who called eugenics "mainly blather" in his column in the *Baltimore Sun* in May 1927. He prevailed upon his friend and fellow Baltimore intellectual Raymond Pearl to write up his reservations about eugenics, publishing them under the title "The Biology of Superiority" in November 1927. Pearl acknowledged the social prejudices underlying the research, and exposed the flimsy science backing it up. Since Pearl was a respected biologist, his article caused a sensation and was picked up by the major news services. Of course, publicly challenging the power structure of the scientific community was not without its risks, and Pearl found that his offer of a professorship at Harvard was quickly retracted.

Other critiques by biologists soon came out, notably by the American geneticist Hermann Muller ("The Dominance of Economics over Eugenics," 1932). These scholars, however, did not necessarily dispense with the foolishly utopian view of a state-guided, scientific approach to love, marriage, and procreation, based on popular prejudices; they merely rebelled against the ways in which the ideas were being implemented at the time. Pearl himself believed that Jews, after centuries of life in crowded ghettoes, had become better adapted to urban life than non-Jews, and he urged that strict quotas be placed on their admission to medical schools, lest their ranks in the professional classes swell excessively at the expense of ordinary Americans. Muller, for his part, tried to convince Josef Stalin to implement a state-sponsored program of eugenic breeding, and barely escaped the Soviet Union with his life in 1937.

It was in Germany that eugenicists were given the opportunity to work with the state most closely to implement their ideas. Adolf Hitler had found inspiration in the compatibility between his political goals and the writings of Madison Grant and the eugenicists. He had read the genetics textbook by Eugen Fischer, Erwin Baur, and Fritz Lenz, who advocated the same social prejudices as their American counterparts. When Hitler came to power in 1932, he promoted like-minded scholars. Eugen Fischer became the director of the Kaiser Wilhelm Institute of Anthropology, Human Heredity, and Eugenics, and he implemented the Nazi policies with such enthusiasm that Franz Weidenreich, a distinguished anatomist who had been forced to emigrate because of his ancestry, later suggested in the pages of the journal *Science* that he be tried as a war criminal.

In 1934, the prestigious journal *Zeitschrift fur Morphologie und Anthropologie* published a special volume in Fischer's honor. In the preface to the volume, two of Fischer's former students wrote, "We stand upon the threshold of a new era. For the first time in world history, the Führer Adolf Hitler is putting into practice the insights about the

Dr. Eugen Fischer. *Fischer, who considered that racial mixing was a threat to European culture, became director of the Kaiser Wilhelm Institute of Anthropology and Genetics.* ARCHIV ZUR GESCHICHTE DER MAX-PLANCK-GESELLSCHAFT, BERLIN DAHLEM.

biological foundations of the development of peoples—race, heredity, selection. It is no coincidence that Germany is the locus of this event: German science provides the tools for the politician." Among the essays that followed were contributions from two Americans, Raymond Pearl and Charles Davenport.

The sterilization laws enacted by the Nazis in 1935 were modeled on the state laws in America, which had been drafted by Charles Davenport's assistant, the geneticist Harry Laughlin. As a result, Nazi-controlled Heidelberg University awarded Laughlin an honorary doctorate in 1936. By then, however, any formal association with the Nazis was sufficiently embarrassing that Laughlin was discouraged from traveling to Germany to accept it in person.

The Nazis were mobilizing the full force of the modern industrial state in support of the eugenic program, and the doctrines of human progress culminating in the Nordic race, that had been promoted for decades in the name of science. The people who felt the full brunt of their efficient technologies in the 1940s were almost precisely the groups initially targeted by Madison Grant in 1916: criminals, the diseased, "weaklings," and "worthless race types". In practice, this meant Jews, Gypsies, homosexuals, and others. Moreover, the sterilization advocated by the scientists was costly and time consuming. To deal with people who were not deemed worthy of reproducing, a hail of bullets or a vial of poison gas was assuredly a more efficient and cost-effective means. If they were not worthy of breeding, why should they be worthy of living?

American support for eugenics waned in America with the accession of the Nazis in Germany. Certainly the stock market crash and the ensuing Depression showed how weakly biological endowments counted in comparison to the life-determining effects of economics and culture. By the end of the 1930s, the Carnegie Foundation had withdrawn its long-standing support for the Eugenics Record Office at Cold Spring Harbor, and full-length criticisms of racist science began to appear in England and America, notably *We Europeans* (1935) by the biologist Julian Huxley and anthropologist Alfred Cort Haddon; *Race: A Study in Superstition* (1937) by the historian Jacques Barzun; and *Man's Most Dangerous Myth* (1942) by the anthropologist Ashley Montagu.

America was not without its deep scientific racist issues, however. Respected anatomists such as Milo Hellman and Adolph Schultz found a relative primitiveness and apishness in the teeth and skeletons of blacks. The physical anthropologist Earnest Hooton of Harvard struggled mightily to differentiate his science from that of his German counterparts, but he was not very successful and clung to theories of genetically based criminality and eugenics long after most American scientists had abandoned them. In a study that continued for decades, medical practitioners in Tuskegee, Alabama, studied black men infected with syphilis and monitored the course of the disease without treating them. In much of America, where segregation was a fact of life, the inherent inferiority and lesser value of black lives (and Native American lives) was widely taken for granted.

THE REFORMATION OF PHYSICAL ANTHROPOLOGY AND HUMAN GENETICS

At the end of World War II, the sciences of physical anthropology (as the study of human physical diversity) and human genetics lay largely in tatters, and both fields had to be reinvented. James Neel provided the inspiration for rebuilding human genetics into a science that focused on real genes rather than imaginary ones, on medical rather than social pathologies, and on the availability of voluntary services for the sake of the family rather than coerced procedures for the good of the state or race. As a founding ancestor, Charles Davenport was quietly buried and Archibald Garrod, who had discovered the Mendelian basis of a metabolic disease in 1902, was installed in his place.

In physical anthropology, Sherwood Washburn took the lead in outlining a new physical anthropology

Ota Benga in the Bronx Zoo, 1906. *Ota Benga, a Congolese pygmy, was put on display at the Bronx Zoo after first coming to the United States to be featured in the anthropology exhibits at the St. Louis World's Fair in 1904.* © WILDLIFE CONSERVATION SOCIETY.

that focused on adaptation rather than classification, evolution rather than typology, real human breeding populations rather than abstract agglomerated races, and common themes of ancient humanity rather than divisive themes of contemporary biological chauvinism. A newer scientific approach to human variation would see the human species, in the words of British physical anthropologist Joseph S. Weiner, "as constituting a widespread network of more-or-less interrelated, ecologically adapted and functional entities."

The rooting of Nazi ideology in the science of race attracted the attention of the fledgling United Nations, which commissioned an international panel of scholars to draft a formal statement summarizing the (nonthreatening) science of race. The anthropologist Ashley Montagu emerged as its principal framer, and the UNESCO Statement on Race was issued in 1950. In twenty-one paragraphs, this statement articulated a view of race in which the cultural forces shaping a human being were far stronger than any biological differences. Thus, "each group arbitrarily tends to misinterpret the variability which occurs as a fundamental difference which separates that group from all others," and "so far as temperament is concerned, there is ... evidence that whatever group differences of the kind there might be are greatly overridden by the individual differences, and by the differences springing from environmental factors." Further, "for all practical social purposes 'race' is not so much a biological phenomenon as a social myth. ... Lastly, biological studies lend support to the ethic of universal brotherhood; for man is born with drives toward cooperation, and unless these drives are satisfied, men and nations alike fall ill."

This language proved too radical for the senior generation of racial scholars, however, and they asked UNESCO to have the document re-drafted. UNESCO capitulated to the pressure, and produced another Statement on Race in 1951. This second statement focused principally on genetics and weakened many of the more forceful assertions of the first. Among the complaints forcing this change was one submitted by the aged former Nazi, Eugen Fischer.

The scientific turmoil at UNESCO, however, was peripheral to racial issues in America. To some extent the key decisions in the civil rights movement of the 1950s, such as *Brown* v. *the Board of Education* (1954), drew inspiration from a generation of Boasian anthropological thought. Ultimately, issues of relative natural endowments and of the pattern and distribution of human biological differences were deemed to be red herrings; the heart of the matter was the guarantee of constitutionally based freedoms to all parts of American society.

THE RADICAL CRITIQUE OF EGALITARIANISM (II)

There was an inevitable backlash to the liberalization of racial thought in the post-Nazi era. As the cold war emerged, a dark secret emerged with it. Back in the 1930s, before America and Germany had gone to war, many Americans held sympathy for Nazi racial views. After all, there was a great deal of continuity between German racial science and its American counterpart. The principal enemies of the Nazis in those days were not the Americans, but the Communists, so many young intellectuals set against Nazi racism naturally tended to gravitate to those who were the strongest opponents of the Nazis—that is, to the Communists. By the 1950s the Nazis had been officially routed, and America's new enemies were now the Communists, and consequently many middle-aged intellectuals who had worked for egalitarian ideals in their youth were now saddled with an embarrassing Communist past.

In 1943 the USO (United Service Organizations) had commissioned a pamphlet by anthropologists to explain race to GIs, and to show them what they were ostensibly fighting for. It was written by two Boasians at Columbia University, Ruth Benedict and Gene Weltfish, and was called "The Races of Man." After extensive distribution of the pamphlet, a group of southern Congressmen, led by Representative Andrew J. May of Kentucky, had it withdrawn and declared subversive for its strongly egalitarian message. A few years later, after Benedict had died, Weltfish was summoned to testify about her Communist past by the House Un-American Activities Committee, after which she was summarily fired by Columbia University. A similar fate befell Ashley Montagu, the principal author of the original UNESCO Statement on Race, who was fired from his position at Rutgers University.

There were also scientists who opposed school integration and the overall goals of the civil rights movement, believing that their positions were validated scientifically. By the early 1960s, however, this group had shrunk to a small, if shrill, minority. Back in 1937, a textile magnate named Wickliffe Draper had set up a philanthropic endowment to support the scientific study of human differences, with a nod towards proving the superiority of the white race. The first president of Draper's Pioneer Fund was the eugenicist Harry Laughlin. By the early 1960s, the Pioneer Fund was supporting psychometric studies purporting to demonstrate the lack of intelligence of blacks. Draper helped underwrite the formation of a journal, the *Mankind Quarterly*, which began publication in 1960 as an outlet for unrepentant racists who felt left out of the liberalized academic mainstream.

The journal's editor was an obscure Scottish nobleman, Robert Gayre, and his associate editors were a psychologist named Henry Garrett and a geneticist named Ruggles Gates. Garrett had testified against school integration and had become convinced that the civil rights movement was the result of a conspiracy of Jews, communists, and anthropologists, all drawing inspiration from Franz Boas. Gates was trained as a botanical geneticist, and because plants commonly profligate outside the accepted taxonomic boundaries of their species, he rejected the interbreeding criterion as evidence of human unity and became the last academic advocate of species status for human races. His book *Human Ancestry* (1948) came with a foreword by his friend Earnest Hooton, who politely disavowed all the ideas that followed.

The *Mankind Quarterly*, edited by Gayre, Garrett, and Gates, caused a sensation with its first issue. The physical anthropologists Geoffrey Harrison, Juan Comas, and Santiago Genoves angrily denounced it in the mainstream scientific literature. An eastern European anthropologist resigned from *Mankind Quarterly*'s editorial board upon discovering its ideological stance; as a Dachau survivor he found the response unsatisfactory and condescending, and therefore criticized the journal, only to be sued by Gayre and Garrett for associating them with Nazi ideologies.

Other prominent segregationists worked to promote a scientific case for their cause. In 1962, Wesley Critz George, an anatomist from the University of North Carolina, authored a study commissioned by the governor of Alabama, called "The Biology of the Race Problem," ostensibly demonstrating the inferiority of black intelligence. The work was assiduously promoted by a propagandist, businessman (founder of Delta Airlines), and sometime historian named Carleton Putnam, whose own segregationist book, *Race and Reason* (1961) echoed Garrett's ideas about the insidious egalitarian cabal of Jews, communists, and anthropologists.

Putnam's work was roundly condemned by the American Anthropological Association at its 1961 meeting. The leading evolutionary geneticist of the era, Theodosius Dobzhansky, also weighed in harshly. Dobzhansky was in an ideal position to criticize the work, for he was not Jewish, not an anthropologist, and an émigré from the Soviet regime. Nevertheless, Putnam and the segregationists had a valuable ally within the anthropological community—Putnam's cousin, the University of Pennsylvania anthropologist Carleton Coon, who was also the sitting president of the American Association of Physical Anthropologists.

Coon's own book, *The Origin of Races* (1962), was being cited by the segregationists even before publication. It purported to demonstrate that Africans had evolved from *Homo erectus* into *Homo sapiens* 200,000 years after Europeans had, which explained their innate backwardness. The scholarly reviews were mixed, with varying degrees of deference paid to Coon's stature in the scholarly community, much querying about the possibility of separate races evolving in parallel across a species boundary, and much private speculation about Coon's political allegiances and motives. Coon maintained a public posture of being apolitical, but he was privately assisting the segregationists.

At the end of the decade, a major beneficiary of the Pioneer Fund, Berkeley psychologist Arthur Jensen, published an article in the Harvard Educational Review that rhetorically asked, "How much can we boost IQ and scholastic achievement?" and answered, predictably, not very much at all. Jensen and his British counterparts, Cyril Burt and Hans Eysenck, were the most prominent remaining proponents of the view that intelligence was principally innate and unalterable. Burt's studies of identical twins separated at birth and subsequently reunited seemed to support these ideas, but by the late 1970s it had become clear that Burt was, to put it mildly, an eccentric scientist whose twins and collaborators were largely products of his imagination. Jensen's and Eysenck's arguments relied heavily on their misinterpretation of a statistic from genetics called "heritability." Prominent geneticists (such as Richard Lewontin and Luca Cavalli-Sforza) and psychologists (such as Steven Rose and Leon Kamin) rose to show the flaws in their reasoning.

Around 1970, Jensen was joined in his crusade by William Shockley, a Stanford University Nobel laureate in physics who parlayed the invention of the transistor into a bully pulpit for his ideas on the inferiority of blacks and the merits of the discarded ideas of eugenics. Shockley also believed that women should have an opportunity to be fertilized by the highest-quality sperm available, and, along with a California tycoon and visionary named Robert Graham, he started a Nobel-laureate sperm bank. Unfortunately for them, most Nobel laureates were smart enough not to want anything to do with Shockley or his ideas, and the sperm bank never produced a Nobel baby (Plotz 2005).

While the present discussion has focused on Euro-American scientific racism, the ideas were also influential to various degrees elsewhere, and the place where they remained in force the longest as formal state policy was in the former British colony of South Africa. Colonial powers there took pains to manipulate the archaeological record, permitting them to deny the attribution of architecture and metallurgy to the ancestors of the local indigenous people. Much scholarly literature in South Africa prior to World War II employed a crude racialized ideology. After World War II, however, with the passage of the laws collectively known as "apartheid," the South African government came to use more anthropologically sophisticated ideas about cultural diversity to rationalize its policies for moving dispossessed blacks to reservations, or homelands. The political transition in the 1990s fostered public reflection on the relationship between European science and anti-African racism. Some acknowledgment of the Africans' early encounters with science was made when the French agreed, in 2002, to repatriate the remains of Sarah Baartman, a Khoe woman who had toured Europe on display and been dissected upon her death by the greatest anatomists of the age, with her remains kept in the *Musée de l'Homme* in Paris for two centuries. Instrumental in the negotiations was the physical anthropologist Phillip Tobias, who had fought against apartheid and its science. Ironically, the apartheid government had also opposed evolution, which has now been embraced by the new government.

SCIENTIFIC RACISM SINCE THE 1970s

One of the ironies about the controversy surrounding the publication of *Sociobiology: The New Synthesis* (1975), by the Harvard entomologist Edward O. Wilson, was that it came with no overt political agenda. Its arguments came from theoretical ecology, its data were from animal behavior, and it said nothing about race, except to raise the possibility that racism (or xenophobia, a Davenport-like neologism meaning "fear of strangers") might be innate. It made rash generalizations about human nature and presented an overly biologized view of human behavior. Observers were justifiably outraged when a protester poured water on Wilson during a scientific meeting, but probably more outrageous was Wilson's own naiveté in not realizing that scientific pronouncements about human behavior are invariably politicized.

Two decades later, this became evident once again, when the Harvard hereditarian psychologist Richard Herrnstein collaborated with conservative political theorist Charles Murray on *The Bell Curve*. This work made a case against social programs directed at the poor, on the grounds that the poor were irremediably stupid, as attested by their low IQs, which the authors claimed are genetically fixed. *The Bell Curve* reiterated Arthur Jensen's arguments (and errors) of the preceding generation, and it cited not only the work of several Pioneer Fund beneficiaries, but several articles published in the *Mankind Quarterly* as well, hardly a mainstream or reputable source. Conservative political activists quickly recognized the value of the book in invoking nature to justify social inequality, just as William Graham Sumner had done a century earlier.

Another quirk of *The Bell Curve* was its citations of the work of a Pioneer Fund beneficiary, the Canadian psychologist Philippe Rushton. In addition, a pre-emptive appendix defended Rushton's work as "not that of a crackpot or a bigot" and "plainly science." Rushton envisions a racial spectrum in which natural selection has produced innately large-brained, law-abiding, civilized, and under-sexualized Asians; innately small-brained, criminalistic, primitive, and licentious Africans; and Europeans as a happy medium. *The Bell Curve*'s mild characterization of these bizarre ideas is not simply an understatement, but is more likely just a simple falsehood (Graves 2002; Lieberman 2001). Rushton had his work reprinted in a digested form and sent to the membership lists of the American Anthropological Association, the American Sociological Association, and other academic organizations, with the financial assistance of the Pioneer Fund, of which he was subsequently made president.

The Bell Curve came as a shock to scholars of human diversity, who thought they had seen the last of these ideas back in the 1960s. It drove home forcefully the lesson that, because the political stakes are high, the scientific study of human diversity requires constant vigilance to prevent its corruption by those who would use science to make people's lives more miserable (which would seem to provide an argument against science generally, if that is indeed its result). Consequently, the

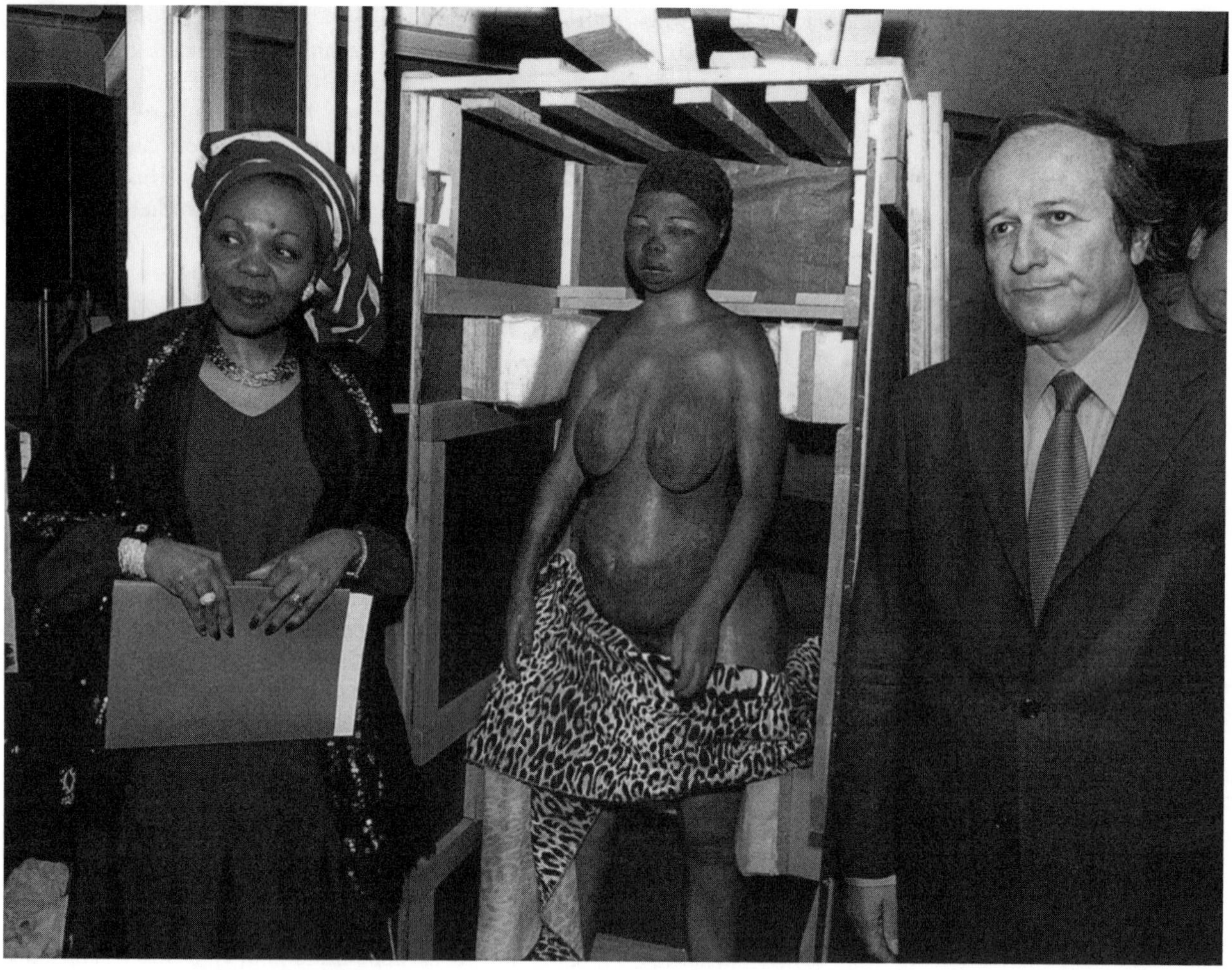

Saartjie Baartman. *Officials stand next to a plaster cast of Saartjie Baartman during a ceremony to mark the return of Baartman's remains to South Africa in 2002.* AP IMAGES.

American Anthropological Association and the American Association of Physical Anthropologists adopted public position statements on race, updating the old UNESCO statements.

At century's end, another version of scientific racism briefly surfaced again. Where the body and mind are commonly juxtaposed against one another, and the minds of whites are taken to be superior to those of blacks, a corollary might be that the bodies of blacks are superior to those of whites. Buffon had responded in the eighteenth century to the popular rumor that blacks were considered more physically hale than whites, and thus more fit for manual labor, while the spectacular success of Jack Johnson in boxing and Jesse Owens in track in the twentieth century suggested an innate physical superiority of "the black athlete"—if one took them not as exceptional, gifted, and well-trained individuals, but as gross avatars or symbols. Paradoxically, as anatomists studied Jesse Owens' legs looking for marks of black superiority, they found none; indeed, they found his feet to be rather "white" (Hoberman 1997).

The gradual entry of blacks into American professional sports, and the opening up of athletics as a professional venue, produced a new crop of excellent black athletes and a new wave of scientific racism to account for their success. The prominence of black football players was accompanied by the underlying sentiment that they could nevertheless not succeed at a "thinking" position such as quarterback. The African-American quarterback Doug Williams subsequently led the Washington Redskins to the National Football League championship in the 1988 Super Bowl. The prominence of black baseball players raised the question of their absence from the managerial ranks in 1987, to which Al Campanis, an executive for the Los Angeles Dodgers, casually responded that perhaps blacks lacked the intellectual abilities for managing (he added that black swimmers also lacked the necessary buoyancy for elite status in that sport). In 1975, Frank

Robinson had become the first black manager in the major leagues, and in 1992 and 1993 Cito Gaston would lead the Toronto Blue Jays to consecutive World Series baseball championships.

Nevertheless, the prominence of blacks in basketball in the 1990s renewed pseudo-scientific suspicions that they were innately endowed, as a group, with athletic prowess. These views were summarized by a journalist named Jon Entine, whose book *Taboo: Why Blacks Dominate Sports and Why We're Afraid to Talk about It* was published in 2000. Entine's answer to black "domination" was racial genetic superiority, and his explanation of the "fear" was an updated version of the old anthropological-Jewish-communist conspiracy. Like all the previous variations on the theme of genetically embedded racial hierarchies, this one was also overtaken by social and historical events—in this case, the collapse of the United States Olympic basketball team in 2004 and the emergence of basketball stars from other parts of the world.

SEE ALSO *Boas, Franz; Chamberlain, Houston Stewart; Eugenics, History of; Exploitation; Galton, Francis; Genocide; Great Chain of Being; Holocaust; IQ and Testing; Jensen, Arthur; Morton, Samuel George; Racial Hierarchy; Slavery, Racial.*

BIBLIOGRAPHY

Allen, Garland E. 1983. "The Misuse of Biological Hierarchies: The American Eugenics Movement, 1900–1940." *History and Philosophy of the Life Sciences* 5 (2): 105–128.

Bachrach, Susan, and Dieter Kuntz. 2004. *Deadly Medicine: Creating the Master Race.* Washington, DC: United States Holocaust Memorial Museum.

Barkan, Elazar. 1992. *The Retreat of Scientific Racism.* New York: Cambridge University Press.

Barzun, Jacques. 1937. *Race: A Study in Superstition.* New York: Harcourt, Brace.

Bowler, Peter. 1995. "Social Metaphors in Evolutionary Biology, 1879–1930: The Wider Dimension of Social Darwinism." In *Biology as Society, Society as Biology: Metaphors*, edited by Sabine Maason, et al. Dordrecht, the Netherlands: Kluwer.

Brace, C. Loring. 1982. "The Roots of the Race Concept in American Physical Anthropology." In *A History of American Physical Anthropology, 1930–1980*, edited by Frank Spencer. New York: Academic Press.

Chase, Allen. 1977. *The Legacy of Malthus: The Social Costs of the New Scientific Racism.* Urbana: University of Illinois Press.

Dubow, Saul. 1995. *Scientific Racism in Modern South Africa.* New York: Cambridge University Press.

Gillham, Nicholas Wright. 2001. *A Life of Sir Francis Galton: From African Exploration to the Birth of Eugenics.* New York: Oxford University Press.

Goddard, Henry H. 1942. "In Defense of the Kallikak Study." *Science* 95: 574–576.

Gould, Stephen Jay. 1978. "Morton's Ranking of Races by Cranial Capacity." *Science* 200: 503–509.

———. 1981. *The Mismeasure of Man.* New York: Norton.

———. 1998. "On Mental and Visual Geometry." *Isis* 89: 502–504.

Grant, Madison. 1916. *The Passing of the Great Race.* New York: Scribner.

Graves, Joseph L. 2002. "The Misuse of Life History Theory: J. P. Rushton and the Pseudoscience of Racial Hierarchy." In *Race and Intelligence: Separating Science from Myth*, edited by Jefferson M. Fish. Mahwah, NJ: Lawrence Erlbaum.

Greene, John C. 1954. "Some Early Speculations on the Origin of Human Races. *American Anthropologist* 56: 31–41.

Haller, John S., Jr. 1970. "The Species Problem: Nineteenth-Century Concepts of Racial Inferiority in the Origin of Man Controversy." *American Anthropologist* 72: 1319–1329.

Haraway, Donna J. 1988. "Remodelling the Human Way of Life: Sherwood Washburn and the New Physical Anthropology, 1950–1980." In *Bones, Bodies, Behavior: Essays on Biological Anthropology. History of Anthropology*, vol. 5, edited by George W. Stocking. Madison: University of Wisconsin Press.

Hoberman, John. 1997. *Darwin's Athletes: How Sport Has Damaged America and Preserved the Myth of Race.* Boston: Houghton Mifflin.

Hooton, Earnest A. 1936. "Plain Statements about Race." *Science* 83: 511–513.

Hrdlicka, Ales. 1914. "Physical Anthropology in America: An Historical Sketch." *American Anthropologist* 16: 507–554.

Isaac, Benjamin. 2004. *The Invention of Racism in Classical Antiquity.* Princeton, NJ: Princeton University Press.

Jackson, John J., Jr. 2001. "'In Ways Unacademical': The Reception of Carleton S. Coon's *The Origin of Races.*" *Journal of the History of Biology* 34: 247–285.

Kevles, Daniel J. 1985. *In the Name of Eugenics.* Berkeley: University of California Press.

Kline, Wendy. 2001. *Building a Better Race: Gender, Sexuality, and Eugenics from the Turn of the Century to the Baby Boom.* Berkeley: University of California Press.

Kuhl, Stefan. 1994. *The Nazi Connection: Eugenics, American Racism, and German National Socialism.* New York: Oxford University Press.

Lieberman, Leonard. 2001. "How Caucasoids Got Such Big Crania and Why They Shrank: From Morton to Rushton." *Current Anthropology* 42: 63–85.

Lombardo, Paul A. 1985. "Three Generations, No Imbeciles: New Light on *Buck v. Bell.*" *New York University Law Review* 60 (1): 30–62.

———. 2002. "'The American Breed': Nazi Eugenics and the Origins of the Pioneer Fund." *Albany Law* 65: 748–828.

Lurie, Edward. 1954. "Louis Agassiz and the Races of Man." *Isis* 45: 227–242.

Marks, Jonathan. 1995. *Human Biodiversity: Genes, Race, and History.* New York: Aldine de Gruyter.

———. 2005 "Anthropology and *The Bell Curve.*" In *Why America's Top Pundits Are Wrong: Anthropologists Talk Back*, edited by Catherine Besteman and Hugh Gusterson, 206–227. Berkeley: University of California Press.

Massin, Benoit. 1996. "From Virchow to Fischer: Physical Anthropology and 'Modern Race Theories' in Wilhelmine Germany." In *Volksgeist as Method and Ethic: Essays on Boasian Ethnography and the German Anthropological Tradition*, edited by George Stocking. Madison: University of Wisconsin Press.

Mencken, Henry L. 1927. "On Eugenics." *Baltimore Sun,* May 15, 1927.

Muller, Hermann J. 1933. "The Dominance of Economics over Eugenics." *Scientific Monthly* 37: 40–47.

Müller-Hill, Benno. 1988. *Murderous Science: Elimination by Scientific Selection of Jews, Gypsies, and Others: Germany 1933–1945.* New York: Oxford University Press.

Odom, H. H. 1967. "Generalizations of Race in Nineteenth-Century Physical Anthropology." *Isis* (58): 5–18.

Paul, Diane B., and Hamish G. Spencer. 1995. "The Hidden Science of Eugenics." *Nature* 374: 302–304.

Pearl, Raymond. 1927. "The Biology of Superiority." *The American Mercury* 12: 257–266.

Plotz, David. 2005. *The Genius Factory: The Curious History of the Nobel Prize Sperm Bank.* New York: Random House.

Proctor, Robert N. 2003. "Three Roots of Human Recency: Molecular Anthropology, the Refigured Acheulean, and the UNESCO Response to Auschwitz." *Current Anthropology* 44: 213–239.

Provine, William B. 1973. "Geneticists and the Biology of Race Crossing." *Science* 182: 790–796.

Snowden, Frank M., Jr. 1948. "The Negro in Ancient Greece." *American Anthropologist* 50: 31–44.

Sommer, Marianne. 2005. "Ancient Hunters and their Modern Representatives: William Sollas's (1849–1936) Anthropology from Disappointed Bridge to Trunkless Tree and the Instrumentalisation of Racial Conflict." *Journal of the History of Biology* 38: 327–365.

Stanton, William R. 1960. *The Leopard's Spots: Scientific Attitudes toward Race in America, 1815–59.* Chicago: University of Chicago Press.

Stocking, George W., Jr. 1966. "Franz Boas and the Culture Concept in Historical Perspective." *American Anthropologist* 68: 867–882.

———. 1987. *Victorian Anthropology.* New York: Free Press.

Tobias, Philip V. 2002. "Saartje Baartman: Her Life, Her Remains, and the Negotiations for their Repatriation from France to South Africa." *South African Journal of Science* 98: 107–110.

Tucker, William H. 1994. *The Science and Politics of Racial Research.* Urbana: University of Illinois Press.

———. 2002. *The Funding of Scientific Racism: Wickliffe Draper and the Pioneer Fund.* Urbana: University of Illinois Press.

Washburn, Sherwood L. 1951. "The New Physical Anthropology." *Transactions of the New York Academy of Sciences, Series II.* 13: 298-304.

Weiner, Joseph S. 1957. "Physical Anthropology: An Appraisal." *American Scientist* 45: 79–89.

Jonathan Marks

SCOTTSBORO BOYS

The Scottsboro Boys case remains one of the most famous examples of racial injustice in the U.S. South during the Jim Crow era. What began with a lie told by two young white women in Alabama to avoid accusations of prostitution, ballooned into perhaps the most infamous legal case involving race in the 1930s, garnering not only national, but also international attention, and even the participation of the U.S. Communist Party. While the accusations landed nine black youths unfairly in prison for years (much of the time under death sentences), the case would commence a slow improvement for African Americans caught up in the southern judicial system, especially for black men accused of the ultimate crime against the repressive racial order of the Jim Crow South—the rape of a white woman.

The case of the Scottsboro Boys began on March 25, 1931. It was near the height of the Great Depression and an estimated 200,000 Americans were living then as virtual vagabonds on the nation's railroads, hopping freight cars from place to place in a desperate search for work. That day, a group of white rail-riders walked into Stevenson, Alabama, claiming some black men had assaulted and thrown them off a Memphis-bound freight train. Authorities promptly stopped the train and pulled off nine young black men. The assault charges they faced quickly grew much more serious when two female rail-riders, Ruby Bates and Victoria Price, accused the black youths of raping them.

The rape of a white woman by a black man was the most serious offense imaginable under Jim Crow. Indeed, thousands of black men were lynched (i.e., extra-legally executed) in the late nineteenth and early twentieth century in the U.S. South after having been accused of raping a white woman. Even worse, for a white woman to point the finger at a black man for rape was tantamount to conviction in the eyes of many white Southerners, and the offense considered so grave that in many localities the alleged perpetrator faced a mob-organized execution (usually by hanging) because an outraged white populace could not wait for justice through normal legal channels, where blacks accused of lesser offenses against Jim Crow usually were dealt with. Virtually all white Southerners in the 1930s, to varying degrees, saw African Americans as barely civilized and believed that black men secretly lusted after white women. They were quite ready to believe any accusation of rape leveled by a white woman against a black man and to deal with such offenders as uncivilized brutes who needed to be done away with quickly for the good of society.

Hence, when the Scottsboro Boys (as the nine young men became known)—Olen Montgomery, Clarence Norris, Haywood Patterson, Ozie Powell, Willie Roberson, Charlie Weems, Eugene Williams, and brothers Andrew and Leroy (Roy) Wright—were taken to Scottsboro, the seat of Jackson County, in far northeastern Alabama, for incarceration and trial, many white Southerners congratulated themselves for what they saw as a moderate, even enlightened response to the gravest of crimes. (Although

The Scottsboro Boys, 1931. *The Scottsboro Boys case remains one of the most famous examples of racial injustice in the U.S. South during the Jim Crow era. The nine men, seen here in an Alabama prison shortly after their arrest, were falsly accused of raping a white woman.* © BETTMANN/CORBIS.

Alabama governor Benjamin Meeks Miller, afraid of a lynching, still felt it necessary to guarantee the safety of the prisoners by sending 119 armed National Guardsmen to Scottsboro).

If Alabama and the white South felt pride at their restrained reaction to the accusations of gang rape of white women by black men, they squandered whatever goodwill garnered outside the region in the initial trials of the Scottsboro Boys. These proceedings were a travesty of justice. They took place in a carnival atmosphere that emphasized rather than concealed the white populace's furious mood, its anger stirred by wildly inflated rumors about the alleged rape. Given their race, poverty, and the horrific nature of the alleged crime, it proved impossible for the Scottsboro Boys to secure competent legal representation. They were forced to go on trial represented by Stephen R. Roddy, an alcoholic lawyer hired with money raised by leading black citizens in nearby Chattanooga, Tennessee. With inadequate representation and having already been convicted in the media, the outcome of the nine boys' trial was a foregone conclusion. Each of the Scottsboro Boys was quickly convicted by all-white juries and sentenced to death, except for thirteen-year-old Roy Wright whose jury could not unanimously decide on a death sentence due to his youth and whose case was declared a mistrial.

With the circumstances of the trials widely reported throughout the United States and abroad, outrage quickly developed outside the South against the verdicts and death sentences levied on the Scottsboro Boys. While many observers expected that the National Association for the Advancement of Colored People (NAACP) would step in to fund and manage the youths' appeals, the U.S. Communist Party, through its front organization, International Labor Defense (ILD), moved quicker to gain the allegiance of the nine men and their families. With the Great Depression causing many Americans to question the future of capitalism as they never had before, the Communists historically were at the peak of their popularity in the United

States, and saw the Scottsboro case as a way to make inroads among African Americans both in the South and elsewhere. As perhaps the only political organization of that era to practice as well as preach racial equality, the Communists were hopeful the case would garner mass support among black Americans and hasten what they believed would be the inevitable revolution of the working class against capitalism in the United States.

The speed with which the ILD took over the Scottsboro Boys' defense stunned the NAACP, which was initially reluctant to involve itself in the case until convinced of the nine young men's innocence. Its efforts to replace the Communists ignited a fight for control that would continue, off and on, for four years. The battle pitted the NAACP's relatively greater resources and respectability against the ILD's ideological fervor and ruthless determination. For example, the Communists made small payments to the families of the Scottsboro Boys and took some of their mothers on speaking tours to the North and abroad as a way of cementing the youths' allegiance. They would later go so far as to try and bribe Victoria Price to recant her original accusation. The fallout of such disasters and their lack of resources would force the ILD in late 1935 to join forces with the NAACP, the American Civil Liberties Union (ACLU), and other more moderate groups into the "Scottsboro Defense Committee." Nonetheless, the Communist Party through the ILD would take the lead role in organizing and funding the defense of the Scottsboro Boys in its early years.

ILD initially hired George W. Chamlee, a maverick Chattanooga attorney with a history of defending leftist radicals in the South, as the new defense counsel for the Scottsboro Boys. They felt the case needed a white Southerner who would have credibility with the Alabama Supreme Court. Chamlee based his appeal there on the inadequate counsel of Stephen R. Roddy in the original trial. While Chamlee's argument before the Alabama Supreme Court failed, it was a necessary step on the way to the U.S. Supreme Court, where the justices agreed to hear the case, *Powell v. Alabama,* and in November 1932 overturned the conviction of the Scottsboro Boys on the grounds of inadequate representation in the original trial.

The victory in the U.S. Supreme Court sent the case back to Alabama for retrial. Given the case's high profile, the Communists were able to retain for the Scottsboro Boys one of the best lawyers available: Samuel Leibowitz, a New Yorker and Romanian-born Jew, considered by many observers, after the retirement of Clarence Darrow, to be the finest criminal defense attorney in the United States. In fifteen years as a practicing criminal attorney, Leibowitz had not yet had a client convicted. Leibowitz took the case pro bono on the condition that he would work independently of ILD, whose role would be limited to fundraising and generating public support for Scottsboro Boys (a limitation the Communists were ill-prepared to accept in practice and one that would inevitably lead to repeated clashes with Leibowitz).

Despite his mounting a first-class defense for his nine clients during the second round of trials in March 1933, Samuel Leibowitz's logic and eloquence were insufficient in the face of white southern prejudice. Although the defense was able to obtain a change of venue in the second trial from Scottsboro to Decatur, Alabama (fifty miles to the west), they were still dealing with all-white juries imbued with the Jim Crow system. Indeed, Leibowitz's attempts to discredit Victoria Price as a witness backfired because the Decatur jury, instead of seeing the clear problems with her account, was instead gravely offended that a New York Jew would dare question a white southern women's assertion that she had been raped by African Americans. Despite the fact that Ruby Bates, Price's co-complainant, recanted her accusations at the second trial and the medical testimony clearly indicated no rape had ever occurred, the jury that decided the fate of the first Scottsboro defendant who was re-tried, Haywood Patterson, quickly convicted him and fixed his sentence again at death.

Surprisingly, while Leibowitz had offended the Patterson jury, he had convinced the judge that presided over the Decatur retrial, James Horton, of the Scottsboro Boys' innocence. The first sign of Horton's sentiments came after Patterson's conviction. The judge suspended further proceedings for the other eight defendants because the inflamed public sentiments evident after the Patterson's conviction would clearly prevent them from getting a fair trial. After a three-month delay, Judge Horton granted a defense motion in June 1933 that Patterson receive a new trial. His sentiments reflected the opinion among a small but growing group of moderate whites in Alabama that were willing to entertain the notion the Scottsboro Boys might be innocent or at least did not deserve the death penalty. Yet the vast majority of white Alabamians remained firmly convinced of the need to convict and execute the nine defendants, and made persons with more moderate opinions pay a price if they exhibited them too publicly. For example, Horton failed to retain his judgeship when he came up for reelection in 1934.

The third round of trials, which began in November 1933, reflected the will of most whites in Alabama to press the proceedings toward the conviction and execution of the Scottsboro Boys, whatever it took. Leading the effort to continue the prosecution was Alabama's attorney general, Thomas G. Knight, who had been a central figure in the case since he had argued his state's case before the U.S. Supreme Court in *Powell v. Alabama*. Knight led the prosecution team personally in Haywood Patterson's retrial and in the third round of trials. He found an ally in

William Washington Callahan, the judge who took over the case when proceedings resumed on November 20, 1933, in Decatur, Alabama. Callahan rejected Leibowitz's motions for a change of venue and his efforts to challenge the exclusion of African Americans from the jury pool in Morgan County, Alabama. He also placed severe restrictions on Leibowitz's ability to question Price on her activities prior to the alleged rape, tantamount to blocking the lawyer's ability to cross-examine her adequately. Callahan also frequently added his own objections to those of Knight, and his instructions to the jury essentially served as a second summation for the prosecution. The judge also tried to use the post-trial procedures to create technicalities to deny Leibowitz's ability to appeal the guilty verdict and Patterson's third death sentence.

In any case, the Alabama Supreme Court rejected Leibowitz's appeal on behalf of Patterson, and the case once again went before the U.S. Supreme Court. The appeal was complicated not only by the procedural roadblock created by Judge Callahan, but also because at this time the attempt of ILD to bribe Price became public. The revelation led to a temporary break in relations between Leibowitz and the ILD, which were repaired in time for the oral arguments before the U.S. Supreme Court in February 1935. Unlike before, the Scottsboro Boys' second appeal to the nation's highest court was based on the exclusion of African Americans from the jury pool in Decatur, Alabama. Leibowitz had carefully made an issue of this practice during jury selection in the trials there. His argument before the justices was bolstered by clear evidence that someone had amateurishly inserted names of potential black jurors to the juror rolls before the Decatur trials presided over by Judge Callahan in an attempt to conceal the longstanding exclusion of African Americans from juries there. Although the Supreme Court refused to make new case law in its decision of the second appeal, it remanded the case back to the Alabama Supreme Court with the clear implication that if the Alabama justices did not order a new trial, it would review the case again. (The Alabama Supreme Court complied.)

Yet the second victory of the Scottsboro Boys in the U.S. Supreme Court did not soften the opinions of most white people in Alabama. As the premier historian of the Scottsboro case, Dan T. Carter, stated of white Alabamians,

> The majority ... had adopted the position that mass electrocution was necessary in order to insure the 'social stability of this section,' observed John Temple Graves, II. It was the 'inflexible if misguided conviction of many Alabamians ... that [even after three rounds of trials] a fresh start be made in the business of getting the accused men to the electric chair'." (Carter 1979, pp. 328–29)

Hence, a fourth round of trials began in Decatur, Alabama, in January 1936, with Patterson going first. Leibowitz, although still chief counsel for the defense, was not as prominent as in the earlier trials because he had by this time become a hated figure among white Alabamians for his uncompromising courtroom style, especially his firm cross-examinations of Price, and the fact he was a New York Jew, something that had been politely overlooked prior to his assault on southern womanhood. Judge Callahan remained in charge and continued making his own objections to questions posed by the defense and generally making no secret of his contempt for them. Yet Patterson's 1936 trial proved something of a breakthrough: when after his inevitable conviction, the jury, rather than sentencing him to death, set down his punishment as imprisonment for seventy-five years.

The prison sentence for Patterson demonstrated that as committed as conservative whites in Alabama were to the conviction and execution of all of the Scottsboro Boys to preserve white supremacy, a more moderate and pragmatic element in the state was willing to engineer a face-saving compromise to end the judicial proceedings once and for all. The negotiations of the compromise remain unclear, but the basic terms quickly took shape. First, prosecution would be dropped against those defendants with the weakest cases against them in terms of their alleged culpability for the assault on the white rail-riders. Second, the convictions against the remaining defendants would stand, but they would be not be sentenced to death and eventually would be pardoned and set free. Furthering the atmosphere for compromise was the sudden death, in July 1937, of Thomas G. Knight. Knight had tied his political career to convicting the Scottsboro Boys, and had even continued to lead the prosecution team after his election as Alabama's lieutenant governor in November 1934. While many white Alabamians, Judge Callahan in particular, wanted to continue with the prosecution of all the Scottsboro Boys for rape, Knight's death removed their most effective advocate.

In other words, Knight's death apparently made possible what became known as the "Compromise of 1937." Despite the fact that Clarence Norris went on trial again for his life on July 12, 1937, and despite the fact he was again convicted and sentenced to death, rumors that a grand bargain involving all the Scottsboro Boys was in the making circulated in the press. These rumors continued even when Charlie Weems was convicted of rape in his 1937 trial and sentenced to seventy-five years, as had been the case with Patterson. They took on reality when Ozie Powell was brought to court for his trial, and Judge Callahan informed him the rape charges against him had been dropped and he would instead be prosecuted for assaulting a deputy sheriff (an incident that had occurred during Patterson's last trial). Powell pled guilty to the assault charge and Callahan sentenced him to twenty years. Charges were then quickly dropped against Olen Montgomery, Willie Roberson, Eugene Williams, and Roy Wright. These four men were quickly whisked by Leibowitz out of Alabama to New York City, where they received a hero's welcome, but then quickly slipped into obscurity (and in some cases continued to live troubled lives).

The pardons for the remaining Scottsboro defendants still in prison were slow in coming. Governor Bibb Graves of Alabama refused quick pardons, but he did commute the death sentence of Clarence Norris to life imprisonment. Evidently, Graves believed that if he released the remaining Scottsboro Boys it would be the end of his political career. As the U.S. Supreme Court refused further appeals and President Franklin Roosevelt declined to exert more than gentle pressure on Graves, the five men left in prison remained incarcerated for years. It would take a world war and fading memories for freedom to become possible for them. Having finally entered the Alabama corrections system, their cases came under the control of the Alabama Board of Pardons and Paroles. It apparently opted for a policy of gradually releasing without fanfare the remaining Scottsboro Boys. The first to bet set free was Charley Weems in November 1943. In January 1944, it paroled Andrew Wright and Clarence Norris. The two men fled the state, in violation of their paroles, were persuaded to return and were re-imprisoned. This episode put a temporary stop to the releases until near the end of 1946, when the board released Powell and re-paroled Norris. Patterson, considered by his jailers the most incorrigible of the Scottsboro Boys, escaped from a work detail in 1948 and successfully eluded recapture, making his way to Michigan, where he permanently gained freedom because the governor of the state refused to extradite him. In 1950, when Wright was re-paroled, the last of the men arrested in 1931 finally went free for good. They, like their compatriots freed in 1937, also faded into obscurity.

Clearly, the resolution of the Scottsboro case was designed in the end for the racist Alabama justice system to save face. Yet it also signaled to the white South that, unlike in the past, people outside the region were watching, not only in the rest of the United States but abroad as well. While racist injustice did not end overnight, change was in the wind, and the Scottsboro Boys helped demonstrate by the 1970s just how much the southern justice system had changed. After NBC in 1976 showed a made-for-television docudrama on the Scottsboro case, Norris, apparently the last surviving Scottsboro Boy, resurfaced asking for a full and unconditional pardon. Alabama governor George Wallace readily gave this pardon. Granted by a politician who had initially made his career as a segregationist but experienced a change of heart, it was a fitting bookend to the case since a "full and unconditional" pardon was generally reserved for those cases where the state recognized the original prosecution and conviction itself had been erroneous.

BIBLIOGRAPHY

Carter, Dan T. 1979. *Scottsboro: A Tragedy of the American South*, rev. ed. Baton Rogue: Louisiana State University Press.

Chalmers, Allan Knight. 1951. *They Shall Be Free*. Garden City, NY: Doubleday.

Goodman, James. 1994. *Stories of Scottsboro*. New York: Pantheon.

Kinshasa, Kwando Mbiassi. 1997. *The Man from Scottsboro: Clarence Norris and the Infamous 1931 Alabama Rape Trial in His Own Words*. Jefferson, NC: McFarland.

Miller, James A., Susan D. Pennybacker, and Eve Rosenhaft. 2001. "Mother Ada Wright and the International Campaign to Free the Scottsboro Boys." *American Historical Review* 106 (April): 387–430.

Norris, Clarence, and Sybil D. Washington. 1979. *The Last of the Scottsboro Boys: An Autobiography*. New York: G. P. Putnam.

Patterson, Haywood, and Earl Conrad. 1950. *Scottsboro Boy*. Garden City, NY: Doubleday.

Donald R. Shaffer

SECOND KLAN

The most notorious white supremacist organization in American history, the Ku Klux Klan (KKK), has assumed various forms over time. The original Klan was organized shortly after the end of the Civil War and engaged in violent activities against African Americans and white Republicans in the South. Four decades later, however, a second Klan, the Knights of the Ku Klux Klan, would appear and evolve into a mass social and political movement that attracted the support of millions of Americans during the 1920s.

ORIGINS OF THE SECOND KU KLUX KLAN

The establishment and success of the second Klan largely resulted from a shift in popular attitudes concerning the original KKK. Although the first Klan had been, by any standard, a lawless terrorist organization, the passage of time had imbued it with a romantic aura that appealed to the racist sensibilities of many white Americans in the early twentieth century. The Klan's improved public image was well shown by the remarkable popularity of Thomas Dixon's novels, *The Leopard's Spots* (1902) and *The Clansman* (1905), both of which presented the KKK as intrepid freedom fighters arrayed against the sinister elements that imperiled Anglo-Saxon civilization. This assessment received academic endorsement from influential scholars who emphasized the alleged mistreatment of white southerners by the Radical Republicans and their black allies during Reconstruction. As historian and future president Woodrow Wilson emphasized, the "white men of the South were aroused by the mere instinct of self-preservation"

(Wilson 1902, p. 58) to take up arms against those who threatened their way of life.

In 1914, the famous movie director David Wark (D.W.) Griffith purchased the film rights to *The Clansman* and began work on his cinematic epic *The Birth of a Nation*. For nearly two decades after its release in 1915, the film remained immensely popular. Never before had the public been exposed to cinematography in a way that so successfully stirred emotions and reinforced racial prejudices. Moreover, many viewers were convinced that the film was not a mere exercise in fiction. Having muted many of the excesses found in Dixon's novel, Griffith argued that *The Birth of a Nation* was solidly grounded in historical fact. As the *New York Times* would favorably note in 1916, Americans in all parts of the country were "being taught to idealize the Klan."

The vogue of the Klan created by the popularity of *The Birth of a Nation* presented an opportunity for a revival of the secret organization. For several years, William J. Simmons, a former Methodist circuit rider and recruiter for men's fraternal societies in Atlanta, had considered starting a new Klan, composing an elaborate ritual and designing the masked costume that would become so well known. In the fall of 1915, shortly before the Atlanta premiere of *The Birth of a Nation*, Simmons, who assumed the title Imperial Wizard, began recruiting members for the new KKK, which he would formally incorporate in the state of Georgia as the Knights of the Ku Klux Klan. Public acknowledgement of the hooded order's revival came on Thanksgiving night of that year, as Simmons and fifteen other Klansmen burned a cross at the summit of nearby Stone Mountain.

The new Klan was at first a mere shadow of its predecessor. Though founded on the principles of "100 percent Americanism" and a militant defense of Protestantism and white supremacy, the group was a fairly typical men's fraternity that concentrated on Masonic-style rituals and the selling of group-rate insurance. American entry into World War I encouraged the Klan to assume a more active role, as its members engaged in the harassment of those they perceived to be enemy aliens and draft evaders, but the KKK's membership remained small, consisting of only a handful of klaverns (local Klan chapters) in Georgia and Alabama. Imperial Wizard Simmons's mediocre leadership skills and chronic financial problems hindered recruiting, and it appeared that the second Klan would probably soon fade away.

REORGANIZATION AND EARLY GROWTH OF THE SECOND KLAN

Desperate to breathe new life into his organization, Simmons in 1920 turned to the Southern Publicity Association, a small public relations firm owned by Edward Young Clarke and Elizabeth Tyler. Skilled salespeople, Clarke and Tyler quickly recognized the Klan's potential for growth, especially if the group more forcefully emphasized its defense of white Protestant Americans against the alleged threat posed by blacks, Catholics, Jews, and immigrants. The early 1920s was an unsettled period still afflicted with the superpatriotism and intolerant zeal of the war years, and longstanding traditions of racism, nativism, and religious bigotry could easily be exploited. Clarke and Tyler also took important steps to improve the Klan's finances and recruiting practices, employing more than a thousand paid recruiters (kleagles) who surreptitiously went from community to community spreading the KKK's message.

Working on commission, kleagles tailored their sales pitch to attract as many recruits as possible. In many instances the KKK's intolerant stance on race and religion was openly emphasized, but recruiters also stressed the hooded order's potential for improving law enforcement, maintaining traditional moral values, and holding corrupt political officials to account. Much of the Klan's early recruiting was done in established men's organizations like the Masons and the Odd Fellows, the kleagles touting the Klan's rich fraternal life and the possibility for making new sales contacts. Thus, while racial and religious intolerance clearly served as the organization's main drawing card, this bigotry was interwoven with a variety of other appeals.

By the summer of 1921 the Klan's improved solicitation procedures began to yield remarkable results, especially in the states of Louisiana, Arkansas, Oklahoma, and Texas, where tens of thousands of new Klansmen entered the fold. In this region, anger over poor law enforcement and a perceived collapse in traditional social morality sustained the organization, with many Klansmen resorting to violent vigilantism. In Texas alone in 1921 there were hundreds of beatings, whippings, and other types of assaults, with both whites and African Americans being targeted. Although the authorities often tried to suppress this violence, it proved difficult to prosecute Klansmen because of the group's tight secrecy and because Klan members on grand juries and in police departments protected their own.

The outbreak of Klan-associated violence in 1921 was extensively detailed in the national press and placed pressure on federal officials to address what appeared to be a deteriorating situation. Shortly after the Joseph Pulitzer–owned *New York World* presented a widely distributed exposé of the Klan that portrayed the group as being inherently lawless, financially corrupt, and violent, the United States House Rules Committee held hearings in October 1921 to determine whether there was a need for governmental action. Despite the best efforts of the KKK's critics, little concrete information came to light, and many Americans concluded that the hooded order had been exonerated of any wrongdoing. As a result, Klan recruiting soared as never before in the months right after the hearings.

NATIONAL EXPANSION

As early as 1920, the Klan had dispatched kleagles to communities outside the South, and by 1922, assisted by the abundance of free publicity resulting from the congressional hearings, their recruiting efforts began to garner impressive results. Several factors contributed to the KKK's expansion to regions where the hooded order had never previously existed. First, and most importantly, the powerful strains of racism, anti-Catholicism, anti-Semitism, and nativism that the Klan exploited were not exclusive to the South. When Klan representatives arrived in the North, Midwest, and West and stressed the need for native-born white Protestants to remain ascendant in America, they found a receptive audience, especially at a time of growing anti-immigration sentiment and anxiety over the increased northward migration of African Americans. Secondly, Americans across the nation, just like southerners, had embraced the romantic and positive image of the Klan presented in *The Birth of a Nation*, and were eager to participate in what appeared to be a novel and exciting movement that stood for admirable values. And thirdly, widespread concerns over rapid social change, a breakdown of effective law enforcement, and political corruption had created a sense among many white Protestant men that some type of forceful action had to be taken to protect their families and communities. Through the Klan, the kleagles stressed, true Americans could band together and oppose the dangerous trends of the times.

From 1922 to 1925, the Klan evolved into a true mass movement, recruiting approximately 5 million men and hundreds of thousands of women, who were organized into the Kamelia and the Women of the Klan, the KKK's two female auxiliaries. In the South, the hooded order encountered the greatest success in Georgia, Alabama, Florida, and Texas, the latter state's membership exceeding 200,000. New York and Pennsylvania together had nearly half a million members, with hundreds of thousands more in Ohio, Michigan, Wisconsin, and Illinois. In Indiana, fully one-fourth of all American-born white Protestant men joined the Klan. In the West, Colorado and Oregon became bastions of pro-Klan sentiment. During this heady period of growth, it seemed that the Klan could very likely become an enduring force in American life.

The Klan's opponents were quick to characterize the hooded order as a movement of fanatical, poorly educated, and economically insecure individuals from the declining villages and small towns of rural America. This, however, was an inaccurate and biased assessment. More than half of all Klansmen resided in urban areas, often large cities like Chicago, Detroit, and Dallas, and the KKK's most prominent leaders were longtime urban residents. Moreover, Klan membership rolls and other official documents reveal that Klansmen were, compared to the overall white male population, significantly above average in terms of socioeconomic standing, being overrepresented in the professions and other prestigious forms of employment. Klansmen typically belonged to mainstream Protestant churches (not small fundamentalist denominations, as was routinely claimed) and were often young family men looking to improve their communities and advance their careers. Nonetheless, these men had willingly joined a secret society that, as numerous undercover reports of Klan activities confirm, lied, conspired, broke the law, and wallowed in the vilest forms of bigotry. That Klan members were otherwise respectable and successful citizens provides strong evidence, therefore, that racism and religious intolerance were not confined to the fringes of society in the 1920s. These dark impulses, to a significant extent, also afflicted the social and economic mainstream.

THE KLAN ENTERS POLITICS

Its phenomenal growth notwithstanding, the Klan found itself beset by internal problems in the fall of 1922. Angered by a morals scandal involving Edward Clarke and Elizabeth Tyler, and displeased by Imperial Wizard Simmons's continued weak leadership, a small group of Klan officials in the group's Atlanta headquarters succeeded in removing Simmons from his post and replacing him with Hiram W. Evans, a dentist from Texas who had previously served as Exalted Cyclops (klavern president) of the Dallas Klan. Soon afterward, Clarke and Tyler ceased their affiliation with the KKK, but Simmons launched a series of lawsuits that kept the Klan in legal turmoil until a final financial settlement was reached in 1924. This internecine squabbling divided the Klan for a period into pro-Simmons and pro-Evans factions, and did little to inspire confidence among the group's rank and file.

The rise of Evans meant that the Klan would become more involved in politics. The new imperial wizard, in contrast to his predecessor, possessed an ability for long-range planning, and it was his hope to turn the Klan into a powerful political machine. Secretly determining which candidates to support and then using Klan votes as a decisive bloc at polling time, the KKK, working within both the Republican and Democratic parties, became an important factor in state politics in Texas, Oregon, Louisiana, Georgia, Alabama, Colorado, and Indiana from 1922 to 1927. One of the hooded order's first political successes took place in Imperial Wizard Evans's home state of Texas, where in 1922 the Klan's candidate, Earle B. Mayfield, defeated former governor James Ferguson for the

Democratic nomination for United States senator. Obscuring his connection to the KKK and stressing Ferguson's past record of corruption and opposition to prohibition and moral reform, Mayfield attracted the support of many non-Klan voters who were unhappy with established politicians and the general direction of American society. Klan leaders such as John Galen Locke in Colorado and David C. (D. C.) Stephenson in Indiana used a similar approach: They built powerful political organizations by exploiting widespread resentment toward what was perceived to be the corrupt and undemocratic policies of government officials and business elites. The general thrust of the KKK's political efforts, therefore, was populist in nature, the secret order posing as the champion of ordinary citizens who wanted to take back control of their country and revitalize it in accordance with the traditional values of native-white Protestantism. This approach was so successful, and intimidating, that neither the Republicans nor the Democrats were willing to denounce the Klan at their national conventions in 1924.

While the Klan's successes in state and national politics were impressive, the organization's political clout was most profoundly felt at the local level. Although on paper the Klan appeared to possess a tightly organized hierarchy, local klaverns operated with considerable independence and modified their programs according to local circumstances. In some communities, like Detroit, the hooded order stressed the alleged peril of African American migration and pressed for segregation in the public schools. In El Paso, Texas, the Klan exploited anger over an inadequately funded public school system, while Klansmen in Denver focused on government corruption and an alleged breakdown in law enforcement. In much the same way that kleagles adapted their sales pitch to attract as many recruits as possible, Klan leaders opportunistically shaped their political programs in the context of the local grassroots issues that could be most successfully exploited. Imperial Wizard Evans openly encouraged this approach, urging that Klansmen not "put into effect any set program, for there are different needs in the various localities." But while the emphasis of Klan political activism varied from community to community, the organization's overall agenda remained clear: the maintenance of native-white Protestant dominance, stricter enforcement of the law (especially Prohibition), and the defense of traditional social and cultural values.

Ultimately, the Klan's entry into politics accomplished little. Despite scores of victories in state and local elections from 1922 to 1927, the hooded order and its allies routinely failed to implement measures that successfully addressed popular concerns over law enforcement, moral issues, public education, and other grassroots issues. Moreover, Klan-backed officials often proved to be just as inept and corrupt as their predecessors. One of the KKK's few legislative successes came in Oregon, where the Klan helped

The Second Klan. *Imperial Wizard Hiram W. Evans leads his Knights of the Ku Klux Klan on a parade in Washington D.C. in 1926. Evans hoped to turn the Klan into a powerful political machine.* THE LIBRARY OF CONGRESS.

secure passage of a bill that required all children age eight to sixteen to attend the public schools, a measure that effectively outlawed parochial education. This law was invalidated by the U.S. Supreme Court in 1925, eighteen months before it was scheduled to take effect.

Increasingly in the mid-1920s, the Klan itself became a political issue. The group's hooded secrecy, its use of anonymous messages and cross-burnings to intimidate opponents, and its use of violence and the threat of violence appeared to many citizens to be inherently un-American and a violation of the principles of free and open government. While the Klan had originally seemed a promising means of reordering American society in accordance with white Protestant values, its deficiencies now clearly seemed to outweigh its virtues.

THE DECLINE OF THE KLAN

From 1925 on, the Klan experienced a steep decline in both membership and influence. The romantic allure that had first sustained the organization had faded away, and open bickering among Klan leaders continued to undermine recruiting efforts. The successful prosecution of Indiana Klan leader D. C. Stephenson for the second-degree murder of a young woman in 1925 further tarnished the KKK's reputation and convinced the Klan's opponents to redouble their efforts to undermine the hooded order. By then, a number of states had passed laws prohibiting the wearing of masks in public, and New York had enacted the Walker Law, which required all secret oath-bound societies to file a list of their membership with the state. At the same time, a variety of anti-Klan organizations, such as the Chicago-based American Unity League, hired undercover informers who acquired Klan membership lists, which were subsequently revealed to the public. In Buffalo, New York, the city's Roman Catholic mayor had an agent break into the local Klan's business office and steal the group's membership records, which were then put on public display and published in pamphlet form. These roughshod tactics proved very effective. Unmasked and exposed, the KKK was no longer the intimidating political and social force it had once been, and members began to depart in droves.

Despite the best efforts of Imperial Wizard Evans, who had moved the Klan's headquarters to Washington, DC, the hooded order's membership steadily dwindled. Even the selection of New York Governor Alfred E. Smith, a Roman Catholic, as the Democratic nominee for president in 1928 was not enough to revive the organization's fortunes, with the result that active Klansmen numbered only 30,000 by 1930. Over the next decade, most klaverns focused on fraternal activities, but occasionally the Klan would publicly denounce labor activists, Communists, and New Deal legislation. In 1939, Evans stepped down as imperial wizard and was replaced by James Colescott, a longtime Klan organizer and former veterinarian from Terre Haute, Indiana. Colescott proved to be an uninspiring leader, and he was unable to restore the Klan to health. He also faced a serious challenge to his leadership when a number of northern klaverns developed a close relationship with the pro-Nazi German American Bund, an alliance opposed by southern Klansmen. The Klan's flirtation with the Bund and its continuing criticism of the government after American entry into World War II attracted the attention of federal authorities, who in 1944 belatedly presented the KKK with a huge tax bill for money the group had earned during its heyday in the 1920s. Unable to pay the bill, the Knights of the Ku Klux Klan liquidated its few assets and formally disbanded.

SEE ALSO *Ku Klux Klan; Race Riots (U.S.), 1917-1923.*

BIBLIOGRAPHY

Chalmers, David M. 1987. *Hooded Americanism: The History of the Ku Klux Klan,* 3rd ed. Durham, NC: Duke University Press.

Goldberg, Robert A. 1981. *Hooded Empire: The Ku Klux Klan in Colorado.* Urbana: University of Illinois Press.

Jackson, Kenneth T. 1992. *The Ku Klux Klan in the City, 1915–1930.* Chicago: Ivan R. Dee.

Lay, Shawn. 1995. *Hooded Knights on the Niagara: The Ku Klux Klan in Buffalo, New York.* New York: New York University Press.

———, ed. 2004. *The Invisible Empire in the West: Toward a New Historical Appraisal of the Ku Klux Klan of the 1920s.* Urbana: University of Illinois Press.

MacLean, Nancy. 1994. *Behind the Mask of Chivalry: The Making of the Second Ku Klux Klan.* New York: Oxford University Press.

Moore, Leonard J. 1991. *Citizen Klansmen: The Ku Klux Klan in Indiana, 1921–1928.* Chapel Hill: University of North Carolina Press.

Wade, Wyn Craig. 1987. *The Fiery Cross: The Ku Klux Klan in America.* New York: Simon and Schuster.

Wilson, Woodrow A. 1902. *A History of the American People,* vol. 5. New York: Harper & Brothers.

Shawn Lay

SECRET ARMY ORGANIZATION

SEE *Organisation Armée Secrète (Secret Army Organization).*

SEX WORK

Sex work is a multidimensional concept used to redefine sex-related services as income-generating labor. In the broadest sense, sex work refers to all aspects of the lawful and unlawful global sex industry—including street prostitution, massage parlors, brothels, escort services, strip clubs, phone-sex operators, pornography, and sex tourism—as well as the particular social, cultural, political, and economic circumstances that make selling sex a viable option. Within the context of race and racism, sex work represents a contemporary manifestation of race-based sexual exploitation with deep historical roots in slavery and colonialism. Structural inequality, race, and gender intersect in myriad ways within systems of global capitalism to produce disparity and desperation.

Although sex work is often a manifestation of women's economic marginalization, exposure to and experiences in sex work are influenced by race as a reinforcing marker of difference. Crosscultural research suggests that the stereotype of male desire is embodied by youthful whiteness with straight blond hair and creamy skin; therefore, women of color experience restricted access to the most lucrative positions within the sex industry. Although white women from the lower economic classes may face unequal access within sex work, they escape the tripartite system of race, class, and gender relegating

Cuban Prostitutes Proposition a Tourist. *Havana prostitutes can make more money in one day from foreign tourists than a professional government employee can earn in a month.* AP IMAGES.

black and brown women to the lowest rungs of the global socioeconomic ladder. In a world in which hundreds of millions of women live in abject poverty, a majority of these marginalized people are additionally affected by processes of racialization that reinforce a binary opposition between whiteness and blackness. Selling sex within this particular system of racial oppression brings sex workers face to face with a neocolonial agenda of white domination, originally established through marketing black bodies as a personal and private commodity in the political economy of slavery.

Women of color frequently enter into sex work as an alternative to low-wage service sector jobs offering no opportunity for advancement. However, negotiating race and racism opens them up to a host of disadvantages. Sex workers report that discrimination within the industry often means they end up walking the streets in dangerous areas, increasing the risk of police harassment and violent attacks. Nonwhite sex workers receive lower wages for sexual services than their white counterparts, yet they are more heavily targeted for fines, arrest, and imprisonment. Adding insult to injury, women of color must constantly contend with the racialized characteristics that define them as less desirable: wearing wigs to hide their kinky hair, altering their speech to sound more white, or dressing more in keeping with accepted notions of ethnic exoticism, thus giving in to the "jungle" fantasy that some white patrons require. As a result, these women suggest that experiences of racial denigration eventually develop into personal insecurities and self-doubt, thereby reinforcing their subordinate position within the industry, society, and their personal lives.

COLONIZATIONS OLD AND NEW

The heavy burden of race and racism facing black sex workers began centuries ago with the enslavement of their African ancestors. For generations the political economy of slavery in the New World exploited sexual labor to satisfy the economic, political, and personal interests of the white owner class. Enslaved men and women, particularly in the U.S. South, reproduced the slave workforce through a calculated system of slave breeding, while desirable females were offered up by the plantation master for additional profits. This system of structural inequality transformed black bodies into economic commodities, thus establishing an ideological foundation for a worldwide reinvestment in the racial inequality and patriarchal capitalism defining the twenty-first century—often referred to as globalization. Many feminist scholars recognize this system as a *recolonization* effort within which race and gender are reasserted economically, socially, and politically. For women of color, these forces translate into greater instability in the formal economy, making informal activities such as sex work unusually appealing.

The developing regions of the Caribbean and Latin America represent a microcosm of this global reality. In an effort to penetrate the world market, many nations have pursued tourism as an economic development strategy, assisted by international lending agencies such as the International Monetary Fund (IMF) and World Bank. The policies mandated by these lending agencies redirect infrastructural investment funds away from social programs toward building a market for the target industry. Once established, the tourist economy offers extremely limited opportunities to the local labor force, which has exaggerated consequences for women and children. Consequently, desperate women find themselves marketing an age-old fantasy of white domination and hypersexuality. With assistance from tourism officials, sex workers in the Caribbean and Latin America have created a booming industry around the exotics of racial difference.

Throughout these regions, whiteness occupies a privileged position in the social hierarchy, while blackness is associated with labor and service. More important, race is continually being reinforced by the exoticization of the black female body to increase tourist revenue. Women of color are portrayed as wildly sexual and animalistic, thus naturalizing their involvement in sex work. In places such as Cuba, Brazil, and the Dominican Republic, this conflation of race and sexuality has become part of the national identity. Popular cultural sentiments only serve to reinforce these racial categories. For example, nearly identical sayings in Brazil and Cuba translate as, "white women for marrying, black women for work, and *mulatas* [mixed-race women] for making love." Categories such as these, while legitimizing white male desires to experience the exotic "other," draw attention to one of the most important aspects of race-making: whiteness as the standard of beauty and purity. The desirability of mixed-race women has everything to do with the characteristics of whiteness they possess and the way those visual characteristics are perfectly mixed with the primal sexuality of blackness. By casting sex workers as naturally hypersexual, tourism advertisements justify the sexual exploitation of women of color. This commodification of otherness must be addressed in light of the glaring human rights abuses associated with marketing sex under the guise of generating tourist revenues.

Sex work, as a political statement associated with the ongoing struggle between exploitation and body politics, continues to gain momentum as an acknowledgment of the sex worker's contributions to the economic market. The unwillingness of most countries to legitimize sex work as a valid means of employment prevents sex workers from adequate protection under the law, while increasing the stigma, isolation, and invisibility of both the industry and the workers. The simultaneous criminalization of sex work sustains a discourse of deviance and immorality that further victimizes disenfranchised workers often caught in desperate economic situations. Global reluctance to engage in meaningful dialogue about the push and pull factors of sex work minimizes the accountability factor for law enforcement officials, governmental agencies, and health care workers. Therefore, sex workers continue to shoulder the blame for their involvement in one of the world's oldest and most controversial professions.

The resulting frustration has prompted worldwide resistance, with empowerment movements framing the issue in terms of international human rights. Sex workers continue to demand recognition as "workers" who contribute their labor to the market, based on articles within both the *Universal Declaration of Human Rights* (adopted in 1948 by the United Nations General Assembly) and the *Convention on the Elimination of All Forms of Discrimination Against Women* (CEDAW) (adopted in 1979 by the UN General Assembly), that proclaim the "inalienable right of all human beings to work and to freely choose their job or profession." Increased dialogue on the issue has introduced a broader debate about human agency, autonomy, and sexual politics.

The historical relationship between sexuality and race offers distinct examples of how women of color have manipulated their sexuality to redefine cultural norms. In the early twentieth century, for example, women of color exploited the black underworld to become "jook joint" women and sex workers in black and white brothels across the United States. Although some view these steps toward economic betterment as a symbol of sexual independence, others suggest they must be firmly positioned within a global reality of gender inequality. As women of color make a place for themselves in areas of the sex industry that have long denied them access, such as strip clubs and pornography, does that signify their power of self-representation or their collusion with a system that views their bodies as a commodity? Can their participation be viewed as a conscious choice when race and gender inequality still define the parameters of employment economics? These are among the most important unresolved debates about the relationships among race, racism, and sex work. What can be asserted without hesitation, however, is that race continues to be a powerful tool in the marginalization and disenfranchisement of women on a global scale.

SEE ALSO *Body Politics; Feminism and Race; Pornography; Poverty; Sexuality.*

BIBLIOGRAPHY

Andersen, Margaret L., and Patricia Hill Collins, eds. 2007. *Race, Class, and Gender: An Anthology*, 6th ed. Belmont, MA: Thomson/Wadsworth.

Ditmore, Melissa Hope, ed. 2006. *Encyclopedia of Prostitution and Sex Work.* Westport, CT: Greenwood.

Gilliam, Angela M. 2001. "A Black Feminist Perspective on the Sexual Commodification of Women in the New Global Culture." In *Black Feminist Anthropology: Theory, Politics,*

Praxis, and Poetics, edited by Irma McClaurin, 150–186. New Brunswick, NJ: Rutgers University Press.

Harley, Sharon, and the Black Women and Work Collective, eds. 2002. *Sister Circle: Black Women and Work*. New Brunswick, NJ: Rutgers University Press.

Harrison, Faye V., ed. 2005. *Resisting Racism and Xenophobia: Global Perspectives on Race, Gender, and Human Rights*. Walnut Creek, CA: AltaMira Press.

hooks, bell. 1992. *Black Looks: Race and Representation*. Boston: South End Press.

Kempadoo, Kamala. 2004. *Sexing the Caribbean: Gender, Race, and Sexual Labor*. New York: Routledge.

Kempner, Martha A. 2005. *Sex Workers: Perspectives in Public Health and Human Rights*. SIECUS Report 33 (2). Available from www.sexworkersproject.org/downloads/SIECUS2005.pdf.

Nagle, Jill, ed. 1997. *Whores and Other Feminists*. New York: Routledge.

Melissa D. Hargrove

SEXISM

Sexism consists of a set of attitudes, beliefs, and practices that assume that women are naturally inferior to men in a variety of ways and that use this alleged natural inferiority to promote, protect, and enforce male privilege and deny women full participation in society. Societies that institutionalize male privilege and women's subordination are said to be "patriarchal" in nature. In such male-dominated societies, male privilege is built into virtually every institution and every aspect of culture, so that women's subordination and men's domination are normalized and experienced as natural. In this way, sexist attitudes, policies, and practices reinforce the status quo through the workings of everyday life.

As with racism, sexism can be conscious or unconscious, intentional or unintentional. What defines sexist behavior is not the motivation behind it but the consequences that flow from it. In this regard, failing to hire a woman in order to protect her from work the employer believes is too dangerous is as sexist as failing to hire her because of a belief that women are not as smart as men. In both cases, women are denied equal opportunity. In the same way, a well-meaning teacher who compliments female students on what they are wearing and male students on what they are doing perpetuates sexist stereotypes, regardless of his or her intentions. Other examples of sexism include applying a double standard to men and women so that sexual behavior considered acceptable for men is considered inappropriate for women; preventing women from competing in sporting events; forcing women to conform to rigid dress codes; limiting or denying women's access to education and training; denying women in the military the opportunity to perform the same duties as their male counterparts; and barring women from positions of leadership in religion, government, business, and other institutions.

RACISM AND SEXISM

The term *sexism* was first used during the 1960s by women activists in the U.S. civil rights movement. These women wanted to draw a parallel between the ways in which black people in the United States were oppressed based on their race or ethnicity and the ways in which women were oppressed based on their sex. In doing so, they hoped to channel some of the moral outrage directed at racism toward the injustices that women endured. In fact, two essays published in 1969 and 1970 bore the telling title "Woman as Nigger." Drawing this parallel had little early success in winning men to the fight against sexism and often led to heated arguments among activists (women as well as men) over which form of oppression was worse.

Ironically, many of the white women who drew the parallel between sexism and racism proved unable or unwilling to recognize the racism within the women's movement. Another unfortunate consequence of drawing this parallel was the implication that racism and sexism were separate and distinct systems of oppression. Thus, the conversation was framed so that it seemed one could either talk about race-based oppression or sex-based oppression, but not both, which often led to the theoretical erasure and practical invisibility of women of color. This misrepresentation continues in the early twenty-first century, insofar as accounts of racial discrimination often tend to focus on the experiences of men of color, while discussions of gender discrimination tend to leave race out. This implies that white women are the only victims of gender discrimination. Further, within communities of color, sexism has sometimes been portrayed exclusively as a white woman's issue. Women of color have often been asked to set aside concerns about sexism and focus all their energy on eliminating racism, and those who have failed to do so have been severely criticized.

In 1969, the activist Frances Beale (who was then New York coordinator of the Student Nonviolent Coordinating Committee's Black Women's Liberation Committee) wrote a now classic essay titled, "Double Jeopardy: To Be Black and Female." Beale explored the ways in which issues of race, ethnicity, gender, and class intersect to oppress black women. The essay was published in *Sisterhood Is Powerful* (1970), a pathbreaking anthology edited by Robin Morgan. The volume also included an article by Eleanor Holmes Norton titled "For Sadie and Maud," which looked at class divisions within the African American community, and an article by Enriqueta Longeaux y Vasquez that examined the situation of Chicana women within the Mexican-American community. These writings, and others that followed, gave rise to the argument that in order to do justice to the complexities of women's lives, it is necessary to recognize the ways in which systems of oppression such as racism, sexism, class privilege, heterosexism, and homophobia intersect. In 1985 the poet and writer Audre Lorde, reacting in part to homophobia within the African American community and racism within the lesbian and gay community, published her essay "There Is No Hierarchy of Oppressions."

WOMEN'S OPPRESSION AND THE POWER OF PATRIARCHY

Discrimination against women based on their sex has been pervasive worldwide throughout recorded history. As UNICEF (The United Nations Fund for Children) reports on its Internet site, although women do two-thirds of the world's work, they earn only one-tenth of the world's income and own less than one percent of the world's property. Globally, women cultivate more than half of all the food that is grown. In sub-Saharan Africa and the Caribbean, they produce as much as 80 percent of basic foodstuffs, yet the great majority of people living in poverty around the world are women. In the United States, the richest nation in the world, the poorest of the poor are women caring for children. As reported by both Christa Wichterich and Jan Pettman, women throughout the world are paid less than men for the same or comparable work, they are denied basic human rights and the basic rights of citizenship, and they are subject to extraordinary levels of violence. According to Human Rights Watch, "millions of women throughout the world live in conditions of abject deprivation of, and attacks against, their fundamental human rights for no reason other than that they are women." In sexist societies, children are raised to believe that physical and mental abilities are correlated with the individual's sex, and they are encouraged to develop those abilities considered appropriate to their sex while ignoring or denying other talents. In such societies—regardless of whether or not they are permitted to work outside the home, move freely in public spaces, or get an education—women are raised to believe that their primary role is to serve as a wife and mother, and to identify their happiness with the fulfillment of these roles. The poet and writer Adrienne Rich, as well as other theorists, have suggested that such societies rely on "compulsive heterosexuality" as a way of constructing and enforcing male-female relations of dominance and subordination. Both girl and boy children are taught that "normal" sexuality occurs between women and men, usually for the purpose of procreation, and severe penalties are imposed on anyone who deviates from this supposed biological norm.

In patriarchal societies, sexist beliefs and assumptions pervade religion, education, science, culture, and even language, so that these institutions all serve to reinforce the existing distribution of power and privilege by either making it appear to be natural or rendering it invisible. Historically, most of the world's major religions have been patriarchal and taught some version of the myth that women were created from or for man, and are thus destined to submit to his rule. Education in such societies teaches an andocentric, or male-centered, curriculum that omits or marginalizes the knowledge and perspective of white women and people of color. The world is presented to children through the eyes of men who are privileged and powerful, so that "women's literature," "African-American women's literature," and "working-class literature" are taught as special-interest fields that inhabit the margins of the discipline. During critical periods in history, science has come forward to provide "scientific evidence" that women of all colors and men of color are biologically and genetically inferior to white males.

Even language has both reflected and perpetuated the status quo by incorporating the sexist and racist biases of patriarchal societies. For example, in many languages where nouns are gendered, there is no female form of the words for doctor, lawyer, or other high-status positions. In English, a man who has relationships with many different women is admired and called a "playboy," while a woman who behaves in a similar fashion is referred to by a derogatory term such as "slut." In some languages, the masculine ending functions as the default, so that groups of children that include both boys and girls become "muchachos." In this way, language is complicit in rendering women invisible. Although taken together, women and men of color constitute the majority of people in the world, in U.S. society the phrase "women and minorities" is used routinely to demote the majority to minority status and portray their interests as being in opposition to the interests and needs of the majority.

STEREOTYPES AND SOCIAL CONTROL

Racism and sexism are similar in that both use stereotypes and ascribed attributes to explain and rationalize the subordination and domination of particular populations. For example, the persistent gap in earnings by race and gender—which shows that white men, white families, and male-headed families have significantly higher annual incomes than all other groups—is explained by perpetuating the myth that women work for "pin money" and by portraying black and Latino men as lazy. Mexicans are said to be suited to field labor because of their height and physiognomy. Women in general, and Asian women in particular, are said to be suited to perform delicate work in the electronics and textile industries because they have tiny hands and are physically dexterous. All women are

Men Pass a Billboard Advertisment for Lingerie, Mexico City, 2002. *Many people in Mexico worry that racism, sexism, and violence against women is increasing.* AP IMAGES.

said to be unsuited to positions of leadership because they are overly emotional.

Ascribing certain attributes to people based on their gender or race effectively absolves the system of responsibility for the unequal treatment and unequal rewards it bestows, while also blaming the victims of sexism, racism, and other forms of institutionalized oppression for their own plight. By constructing men and women as different in this way, the unequal distribution of wealth and opportunity is made to appear natural, a consequence of men and women's different natures rather than the result of discriminatory practices and specific policy decisions made by those in power.

As the historian William Chafe and the sociologists Sandra and Daryl Bem have pointed out, discrimination can only frustrate choices that have already been made. A more damaging form of social control frustrates the very ability to choose. In sexist and racist societies, women of all colors and men of color are taught to internalize a set of negative stereotypes that reconcile them to their socially constructed subordination and teach them forms of behavior that reinforce the prevailing social and economic relations of society. These lessons are often taught to women by other women, and to people of color by other people of color, making it more difficult to recognize their oppressive and harmful nature. While these lessons reflect the internalized sexism and racism of those offering the instruction, they also sometimes grow out of a desire to protect those who are most vulnerable. In both cases, however, members of the subordinate group end up reinforcing the status quo.

While some versions of sexism attribute certain "special" qualities to some women, usually associated with their childbearing function and their supposedly tender nature, even the ways in which women are supposedly superior to men are used to subordinate women in sexist societies. In the United States, for example, men who sought to deny women the right to vote during the late 1800s maintained that women had greater moral sensibilities and more delicate natures than men. They also argued, however, that because voting routinely took place in saloons and barber shops, women should be denied the right to vote in order to protect them from the crass and corrupt world of politics. Yet while white women, particularly those who are economically privileged, have been socially constructed in ways that portray them as both better and worse than men in some respects, women of color have consistently been portrayed as inferior to men of all colors by virtue of their sex and as inferior to white women by virtue of their race.

Societies have differed greatly over exactly which qualities and abilities are "naturally" male and female. It is not sex alone, however, but also differences in race and class that have played a significant role in determining what kinds of activities are considered appropriate to men and women. In some parts of the world, farming is viewed as a male occupation, while in others it is women who have primary responsibility for agriculture. In some countries, only men go to market and engage in buying and selling, while in others doing so is a female occupation. In the United States, the wives and daughters of white middle-class males were once said to be too delicate for physical labor by virtue of their sex, while at the same time African-American women held in slavery were forced to perform heavy manual labor from sunrise to sunset, and white working-class women and girls were forced to labor for as much as twelve or sixteen hours in dark, airless, factories.

VIOLENCE AND SOCIAL CONTROL

In examining the forms of social control that have kept both racism and sexism in place, it is impossible to overstate the role played by physical violence and the threat of such violence. According to the World Health Organization (WHO), violence against women is condoned in almost every society in the world. The United Nations Development Fund for Women (UNIFEM) reports that violence against women is so widespread that one out of every three women will suffer some form of violence in her lifetime. Throughout much of U.S. history, men and women of color have been subject to vicious and irrational physical attacks, including lynchings, rapes, and bombings, by the white community. These attacks have often gone unacknowledged and unprosecuted. Women of all racial and ethnic groups, and of all classes, live in a world where sexual harassment, rape, and assault are ever-present dangers. Data collected by UNIFEM suggest that half of the women in the world that die from homicide are killed by their husband, former husband, or partner, making domestic violence epidemic. Every year, some two million girls between the ages of five and fifteen are trafficked, sold, or forced into prostitution worldwide. In this way, violence, or the threat of violence, plays a critical role in maintaining and reinforcing gender and race subordination and perpetuating white privilege and male privilege.

SEE ALSO *Feminism and Race; Heterosexism and Homophobia.*

BIBLIOGRAPHY

Anzaldúa, Gloria. 1990. *Making Face/Making Soul, Haciendo Caras: Creative and Critical Perspectives by Feminists of Color.* San Francisco: Aunt Lute Foundation Books.

Bem, Sandra, and Darryl Bem. 1978. "Homogenizing the American Women: The Force of an Unconscious Ideology." In *Feminist Frameworks*, edited by Alison Jaggar and Paula Rothenberg Struhl. New York: McGraw-Hill.

Bird, Caroline, and Sara Welles Briller. 1968. *Born Female: The High Cost of Keeping Women Down.* New York: David McKay.

Chafe, William. 1977. "Sex and Race: The Analogy of Social Control." In *Women and Equality: Changing Patterns in American Culture.* New York: Oxford University Press.

De Beauvoir, Simone. 1952. *The Second Sex.* Translated by H. M. Parshley. New York: Knopf.

Eisenstein, Zillah. 1996. *Hatreds.* New York: Routledge.

Faludi, Susan, 1991. *Backlash: The Undeclared War against American Women.* New York: Crown.

Friedan, Betty. 1963. *The Feminine Mystique.* New York: Norton.

Human Rights Watch. "Women's Rights." Available from http://hrw.org/women.

Johnson, Allan G. 2005. *The Gender Knot: Unraveling Our Patriarchal Legacy.* 2nd ed. Philadelphia, PA: Temple University Press.

King, Deborah. 1995. "Multiple Jeopardy, Multiple Consciousness: The Context of a Black Feminist Ideology." In *Words of Fire: An Anthology of African American Feminist Thought,* edited by Beverly Guy-Sheftall, 294–317. New York: The New Press.

Lakoff, Robin. 1975. *Language and Woman's Place.* New York: Harper & Row.

Lorde, Audre. 1984. "There Is No Hierarchy of Oppressions." In *Sister Outsider: Essays and Speeches.* Freedom, CA: The Crossing Press.

Moraga, Cherrie, and Gloria Anzaldúa, eds. 1981. *This Bridge Called My Back: Writings by Radical Women of Color.* Watertown, MA: Persephone Press.

Morgen, Robin, 1970. *Sisterhood Is Powerful: An Anthology of Writings from the Women's Liberation Movement.* New York: Vintage Books.

Morrison, Toni, ed. 1992. *Race-ing Justice, En-gendering Power: Essays on Anita Hill, Clarence Thomas, and the Construction of Social Reality.* New York: Pantheon.

Pettman, Jan. 1996. *Worlding Women: A Feminist International Politics.* New York: Routledge.

Rich, Adrienne. 1986. "Compulsory Heterosexuality and Lesbian Experience." In *Blood, Bread, and Poetry: Selected Prose 1979–1985.* New York: Norton.

Rubin, Gayle. 1969. "The Woman as Nigger." In *Masculine/Feminine Readings in Sexual Mythology and the Liberation of Women,* edited by Betty Roszak and Theodore Roszak. New York: Harper & Row.

Spender, Dale. 1980. *Man Made Language.* London: Routledge & Kegan Paul.

UNICEF. 2007. *The State of the World's Children 2007—Women and Children: The Double Dividend of Gender Equality.* Available from http://www.unicef.org/sowc07.

Weisstein, Naomi. 1970. "The Woman as Nigger." In *Voices from Women's Liberation*, edited by Leslie B. Tanner. New York: Signet Books.

Wichterich, Christa. 2000. *The Globalized Woman Reports from a Future of Inequality.* London: Zed Books.

Paula Rothenberg

SEXUALITY

Sexuality can be broadly defined to encompass a wide array of sexual relations, including sexual politics, sexual activities, eroticism, sexual identity, and sexual meaning. Although sexuality is often discussed in terms of biological sex or gender, it is important to note that sexuality and gender form the basis of what Gayle Rubin, in "Thinking Sex: Notes for a Radical Theory of the Politics of Sexuality," calls "two distinct arenas of social practice" (Rubin 1984, p. 308).

Similar to the ways in which gender has been culturally constructed throughout history, sexuality should also be viewed as a cultural phenomenon. The meaning and place of sexuality in cultural relations is not only informed by gender ideology, but also by other intersections of social inequality, such as class and race. Ideas about sexuality have been central to racial ideologies and the social practices associated with institutionalized racism throughout the world. Historically, racialized sexuality has played a significant role in the transnational dynamics of colonialism and postcolonialism, the global diaspora, migration, and global capitalism.

GENDER VALUES IN COLONIAL SOCIETIES

In colonial contexts, sexual policies were often used by colonizers to subordinate the colonized by punishing what was viewed as immoral behavior, instilling concubinage as common law, or privileging monogamy. In colonial North America, what European colonizers viewed as immoral sexual behavior by Native Americans (i.e., nudity, lack of shamefulness associated with sexual activities, the non-institutionalization of marriage) was often used to rationalize the stealing of land, the breaking of treaties, and the outright genocide of entire populations of people. These policies continued throughout the nineteenth and twentieth centuries as Christian missionaries urged Native Americans to abandon traditional ways and adopt the nuclear family. Hence, Christianity and racist ideology were tools in the oppression and exploitation of Native American peoples. They also allowed whites to rationalize controlling Native American women's bodies and their sexualities. As the twentieth century progressed, Indian boarding schools attempted to achieve these goals by teaching girls the values of domesticity and purity. The pattern of imposing Euro-American sexual and gender values upon other racial groups has existed for centuries, and these impositions have significantly impacted the way nonwhite bodies are viewed sexually.

SEXUALITY AND SLAVERY

As such, sexuality was also central to the institution of slavery in the American colonies, as blacks and whites were differentiated in sexual terms and interracial sexual relations were contained. By assigning sexual stereotypes to enslaved Africans (e.g., that Africans were hypersexual, aggressive, and beastlike), European colonists were able to justify their economic and social control of blacks. The focus on the enslaved Africans' darker skin color and what was viewed as animalistic sexuality also prompted white European colonists to conclude that those of African descent were of a different breed, or "race," than Europeans. It was therefore posited that whites and blacks should not interbreed, and it was considered "natural," and even imperative, for whites to dominate blacks. Even after the American Revolution, the institution of slavery continued, along with its racial and sexual stereotypes.

Because enslaved African-American men were frequently regarded as aggressive and beastlike, they were also viewed as overt sexual threats to the chastity of white women. White men suddenly became the protectors of femininity, asserting their masculinity by protecting white women from the sexual threat of African-American men. Enslaved African-American women, on the other hand, were often stereotyped and dichotomized as either nonsexual, nurturing, nonthreatening "Mammies" that were expected to care for white masters' children, or as hypersexual "Jezebels" that lured white slave-owning men into their beds. Both of these stereotypes of black enslaved women were used to subjugate and exploit them economically and reproductively: Mammies were expected to nurture and selflessly raise white children, while Jezebels were expected to produce more enslaved labor through the exploitation of their reproductive abilities.

The Jezebel stereotype played on the white notion of the hypersexuality of the black female. Thus, a female slave was blamed for any sexual relationship she might have with a white man. Her desire for sexual relationships suddenly became her reason for existence—without sex she had no purpose. She was at fault for her own sexual exploitation and eroticization in society. For white society, the black woman fit into these two dichotomies: She was either hypersexual and a threat to white society, or she was mothering and completely desexed. These sexual stereotypes significantly affected the way society viewed the bodies of both black and white men and women in the nineteenth century, and the repercussions of the stereotypes can still be witnessed in the early twenty-first century.

Sexual stereotypes often transform society's ideas about the body as a physical entity. For instance, the historical notion that black men and women were socially viewed as overtly sexual allowed American white society to view their bodies as sexual objects. Once other aspects of the human form have been omitted and attention is diverted to the body as merely a sexual entity, the body—and entire groups of people—can be socially and economically exploited.

Both historically and contemporarily, the bodies of nonwhite groups have been viewed as directly sexual in comparison to white society. This dichotomy has made it possible for white society to appropriate the labor and resources of other racial groups considered inferior to them. During the colonial period, entire racial populations began to be sexually exploited based on the notion that white society was sexually superior. White men were viewed as protectors of the home thus creating the idea that their sexuality was necessary in order to create family unity and strength. As a result, upper-class white women were viewed as genteel, and their sexuality was viewed as pure in comparison to both women of color and poor white women.

SEXUALITY IN THE MODERN WORLD

Contemporary ideas of sexuality continue to be influenced by historical perspectives. Stereotypical notions of sexuality, whether positive or negative, influence ideological perspectives. Racial groups are still separated by different sexual ideologies, while white society continues to be held in high esteem based on historically established sexual stereotypes. Socially conservative views place white society in a position hierarchically superior to other racial groups. White men continue to be portrayed as sexually superior, although not overtly sexual, and white women are still considered to be sexually subordinate and in need of sexual protection and instruction by men in general, especially those women who are considered to be part of the middle and upper classes.

Popular contemporary culture influences ideas of black sexuality as well. Black men and women continue to be viewed as highly sexual, and interracial relationships are still often considered taboo. Although these types of relationships are beginning to be much more prevalent, in American society there is still a greater propensity toward sexual relationships between individuals in the same racial group. In addition, the strict differences between the portrayal of white and black social groups significantly impact the way that other racial groups are viewed sexually.

THE SEXUAL HIERARCHY

When a sexual hierarchy is established, racial groups are often situated along a sexual continuum. In western societies, white sexuality and white bodies are placed at the top of this sexual pyramid. Intersections of gender and class also frequently affect the position of individuals along this continuum, with white women and lower-class whites below white men of all classes and white women belonging to the upper and middle classes. Although many European citizens are viewed as racially white, American society situates these groups into a separate racial category hierarchically. These groups of European whites are placed directly beneath American whites in the sexual continuum. Beneath this group is the Asian population. This group includes not only citizens of Asian countries, but also Asian Americans. As Cynthia Enloe states in *Bananas, Beaches, and Bases: Making Feminist Sense of International Politics*, while Asian women's sexuality is not viewed as stereotypically overt, Asian women have often been sexually exploited because they have been viewed as sexual objects to serve foreign men (1991, p. 44). Contemporary research regarding prostitution in Asian countries has exposed a sexually eroticized idea of Asian femininity, and many men in other countries continue to view this racial group as sexually exotic. Red-light districts in Eastern countries grew significantly during colonization, and they continue to grow during postcolonial times as Asian female bodies continue to be sexualized.

Other racial groups, including but not limited to Africans, African-Americans, Latin Americans, and Middle-Easterners, are positioned at the bottom of the sexual continuum. Their sexualities are not only highly exploited, they are also viewed as socially inferior to other groups. The sexualities of these groups have been significantly affected by the historical reconstruction of sexual ideologies, and sexual inequalities clearly go hand in hand with inequalities based on race.

One assumption that is made within this sexual continuum is that heterosexuality is hegemonic and compulsory. Groups that situate themselves outside of heterosexuality are also placed at the bottom of the sexual continuum. Hegemonic heterosexuality supercedes race and impacts views of even white society. People who situate themselves outside of heterosexual hegemony, even whites, find themselves among the downwardly mobile in the sexual continuum based on society's constructed sexual ideology. This constructed social norm affects all racial groups, both inside and outside the United States.

Transnationalism and globalization have also been significantly influenced by this sexual continuum. Western sexual ideologies have been transposed on multiple cultures, and as the worldwide media expands, so do Western ideas of sexuality and the sexual continuum. Transnationalism and globalization have allowed the sexual hierarchy to become widespread and multiregional, influencing not only American ideas of sexuality but foreign sexual ideologies as well.

The sexual continuum has also led to the global ideology that bodies are objects of consumerism. The rise of the pornography and sex-work industries exposes the transnational marketing of the body as a commodity. The idea that the body as a sexual object can become a marketable item has been heavily influenced by ideas about racially stereotyped sexualities. Although heavily influenced by colonialism, the notion that white sexualities are superior to the sexualities of nonwhites has only increased with the expanse of global capitalism.

Ideas about sexuality have been significantly influenced in the global arena by intersections of race, gender, and class. Racialized sexuality has changed the way that human bodies are viewed cross-culturally and in the transnational arena. Historical notions of colonialism and racial hierarchy have not only changed the way that bodies are viewed, they have also changed the way that sexuality as a whole is viewed. Colonialism and domestic purity have allowed sexuality to be dissected into racial categories that still exist. In particular, transnational dynamics and the shift towards global capitalism dramatically affect the way that sexual hierarchies are continued worldwide. Further, hegemonic notions of sexuality are still transposed on multiple racial groups, eliminating the possibility for racial sexual equality. This inequality affects all people by establishing unconquerable notions of an ideal sexuality.

SEE ALSO *Gay Men; Heterosexism and Homophobia; Institutional Racism; Lesbians; Transnationalism.*

BIBLIOGRAPHY

Collins, Patricia Hill. 1999. "Producing Mothers of the Nation: Race, Class, and Contemporary U.S. Population Policies." In *Women, Citizenship, and Difference*, edited by Nira Yuval-Davis and Pnina Werbner, 118–129. London: Zed Books.

D'Emilio, John D., and Estelle B. Freedman. 1997. *Intimate Matters: A History of Sexuality in America*, 2nd ed. Chicago: University of Chicago Press.

Enloe, Cynthia. 1991. *Bananas, Beaches, and Bases: Making Feminist Sense of International Politics*. Berkeley: University of California Press.

Mies, Maria. 1986. *Patriarchy and Accumulation on a World Scale: Women and the International Division of Labour*. London: Zed Books.

Mohanty, Chandra Talpade. 1999. "Women Workers and Capitalist Scripts: Ideologies of Domination, Common Interests, and the Politics of Solidarity." In *Feminist Approaches to Theory and Methodology: An Interdisciplinary Reader*, edited by Sharlene Hesse-Biber, Christina Gilmartin, and Robin Lydenberg. New York: Oxford University Press.

Mullings, Leith. 1986. "Uneven Development: Class, Race, and Gender in the United States before 1900." In *Women's Work: Development and the Division of Labor by Gender*, edited by Eleanor Leacock, Helen I. Safa, and contributors, 41–57. South Hadley, MA: Bergin and Garvey.

Rubin, Gayle. 1984. "Thinking Sex: Notes for a Radical Theory of the Politics of Sexuality." In *Pleasure and Danger: Exploring Female Sexuality*, edited by Carole S. Vance, 267–319. Boston: Routledge and Kegan Paul.

Welter, Barbara. 1966. "The Cult of True Womanhood, 1830–1860." *American Quarterly* 18 (2): 151–174.

Tanya A. Faberson

SHEPPARD, WILLIAM
1865–1927

William Henry Sheppard, born in Waynesboro, Virginia, on March 8, 1865, cofounded the American Presbyterian Congo Mission (APCM) and became an important critic of the brutal colonial regime of King Leopold II of Belgium. When he was fifteen, his parents—Sarah Frances Martin Sheppard, a bath attendant, and William Henry Sheppard Sr., a barber—sent him to Hampton Normal and Industrial Institute in Hampton, Virginia. At Hampton, he was taught by Booker T. Washington, who would soon become the founding principal of Tuskegee Institute in Tuskegee, Alabama.

After completing his seminary education at Tuscaloosa Theological Institute (later renamed Stillman Institute) in Alabama in 1886, Sheppard began lobbying the southern Presbyterian Church (U.S.) to establish a mission in Africa. However, the church refused to commission Sheppard until a white minister was found to accompany him. Finally in 1890, Samuel Norvell Lapsley, the twenty-three-year-old white son of a well-connected Alabama judge, agreed to travel with Sheppard to establish the APCM. The pair set up a station in the town of Luebo at the junction of the Lulua and Kasai Rivers. Following Lapsley's untimely death in 1892, Sheppard, the APCM's senior missionary, traveled to the famously hidden Bakuba capital of Mushenge, where he was welcomed as the reincarnated heir to the throne. Sheppard's frequent recounting of his royal welcome resonated among African Americans and others he addressed at U.S. colleges and churches during his 1893 to 1894 furlough. Beyond sharing information about Africa with his audiences, during this trip he recruited four other African Americans to the APCM, including Henry Hawkins, Maria Fearing, Lillian Thomas, and his fiancée Lucy Gantt. Gantt, a graduate of Talladega College in Alabama and a professional singer, married Sheppard in 1894 before their departure. For the next decade, the APCM was a majority-black, albeit racially integrated mission representing a segregated U.S. church in central Africa.

At the 1884–1885 Berlin Conference, the European powers and the United States approved King Leopold II's claim on the Congo state. During the early 1890s, as Sheppard was shaping the APCM, Leopold's regime was codifying its brutally exploitative system of rubber production. By militarily enforcing compulsory labor, the state was able to increase its export income more than a hundredfold over a decade. Meanwhile, African resistance developed, including mass migration away from state-controlled regions and the assassination of state agents. In September 1899 Sheppard produced one of the first outside eyewitness accounts of the state practice of hand severing; in early 1900 his observations were reported in the Presbyterian Church's *Missionary* and Hampton Institute's *Southern Workman*. Sheppard's report became vital to the work of the Congo Reform Association (CRA), an organization founded in Liverpool, England, in 1903 by shipping company employee E. D. Morel in opposition to Leopold's regime. In his historical account of the international response to Leopold's Congo regime, Adam Hochschild (1999) suggests that the Congo reform movement was a crucial bridge between nineteenth-century antislavery movements and late-twentieth-century international human rights campaigns. Sheppard's report was sent to Mark Twain and Booker T. Washington, who both cited it and served as vice presidents of the American branch of the CRA. In 1905, as activists were trying to get Theodore Roosevelt involved, Sheppard met with the president at the White House.

In 1909 Sheppard was again in the international spotlight when Belgium (which took control of the state in 1908) charged him with libel for reporting in the APCM's *Kassai Herald*, "There are armed sentries of chartered trading companies, who force the men and women to spend most of their days and nights in the forests making rubber, and the price they receive is so meager that they cannot live upon it." The *Compagnie du Kasai*, claiming it was not chartered, filed a suit that forced Sheppard and *Herald* editor William Morrison to travel for several months to the trial in Leopoldville (Kinshasa). Sheppard, who became the sole defendant when charges against Morrison were dropped, was represented by Emile Vandervelde, a prominent Belgian Socialist Party member. At the trial, which was attended by U.S. and British consular officials, Sheppard's accusations were corroborated, resulting in his acquittal. The *Compagnie du Kasai* was ordered to pay court costs.

Despite his unqualified vindication, Sheppard was nonetheless forced to retire by a mission board that was increasingly uncomfortable with the work of its African American missionaries. Between 1908 and 1910, the three senior male missionaries—Sheppard, Hawkins, and Joseph Phipps, all of whom were black—faced charges of adultery, which forced their retirements. Whereas eleven blacks were appointed to the APCM during its first twenty years, the Presbyterian Church appointed only one black person during the next fifty years (and in her case only because she married a recently widowed active missionary).

After quietly confessing to sexual misconduct and serving a one-year suspension from the church, Sheppard was appointed pastor of Grace Church in Louisville, Kentucky, in 1912. Under his direction, the congregation and its programs expanded dramatically. While in Louisville, Sheppard maintained a strong relationship with Hampton, where he continued to give public addresses. In addition to speeches on campus, in 1911 he coheadlined a fundraising tour on its behalf with Booker T. Washington. He sold his visual art collection to Hampton, where it has educated generations of students. Nationally, Sheppard was a prominent public figure who published articles, children's books, and in 1917 *Presbyterian Pioneers in the Congo*. He was profiled in the National Association for the Advancement of Colored People's (NAACP) *Crisis* in 1915 and addressed an NAACP conference on Africa in 1919. Through his activities, speeches, writings, and art collection, Sheppard influenced writers, visual artists, political activists, and religious leaders. He served as pastor of Grace Church until his death on November 27, 1927. In Louisville, Lucy Gantt Sheppard was a social worker and directed the Grace Church choir. She remained active until her death at the age of eighty-eight on May 26, 1955.

BIBLIOGRAPHY

Hochschild, Adam. 1999. *King Leopold's Ghost: A Story of Greed, Terror, and Heroism in Colonial Africa*. New York: Mariner Books.

Kennedy, Pagan. 2002. *Black Livingstone: A True Tale of Adventure in the Nineteenth-Century Congo*. New York: Viking.

Phipps, William E. 2002. *William Sheppard: Congo's African American Livingstone*. Louisville, KY: Geneva Press.

Sheppard, William H. 1917. *Presbyterian Pioneers in Congo*. Richmond, VA: Presbyterian Committee of Publication.

Ira Dworkin

SICKLE CELL ANEMIA

Sickle cell anemia is a severe and commonly fatal anemia, or failure of oxygen transfer. Its name derives from the fact that the red blood cells (RBCs), the transporters of oxygen, which are normally lozenge shaped, collapse into characteristic sickle-shaped cells under the influence of the disease. These red blood cells have drastically reduced ability to transport oxygen and a reduced life expectancy (10–12 days instead of the normal 120 days). The condition is often punctuated by painful "crises" resulting from the fact that the sickle shaped cells are elongated and relatively stiff and may periodically block capillaries because they clump, or agglutinate. The condition was first described in Western medicine by James Herrick in a series of publications between 1910 and 1912.

SYMPTOMS AND CAUSES

A wide range of symptoms may result, ranging from the weakness and lassitude characteristic of anemia to acute and/or chronic pain. Specific symptoms include shortness of breath, jaundice, poor physical development, small slender bodies, delayed sexual maturity, swelling of hands and feet, impaired mental function, and rheumatism. It may also cause local failure of blood supply, possibly resulting in blindness, strokes, and damage to the heart, brain, lungs, spleen, gastrointestinal tract, and kidneys. In addition, it can cause painful priapism, resulting in damage to the penis. One of its most dangerous consequences is reduced resistance to infection, particularly influenza, pneumonia, and meningitis. Fewer than 10 percent of individuals with sickle cell anemia survive to adulthood, and their evolutionary fitness or reproductive success (compared to average fitness, defined as 1.0) is about 0.1.

Sickle cell anemia was the first genetic disease whose molecular basis was identified. The condition is the result of having two copies (i.e., the homozygote condition) of the HbS allele (variant) of the gene for the production of hemoglobin, a complex molecule of four polypeptide (amino acid) chains. Hemoglobin is found in red blood cells and is the molecule that grabs oxygen from the lungs and transports oxygen in the blood for use in the body. The HbS allele results from a point mutation of the HbA allele, resulting in the substitution of amino acid valine for glutamic acid in position six on the beta chain of the hemoglobin molecule. The codon change is a substitution of GTG for GAG.

HbS is a classic autosomal recessive trait. The alleles are distributed in a normal Mendelian manner such that heterozygote parents (i.e., each with one copy of the allele) will produce homozygote "normals," sickle cell carriers, and homozygotes with full-fledged sickle cell disease in a ratio of 1:2:1. On average, 25 percent of children born to two heterozygote parents will have the disease. Homozygous individuals are heavily afflicted, whereas heterozygotes possess both types of hemoglobin and function normally unless placed in conditions of high oxygen stress such as heavy labor, athletics, or high-altitude activity. It is now known that the disease is carried by about one in twelve African Americans, resulting in sickle cell anemia in one of 500 births to African Americans, although the rate is gradually declining.

The mutation(s) may have occurred separately several times: in as many as four locations in Africa and an additional one in India or Arabia. However, that interpretation remains controversial. The allele may also have radiated outward from a center in West Africa or, conversely, into Africa from the Middle East. The modern distribution of the allele results in significant part from patterns of trade and travel under Muslim and then Christian dominion of areas of the Middle East and Africa. In the early twenty-first century it occurs with the highest frequency in Central Africa, where 30 percent or more of the population can be carriers, as well as in northeast and northwest India, Turkey, and Saudi Arabia. It also reaches high frequencies in parts of Greece and is found elsewhere in Mediterranean Europe.

SICKLE CELL ANEMIA AND MALARIA

The persistence of such a deleterious allele posed an evolutionary paradox for biological scientists: Why doesn't the allele simply disappear through natural selection? The solution to the paradox was first addressed by Anthony C. Allison in the 1950s and has since received considerable attention from other scholars, notably F. B. Livingstone. As a result of this attention, the sickle cell allele has emerged as the first and still best understood example of the role of infectious disease and human behavior in natural selection; it remains the model on which interpretation of other genetic disorders such as Tay-Sachs disease and cystic fibrosis is based.

All three are examples of "balanced polymorphisms" in which an allele deleterious in homozygotes is maintained in a population because in the heterozygote form it provides protection from an infectious disease. In the case of the sickle cell trait, the heterozygote HbS-HbA tends to resist malaria, itself one of the most significant debilitating and often fatal diseases affecting human beings throughout history. Malaria has been a major force in human evolution. The sickle cell trait is an example of how rapidly the spread of a disease can result in significant evolutionary change in the human species. Individuals possessing the allele are less likely to harbor the malarial parasite in significant numbers in comparison to homozygote normals. They live longer and are less affected by symptoms of malaria. Heterozygote women may be more fertile; men may also be more fertile because high fevers associated with malaria can reduce spermatogenesis. In malarial areas, both the homozygote HbA and the homozygote HbS are selected against. For every 100 heterozygote survivors in malarial areas, there are only about 88 HbA homozygote survivors and only 14 HbS homozygote survivors. The relative success of the heterozygote results in perpetuation of the HbS allele. (Tay-Sachs disease may be a similar response to tuberculosis, cystic fibrosis, cholera, typhoid, or other intestinal infection.)

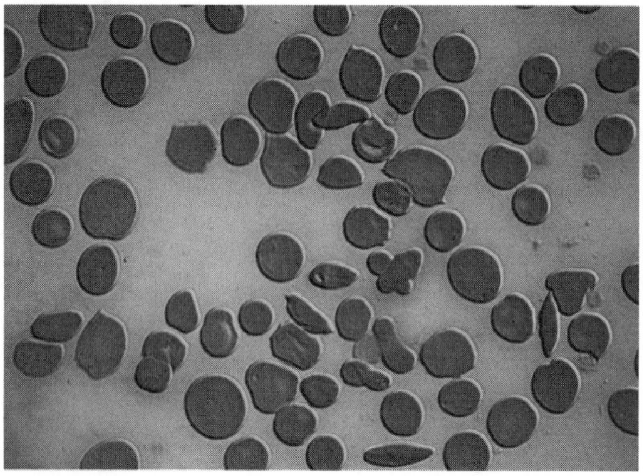

Sickle-Cell Red Blood Cells. *Both normal red blood cells and deformed cells can be seen in this sample of blood taken from a person with sickle cell anemia.* DR. DAVID M. PHILLIPS/VISUALS UNLIMITED/GETTY IMAGES.

The relationship between the sickle cell allele and malaria has been demonstrated sequentially in three ways. First, it has been shown that allowing for some movement of populations and malarial zones, the geographical concordance of HbS (and/or other forms of abnormal protective forms of hemoglobin, including HbC, HbE, HbO, variants of the Duffy blood group, various forms of thalassemia, and the enzyme G6PD, or glucose 6 phosphate dehydrogenase) with malaria is striking and too detailed to reflect mere chance. Figure 1 depicts the broad geographical correlation of the allele and the disease. The detailed correlation in specific locations such as various altitudes adds to the strength of the correlation. Allison (1954), for example, reports that there is no indigenous group in Africa with a high percentage of the S allele in which malaria is *not* present. It is, for example, rare in highlands and dry areas inhospitable to Anopheles mosquitoes. It is also less common where swidden agriculture is not the norm.

Second, the fitness effects of the HbS allele (as above) have been demonstrated repeatedly. Third, it has been shown that the structure of the sickled red blood cell is less able to support the growth of the protozoan malarial parasite, demonstrating the mechanisms by which heterozygotes are protected against malaria.

The history of the sickle cell allele is bound to that of the spread of malaria, which is in turn bound to the emergence of agricultural economies in the afflicted areas within the last 6,000 years, when falciparum malaria spread in an explosive manner. In West Africa it spread probably in association with the expansion of Bantu farmers into areas previously devoted to hunting and gathering in the last 2,000 to 3,000 years.

Forest clearance associated with farming created the mix of light and shade that in humid climates is highly favorable to Anopheles mosquitoes, which are the most efficient vectors of falciparum malaria. In addition, large populations and the sedentary communities that emerged with farming provided a larger pool of susceptible people, permitting the disease to become endemic. Farming also created layers of highly impenetrable lateritic soils, which in turn led to more standing water where mosquitoes could breed. It also tended to remove or displace other mammals as potential victims of mosquitoes, which then focused the attention of the mosquitoes on human beings.

MODERN-DAY ISSUES

Sickle cell anemia is also in some sense a dietary deficiency disease, at least in the United States. Its effects are mitigated to a significant degree by diets rich in cyanate and thiocyanate, which are typically found in tropical foods such as yams, manioc (cassava), sorghum, and some millets that are rarely eaten in the United States. Symptoms are often worse in the United States than in areas where these foods are more often consumed. The sickle cell trait has been found to be more common in areas of Africa where these foods are eaten, presumably because they reduce the severity of the symptoms, thus changing the balance of selective pressures. Yams, however, also reduce resistance to malaria, often resulting in patterns of yam consumption in Central Africa carefully balanced with seasonal malaria.

In the United States and other areas with the benefits of modern biomedicine, the symptoms of this disease can be alleviated by a therapeutic diet rich in cyanates and antioxidants. It has become possible to identify the presence of the gene by a simple blood test. Prenatal testing of fetuses for the presence of HbS and genetic counseling for heterozygote parents are available. Since 1984 it has been possible to fight HbS with bone marrow transplants from "normal" homozygotes. As of 1995 there has also been a therapy, hydroxyurea, that effectively treats symptoms.

Although often considered a "racial" concomitant of dark skin, sickle cell genetics actually provides one of many pieces of evidence demonstrating that biologically, "races" do not exist. Sickle cell hemoglobin is not limited to individuals of dark skin, and its correlation with dark skin is actually weak. Even in populations where it is endemic, such as in malarial regions of West Africa, no more than 10 to 30 percent of hemoglobin alleles are of the HbS form. The comparable figure in African Americans is no more than 5 percent. In other areas of Africa where malaria is less of a problem, the allele occurs in far lower frequencies or not at all. It does not occur among unrelated dark-skinned populations of Oceania or

Australia. That is, the overwhelming majority of dark-skinned people, even those from or derived from West Africa, do not carry the allele. Conversely, the allele is known in malarial areas north of the Mediterranean, from southern Europe to India, among populations normally considered "white." It is interesting to speculate that if Mediterranean populations from Spain, Portugal, Greece, Italy, or Turkey had been the main colonizers of the New World, and if they had obtained their slaves from some areas of North and South Africa or Australia, the sickle cell trait might be associated with light rather than dark skin.

SEE ALSO *Diseases, Racial; Life Expectancy; Tay-Sachs and "Jewish" Diseases.*

BIBLIOGRAPHY

Allison, Anthony C. 1954. "Protection Afforded by the Sickle Cell Trait against Malarial Infection." *British Medical Journal* 1:290–294.

———. 2004. "Two Lessons from the Interface of Genetics and Medicine." *Genetics* 166 (4): 1591–1599.

Livingstone, Frank B. 1958. "Anthropological Implications of Sickle Cell Gene Distribution in West Africa." *American Anthropologist* 60 (3): 533–562.

Molnar, Stephen. 2005. *Human Variation: Races, Types, and Ethnic Groups*, 6th ed. Upper Saddle River, NJ: Pearson Prentice Hall.

Weiss, Kenneth M. 1993. *Genetic Variation and Human Disease: Principles and Evolutionary Approaches.* Cambridge, U.K.: Cambridge University Press.

Mark Nathan Cohen

SINGLETON, BENJAMIN "PAP"
1809–1892

Benjamin "Pap" Singleton called himself "the Moses of the Colored Exodus." Singleton became a black separatist and, along with Henry Adams, a leader in one of the largest internal migrations of African Americans in U.S. history. In 1879–1880, he served as a spokesperson for the "Exodusters," formerly enslaved blacks who moved from Tennessee, Kentucky, and other southern states, to settle mainly in Kansas. In a U.S. Senate report (1880), formerly enslaved Henry Adams of Louisiana stated that as early as 1874 blacks from several Deep South states had organized a semisecret "colonization council," which reportedly enrolled upwards of 98,000 persons desiring to migrate westward. Singleton, though, was very open about his activities, often conducting meetings in churches. Hence, he was much better known than Adams, whose group may have motivated more people to emigrate than Singleton.

By the time Singleton became the public voice of emigration, he was in his sixties and gray-haired; his age and pleasant manner gained him the nickname "Pap." He claimed credit for establishing eleven colonies of African Americans in Kansas, but the record shows only two communities, in Dunlap County and Morris County. In 1880 he informed a special U.S. Senate committee seeking the causes of the migration that he had brought 7,432 people out of the South, and he proudly but erroneously proclaimed, "I am the whole cause of Kansas migration!"

Singleton was born in Nashville, Tennessee, to an enslaved mother. He fled slavery and went to Canada via the Underground Railroad. He soon returned to the United States and found a job in Detroit. After Emancipation, he went back to Tennessee and encountered ongoing economic oppression and white violence against African Americans. He continued to work in cabinetry and carpentry. In his work making coffins, he saw the bodies of black men and women whom whites had sexually assaulted and lynched. Well-to-do whites who controlled the economy exploited black workers, creating and perpetuating black poverty and hunger. A major crop failure in 1868 in the South intensified the hardship of many newly freed southern blacks. With the withdrawal of federal troops from the region in 1877, oppression of blacks intensified.

Singleton had once hoped that African Americans in the South could develop economic security by saving money, purchasing homes, and moving out of sharecropping. He helped create the Tennessee Real Estate and Homestead Association, which later became the Edgefield Real Estate and Homestead Association. This association vainly sought local land inexpensive enough for blacks to purchase. This effort failed, and Singleton soon began to believe that blacks should settle in new communities separated from whites, and thereby avoid white violence, oppression, and economic competition. He felt that life for southern blacks would begin to improve but, that in the short term, leaving was the best option. Singleton asserted that God had given him the message to lead blacks out of the South. In contrast to Henry Adams, who spent time in dialogue learning people's needs and opinions, Singleton asserted that he had been told by God to advocate for creating African American settlements outside the South.

Working alongside clergyman Columbus Johnson, also of Tennessee, Singleton selected Kansas as the most attractive destination for new black settlement. It appeared to have a pleasant climate and affordable public lands. Despite opposition from some black politicians, Singleton believed the new colonies would "consolidate the race" and create African American economic independence. Singleton's promotional pamphlets often contained appealing pictures of lush farm and attractive dwellings. The circulars also contained "exodus" songs such as "The Land that Gives Birth to Freedom." Kansas was presented as the Promised Land. The movement into Kansas was dramatic. In 1860, there were only 625 free blacks and two enslaved blacks in the state. By 1870, there were 17,108 blacks, and in 1880, 43,107. The migrants came not only from Tennessee, but also from Louisiana and Mississippi.

The colonies in Kansas did not live up to the advertising, and many migrants struggled greatly, some returning to the South. In his later years Singleton continued to work for black progress. In 1881 he founded and became president of United Colored Links, which aimed to use black resources to help blacks break into trades from which whites had excluded them, to help the community's poor, and to promote black progress.

The black and white working class had little solidarity in this period in Kansas because of the racism of white workers and the racially divisive tactics of factory owners, who paid black laborers lower wages and used them as "scabs." Although the Links tried to work with white labor groups to end the bar against black membership in labor organizations, the Links ultimately sought to unite blacks to form a separate, distinct, but coexisting black society.

Financial strain and other factors led to the dissolution of the United Colored Links. White discrimination, racism, and economic blockage continued to plague blacks in both the South and North, and Singleton began to believe that blacks could not achieve full success and security in the United States. Singleton then founded the United Transatlantic Society, a black separatist group that advocated migrating to Africa, considering both Liberia and Ethiopia as potential destinations. This organization did not succeed in relocating anyone to Africa, in large part because of the great cost of transoceanic travel. Despite his many setbacks, Singleton continued to fight for better conditions for blacks until the end of his life. He died in 1892 in St. Louis, Missouri.

BIBLIOGRAPHY

Fleming, Walter L. 1909. 'Pap' Singleton, the Moses of the Colored Exodus." *American Journal of Sociology* 15 (1): 61–82.

Garvin, Roy. 1948. "Benjamin, or 'Pap,' Singleton and His Followers." *Journal of Negro History* 33 (1): 7–23.

Meacham, Mike. 2003. "The Exoduster Movement." *Western Journal of Black Studies* 27 (2): 108–117.

Painter, Nell Irving. 1977. *Exodusters: Black Migration to Kansas after Reconstruction*. New York: Knopf.

U.S. Senate. 1880. *Report and Testimony of the Select Committee of the United States Senate to Investigate the Causes of the Removal of the Negroes from the Southern States to the Northern States*. 3 vols. 46th Cong., 2nd sess., Senate Report 693.

Michelle VanNatta

SKIN COLOR

The skin of modern humans, *Homo sapiens*, varies from near ebony black to ivory white. Skin color is important to people because it is one of the most highly visible aspects of a person's external appearance. As one of the most obvious and geographically variable aspects of the human phenotype, skin color long served as the primary basis for classification of people into what were considered distinct biological groups, which were designated variously as species, subspecies, or races. Research findings from anthropology and genetics now demonstrate that a person's visible skin color is useless as a marker of unique genetic identity and that it is invalid as a basis for classifying people into biologically distinct groups. Despite this fact, skin color continues to be used in many countries and in many social contexts to evaluate a person's group affiliation or social worth, often with prejudice.

Human skin color is determined by several pigments, the most important of which is melanin. Human skin contains the two types of melanin found in all mammals, the brownish-black eumelanin and the reddish-yellow pheomelanin. Eumelanin imparts color to darker skin and tanned skin, and is an extremely dense, virtually insoluble, high-molecular-weight polymer attached to a structural protein. Pheomelanin is largely responsible for freckles but is otherwise present in very small quantities in the skin; it is best known for giving red hair its color. Melanin is produced in specialized cells within the epidermis (the top layer of skin cells) called melanocytes. Melanocytes produce melanins in specialized cytoplasmic organelles called melanosomes, which vary in size and degree of aggregation depending on skin type and pigmentation (Figure 1). Natural melanin compounds absorb, scatter, and reflect light of different wavelengths, from the ultraviolet (UV) through the visible range. These processes are influenced by the density and distribution of melanosomes within skin cells and the presence in darker skin of flecks of melanin pigment ("melanin dust") in the superficial parts of the epidermis. When present in high concentrations in the skin, eumelanin provides protection against sunburning and other harmful effects of UV radiation (UVR). Melanin also helps to prevent damage to DNA in the skin by inhibiting destructive oxidative processes caused by UVR.

Accurate measurement of skin color is required in many scientific and medical settings. Skin color was for many years simply described as "white," "yellow," "black," "brown," and "red." During the early twentieth century, these imprecise descriptions gave way to color-matching methods, which utilized colored tablets or tiles of different colors and hues. Because these methods could not be consistently reproduced, the more objective method of reflectance spectrophotometry was widely adopted soon after its

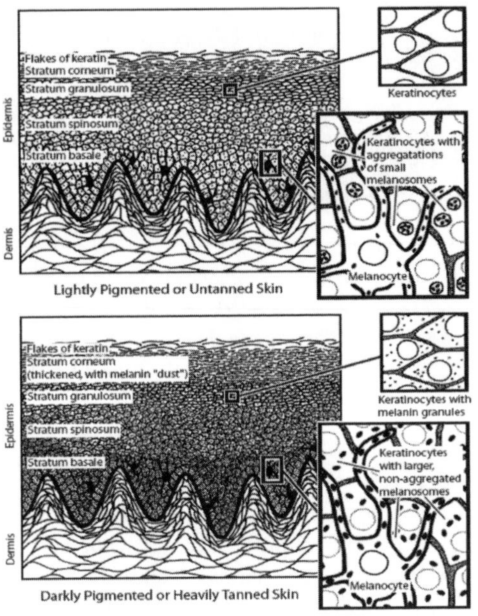

Figure 1. *Schematic rendering of cross-sections of lightly pigmented and darkly pigmented human skin, showing its laminar structure and mail cell types. Darkly pigmented skin contains larger melanosomes (melanin-containing organelles) and "melanin dust" in the epidermis.* © JENNIFER KANE, 2007.

introduction in the early 1950s. This method utilizes a light source of known wavelength that is shown upon the surface of the skin. A detector on the apparatus then measures the amount of light reemitted or reflected by the skin. The resulting measurement is called skin reflectance. This procedure is carried out on skin that is not routinely exposed to sunlight, with the inner surface of the upper arm being preferred.

In recent years, several new and highly portable types of spectrophotometers and other measurement devices have been introduced to measure skin color in the field, laboratory, and doctor's office. Unexposed skin provides information on a person's constitutive skin color, that is, the genetically determined skin color not affected by exposure to the sun. In most people, the skin darkens (tans) to greater or lesser extents with sun exposure. This temporary darkening imparts a person's facultative skin color. In clinical settings, the need to assess skin color quickly and without complex instrumentation led to the creation of skin phototypes, ranging from Type I (very sensitive, easily burned, with little or no potential for tanning) to Type VI (insensitive, never burns, and deeply pigmented).

Among the indigenous peoples of the world, skin color varies continuously and forms a natural cline, or gradient, from darkly pigmented peoples near the equator to lighter ones closer to the poles. This distribution led early observers to think that skin color must be related to the distribution of sunlight on the Earth's surface, and most research on the evolution of skin color has been concerned with identifying the nature of the relationship between sunlight and skin color.

THE EVOLUTION OF SKIN COLOR

Human skin is distinguished mainly by its naked appearance, its greatly enhanced abilities to dissipate body heat through sweating, and the great range of genetically determined skin colors that it exhibits. Although skin is rarely preserved in the fossil record, many aspects of the evolution of human skin and skin color can be now reconstructed using comparative anatomy, physiology, and genomics. The evolutionary lineage leading to humans separated from that leading to chimpanzees, our closest relatives, about six million years ago. The skin of this species probably had lightly pigmented skin covered with dark hair, as chimpanzees and most other Old World anthropoid primates do. As the human lineage evolved, important changes occurred in body shape and proportions, and in brain size.

The earliest members of the genus *Homo* living in equatorial Africa from about 2 to 1.5 million years ago exhibited larger bodies, relatively larger brains, and relatively longer lower limbs than their predecessors. Their activity levels are thought to have been correspondingly higher and their range of daily travel longer than those of their ancestors. This situation would have required that their skin be functionally naked and endowed with a high density of sweat glands in order to facilitate heat loss and protect the brain from hyperthermia, especially during periods of exertion in hot environments. The dense, hairy coats of other mammals protect their skin from UVR-induced damage because the hairs themselves absorb or reflect most short-wavelength solar radiation. Lacking this protection, the mostly naked skin of early *Homo* became darker, because the greatly increased melanin content helped to protect the body from the harmful effects of UVR. The ancestral stock from which all later humans evolved was, thus, darkly pigmented. This interpretation has recently been supported by genetic evidence demonstrating that strong natural selection acted over one million years ago to produce darkly pigmented skin in early members of the genus *Homo* (Rogers, Iltis, and Wooding 2004).

Skin pigmentation among indigenous populations of modern humans shows remarkable regularity in its geographic distribution. Darker skins occur in more tropical regions and lighter skin in temperate regions, although this gradient is less intense in the New World as compared to the Old World. In 1958, Hubert von Walter was the first to suggest that the pigmentation gradient observed was linked to the intensity of UVR, and he established this relationship by calculation of correlation coefficients between skin color and estimated UVR. More recent studies utilizing remotely sensed data gained from earth-orbiting satellites established a conclusive correlation UVR and skin reflectance. Further, skin color is more strongly correlated with UVA, which is consistently higher throughout the year at all latitudes than with UVB. Using the known relationship between environmental parameters (primarily UVR) and skin color in indigenous human populations, it is possible to derive a map of predicted human skin colors (Figure 2). This map depicts an idealized situation in which humans are assumed to have lived in their respective regions for the same lengths of time and have followed similar cultural practices that could affect their skin color. Populations of native peoples in the Americas tend to be lighter than those in the Old World mostly because they have not inhabited their lands for as long a time. The pace and extent of human migrations in the last 500 years have also contributed to departures from the idealized pattern. Specifically, there are now many lightly pigmented people living in regions with high UVR levels that were originally inhabited only by darkly pigmented people, and many darkly pigmented people living in regions with low UVR levels that were originally inhabited only by lightly pigmented people.

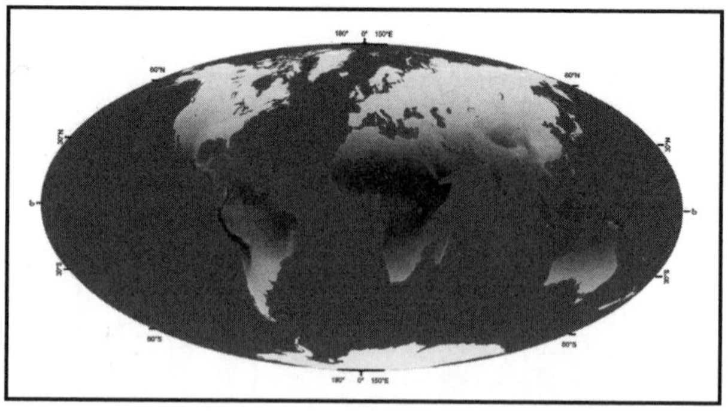

Figure 2. *The distribution of predicted human skin color as determined from the known relationship between skin reflectance in indigenous human populations and environmental factors, the most important of which being UVR.* © GEORGE CHAPLIN, 2007.

Melanin pigmentation is adaptive and has been maintained by natural selection, but until recently a consensus had not been reached as to why differences in melanin pigmentation among human populations evolved and have been maintained. Many ideas about the adaptive value of skin color have been brought forward in the last century. Dark skin was thought to protect against sunburn and skin cancer, to enhance immune protection of the body, or to serve as concealment in forest environments. Light skin was thought to facilitate vitamin D production in the skin or to help resist cold injury. None of these explanations alone, however, satisfies the criteria for a true evolutionary adaptation. In order for skin color to be considered a true biological adaptation, differences in survivorship and reproductive success between people of different skin colors under the same environmental conditions must be demonstrated.

Current understanding of the evolution of skin color is that varying degrees of melanin pigmentation evolved in *Homo sapiens* to regulate the penetration of UVR into the skin. The amount of melanin present represents enough to prevent the breakdown of certain light-sensitive compounds while permitting the production of others. This theory is based on two equally important facts. The first is that the B vitamin folate (folic acid) is destroyed by UVR (UVA), and that folate deficiency endangers successful reproduction in both females and males. This is because folate is necessary for production of all DNA in the body and is therefore required for all cell division. Rapid cell division is required during development of the human embryo and fetus and during the production of sperm. A lack of sufficient folate compromises cell division and can lead to serious or fatal birth defects and the slowing or cessation of sperm production. The second important fact is that vitamin D_3 is produced in the skin by wavelength UVR (UVB) and that severe vitamin D deficiencies adversely affect survival and eventual reproductive success by interfering with uptake of calcium from the diet. Vitamin D is important for building and maintaining the bones of the skeleton and for maintaining a strong immune system. Insufficient amounts of vitamin D during early childhood inhibit proper skeletal development, leading to rickets, while deficiencies later in life lead to bone thinning (osteomalacia) and compromised functioning of the immune system.

Evolution has, therefore, produced two clines of skin pigmentation. The first grades from darkly pigmented skin at the equator to lightly pigmented skin near the poles and can be thought of as the cline of folate protection. The second grades from lightly pigmented near the poles to darkly pigmented at the equator and can be referred to as the cline of vitamin D production. Loss of melanin pigmentation was important for humans living outside of the tropics because the large quantities of melanin present in dark skin greatly slow the process of vitamin D_3 production in the skin. In the middle of the two clines are people with enhanced abilities to gain and lose facultative pigmentation (a tan) according to seasonal UVR levels.

Adaptive explanations for human skin pigmentation have dominated the literature, but some authorities downplayed or discounted the role of adaptation by natural selection in determining human skin color. Some have emphasized the role of sexual selection, especially by way of explaining the lighter constitutive pigmentation of women relative to men. Others have argued that loss of melanin pigment in the skin of people outside of tropical latitudes occurred not because lighter skin color was selected for but because selective pressures for deep pigmentation were relieved as people inhabited increasingly high latitudes where dark pigmentation was no longer required as a shield against UVR.

The evolution of skin pigmentation in humans has been determined by many factors, the most important being UVR. Through human history, however, the number of factors influencing human skin pigmentation has increased, and culture has reduced the scope for the action of natural selection on human skin. Cultural behaviors such as wearing clothes and using shelters have become more common through time and have affected the evolution of skin pigmentation because they have tended to reduce individual UVR exposure. In early prehistory, people had a simpler material culture and had fewer cultural trappings to buffer themselves against the environment. Under these conditions, natural selection promoted biological adaptations to the environment, such as changes in skin coloration and body proportions. With increasing cultural complexity, nonbiological solutions to environmental problems became more common.

In the early 2000s the genetic basis of human skin pigmentation is not yet well understood, but this situation is rapidly improving with advances in comparative and functional genomics. Skin pigmentation is a trait determined by the interaction of many genes with the environment, and determining the relative importance of variant forms of genes in different environments has been challenging. The greatest attention so far has been focused on the nature and function of the melanocortin-1 receptor (MC1R) gene in people of different skin colors. The MC1R gene is one of the major genes involved in the determination of human hair and skin pigmentation. It is characterized by high levels of variation in light-skinned individuals outside of Africa and lower levels of variation in dark-skinned individuals within Africa. Natural selection favored people with sun-resistant forms of the MC1R gene, probably when humans first became hairless in tropical Africa. Later movements of modern people into the less sunny climes of Eurasia favored variant forms of the gene that did not produce dark skin.

The timing and nature of movements of groups of early *Homo* species and of *Homo sapiens* in prehistory suggests that human populations have moved in and out of regions with different UVR regimes over the course of thousands of years. Natural selection, therefore, would have favored the evolution of dark and light skin pigmentation in disparate places at different times, resulting in the independent evolution of dark and light skin phenotypes and recurrent episodes of repigmentation and depigmentation. This hypothesis is supported by genetic evidence, which indicates that the lightly pigmented skin characteristic of northern Europeans evolved as the result of a mutation in a gene that affects the properties of melanin-containing organelles within skin cells. The absence of the same mutation in lightly pigmented northern and eastern Asians denotes that the depigmented skin of these peoples evolved independently (Lamason et al. 2005).

SKIN COLOR AND RACE

Throughout history and in most countries, skin color has been the primary characteristic used to classify people into purportedly genetically distinct geographic groups or races. The biological basis of skin pigmentation in humans strongly argues against the use of the trait in this way. Skin pigmentation is adaptive, and its evolution in specific populations has been strongly influenced by environmental conditions in specific places. Highly adaptive characteristics are not useful for classifying people or other organisms because they often recur under similar environmental conditions; that is, they evolve in parallel. Genetic evidence indicates that the evolution of pigmentation genes has been driven by natural selection working to produce adaptive responses in different environments, suggesting that similar skin colors have evolved independently in human populations inhabiting similar environments. Darkly or lightly pigmented skin, therefore, provides evidence only about the nature of the past environments in which people have lived, not their membership in a unique group or race.

Skin color continues to influence human affairs because people are strongly visually oriented and are highly culturally attuned to noticing even small differences in external appearance. The existence of differences between so-called human races based on skin color is the result of an exaggerated perception and heightened sensitivity to a visually obvious attribute of human appearance. Different skin colors have taken on different cultural values in different places throughout history, and human societies have tended to maintain culturally ingrained values about individual worth based on skin color. This remains one of the most sinister forces affecting human affairs throughout the world today.

SEE ALSO *Clines; Genetic Variation Among Populations; Human and Primate Evolution; Human Biological Variation; Human Genetics.*

BIBLIOGRAPHY

Aoki, Kenichi. 2002. "Sexual Selection as a Cause of Human Skin Colour Variation: Darwin's Hypothesis Revisited." *Annals of Human Biology* 29 (6): 589–608.

Brace, C. Loring. 1963. "Structural Reduction in Evolution." *American Naturalist* 97 (892): 39–49.

Chaplin, George. 2004. "Geographic Distribution of Environmental Factors Influencing Human Skin Coloration." *American Journal of Physical Anthropology* 125 (3): 292–302.

Frost, Peter. 1988. "Human Skin Color: A Possible Relationship Between Its Sexual Dimorphism and Its Social Perception." *Perspectives in Biology and Medicine* 32 (1): 38–58.

Holick, Michael F. 2001. "A Perspective on the Beneficial Effects of Moderate Exposure to Sunlight: Bone Health, Cancer Prevention, Mental Health and Well Being." In *Sun Protection in Man*. Vol. 3. Edited by P. U. Giacomoni, 11–37. ESP Comprehensive Series in Photosciences. Amsterdam: Elsevier.

Jablonski, Nina G. 2004. "The Evolution of Human Skin and Skin Color." *Annual Review of Anthropology* 33: 585–623.

———, and George Chaplin. 2000. "The Evolution of Skin Coloration." *Journal of Human Evolution* 39: 57–106.

Lamason, R. L., M. A. Mohideen, J. R. Mest, et al. 2005. "SLC24A5, a Putative Cation Exchanger, Affects Pigmentation in Zebrafish and Humans." *Science* 310: 1782–1786.

Makova, Katherina, M. Ramsay, T. Jenkins, and W.-H. Li. 2001. "Human DNA Sequence Variation in a 6.6-kb Region Containing the Melanocortin 1 Receptor Promoter." *Genetics* 158 (3): 1253–1268.

Rana, B. K., D. Hewett-Emmett, L. Jin, et al. 1999. "High Polymorphism at the Human Melanocortin 1 Receptor Locus." *Genetics* 151: 1547–1557.

Rogers, Alan R., David Iltis, and Stephen Wooding. 2004. "Genetic Variation at the MC1R Locus and the Time Since Loss of Human Body Hair." *Current Anthropology* 45 (1): 105–108.

Sturm, Richard A., Rohan D. Teasdale, and Neil F. Box. 2001. "Human Pigmentation Genes: Identification, Structure and Consequences of Polymorphic Variation." *Gene* 277 (1–2): 49–62.

Walter, Hubert von. 1958. "Der Zusammenhang von Hautfarbenverteilung und Intensitat der ultravioletten Strahlung." *Homo* 9 (1): 1–13.

Wheeler, Peter E. 1984. "The Evolution of Bipedality and Loss of Functional Body Hair in Hominids." *Journal of Human Evolution* 13: 91–98.

Nina G. Jablonski

SKINHEADS

SEE *English Skinheads; Neo-Nazis.*

SLAVE CODES

Slave codes were elaborate sets of laws or statutes passed to regulate slavery in all its aspects. In civil-law societies, they were organized into specific codes, such as *Le Code Noir* in French Louisiana, which brought together all the laws and regulations pertaining to enslaved persons and free blacks. In the rest of the United States, however, the slave codes were more amorphous. The entire corpus of laws regulating slavery would be considered the "slave code" for a particular state, though no state ever published all of its laws pertaining to slavery in any one place.

The *Code Noir* and other civil slave codes were based on Roman law, which contained a number of well-developed provisions regulating the status of enslaved persons. However, Roman slavery differed from chattel slavery in the Americas in several key ways. First, Roman slavery was nonracial in character. Race did not determine who could be enslaved, nor did it describe the limits of personal capabilities in the way that proslavery ideology did in the British mainland colonies and the United States from the late seventeenth century to the end of the Civil War. Second, the state of enslavement resulted from a variety of universal causes, including capture during wartime, satisfaction of debt, and punishment for a crime. Finally, under the Roman code, enslaved persons retained a number of rights, including the right to own property and the right to purchase one's own freedom. However, at the same time, Roman law placed no limits on the punishments a master might inflict on a slave and allowed the master to kill a slave without fear of any legal sanction. Third parties who killed Roman slaves could only be charged with destruction of property. Furthermore, if a slave was used as a witness in a trial the law *required* that the slave be tortured before his testimony would be accepted. In the United States, some masters (as well as third parties) were punished for murdering slaves, there were limits on the kinds of punishments slaves could receive, and it was illegal for the courts to order that slaves be tortured.

EARLY DEVELOPMENT OF SLAVE CODES

The mature slave codes of the late antebellum South were products of years of statutory development. These codes regulated free blacks as well as those who were enslaved, and they often had provisions that affected whites as well. Many antebellum statute books had entire sections devoted to slavery. For example, the Georgia Code of 1845 contained forty-nine pages under the general title "Slaves and Free Persons of Color." Similarly, Title 30 of the Virginia Code of 1849, contained five separate chapters, gathered under the heading "Slaves and Free Negroes." Both of these codified sections contained scores of statutes that had been passed over many years and were now put together in one convenient place. Yet even these sections did not contain all the laws in force that dealt with slavery. Thus, the 1845 Georgia code had more than seven additional pages on "Offences Relative to Slaves," whereas other parts of the code also had references to slaves and free blacks.

The first Africans arrived in the British North American colonies in the early seventeenth century. Traditional chronologies date the arrival of blacks in Virginia as occurring in 1619. Initially, these blacks were treated as indentured servants, and some gained their freedom. Gradually, however, some blacks were reduced to slavery, while others remained free. Starting in the 1660s, Virginia began to pass laws to regulate slavery, but these laws were scattered and not part of any coherent legislative program.

The early laws of Virginia and the other colonies tended to regulate race and labor, as much as slavery itself. In 1640 the Virginia legislature passed a law requiring that "All persons except negroes to be provided with arms and ammunition or be fined at pleasure of the Governor and Council." The law was designed to provide for a defense against Indian attacks, and "all persons" clearly referred to adult white males. The law did not prohibit blacks from carrying guns, but it did not require them to do so. This law may reflect a fear of Africans because they were unwilling immigrants to the New World, or simply because they were black. It may also reflect a belief that providing guns to Africans should not be mandatory because as non-Europeans they would not know how to use them. The fact that the law did not prohibit blacks from owning weapons suggests that there was a complex view of blacks at the time. Two years later the Virginia legislature provided for a tax on all male workers and all black female workers. This again may reflect racism, or it may merely point to the reality that black women were performing the same agricultural labor as white and black men. Whether or not it was intended to discriminate, this law had the effect of insuring that most black female workers would be sent into the fields, since their masters would be taxed as if all black female workers were field laborers. Some years later, Virginia applied the same tax rule to white female servants who actually did work in the fields. However, this law meant that the masters of white female servants could avoid the tax by keeping them out of the fields.

These early laws illustrate how race affected how people were treated, even before there was a system of slavery in the colonies. The net result of these early laws was to slowly stigmatize blacks to the point where all whites would begin to view them as different and inferior. Slavery did not begin to emerge in Virginia as a coherent system of labor and race control until the 1660s. Over the next three decades the legislature passed laws regulating slavery and race on a piecemeal basis. In 1662 the legislature decreed that the children of black women would inherit the status of their mothers, even if their fathers were free blacks or free white men. In 1667 the legislature declared that baptism would not lead to the emancipation of blacks already being treated as slaves. Three years later the legislature declared that free blacks (who at that point outnumbered slaves) could never have or control white indentured servants. In 1680 the legislature prohibited blacks from owning guns or swords, while also authorizing the killing of slaves who ran away and refused to return.

CONSOLIDATION OF SLAVE CODES IN VIRGINIA

These laws set a pattern that other colonies would follow up until the American Revolution and that the slave states would continue to follow afterwards. By 1705, Virginia had enough laws regulating slaves and free blacks to constitute a slave code. That year the legislature attempted to adopt a consolidated slave code with the passage of "An Act concerning Slaves and Servants." Running more than fifteen pages with forty-one sections, the law reenacted almost all of the colony's existing legislation regarding blacks and slaves. The law also purported to repeal all previous regulations of slaves and blacks not incorporated into the new act. This was the first comprehensive slave code in the American colonies. It may also be one of the few instances where an American slave code attempted to consolidate all the legislation of a jurisdiction on the subject of slavery and blacks.

However, this important consolidation of the colony's laws on slavery and blacks was probably not intended to be completely comprehensive. For example, the very first law passed in this session was titled "An Act for Laying an Imposition on Liquors and Slaves." This law regulated the importation of slaves and set out the taxes to be levied on them for the years 1706 through 1708. It seems unlikely that the legislature passed this elaborate revenue-raising bill at the beginning of its session only to intentionally repeal it later in the session. This example illustrates the persistent confusion over laws involving slavery in the colonial period. This sort of confusion would continue in the antebellum period. Similarly, another act passed that year prohibited mulattoes, blacks, and Indians from holding public office in Virginia. Again, it does not seem likely that the legislature passed this ban at the beginning of the session only to repeal it as part of the slave code later in the session. The same is probably true for "An Act concerning Tithables" passed before the legislature adopted the slave code. This act made all "negro, mulatto, and Indian women" responsible for paying taxes to support the colonial government; otherwise their owners or masters were required to pay the tax on their behalf. Most important of all, in 1705 the legislature passed "An act for the speedy and easy prosecution of Slaves, committing Capitall Crimes." Surely the later act regulating slaves and servants was not intended to repeal this law.

These laws, and others passed in 1705 before the 1705 slave code, suggest the virtual impossibility of ever consolidating all the laws and regulations of slaves, slavery, and free blacks into any single law. Even if the legislature had somehow accomplished this, and if the 1705 slave code had consolidated all existing legislation on slavery, the effort would have been short-lived. The new slave code was listed as "Chapter 49" in the statutes of 1705. Chapter 50, the very next law passed that term, was "An act to prevent killing Deer at unseasonable times." This law had two sections that dealt with slaves. The first imposed a fine for masters who ordered their slaves to kill deer out of season. The second provided for the whipping of slaves who killed deer out of season on their own accord. Thus, immediately after Virginia supposedly passed a comprehensive and complete slave code to regulate slavery, the colony began to enact new laws that went beyond the code to regulate slaves.

THE PURPOSE OF SLAVE CODES

The experience of Virginia in 1705 would be repeated by every American slave jurisdiction until slavery disappeared. Slave states passed laws regulating slavery at almost every session. These involved taxation, sale, punishment, and policing. The laws were all designed to accomplish three things.

First, the laws were aimed at preventing slave insurrections and rebellions. Because slavery relied ultimately on force, the law had to be forceful. Early slave laws, repeated until the end of slavery, made certain that masters, overseers, and other whites would not be prosecuted if they killed slaves through "moderate coercion," or if they killed slaves who were resisting authority. The laws made it an offense, sometimes a capital offense, for a slave to strike a master or overseer. The laws also regulated the gathering of slaves and their access to weapons or poisons. Along these lines, the laws of the late antebellum period limited gatherings of slaves and free blacks, regulated the religious services of free blacks, prevented free blacks from entering slave states, and prohibited slaves, and sometimes free blacks, from learning to read.

Second, the laws sought to regulate race. This was in part a safety measure, but it was also necessary to justify slavery within a republican society that proclaimed all people to be "equal." Thus, the codes insured that blacks, whether enslaved or free, would be subordinate to whites in all ways. Early laws banned interracial marriage but allowed white men to have unfettered access to black women by making it impossible for black woman, bound or free, from ever testifying against a white. Marriage of enslaved persons was a legal impossibility, and enslaved families were thus entirely at the mercy of masters and the vagaries of the law. The division of property at the death of a master, a bankruptcy, the need to move, or simply a shortage of cash could destroy slave families. Some free blacks voted in the South in the Revolutionary period, and they continued to vote in North Carolina and Tennessee until the mid-1830s, but otherwise blacks had no political rights. They could not hold office, serve on juries or in the militia, testify against whites, or hold certain jobs that might endanger the white community. The slave codes, supported by the courts, made race a presumption of slave status.

Finally, the codes were designed to maximize the profits of masters. The object of the codes was to suppress slaves and blacks so that they could be exploited. The codes protected the property interests of the masters, allowing them to sell, barter, or even give away slaves. Because the laws did not generally recognize slave families, the sale of a slave was a simple matter. Some states prohibited selling infants away from mothers, but such laws could only be enforced in public markets. The codes allowed for private sale without a need to even register the sale.

By 1860 the fifteen slave states had elaborate laws, never easily consolidated, that regulated slavery and allowed masters almost total autonomy over their slaves. Short of murdering a slave or mutilating one, masters could punish slaves as they wished, use and abuse slaves with impunity, and sell slaves with more ease then they could sell real estate. Significantly, one of the major issues of the 1850s was the demand of the South that Congress pass a slave code for the federal territories. Without a law to enforce their property relationship and to suppress slaves to keep them in line, the master class knew slavery could not survive in the territories. Slavery required a legal system that could protect it and preserve it. The slave codes accomplished this.

BIBLIOGRAPHY

Finkelman, Paul, ed. 1997. *Slavery and the Law*. Madison, WI: Madison House.

Morris, Thomas D. 1996. *Southern Slavery and the Law, 1619–1860*. Chapel Hill: University of North Carolina Press.

Paul Finkelman

SLAVE TRADE IDEOLOGY

The institution of slavery, which defined the lowest possible social status in colonial America, required the approval of the prevailing political elites. The transatlantic slave trade therefore rested upon a composite ideological foundation that reflected the core values of the ruling classes of European maritime societies, the African coastal societies, and the colonial elites of the Americas.

The international slave trade of the fifteenth and sixteenth centuries was part of the explosive intellectual, political, and territorial expansion of western Europe, of which the Renaissance was the intellectual expression. The ensuing colonization of the Americas represented its political expression, while the resources of Africa and other colonized parts of the world, including their human capital, were plundered to maximize the economic potential of the so-called New World. Regardless of what is said about the multifarious gradations of black-on-black bondage and its alleged humane mildness, the fact remains that millions of black people were available for acquisition by other people in exchange for things deemed of value. This essay focuses on the potentials for and actual process of exchange far more than the morality of it. The process itself involved vast numbers of purchasers dealing with even greater numbers of sellers. According to the Trans-Atlantic Slave Trade Database, compiled by the W. E. B. Du Bois Institute for African and African American Research, between 25,000 and 35,000 European voyages took something of value to Africans between 1450 and 1867. These ships came away with enslaved human cargoes, containing among others Igbos and Yorubas from Nigeria, Ewes and Minas from Ghana, the Mbundu of Angola or Makua natives from Mozambique on the other side of the continent. In general, Europeans could make their purchases of captives at barracoons and forts only a short distance from their vessels anchored in sight of land.

GANG OF 25 SEA ISLAND

COTTON AND RICE NEGROES,

By LOUIS D. DE SAUSSURE.

On *THURSDAY* the 25th Sept.. 1852, at 11 o'clock, A.M., will be sold at RYAN'S MART, in Chalmers Street, in the City of Charleston,

A prime gang of 25 Negroes, accustomed to the culture of Sea Island Cotton and Rice.

CONDITIONS.—One-half Cash, balance by Bond, bearing interest from day of sale, payable in one and two years, to be secured by a mortgage of the negroes and approved personal security. Purchasers to pay for papers.

No.		*Age.*	*Capacity.*	*No.*		*Age.*	*Capacity.*
1	Aleck,	33	Carpenter.	16	Hannah,	60	Cook.
2	Mary Ann,	31	Field hand, prime.	17	Cudjoe,	22	Prime field hand.
3—3	Louisa,	10		3—18	Nancy,	20	Prime field hand, sister of Cudjoe.
4	Abram,	25	Prime field hand.				
5	Judy,	24	Prime field hand.	19	Hannah,	34	Prime field hand.
6	Carolina.	5		20	James,	13	Slight defect in knee from a broken leg.
7	Simon,	1½		21	Richard,	9	
5—8	Daphne, infant.			22	Thomas.	6	
				5—23	John,	3	
9	Daniel,	45	Field hand, not prime.				
10	Phillis.	32	Field hand.	1—24	Squash,	40	Prime field hand.
11	Will,	9					
12	Daniel,	6		1—25	Thomas,	28	Prime field hand.
13	Margaret,	4					
14	Delia	2					
7—15	Hannah,	2 months.					

Broadside Announces the Sale of 25 Slaves. MANUSCRIPTS, ARCHIVES AND RARE BOOKS DIVISION, SCHOMBURG CENTER FOR RESEARCH IN BLACK CULTURE, THE NEW YORK PUBLIC LIBRARY, ASTOR, LENOX AND TILDEN FOUNDATIONS.

The basic argument here is that certain preexisting traditional ideological foundations and economic practices in place in Africa coincided with the European demand for highly regimented and effective colonial labor force not to be found among white indentured workers or coerced Native Americans laborers. In particular, the types of bondage transactions developed in traditional African societies unwittingly suited the process by which European colonial labor demands were addressed. In addition, the accelerated intensity of European exploitation of African economic practices was a consequence of large-scale state-sponsored mercantilism and the unprecedented maritime capabilities of the Europeans. The striking differences in technology, in coloration, and cultures between Europeans and Africans were codified and stratified by Europeans in the social construction of the concept of "race" as a biological fact of nature. Europeans and Africans thus were seen as polar opposites with attributes of the European world being most positive and those of the African world the least positive, perceptions resulting in the concomitant behaviors that maintained this construction. The elitist ideologies of all three continents—European, African, colonial New World—placed enslaved Africans on the very margins of their respective systems of rights. Enslaved Africans were treated as rightless when held in the forts or baracoons on the African coasts, treated as rightless when purchased by slave traders and sold as rightless in the New World. In the slave trade per se, all business parties were engaged in buying and selling rights over the enslaved, the latter being without legal voice or rights. In the case of enslavement by military conquest, the victors were under no obligation to honor the rights of the vanquished. Indeed, such rights became the property of the victorious, who could and did sell them to third parties.

Whereas transactions involving rights in people and rights to people were continent-wide in Africa, the moral sense of responsibility for others was local and limited to individual identity, kinship or affinity groups. Many scholars forget that traditional Africa comprised many, many diverse political groups and locations, and they erroneously analyze it as a single entity. They frequently presume similarities of condition and status of blacks in the Diaspora to be merely continuities of African continental homogeneity. Common economic practices, however, do not mean uniformity of cultures or of cultural values, otherwise transactions beyond one's primary group would not be possible. The slave trade was based on common factors of acquisition and economic availability on all sides of the continent. That is, however, initially acquired by sellers, humans were available for commercial exchange. Likewise, Europeans acquired Africans for slave labor because they were available for a number of reasons: European religious ideology permitted the enslavement of God-cursed Hamitic "pagans"; and European beliefs that sub-Saharan Africans, bond or free, were an inherently different and inferior species of humankind whose coloration was an obvious indicator, blackness being associated with negativity of quality, value and condition.

The transatlantic slave trade of hundreds of thousands of enslaved was of an unprecedented scale and intensity that dwarfed the annual 5,000 to 10,000 captives headed for Arabia or India. The usual explanation of the availability issue is that Europeans stimulated intertribal warfare on a massive scale with the losers enslaved for European purchasers. Left unexplained is how ship captains, many of whom had never been to Africa, from the relative security of their ships, and later, ground settlements, were able to persuade free Africans to make slaves of other free Africans. Or how they *created* numerous situations where an Olaudah Equiano could be kidnapped and sold several times before final sale to a European buyer. Assuming the conventional instigation, divide and conquer theory of slave acquisition, how did the European sea captains, with often derelict crews, overcome the multiple barriers of communication, transportation and distance to in effect "control" the behaviors of their African slave procurers, especially from sources hundreds of miles inland? In short, how could so few command so many with such astonishing success among so many politically disparate groups?

If theories of unilateral European control of the slave trade as *process* are accepted, then one is looking at history's most persuasive human beings. If one accepts theories of cupidity and economic greed, then what accounts for their reduction of others to the level of chattel slaves, a reduction made permanent through sale? These questions will be examined in an effort to provide a perhaps more rationale explanation of the nature and volume of economic transactions that comprised the slave trade.

ACQUISITION: AN INTRODUCTION

The European labor demands were driven by the highest political authorities in Spain, Portugal, France, England and Holland, and the work of acquiring this labor was carried out by professional slavers. Correspondingly, enslaved Africans were made available by the highest authorities of various regions of Africa, including the kingdoms of Wolof, Igala, Oyo, Anziku, Ashanti, and Dahomey. The elites of settler communities in the New World were the ultimate customers of this inhuman trade. Often forgotten is that the European acquisition of economically available Africans was undertaken on a ship-by-ship basis. From this perspective of acquisition, a remarkably few Europeans on the beaches of Africa obtained astonishingly large numbers of Africans in relatively brief periods of time. The following excerpt from the 1675 report of Captain Peter Blake of the Royal African Company is not unusual in its description of the almost casual manner in which he worked to obtain a satisfactory number of enslaved Africans:

> *Monday 30*: ... came in sight of the towne of Assence. ... Sent my pinase, with six of my passentg'rs to cape Corso with all the lett'rs and pap'rs belonging to the Agent. ... *Tuesday 31st:* ... several canoes came aboard from this towne to whom I sold severall goods for gold and slaves. ... *Sept'r 1675, Wednesday 1st:* severall canoes came ... to whom I sold severall goods for gold and slaves. (Donnan 1930)

Many accounts exist of negotiations between Europeans and African for slaves. In a journal entry made in 1746, a Captain Thomas Phillips complained about having to purchase the local king's slaves: "the worst in the trunk, ... ere they would shew us any other," Phillips wrote, adding:

> we paid more for them than any others, which we could not remedy, it being one of his majesty's prerogatives. ...When we had selected from the rest such as we liked, we agreed in what goods to pay for them, the prices being already stated before the king, how much of each sort of merchandize we were to give for a man, woman, and child, which gave us much ease, and saved abundance of disputes and wranglings, and I gave the owner a note, signifying our agreement of the sorts of goods. (Dow 2002 [1927], p. 61).

Phillips then had to pay taxes to the king's representatives, a stipend to the "sand captain" (the local African security man who kept watch over the growing assemblage of slaves), and supply gold to the seven African canoemen who ferried manacled slaves to his ship, the *Hannibal*. This type of interaction occurred hundreds of thousands of times over the 300-odd points of sale between Senegal and Madagascar.

Phillips's report does not state the number of European seamen on the *Hannibal,* although by the mid-1700s European governments and chartered trading companies had began prescribing the ratio of sailors to the size of the ship, with a doubling of the number if the ship was engaged in the transatlantic slave trade. David Moore, in his account of the *Henrietta Marie* salvage project, notes the following: "In 1702, the frigate *Angola,* tonnage (capacity) of 125, carried a crew of 24; the 1706 galley *Grayhound,* tonnage 100, carried a crew of 20 seamen, in addition to the captain, quartermaster, doctor, book keeper and black 'linguister' or translater [sic]." (Moore 1989, p. 41). The 120-ton *Henrietta Marie* itself, which foundered in Key West in 1700, had a crew of eighteen to twenty basically poor whites and a cargo of 205 slaves. In writing of the battles for a share of the slave trade between the Portuguese and Spanish (and later the French), Basil Davidson noted that "out of these grim rivalries, in small ships and with small crews, ... wrecked and ruined by one another in sudden battles from the coast of Senegal to the Bight of Benin, there nonetheless emerged a pattern of commercial exchange and, gradually, a recognized order of behavior" (Davidson 1961, p. 53). This "recognized behavior" was essentially persuasion rather than coercion. In actual practice, European slavers generally purchased slaves already in captivity, as Captain Phillips and many others reported.

Some African societies refused to be a part of the transatlantic slave business, most notably, at least for a time, Queen Nzinga Mbande of the Ndongo Kingdom, whose Imbangala mercenary warriors valiantly battled Portuguese slavers in the 1620s. Ironically, Nzinga later became "a Dutch ally, and undertook several small wars locally in order to provide the Dutch with more slaves than she could otherwise supply" (Thomas 1997, p. 184).

AVAILABILITY

In treating the issue of availability, it is necessary to note the various ways in which individuals were designated "unfree." Orlando Patterson, an international authority on global slavery, has identified at least eight different ways that individuals could become unfree: by military defeat, by community assault or kidnapping, as payment of tax, as payment of a debt, by judicial decree, by abandonment (of minors), by voluntary self-enslavement, and by being the offspring of a slave. If unfree Africans were not technically considered slaves by their overlords, after they were bought by Europeans slavers and placed into the international streams of commerce, they clearly became chattel, regardless of the words or concepts used by their sellers.

Stressing the "mildness" of the original African bondage system does not cancel the fact that these pawns, clients, vassals or fictive kinmen were sold to Europeans. Along with a host of other scholars, Patterson holds that the vast majority of Africans in the slave trade were captured in war or were kidnapped. These two sources provided more slaves than all the others combined, except perhaps birth.

The near universal prevalence of warfare as a means of creating unfree categories of individuals rests on a simple ideological foundation: In traditional warfare, the winner literally owns the loser, the victor having held off killing the vanquished. The loser owes the winner everything, including life itself. In traditional Africa, as elsewhere, the defeated males were often massacred, while the women and children became social outsiders whose "rights" were the prerogatives of the groups now controlling them. These prerogatives may include the ability to "own" others, to "own" material goods, or to marry and create families and to be considered adopted kinsmen. In many societies, a military victory was interpreted as a godly blessing for the winner and a reward for righteous conduct. This is the idea behind the concept of just and unjust wars. However, in wars of acquisition in traditional Africa, this European concept of a "just war" did not apply. In the Ganda kingdom in Uganda, for example, "it was in war ... that lay the sources of their wealth such as livestock, slaves and ivory; in sum, the very things of which there is a shortage in Buganda"(Davidson 1969, p. 238).

RIGHTS AS COMMODITIES

It has been argued that traditional Africa was perhaps unique in its concept of the nature of rights. Here, "rights" had a dualistic aspect, in that they could: (1) be "owned" or recognized as belonging to the individual in accordance with his or her group membership status and under certain rules, or (2) be treated as commodities available for negotiated exchange. Suzanne Kopytoff and Igor Miers, who are close students of bondages in Africa, have this to say about rights: "When the question of rights-in-persons is considered in relation to African cultures, it becomes clear, first that such rights tend to be explicitly recognized and precisely defined in law; second, that they are the subject of complex transaction; and finally, that the position of the so-called 'slave' can only be understood in the general cultural context of these rights" (Miers and Kopytoff 1977, p. 7).

In examining the precision, explicitness, variability and transferability of rights in traditional African cultures, anthropologists have concluded that few if any societies surpassed these societies in marketing such rights, which were seen as transferable in whole or in part. This meant

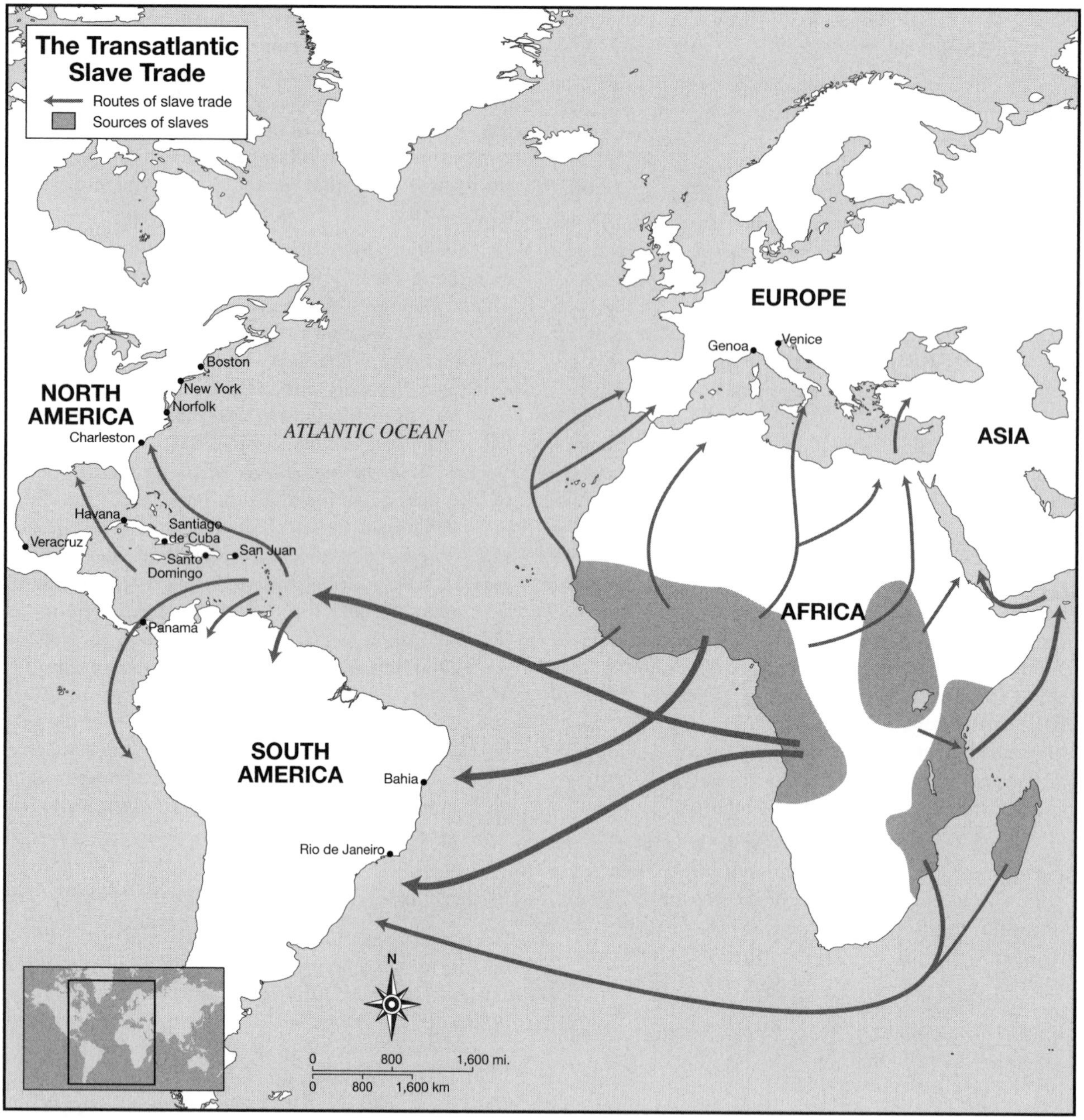

The Trans-Atlantic Slave Trade. *During a period of nearly four hundred years about ten million Africans were forced to become slave laborers in the Americas.* MAP BY XNR PRODUCTIONS. GALE.

that many different levels of status and service existed as a consequence of the sale of rights, the lowest possible level being that of chattel slavery, where individual rights were totally transferred from a seller to a purchaser.

In kin-based societies where persons were also assets, the details of group membership rights are matters of customary laws of exchange, the ultimate purpose being that of conserving original values while effecting change. This point is best illustrated in the case of traditional marriages throughout continental Africa. Traditional Africans saw marriage as an occasion for the negotiated exchange of assets (both bride wealth and bride price), not only between the prospective bride and groom, but also between their corporate bodies or clans. "Bride price" refers to the value of the items involved in the bride wealth. Rights related to sexual expression and to individual and clan claims on children were altered under customary rules and modified by circumstance to determine the new conditions of kinship and "belonging." During the slave trade era, "lobola," or bride price, was measured in cattle—the number of cattle required depended on the bride's particular assets, skill level, previous role in her family, and other factors. Details were determined by custom, and families planned years in advance to comply with them. Whereas in the early twenty-first century cash is as likely to be used as cattle, such practices are still followed in some societies. Jan Vansina, the author of *Kingdoms of the Savanna,* notes that in the traditional Kongo, "the Bolia and Kuba . . . have a type of marriage whereby in return for a great amount of bride wealth, the children or some of the children are detached from the descendents of the mother and become members of the father's lineage." Depending on the group custom, bride wealth rules may require, for example, that "men and their spouses and children . . . shift from the village of the husband's father to that of his mother's brother" (Vansina 1966, p. 25). If there are several daughters, each of whom is planning to marry, the transfer of clan membership presents bride wealth and bride price negotiators with a complicated scenario, the contents of which must meet the requirements of custom and satisfy the expectations of the groups involved.

Here, the concept of "belonging" is helpful in understanding traditional African practices of human exchange. If one were a full kinship member of a group, then one's person and one's rights were considered as "belonging in" the group, and as such they were basically not automatically subject to commodity exchange away from the group. Within the group was focused the intense religious devotion to the welfare and moral conduct of its members toward one another and toward peaceful outsiders. Full kinship, and hence full membership, rested on birth, marriage, and ritualistic total adoption or fictive inclusion. In between full inclusion and total exclusion of rights were many levels of subordination with customary "rights" attached to each level.

These rights could be modified, depending on given circumstances, by juridical decision, by in-group rules of "loaning" or pawning group members to other groups to satisfy an obligation, or by "self-sale" to a group for survival. "Belonging to" a group, on the other hand, stressed an external, outsider attachment to a given group. If one "belonged to" a kin group as a non-kin person, then in certain situations the rules of the commodity system could be applied. The remarkable thing about rights-in-persons transactions is that they appear to have been peaceful, with revolts of dependents being quite rare. The critical point is that once detached from a "belonging in" or a "belonging to" group, the affected person sold had no third party clan or community protection. Rights were detachable assets and could be treated as property in and of themselves. No continent-wide rule or agency existed to supervise human commodity rights transactions between European purchasers and African sellers.

PEOPLE POSSESSION AS POWER

In precolonial African societies, the larger the group, the greater a person's individual status was in the context of other groups. If kinship was the cement holding together African lineages, "in the struggle for prestige, what was critical in *all* African societies was the number of dependents an ambitious man could acquire" (Patterson 1982, p. 83 [emphasis in original]).

Increases in group size were a function of natural increase among members within the group and of the numbers of individuals who were acquired by the group. Group enlargement also occurred as a result of peace negotiations. Ironically, the greater the size of a given group, the greater the ease with which it could reduce smaller groups to feudalistic vassalage and certain individuals to chattel slavery. The larger the group, the greater its prestige. This kind of situation might be defined as "wealth-in-people."

Not only did traditional African societies value wealth-in-people as defining the intrinsic status of the group, but such societies appreciated people-as-wealth from a commodity standpoint. Regardless of the size of the social groups involved, and virtually independent of their relations with one another, people as exchange commodities were a common part of precolonial social systems throughout most of the African continent. The practice was quite common, whether in Senegal on the west coast or Kenya on the east, and whether in small kin-based social formations of a thousand souls or within large states such as the fifteenth-century Songhai Empire, whose boundaries could contain modern France and part of Spain. In the fourteenth century, Mansa Musa, ruler of ancient Mali (the predecessor state to Songhai), went to Mecca with an entourage of a reported 500 slave porters carrying supplies and exchange goods, bankrupting himself in the process.

Dependent persons without rights in traditional Africa were not only a form of wealth in and of themselves, they were also a source of additional wealth through their labors. According to John Thornton, who has looked rather closely at traditional bondage practices in Africa, "If Africans did not have private ownership of one factor of production (land), they could still own another, labor" (Thornton 1992, p. 85). Thornton argues that the relative absence of individual private ownership of land as wealth facilitated the view that ownership of labor was wealth. Land itself was the joint property of the group and was vested in the king or official head of the group. Persons possessing control or ownership of dependents, bond or otherwise, could profit by working communally held lands. The rulers, especially on the Gold Coast, used slaves as part of the apparatus of government. They were "used by state officials as a

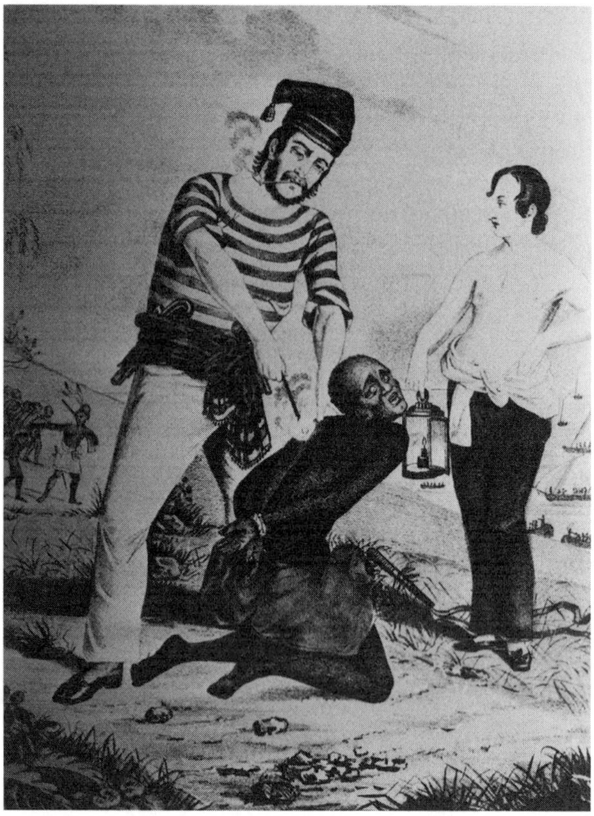

Branding Slaves on the Coast of Africa. *A slave is branded prior to embarkation.* © BETTMANN/CORBIS.

dependent and loyal group, both for the production of revenue and for performing military service in the struggles between kings or executives . . . and other elite parties who sought to control royal absolutism" (Thornton 1992, p. 89).

All of the practices involving the acquisition and use of detachable dependents with attenuated or nonexistent rights contributed to the formation of a commercial ideology and mindset that made enslaved Africans available for exchange to lands east, north, and west of the African landmass, so that dependent Africans were soon found in India, China, and even Russia. The great tragedy, then, of traditional African social history is that its varied societies universally recognized commercial property rights in dependent persons far more than universal human rights. For traditional African societies, freedom was limited to persons "belonging in" their corporate groups. In practice, this meant that the market for rights as commodities was the whole world, whereas the venue for freedom was only one's own defining local unit of humanity. African bondsmen were available to those who had the means to acquire them. The African proprietors of rights in and over other Africans treated the latter as gold.

The Europeans, meanwhile, in their accumulation frenzy to supply colonial labor demands, treated African availability as a gold rush, literally cashing in on the African conception of people-as-wealth. Their acquisitive greed stimulated African acquisitiveness regarding certain European trade goods: cloth, iron bars, guns, alcohol, basins, beads, mirrors, and so on, for the African ruling elites, stimulating commercial transactions that set in motion millions of human souls on thousands of ships over hundreds of years. Neither European purchasers nor African sellers could have existed without the other, sharing the ideology that some people of Africa could be treated as commodities. In retrospect, greed may be seen as the only common link between Africans and Europeans in the watershed years of the fifteenth and sixteenth centuries. This greed may have boomeranged on Africa, but it propelled Europe toward global power.

EUROPEAN ECONOMIC IDEOLOGY: MERCANTILISM

The international transatlantic slave trade lasted nearly 500 years, and the principal ideology that governed the European aspect of it was mercantilism or state coordination of private economic transactions, which was as important to the ideology of the slave trade as the ideology of transferable rights was to African participation in it. Both were ideologies of acquisition and wealth production. In the fifteenth and sixteenth centuries, mercantilism was the belief that the state should coordinate all aspects of its economy in order to maximize its political power in an international environment of multistate competition among sovereigns claiming a divine right to rule.

The term *mercantilism* is a product eighteenth-century thought, when it was retroactively applied to historical analyses of the preceding two centuries by Adam Smith, Edward Ricardo, and Jeremy Bentham in their economic *laissez faire* arguments. The ruling elites of Spain, Portugal, England, France, and Holland, all maritime nations, were convinced that only by controlling the productive energies of their respective social systems could they achieve the power to prevail in economic and military contests among themselves. Gold and silver were required for funding large mercenary military forces on land and building a navel presence at sea. This meant that buying and selling commodities of any sort had to be done for the purpose of increasing rather than decreasing the gold supply within the nation. Of course gold was the original European interest in Africa. For the mercantilists, a healthy economy called for a balance of trade, or a situation in which the net result of the economic transactions of a nation was that it gained more gold and silver than it lost. To achieve this balance, a given nation was expected to export more goods than it imported. Tariffs or taxes on imported goods were also used to achieve this balance. Under mercantilism, a great value was placed on the control of import-export items, as well as on the sources of gold and silver.

NAVAL CAPABILITIES

The movement of gold and silver, and of slaves and the by-products of slave labor, called for a strong naval presence. If mercantilism dictated economic collaboration within a society, then naval capabilities were necessary to move items of wealth, whether it was gold or human capital in the form of enslaved Africans. Mercantilism was the master ideology of the age of European expansion, and it directed and concentrated social energy with unprecedented precision. Whatever the form of these commodities, the wealth of nations depended on the conscious supervision of economic activities, including productive European domestic and African foreign labor. Enslaved colonial Africans worked out of sight of the peoples of the mainland of participating nation-states, a fact that may have contributed to spread of the concept of freedom for the average European and bondage for the average African in the Americas. Thus, the color line was drawn several centuries before W. E. B. DuBois, the eminent African American polymath, declared it to be "the problem of the twentieth century." In the context of mercantilism, the institution of slavery was a secondary institution, a means to an end much larger than itself. It was an extremely controlled support of mercantilism.

EUROPEAN ABSOLUTISM AND ELITISM

The sixteenth-century European seafaring societies bordering the Atlantic Ocean had several things in common, including several natural advantages. England, Holland, France, Spain, and, above all, Portugal, possessed extremely long and easily accessible waterfronts, a situation that helped to sharpen their maritime skills. These societies also had geographic size sufficient to support investments in the transatlantic slave trade, and all but one was headed by an absolute monarch (Elizabeth I in England, Louis XIV in France, Dom Joâo III in Portugal and Charles V and different Phillips in Spain). The West India Company, established in 1621, was a principal transatlantic conveyer of slaves, governed by a Council of Nineteen, whose members were usually of one mind in matters of trade.

The trading company was the instrument of commerce and settlement, operating with delegated authority and partial funding from the state. Portugal, Spain, France, England, Holland, and even Sweden set up trading companies with varying levels of authority and autonomy to link colonies to the home country. To cite their names is to conjure up the age of exploration and settlement: the Casa de Contracio (Portugal, 1510), the Caracas Company (1628), the Dutch West India Company (1621), Compagnie des Cent-Associés (Company of a Hundred Associates, 1628), the Massachusetts Bay Company (1629), the Brazil Company (Portugal, 1649), the English Company of Royal Adventurers (1660), the Hudson Bay Company (1670), and the Royal African Company (1672), among others. In one way or another, the political and mercantile elites dominated these companies, whose existence represented sums of money and other resources far beyond the reach of a single merchant. The companies were de facto representatives of their governments as well as agents of private investors. In international trade, they were cargo carriers; the Royal African Company, for example, transported several hundred enslaved Africans across the Atlantic Ocean. Like the triangle of trade itself, these companies had three places of business: the home office, the African station or garrison, and the office of agents on the various islands, on the American mainland, or in the Brazilian coastal cities.

Companies established to underwrite the international business operations, including the use of slaves, initially were headed by the political and financial elites of their sponsoring countries. When the Royal African Company was organized, among its twenty-plus investors were the Duke of York (for whom New York is named); Sir George Carteret, the commissioner for Trade and Plantations; and the philosopher John Locke. The chief personnel of England's Company of Royal Adventurers in 1660 included four members of the royal family itself, four barons, five earls, and two dukes. Queen Elizabeth I initially opposed slavery, but in 1564 she became an investor in slaving expeditions. When the French West India Company was organized in 1664, King Louis XIV himself set aside 3,000,000 livres to cover its expenses, including the purchase of African slaves for its Caribbean operations. His finance minister, Jean Baptiste Colbert, was its principal director. In Spain the "House of Contracts" was a subdivision of the Treasury Department, which reported directly to the king. The rulers of Spain and Portugal were direct participants in the operations of the colonial slave holdings, each receiving tax revenue from the slave acquisition agreements, or *asientas*. The Dutch Council of Nineteen hired the upper-status managers of the West India Company.

In short, colonial territories were held to be the possessions of kings and queens and by extension of the societies that established them. Mercantilism brought together rulers and their agents, agricultural and manufacturing sectors, and entrepreneurs and shippers on both sides of the Atlantic. Iberian, French, English, or Dutch companies were the micromanagers and movers of settlers and slaves, of gold and silver, of tobacco and other agricultural products such as sugar, coffee, rice, and cotton, and of forestry products such as timber. They transported the first generations of European settlers, including indentured servants and enslaved Africans to do the work of producing the goods and services for the trade side of the triangular system. In the context of mercantilism, the historian Niels Steensgaard wrote: "The specific north-west European contribution to the organization of European expansion became the companies, a unique form of co-operation between merchant entrepreneurs and government interests" (1981, p. 263). The entire trade system, however, depended on tightly controlled labor.

Such was the powerful combinations behind their seagoing agents dealing with African fragmented authorities representing social formations ranging from several hundreds to hundreds of thousands of persons "belonging in" them, the Ashanti and Dahomey kingdoms being examples of the larger size groups.

Some fifty years before Christopher Columbus dropped anchor in San Salvador in 1492, precolonial sugar cultivation shifted from a multicultural, multicolored workforce of Greek, Jewish, Islamic, and Cypriot slaves in the Middle East and the Mediterranean regions to an all-black enslaved labor force producing sugar on the West African Islands of Fernando Po and São Tomé and Principe, as well as the Cape Verde Islands and the Madeira and Canary Islands in the Atlantic Ocean. By the middle of the fifteenth century, Islamic and Christian slaveholders had adopted the ideology of the Hamitic curse, which lent a biblical imprimatur to consigning blacks to bondage, even as their own faiths began prohibiting, in theory, their enslavement of their fellow Christians, even as they continued to engage in internecine wars that usually ended in some sort of peace without enslavement of losers.

Before sugar cane cultivation became the key commodity of the slave trade, the people of the Iberian Peninsula were already accustomed to seeing blacks as a servile race of laborers. As early as 1450, the city of Lisbon, Portugal, contained an estimated 10,000 enslaved African domestics and porters. The Spanish cities of Seville and Cadiz contained large numbers of both Moslem and pagan blacks, some enslaved and some free. Religious creed, non-Iberian cultural backgrounds, and a lack of wealth appear to have been more influential than color per se in determining status. But with the advent of an all-black, all-slave workforce on the sugar plantations, a conflation of creed, culture, condition, and color took place. Henceforth, any African outside of Africa itself was presumed to be a slave.

Enslaved black laborers thus represented the personification of a host of negatives long associated with ideologies and traditions that represented blackness as evil, God's curse, the devil, beauty's opposite, and nighttime fears. The separation of blacks from other categories of humankind was seen as absolute. The black ideological color line existed in the European popular mind long before it appeared in European overseas commodity production. In large measure this pre-existing concept accounts for the speed with which colonial powers acquired and sprinkled the New World with enslaved Africans. This color line, in turn, rested on an ideological predisposition toward black servitude that was jolted into prominence by the almost convulsive energy of colonization. This color line has lingered ever since, embedded in the cultural memory of Western civilization. This rigorously enforced line, once literally a matter of life or death, has given the social construct of "race" a power that confounds reason.

BIBLIOGRAPHY

Davidson, Basil. 1961. *The African Slave Trade: Precolonial History, 1450–1850.* Boston: Little Brown.

———. 1969. *The African Genius: An Introduction to African Cultural and Social History.* Boston: Little, Brown.

Davis, David B. 2006. *Inhuman Bondage: The Rise and Fall of Slavery in the New World.* New York: Oxford University Press.

Donnan, Elizabeth. 1930. *Documents Illustrative of the History of the Slave Trade to America*, 11 vols. Washington, DC: Carnegie Institution.

Dow, George Francis. 2002 (1927). *Slave Ships and Slaving.* Mineola, NY: Dover Publications.

French, Howard W. 1998. "The Atlantic Slave Trade: On Both Sides Reason for Remorse." *New York Times* April 5.

Jordan, Winthrop. 1968. *White over Black: American Attitudes toward the Negro, 1550–1812.* Chapel Hill: University of North Carolina Press.

Miers, Suzanne, and Igor Kopytoff. 1977. *Slavery in Africa: Historical and Anthropological Perspectives.* Madison: University of Wisconsin Press.

Moore, David D. 1989. "Anatomy of a Seventeenth-Century Slave Ship: Historical and Archaeological Investigations of the Henrieta Marie, 1699." Master's thesis, East Carolina University Maritime Studies Program.

Patterson, Orlando. 1982. *Slavery and Social Death: A Comparative Study.* Cambridge, MA: Harvard University Press.

Steensgaard, Niels. 1981. "The Companies as a Specific Institution in the History of European Expansion." In *Companies and Trade: Essays on Overseas Trading Companies during the Ancien Regime*, edited by Leonard Blussse and Femme Gaastra. Leiden, The Netherlands: Leiden University Press.

Thomas, Hugh. 1997. *The Slave Trade: The Story of the Atlantic Slave Trade, 1440–1870.* New York: Simon & Schuster.

Thornton, John. 1992. *Africa and Africans in the Making of the Atlantic World, 1400–1680.* Cambridge, U.K.: Cambridge University Press.

Tishksen, Joel E. 2000. "Central Africa: Peoples and States." In *Africa*, Vol. 1: *African History before 1885*, edited by Toyin Falola, 213–214. Durham, NC: Carolina Academic Press.

Vansina, Jan. 1966. *Kingdoms of the Savanna.* Madison: University of Wisconsin Press.

Walzer, Michael. 1977. *Just and Unjust Wars: A Moral Argument with Historical Illustrations.* New York: Basic Books.

Russell L. Adams

SLAVERY, RACIAL

In specific historical contexts, when some human societies began to accumulate surplus wealth and disperse it unequally among various class strata, slavery became possible. For hunting and gathering bands and most horticultural societies, the human needs for balanced reciprocity and generalized cooperation militated against the formation of slave relations. Nor did all state societies have slavery, but a socially stratified state society is a historical requirement for institutionalized slavery. Moreover, in early instances of localized slavery, it was not especially "racial," because long-distance transport, globalization, alienation, and racial diversity were generally not present.

DEFINITIONS AND HISTORICAL FOUNDATIONS

Usually, slavery appears in class societies that create individuals and populations that are being punished, captured, transformed into an economic resource, or a combination of all three. Slavery always involves coercion because it is an involuntary relationship between human groups. One may gloss this relationship by defining slaves as "prisoners of war" insofar as "war" can be defined ecologically, economically, socially, politically, militarily, or on the basis of racial or ethic categories and gender. Slavery has existed for roughly 4,000 or 5,000 years under specific circumstances in which it grows, thrives, or declines.

Even when ancient slavery was institutionalized, it was usually on a small scale and practiced by high-status minority groups. Often, early slavery was closer to indenture and provisional servitude, as certain rights and responsibilities existed for slaves and slavery was not necessarily a lifetime status. As human groups moved into imperial and conquest modes, slavery increased. Indeed the Western term *slave* is derived from "Slavic," the source of captives in the expanding Roman Empire. Nascent Rome first captured local rivals such as the Latins, Etruscans, and Sabines and coerced them to pay "tribute" and become subordinate "tribes" of Rome. When Rome expanded across the Adriatic Sea to the Slavic people, the subordinated status of "othered" groups became permanent. Captives from these Slavic lands entered the Roman political economy in perpetual servitude for cash exchange to work on large-scale agricultural estates and mines, in domestic service, as concubines, to provide labor on galleys or plantations, and in gladiatorial combat.

The process of "othering" slaves on the basis of their lands, language, gender, property, sexuality, or ethnicity, and later on the basis of socially constructed "race" occurs only when greater distances for slave origins become substantial factors. Slave systems that are based on "race" require not only state formation but also large-scale "globalized" states in which racio-ethnic "othering" takes place and the slave's hope of returning to his or her place of origin is minimal at best.

In ancient Egypt, certainly by the imperial New Kingdom (1500–1000 BCE), if not much earlier, slaves were clearly "othered" in the graphic images that depicted ethno-racial plurality and in lexical references to "vile" and otherwise "despicable" Nubians and Africans who were under their colonial occupation. This important issue has been carefully explored by Fluehr-Lobban and Rhodes in *Race and Identity in the Nile Valley* (2004). In Mesopotamia the cuneiform glyph for a female slave was composed of the symbol for "woman" from a "foreign land," and the famed Code of Hammurabi indicated very specific legal rights, duties, and punishments for slaves versus free versus nobility.

An interesting instance of slavery in the Greek "Golden Age" occurs with the famed slave storyteller known as Aesop. He was expressly known as a slave of foreign rather than domestic origins who was "ugly." His name reflects the general reference to his "Ethiopian" or Nubian origins. His death was essentially an informal lynching. In this example, one may condense the defining features of an imperial state society, including "othering" and denigrating on the basis of race.

Incidentally, the Nubian (Sudanic) word for slave was *nogor*, possibly the source of the Latin word "Negro." There were other words for the color black, but this word was used just for "black people." Even in the early twenty-first century, for example, French has the terms *noir* and *negre*, both meaning "black" but one used for the color and one for people. In American English "black" is neutral or positive but *nigger* is highly negative or problematic.

Certainly the Greeks were not the first in the Old World to reach this point in slave relationships, nor were the subsequent Romans. At the start of their empires, slavery was "racial" in a limited sense because the slave populations were largely of European origin, though they were distinguishable by language. When these empires reached their fullest geographical extents and conquered "racially" diverse peoples, then the coercive power of slavery could be "racial."

Earlier areas that passed through this process included the Nile Valley, Mesopotamia, ancient China,

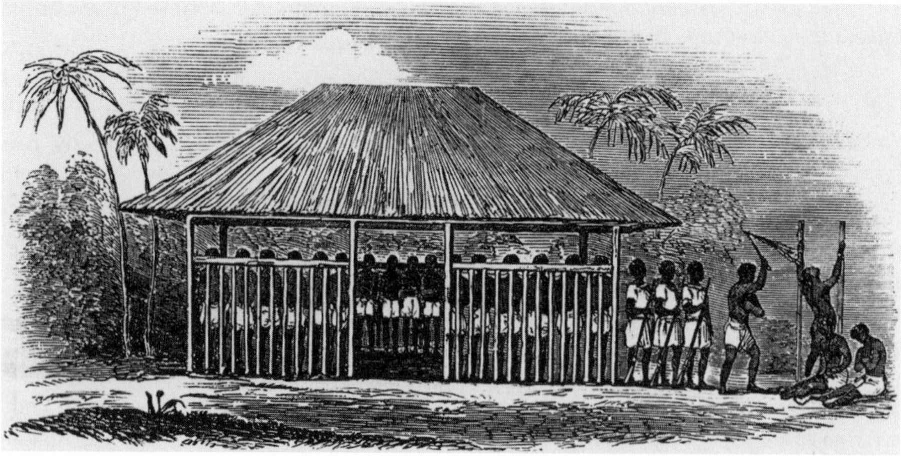

Slave Barracoon in Africa. *African tribes used huts called barracoons to hold captured slaves before they were sold to Europeans. Slaves were typically chained together at the neck or ankles. This illustration also shows a slave being whipped, probably as punishment for trying to escape.* TIME LIFE PICTURES/MANSELL/TIME LIFE PICTURES/GETTY IMAGES.

the Indus Valley, Europe, and the Middle East, especially the Phoenician, Greek, and Roman empires at the high points of their commercial power and military greatness. Later examples can be found in New World societies such as the Incans, Mayans, and Aztec.

Taking note of the Egyptian example, despite some protestations that it was not a slave society, there is abundant linguistic, textual, and archaeological evidence that slaves did certainly exist, especially by foreign capture when military tribute was commonly enumerated in slaves, livestock, and natural resources seized from the peripheries of their expansive empire. The same holds true for ancient Mesopotamia, whether in Assyria, Babylon, or other state formations of that region. For the relatively small-scale city-states of medieval Europe, imperial conquest could not be so easily sustained, so the status of slaves often devolved to serf and feudal servitude. During medieval "religious" and imperial crusades, slavery was restored on a grander scale both by Christian Europeans and the Muslim of the Middle East.

Among the savanna kingdoms in Africa, such as Ghana, Mali, Songhai, and the East African states of Kilwa, Zanzibar, and Mogadishu, slave raiding and trading was an essential part of the domestic and export economies. While these trades started earlier than the European slave trading of the fifteenth through the eighteenth centuries and lasted longer (and even still exist), in general they were not usually linked to large-scale plantation production of cotton, sugar, and tobacco. Instead, the African and Arab experiences with slavery were more associated with domestic service, concubines, and military service. Moreover, de facto slave status gradually diminished for individuals within the incorporative nature of Islamic societies, while de jure slavery in the New World was often castelike and permanent over generations.

In the context of late medieval imperial expansion, New World exploration, Arab world circumnavigation, and religious justification, large-scale, racially based slave systems took root. The watershed year of 1492 was a tipping point in Euro-African relations with the voyages of Columbus, West African exploration, and the termination of centuries of Moorish occupation with the expulsion of Arabs and Jews from Iberia. The experimental foundation of the political economy of racially constructed slavery was put into place in the Canary Islands as early as 1441 with genocide against the native Guanache population and the installation of a sugar plantation economy run with slave labor. In the case of medieval Ghana, Europeans glossed this savanna kingdom as the "Land of Gold" or the "Land of the Blacks," echoed in the Arabic term *Bilad as-Sudan* (the land of the blacks). To the extent that the crusading Christian worlds were warring against the "infidel" Muslim worlds, taking slave captives and other items of wealth was justified as military booty that could be used to economic advantage.

As Europeans sailed down the West African coastline, their commodity-based nomenclature gives some mute testimony to their interests with references to the "Pepper Coast" (Sierra Leone), the "Grain Coast" (Liberia), the "Ivory Coast" (still the same name), the "Gold Coast" (Ghana), the "Slave Coast" (today's Benin and Nigeria), and the "Shrimp Coast" (Cameroon). From these places some of the human and natural resources for European and New World development could be found, along with markets for European manufactured goods such as cloth, firearms, metal ware, and alcoholic spirits.

EURO-AFRICAN SLAVE TRADE: RISE AND EVOLUTION

The one-way Atlantic crossing from Africa to the New World known generally as the Middle Passage took untold millions from African homelands to shortened lives in American mines, plantations, docks, and estates. Sometimes it was termed "the world's longest graveyard," because the mortality rate in the Middle Passage varied by the length of the voyage, the degree of "tight-packing" or "loose-packing," health conditions, mutinies, and so forth. Some ships were lost altogether; others came through with cargoes largely intact. On average, scholars calculate that about one in five slaves boarded in West Africa did not reach the New World alive. Other calculations note that for every slave boarded, at least another one died in resistance to the slave raiding of Africans or Europeans. For those reaching New World markets, life was often very harsh and brutally shortened.

A great and long debate has been under way about the total number of Africans involved the Middle Passage diaspora. Probably the strongest, most defensible and conservative numbers are those offered by Phillip Curtin (1969): from 10 million to 15 million. However, for parts of this history, the Atlantic slave trade was openly illegal; hence, official records were not kept. Other records were simply lost. Given the many centuries, nationalities, and contexts involved, it is clear that the numbers were much higher, especially if the factors of mortality before boarding and the Middle Passage were included more effectively or accurately. This statistic will never be known precisely.

If the Atlantic slave trade began in 1441 when African slaves were first taken by Europeans from the area of modern Mauritania to Portugal or the Canary Islands, it was another fifty years before they crossed the Atlantic Ocean. Although the early sailors for the Spanish and English Crowns sometimes locally enslaved Native Americans, it was in 1502 that the first African slaves were brought to the New World by Spanish slavers.

More prominent in American history were the events in August 1619, when twenty "Negroes" were brought to Jamestown, Virginia, as enslaved Africans (indentured servants) on a Dutch man-of-war. White indentured servitude was also legal in Virginia. English indenture obligations initially lasted four to seven years for whites or "Negroes" but was later extended to life for Africans. By 1629 Governor John Winthrop of Massachusetts owned slaves, and in the chartering of the Massachusetts Bay Company, only propertied free white men were allowed to participate. From the 1630s to the 1660s there was steady privatization of Indian land in New England, where the population of Indians was steadily reduced by warfare, execution, displacement, slavery, and disease as some 20,000 English settlers arrived between 1630 and 1642. Also in this period, Scottish slaves were exiled from Scotland to the New World as the English extended their empire upon the backs of the Celtic and Pictish peoples.

In June 1636, Roger Williams founded a settlement in Providence, Rhode Island, for political opponents of the Massachusetts Bay Colony. Initially, he recognized the property rights of Native Americans, who were "paid" for the privatization of their land. It appears that the Indians had a different understanding of this "transfer," because the concepts of "private" and "perpetuity" could not easily be translated. In neighboring Connecticut in 1636 the Pequot war/massacre/ethnic cleansing took place when settlers attacked a Pequot fort; while seven Pegquot were captured, seven escaped, and more than 700 were killed. The scene of carnage was upsetting to the young English soldiers, who reported that "great and doleful was the bloody sight." Williams wrote to Winthrop asking about what to do with captured Pequots; subsequently, some 1,400 Pequot men, women, and children were sold and exported from New England as slaves to Bermuda and the Bahamas. Williams provided key intelligence about the attack, because he was then allied with the Pequot rivals, the Narragansetts. Thus, some of the earliest racial slavery in the American colonies was based on the military subjugation, genocide, ethnic cleansing, and commercial exportation of native peoples as slaves. Some costs of financing the militias were through the sale of captives. Addressing this practice in 1641, Massachusetts legalized slavery for "lawful captives taken in just wars and such strangers as willingly sell themselves, or are sold to us." In 1642 "man-stealing" was made a capital offense in Connecticut.

The legal and moral contestation of racial slavery existed from the start. Needless to say the slaves as well as some moral leaders were opposed to this practice, but because they were excluded from legislative bodies, their voices were muted. In 1644 eleven slaves petitioned against slavery in Dutch New York. Each was given a tract of land. In 1645 there were antislavery protests in Massachusetts. These events indicate there was a struggle against slavery the moment it was started. Despite the legal status of the institution, these were laws for a group of wealthy white men. It is factually incorrect to dismiss slavery as broadly acceptable because it was legal while various groups actively opposed it. These contradictions can be seen in the first slave ship departing directly for Africa from Boston, *Rainbow*, under Captain Smith, which was forced to forfeit the slaves and return them to Africa. The questionable status of slaves is also apparent when slavery was made legal in Connecticut in 1650 and in Rhode Island in 1652, but only for a ten-year period or until the slave was twenty years

Scene in the Hold of the "Blood-Stained Gloria." (Middle Passage.)

Cargo Hold of a Slave Ship. *The conditions aboard a slaving vessel were generally poor and it is estimated that one-fifth of all slaves died in the passage to the Americas.* MANUSCRIPTS, ARCHIVES, AND RARE BOOKS DIVISION, SCHOMBURG CENTER FOR RESEARCH IN BLACK CULTURE, THE NEW YORK PUBLIC LIBRARY, ASTOR, LENOX AND TILDEN FOUNDATIONS.

old. In principle, this made slavery a temporary status, but the act was not enforced.

In 1655 the first known Dutch slave ship, the *Wittepaert*, imported slaves from Africa to New York. When the first Quakers arrived in Rhode Island in 1657, they were morally uneasy about slavery, yet some Friends had slaves. The legal threshold from term indenture to racially based slave systems was crossed in 1661 when the Virginia Slave Statues made slave status hereditary. In 1663 slavery was made legal in Maryland, but resistance is also clear when a Virginia slave conspiracy was broken up. Further clarification of Maryland law in 1664 said that baptism did not affect slave status, and it became illegal for white women to marry blacks. In 1665 slavery was made legal in New York.

THE ECONOMICS OF NEW WORLD SLAVERY

The heyday of American slavery was the eighteenth century with sustained imports of slaves directly from Africa or from the Caribbean for use in domestic service or plantations for the production of rum and molasses from sugar cane, for raising tobacco and cotton, and harvesting lumber, pines stores, and turpentine. This was the birth of economic globalization and the use of slaves for agricultural production was only one part of the entire Triangle Trade. In turn, this spawned maritime insurance businesses and ship handling; iron mining, forging, and iron mongering industries that produced ship hardware; cleats brackets, bands, barrel bands, anchors, chains and shackles; farming and maritime tools; and firearms and cannons.

Closely related and integrated were the diverse ship building industries of logging and milling, carpentry, planking, fittings, mast hauling, furniture, barrel-making, rope and cordage industries, canvas and sail-making. For the crews, slaves and for trade items there were victuals and supplies, such as salt fish (tons of salt cod were used a slave food), salt beef and pork, vegetables, such as potatoes, water and rum, bread and hard biscuits. Another interconnected spin-off was in various farming and agriculture activities that exported horses for plantation overseers and trade, and cheeses for trade and consumption.

One of the most deeply damaging elements of the Triangle Trade was rum. It required slave labor to grow and harvest the sugar cane and even more slave labor to crush the cane and turn it into molasses treacle. At this stage it could be barreled and shipped to Rhode Island for distillation into rum. Dozens of rum distilleries existed in this colony where about half of all production was for local consumption in homes and saloons. The other half was sent back for the export trade to exchange for more slaves according to established bartering rates. African traders also consumed part of the shipment sent from Rhode Island.

A similar tale can be told for the textile industry in New England in which local wool or slave-produced cotton was brought into the nascent mills to make cloth for Americans but also to make "Guinea Cloth" and some woolen cloth for re-export back to Africa as trade items to acquire more slaves, thus completing the circuit once again. Equally, the case of cheap metal ware such as pots, pans, tins, knives, beads and glassware stimulated local manufacture while producing surplus items for global exchange and especially brought into play for the trans-Atlantic slave trade.

RACISM AND SLAVERY

Throughout the colonies, interesting aspects of racism and slavery can be seen. In 1698 it was feared that "too many Negroes" had been imported to South Carolina but the importation of white servants was encouraged. Little effect was observed. In Greenwich, Rhode Island, the will of Giles Peace recorded that a slave, his "Negro girl," be left to his wife. William Randall of Providence freed his slave Peter Palmer in 1702, and in 1705 sexual relations between "the races" was made illegal in Massachusetts. In short, the human relations between races under slavery ranged from compassionate, to confused, to practical, but the foundational features of slavery were still based on violent coercion or occasionally on resistance. On April 7, 1712, there was a major slave revolt in New York in which nine whites were killed; soon after, on May 3, twenty-one slaves were executed.

By 1708 the Negro population in Rhode Island was 426, of which 220 lived in Newport, where a duty tax of three pounds was placed on every Negro imported to Rhode Island. This was to raise local revenue and discourage the further growth of the Negro population. There was a refund if the Negroes were reexported. In 1714 slavery was made legal in New Hampshire, and at the same time Judge Samuel Sewell of Boston published "The Selling of Joseph," an early antislavery tract.

By the early eighteenth century the slave population in the United States was substantial. Although it had declined in the North, it had increased tremendously in the South as "King Cotton" and interior expansion of slave plantations were actively underway. In some southern colonies the slave population greatly exceeded that of whites.

In 1715 slavery was made legal in North Carolina as cotton and tobacco production expanded and labor demands increased, but in 1716 Quakers in New Jersey condemned the slave trade. Many, but not all, Rhode Island Quakers agreed. The first abolitionist action of these Quakers was to ban members who did not free their slaves. Clearly, making slavery legal did not make it morally correct. But the wealth that could be gained from making use of slave labor made moral vision cloudy. In 1718 the first slaves arrived in Bristol, Rhode Island, directly from the West Indies. In fact, Bristol ships carried about a fifth of the slave cargoes into Charleston, South Carolina, which was closely connected to Rhode Island socially and commercially. Aside from the direct wealth in buying and selling slaves and the wealth that slave labor produced, substantial amounts of tax revenue were generated from commercial and commodity sales. In short, it was not only individuals and companies that invested but colonies and states as well.

A few headlines from the eighteenth century illustrate the contested terrain of slavery and racism: On June 13, 1727, an Indian slave named Peter, in Portsmouth, Rhode Island, was branded and whipped in Newport for firing a bullet through his master's hat. In 1733, Elihu Coleman, a Newport Quaker, expressed his opposition to slavery. In 1735 a Negro couple in Boston saved money to sail from Newport back to Africa. In 1736 the sloop *Mary* owned by James Brown sailed from Providence for slaves in Africa. In 1739 the African Freedmen Society was formed in Providence. In 1741 amid fears of another slave revolt in New York, thirty-one slaves and five whites were executed. In 1748 the first cotton was exported from Charleston to England, seven bails valued at $875. In 1749 slavery was made legal in Georgia. In 1750 the Rhode Island General Assembly passed a law prohibiting slaveholders from allowing their slaves to dance or to have gaming and other diversions. The fine was fifty pounds or one month in jail. Meanwhile, Governor Robinson of Rhode Island owned twenty slaves, half of the population of Virginia consisted of slaves, and two-thirds of the population of South Carolina consisted of slaves.

THE REVOLUTIONARY ERA

Not surprisingly, a black Boston seaman and whaler, Crispus Attucks, forty-seven years of age, was the first to die in the growing protest against the British. Attucks was a runaway slave in Massachusetts and may have been part

Native American. All of the first citizens killed were workers. The seeds of the future revolution were planted, and issues of class, race, and slavery came to the fore during these revolutionary times.

Another explosive moment occurred on June 10, 1772, with the burning of the British customs ship *Gaspee* in Narragansett Bay. The American attack was led by John Brown, a leading maritime merchant and slave shipper. His slave, Aaron Briggs, helped row out to the grounded ship to sink it and wound the British captain. The Brown rebel group was annoyed with British taxes and interference with their commerce in slaves and rum. Also of note, on August 23, 1772, a legal marriage took place between a slave called "Mingo" belonging to Colonel Silas Niles and "Dinah" belonging to Jeremiah Niles in South Kingston.

Against this turbulent backdrop, on April 20, 1773, Peter Bestes, Sambo Freeman, Chester Joie, and Felix Holbrook circulated a petition against slavery in Boston. At last, on June 28 no Rhode Island Quakers held slaves, and on November 10, 1774, Moses Brown freed his remaining slaves to join the Quakers. Brown and Samuel Slater turned to the textile business, but even so they processed slave-grown cotton from the South, and "Guinea cloth" was used for clothing and trading for slaves. Samuel Hopkins launched plans to missionize and colonize Africa; he was joined by Dr. Ezra Stiles, a Congregationalist of Newport. Following intense lobbying by the Quakers, slave imports were officially restricted in Rhode Island. Jacob Shoemaker willed his six Negroes to the town of Providence. The census in 1774 indicated 16,034 blacks were living in New England, both slave and free.

The revolutionary storm gathered strength and on April 14, 1775, another abolitionist group formed in Philadelphia. On April 19, 1775, white and black Minutemen fought the British at Lexington and Concord, and again on June 17, 1775, at the Battle of Bunker Hill. The black population (slave and free) of the colonies was at least 20 percent, but by this time 90 percent of the black population was living in the South. Black enlistment in the Revolutionary army was opposed, but the need for soldiers prevailed. On November 7, 1775, the British Lord Dunmore offered freedom to slaves if they would fight for the British. Pressure mounted on reluctant George Washington to muster black troops, both slave and free, to fight on the American side. Approximately 5,000 blacks fought on the American side. with many recognized for bravery.

When the Declaration of Independence was proclaimed on July 4, 1776, the armed struggle against British colonialism was irreversible. The fifty-six signers of the Declaration were all white men, including twenty-five lawyers, eight merchants, six physicians, and five wealthy farmers. In the first draft of the Constitution, slave plantation owner Thomas Jefferson abolished the slave trade, but the final draft omitted this reference. The struggle for freedom and democracy was for a wealthy, male, white minority group; the majority voices of women, free and enslaved blacks, Native Americans, and indentured whites had little expression. In various respects, some of these contradictions are still with America in the early years of the new millennium.

While the war unfolded, in 1777 Vermont became the first colony to abolish slavery, while some slaves in New Hampshire and Connecticut petitioned for their freedom to their legislatures. Rhode Island officially banned the exportation of slaves from the colony. The human and legal struggles were clearly intensifying. A case in point is the Black Battalion in Rhode Island.

THE RHODE ISLAND BLACK BATTALION

Out of military necessity, on January 19, 1778, General Varnun asked permission of General George Washington to use slaves in the army. By February 2, legislation was passed to raise the Rhode Island Black Battalion. On July 6 the first call-up took place for the Black Battalion, and on July 28 the Black Battalion was sent to Providence to serve under General Sullivan. By August 24, 1778, 755 blacks were under the direct command of George Washington. Some of these slaves were actually purchased by the colony treasury from their owners with the possibility that they would be returned to slave status when the conflict was resolved. However, in a remarkable case of combat courage and holding the line, on August 29 the Black Battalion defeated Hessian mercenary troops at Bloody Run Brook in Portsmouth, or the Battle of Rhode Island. Inevitably, the struggle of wealthy white men led to the sacrifices of enslaved blacks.

Paul Cuffe, son of a slave father and a Native American mother from Cuttyhunk, Massachusetts, rose to major commercial success as an owner of a fleet of five coastal cargo ships. He was a supporter of the back-to-Africa movement. Inspired by the revolutionary principles of "no taxation without representation," on February 10, 1780, Cuffe, with his brother John Cuffe, and five others petitioned the General Court in Dartmouth, Massachusetts, with this complaint: If they could not vote as black people, then they would not pay taxes. These glaring contradictions were addressed when slavery was abolished in Massachusetts and New Hampshire.

On February 13, 1784, the Rhode Island Assembly passed a law, the Gradual Abolition Act, that all children of slaves born after March 1784 were considered free. It was followed on February 23 by the Negro Emancipation Act. The law was further clarified on March 1, when the

General Assembly passed a law that all slaves were free at age twenty-one for males and eighteen for females.

In 1789 the Providence Abolitionist Society was formed and Benjamin Franklin helped to create the Pennsylvania Society for the Abolition of Slavery. *The Life of Olaudah Equiano or Gustavus Vassa*, a former slave, was published to support the abolitionist cause.

In 1790 an Anti-Slavery Society was founded in Connecticut. Antislavery societies were founded in New Jersey and Pennsylvania the following year. In 1793 the Fugitive Slave Law was passed. The invention of Eli Whitney's cotton gin increased cotton production and the demand for slaves.

By 1800 the U.S. slave population reached one million, and there was a slave revolt in Virginia that year. In 1831 Nat Turner of Virginia led the most violent of Northern American slave revolts, which took the lives of some fifty-five whites. Ex-slave Denmark Vesey of South Carolina made plans for a massive uprising in 1833 but the plot was discovered and he was hanged in 1832. It is estimated that more than 250 insurrectionary efforts by slaves were made between 1700 and 1860. From 1830 forward an abolition movement involving whites and northern free blacks attempted to use nonviolent means to end slavery. Outstanding among the many antislavery workers were William Lloyd Garrison, the editor of the *Liberator,* and Frederick A. Douglass, ex-slave, master orator, brilliant polemicist, and founding editor of *The North Star*. Primary subscribers and supporters of these two newspapers were members of the black communities.

In 1857 the U.S. Supreme Court in the case of *Dred Scott v. Sanford* attempted to settle the question of the legitimacy of slavery and the status of free blacks. In this case, Dred Scott and his family were taken from the slave section of southern Missouri to the free state of Illinois as a possession of a U.S. military officer. When Scott was returned to Missouri, his abolitionist lawyers sued for his freedom, on the ground that Scott's residence in a free state had nullified his slave status. The Court attempted to address major constitutional issues regarding slavery in the United States. It held that the management of slaves was a state matter, that the Founding Fathers never intended the Constitution to be extended to persons of African descent, and thus, that Scott had neither legal standing nor any other rights American citizens were bound to respect.

Within three years, however, the issue of slavery overran the judicial system and split the nation with the Civil War. After four years of bitter fighting and 600,000 casualties, the war ended on the side of black freedom. On December 18, 1865, the Thirteenth Amendment was adopted, legally ending the enslavement of some 4 million blacks, including the 140,000 ex-slave soldiers who took part in America's war of emancipation.

Slavery ended in Haiti in 1803 for 500,000 blacks after two large contingents of Napoleon's finest troops were defeated. Slavery ended peacefully in Brazil in 1888, with the emancipation of 730,000 enslaved Africans, the remnant of a much larger number. Between 1542 and 1888, nearly 8 million slaves had been imported to Brazil, which to this day contains the largest African-descended population in the Western hemisphere. With Ethiopia being the last African country officially ending slavery in 1936 and Saudi Arabia in 1962, nowhere on the globe is there now legal support for the institution of chattel slavery.

CONCLUSION

It is undeniable that slavery played a deep role in with the creation of the United States. The complex efforts to negotiate, legitimate, adjudicate, mediate, moralize, and justify it were doomed to fail as long as a political metaphor of freedom and equality was discernable in religious and political thought. To the extent that racism lubricated the repressive ideology, political economy, and practices of slavery in the Americas, one can conclude that slavery and racism in America were entwined. The residual features of this deeply rooted interplay are being processed as travels on this troubled and twisted road continue.

SEE ALSO *Abolition Movement; American Anti-Slavery Society; Dred Scott v. Sandford; Emancipation Proclamation; Language; Plantations; Slave Trade Ideology.*

BIBLIOGRAPHY

Aptheker, Herbert. 1966. *Nat Turner's Slave Rebellion.* New York: Humanities.

Bennett, Lerone, Jr. 1975. *The Shaping of Black America: The Struggles and Triumphs of African-Americans, 1619–1990s.* New York: Penguin.

Curtin, Philip D. 1969. *The Atlantic Slave Trade: A Census.* Madison: University of Wisconsin Press.

Davis, David B. 2006. *Inhuman Bondage: The Rise and Fall of Slavery in the New World.* New York: Oxford University Press.

Everett, Susanne. 1991. *History of Slavery.* Greenwich, CT: Brompton.

Finkelman, Paul, and Joseph C. Miller. 1998. *Macmillan Encyclopedia of World Slavery*, 2 vols. New York: Simon and Schuster.

Fluehr-Lobban, Carolyn, and Kharyssa Rhodes, eds. 2004. *Race and Identity in the Nile Valley: Ancient and Modern Perspectives.* Trenton, NH: Red Sea Press.

Gates, Henry Louis, Jr. 1987. *The Classic Slave Narratives.* New York: New American Library.

Jones, Howard. 1987. *Mutiny on the* Amistad: *The Saga of a Slave Revolt and Its Impact on American Abolition, Law, and Diplomacy.* New York: Oxford University Press.

Manning, Patrick. 1990. *Slavery and African Life: Occidental, Oriental, and African Slave Trades.* New York: Cambridge University Press.

Meillassoux, Claude. 1991. *The Anthropology of Slavery: The Womb of Iron and Gold.* Trans. Alide Dasnois. Chicago: University of Chicago Press.

Meltzer, Milton. 1993. *Slavery: A World History.* New York: Da Capo Press.

Solow, Barbara L., ed. 1993. *Slavery and the Rise of the Atlantic System.* New York: Cambridge University Press.

Richard A. Lobban Jr.

SLAVERY AND RACE

Slavery has been an important phenomenon throughout history. Different societies made use of slave labor, from ancient civilizations to Islamic societies, as well as in India, Asia, Africa, and the Americas. Only during the modern era, however, did slavery become associated with Africans. After the establishment of European colonies in the New World, slavery was the mainstay of their economies, including that of Brazil, the Caribbean islands, and North America. Africa became intimately connected with the history of slavery, as the source of slaves and also as an important stage for the establishment of slave societies.

DEFINITIONS OF SLAVERY

Slavery is a form of extreme exploitation. Slaves are defined as economic property. They are social outsiders who are alien by origin or who had been denied their heritage through judicial or other sanctions. With slaves, coercion could be used at will, and their labor power was at the complete disposal of the master. They did not have the right to their own sexuality and, by extension, to their own reproductive capacities. Slave status was inherited unless provision was made to ameliorate that status.

Slavery was fundamentally a means of denying individuals the rights and privileges of a particular society so that they could be exploited for economic, political, and/or social purposes. Usually these people were "outsiders" who were perceived as ethnically different. A person who spoke the same language as his master, without an accent, who shared the same culture, believed in the same religion, and understood the political relationships that determined how power was exercised was far more difficult to control than an outsider, although in some cases people who belonged to the same society could be reduced to the status of slave. When differences in culture or dialect were relatively unimportant, the level of exploitation and the social isolation of slaves were usually limited; such situations suggest that slave holdings were small and that political and economic stratification was minimal. Certainly, the most developed forms of slavery were those in which slaves were removed a considerable distance their birthplace, thereby emphasizing their alien origin. This uprooting was as dramatic as the transport of Africans across the Atlantic Ocean or the Sahara Desert or as dramatic as the seizure of people who lived only a hundred kilometers or less from the home of the enslavers. Both situations helped to define the slave as an outsider, at least in the first instance. Over time, cultural distinctions tended to blur, so that the extent to which alien origin was a factor varied.

When social structures and economics were more complex, then the identification of slaves as outsiders also became more pronounced, so that the acculturation that invariably occurred did not affect the ability of masters to exploit the labor and services of their slaves. For Muslims, religion was a means of categorizing slaves. Those recently acquired were usually not Muslims, or were nominally so. For Europeans in the era of overseas expansion, slaves were perceived as racially distinct and even more clearly defined as outsiders. This meant that European societies could severely limit their acquisition of rights. Other more subtle distinctions were made, including differences in dialect, the accent of people who had just learned a new language, facial and body markings, perceived physical characteristics, and, most common of all, collective memory.

Slavery was fundamentally tied to labor and not infrequently to social prestige. It was not the only form of dependent labor, but slaves could be made to perform any task in the economy. They often performed the most dangerous, menial, and laborious tasks of a given society. In the case of slaves, the concept of labor was not perceived as separate from the slave as a person. The slave was a speaking instrument of work, and coercion could be used to force compliance with particular orders. Slavery could and did exist alongside other types of labor, including serfdom, in which people were tied to the land rather than to the person of the landlord, and their obligations to the landlord were fixed by custom. Other forms of dependent labor arrangements included clientage (voluntary subordination without fixed remuneration for services), wage labor (in which compensation for work was paid), pawnship (in which labor was perceived as interest on a debt, with the pawn as collateral for the debt), and communal work (often based on kinship or age grades, in which work was perceived as reciprocal activity based on past and future exchanges). These forms of labor could involve coercion, too, but usually not to the point that they were indistinguishable from slavery.

A primary feature of slavery was the absolute lack of choice on the part of slaves. Their masters controlled their productive capacities, as well as their sexual and reproductive capacities. When slaves constituted a significant proportion of any population, then sexual access and reproduction involving free persons were strongly controlled. Women (and men too) could be treated as sexual objects; the ability to marry could be closely administered; and males could be castrated. The significance of sex is most strikingly revealed in the market price of slaves. In Muslim, Hindu, and ancient Chinese societies, eunuchs were often the most costly. Pretty women and girls cost more, their price depending upon their sexual attractiveness. These two opposites—castrated males and attractive females—demonstrate most clearly the master's power over slaves' sexual and reproductive functions. Slaves lacked the right to engage in sexual relationships without the consent of their masters. Their children, when slaves were given the opportunity to have children, were not legally their offspring but the property of the master of the mother. Biologically, they were the offspring of the slaves, but the right to raise the children could be denied. Instead, slave children could be taken away, and even when they were not sold, they could be redistributed as part of marriage arrangements, trained for the army or administration, or adopted by the master's family. Slaves thus had no legal relatives—neither parents nor siblings nor children.

Those born into slavery clearly had a different experience from those who had been enslaved later in life. For example, in the case of enslaved Africans in the Western Hemisphere, Africa-born slaves were termed *bozales* and those born in the New World were called *creoles.* Parents might tell their children of their enslavement, but this was not the children's experience. Children could also learn about enslavement from new captives, and they were educated into a society in which such acts were well known. Legally, they could be separated from their parents and sold, although some slave laws such as the Spanish *Siete partidas* encouraged the preservation of intact slave families. The violence behind the original act of enslavement remained, although for the descendents of slaves it was transformed from a real act to a threat. As such, violence was still a crucial dimension of social control.

Slaves tended not to maintain their numbers naturally, and slave populations usually had to be replenished. One reason for this situation was the relatively short life span for many slaves. Death could result from particularly harsh work, and funeral sacrifices and unsuccessful castration operations also took their toll. Travel conditions for slaves destined for distant markets were also a factor; individuals were moved from one disease environment to another and rations were often inadequate.

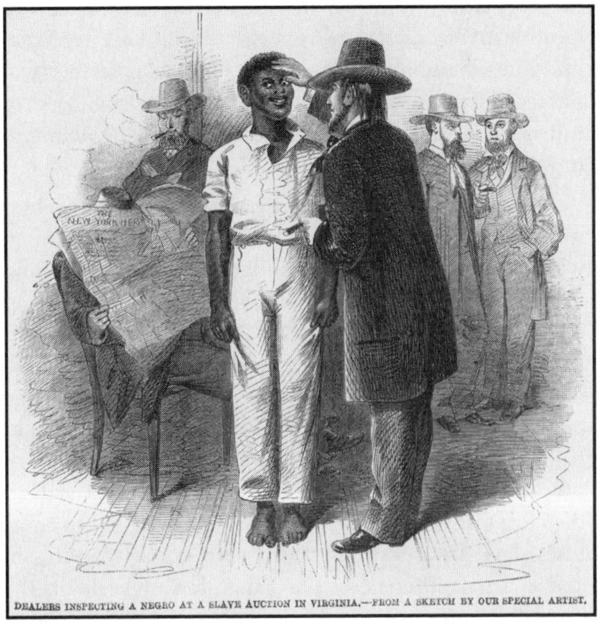
DEALERS INSPECTING A NEGRO AT A SLAVE AUCTION IN VIRGINIA.—FROM A SKETCH BY OUR SPECIAL ARTIST.

Inspecting a Slave at Auction. *Slavery is based on the idea that people can be owned as property.* **PICTURE COLLECTION, THE BRANCH LIBRARIES, THE NEW YORK PUBLIC LIBRARY, ASTOR, LENOX AND TILDEN FOUNDATIONS.**

Another reason for decline was the demographic imbalance between the sexes in slave populations, namely, fewer slave women than slave men. Moreover, when slave women were concentrated in the hands of powerful men who recognized their children as free, such as with concubines in Muslim societies, the proportion of slaves in society may well have had a tendency to decline without affecting the number of people. In some situations, when the status of concubines and slave wives changed to freed, often leading to assimilation or full emancipation, the size of the slave population decreased accordingly. In patrilineal societies the children of slave wives and concubines by free fathers were often granted a status that was completely or almost free. Under Islamic law, for example, this was most pronounced. Concubines could not be sold once they gave birth, and they became free on the death of their master. The children of such unions were free on birth. These features of gradual assimilation or complete emancipation contrasted with slavery as an inherited status, but still illustrate the master's power to manipulate sexual and reproductive functions for his own purposes.

SLAVERY AS A GLOBAL PHENOMENON

The best way to approach the overlapping topics of slavery and race is to disaggregate the two ideas. Slavery is best treated historically, that is, what happened over the long sweep of history in terms of the prevalence and location of major slavery concentrations. This approach illustrates the ubiquity of slavery. Race, as it connects to slavery, is peculiar to time and place, particularly to Europe and its colonies since the age of Enlightenment in the eighteenth century.

In ancient times, slavery had little to do with physical appearance. In ancient Greece, slavery was associated with foreigners, or those considered "barbarians." Anyone from outside the Greek world was subjected to enslavement, including Africans, central Europeans, and Asians. The regions that regularly supplied the Greek market with slaves were Scythia and Illyria in Europe and Syria and Persia to the east. Slaves were brought from northeastern Africa as well. Slavery was also a product of warfare: Prisoners of war were enslaved by their captors and employed as manual laborers. In most cases slavery was also associated with ethnicity, religion, and cultural differences. The expansion of Islam in the seventh century extended and further codified existing forms of slavery that had dominated the Mediterranean region. Under Islam, religion was a key factor in defining slave status—Muslims being theoretically protected from enslavement—and populations who were not Muslim were subjected to assault, enslavement, the payment of special taxes, and other religiously sanctioned discrimination. In this case, slavery was not correlated to skin color. For Muslims, slavery was restricted to non-Muslims. Christians, Jews, and pagan populations could be enslaved.

Slavery was not a racial institution but rather an institution of conquest. Slaves were brought from subjugated territories. Muslim scholars developed theories about the good and bad qualities of different groups of people, including a taxonomy of slaves that categorized them according to both their origins and their educational backgrounds. Ibn Butlan (d. 1066 AD) argued that the determining factor in the differences in human character was geographical location. He accordingly viewed as opposites the characteristics of Easterners and Westerners, as well as Northerners and Southerners. He considered the Armenians the worst of the whites, while he considered the Zanj the worst of the blacks. "They are similar in the strength of their stature, their propensity to destruction, and their toughness" (Ibn Butlan 1393/h-1973, p. 378). There was, however, space to discredit some of the stereotypes associated with blacks. The Muslim theologian al-Jahiz (c. 776–868 or 869 AD), for instance, challenged these views in his epistle on the relative qualities of blacks and whites.

The Christian justification of slavery hinged on racial categories, in which the Biblical reference to the curse of Noah was invoked to explain why Africans were slaves. According to legend, the curse on the "sons of Ham" explained the color of the skin of Africans, and the curse meant that black people were degraded and their punishment a "natural" slavery. Slavery, however, was not associated specifically with Africans or blacks.

During the Middle Ages most slaves serving in western Europe were of "Slavic" origins from central and eastern Europe. The term *slav* gave way to *sclavus*, the root of *schiavo*, *esclavo*, *esclave*, *sclau*, *sklave*, and *slave* in various European languages. In Germany during the tenth century, *sclavus* had become synonymous with *slave*. In Europe Italian merchants continued to buy large numbers of Slavic prisoners along the Dalmatian coast. During the thirteenth century, western Europeans began to intercept people from Caucasia to the eastern Balkans, under foreign rule, to force them into slavery. These captives were Armenians, Circassians, Georgians, Abkhazians, Mingrelians, Russians, Tartars, Albanians, and Bulgarians—a very multicultural group. These "slavs" were exported to Mediterranean markets, mainly Egypt, Syria, Cyprus, and Sicily, where local traders were willing to pay a good price for their services. Targeting "slavs" led to the transformation of the term into a synonym for chattel slavery. The term began to be applied to others as well, including Muslim captives seized in the Iberian Peninsula. The term, then, lost its original meaning, which was associated exclusively with people of Slavic descent and came to signify any captive. Nevertheless, slavery continued to be conceived as appropriate only for outsiders, pagans, and infidels, who shared the supposed characteristics of "slavs." In Portugal, on the periphery of the Slavic slave trade but increasingly involved in religious warfare with Muslim North Africa, the word *escravo* was used alongside such terms as *mouro*, *guineu*, and *negro*. Later on, the French *nègre* and the English *black* became virtually synonymous with *slave*.

Europeans were aware of African slavery long before they settled their colonies in the Americas. The trans-Saharan routes unifying North and sub-Saharan Africa had brought African slaves to the Mediterranean world. Slaves were traded through North Africa to supply markets in southern Europe and in the Arabian Peninsula. African slaves also became an important source of labor in both Spain and Portugal, working side by side captured Muslims. Slavery was still not seen in racial terms and was not limited to Africans and their descendents. Europeans, in this case, mainly Portuguese, bought and traded non-Christians, moving them from Europe and Africa to the Atlantic islands. Domestic slavery was also employed along the Iberian Peninsula, but again, bondage had nothing to do with physical attributes. For Iberians, slavery was associated with non-Christians, either pagans or Muslims. Slavery, however, was utterly transformed by the European expansion to the Americas.

Initially, European commercial expansion was motivated by the quest for gold and spices—the profits of trade. The Portuguese were more interested in reaching the sources of gold in sub-Saharan African than in buying slaves. The initial European maritime contacts with West Africa were forged to acquire gold and other commercial commodities that were already being traded across the Sahara to North Africa by Muslim traders. Portuguese intentions were to bypass these merchants. During their maritime explorations, however, the Portuguese settled a series of islands in the Atlantic from the Azores to São Tomé. Plantations were established on the islands to supply the nascent European demand for sugar. The Azores, Canary Islands, Cape Verde, and São Tomé were ideal locations for trading ventures along the African coast. Portugal's small population limited these ventures. The Portuguese Crown was able to relocate only a few artisans and other workers, who aspired to escape manual labor and achieve access to land. Captives from the Canary Islands supplied the needed labor. They were employed in the construction of public works, including irrigation canals. From very early on, African slaves were brought to the various islands. The Atlantic islands were the prototype for the sugar plantation economies established in the Americas. From the beginning, sugar production was dependent on African slave labor.

THE TRANSATLANTIC SLAVE TRADE AND THE RACIALIZATION OF SLAVERY

In 1498, just a few years after the arrival of Christopher Columbus in the Americas, the Spanish Crown began importing African slaves to work on sugar plantations in its American colonies. The first recorded use of African slaves in Spanish America was in 1502. A series of laws were established in order to control the slave trade between Africa and the Spanish colonies in the Americas. These laws not only established a House of Commerce, which controlled the trade, they also favored the importation of Africans instead of the use of Amerindians as slaves. Between 1502 and 1650, most of the slaves imported into the Americas went to Spanish colonies. Differing from the Portuguese, British, and French, who increased their importation in the eighteenth century, the core of the African slaves imported into mainland Spanish America arrived in the early period of colonization. Africans were used on agricultural plantations, particularly sugar, but also in mining operations. By 1650, after the Spanish had discovered silver mines in the viceroyalties of New Spain and La Plata, it is estimated that there were 35,000 African slaves in modern Mexico and 100,000 in Peru.

In the sixteenth century, stimulated by the profits of sugar exports to Europe, the Portuguese Crown imported sugarcane from the islands of Madeira and São Tomé in order to establish sugar plantations along the Brazilian coast. Amerindian and African labor were used side by side in Brazil. However, the constant conflict between the Portuguese authorities and the indigenous population, and the condemnation of enslavement of Native Americans, stimulated the importation of African slaves. The Portuguese Crown, in an effort to drain Portuguese prisons, started to deport prisoners and outlaws to Brazil. Nevertheless, the belief that Europeans should not be enslaved was already strong by the mid-sixteenth century. By 1600, half of the slave population in Brazil was African born, and this number increased in the following decades. The slave trade was so profitable for the Portuguese Crown that by 1650 Portuguese America had superseded the Spanish territories as the major importer of African slaves.

The increasing wealth of the Portuguese monarchy, through the profits of the slave trade between Africa and the Americas, as well as sugar production, drew the attention of the British, Dutch, and French elites to the opportunities that the Americas offered. Still, slavery and servitude were not exclusive to Africans. Between 1654 and 1685, 10,000 indentured servants sailed from Bristol alone, chiefly for the West Indies and Virginia. Two-thirds of the immigrants to Pennsylvania during the eighteenth century were white servants; in four years, 25,000 came to Philadelphia alone. It has been estimated that more than 250,000 persons were of this class during the colonial period and that they probably constituted one-half of the all-English immigrants, the majority going to the middle colonies. Some of these white immigrants were indentured servants, so-called because before departure from their homeland, they had signed a contract, indented by law, binding them to service for a stipulated time in return for their passage. Still others, know as "redemptioners," arranged with the captain of the ship to pay for their passage on arrival or within a specified time thereafter; if they did not, they were sold by the captain to the highest bidder. Others were convicts, sent out by the deliberate policy of the home government to serve for a specified period.

This white servitude is of cardinal importance for an understanding of the development of slavery in the New World and the idea of races. That whites were employed as indentured laborers contradicts the idea that whites could not stand the strain of manual labor in the climate of the New World and that, for this reason, the European powers had to turn to Africans. African slavery had nothing to do with climate; it was only a solution to the labor problem. Sugar meant labor—at times that labor has been slave, at other times nominally free; at times black, at other times white, brown, or yellow. Despite the early experiments with local Amerindian labor, by the end of the sixteenth century the link had been forged between African slave labor and sugar cultivation on plantations. Thereafter, Europeans and local-born planters consistently preferred Africans as laborers on sugar plantation. Later planters came to think that African slaves and their descendents were the only appropriate form of labor for work on plantations, whatever the crop.

In the seventeenth century more European states joined the slave trade. Despite Spanish and Portuguese control over the trade between Africa and the Americas, private and state representative merchants of other European monarchies enrolled in the lucrative trade. The Dutch were present in different regions of the Americas, from New Amsterdam to Guyana, passing through the island of Curaçao in the Caribbean. After the Dutch took control of Olinda and Recife, in northeastern Brazil, in 1630, they obtained control over sugar production in the Americas. However, they did not control the supply of slaves. The solution was to conquer, in 1637, the Portuguese-controlled Elmina fort along the Gold Coast—one of the most important slaving ports in West Africa. A few years later, in 1641, the Dutch also seized other Portuguese holdings in Africa such as the ports of Luanda and Benguela and the island of São Tomé. Dutch imperial pretensions were complete with the conquest of São Luis do Maranhão, in northeastern Brazil. For twenty years, the Dutch controlled the slave trade between Africa and the Americas. They occupied the space left by the Portuguese Crown, which was divided by internal political problems. Since its unification with the Spanish Crown, in 1580, the Portuguese monarchy had been in decline. It recovered only after the two crowns were once again divided in 1640. Soon after that, in 1648, Portuguese and Luso-Brazilian troops conquered Luanda, and by 1654 the Portuguese again controlled northeastern Brazil. In the last years of the seventeenth century gold was found in Minas Gerais, in Brazil. This led to an increase in the volume of African slaves imported in order to work in mines. After a few decades away from the slave trade business, Portuguese and Brazilian brokers were back on the African coast. The importation of slaves increased in order to supply the nascent mining industry in the interior and the expanding sugar cane production along the coast.

The English and the French were not far behind. The English were drawn to West Africa by the Portuguese and Spanish successes. Their initial efforts were mainly privateering raids, but by the early seventeenth century the English began to trade seriously in the region, thanks in part to the acquisition of colonies in the Americas. In the 1630s sugar production was introduced into the British colony of Barbados, as an adventure of private merchants looking for quick profits. Even without state support, a group of settlers found economic support among British merchants interested in the importation of agricultural goods, especially tobacco from Virginia and sugar from Barbados. The main problem was the labor supply in the colonies. At first, free labor, especially of immigrants escaping religious persecution, was used in North American territories. Soon, however, the profits of the slave trade were found to be very attractive, and the British plantation owners proceeded to organize and finance expeditions to the African coast. The English slave trade was organized initially through state-backed monopoly companies. From the beginning, however, interlopers sought to penetrate these trading restrictions. Like others before, the English found that the key to the expansion of their slave trading was to be found in the Americas. The settlement of West Indies islands, notably Barbados and Jamaica, and the development of the Chesapeake colonies, laid the foundations for British colonial demand for imported labor. After experiments with different kinds of labor, local settlers in all these places turned to African slaves. In the Caribbean the importation of African slaves started in the 1640s, but in Virginia and Maryland African slave labor became predominant only by the end of the seventeenth century. Noticing the potential profits in the slave trade business, the British Crown in 1672 created the Royal African Company, which held a monopoly over the slave trade. By 1689, however, independent traders were able to break the monopoly and bring more slaves to the British colonies than the Royal African Company could supply. In the last two decades of the seventeenth century the trade in African slaves increased sharply. It is estimated that 20,000 slaves disembarked in the North American colonies in this period. As in the other American colonies, male slaves were preferred over females and children. From the slave owners' perspective, females and children were not as profitable as male slaves.

SLAVERY AND RACIAL CATEGORIES

In most societies, slaves did not differ radically in physical shape and color from the freeborn population, and yet over time slavery and race became closely linked, especially in reference to Africans. Rome enslaved people from elsewhere in the Mediterranean and then later from north of the Alps. In the Arab world, slaves could be blonde-haired people from the Slavic world or black people from south of the Sahara. And there were many slaves in the medieval period who came from eastern Europe. Both Christianity and Islam banned the sale of coreligionists, although this rule was not always enforced. They enslaved each other and felt free to enslave peoples seen as pagans or barbaric, that is, people who were different from themselves. By the fifteenth century, Portuguese and other southern Europeans began receiving increasing number of slaves from West Africa, and from that time on, slavery began to be associated with Africans.

In the sixteenth century, European conquest and exploitation of the resources of the Americas had a devastating impact on the indigenous population, with the result that there was a severe decline in population as a consequence of new diseases and harsh policies. Hispanic America Catholic missionaries, such as Bartolomé de Las Casas (1474–1566), were horrified by the treatment of native peoples and persuaded the Spanish Crown to ban their enslavement, although Amerindians continued to be enslaved well into the eighteenth century. Slaves were still thought to be necessary. Because Europeans were not willing to enslave each other and lacked the military capacity to enslave Muslims in large numbers, the Portuguese and then other Europeans turned to Africa for the labor they needed to open up commercial agriculture on the islands off the African coast, in Brazil, and in the Caribbean and to conduct mining operations in Hispanic America and Brazil.

The association between Africans and slavery resulted in a high level of prejudice against blacks during and after slavery. It became a common misconception that the enslavement of Africans must have arisen as the result of racial differences. In his 1944 book *Capitalism and Slavery*, the historian Eric Williams forcefully argued that this was not the case. Slavery caused racism, but economic motives, not racial impulses, caused slavery. The rise of plantation slavery was tied to the development of capitalism; the decision to import large numbers of Africans and to hold them in hereditary bondage was based on the fact that enslaved Africans were cheaper than any other form of labor then available.

Many scholars maintain that the concept of "race" is a modern invention, the result of European imperial expansion from the sixteenth century onward, and especially gaining currency in the eighteenth century. Hence, the practice of racial classification began only a few hundred years ago, and the concept became fully developed only during the Enlightenment, when European intellectuals and political leaders became increasingly confident that experience and reason enabled them to explain all natural phenomena. Europeans were struck by physical differences between themselves and Africans and believed that these differences demanded explanation. This focus on somatic differences was in sharp contrast with the casualness of ancient Greeks about their physical differences from Nubians. In ancient times, it seems, people apparently were less concerned about such differences.

According to modern science, physical differences among people are superficial, especially skin color. Not only is it impossible to classify people in neatly divided groups, but the mixing of peoples that has taken place in all parts of the world means that all people are more closely related to each other than they are different. There is also no evidence to link visible physical characteristics with moral, temperamental, or intellectual differences. Nevertheless, once developed, racist ideologies have provided justifications for discrimination, segregation, and colonial rule.

"SCIENTIFIC" RACISM AND SLAVERY

Most nineteenth-century Westerners came to believe, based on the widespread concept of scientific races, that there were three basic racial groups—Caucasoids, Negroids, and Mongoloids. Western scientists, however, did not agree on the total number of races that could exist on Earth, although they all shared the assumption that distinct racial groups existed. The most notable and eminent scientists of the nineteenth century supported the idea of human beings divided by races, including the French diplomat and writer Arthur Gobineau, the Americans Josiah Clark Nott and George Robins Gliddon, and the German philosopher Arthur Schopenhauer. Their work is usually called "scientific racism."

Differences among people, including differences among communities within a single society, are fundamental to the way people are classified. Since the end of the eighteenth century, race and nationalism became important factors in such classifications. Instead of situational features, slavery became associated with race, which had acquired a biological meaning. Slavery preceded racism against blacks, but during the nineteenth century racist ideas were generated to justify the enslavement of Africans. The European expansion and occupation of new lands produced a new world divided along color lines. A new worldview was in place, corroborated by Western scientists. According to this new worldview, whites were superior to any other group of people. Subjugated people were portrayed as inferior. Africans became associated with slavery, savagery, paganism, immorality, primitiveness, and wretchedness.

In the context of African history, the interrelationship of internal forms of slavery and servility with the export trade in slaves is an important consideration and topic of debate among scholars. The transatlantic and trans-Saharan slave trades removed millions of enslaved Africans from their homelands. The relative impact of the external trade in slaves to internal developments within Africa is also a subject of debate. Most estimates of the number of enslaved Africans who were shipped to the Americas center on twelve million; the number of people sent as slaves across the Sahara Desert, the Red Sea, and the Indian Ocean have been more difficult to establish, but the scale of this trade was historically very large.

The political developments of the several centuries before the institution of formal European rule resulted in the massive enslavement of people in Africa. The emergence of new states along the Atlantic coast of Africa and in its immediate hinterland was closely associated with the development of the transatlantic slave trade. Dahomey (later Benin), for example, emerged as a state whose structure required the enslavement of people. Slaves were killed in public ceremonies associated with the political power of the Dahomean monarchy; were sold to Europeans to raise essential revenue for the state; or, after the ending of the transatlantic trade in slaves, were settled on plantations in Dahomey to produce palm oil and harvest palm kernels. A series of Muslim holy wars, which began in the Senegambia region in the late seventeenth century and spread across the savanna as far as the Red Sea by the end of the nineteenth century, also accounted for great numbers of slaves.

Even though forms of slavery existed in Africa before the maritime arrival of Europeans and long before the emergence of the American slave systems, the European demand for African slaves had a transforming impact on African societies. The imposition of a racially defined slavery system changed the understanding of slavery. In the Americas, for the first time, slavery targeted a single group, and it was based on physical attributes, rather than being situational and tied to capture in war.

SEE ALSO *African Enslavement, Pre-Colonial; Language; Nott, Josiah; Plantations; Skin Color.*

BIBLIOGRAPHY

Davis, David Brion. 1966. *The Problem of Slavery in Western Culture.* Ithaca, NY: Cornell University Press.

———. 2006. *Inhuman Bondage: The Rise and Fall of Slavery in the New World.* Oxford: Oxford University Press.

El Hamel, Chouki. 2002. "Race, Slavery, and Islam in Maghribi Mediterranean Thought: The Question of the *Haratin* in Morocco." *Journal of North African Studies* 7 (3): 29–52.

Eltis, David. 2000. *The Rise of African Slavery in the Americas.* Cambridge, U.K.: Cambridge University Press.

Hall, Bruce S. 2005. "The Question of 'Race' in the Pre-colonial Southern Sahara." *Journal of North African Studies* 10 (3–4): 339–367.

Ibn Butlan, Shaykh Abu al-Hasan al-Mukhtar b. al-Hasan b. 'Abdun. 1393/h-1973. "Risala Jami'a li-funun nafi'a fi shira 'l-raqiq wa taqlib al-'abid." In *Nawadir al-Makhtutat*, N. 4, edited and with introduction by Abd al-Salam Harun, 2nd ed., vol. 1, 333–389. Cairo: Mustafa al-Babi al- Halabi and sons.

Lewis, Bernard. 1971. *Race and Color in Islam.* New York: Harper and Row.

———. 1990. *Race and Slavery in the Middle East: An Historical Enquiry.* New York: Oxford University Press.

Lovejoy, Paul E. 2000. *Transformations in Slavery: A History of Slavery in Africa*, 2nd ed. Cambridge, U.K.: Cambridge University Press.

Manning, Patrick. 1990. *Slavery and African Life: Occidental, Oriental, and African Slave Trades.* Cambridge, U.K.: Cambridge University Press.

Miller, Joseph C., ed. 1999. *Slavery and Slaving in World History: A Bibliography.* 2 vols. Armonk, NY: M.E. Sharpe.

Williams, Eric. 1944. *Capitalism and Slavery.* Chapel Hill: University of North Carolina Press.

Willis, John Ralph, ed. 1985. *Slaves and Slavery in Muslim Africa.* 2 vols. London: Cass.

Paul E. Lovejoy
Mariana P. Candido
Yacine Daddi Addoun

SMITH, JAMES McCUNE
1813–1865

James McCune Smith was born in New York City on April 18, 1813, to an enslaved mother. Both his father, who worked as a merchant, and his mother were former slaves. He went on to become one of the most important, yet historically neglected, figures in antebellum African-American history. As a physician, scientist, essayist, and spokesman on behalf of free blacks, he widely influenced the African-American movement to abolish slavery and create equality for free people of African descent.

Smith was educated at the African Free School in New York City, an institution founded by white abolitionists in the post-Revolutionary period that schooled a host of young African-American men who later became important public figures, including Henry Highland Garnet, Samuel Ringgold Ward, Alexander Crummell, and Ira Aldridge. The Free School offered a liberal arts education designed to demonstrate African Americans' intellectual equality with whites. In 1832, after being denied admission into several American colleges, Smith enrolled at the University of Glasgow in Scotland, where he eventually earned a bachelor of arts, a master's, and a medical degree. The Glasgow Emancipation Society—one of many institutions in Great Britain that reflected popular antislavery sentiment—helped sponsor his education and served as a forum for his abolitionist activities while in college.

In 1837, after completing his studies in Paris, Smith returned to the United States. By virtue of his education and literary abilities, he quickly became an exceptional figure in New York's African-American community. He opened a pharmacy on West Broadway and ran a racially integrated medical practice, the first in the United States run by a university-trained black physician. The Colored Orphans Asylum, which after the Free School was the most important benevolent institution for African Americans in New York, benefited from his work there as a physician starting in the 1840s. In addition, he participated in many efforts to build institutions among African Americans, and he played a leading role in the establishment of literary and educational societies, mutual relief organizations, and antislavery agencies. In the early 1850s he helped found the National Council of Colored People, one of the pioneer national efforts to organize African Americans, and in the mid-1850s he helped found the Party of Radical Political Abolitionists.

Smith's intellectual legacy stems from his work as an essayist, thinker, and activist. His notable publications included *A Lecture on the Haytian Revolution* (1841), *The Destiny of the People of Color* (1843), and introductions to Frederick Douglass's second autobiography (*My Bondage and My Freedom* [1855]) and Henry Highland Garnet's *Memorial Discourse* (1865). He also published several essays reflective of his scientific training, writing on topics such as phrenology, longevity, climate, and race. He enjoyed editorial stints at three black newspapers—*The Colored American, The Northern Star and Freemen's Advocate*, and *Douglass' Monthly*—and contributed regularly to the black press, penning several important essays for *The Anglo-African Magazine* and a column for *Frederick Douglass' Paper.*

Smith's thinking reflected the diversity of his interests and the breadth of his training. He took strong stands against black migration to another country, for black education of all sorts, and against racial theories that declared all people of African descent a separate and inferior part of creation. Twin themes, often held in delicate tension, dominated his approach to racial activism. On the one hand, he strongly advocated a program of self-help and racial uplift that promised to "elevate" African Americans in the eyes of whites and roll back the tide of prejudice. On the other hand, he argued that only an independent black independent movement could vindicate the "manhood" of the race and achieve meaningful equality.

Smith's self-help doctrine called for industrial and classical education for black youth to assist in inculcating positive habits and behaviors for racial uplift. He feared that the conduct of uneducated African Americans strengthened discrimination, believing that only their "moral excellence" could refute the pervasive prejudice besetting them. At times, Smith expressed frustration with the pace of the black non-elite's self-elevation, calling those like himself "leaders of an invisible people." Smith sought to shake off the patronage of white abolitionists and place African Americans at the center of their own freedom struggle. "The battle against caste and Slavery," he wrote to his fellow African Americans, "is emphatically our battle; no one else can fight it for us, and with God's help we must fight it ourselves."

The tensions in Smith's thinking—between the need to demonstrate blacks' equality by accepted measures of civility versus the need for blacks to act independently on their own behalf—inhered in much antebellum black protest thought. Ultimately, though, the two impulses complemented each other rather than conflicted with each other. While black activists such as Smith did rely on standards of "respectability" and "civilization" derived from a world dominated by prejudiced whites, they did not see these virtues as exclusively "white," but as universal, and they claimed them as their own. The path to equality lay not in subservience or the uncritical adoption of "white" standards, but in embracing and embodying those elements of the American creed that stressed manly independence and the capacity for self-governance. Only this route would change public perceptions of blacks, refute prejudice, and secure for African Americans a meaningful equality.

When the Civil War broke out, Smith saw, as did his colleagues, unparalleled opportunities for African Americans to enact this philosophy. Along with notables such as Frederick Douglass and Martin Delany, he lobbied relentlessly for the chance for African Americans to demonstrate their loyalty to liberty and their capacity for civic participation through military service. He believed that slavery would truly die not merely through the war alone, but through a thorough and equitable redistribution of Southern wealth into the hands of the four million freedpeople whose labor had been so long expropriated. Smith's desire for a "quite Professorship" was granted in 1863 when Daniel Alexander Payne, a longtime colleague and a bishop in the African Methodist Episcopal Church, offered him a position at the abolitionist-sponsored Wilberforce College in Ohio. Unfortunately, he never lived to occupy the post. On November 17, 1865, he died of heart disease at the age of fifty-two.

SEE ALSO *Antebellum Black Ethnology.*

BIBLIOGRAPHY

Blight, David W. 1985. "In Search of Learning, Liberty, and Self Definition: James McCune Smith and the Ordeal of the Antebellum Black Intellectual." *Afro-Americans in New York Life and History* 9 (2): 7–26.

Dain, Bruce R. 2002. *A Hideous Monster of the Mind: American Race Theory in the Early Republic.* Cambridge, MA: Harvard University Press.

Stauffer, John. 2001. *The Black Hearts of Men: Radical Abolitionists and the Transformation of Race.* Cambridge, MA: Harvard University Press.

Patrick Rael

SOCIAL CLASS AND MORTALITY

Racial, ethnic, and class disparities in health outcomes are wide and persistent, and they cut across the full range of indicators of disease prevalence and mortality rates in all nations of the world. Populations understood by social and political convention to constitute distinct "racial" or "ethnic" minorities are, in general, sicker and die sooner than their majority counterparts. These patterns have been evident for as long as researchers have investigated the issue, and even a cursory examination of, say, the health of blacks in the United States and South Africa, or of indigenous people in New Zealand, Canada, or the Commonwealth of Dominica, bears this out. Despite a considerable amount of research in the United States in the early twenty-first century that seeks to understand how "racial" differences—whether in a genetic or, categorical sense—might explain health inequalities, it is clear that these health inequalities reflect the relatively unequal social position that racial and ethnic minorities almost invariably inhabit.

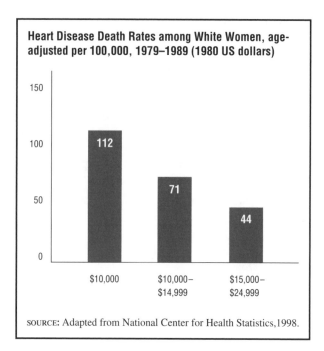

Heart Disease Death Rates among White Women, age-adjusted per 100,000, 1979–1989 (1980 US dollars)

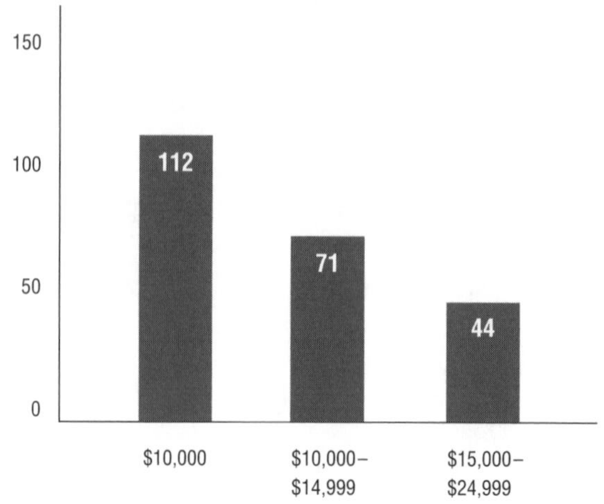

SOURCE: Adapted from National Center for Health Statistics,1998.

Figure 1.

GENETIC FACTORS

There are a number of reasons why health disparities between and within countries cannot be genetic in nature. "Racial" categories are social and political constructions: They do not reveal much about underlying human variation at the level of the gene. As Richard Lewontin and others have pointed out, there is more genetic variation within the so-called races than between them (see Lewontin 1972). From the standpoint of genetic variation, for example, two "blacks" of sub-Saharan Africa could be further apart from each other genetically than they are from two Swedes selected at random. A second and related point is that, from the standpoint of genetic variability, Africans are more genetically diverse than non-Africans, and thus subsume the genetic diversity found among people in the rest of the world (Marks 2002). Third, the leading causes of death in most countries are not the outcome of single-gene mutations, such as those that produce sickle-cell disease, cystic fibrosis, or Tay-Sachs disease; rather, the leading causes of death reflect a complex interaction between (multiple) genes and the social and physical environment (Cooper et al. 2003).

The "social gradient" pattern of morbidity and mortality also argues against a genetic explanation. For more than 150 years, researchers have known that when mortality rates associated with various causes are plotted against measures of class or socioeconomic status—typically income, education, or occupation—a graded pattern emerges, with mortality increasing as socioeconomic status decreases. Figure 1 shows heart disease-related mortality rates among white American women plotted against income.

This graph shows what has been known for some time: that worse health outcomes are not a simple matter of rich and poor, but rather that risk for death (or disease) is continuous along a socioeconomic continuum. Each step up the social ladder corresponds to better health outcomes.

BEHAVIORAL FACTORS

Health related behavior—e.g., smoking, diet, and physical activity—is certainly one fact that explains disparities in health outcomes between populations that differ in terms of socioeconomic status, but two points are worth emphasizing: First, class, or socioeconomic status, predicts health-related behavior; and second, in empirical studies that weigh health behaviors against measures of social status, the results suggest that no more than 30 percent of the variation can be explained by behaviors such as smoking and physical activity (see Marmot 2004). When statistical analyses weigh the contribution of various factors, socioeconomic status explains more of the disparity than all health-related behaviors combined.

SOCIAL STATUS

Researchers in public health and other disciplines suggest that social status is fundamental to health disparities, but it is also clear that measures of socioeconomic status

Heart Disease Death Rates among Black and White Women, age-adjusted per 100,000, 1979–1989 (1980 US dollars)

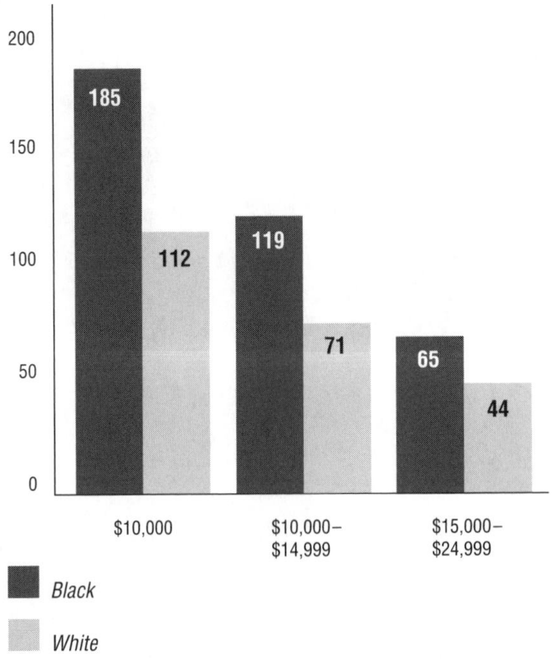

SOURCE: Adapted from National Center for Health Statistics, 1998.

Figure 2.

might not fully capture these differences. Figure 2 shows heart disease death rates among black American women compared to white American women at the same income points. These bar graphs show a clear gradient in heart disease death rates among white and black women at various points along the income ladder. For both groups, more money means better health. This figure also shows that at comparable points of income, black women have higher mortality rates.

Researchers have found similar patterns in countries around the world. In New Zealand, for example, it is well established that the indigenous people of that country, the Maori, have worse health than non-Maori people. However, in studies that have examined health outcomes in terms of smoking and socioeconomic deprivation, researchers have seen an "independent effect" of ethnicity. Adjusting for smoking and for measures that gauge deprivation (housing, access to a car, and so forth) explains some of the ethnicity health gap, but does not account for all of it (see Blakely et al. 2006).

A study of infant health in Brazil provides additional evidence that health status is a function of racial and class identity. In 2001 Fernando Barros and colleagues conducted a cohort study in Pelotas, southern Brazil, and found that children with one or two black parents had a higher prevalence of poor health indicators—such as low birth weight and infant mortality—than children who had two white parents. Socioeconomic measures and other variables explained a good portion of the inequalities in health indicators, but not all (Barros et al. 2001). This study, and others, lend support to the view that health is a function of social status, but they also point out the need for understanding social status both in terms of race (or ethnicity) and social class.

DETERMINANTS OF SOCIAL STATUS

What are the determinants of these social gradients? Access to and quality of health care is certainly part of the story. In the United States, blacks are much more likely than whites to lack health insurance. Studies further suggest that racial and ethnic minorities cannot expect equal treatment in the clinical setting, even when patients are similar in all the important ways, such as age, insurance status, and comorbidity. Around the world, aboriginal health is affected, to varying degrees, by the insufficient/inadequate availability of health services, especially in rural areas. Still, whereas disparities in health care access and treatment are vital with respect to diagnosing and treating chronic conditions, access to health services does not prevent the onset of many conditions that lead to premature death. In other words, health care matters when an individual gets sick, but it does not determine whether he or she is afflicted in the first place.

PSYCHOSOCIAL FACTORS

A significant body of research suggests that relative inequality "gets under the skin" through a variety of pathways, some material—e.g., exposures that make people sick regardless of perception—and others pyschosocial, such as illness induced by subjective evaluation of one's social position. In many places worldwide, poor health outcomes reflect deprivation in the form of poor sanitation, more polluted environments, inferior housing, and various features of the social and physical environment. In countries that have passed a certain threshold of development, relative deprivation might impact health through pyschosocial processes: The physiological effects of feeling poor can affect health. Research by Nancy Adler and colleagues in 2000 found, for instance, that subjective evaluations of socioeconomic status predicts levels of stress hormones, patterns of cardiovascular function, incidences of obesity, and other physiological outcomes.

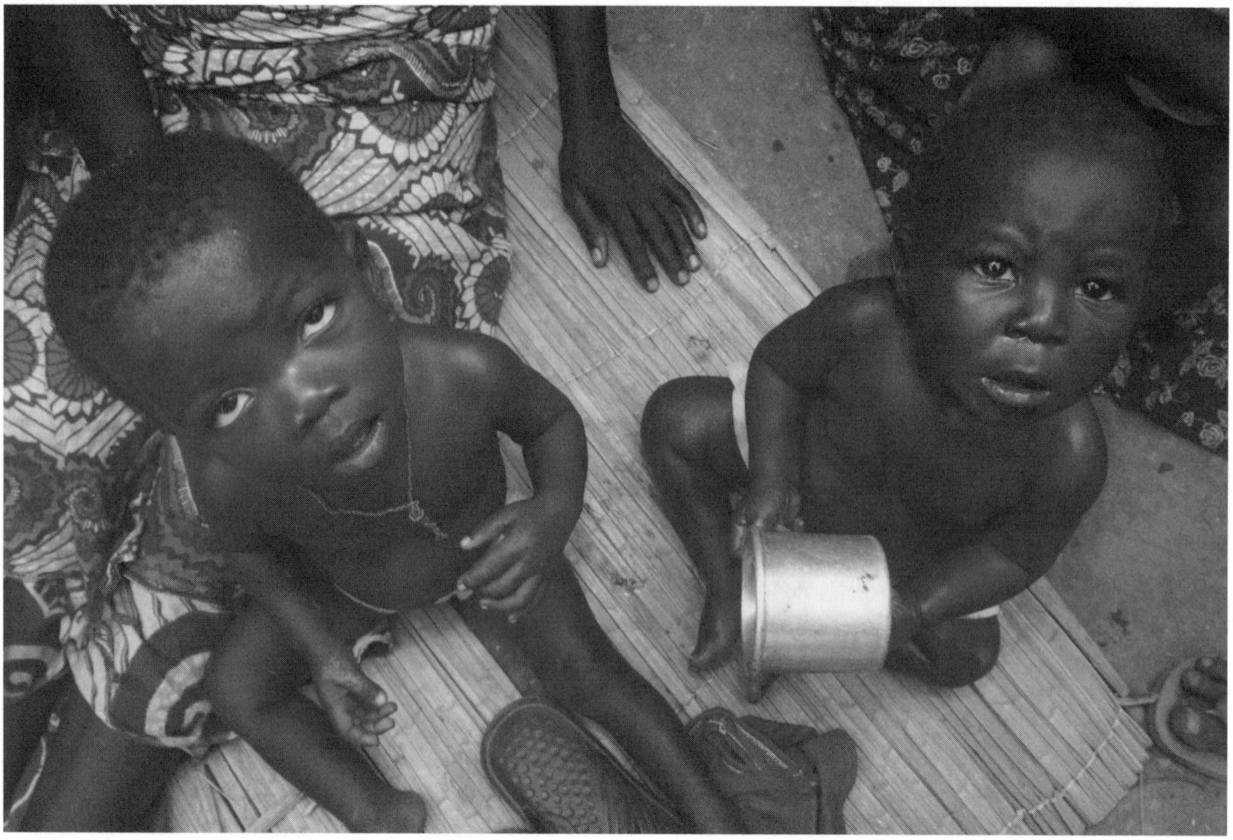

Hungry Angolan Children, June 2002. *A mother and her two children wait to receive food in Nabuangongo, Angola. Famine has been a fact of life in parts of Africa for decades, making many people dependent on international food shipments.* AP IMAGES.

In studies of poor black communities in the American South, the medical anthropologist William Dressler found that, among poor black Americans in a southern community, falling short of the lifestyle that a particular community emphasized (e.g., having certain material items) affected levels of blood pressure. In a 1998 study of subjects from a Brazilian city, Dressler and colleagues (1998) similarly found an inverse relationship between distance from a culturally defined sense of lifestyle and arterial blood pressure, depressive symptoms, and perceived stress.

These and other studies that examine how chronic stress affects health suggest how the material and pyschosocial factors might be linked. Humans may be well equipped to deal with acute stress, but chronic stress clearly increases the risk or severity of a number of diseases, such as Type 2 (adult-onset) diabetes, for example. A broad scientific literature has shown that individuals are at greater risk for stress-sensitive diseases when they (1) feel that they have little control over the source of stress; (2) have no way to predict the duration and intensity of the stress; (3) have few outlets that help deal with the frustration caused by the stress; (4) see the source of stress as evidence that circumstances are getting worse; and (5) lack social support. Moreover, exposure to stress, and the resources that mitigate stress, are not distributed evenly. Moving from high socioeconomic status to low socioeconomic status generally means greater exposure to a variety of stressors—neighborhoods marked by high violence, job and housing insecurity, and so forth—and fewer of the resources that help mitigate them (see Sapolsky 2005).

Many researchers theorize that chronic exposure to racial and ethnic discrimination might affect health in stress-related ways (e.g., Mays et al. 2007). Whereas the overall results have been mixed, a number of studies have found that individual perception of race-based discrimination is associated with higher blood pressure and poorer self-rated health (Kreiger and Sidney 1996). Perceptions of racial discrimination have also been shown to affect birth outcomes (see Kreiger and Sidney 1996, Collins et al. 2000).

These studies suggest, again, that the fundamental sources of health disparities are neither rooted in the genes nor explained by health-related behavior. Morbidity and mortality patterns reflect social status. Inferior status for racial and ethnic minority populations started with slavery and/or colonialism, and in the early twenty-first century it reflects continuing discriminatory practices and unequal access to vital resources that are relevant to health. Health inequalities in terms of race, ethnicity, and class are, therefore, fundamentally rooted in current and past political and economic practices that generate social stratification.

BIBLIOGRAPHY

Adler, Nancy E., Elissa S. Epel, Grace Castellazzo, and Jeannette R. Ickovics. 2000. "Relationship of Subjective and Objective Social Status with Psychological and Physiological Functioning in Preliminary Data in Healthy White Women." *Health Psychology* 19 (6): 586–592.

Barros, Fernando C., Cesar G. Victora, and Bernardo L. Horta. 2001. "Ethnicity and Infant Health in Southern Brazil: A Birth Cohort Study." *International Journal of Epidemiology* 30 (5): 1001–1008.

Blakely, Tony, Martin Tobias, Bridget Robson, et al. 2005. "Widening Ethnic Mortality Disparities in New Zealand 1981–99." *Social Science & Medicine* 61 (10): 2233–2251.

Blakely, Tony, Jackie Fawcett, Darren Hunt, and Nick Wilson. 2006. "What Is the Contribution of Smoking and Socioeconomic Position to Ethnic Inequalities in Mortality in New Zealand?" *Lancet* 368 (9529): 44–52.

Collins, James W., Jr., Richard J. David, Arden Handler, et al. 2004. "Very Low Birthweight in African American Infants: The Role of Maternal Exposure to Interpersonal Racial Discrimination." *American Journal of Public Health* 94 (12): 2132–2138.

Cooper, Richard S., Jay S. Kaufman, and Ryk Ward. 2003. "Race and Genomics." *New England Journal of Medicine* 348 (1): 1166–117069.

Din-Dzietham, Rebecca, Wendy N. Nembhard, Rakale Collins, and Sharon K. Davis. 2004. "Perceived Stress Following Race-Based Discrimination at Work Is Associated with Hypertension in African-Americans. The Metro Atlanta Heart Disease Study, 1999–2001." *Social Science & Medicine* 58 (3): 449–461.

Dressler, William W. 1990. "Lifestyle, Stress, and Blood Pressure in a Southern Black Community." *Psychosomatic Medicine* 52 (2): 182–198.

———, Mauro C. Balieiro, and Jose E. Dos Santos. 1998. "Culture, Socioeconomic Status, and Physical and Mental Health in Brazil." *Medical Anthropology Quarterly* 12 (4): 424–446.

———, and José Ernesto Santos. 2000. "Social and Cultural Dimensions of Hypertension in Brazil: A Review." *Cadernos De Saude Publica* 16 (2): 303–315.

House, James S., and David R. Williams. 2000. "Understanding and Reducing Socioeconomic and Racial/Ethnic Disparities in Health." In *Promoting Health: Intervention Strategies from Social and Behavior Research*, edited by Brian D. Smedley and Leonard S. Syme. Washington, DC: National Academy Press.

Kawachi, Ichiro, Norman Daniels, and Dean E. Robinson. 2005. "Health Disparities by Race and Class: Why Both Matter." *Health Affairs* 24 (2): 343–352.

Krieger, Nancy, and Stephen Sidney. 1996. "Racial Discrimination and Blood Pressure: The CARDIA Study of Young Black and White Adults." *American Journal of Public Health* 86 (10): 1370–1378.

Krieger, Nancy, Kevin Smith, Deepa Naishadham, et al. 2005. "Experiences of Discrimination: Validity and Reliability of a Self-Report Measure for Population Health Research on Racism and Health." *Social Science & Medicine* 61 (7): 1576–1596.

Lantz, Paula M., John W. Lynch, James S. House, et al. 2001. "Socioeconomic Disparities in Health Change in a Longitudinal Study of US Adults: The Role of Health-Risk Behaviors." *Social Science & Medicine* 53 (1): 29–40.

Lewontin, Richard C. 1972. "The Apportionment of Human Diversity." *Evolutionary Biology* 6: 381–398.

Link, Bruce G., and Jo C. Phelan. 1995. "Social Conditions as the Fundamental Causes of Disease." *Journal of Health and Social Behavior,* Special Issue: *Forty Years of Medical Sociology: The State of the Art and Directions for the Future*: 80–94.

Lynch, John W., George A. Kaplan, and J. T. Salone. 1997. "Why Do Poor People Behave Poorly? Variation in Adult Health Behaviours and Psychosocial Characteristics by Stages of the Socioeconomic Lifecourse." *Social Science and Medicine* 44 (6): 809–819.

Marks, Jonathan M. 2002. *What It Means to Be 98% Chimpanzee*. Berkeley: University of California Press.

Mays, Vickie M., Susan D. Cochran, and Namdi W. Barnes. 2007. "Race, Race-Based Discrimination, and Health Outcomes among African Americans." *Annual Review of Psychology* 58: 201–225.

National Center for Health Statistics. 1998. *Health, United States, 1998, with Socioeconomic Status and Health Chartbook.* Hyattsville, MD: U.S. Public Department of Health and Human Services. Available from http://www.cdc.gov/nchs/data/hus/hus98.pdf.

Sapolsky, Robert. 2005. "Sick of Poverty." *Scientific American* 293 (6): 92–99.

Wilkinson, Richard G. 2005. *The Impact of Inequality: How to Make Sick Societies Healthier*. New York: New Press.

Dean E. Robinson

SOCIAL PROBLEMS

Race, racism, and social problems intersect in many ways. First, social problems are not randomly or evenly distributed; some groups of people are affected by social problems more often and more severely than others. Second, race and racism are important factors in how problematic situations are defined and dealt with. Third, racism itself is an issue that is defined and debated as people interpret the potential causes, effects, and solutions to social problems.

WHAT ARE SOCIAL PROBLEMS?

The concept of *social problems* refers to major societal issues or conditions that have harmful effects on large numbers of people. Strictly speaking, though, there is no consensus on a definition of social problems, for it is difficult to specify precisely what constitutes "major issues," "large numbers of people," or even "harmful effects." Moreover, the word *social* implies a human component, a focus on situations that are created and potentially solved by people, though it is difficult to distinguish socially created conditions from those that are exclusively "medical problems" or "natural disasters," because much of what human beings do influences their health and their experiences with the natural world (e.g., hurricanes, earthquakes, and floods).

Another complexity is that social problems can be approached in at least two ways: as objective situations or as interpretations. Some scholars study problems by attempting to find facts. What is the nature and extent of the problem? What causes the problem? What are the effects of the problem? What are the solutions to the problem? Other scholars study problems by focusing on interpretation. They study how different people make claims (interpretations) about the nature, extent, causes, effects, and solutions of putative problems. In practice, many scholars combine the objectivist and subjectivist approaches by alternating between treating problems as discernibly real or factual and treating them as ambiguous situations that are "defined into being" via interpretative views.

SOCIAL PROBLEMS ARE NOT EVENLY DISTRIBUTED

Objectively speaking, social problems can have wide-reaching implications and effects. Issues such as poverty, crime, and environmental decline either directly or indirectly touch the lives of nearly everyone. However, it is usually an oversimplification to assert that a social problem "crosses all lines" or "knows no boundaries." Social problems are not randomly or equally distributed. The location and impact of social problems are somewhat patterned and predictable, and they affect some groups more than others.

The majority of poor people in the United States are white. However, in terms of percentages rather than absolute numbers, whites as a group tend to be afflicted with poverty at a much lower rate than other groups. In the 1990s, for example, poverty rates for African Americans and Hispanics (approximately 20–30%) were generally two or three times higher than what they were for whites (around 10%). Due in no small part to poverty, crime victimization is also differentially distributed by race and neighborhood. African Americans are more likely than whites to be robbed, burglarized, assaulted, and murdered. Health problems, too, are not random. White Americans, on average, live several years longer than African Americans, and they tend to receive superior medical treatment. Lastly, whereas it would seem that an issue such as environmental decline would have no racial component, many believe this is not the case. In major cities such as Los Angeles, for example, people of color tend to live in areas with the greatest air pollution. Some argue that environmental hazards (such as toxic-waste disposal sites) are disproportionately located near the communities of minorities rather than whites.

Similar examples can easily be found with respect to education, housing, employment, and other aspects of social life. Major social problems tend to be distributed unevenly along racial lines, rather than emerging randomly or equally across all groups.

Occasionally, the argument "this is a problem that affects everyone" can be a useful strategy for eliciting support, motivating volunteers, and prompting new policies. In many instances, though, this "universalization" of social problems can remove attention and resources from those who suffer the most from a problem, which often means the poor and people of color. For that reason and others it is important to keep in mind exactly who is affected by a social problem, and to what degree.

RACE, RACISM, AND THE DEFINITION OF SOCIAL PROBLEMS

The study of social problems is challenging because there is often little consensus on how to define any given societal situation. Does a problem exist? What kind of a problem is it? What are its causes, effects, and solutions? Different individuals, working from different perspectives, can answer all of these questions differently. For interpretive scholars, problems are "defined into being" as people think and talk about them. Problems arise and are given meaning when activists, politicians, reporters, and others interpret ambiguous situations as troubling in one way or another.

A clear example of the interpretation of problems that involves race and racism is the case of "drapetomania," which was conceived as a widespread problem involving many African Americans. In 1851, Samuel Cartwright (a doctor at the University of Louisiana) published an article in a medical journal describing drapetomania as a "disease of the mind" that compelled slaves to flee their masters. For Cartwright, the problem at hand was not slavery itself, which he described as a proper, natural, God-given role for "Negroes"; instead, the problem as he interpreted it was the fleeing of slaves from their service. The treatment and prevention of this ailment, according to Cartwright, was to continuously remind slaves of their (submissive) place, while still treating them in a kindly manner. This could be done by providing adequate food and shelter but restricting the use of alcohol and limiting social activities at night. By doing so,

Hurricane Katrina Victims at the New Orleans Convention Center, 2005. *Some commentators have speculated that race and racism played a role in the government's sluggish response to Hurricane Katrina.* AP IMAGES.

Cartwright argued that southern slave owners could help reduce the social problem of runaway slaves.

It seems painfully obvious that drapetomania is a highly questionable and racist interpretation, rather than a factual diagnosis, of a social issue. The "problem" at hand could very easily be defined as slavery itself, not people fleeing from slavery; and the cause of fleeing could be seen not as a "disease of the mind" but as a "normal" or "natural" desire to be free.

The identification of more modern problems also seems influenced by racism. Beliefs that certain groups are lazy, intellectually inferior, or immoral often seem to influence whether problems are noticed and how they are interpreted. For example, the reduction of poverty does not seem to be a high priority in American politics, and even when it is, the victims are often blamed for their own plight. The image of the African-American "welfare queen"—whose culture and behavioral choices purportedly lead to her own poverty and her continuing reliance on government aid—has often pervaded discussions of welfare reform, despite the inaccuracies of the stereotype. Drawing attention to the supposed problem of welfare abuse shifts the debate from the historical and structural causes of poverty to the issue of "how to get people off government aid." Similarly, illegal immigration has been portrayed as a serious (if not apocalyptic) problem through the presentation of images of immigrants as criminal, pathological, potentially terrorist, freeloading individuals who are eager to use publicly funded social services. Obviously, not all analysts agree with this interpretation of immigrants, their reasons for migrating, and their status as a society-threatening problem. Rather, many see immigrants as hard-working individuals who are trying to support themselves and their families in the face of interregional inequality, and who are making positive contributions to American society in the process.

RACISM AS A CONTESTED INTERPRETATION

It would be intellectually dishonest not to acknowledge that racism is itself an interpretation. Like race, racism is a concept that can be defined and used in different ways. It is something that often must be inferred from statements and actions, and these are usually open to multiple interpretations. When Hurricane Katrina struck New Orleans in 2005, most agreed that the devastation was exacerbated by the slow reaction of the federal government. Some commentators speculated, however, that race and racism played a role in the government's sluggish response, given the racial (and economic) makeup of the city of New Orleans. Others vehemently disagreed with this viewpoint, citing inexperience, poor communication, difficult on-scene conditions, and other causal explanations.

Thus, while race and racism play large roles in the occurrence and interpretation of many social problems, the exact nature and extent of their impact is often an emotionally charged subject that is open to debate.

SEE ALSO *Children, Racial Disparities and Status of; Education, Racial Disparities; Ethnic Cleansing; HIV and AIDS; Poverty; Violence against Women and Girls.*

BIBLIOGRAPHY

Collins, Sheila. 1996. *Let Them Eat Ketchup! The Politics of Poverty and Inequality*. New York: Monthly Review Press.

Feagin, Joe. R., and Pinar Batur. 2004. "Racism in Comparative Perspective." In *Handbook of Social Problems: A Comparative International Perspective*, edited by George Ritzer. Thousand Oaks, CA: Sage Press.

Foster, John. 1999. *The Vulnerable Planet: A Short Economic History of the Environment*, rev. ed. New York: Monthly Review Press.

Heiner, Robert. 2006. *Social Problems: An Introduction to Critical Constructionism*, 2nd ed. New York: Oxford University Press.

Lindsey, Linda L., and Stephen Beach. 2002. *Sociology*, 2nd ed. Upper Saddle River, NJ: Prentice Hall.

Szasz, Thomas S. 1971. "The Sane Slave: An Historical Note on the Use of Medical Diagnosis as Justificatory Rhetoric." *American Journal of Psychotherapy* 25 (2): 228–239.

Wagner, David. 1997. "The Universalization of Social Problems: Some Radical Explanations." *Critical Sociology* 23 (1): 3–23.

Welch, Michael. 2002. *Detained: Immigration Laws and the Expanding I.N.S. Jail Complex*. Philadelphia, PA: Temple University Press.

Scott R. Harris

SOCIAL PSYCHOLOGY OF RACISM

The concept of race has historically derived from beliefs about the biology of group differences. However, contemporary views of race reject the validity of any biological basis of race, and in the early twenty-first century it is most common to view race as constructed from the social fabric of societal beliefs and actions. The social construction of race contributes to the cultural meanings that are widely shared as stereotypes. The meanings of race, therefore, vary over time as a result of newly constructed beliefs, ideologies and stereotypes.

Racism has been defined in many different ways, but four features of these definitions are most significant. First, racism is a form of dominance in which one racial group enjoys control over the outcomes of another racial group. The dominant racial group exercises its power to the persistent disadvantage of the subordinate group. Second, the beliefs that sustain and rationalize group dominance presume the superiority of the in-group and the inferiority of the out-group. Third, racism is a multilevel phenomenon that is expressed by individuals (micro level), is critically influenced by institutions (meso level), and deeply embedded in the entire culture (macro level). Influences among the levels are bidirectional and evolve and change over time. Fourth, racism contributes directly and indirectly to persistent racial inequality.

Individual-level racism is most similar to racial prejudice and is based on persistent in-group preference. It differs from prejudice in that dislike or discomfort with out-group members is further complicated by feelings of in-group superiority. At the individual level, negative attitudes, feelings, or behaviors are directed at the targets of racism. These negative expressions of racism may be intentional, as in *dominative* racism, or unintentional (or without awareness) as in *aversive* racism. Discrimination is an aspect of individual-level racial dynamics in that it captures the disparity in behaviors directed at members of one's own and another racial group. The most common forms of discrimination involve more negative or less positive behaviors directed at out-group members relative to in-group members. Prejudice is usually linked to negative stereotypes held about an out-group and applied to behavior directed at members of that group, regardless of whether or not they fit the group stereotype.

Institutional-level racism perpetuates and exacerbates racial inequality. Institutional racism occurs when standard practices create or sustain racial inequality. Slavery and the evolution of Jim Crow discrimination, (as well as the beliefs that sustained them), have played a critical and cumulative role in creating and maintaining racial inequality. Prior to passage of the Civil Rights Act (1964) and the Voting Rights Act (1965), widespread systematic racial discrimination in housing, banking, and education conspired to disadvantage black people in America. Real estate and banking practices and policies played a major role in creating and maintaining racial segregation. These practices and policies insured that blacks had a harder time buying homes and that the homes they did buy were in neighborhoods where property values were lower and driven downward. Further, blacks were disadvantaged by mortgage interest rates that were appreciably higher, imposing an additional financial burden due to race. Home ownership is the single most effective source of wealth accumulation in the United States. Thus, systematic racial discrimination in real estate and banking has accounted for billions of dollars of lost wealth for blacks. Added to the loss of real estate assets is the loss of tax breaks afforded homeowners. In

March from Selma, 1965. The Voting Rights Act was passed by Congress shortly after State troopers violently broke up the civil rights voting march in Selma, Alabama on March 7, 1965. AP IMAGES.

this way, cumulative racism plays a major role in socioeconomic racial inequality in America.

Cultural racism offers a worldview in which attributes such as character, behavior, social organization, and cultural expression of out-groups are denigrated and in-groups are exalted. The presumptive inferiority of blacks from slavery times on was woven into the fabric of American mythology. For example, Abraham Lincoln opined that "there is a physical difference between the white and black races which ... will ever forbid the two races living together on terms of social and political equality ... [but] while they do remain together there must be the position of superior and inferior and I ... am in favor of having the superior position assigned to the white race." (Nicolay and Hay 1890, pp. 457–458). The mythology of racial superiority and inferiority is passed down from generation to generation, and it is reflected in the language, speech, symbols, and practices of American society. It is suffused throughout the culture and informs institutional practices and individual beliefs and behaviors, thus maintaining an infrastructure that perpetuates racial inequality, whether it is intentional or not.

Racism has significant effects on its targets. In the 1950s the social indicators of racial segregation were judged to produce an inherently unequal psychological world for black children. Research and theory suggested that damaged self-esteem was an inexorably psychological consequence of culturally sanctioned racism (Kardiner and Ovesy 1951). Subsequent research, however, challenged this deterministic conclusion by showing a wide range of factors that help targets of racism cope with disadvantage and develop self-protective racial identities (Sellers et al. 1997). Individual and collective mechanisms that confer psychological resilience have also been identified.

PREJUDICE AND STEREOTYPES

Racism, as it is found in individuals, has three components: stereotypes, prejudice, and discrimination. Stereotypes are beliefs about the characteristics possessed by members of a group. They embody the cognitive component of racism and exist at both the cultural and individual levels. At the cultural level, stereotypes are beliefs that members of one culture or group hold about the characteristics of another culture or group. At the individual level, stereotypes reflect an individual's beliefs about the characteristics found in a group. Individuals engage in stereotyping when they designate certain characteristics as especially prevalent in certain groups, or when they base their impression of a person on the characteristics believed to be associated with that person's group identity. Stereotypes can be positive or negative. For example the cultural stereotype of blacks in America includes positive (e.g., athletic) and negative (e.g., hostile) characteristics. The accuracy of stereotypes can also vary, but they are most often viewed as overgeneralizations. For example, even though whites may correctly believe that more blacks than whites play professional basketball, they may over generalize this belief by overestimating the number of blacks who play basketball.

Prejudice is the emotional component of racism. It is a negative attitude that is directed at a group and its members. There is no simple correspondence between prejudice and stereotypes. Unsurprisingly, as an individual's endorsement of negative stereotypes increases, so does his or her prejudice, though the overall strength of this relationship is only moderate. Also, when prejudice and stereotypes change, they do not necessarily change together. Favorable intergroup contact reduces prejudice more than it changes stereotyping. Conversely, stereotyping can be reduced by informing people that their peers do not endorse stereotypes, but this does not always simultaneously reduce prejudice.

Discrimination is the behavioral manifestation of racism. When whites act more favorably towards whites than towards blacks, discrimination is occurring. Comparing the prejudice-discrimination relationship with the stereotyping-discrimination relationship reveals a further discrepancy between stereotypes and prejudice. The prejudice-discrimination relationship is stronger than the stereotyping-discrimination relationship. Yet there may be important exceptions to this. Studies using video-game simulations have investigated the influence of race on the kind of rapid decisions that police must make when confronting suspects. These studies reveal that whites accidentally shoot unarmed blacks more often than they accidentally shoot unarmed whites. This effect is not associated with prejudice, however, and even blacks shoot armed blacks quicker than they shoot armed whites (Correll et al. 2002). Rather, this effect appears to result from activation of the stereotype that blacks are violent and criminal. In sum, prejudice and stereotyping are related, but they can be influenced independently and can display different relationships with discrimination.

Although stereotyping and prejudice are related, researchers are still learning about the nature of this relationship. Many recent cognitive theories of intergroup relations have viewed stereotypic beliefs as a cause of prejudice. However, other accounts of intergroup relations have viewed stereotypic beliefs as a result of prejudice. There is probably some truth to both propositions. At the societal level, racial inequalities (e.g., on average, blacks earn less than whites) are justified by culturally shared stereotypes (e.g., blacks earn less because they are lazy), which perpetuate racial inequality (e.g., blacks are overlooked for high-paying jobs because they are assumed to be lazy). Similarly, once stereotypes and prejudices are formed in an individual's mind, they can reinforce one another. For example, the prejudiced person may stereotypically interpret a black's difficulty in finding work as resulting from laziness, which then serves to reinforce his prejudice. Indeed, highly prejudiced individuals more strongly endorse the cultural stereotype of blacks than do low-prejudiced individuals (Devine 1989). They also tend to ignore information that disconfirms stereotypes, while low-prejudiced individuals pay attention to information that disconfirms stereotypes (von Hippel et al.1995).

Although stereotypes and prejudice often have mutual influences on each other, they may also arise independently of one another. It may, therefore, be more informative to examine the sources of both stereotypes and prejudice than to try to answer the question of which comes first. The fundamental source of intergroup problems lies in social categorization. People have a natural tendency to think in social categories. For example, dark-skinned people with African features are thought of as black, while light-skinned people with European features are thought of as white. However, even this basic schema of racial categorization can be altered. Under certain circumstances, both whites and blacks will categorize light-skinned blacks and dark-skinned blacks into separate groups, underscoring the point that race is a social construction.

Social categorization occurs because it has practical value. Social categories simplify the social world and make it predictable. Placing individuals into social categories is simplifying because it obviates the need to form complex individuated impressions of others. Categories make the social world predictable because once a category is formed it becomes associated with certain characteristics. These characteristics form a stereotype that allows one to predict another's behavior simply by observing their membership in a particular category. Research consistently shows that stereotyping follows from categorization. For example, accentuating ethnicity by depicting a Chinese woman eating Chinese food increases activation of the Chinese stereotype, while accentuating gender by depicting a Chinese woman putting on makeup increases activation of the female stereotype (Macrae et al. 1995).

Social categorization does not only give rise to stereotyping, it also forms a foundation for prejudice. Categorization creates in-group–out-group (we-they) distinctions, and because of a motive to evaluate one's own group more positively than other groups, these distinctions generally lead the in-group to be liked more than the out-group. This motive is so ubiquitous that even when groups are created arbitrarily, such that there is no prior history of conflict and no pre-existing negative stereotypes of the out-group, bias in favor of the in-group still develops (Tajfel and Turner 1986). When an in-group–out-group distinction occurs in combination with conflict, bias favoring the in-group can be replaced by hatred of the out-group, and even this more vicious form of prejudice can develop in the absence of pre-existing negative stereotypes. Yet stereotypes may quickly develop as a way to make the in-group appear more positive than the out-group and sustain feelings of hostility.

Psychologically, conflict leads to prejudice by first creating a sense of threat. Threat can result from conflicts over tangible resources (e.g., jobs) or from perceived differences in values, such as a perception among some whites that blacks violate the American value of having a strong work ethic. Threat can also stem from anxiety and negative stereotypes. The prospect of interacting with members of an out-group can create anxiety, which acts as another type of threat that leads to prejudice. Similarly, negative stereotypes may exert a causal influence on prejudice when they create a sense of threat. For instance, the belief that blacks are unfair beneficiaries of affirmative action can be threatening to whites, thus creating negative emotions that give rise to prejudice.

Four Roses Advertisement. *A lawn jockey is used in a vintage advertisement for Four Roses Whiskey. Many Americans find the lawn jockey to be racially offensive.* AP IMAGES.

REDUCING PREJUDICE AND COMBATING RACISM

At the individual level, attempts to reduce racial prejudice typically involve educational strategies to extend knowledge and appreciation of other groups, or to emphasize the message that prejudice is wrong (e.g., in mass media campaigns). Alternatively, for more contemporary, subtle forms of prejudice (e.g., aversive racism) some strategies attempt to make people aware of inconsistencies in their nonprejudiced self-images and values and their discriminatory behaviors, hoping to motivate more favorable attitudes and behaviors. Other techniques are aimed at changing or diluting stereotypes by presenting stereotype-disconfirming information. Research has shown that this technique is primarily effective at changing the stereotype of the group when the information concerns a broad range of group members that are perceived to be typical of their group (Rothbart and John 1985).

Mere contact between groups can also reduce intergroup conflict and bias, but it is even more effective when it occurs under specified conditions (including equal status between the groups, cooperative intergroup interactions, opportunities for personal acquaintance, and supportive egalitarian norms). Research has attempted to explain the psychological processes by which these conditions of contact reduce bias, thereby allowing interventions to focus on specific psychological processes. One framework proposes that the features specified by the "contact hypothesis" (e.g., equal status, cooperative interaction, self-revealing interaction, and supportive norms) share the capacity to decategorize group boundaries and promote more differentiated and personalized conceptions, particularly of out-group members (Brewer and Miller 1984). With a more differentiated representation of out-group members comes recognition that there are different types of out-group members (e.g., professional hockey players that are both sensitive and tough), thereby weakening the effects of categorization and the tendency to perceptually minimize and ignore differences between category members. Group members start to "attend to information that replaces category identity as the most useful basis for classifying each other" (Brewer and Miller 1984, p. 288).

In contrast to the decategorization approach, the "common in-group identity model" (Gaertner and Dovidio, 2002) proposes that the conditions of contact reduce intergroup bias and conflict because they lead members to recategorize perceptions of both groups, from "us" and "them" to a more inclusive "we." This induces more positive attitudes toward out-group members through processes involving bias favoring the in-group.

Specifically, it is hypothesized that intergroup interdependence and cognitive, perceptual, linguistic, affective, and environmental factors can either independently or in concert alter an individual's cognitive representations of the aggregate. These resulting cognitive representations (i.e., one group, two subgroups within one group, two groups, or separate individuals) then result in the specific cognitive, affective, and overt behavioral consequence. In addition, it is proposed that common in-group identity may be achieved by increasing the salience of existing common superordinate memberships (e.g., a school, a company, a nation) or by introducing factors (e.g., common goals or fate) that are perceived to be shared by members. The development of a superordinate identity does not necessarily require people to abandon their previous group identities. Instead, they may possess dual identities, conceiving themselves as belonging to both the superordinate group and to one of the original groups included within the new larger group. Thus, even when racial or ethnic identity is strong, perceptions of a superordinate connection can enhance interracial trust and acceptance. Support for the effectiveness of this model is derived from laboratory and field experiments as well as surveys in natural settings (e.g., a multiethnic high school) and an intervention in an elementary school (Houlette et al. 2004).

Decategorization and recategorization both emphasize altering how group boundaries are represented. Yet some approaches posit that intergroup relations will be harmonious when group identities remain strong as long as the groups interact within a cooperative context (Brown and Hewstone 2005). People like to belong to groups that are both unique and positively evaluated. When groups lose their distinctiveness, intergroup bias often increases as group members strive to reassert their uniqueness by enhancing evaluations of the in-group over those of the out-group. Thus, maintaining group distinctiveness within a cooperative intergroup relationship can reduce intergroup bias. In addition, the salience of intergroup boundaries provides an associative mechanism through which changes in out-group attitudes that occur during intergroup contact can generalize to the out-group as a whole.

Two striking features of racism are its tenacity and omnipresence. Group-based inequality is a persistent feature of civilization. Even in the United States, a nation founded on principals of equality, racism continues to exist both at the societal and individual level. As the public has come to renounce racism, its manifestations have become less obvious—housing discrimination has supplanted slavery, and subtle preferences for the racial in-group have remained even as overt expressions of hatred have diminished—but not less real. The problem arises from a combination of a basic human tendency to categorize people into groups and a history of the dominant group passing on disadvantage to subordinate groups, which has created a self-sustaining hierarchy. In individuals, categorization leads to in-group favoring bias and stereotyping, which can be exacerbated by societal conditions (e.g., employment discrimination) that make subordinate groups appear less valuable than the dominant group. Social hierarchy further serves to encourage stereotypes that justify inequality. Moreover, as progress toward equality occurs, dominant group members may experience threat as subordinate group members increasingly "take" good jobs and influence cultural values, thereby leading to open expressions of prejudice.

It is against this backdrop that attempts to reduce racism must operate. Different approaches are suited to attacking different aspects of the problem. Contact structured to encourage either decategorization or recategorization attempts to undermine social categorization, which provides the psychological foundation of racism. Other approaches seek to leave categorization intact while altering beliefs and attitudes about racial out-groups or by helping well-intentioned individuals recognize and change their own subtle racial biases. Finally, education and persuasive messages about the unacceptability of racism can create a change in individual levels of prejudice while simultaneously facilitating change at the societal level by creating racially tolerant norms. Racism is a complicated problem, and a complete solution requires careful consideration of all its complexities.

BIBLIOGRAPHY

Allport, Gordon W. 1954. *The Nature of Prejudice*. Cambridge, MA: Addison-Wesley.

Brewer, Marilyn B., and Norman Miller. 1984. "Beyond the Contact Hypothesis: Theoretical Perspectives on Desegregation." In *Groups in Contact: The Psychology of Desegregation*, edited by Marilyn B. Brewer and Norman Miller, 281–302. New York: Academic Press.

Brown, Rupert J., and Miles Hewstone. 2005. "An Integrative Theory of Intergroup Contact." In *Advances in Experimental Social Psychology*, Vol. 37, edited by Mark P. Zanna, 255–343. San Diego, CA: Elsevier Academic Press.

Civil Rights Act of 1964 (*Pub. L.* 88–352, 78 *Stat.* 241, *July 2, 1964*).

Correll, Joshua, Bernadette Park, Charles M. Judd, and Bernd Wittenbrink. 2002. "The Police Officer's Dilemma: Using Ethnicity to Disambiguate Potentially Threatening Individuals." *Journal of Personality and Social Psychology* 83: 1314–1329.

Devine, Patricia G. 1989. "Stereotypes and Prejudice: Their Automatic and Controlled Components." *Journal of Personality and Social Psychology* 56: 5–18.

———, and Andrew J. Elliot. 1995. "Are Racial Stereotypes Really Fading? The Princeton Trilogy Revisited." *Personality and Social Psychology Bulletin* 21: 1139–1150.

Eberhardt, Jennifer L., Philip A. Goff, Valerie J. Purdie, and Paul G. Davies. 2004. "Seeing Black: Race, Crime, and Visual Processing." *Journal of Personality and Social Psychology* 87: 876–893.

Gaertner, Samuel L., and John F. Dovidio. 1986. "The Aversive Form of Racism." In *Prejudice, Discrimination, and Racism*, edited by John F. Dovidio and Samuel L. Gaertner, 61–89. Orlando, FL: Academic Press.

———. 2000. *Reducing Intergroup Bias: The Common Ingroup Identity Model.* Philadelphia: Psychology Press.

Houlette, Melissa A., Samuel L. Gaertner, Kelly M. Johnson, et al. 2004. "Developing a More Inclusive Social Identity: An Elementary School Intervention." *Journal of Social Issues* 60: 35–55.

Jones, James M. 1997. *Prejudice and Racism*, 2nd ed. New York: McGraw-Hill.

Kardiner, Abram, and Lionel Ovesy. 1951. *The Mark of Oppression.* New York: W. W. Norton.

Macrae, C. Neil, Galen V. Bodenhausen, and Alan B. Milne. 1995. "The Dissection of Selection in Person Perception: Inhibitory Processes in Social Stereotyping." *Journal of Personality and Social Psychology* 69: 397–407.

Massey, Douglas S., and Nancy Denton. 1993. *American Apartheid: Segregation and the Making of the Underclass.* Cambridge, MA: Harvard University Press.

Pettigrew, Thomas F., and Linda R. Tropp. 2006. "A Meta-Analytic Test of Intergroup Contact Theory." *Journal of Personality and Social Psychology* 90: 751–783.

Rothbart, Myron, and Oliver P. John. 1985. "Social Categorization and Behavioral Episodes: A Cognitive Analysis of the Effects of Intergroup Contact." *Journal of Social Issues* 41: 81–104.

Sellers, Robert M., Stephanie J. Rowley, Tabbye M. Chavous, et al. 1997. "Multidimensional Inventory of Black Identity: A Preliminary Investigation of Reliability and Construct Validity." *Journal of Personality and Social Psychology* 73 (4): 805–815.

Tajfel, Henri, and John C. Turner. 1986. "The Social Identity Theory of Intergroup Behaviour." In *Psychology of Intergroup Relations*, edited by Stephen Worchel and William G. Austin, 7–24. Chicago: Nelson-Hall.

U.S. Department of Justice, Civil Rights Division 1965. *The Voting Rights Act of 1965.* Washington, DC: United States Government Printing Office.

Von Hippel, William, Denise Sekaquaptewa, and Patrick Vargas. 1995. "On the Role of Encoding Processes in Stereotype Maintenance." In *Advances in Experimental Social Psychology*, vol. 27, edited by Mark P. Zanna, 177–253. San Diego, CA: Academic Press.

Eric W. Mania
James M. Jones
Samuel L. Gaertner

SOCIAL WELFARE STATES

Social welfare states implement governmental policies and practices developed to address or insure the protection and basic needs of vulnerable populations, such as people with mental or physical disabilities, the chronically ill, children, the elderly, and the poor (including low-income workers, or the working poor). According to James Leiby, the author of *A History of Social Welfare and Social Work in the United States* (1978), the term *welfare state* developed in the 1940s in England as a euphemism for what was then known as "charity and correction," a form of public assistance provided to the very poor (paupers) or those with serious disabilities (the defective). From its inception, the general structure of the welfare state has typically reflected policymakers' definition of need, rather than the reality of need as a lived experience. Thus, despite its humanitarian implications, the welfare state is a highly contested and stigmatized concept because of its relationship to poverty.

WELFARE, POVERTY, AND RACISM

In industrialized societies, poverty is more often viewed as a consequence of defective character, behavior, and morality than a result of the unequal distribution of wealth. Since the early 1800s, beliefs about the nature of poverty have influenced the categorization of the poor as either "deserving" or "undeserving." Michael Katz argues that in both America and England, distinctions were made between poverty as an unavoidable evil and pauperism as a consequence of immorality. Even in the early twenty-first century, the notion of the "unworthy poor" is accompanied by numerous morality-based stereotypes. African Americans and other people of color who live in low-income communities are blamed for poverty, crime, and other social ills. These stereotypes justify the ill treatment of the poor and shape the policies that govern their lives. Yet social marginalization and restrictive, punitive policies actually contribute to the perpetuation of poverty. These powerful forces actually ensure that poor people will accept low-wage employment. Thus, the welfare state is intricately connected to the maintenance of a low-wage work force.

The welfare state is also a highly racialized and gendered concept. Numerous stereotypes about poor people and welfare reflect the belief that people of color (particularly women of color) saturate and abuse the welfare system. In the United States, for example, the welfare state is strongly associated with inner-city African-American and Latino families headed by women. Kenneth Neubeck and Noel Cazenave call this "welfare racism," citing American public opinion polls indicating the general belief that most welfare recipients are African-American teenage mothers who continue to have children just to avoid gainful employment. These scholars argue that the percentage of African American families receiving welfare in the late 1990s was nearly identical to the percentage of white families receiving welfare. Yet many white Americans viewed public assistance—particularly the Aid to Families with Dependent Children (AFDC) program—as a "black program." Neubeck and Cazenave contend that, over the decades, powerful politicians "forged and exploited the link between 'race' and 'welfare' to such a degree that the two terms are now politically and culturally inextricable" (Neubeck and Cazenave 2001, p. 3).

WELFARE IN PRACTICE

Social welfare states reflect the historical, complex, and ever-changing interplay between social practices, politics, economics, and family life. Although models of social welfare vary widely from one country to another, in most industrialized nations the welfare state provides minimum forms of relief or assistance for people living in poverty. Moreover, in every welfare system there is a vast difference between the stated goals and intentions of the system and the actual social support provided.

In Britain, for example, the social welfare state is theoretically characterized as a system providing services and protection as a right of citizenship. In practice, however, social services in Britain are neither comprehensive nor generous. Throughout Europe, welfare systems are similarly troubled and complex. Social policies are influenced by finite resources as well as politics and racial ideologies, and people who must remain connected to these systems also generally remain in perpetual poverty.

SOCIAL SECURITY AND THE WELFARE STATE

Social welfare in the United States refers to a complex system of both entitlement programs and relief programs, most of which emerged in the 1930s. In this two-tiered system, the only stigmatized programs are those that assist poor citizens. Most direct government aid goes to people who are not poor, and these aid programs are considered "entitlements." This was the original intent of the Social Security Act of 1935, which was created during the New Deal era. Preceded by the stock market crash of 1929 and the decade-long Great Depression, this legislation was the first permanent social assistance program in the United States and the foundation of America's current welfare state.

The main purpose of Social Security was to provide assistance for men who were unemployed due to the Depression. The legislation included work relief provisions and social insurance to avert future economic hardships for these men and their families. However, several scholars have shown that the proposed programs in the Social Security Act excluded most Americans, particularly blacks and women. Social Security legislation provided federal subsidies to the states to enhance state and local employment programs, but there were no directives preventing states from discriminatory practices in the provision of assistance.

Moreover, Social Security was never meant to be a comprehensive assistance program. It was designed to promote employment and ensure a low-wage workforce.

A relatively small segment of the Social Security Act was the Aid to Dependent Children (ADC) program that assisted single-mother families not covered by Social Security. (ADC became AFDC in 1960, and in 1996 it underwent a number of changes and became the Temporary Assistance for Needy Families [TANF] program.) Conceptualized as a temporary program, ADC was funded by states through property taxes, and it is still considered to be public charity. It was also discriminatory because of the belief that only widowed white mothers were deserving of assistance. African-American women were not deemed virtuous enough to qualify for assistance.

The ADC program of 1935 was not the first means-tested assistance program for American women, and it was not the first program to be influenced by a Victorian sense of morality. In the early twentieth century, white women's groups organized a mothers' pension movement, advocating that impoverished women be allowed to remain at home to raise their children, just as married, middle-class mothers were expected to do. Promoting children as an important national asset, the movement framed mothers' work as a critical component in nation-building.

Although legislation was passed approving mothers' pensions in most states, there were no legislative requirements attached, and relatively few poor women were helped by this program. Those who did receive mothers' pensions were widowed white women, and few activists or governmental officials ever considered the plight of impoverished African-American mothers and their children. These women remained in the low-wage workforce, cleaning the homes of white families and leaving their children behind to grow up on their own. Consequently, the first significant attempt to provide public assistance to the truly needy was tainted by both sexism and racism, reflecting the nation's hostile attitude toward African-American women in particular. The same gendered racism would influence the administration of ADC and the public assistance programs that would follow it.

WELFARE AND CIVIL RIGHTS

The 1950s and 1960s brought about unprecedented and dramatic transformations in American race relations. As they fought to dismantle racial discrimination, most civil rights activists understood that economic marginalization was an effective and destructive social weapon, and that it had crippled most black American families for centuries. The 1963 March on Washington for Jobs and Freedom underscored the devastation wrought by the intersection of racial and economic oppression. By the 1960s poverty was an uncontrolled epidemic, affecting more than 17 percent of Americans. Many of the impoverished were African Americans who, in the 1940s and 1950s, had migrated from the rural South to urban communities in the North seeking economic opportunities that had never materialized.

At the core of the 1960s urban unrest was the rage, disappointment, and misery experienced by African Americans who left blighted slums day after day to work in abysmal jobs for low wages that barely paid the rent on their decrepit dwellings. This unrest, coupled with a civil rights movement that had turned its focus toward the urban North, gave rise to a relief movement similar to the Depression era relief movements. In both eras, the masses challenged the government to consider its responsibilities to the economic well-being of its people. Other factors influencing and supporting the growing demands for social support included President Lyndon Johnson's War on Poverty and the development of the National Welfare Rights Organization. Declaring a War on Poverty in his 1964 State of the Union address, Johnson influenced the development of legislation that prohibited racial and gender discrimination in employment and programs that addressed hunger, housing, job training, and community development. The National Welfare Rights Organization, which remained active until the mid-1970s, sought to educate the urban poor on their rights to freedom from systemic tyranny in the forms of oppressive welfare policies and practices. One of the results of these combined efforts was a significant rise in the relief rolls. In their book *Poor People's Movements* (1977), Frances Fox Piven and Richard Cloward contend that "in 1960, 745,000 families received assistance; in 1968, the number reached 1.5 million. Then, between 1968 and 1972, the rolls surged to 3 million families. … Money payments, less than $1 billion in 1960, reached $6 billion in 1972" (1977, p. 275).

Although most civil rights leaders were reluctant to fully support black participation in AFDC and other social welfare programs, quality of life did improve for the chronically poor, who now had access to a range of programs that could guide them out of poverty. The welfare state continued to be a source of much debate and controversy, however, and legislation directing policies and practices fluctuated with each new administration.

WELFARE REFORM

In the last years of the twentieth century, the American welfare state remained generally ineffective, uneven, and racialized. In 1996 President Bill Clinton, who had run for office on a platform promising to "end welfare as we know it," signed the Personal Responsibility and Work Opportunity Reconciliation Act (PRWORA). Clinton's focus on welfare reform mostly pertained to the AFDC program (which became TANF). The legislation included work requirements and time limits on assistance. Well into the twenty-first century, entitlements assisting those who are not the poorest of the poor remained intact, and the American social welfare state remained a two-tiered system that continued to define citizenship in the context of race and class.

SEE ALSO *Civil Rights Movement; Demographics and Race; Multiculturalism; Poverty; Racial Formations; Sexism; South African Racial Formations; United Kingdom Racial Formations.*

BIBLIOGRAPHY

Katz, Michael. 1996. *In the Shadow of the Poorhouse: A Social History of Welfare in America*, rev. ed. New York: Basic Books.

Leiby, James. 1978. *A History of Social Welfare and Social Work in the United States.* New York: Columbia University Press.

Neubeck, Kenneth, and Noel Cazenave. 2001. *Welfare Racism: Playing the Race Card against America's Poor.* New York: Routledge.

Piven, Frances Fox, and Richard Cloward. 1977. *Poor People's Movements.* New York: Pantheon.

Cheryl R. Rodriguez

SOLDIERS OF COLOR

African-American and Mexican-American soldiers have consistently experienced unequal treatment in the U.S. military. However, the types of experiences that African Americans and Mexican Americans have had differed. A major difference is that, up until the Korean War, African Americans were either excluded from the U.S. armed forces or segregated within them. Mexican Americans, however, have been integrated into all branches of the military since the 1860s. Individual Mexican Americans, however, have experienced racism, based either on dark skin color or poor English-speaking abilities, while in the military. For both African-American and Mexican-American soldiers, group segregation and racism have occurred once they left the military and reentered American society.

AFRICAN AMERICANS IN COLONIAL AND REVOLUTIONARY FORCES

African Americans have participated in all U.S. wars since colonial times. In the early American colonies, both able-bodied white and black men (free or slave) were supposed to participate in militia units when warfare broke out with Native Americans. In peacetime, however, African Americans were excluded from service due to fears of armed slave insurrections and doubts about the ability of African Americans to learn military skills. Thus, African Americans served only in times of crisis and emergencies. Their training was in the use of hatchets and pikes but not firearms. On some occasions, however, African Americans were fully armed and fighting side by side with European Americans against Native Americans. African Americans joined militias even if it was temporary, because it could mean an improvement in civil status, often receiving the same pay as European Americans, and sometimes offers of freedom by some local governments in exchange for killing or capturing an enemy. In April 1775, General George Washington issued orders not to enlist African Americans, but when the British recruited African Americans in December, Washington amended his orders and allowed African Americans to serve. Thus, the Continental Army was integrated, and, on average, forty-two African-American soldiers served in every brigade. The Continental Navy was also integrated, due to manpower shortages and the considerable experience of African-American seamen. About 5,000 African Americans served in the Continental forces, and about 1,000 served with the British. Some African Americans gained their freedom as a result of their service. Many who enlisted with the British were re-enslaved. As an ally of the American revolutionaries, Spain ordered General Bernardo de Galvez, then the governor of Louisiana, to take troops to participate in the Gulf campaigns of the American Revolution from 1779 to 1781. Two thousand of these soldiers were Mexican Indians.

POSTREVOLUTIONARY FORCES

After the American Revolution, the Mexican Indian soldiers returned to their bases in New Spain (Mexico), while the African Americans were excluded by law from militias (except in Louisiana). At the beginning of the War of 1812, African Americans were told they could not serve in the U.S. Army and Navy. By 1814, however, they were allowed to enlist. Andrew Jackson had about 600 African-American troops fighting with him at the Battle of New Orleans, and it is estimated that 10 percent of the naval crews serving in the war were African Americans. The navy imposed a 5 percent quota on free African-American enlistment after the war during peacetime. Slaves could not serve in the navy. By 1820–1821, orders were added to General Regulations that once again excluded all African Americans. State militias also limited their services. Only "free white male citizens" could be in the artillery, infantry, cavalry, dragoons, riflemen, and grenadiers. Hundreds of African Americans, primarily slaves, did in fact serve in the army and navy, but only as laborers, dock hands, cooks, coopers, carpenters, personal servants of officers, and other similar jobs.

During the Mexican War (1846–1848), African Americans were still excluded from the ranks. But African Americans who could pass the "color line" did serve in the army until their ancestry was questioned, whereupon they were typically cashiered from the army. Slaves took part as servants to officers. Mexican guides were hired by the American army during its campaigns in Mexico, and there were a few native Californios and New Mexicans that served in the U.S. Army, but for the most part Mexicans fought against the Americans.

AFRICAN-AMERICANS IN THE CIVIL WAR

The Civil War (1861–1865) was the first war in which both African Americans and Mexican Americans served as soldiers. But their service continued to be more dissimilar than similar. About 186,000 African Americans served in the Union Army as part of the U.S. Colored Troops. They did not serve as Regulars but in volunteer cavalry, artillery, and infantry units. They served in segregated units, usually under the command of white officers. At the start of the Civil War, African Americans were not allowed to enlist, but manpower shortages and the Confederate use of slaves as laborers, cooks, teamsters, and farmworkers led to a change in policy about enlisting African Americans. At first, slaves who entered the lines of the Union Army (called the "contrabands of war") were used as workers. In 1863 the Emancipation Proclamation called for the enlistment of African-American troops, and the 54th Massachusetts Infantry Regiment was formed. However, the African-American soldiers who enlisted protested the dual-wage system, by which European-American soldiers were paid $13 plus $3.50 for clothing, while African Americans were paid $7 plus a $3.00 allotment for clothing. Their efforts were successful, and in 1864 all soldiers got the same pay and allotment monies.

Even though African-American soldiers were not trained sufficiently, they saw action in every theater of war. About 38,000 of them lost their lives. A major concern was where commanding officers would place the African-American troops in battle. William Carney, an African American soldier of the 54th Massachusetts, won a Medal of Honor for not letting the American flag drop to the ground, though he did not receive his medal until the 1890s. This would not be the first time that African-American soldiers would be denied medals during a war, only to have some soldiers acknowledged for bravery under fire by a later generation of American politicians. About 10,000 Mexican Americans served in the Civil War, on both the Union and Confederate sides. They were placed in integrated units serving in Alabama, Louisiana, Texas, California, and the New Mexico and Arizona territories. Some Mexican Americans made the officer corps, and the highest-ranking Mexican American was a colonel in the Confederate Army.

After the Civil War, African-American soldiers were not allowed to march in victory parades. Under the reorganization of the Army that took place between 1866 and 1869, the U.S. Colored Troops became army Regulars, but they were committed only to the remote parts of the U.S. West. They were formed into the 9th and 10th Cavalry and the 24th and 25th Infantry. It was during this period that African-American soldiers became known as "Buffalo Soldiers." Although they had very low rates of desertion, they received inferior equipment and horses, and poor barracks housing in forts. Mexican-American soldiers were part of the frontier army as well, primarily serving in the New Mexico and Arizona territories and Texas.

African-American troops again saw service in the Spanish American War and the Philippine War. Colonel Theodore Roosevelt congratulated them in helping to save his troops, but later, while campaigning for office, he said that African-American troops were cowardly. During the Philippine War, some African-American soldiers, after constantly being humiliated by the racist behavior of European-American soldiers and officers, deserted the U.S. Army and found common cause with the Filipino insurgents. Only a handful of Mexican Americans served in integrated units during the Spanish American War, and only one Mexican American was an officer during the conflict.

After 1900, the U.S. military was completely segregated. With the approach of World War I, the United States needed to prepare for wartime manpower needs, which included using African Americans during times of crisis and during emergencies. In 1917, the 24th Infantry was stationed in Houston, Texas, but many residents did not like having armed African-American soldiers in their midst, and a riot ensued. Southerners thought that African-American soldiers would be a determent to racial harmony in the military, and southern politicians protested their inclusion in the Selective Service Act of 1917. Nonetheless, African Americans were soon to be drafted. To appease the southern politicians, draft applicants had to indicate their race on the form. That way, African-American draftees could be segregated when and if they were called up.

The most experienced black units, the 9th and 10th cavalry and the 24th and 25th infantry, were not allowed to fight in World War I. Instead, draftees were formed into the 92nd and 93rd Divisions. By 1918, about 367,000 African Americans had been drafted, and about 200,000 served in Europe. The 93rd Division was sent to France, and under French command they received training and engaged in combat. The 92nd Division also performed well in combat, but its soldiers were chastised as being inferior for not taking an enemy position. The U.S. military did not see a need for African-American soldiers in combat units, mostly based on European-American officers' negative views about their fighting abilities. Things only got worse for African Americans when they returned to the states after World War I. Some African Americans were lynched for wearing service uniforms in Mississippi and Georgia, even though they had served in the military.

Mexican Americans also fought in World War I. Exact numbers are not known, however, because the U.S. military did not segregate Mexican Americans in separate units. One Mexican American, David Barkeley, was made a first lieutenant and received a Medal of Honor. He had enlisted in Laredo, Texas, using only his Anglo first and last names, because he knew that if he used his mother's last name, Cantu, he would neither get to be an officer nor be eligible for high military honors.

By the time of World War II, African Americans were no longer considered desirable as fighting troops, primarily because of biased views about their combat performance in World War I. African-American combat units were limited principally to the 92nd and 93rd Infantry Divisions. Two African-American fighter squadrons, known as the "Tuskegee Airmen," were created, however, and both achieved outstanding combat records. About one million African Americans served during World War II, and about 300,000 to 500,000 Mexican Americans served during this war. Mexican Americans served in all theaters of war, primarily in the lower ranks, and thirteen of them received the Medal of Honor. The 141st Infantry had a high concentration of Mexican Americans, saw 361 days of combat, and sustained more than 6,000 casualties. Upon returning home, some Mexican-American soldiers (including the Medal of Honor winners) and African Americans were not allowed to eat in restaurants that catered to white customers, and they had to return to living in segregated areas. In 1948,

African American Soldiers Leave for WWI. *After 1900, the United States military was completly segregated. It would remain this way until the Korean War.* NATIONAL ARCHIVES, U.S. WAR DEPARTMENT GENERAL STAFF.

the body of Felix Longoria, an army private, was returned to Three Rivers Texas from the Philippines. However, his family was not allowed to use a chapel in the segregated "white" cemetery. This degrading incident spurred the formation of the G.I. Forum, a prominent Latino advocacy organization.

FROM SEGREGATION TO DESEGREGATION

In 1948, President Harry S. Truman issued Executive Order 9981, which desegregated the military. There was resistance from the armed forces, however, and it would take until the mid-1960s to address lingering restrictions on assignments and deployments. The Vietnam War was the first U.S. war in which African Americans were integrated at all levels of the military. Yet while they made up more than 10 percent of the army, their casualty rate was 13 percent. African Americans made up 60 percent of the complement of some infantry platoons and airborne units. Conflicts flared in all the services between African Americans and European Americans, especially in the rear areas. Twenty percent of Hispanics that fought in the Vietnam War were killed, while 33 percent were wounded. Mexican Americans, meanwhile, were disproportionately drafted in relation to their population in the U.S.

After the Vietnam War, African Americans were overrepresented in the all-volunteer armed forces. Yet for African-American officers, and even more so for Mexican Americans, promotion rates lagged behind the military's overall officer promotion rates. A 1997 Defense Manpower Data Center survey, to which more than 40,000 service members responded, found wide gaps between how European Americans and minorities perceived treatment of racial incidents. Seventeen percent of European-American soldiers, 38 percent of Hispanic soldiers and 62 percent of African-American soldiers thought that the military did not pay enough attention to the problem of race discrimination. In the first Gulf War (1990–1991), out of 30,000 women in the U.S. military about 44 to 48 percent were African American. At the beginning of the second Gulf War, in 2003, African Americans made up 12 percent of the U.S. population but 20 percent of the U.S. military. At that time, African Americans were underrepresented as combat soldiers, as pilots for the U.S. Air Force and Navy, and in the Green Berets. Mexican Americans and Latinos constituted 13 percent of the U.S. population and about 10 percent of total U.S. troops. They were underrepresented in all branches of the military and in the officer corps. More than 36,000 of these soldiers were noncitizens, and about 32 percent from Mexico and South America. Noncitizens cannot become officers or obtain security clearances. Data from 2006 indicated that Mexican Americans made up more than 37 percent of all active duty Marines and experienced high casualty rates as combat soldiers in Iraq. High numbers of Latinos were in the forces deployed in Iraq and reflect higher numbers of Latinos in the Marines, with lower numbers in the other branches.

A lingering tradition of racism in some quarters of the military is given as one reason for the racial divide. The history of African Americans and Mexican Americans have some dissimilarities, but by the time of the Vietnam War both groups were incorporated into all branches of the U.S. military, though often at lower ranks, with few making it into the officer corps. Until the Vietnam War, both African-American and Mexican-American soldiers believed that suspending civil rights struggle in civilian society and fighting as Americans would help them gain more rights. However, during the Vietnam War and thereafter, both groups refused to delay or postpone civil rights activism during wartime. Increasingly, leaders from these communities emerged who did not serve in the U.S. military, and they often protested the services of African Americans and Mexican Americans as needless "cannon fodder."

SEE ALSO *Buffalo Soldiers; Occupational Segregation.*

BIBLIOGRAPHY

Carroll, Patrick James. 2003. *Felix Longoria's Wake: Bereavement, Racism, and the Rise of Mexican American Activism.* Austin: University of Texas Press.

Mershon, Sherie and Steven Schlossman. 1998. *Foxholes and Color Lines: Desegregating the U.S. Armed Forces.* Baltimore, MD: John Hopkins University Press.

Moore, Brenda L. 1996. *To Serve My Country, to Serve My Race: The Story of the Only African American WACS Stationed Overseas during World War II.* New York: New York University Press.

Morin, Raul. 1963. *Among the Valiant: Mexican-Americans in WW II and Korea.* Alhambra, CA: Borden Publishing.

Moskos, Charles, and John Sibley Butler. 1996. *All That We Can Be: Black Leadership and Racial Integration the Army Way.* New York: Basic Books.

Natty, Bernard C. 1986. *Strength for the Fight: A History of Black Americans in the Military.* New York: Free Press.

Sandler, Stanley. 1992. *Segregated Skies: All-Black Combat Squadrons of WW II.* Washington DC: Smithsonian Institution Press.

Thompson, Jerry D. 1986. *Mexican Texans in the Union Army.* El Paso: Texas Western Press.

Ybarra, Lea. 2004. *Vietnam Veteranos: Chicanos Recall the War.* Austin: University of Texas Press.

Elizabeth Salas

SOUTH AFRICAN RACIAL FORMATIONS

South Africa's racial policies during and prior to the apartheid era (1948–1994) have left a lasting legacy that still bedevils post-apartheid society and politics. These policies became notorious for the level of disparity between racial groups, the extent to which assumed racial distinctions were legally enacted, and for the pervasiveness of the social control that governed relations between the groups. As a result, South Africa offers one of the classic examples of the social construction of racial boundaries, and of the use of assumed biological differences to structure every aspect of society. Racial ideology was used as part of a social and political agenda to limit access of native Africans to scarce resources in order to privilege a small group of whites. This approach was so successful for such a long time, and to such a degree, that South Africa's racial policies before the collapse of apartheid came to epitomize racism as an ideology and racialism as a set of practices. However, the introduction of apartheid in 1948, following the electoral victory of the Afrikaans National Party, was not the beginning of South Africa's racial formations.

THE COLONIAL ROOTS OF SOUTH AFRICA'S RACIAL FORMATIONS

Colonization took a different form in South Africa than it did in other societies, but it was the single overriding factor that helped to create the kind of society in which there was rigid racial division. This division was culturally reproduced over the centuries, and wealth, resources, and political power were structured around it, leading to intense social conflict.

Africa was a trading post for the spice sea routes to the East, first permanently colonized by whites for such purposes in 1652, and it provided an opportunity for settlers to escape war, persecution, or poverty in Europe. Along with colonization came Christian intolerance, with Africans seen as the personification of evil, and European notions of civilization, with Africans being supposedly primitive and culturally inferior. The southern tip of Africa was most suited to European settlement, with the Dutch being the first settlers in the area. They were led by Dutch surgeon and pioneer Jan van Riebeeck (1619–1677), an iconic figure for white settlers in South Africa, who were known as Trekboers, from the Dutch *boer,* meaning "farmer," and *trek*, meaning "to pull" (in this case farm wagons). They were also known simply as Boers or Afrikaners.

The settlement needed both land and labor. The first need, for land, led to wars of conquest and dispossession of the indigenous population; the second need, for labor, led to the importation of slaves from the Dutch East Indies. Slave ownership and a frontier mentality were central experiences of the lifestyle of the early settlers. The Trekboers were organized as military commando communities as much as farm settlements, and they justified slave ownership on moral grounds. Toward the end of the nineteenth century, one Afrikaner author wrote that black people carried the mark of Cain: It was God that had made them, as scripture says of Cain's descendants, "drawers of water and hewers of wood." In effect, they were seen as divinely suited as servants of the white "race." The writer doubted whether Kaffers (the derogatory term for African peoples) had souls (Reader 1998, p. 481). This did not, however, stop the Boers from engaging in furtive miscegenation, from which came the "colored" community.

The British took the Cape Colony from the Dutch in the early 1800s, first by force and then by treaty. Britain first wanted the Cape merely as a stepping off point for its growing trade routes. Thus, they wanted to minimize further development, and they instructed settlers to keep themselves absolutely separate from Africans, who were, meanwhile, subject to military campaigns by British forces to solidify earlier land dispossession. However, by 1820, Britain started to plant settlers in the Cape, and they quickly established themselves as merchants rather than farmers. British traders ventured from the Cape into Natal, with more military campaigns ensuing to effect British control. But the impact of British policy on the Trekboers was as influential as it was on Africans—putting an end, for example, to Afrikaner slave ownership. Given that slavery was supposedly divinely ordained, Afrikaners perceived the British government's abolition of slavery as contrary to God's law and against the natural distinctions of "race" and religion, and it led directly to the Great Trek by Afrikaners into what came to be called the Orange Free State and Transvaal. Their trek into Natal in the hope of an alliance with the Zulu nation against the British resulted in the massacre of many innocent trekkers (including the murder of Piet Retief [1780–1838], the leader of the Great Trek) and the infamous Battle of Blood River. When they reached their new territories, the Trekboers met their need for labor in the same way they had in the Cape, by the seizure of Africans.

However, the discovery of gold and diamonds transformed Afrikaans society out of all recognition. As far as Britain was concerned, the discovery of gold and diamonds in Afrikaner-held territory could not have been more unfortunate, but they soon took it over, annexing first what became known as Griqualand West (for diamonds) and then eventually moving on the Transvaal (for gold). The discovery of gold and diamonds inflamed British colonial administrator Cecil Rhodes's (1853–1902) imperial designs for British interests in southern Africa, but it is more important for the profound social changes that followed the development of mining. The mines intensified the shortage of labor, leading to the use of convict labor and the development of the migrant labor system. With migrant labor came the mine compounds, the development of African townships (called, at the time, "locations") without a sustainable infrastructure as dormitories for workers, and the infamous Pass Laws, which restricted African people's residence rights and gave the police significant powers to exclude them from white areas. And as the regulation of labor increased, so did the number of offenses committed by workers, leading to the development of crude forms of policing (see Brewer 1994), while simultaneously increasing the supply of convict labor. The polarization of racial attitudes went hand in hand with the implementation of this official racial segregation, which gave twentieth-century apartheid solid roots in British policy in the nineteenth century.

The development of the South African state in 1910, through the union of the provinces of Transvaal, Orange Free State, the Cape, and Natal, was a way of managing cooperatively both Boer and British interests, but for Africans it meant the consolidation of colonial dispossession and inequality. The reconciliation of Boer and Briton under Generals Louis Botha (1862–1919) and Jan Smuts (1870–1950) resulted in a common "native policy," but the narrower Afrikaner nationalism of people such as General James B. Hertzog (1866–1942), which eventually culminated in an election victory for the National Party in 1948, pushed the country's racial policies in an even tougher direction. The Natives' Land Act of 1913 contained the essentials of South Africa's later apartheid policy, guaranteeing in law the dominance of whites. This system of laws was underpinned by the militarization of policing and other forms of social control, and by a cultural and religious critique that justified inequality and injustice on racial and scriptural grounds biology and the Bible were thus in collusion to support apartheid.

APARTHEID'S RACIAL FORMATIONS

When Afrikaner nationalists came to power in 1948, they built on the former "race" policies of the British. Apartheid (literally meaning "apartness") evolved over the years as racial distinctions became more finely defined in law to accommodate more and more groupings, and as the degree of social control intensified as the white population came to feel increasingly threatened. It is common to distinguish between early and late periods in the development of apartheid (Posel 1991), with the juncture occurring around 1960 with the development of what the National Party government called "Separate Development."

The Population Registration Act of 1950 racially classified all South Africans into four categories: White, Asian, Colored, and Native (later called Bantu), with "Natives" eventually subdivided ethnically into various cultural groups, thus merging "race" with ethnicity to compensate for the inadequacies of biology to sufficiently support political distinctions among the African population. Africans were split into Zulu, Xhosa, Tswana, Sepedi (or North Sotho), Seshoeshoe, Swazi, and Venda. Various proclamations to the act over the years led to further subdivisions of Coloreds. The system was very rigid, for although it was possible for people to move from one group to another if their physical features made it feasible, this was very rare (and often done only after humiliating scrutiny). Various nationalities were made "honorary Whites" (such as Japanese and Koreans) as the government sought political allies and trading partners throughout the world. Population ratios have varied little over the years, however, with Africans comprising around seven out of every ten people, Whites around one and a half, Coloreds one, and Asians about a half.

The whole purpose of this racial classification was to use "race" as the mechanism to allocate resources and land unequally to the privilege of whites. Territorial segregation was enforced by the 1950 Group Areas Act, with black groups confined to designated areas and permitted into so-called White areas only for employment. Forced removals uprooted people from areas where their families had lived for generations if they happened to be in an area that had been designated for another racial group. This segregation was supported by the infamous Pass Laws, which required people to carry documentation proving their right to be in an area otherwise designated for a different racial group. The 1953 Bantu Education Act segregated the "races" in schooling. Miscegenation was strictly controlled by the 1949 Prohibition of Mixed Marriages Act and various Immorality Acts that made sexual relations between the "races" illegal. The provisions of the Reservation of Separate Amenities Act of 1953 created "common areas" for each group, which controlled all sorts of possible social interactions. The act led to separate buses (or demarcated spaces on shared buses), toilets, bathing beaches, post offices, shops, health facilities and the like, and even to separate waiting lines for shared services. This social apartness epitomized apartheid.

Cultural apartness however, was the least of the purposes of apartheid. Material deprivation coincided with race, space, and territory, as black areas were under-resourced; education, housing, welfare, health, and employment opportunities were unequally distributed; and political power was in white hands. By 1959 various homelands (called Bantustans) were created for the separate development of Africans, who were given parliamentary representation and voting rights, as well as employment, housing, and other social rights, in their "own" areas. This was an even more ruthless attempt at social engineering, as an ambitious policy was introduced to strip Africans of their South African citizenship and force them to become citizens of contrived states. While some "citizens" of these states could legally work in so-called White areas, they often lived in African townships that bordered the white areas or were allowed to live as temporary residents subject to significant restrictions and monitoring. These putative ethnic homelands were controlled, financed, and buttressed by the National Party government and became second-class states with little employment opportunities, inferior schools, and powerless political assemblies. They did not achieve their purpose to stop the tide of people moving to the white areas illegally in search of work.

Illegal encroachment only intensified the policing of racial boundaries in white areas, as repressive measures were reinforced in order to try to maintain the exclusivity of white districts. The 1950 Suppression of Communism Act had such a broad definition that it included many routine forms of opposition. The 1950 Internal Security Act provided for detention without trial of someone not even suspected of a criminal offense, so long as the minister of justice was satisfied that the person threatened public order. Most forms of political organization among blacks were banned under the 1960 Unlawful Organizations Act or amendments to the Riotous Assemblies Act (first introduced in 1914 to control Afrikaner support for Germany in the First World War). The many internal security laws gave almost unfettered power to the police and military. Violent repression, deaths in detention and prison, and indiscriminate harassment and victimization against blacks

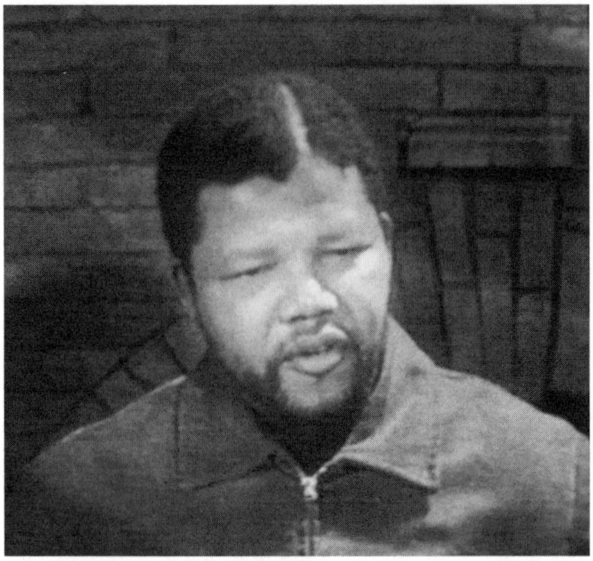

Nelson Mandela, early 1960s. *African National Congress (ANC) leader Nelson Mandela was imprisoned for 27 years.* WALTER DHLADHLA/AFP/GETTY IMAGES.

became the marks of policing (Brewer 1994). The tragic death of Steve Biko (1946–1977), the Black Consciousness leader, in police custody in 1977 was only one of very many deaths (Brewer 1986, pp. 111–115).

REPRESSION AND RESISTANCE

Apartheid's racial formations brought conflict and violence into the heart of society. Black political opposition has a proud history of nonviolent protest, but such tactics manifestly failed to prevent the gradual exclusion from all representative politics, first for Africans and eventually for all nonwhite groups. Incidents of collective protest occurred, such as those at Sharpeville in 1960, but the banning of the African National Congress shortly afterwards, and the imprisonment or exile of its leaders, including Nelson Mandela, effectively ended political protest in the 1960s, leading to a long quiescent period. Violence remained, however, in specific forms. There was structural violence against black South Africans in the form of extreme social exclusion, poverty, and unemployment; there was state violence reflected in the severe repression of black people; and there was criminal violence in black areas, with high rates of murder, rape and violent assault. The strains and tensions within apartheid and the migrant labor system manifested themselves in high levels of drunkenness, family breakdown, domestic abuse, and violent crime (on the negative effects of migrant labor, see Dunbar, Moodie, and Ndatshe 1994).

The political conflict that ignited in South Africa after the 1976 Soweto uprising, which spread rapidly through the urban townships, produced a different kind of violence. Political violence after 1976 took five forms: (1) an intermittent and low-intensity campaign of insurgency by *Umkhonto We Sizwe*, the armed wing of the ANC; (2) collective unrest in the townships to make them ungovernable; (3) violence from the security forces and their surrogates, at first to confront black protest and subsequently to disrupt transitional negotiations; (4) politically motivated black-on-black violence between the ANC and Chief Buthelezi's Inkatha movement, later called the Inkatha Freedom Party (Mare and Hamilton 1984); (5) and random black-on-black violence between warlords, criminal gangs, migrants, and hostel dwellers, which was linked to the pathological conditions of apartheid but also often exploited both by political groups and the security forces and their surrogates. This social dislocation easily transformed into ordinary criminal violence, which rose dramatically as political violence intensified. For example, it is estimated that between 1983 and 1992 there were 15,843 deaths attributable to political violence in South Africa, with two-thirds happening after 1990, but in the same nine-year period there were seven times more nonpolitical murders (Kane-Berman 1993). By 1995, "ordinary" murders had nearly doubled compared to 1991, representing more than the total number of deaths caused by political violence in the decade between 1983 and 1994. Fifty-two people were murdered every day in South Africa in 1995. Indeed, South Africa's murder rate in 1995 was six times higher than in the United States (du Toit 2001). Thus, apartheid made South Africa an extremely violent society.

THE RAINBOW NATION AND APARTHEID'S LEGACIES

In 1990, South Africa's president, F. W. de Klerk, began a process of reform that culminated in the release of Nelson Mandela, the removal of the ban of the ANC, and the development of a new constitution ending white-minority rule. The first nonracial elections were held in 1994, and the ANC was voted into power, with Mandela, the Robben Island prisoner of twenty-eight years, becoming the first nonracial president. The reform process up until the de Klerk government had permitted economic liberalization, but only in the context of the maintenance of white political control. De Klerk's vision was to cede political control of the state in the hope of maintaining white command of the economy; Mandela's was to avoid complete disintegration so as not to inherit a failed state and economy (Brewer 2003). The ANC jettisoned its socialist rhetoric, pursued pro-Western capitalist economic and fiscal policies, and diligently implemented its tradition of nonracialism, thus relieving white fears of majority rule, while the National Party

Protesting Proposed Name Change of Pretoria. *In 2005 South Africa proposed to change the name of its capital city, Pretoria, to the African Tshwane. Opponents feared that renaming the city would cause a racial divide among citizens.* AFP/GETTY IMAGES.

gave up the state to become a small minority party without prospect of ever forming the government again.

That the National Party should do this willingly may seem puzzling. However, it did so under extreme external pressure from economic sanctions and diplomatic interventions, although these had always been resisted in the past. The internal pressures were mounting by the end of the 1980s, as the townships were proving ungovernable as a result of violent political protests against apartheid. However, the Sharpeville (1960) and Soweto (1976) protests show that the state had withstood black protest before. For the most part, apartheid collapsed under the contradictions of its own racial policies. There were too few whites to run the economy and state without the need for massive black labor, personnel, and human skills, so apartheid's strict regulation of the races became counterproductive to the needs of a modern polity and economy. The various liberalizations since 1976 that opened up access to certain resources in certain spaces for certain racial minorities only set up expectations of greater change as a black middle class developed, making white political control itself the main problem.

However, while it was easy for the new ANC government to quickly dismantle the pillars of apartheid, the extent of discrimination in the past was so immense that economic redistribution has only very slowly addressed the central inequalities. The African population, in particular, is so large and poor that apartheid's effects will endure long after its abolition. There is also a residue of racism after centuries of racial classification, which has been imprinted on people's ways of thinking and on their cultural values. The violence that characterized apartheid also still bedevils the "Rainbow Nation," giving it very high levels of violent crime. That most people nonetheless remain committed to reconciliation and to establishing a new identity as South Africans is testimony to the relatively peaceful way in which apartheid crumbled, to the enduring legacy of the ANC government's historical commitment to the principles of nonracialism, and to the fact that the African community values political control of the state and majority rule above economic redistribution. This suggests that for all its social segregation and economic privations, apartheid was experienced primarily as a form of political exclusion, and that poverty levels have not diminished the sense of freedom and dignity that followed its destruction.

SEE ALSO *African Economic Development; Anti-Apartheid Movement; Apartheid; Black Consciousness; Children, Racial Disparities and Status of; HIV and AIDS; Mandela, Nelson; Racial Formations; Social Welfare States; White Settler Society.*

BIBLIOGRAPHY

Adam, Heribert, and Hermann B. Giliomee. 1980. *The Rise and Crisis of Afrikaner Power.* Cape Town, South Africa: David Philip.

Brewer, John D. 1986. *After Soweto: An Unfinished Journey.* Oxford: Clarendon Press.

———. 1994. *Black and Blue: Policing in South Africa.* Oxford: Clarendon Press.

———. 2003. *C. Wright Mills and the Ending of Violence.* London: Palgrave.

Du Toit, P. 2001. *South Africa's Brittle Peace: The Problem of Post-Settlement Violence.* Ethnic and Intercommunity Conflict Series. London: Palgrave.

Gerhart, Gail. 1978. *Black Power in South Africa: The Evolution of an Ideology.* Berkeley: University of California Press.

Kane-Berman, John. 1993. *Political Violence in South Africa.* Johannesburg: South African Institute of Race Relations.

Karis, Thomas, and Gwendolen Carter. 1972–1977. *From Protest to Challenge: A Documentary History of African Politics in South Africa, 1882–1990.* 4 vols. Stanford, CA: Hoover Institute Press.

Lodge, Tom. 1983. *Black Politics in South Africa Since 1945.* London: Longman.

Mandela, Nelson. 1994. *Long Walk to Freedom: The Autobiography of Nelson Mandela.* Boston: Little, Brown.

Maré, Gerhard, and Georgina Hamilton. 1984. *An Appetite for Power: Buthelezi's Inkatha and South Africa.* Johannesburg, South Africa: Ravan Press.

Moodie, T. Dunbar, and Vivienne Ndatshe. 1994. *Going for Gold: Men, Mines, and Migration.* Berkeley: University of California Press.

Posel, Deborah. 1991. *The Making of Apartheid, 1948– 1961.* Oxford: Clarendon Press.

Reader, John. 1998. *Africa: A Biography of the Continent.* London: Penguin.

South African Truth and Reconciliation Commission. 1998. *TRC Report,* vols. 1–5. Cape Town: Juta. Available from http://www.info.gov.za.

Wilson, Monica, and Leonard Thompson. 1971. *The Oxford History of South Africa.* New York: Oxford University Press.

John D. Brewer

SOUTHERN POLITICS, 1883–1915

This essay explores the social and political struggles and experiences that characterized the southern United States with regard to politics from 1883 to 1915. Sometimes called the "nadir," or the worst period of race relations in America, this period begins with the U.S. Supreme Court decision in the *Civil Rights Cases* of 1883, which canceled previous civil right legislation and permitted racist vigilante groups such as the Ku Klux Klan with impunity despite the equal rights protections of the Fourteenth Amendment. The case that most stands out in this period is the landmark Supreme Court case *Plessy v. Ferguson* (1896). At issue in this case was a Louisiana law of 1890 that required passenger trains operating within the state to provide "separate but equal" accommodation for "whites and colored persons." The Court held that segregation of the races did not violate the equal protection clause of the Fourteenth Amendment because people of each race received equal treatment. Booker T. Washington condoned the principle of "separate but equal" and became an international celebrity.

JIM CROW LAWS

Between the 1871 amnesty of ex-rebels against the federal government and 1876, the southern Democratic Party regained control of Alabama, Arkansas, Georgia, Mississippi, North Carolina, Tennessee, Texas, and Virginia. Disputes over presidential electoral vote totals in Florida, Louisiana, and South Carolina led to the Compromise of 1876, which was settled by the South ceasing to challenge the election of referees. This electoral victory gave the twenty-year-old Republican Party its third president. It also freed the party from dependence on a southern base of new black voters whose numbers were being reduced through violence from white supremacist vigilante groups, through the maneuvers of white election officials, and finally, through the adoption of "grandfather clauses," or rules exempting would-be voters from literacy tests if they could prove that their grandfathers had voted prior to January 1, 1867, a year before blacks became citizens. The grandfather-clause voting requirement was widely employed until the U.S. Supreme Court declared this practice unconstitutional in the case of *Guinn v. United States* in 1915.

The *Civil Rights Cases* of 1883 represented a conservative U.S. Supreme Court's stand at the beginning of a new era in the South, and its agenda was set by states enacting Jim Crow laws calling for segregation of the races. A few examples illustrate this point. In 1872, West Virginia legislators passed a law restricting jury duty to "all white male persons who are twenty-one years of age." In 1875, the Tennessee legislature gave to owners of public accommodations of any sort the right to choose their customers, a right that "shall be as perfect and complete as that of any private person over his private house, carriage or private theatre, or places of amusement for his family." In 1877 Georgia lawmakers enacted a law stipulating that "separate schools shall be provided for white and colored races." Mississippi enacted a similar law in 1878. In the early 1880s, similar state and local segregation laws were adopted across the South, allowing southern whites to deny blacks social, educational, economic, and political equality. The majority of southern states enacted Jim Crow laws that forbade interracial marriage and cohabitation and allowed the segregation of the races in nursing homes, buses, railroads, restaurants, pool houses, toilet facilities, prisons, hospitals, burial grounds, restaurants, parks, sports arena, beer parlors, housing, transportation, educational institutions, libraries, telephone booths, lunch counters, libraries, movie theaters, and other public accommodations.

THE *CIVIL RIGHTS CASES* OF 1883

Between 1875 and 1883 seven incidents summarized as the *Civil Rights Cases* were fundamental to the politics of the South. According to Rayford W. Logan (1965), these cases "included the denial of hotel accommodations to Negroes in Kansas and Missouri; the denial of a seat to a Negro in the dress circle of a theatre in San Francisco; the denial to a person (presumably a Negro) of the full enjoyment of the accommodations of the Grand Opera in New York; the refusal of a conductor on a passenger train to allow a colored woman to travel in the ladies' car of the Memphis and Charleston Railroad Company" (p. 116). The Court ruled that such actions were constitutional under the Fourteenth Amendment's equal protection clause because the amendment specified private individual actions and because Congress was not authorized to make general rules, but only corrective regulations.

The dying breed of Southern Unionists in the Republican Party began switching to the Democrats in this period, concluding as did one Mississippian that "no white man can live in the South in the future and act with any other than the Democratic party unless he is willing and prepared to live a life of social isolation and remain in political oblivion" (Davidson et al. 1990, p. 637). In the party platforms of the elections of 1884, 1888, 1892, 1896, and onward, both parties verbally celebrated the sanctity of the ballot and the value of freedom regardless of race or previous condition, but in reality did little to protect blacks politically or personally.

The rise of white agrarian unrest was abetted by the depressions of the 1880s and early 1890s and by the rise of small-scale farms personally worked by their white owners or more commonly with black sharecroppers. The period also saw more and more small-town merchant suppliers placing liens on crops for goods sold, higher prices for supplies the farmers bought, and a decline in prices for the crops they sold, and similar developments. This small farmer constituency called for government regulation of banks and railroads, the extension of credit and a more flexible fiscal policy, the establishment of subtreasuries, and the establishment of produce warehouses or grain elevators to hold crops until prices rose to yield a fair profit.

Because at least 85 percent of the African American population worked in agriculture, their presence could hardly be ignored in any effort to deal with the economic hardships now common to all. Thus, a class aspect of agrarian unrest was added to the conundrum of race, proportionately most of the rural workers being black.

THE RISE OF POPULISM

Black workers, especially farmers, had good success in joining the Southern Farmers' Alliance (SFA), founded in Texas in 1877 by R. M. Humphrey. Although like all workingmen's organizations of the era, the SFA kept the locals of the alliance racially separate, blacks flocked to the movement via the Colored Farmers' National Alliance and Cooperative Union. In its statement of purpose, the alliance said that "the object of this corporation shall be to elevate the colored people of the United States … to labor more earnestly for the education of themselves and their children, especially in agricultural pursuits … to be more obedient to the civil law, and withdraw their attention from political partisanship." By the 1890s, every southern state had local Colored Farmers' Alliance units. According to Humphrey, the numbers included Alabama, 100,000; Georgia, 84,000; South Carolina, 90,000; Mississippi, 90,000; Texas, 90,000; Arkansas, 20,000; Louisiana, 50,000; Virginia, 50,000; Kentucky, 25,000; Tennessee, 60,000; and North Carolina, 55,000. The sum of these numbers in the states listed nearly equals that of the 600,000 blacks who voted as citizens in the first presidential election after slavery.

Although their state and local units were color coded, the Farmers' Alliance national conventions were remarkably open on the issues of race and gender; an observer of a score of black male delegates felt compelled to also note "wimmin is everywhere" (Davidson et al. 1990, p. 785). Humphrey himself claimed that 300,000 females were among the 1,200,000 members of the national Colored Farmers' Alliance. One hundred black delegates were present at the St. Louis alliance convention in 1892, when the movement decided to go explicitly political with a new entity called the People's Party (Populist Party). Many of the delegates had political histories in the Republican and Democratic Parties. By the election of 1896, many activists resolved the contradictions by voting as Populist Party members in the election of 1896. Here and there blacks again won local election as fusion candidates, either Republican/Populists or Democrat/People's Party candidates. The wall between economics and politics, always porous, collapsed. Black political activism was met with cynical manipulation and strong resistance from southern whites within the movement. Class could not surpass race.

In some places, the Populist Party's strength was great enough to garner the support of established Democratic politicians such as Benjamin "Pitchfork" Tillman of South Carolina and Thomas Watson of Georgia, each of whom advanced himself as a champion of the working poor regardless of race. Tillman posed as a friend of white farmers to enable him take over the South Carolina Farmers' Alliance by adopting its platform, thus leaving it nothing to say. In 1890, he was elected governor of South Carolina. Once in power he repudiated black participation in electoral politics. Tillman organized the state constitutional convention in 1895, which relied strongly on Jim Crow laws to disenfranchise most of South Carolina's black men. In 1900, Tillman was quoted as boasting: "We have done our level best to prevent blacks from voting. We have scratched our heads to find how we could eliminate the last one of them. We stuffed ballot boxes. We shot them. We are not ashamed of it" (Logan 1997, p. 91). He was philosophically opposed to the emergence of a mass or people's party, as he feared that its national program for agricultural renewal would eventually bring about the empowerment of southern blacks.

Thomas E. Watson, elected to the Georgia legislature in 1882, also found ideological cover under the social and political climate in the South. His use of the Farmers' Alliance/Populist platform helped to catapult him into the U.S. Congress in 1890. While in Congress, he abandoned the Democratic caucus and attended the first Populist Party congressional caucus as the only and first Southern Alliance democrat to do so. As a populist, Watson helped unite agrarian (rural) farmers in the South across racial and class lines. He also supported the right of African American men to vote. As his attempts to use biracial politics to build a progressive majority coalition failed, he blamed black political activism for that failure. Indeed, with Populist James Baird Weaver as its presidential nominee, the party won a million votes but in the process built the Democratic Party in the South.

Determined to regain the support of the largely antiblack majority, Watson transformed himself into an ardent racist. He saw that the Democratic Party conservatives were determined to end black political participation, which they termed "Negro domination." In local elections, the Populists elected three governors, five senators, ten congressmen, and nearly 1,500 members of state legislatures. In the elections of 1896, the Populist Party lost overall, even though blacks won control of several local governments, most notably that of Wilmington, North Carolina, only to literally be driven out of office in the riots of 1898. White populists became Democrats, and the Democrats became advocates of a solid South, all white. Black disfranchisement became an openly promoted objective. Of the black male, Watson wrote, "In the South, we have to lynch him occasionally, and flog him, now and then, to keep him from blaspheming the Almighty, for his conduct, on account of his smell, and his color." He also declared that "lynch law is a good sign; it shows that a sense of justice yet lives among the people" (Crowe 1970). Editors such as Hoke Smith of the *Atlanta Journal* published racially inflammatory writings that helped to create a climate for the infamous Atlanta Riot of 1906. When blacks were finally eliminated from political influence, Watson again supported the Populist Party's economic program, becoming its presidential candidate in 1904 and 1908 when blacks were no longer visible in party circles.

INTO THE NEW CENTURY

At the height of racist politics in the South, politicians such as Mississippi governor James K. Vardaman (1904–1908) rode to power in a landslide victory, propelled by white racial fears in 1903. The time was ripe for advocates of black oppression. Vardaman denounced the education of blacks. He called it nothing but a form of "kindness that would make blacks unfit to serve whites." He generally characterized blacks as "lazy, lying and lustful animals for which no amount of training can transform into tolerable citizens," a sentiment that was both popular and well received among southern whites. Vardaman even went as far as stating that whenever convenient and "necessary it would be a good idea to lynch blacks in the state of Mississippi in order to maintain white supremacy" (Lopez 1965).

Against a background of triumphant white supremacy, on September 18, 1895, Booker T. Washington made his famous racial compromise speech in Atlanta, Georgia, at the Cotton States and International Exposition held to celebrate the South's recovery from the Civil War. In this address, Washington urged blacks to eschew political activity, saying that "in all things that are purely social, we (blacks and whites) can be as separate as the fingers, yet one as the hand in all things essential to mutual progress." This address made him a national figure and the most powerful African American of his time. Although many southern whites embraced his speech, most prominent blacks, such as writer and sociologist W. E. B. Du Bois, did not. Du Bois not only disagreed with Washington's ideas and public utterances but condemned outright his philosophy and strategy with respect to fighting black exploitation and oppression. Du Bois further challenged Washington's leadership through the platform of the Niagara Movement, which demanded economic and educational equality for blacks, and an end to discrimination in public facilities.

Although the Niagara Movement was not directly responsible for the formation of the National Association for the Advancement of Colored People (NAACP), it was hailed as a catalyst, at least for establishing a precedent that brought together black and white intellectuals opposed to the coexistence strategies of Booker T. Washington. The Niagara Movement met in New York in 1909 to discuss the formation of a new organization whose goal would be to improve the social, economic, and political condition of blacks. These efforts culminated in the establishment of the NAACP in 1910. Although the founding members were overwhelmingly white, they elected Du Bois as one of their members.

A series of other events gave impetus to the racial relations status quo in the South. In the landmark Supreme Court case *Guinn v. United States* (1915), the Court ruled unconstitutional an Oklahoma law that provided an exemption that served no discernable purpose other than to favor white voters at the expense of black citizens' right to vote. This verdict severely curtailed the challenges of Jim Crow laws. It also helped to enforce sweeping segregation laws in the southern states in particular and the United States in general, supposedly in perpetuity.

BIBLIOGRAPHY

Bobo, Lawrence, and Franklin D. Gilliam Jr. 1990. "Race, Sociopolitical Participation, and Black Empowerment." *American Political Science Review* 84 (2): 377–393.

Chavez, Linda. 1989. "Tequila Sunrise: The Slow but Steady Progress of Hispanic Immigrants." *Policy Review* 48 (Spring): 64–67.

Crowe Charles. 1970. "Tom Watson, Populists, and Blacks Reconsidered." *Journal of Negro History* 55 (April): 99–116.

Davidson, James West, Mark H. Lytle, Christine Leigh Heyrman, William E. Gienapp, and Michael B. Stoff. 1990. *Nation of Nations: A Narrative History of the American Republic.* New York: McGraw-Hill.

Hajnal, Zoltan L. 2001. "White Residents, Black Incumbents, and a Declining Racial Divide." *American Political Science Review* 95: 603–617.

Ivers, Gregg, and Karen O'Connor. 1990. "Minority Set-Aside Programs in the States after *City of Richmond v. J.A. Croson Co.*" *Publius* 20 (3): 63–78.

Lamb, Charles M. 1981. "Housing Discrimination and Segregation in America: Problematical Dimensions and the Federal Legal Response." *Catholic University Law Review* 30: 363–430.

Logan, Rayford W. 1965. *The Betrayal of the Negro: From Rutherford B. Hayes to Woodrow Wilson.* New York: Collier.

Lopez, Clara S. January 1965. "James K. Vardaman and the Negro: The Foundation of Mississippi's Racial Policy." *Southern Quarterly* 3 (January): 155–180.

McLemore, Nannie Pitts. 1967. "James K. Vardaman, a Mississippi Progressive." *Journal of Mississippi History* 29 (February): 1–11.

Mladenka, Kenneth R. 1989. "Blacks and Hispanics in Urban Politics." *American Political Science Review* 83: 165–191.

Perry, Huey L. 1990. "Recent Advances in Black Electoral Politics." *PS: Political Science and Politics* 23, (2): 133–160.

Rogers, Harrell R. 1981. "Civil Rights and the Myth of Popular Sovereignty." *Journal of Black Studies* 12 (1): 53–70.

Scavo, Carmine. 1990. "Racial Integration of Local Government Leadership in Small Southern Cities." *Social Science Quarterly* 71: 362–372.

Tolbert, Caroline J., and Rodney E. Hero. 1996. "Race/Ethnicity and Direct Democracy: An Analysis of California's Illegal Immigration Initiative." *Journal of Politics* 58: 806–818.

Ngozi Caleb Kamalu

SOUTHERN POVERTY LAW CENTER

Founded by two white Alabama lawyers in 1971, the Southern Poverty Law Center (SPLC) is in the early 2000s one of the best-known civil rights organizations in America. The SPLC, based in Montgomery, Alabama, initially focused strictly on legal matters related to the Fourteenth Amendment to the U.S. Constitution, which mandates equal protection under the law to all American citizens. In the 1980s the center pioneered new legal avenues of attack against the Ku Klux Klan and other hate groups, and it also created a new department to monitor the activities of these organizations and publish information about them. In the early 1990s it launched Teaching Tolerance, a major initiative to provide teachers with free high-quality classroom materials aimed at undermining prejudice and supporting racial tolerance and diversity. Late in the decade, the SPLC created a Web site that was more broadly aimed at Americans of all ages. In 2005 it opened the Civil Rights Memorial Center, including a monument dedicated to the martyrs of the civil rights movement. The memorial, which was dedicated on November 5, 1989, was created by famed designer Maya Lin.

The origins of the SPLC stretch back to 1969, when the YMCA in Montgomery was in its one-hundredth year as a segregated institution. After the YMCA refused to admit two black youngsters to its summer camp, the attorney Morris Dees, who would co-found the SPLC with Joseph J. Levin Jr., filed a class action lawsuit against the organization. A federal judge, noting a secret agreement between the YMCA and city for the organization to run recreational facilities, ruled that the YMCA had been invested with a "municipal character" and was therefore subject to laws affecting public bodies. In the end, U.S. district judge Frank Johnson ordered the organization to halt its discriminatory practices.

In January 1971, Dees and Levin opened the SPLC; they had some old furniture, one typewriter, a line of credit, and no other financial support. The first fund-raising letter they sent out was on behalf of a black man charged with the murder of a white schoolteacher. The trial judge had pronounced the man "probably guilty," a characterization repeated in headlines in the *Montgomery Advertiser.*

In the years that followed, the SPLC's lawyers took *pro bono* cases that few others had the resources or energy to pursue. Refusing lawyers' fees or any part of the monetary awards it won for its plaintiffs, the SPLC helped to implement the Civil Rights Act of 1964 and the Voting Rights Act of 1965. Early lawsuits resulted in the reapportionment of the Alabama legislature, the integration of the formerly all-white Alabama Department of Public Safety, and the reform of barbaric state prison conditions. Cases in the 1970s and 1980s won equal rights for women in the armed forces, ended involuntary sterilization of women on welfare, gained monetary awards for textile workers with brown lung disease, and developed comprehensive strategies for lawyers defending capital cases. A number of SPLC cases resulted in landmark decisions in the U.S. Supreme Court that had far-reaching effects.

A resurgence of the Klan in the late 1970s sparked a whole new series of cases. After Klansmen violently attacked peaceful civil rights marchers in Decatur, Alabama, in 1979, SPLC's lawyers brought the center's first civil lawsuit against a major Klan organization. The case also led to the creation, in 1981, of a new SPLC department called Klanwatch (later renamed Intelligence Project) to investigate and monitor organized white-supremacist activity throughout the country. Similar cases followed. Using a legal theory sometimes referred to as "vicarious liability," SPLC lawyers have since won civil judgments against forty-six individuals and nine major white supremacist organizations. The results were often dramatic. Beulah Mae Donald, whose son was lynched by Klansmen, was deeded a Klan headquarters building and purchased her first home with proceeds from its sale. The college education of an Ethiopian youth, Henok Seraw, was paid for with a judgment against White Aryan Resistance and its principals, who were held liable for the murder of Seraw's father. A black South Carolina church burned to the ground by a Klan group was awarded the largest-ever judgment against a hate group, $37.8 million (a judge later reduced that amount to $21.5 million). Two individuals who were terrorized by gun-wielding thugs from the Aryan Nations won a judgment that resulted in the neo-Nazi group's leader being forced to auction off its Idaho headquarters compound. Other lawsuits halted the harassment of Vietnamese shrimp fishermen by the Klan in Texas and paramilitary training that was being offered by the Klan-related White Patriot Party in North Carolina. Though each case differed in its particulars, all of them were based on the notion of holding white supremacist leaders responsible for the criminal actions of their followers.

Since the mid-1990s, the SPLC's legal department has concentrated on high-impact cases on behalf of those who typically have few defenders. These have included a number of cases related to prison conditions, such as the reintroduction of chain gangs in Alabama, the use of the barbaric "hitching post" as punishment for prisoners refusing to work, and abominable medical services in penitentiaries (a federal judge found, in a 1976 case brought by the SPLC, that Alabama's prisons were "wholly unfit for human habitation"). Several cases have focused on the brutal treatment of children in juvenile-offender facilities, notably in Louisiana. In 2004 the SPLC created a new legal program, the Immigrant Justice Project, meant to protect the rights of legal and undocumented immigrants. Some of the project's first cases were brought against exploitative forestry companies.

Klanwatch, which essentially started as the investigative arm of the SPLC's legal department, began publishing a small newsletter when it launched operations in 1981. This publication was meant to inform law enforcement officials about developments on the radical right, particularly with regard to the Klan. Over the years, the newsletter grew into a major investigative magazine, going from a short black-and-white format to a full-color glossy periodical in 1999. The magazine also expanded its bailiwick greatly, taking in whole new sections of the radical right, including the militia movement, tax protesters, black separatists, neo-Nazis, the anti-immigration movement, the neo-Confederate movement, and much more. By 2005, the magazine, *Intelligence Report*, had won numerous journalistic and design awards and was read by more than 300,000 people around America.

Between its legal cases against hate groups and the work of its Intelligence Project (the renamed Klanwatch), the SPLC was so effective that it enraged literally hundreds of white supremacist criminals. In 1983 the SPLC's first office was destroyed by Klan arsonists who broke in at night, then sprayed the area with gasoline and ignited it. Dees and others at the SPLC were targeted for death on several occasions. By 2005, more than twenty individuals had been sent to federal prison for their role in a series of plots aimed at destroying the center or assassinating Dees.

The third major program area of SPLC, after the legal department and the Intelligence Project, was created in 1991. Teaching Tolerance was meant to foster multiculturalism and tolerance among future generations, specifically by targeting educational material to teachers of kindergarten and the twelfth grade. It produced the first issue of *Teaching Tolerance* magazine, which would go on to win numerous educational and other awards, in 1992. By 2005, the magazine was being distributed free of charge to more than 600,000 educators nationwide. Teaching Tolerance also has produced a series of curriculum kits, including a film and teacher's guide, that are in use in more than 80,000 schools. Two of these films, *A Time for Justice: America's Civil Rights Movement* and *Mighty Times: The Children's March*, won Oscars for best short documentaries. Another educational film in the same series, *Mighty Times: Legacy of Rosa Parks*, won an Emmy Award. A spin-off project, the Tolerance.org Web site, was created as a separate department in the late 1990s, but it was eventually subsumed under Teaching Tolerance. On the site, one can find articles from SPLC and other publishers about tolerance, racism, and related themes.

The SPLC has also worked to ensure that the martyrs of the civil rights movement, and all that they accomplished, will never be forgotten. In the late 1980s it asked Maya Lin, the designer of the Vietnam Veterans Memorial in Washington, D.C., to design the Civil Rights Memorial. The monument, made of black granite and dedicated to some forty people who died between 1954 and 1968, has become a major

Civil Rights Memorial. *The Civil Rights Memorial Center outside the Southern Poverty Law Center incorporated a major memorial monument to the martyrs of the civil rights movement created by famed designer Maya Lin in 1989.* AP IMAGES.

tourist attraction in Alabama, drawing visitors from around the country and the world, along with daily busloads of schoolchildren. In 2005 the SPLC opened the adjoining Civil Rights Memorial Center, the organization's first public facility. The new center features an SPLC-made film; exhibits on civil rights, hate groups, and the international struggle for human rights; and a classroom for instruction.

SEE ALSO *Chain Gangs; Civil Rights Acts; Hate Crimes; Intelligence Project; Ku Klux Klan; Neo-Nazis; Voting Rights Act of 1965.*

BIBLIOGRAPHY

Dees, Morris. 1993. *Hate on Trial: The Case against America's Most Dangerous Neo-Nazi.* New York: Villard.

———. 1995. "Courtroom Victories: Taking Hate Groups to Court." *Trial* 31 (2): 20–29.

Dees, Morris, with Steve Fiffer. 1991. *A Season for Justice: The Life and Times of Civil Rights Lawyer Morris Dees.* New York: Scribner.

Gannon, Julie. 1995. "'We Can't Afford Not to Fight'; Morris Dees Takes Bigotry to Court." *Trial* 33 (1): 18–24.

Mark Potok
Heidi L. Beirich

STANDARDIZED TESTS

Standardized tests have a long history in American education. Beginning in the late nineteenth century, these tests were largely used to make decisions about college admission and high school graduation. Following World War II, standardized tests were administered more broadly. Many educators welcomed the tests as tools that would create empirical data about student performance, thus making educational decision-making processes more objective and scientific. After the *Brown v. Board of Education* decision in 1954, however, tests began to serve a different function. As increasing numbers of African-American and Latino students were integrated into white schools, standardized tests began to serve gatekeeper functions against minority students. In the early 1970s, the College Board, the governing body for the Scholastic Aptitude Test (SAT), began to keep statistics on race. What was largely suspected was then made evident: There was a significant gap between the test scores of blacks and whites. In addition, this gap was not confined to the SAT but manifested across the standardized test world, and while shrinking at times, it has failed to narrow significantly. Furthermore, due to political and social changes in the 1980s and 1990s, standardized tests are having a greater impact on the lives of American students than ever before. The negative impact on African American and Latino students has been significant.

NO CHILD LEFT BEHIND

No Child Left Behind (NCLB) became national law on January 8, 2002. The purpose of the legislation was to increase American academic standards and performance and to shrink the performance gap between minority and white students. The law has been met with sharp criticism from parents, students, administrators, politicians, teachers, and concerned communities. A key point of contention is the sole use of standardized tests to make critical decisions about students' education. The law requires that, as of the 2005–2006 school year, students be tested in reading and mathematics in the third and eighth grades, with science tests added in the 2007–2008 term. Before implementation of NCLB, only six states tested students at this rate. NCLB mandates these tests despite caveats from the preeminent guide for determining test validity, the *Standards for Education and Psychological Tests*, which states no long-term decisions for a student's education should be made as a result of one score.

The pressure to increase scores on high-stakes tests has affected all of American education, but it has had a particularly significant effect on the overall education experience of African Americans and Latinos. Teachers are more likely to "teach to the test," spending valuable classroom time on test preparation in an effort to meet testing goals. Research has demonstrated, however, that this preparation actually has negative effects. Some schools suspend the established curriculum for a month or more to prepare for these tests. Moreover, teachers who have a large percentage of students of color report that standardized tests affect their teaching styles more than those who teach predominantly whites.

Those students who fail the third- or eighth-grade tests are forced to repeat the grade. Theoretically, this would offer another opportunity to learn the skills and subject matter necessary for academic success at the next level. Retention, however, is highly correlated with dropout rates. Since instituting high-stakes tests, the state of Texas has forced African-American and Latino students to repeat grades at a rate almost twice that of whites. Moreover, the dropout rates for those students held back are more than twice those of students who have never been kept back.

Student success on high-stakes tests is highly correlated with teacher experience. Students of color, however, are more likely to be taught by teachers who have less education than teachers of white students. A Stanford University study found that, nationwide, in schools with the highest concentrations of students of color, students have less than a 50 percent chance of being taught math or science by a teacher who has credentials in those fields. A study in California found that schools with the lowest passing rates on California's high school exit exam have high minority enrollment and double the amount of uncertified teachers. Those students who need strong, capable teachers the most, and who are most prone to the negative effects of high-stakes testing, are thus less likely to get the help they need.

Moreover, for students who are not motivated by tests, the inclusion of more test-specific materials and curricular changes has a negative ripple effect. Increased test pressure for a student who is not motivated by test outcome can serve to cast the tests, and subsequently the entire educational enterprise, in a negative light, thus making academic achievement a low priority and ultimately leading to what Jason Osborne calls academic disidentification. This means that students, to preserve their self-esteem, stop identifying with academic success and disengage from the academic process altogether.

There are also funding implications tied to testing. California and Texas award schools incentive funding for performance on standardized tests. But schools with high concentrations of students of color tend to receive half of the performance awards as school with high concentrations of whites. At first, this may appear to be the just result of a meritorious policy. But there is a correlation between academic performance and school funding. So the performance awards then serve to exacerbate the problem of performance at the schools by not distributing critical funds to those schools that need it most.

Perhaps most discouraging is that the law's efficacy and the mandated tests' effectiveness are highly questionable. According to National Assessment for Educational Progress, the pressure of NCLB and mandated tests produced no significant gains in reading scores at any grade level in 2003.

TRACKING

Most American public schools have some method of differentiating instruction according to perceptions of ability. The common method is a three-tiered tracking system, with gifted, general, and special education tracks. Grades and teacher input highly affect placement, but only within the general track. For the special education and gifted tracks, however, tests are relied upon most heavily. Therefore, lower performance on IQ tests directly contributes to the disproportional representation of African Americans and Latinos on these tracks. Students of color are overrepresented in special education classes in forty-five out of fifty states. Africans Americans are four times as likely to be designated mentally retarded or "special needs" than whites in five states.

A chief indicator of college success is the rigor of one's secondary curriculum. When students are deprived of this level of education, their chances of success in college are sharply diminished. African-American and Latino students are less likely to attend schools where advanced or honors/accelerated curricula are taught. Even in schools with such curricula, students of color are less likely to been enrolled in these classes. An over-reliance on test scores to make the determination is a likely culprit. Studies have demonstrated that racial bias on the part of teachers and administrators also plays a significant role in the selection process. In a study of a San Jose school, Latino students were half as likely to take accelerated courses as whites with similar scores.

More subtle forms of tracking still persist in schools that have abolished traditional test-based tracking systems. Parents of middle-class students often successfully make demands of administrators to have their students placed with highly qualified teachers with fewer students of color. As a result, schools that are racially diverse often harbor hidden in-school stratification systems.

THE SAT

Since the College Board began to keep data on race, the gap that exists between African American and Latinos and whites has been a lightning rod, drawing attention from parents, politicians, and educators alike. The problem is persistent and remains salient due to a myriad of reasons. African Americans tend to score, on average, 100 points less on the Scholastic Aptitude Test (SAT) than whites.

One of the chief predictors for success on the SAT, as is the case with postsecondary success, is the rigor of the secondary curriculum. But given the presence of test-based tracking systems, many African Americans are situated on tracks that do not offer instruction in higher-order skills, making success on the SAT problematic in the extreme.

The SAT, despite subtle class-related challenges, is considered by most researchers to be a valid test. The problem occurs with its use. Many colleges and universities rely too heavily on the SAT in making determinations about admissions. This over-reliance has put diversity efforts in jeopardy. Opponents to affirmative action and other programs designed to make adjustments for a history of American racist policies and institutions have used this over-reliance to challenge the constitutionality of affirmative action.

On the opposite end of the spectrum, African Americans who attend elite postsecondary institutions tend to have lower freshman grade point averages than whites with comparable SAT scores. The reasons for this phenomenon are unclear. However, the fact remains that the SAT alone, in those situations, does not conclusively predict success at those schools. Other factors must be examined to explain this difference in performance.

The Stanford University psychologist Claude Steele has researched African-American test performance and discovered a condition he terms "stereotype threat." Steele found that among the most capable African-American students, test performance is negatively impacted by a desire to avoid being characterized by prevailing perceptions and stereotypes of intellectual inferiority. For those students who are most invested in academics, the possibility of failure creates inordinate psychological and even physiological stresses, which impair performance. Steele also found that even asking students to state their race on a standardized test is enough to reduce notions of efficacy and cause a decline in performance.

High-stakes standardized tests are becoming hardened fixtures in American education, and they are used to make long-term determinations about the educational futures of students. While there are inherent problems in test design, more problems occur in the systems in which these tests exist. Students of color will continue to languish in this system as long as tests play a considerable role in decisions concerning their futures.

BIBLIOGRAPHY

Jencks, Christopher, and Meredith Phillips. 1998. *The Black-White Test Score Gap.* Washington, DC: Brookings Institution Press.

Osborne, Jason W. 1997. "Race and Academic Disidentification." *Journal of Educational Psychology* 89 (4): 728–735.

Ramist, Leonard, Charles Lewis, and Laura McCamley-Jenkins. 1994. *Student Group Differences in Predicting College Grades: Sex, Language, and Ethnic Groups.* College Board Report No. 93-1. New York: College Board.

Steele, Claude M., and Joshua Aronson. 1995. "Stereotype Threat and the Intellectual Test Performance of African

Americans." *Journal of Personality and Social Psychology* 69: 797–811.

Bruce Webb

STEREOTYPE THREAT AND RACIAL STIGMA

Stereotype threat is a term given to the psychological experience of being confronted with a negative stereotype associated with a particular social identity. The term was coined in 1995 by Claude Steele and Joshua Aronson, who defined it as an uncomfortable apprehension arising from awareness of a negative stereotype in a situation in which the stereotype is relevant and therefore confirmable through the target's behavior. Stereotype threat is a predicament that can beset anyone. Thus, a white male in the presence of blacks may worry that he will inadvertently say something perceived as racist; an elderly man who has misplaced his keys may worry that others think he is senile; a southerner may worry that her drawl makes her sound unsophisticated, and so on.

Steele and Aronson (1995) argue that African Americans, who historically have been stereotyped as intellectually inferior to other groups, are likely to experience stereotype threat whenever they find themselves in situations where intellectual abilities are relevant, such as during standardized tests or in other academic situations. Their initial experiments confirmed that when African-American college students were given a standardized test, they experienced greater anxiety, increased cognitive activation of stereotypes, and lower test performance when the test was presented as a way to evaluate their intelligence. The same test presented in a non-evaluative manner, however, produced little anxiety or cognitive activation of stereotypes and resulted in significantly better test performance among African-Americans. The manipulation of stereotype threat had no significant effect on white students, however.

By contrast, *racial stigma* is an attribute that marks or discredits an individual, one that reduces him or her "from a whole and usual person to a tainted, discounted one" (Goffman 1963, p. 3). Racial stigma is not completely trans-situational. Rather, a stigma is defined by the particulars of the situation, in the sense that an attribute such as black skin may be viewed negatively in some contexts (e.g., the academic arena) but positively in others (e.g., the basketball arena), because of the specific attributes a culture attaches to specific social identities. Although perceptions of African Americans have steadily improved since the 1960s, they continue to perform worse, on average, in school and on standardized tests than other groups. Thus, blackness continues to be a stigma in educational contexts. The same can be said for females in the domain of mathematics and science, despite the fact that women have made significant strides in these domains, and that the roles and opportunities available to women have expanded considerably since the mid-1900s.

Stereotype threat begins with a person's knowledge that certain social identities are stereotypically associated with a stigmatized status in a given situation. Because the stereotype alleging African-American intellectual inferiority has been promulgated in America at least since the introduction of slavery, it is widely known throughout American society. Blackness can thus be stigmatizing in any context where intellectual ability is relevant or thought to be relevant. In many studies on stereotype threat, it is the relevance of intelligence to some activity that is manipulated. Thus, just as Steele and Aronson found that labeling an academic task as a measure of intelligence undermined performance, so too did labeling a sports activity as a measure of intelligence interfere with athletic performance (Stone et al. 1999).

Stereotype threat is an experience that is not limited to racial groups. For example, significant underperformance in response to stereotype threat has been demonstrated in a wide variety of groups. It is thus a general process, one not tied to any particular social identity; any group for whom a negative stereotype exists, or for whom some allegedly superior comparison group exists, can be vulnerable. So while white males are not stereotyped as being bad at math, they have been shown to perform less well on math tests when explicitly reminded of the stereotype of Asian mathematical superiority (Aronson et al. 1999). Significant stereotype threat effects (underperformance on some kind of ability test) have been documented among a wide variety of social groups (Aronson and Steele 2005), including African Americans on verbal and IQ tests; Latinos on verbal tests; women in the domain of math and science; elderly individuals in the domain of short-term memory; low-income individuals in the domain of verbal abilities, and white males in the domains of athletics (when compared to African Americans), mathematics (when compared to Asians), and social perceptiveness (when compared to women).

The effects of stereotype threat on intellectual performance appear to be mediated by a number of psychological processes. For example, experiments that vary the amount of stereotype threat find that a high level of stereotype threat results in higher blood pressure, faster heartbeat, higher cognitive load, higher self-reported anxiety, and a greater number of negative thoughts—all of which are capable of interfering with intellectual performance.

In the academic arena, various individual differences exist that appear to be risk factors for underperformance. Individuals who do not care much about academics or athletics are less likely than those who do to be bothered by the allegation that they lack ability in these areas. Experiments show that the greatest test-performance pressure occurs among those students who care a good deal about doing well (Aronson et al. 1999); if a given individual does not care about the evaluative domain in question—if they are not especially invested in academic achievement, for example—they will be less likely to find the relevance of a stereotype bothersome or disruptive to performance. Likewise, if a person does not feel any particular connection to the social group they belong to, they probably will not feel much pressure to disprove the negative stereotype about that group. In a 2005 study, Kay Deaux and her associates found that black Americans who are fairly recent immigrants from other countries do not identify with African-American culture as much as American-born blacks or those whose parents immigrated less recently. The degree to which such individuals identified with African-American culture significantly predicted their underperformance on an evaluative test, strongly suggesting that it is African-American culture, rather than genetic predisposition, that makes blacks vulnerable to underperformance.

Other risk factors include individual differences in areas related to mistrust. That is, some individuals tend to be more aware of prejudice and more bothered by its presence in their lives than do others. Such individuals enter situations anxiously, expecting people to perceive them and treat them differently based on their race, ethnicity or gender. All things being equal, individuals who have a high measure of this kind of cultural mistrust tend to perform worse on standardized tests, have a harder time adjusting to integrated academic colleges, and receive lower grades than their more trustful counterparts.

Stereotype threat has been viewed as a very positive development in the social-science literature because it convincingly attributes racial differences in test performance and school achievement to tractable, situational factors. It thus stands as one of the most compelling counterarguments to the point of view put forward in the controversial book *The Bell Curve* (1994), in which Richard Hernnstein and Charles Murray attribute African Americans' lower average IQ test scores and school achievement to genetically based differences in intelligence between racial groups. The stereotype-threat research casts doubt on this interpretation by demonstrating how testing and schooling situations are experienced differently for individuals of color, and how these differences can powerfully undermine performance. A number of research studies based on Steele and Aronson's research have shown that test performance and school achievement can be significantly improved with simple interventions. For example, Aronson and his colleagues found that teaching minority students that their intelligence is not fixed—that it is malleable and can be expanded with hard work—significantly reduced the achievement gap on both standardized tests and grade point averages (Aronson and Steele 2005). Similarly, Cohen, et al. (2006) found that stereotype threat could be reduced by affirming the self-concepts of minority students, a simple intervention that resulted in a substantial reduction of the black-white achievement gap among low-income adolescents. These interventions, derived from the stereotype threat formulation, provide a hopeful antidote to the pessimistic theories that attribute racial gaps primarily to intractable social forces and fixed, biological group differences in intellectual endowment.

SEE ALSO *Education, Racial Disparities; Social Psychology of Racism.*

BIBLIOGRAPHY

Aronson, Joshua, et al. 1999. "When White Men Can't Do Math: Necessary and Sufficient Factors in Stereotype Threat." *Journal of Experimental Social Psychology* 35: 29–46.

Aronson, Joshua, and Claude M. Steele. 2005. "Stereotypes and the Fragility of Human Competence, Motivation, and Self-Concept." In *Handbook of Competence and Motivation,* ed. Andrew Elliot and Carol Dweck. New York: Guilford.

Cohen, Geoffrey L., et al. 2006. "Reducing the Racial Achievement Gap: A Social-Psychological Intervention." *Science* 313: 1307–1310.

Deaux, Kay, et al. 2005. *Becoming American: Stereotype Threat Effects in Black Immigrant Groups.* Unpublished Manuscript, Graduate Center, City University of New York.

Goffman, Erving. 1963. *Stigma: Notes on the Management of Spoiled Identity.* Englewood Cliffs, NJ: Prentice-Hall, Inc.

Herrnstein, Richard, and Charles Murray. 1994. *The Bell Curve: Intelligence and Class Structure in American Life.* New York: Free Press.

Massey, Douglas S., Camille Z. Charles, Garvey Lundy, and Mary J. Fischer. 2003. *The Source of the River: The Social Origins of Freshmen at America's Selective Colleges and Universities.* Princeton, NJ: Princeton University Press.

Mendoza-Denton, Rodolfo, Valerie Purdie, Angelina Davis, and Janina Pietrzak. 2002. "Sensitivity to Status-Based Rejection: Implications for African American Students' College Experience." *Journal of Personality and Social Psychology* 83 (4): 896–918.

Steele, Claude M., and Joshua Aronson. 1995. "Stereotype Threat and the Intellectual Test Performance of African-Americans." *Journal of Personality and Social Psychology* 69 (5): 797–811.

Stone, Jeff, Christian I. Lynch, Mike Sjomeling, and John M. Darley. 1999. "Stereotype Threat Effects on Black and White Athletic Performance." *Journal of Personality and Social Psychology* 77: 1213–1227.

Joshua Aronson

STEREOTYPING

SEE *Social Psychology of Racism.*

STERILIZATION

SEE *Forced Sterilization; Forced Sterilization of Native Americans.*

STODDARD, T. LOTHROP

1883–1950

In the opening pages of *The Great Gatsby*, F. Scott Fitzgerald's classic Jazz Age novel about wealthy "careless people," the character Tom Buchanan is depicted as an arrogant, immoral bully and a white supremacist. "Have you read 'The Rise of the Colored Empires' by this man Goddard?" he asks the novel's narrator, noting that "it's a fine book and everybody ought to read it. The idea is if we don't look out the white race will be—will be utterly submerged. It's all scientific stuff; it's been proved." While Buchanan might have been a product of Fitzgerald's imagination, every well-informed reader at the time recognized his comment as a reference to *The Rising Tide of Color against White World-Supremacy* by T. Lothrop Stoddard.

Born in Brookline, Massachusetts, Stoddard was descended from a prominent New England family that traced its roots back to colonial America. His father, John Lawson Stoddard, had traveled throughout the world and become a household name in the United States due to his popularity as a speaker on the exotic sights of far-off lands (his lectures are still available).

A lawyer and historian with a doctorate from Harvard, Lothrop Stoddard earned his own reputation as one of the racist intelligentsia in the first half of the twentieth century, second in importance only to the eugenicist Madison Grant. These nativists, who tended to be from Brahmin backgrounds that emphasized the importance of "good breeding," were concerned about the flood of new immigrants from southern and eastern Europe. A number of them, including Stoddard, testified before the House Committee on Immigration and Naturalization in the hearings leading to passage of the Immigration Act of 1924. Some of these activists were naturally drawn to the eugenics movement, which concluded that the peoples of northern Europe who had settled the United States were genetically superior to the more recent arrivals, and they became well known as authorities in the field, despite having no formal scientific training. Stoddard himself was a member of the Galton Society, an organization of racial determinists formed as an alternative to the American Anthropological Association, which was perceived as increasingly dominated by Jews and Bolsheviks.

While Stoddard was one of the most prominent racial propagandists, the belief in the fundamental importance of race in human affairs and national well-being was commonplace at the time. Popular magazines as well as a number of academics and intellectuals expressed concern over the presence of so many hyphenated Americans and encouraged a view of racial competition in which whites in general and Nordics in particular had to act out of racial solidarity.

Among the many books Stoddard wrote, *The Rising Tide of Color* was by far the most influential. Published in 1920, it offered a view of World War I as "a headlong plunge into race suicide" that pitted whites against each other and fractured their racial solidarity, much to the advantage of the colored world, which watched from the sidelines with "the light of undreamed-of hopes" in their eyes. Although Stoddard regarded the Nordics as far superior to the other European subraces (the Alpines and Mediterraneans) he nevertheless found it imperative for these three groups to unite in the face of the threat posed by other races, and from the "yellow race" in particular. Stoddard dismissed blacks as inferior savages, and it was "Asiatics" whom he perceived as whites' most serious competitors in the struggle to control Africa and "mongrel-ruled" Latin America. Among the Asiatics, Stoddard believed that the Japanese were the greatest danger, having already defeated "one of the great white Powers" in the Russo-Japanese War of 1904. However, he saw an additional threat to whites emerging from the Great War: The leaders of Bolshevism, "the traitor within the gates," were attempting to foment a race war as a tactic in its assault on civilization by urging "discontented colored men" throughout the world to seek revenge. In *The Revolt against Civilization,* published in 1922, Stoddard elaborated on Bolsheviks as comprising hereditary defectives led by alienated Jews.

As the passage from *Gatsby* suggests, *The Rising Tide of Color* was well known and widely cited at the time. An editorial in the *Saturday Evening Post* recommended that "every American should read" the book, and in a speech in Birmingham, Alabama, President Warren Harding cited Stoddard's book as evidence that the race issue in the United States was only a "phase" of a problem that the whole world had to confront.

Stoddard also viewed the "Jewish Question" as a matter of race, which led him to propose the Khazar theory of Jewish racial background, which posits that modern Jews are not descended from the ancient Hebrews. Instead this pseudo-anthropological approach (which is still promoted by neo-Nazi groups) maintains that the Jews were originally a tribe of nomadic Semites, and that they intermingled genetically with many other peoples during their sojourns. Eventually, two subgroups emerged: the Sephardim around the Mediterranean, and the Ashkenazim in eastern Europe. The Sephardim, the "aristocracy of Jewry," were characterized by a slender build, finely-cut features, and a generally "harmonic"(i.e., racially unmixed) make-up. The first Jews to come to America were nearly all Sephardim, according to Stoddard. In contrast, he claimed, the Ashkenazim—who had immigrated only recently but in very large numbers, so that they now constituted some 90 percent of the American Jewish population—were short, thick-set, and coarse-featured, reflecting their greater "mixture of diverse bloods," especially with the Khazars of southern Russia, whose fusion with the Jews was responsible for the profound differences, not only in physical appearance but also in temperament and mentality, between Ashkenazim and Sephardim. Thus, the traits of the Ashkenazim were incompatible with traditional American ideals and values.

In 1940—before implementation of the Final Solution but well after the Jews had been herded into ghettos and their property confiscated by the Third Reich—Stoddard traveled through Germany, observing daily life and meeting with the Nazi regime's leading scientists and top officials, including Heinrich Himmler, Joseph Goebbels, and Hitler himself. In the published account of his experiences, *Into the Darkness,* Stoddard concluded that both *Mein Kampf* and the Nazi state were based on sound eugenic principles. Inside Germany, he reported, the Jewish problem was regarded as a passing phenomenon, and more attention was being paid, properly, to regeneration of the Germanic stock, which had lost some of its finest racial elements because of the Great War and the reduced birth rate during the postwar depression.

During the interwar period, Stoddard's books were standard reading at military institutions such as the Army War College, the Navy War College, and the Army Industrial College, and Stoddard himself was often asked to lecture to their students on topics such as race and world affairs. Ironically, just before the entry of the United States into World War II, Stoddard's name was placed on a list of persons to be investigated by army intelligence in case of war.

In the early twenty-first century, Stoddard's ideas are still praised, and his books promoted, by numerous contemporary organizations with racist or neo-Nazi sympathies, such as National Alliance, Stormfront, and American Renaissance.

BIBLIOGRAPHY

Bendersky, Joseph W. 2000. *The "Jewish Threat": Anti-Semitic Politics of the U.S. Army.* New York: Basic Books.

Stoddard, T. Lothrop. 1920. *The Rising Tide of Color against White World-Supremacy.* New York: Charles Scribner's Sons.

———. 1922. *The Revolt against Civilization.* New York: Charles Scribner's Sons.

———. 1926. "The Pedigree of Judah." *The Forum* 75 (3): 8–20.

———. 1940. *Into the Darkness.* New York: Duell, Sloan and Pearce.

William H. Tucker

STOWE, HARRIET BEECHER
1811–1896

Harriet Beecher Stowe was born in Litchfield, Connecticut, on June 14, 1811. She authored several books, two of which were abolitionist novels: *Uncle Tom's Cabin: Or Life of the Lowly* (1852) and *Dred: A Tale of the Great Dismal Swamp* (1856). Stowe's other works relevant to the study of race include *A Key to Uncle Tom's Cabin* (1853) and *Sojourner Truth or the Lybian Sybil* (1863). While *Dred* is Stowe's more radical novel, *Uncle Tom's Cabin* has made the largest impact on the construction and study of race and racism because of its popularity and its consequent role as a site of controversy in the field.

Stowe was one of twelve children in a family of several noted abolitionists, including her father, the Calvinist minister Lyman Wheeler Beecher, and her brother, Henry Ward Beecher, a minister renowned for his militant abolitionism. Stowe grew up in Hartford, Connecticut, and Boston, but the family's move to Cincinnati, Ohio, in 1832 was most important to her antislavery novels. A major haven for runaway slaves from Kentucky and other slave states, Cincinnati was also where a white mob destroyed the presses of an abolitionist newspaper in 1836. In Cincinnati, Harriet Beecher married the minister Calvin Stowe and became the mother of seven children, one of whom died in infancy. Stowe returned to live in New England in 1850.

Stowe's literary style has been called romantic racialism, and it drew on eighteenth-century categories of race that treated peoples from different geographical areas as differing in character. Stowe is contradictory on whether she saw racial categories as unchanging or as comprising a general sprit that could be shaped by environment. *Uncle Tom's Cabin* presents its hero, whom she treats as humble, loyal, and spiritual, as a representative of African character. Yet *Dred* imagines African spirituality as subject to change and allied with prophecy and a just vengeance. As with many white abolitionists, Stowe's antislavery stance did not presuppose a belief in equality.

Uncle Tom's Cabin has been controversial because it entwines complex power relations of race, gender, and class and includes contradictions. Equally important, the novel achieved unprecedented popularity. Within a year of its publication, it sold 300,000 copies in the United States and more in Great Britain. It was also translated into many languages. *Uncle Tom's Cabin*, a sentimental and melodramatic novel, traces the path of Uncle Tom, who, refusing to flee slavery, is sold away from his family until he is bought by the evil Simon Legree. Legree finally murders Tom when Tom heroically refuses to reveal the whereabouts of escaping slaves but, like a Christian martyr, submits to Legree's blows without defending himself. The novel also traces the path of intelligent, strong-willed slaves who escape, notably George and Eliza Harris and Cassy. Yet these are characters of mixed ancestry, seen by Stowe and many of her contemporaries as inheriting intelligence and will from their white lineage. The novel also includes Topsy, a comic and mischievous slave child drawn from minstrel shows as a foil to the serious and spiritual white heroine, Little Eva.

Initially, the most pointed challenge to *Uncle Tom's Cabin* came from slavery's advocates, who charged that Stowe knew about neither African-descended people nor the purportedly benevolent, paternal institution of slavery. The most vicious responses attacked Stowe as unwomanly for writing on political issues and in tones suitable for the pulpit. At the other end of the political spectrum, Martin R. Delaney, the noted African-American writer and activist, objected to the novel's ending, which, tapping the American Colonization Society's agenda, sent its fugitive slaves away to Liberia. Frederick Douglass praised *Uncle Tom's Cabin* as valuable to abolitionism but countered Tom's passivity in the hero of his own 1852 novella, *The Heroic Slave*. At the same time, *Uncle Tom's Cabin* was widely praised by many readers black and white.

Stowe also wrote *A Key to Uncle Tom's Cabin*, which attempted to establish a factual basis for her characters and events by citing newspaper articles, advertisements for slave auctions and fugitive slaves, and witnesses to slavery. Stowe's second novel, *Dred*, responds to criticisms of *Uncle Tom's Cabin* from slavery's advocates, and as Robert S. Levine argues in "The African-American Presence in Stowe's *Dred*" (1996), she also responds to her African American critics. *Dred* incorporates discussion of sources within it and features a rebel slave loosely based on Nat Turner, whose vengeance she treats as justifiable.

American culture has given the characters and plot of *Uncle Tom's Cabin* a long symbolic life beyond Stowe's novel. As Eric Lott observes in *Love and Theft* (1993), competing pro- and antislavery plays took up Stowe's characters during the 1850s to enact the developing sectionalism that would produce the Civil War. In the late nineteenth-century backlash to reconstruction, traveling "Tom Shows" toured the nation with exaggerated versions of Topsy and entertaining versions of Uncle Tom.

Between World War II and the twenty-first century, as writers and scholars grappled with issues of race and gender under new historical circumstances, Stowe's novel came to serve as a source of controversy over racism and of inquiries into race and gender. Key historical contexts were the civil rights movement and the Black Power movement, second-wave feminism, and the presence in academia of African-American men and women and feminist scholars in debate and conversation with one another. Amid its radicalism, *Uncle Tom's Cabin* made otherwise indifferent people feel the horror and sense the injustice of slavery. Stowe wrote a dozen other books, but this one book was so powerful that it has survived in the nation's memory.

SEE ALSO *Abolition Movement.*

BIBLIOGRAPHY

PRIMARY WORKS

Stowe, Harriet Beecher. 1994 (1852). *Uncle Tom's Cabin: Or the Life of the Lowly.* Edited by Elizabeth Ammons. New York: Norton.

———. 2000 (1856) *Dred: A Tale of the Great Dismal Swamp.* Edited by Robert S. Levine. New York: Penguin.

SECONDARY WORKS

Ammons, Elizabeth, ed. 1980. *Critical Essays on Harriet Beecher Stowe.* Boston: G. K. Hall.

Hedrick, Joan D. 1994. *Harriet Beecher Stowe: A Life.* New York: Oxford University Press.

Levine, Robert S. 1996. "The African-American Presence in Stowe's *Dred.*" In *Criticism and the Color Line: Desegregating American Literary Studies*, edited by Henry B. Wonham, 171–190. New Brunswick, NJ: Rutgers University Press.

Lott, Eric. 1993. *Love and Theft: Blackface Minstrelsy and the American Working Class.* New York: Oxford University Press.

Sundquist, Eric, ed. 1986. *New Essays on* Uncle Tom's Cabin. Cambridge, NJ: Cambridge University Press.

Warren, Kenneth W. 2004. "The Afterlife of *Uncle Tom's Cabin.*" In *The Cambridge Companion to Harriet Beecher Stowe*, ed. Cindy Weinstein, 219–234. Cambridge, NJ: Cambridge University Press.

Ellen J. Goldner

SUBSPECIES

A subspecies is a taxonomic category applied to geographically, genetically, or physically distinct interfertile populations (those capable of interbreeding). Evolutionary theory dictates that species formation is a process, and it therefore may be analyzed or interrupted at various stages of completion. Charles Darwin summarized his argument in *The Origin of Species* with the conclusion that "species are not immutable; but that those belonging to what are called the same genera are lineal descendants of some other and generally extinct species, in the same manner as the acknowledged varieties of any one species are the descendants of that species."

A population is considered a full taxonomic species if it has evolved a tendency to see its own members as a pool of potential mates (or competitors for mates), in contrast to members of other animal groups. Local distinct populations, as partially formed taxonomic entities, have been variously called breeds, varieties, or races. Defining *subspecies* in terms of lacking the attributes of a species creates a flexible scale without any clear criteria, and consequently makes the concept difficult to apply rigorously.

Nevertheless, there are some primate species that live in complex structured populations that are amenable to the designation of "taxonomic subspecies." The best known is the savanna baboon (*Papio hamadryas ssp.*), whose formal varieties are the yellow baboon (*P. h. cynocephalus*), chacma baboon (*P. h. ursinus*), olive baboon (*P. h. anubis*), guinea baboon (*P. h. papio*) and hamadryas baboon (*P. h. hamadryas*). Each is distinctive in appearance, and hybridizes with other subspecies along a border wherever they come in contact. Some primate species have subspecies with distinctions of the chromosomes, or karyotypes, including *Eulemur fulvus* (brown lemur), *Hylobates lar* (gibbon), and *Aotus trivirgatus* (night monkey).

Biological variation within the human species is patterned differently and is much smaller in its extent than can be identified in the generally acknowledged subspecies of great apes. Nevertheless, the common cultural process of naturalizing difference (i.e., rationalizing differences in social status and power by recourse to differences in biology) has often led physical anthropologists to attempt to identify subspecies among living humans.

One argument for the existence of human subspecies might be if interracial offspring were rare, distinctive, less viable, or less fertile than intraracial offspring. Indeed, the viability of interracial unions was considered to be an open question in human biology in the early decades of the twentieth century. Two infamous works of this period that suggested that race-crossing was biologically harmful were Eugen Fischer's study on a South African "coloured" community (1912), and "Race Crossing in Jamaica" by Charles Davenport and Morris Steggerda (1929). The latter work, in particular, was widely regarded as ineptly executed and argued, even by other like-minded eugenicists.

Of somewhat longer-lasting value was Harry Shapiro's careful study of the descendants of the English crew of the H.M.S. *Bounty* and their Tahitian wives on Pitcairn Island. Shapiro studied the biological and cultural syncretism and concluded that there were no harmful effects of race-crossing. After World War II, this came to be taken as axiomatic in physical anthropology, and it has since become recognized that there is a single extant subspecies of *Homo sapiens*. The modern disagreement is over whether Neandertals should be considered a different (though extinct) subspecies or a different species.

SEE ALSO *Human Biological Variation.*

BIBLIOGRAPHY

Darwin, Charles. 1909. *The Origins of Species.* New York: P.F. Collier & Son Company.

Marks, Jonathan. 1997. "Systematics in Anthropology: Where Science Meets the Humanities (and Consistently Loses)." In *Conceptual Issues in Human Origins Research*, edited by G. A. Clark and C. Willermet, 45–59. New York: Aldine de Gruyter.

Provine, William B. 1973. "Geneticists and the Biology of Race Crossing." *Science* 182: 790–796.

Simpson, George G. 1961. *Principles of Animal Taxonomy.* New York: Columbia University Press.

Jonathan Marks

SUBSTANCE ABUSE

In the 2000 U.S. census, approximately 4.1 million people reported their race as "American Indian or Alaska Native." While that constitutes only 1.5 percent of the United States population, the U.S. Department of Health and Human Services reports that American Indians and Alaska Natives account for 2.1 percent of all admissions to publicly funded substance-abuse treatment facilities, with 40 percent of these individuals being referred to such programs by the criminal justice system. This clearly demonstrates that substance abuse continues to be a persistent and growing issue among the Native American population.

NATIVE AMERICANS AND ALCOHOL

Historically, the introduction of intoxicating substances, especially alcohol, among indigenous populations often served the colonial designs of European nations. Alcohol became an important vehicle with which to appropriate resources, weaken the structure of indigenous societies, and destroy indigenous resistance to European colonialism. The overconsumption of alcohol also served to reinforce European beliefs about the inferiority of indigenous peoples, thereby bolstering the belief in "white" racial superiority. As Robert Berkhofer points out in *The White Man's Indian* (1979), alcohol abuse provided concrete evidence of Indian degeneracy and criminality, leading to the public stereotype of the "drunken Indian."

According to Gilbert Quintero, associate professor of anthropology, University of Montana, nonnative beliefs about Indian drunkenness constitute:

> A form of colonial knowledge ... that creates standardized categories and oppositional differences that distinguish the colonizers from the colonized. In addition, colonial knowledge functions to keep the colonized in a subjugated position relative to the colonizer. It does so primarily by attributing devalued characteristics and features to a specific group of people that is usually recognized as somehow distinct, usually in racial, cultural, or historical terms. (Quintero 2001, p. 57)

Despite the proliferation of scientific research about American Indian drinking, the myth persists that indigenous peoples are predisposed to addiction and that there are biophysical reasons for their inability to control their addictive behaviors. In some respects, the argument that there is a genetic basis to explain excessive alcohol consumption among Native Americans continues to serve the stereotypes of racial inferiority and degeneracy, especially when held up against reported data and beliefs about white alcohol consumption and behaviors. In addition, for some this argument can ostensibly be extended to other forms of substance abuse. There is, in fact, data to establish genetic contributions to alcoholism and other substance abuse addictions. This biogenetic predisposition is not exclusive to Native populations, however, but also exists among all ethnic populations. Evidence specific to American Indian addictions, especially alcohol, reveals that there is more in-group variation than between-group variation, indicating that environmental variables play a significant role in the manifestation of Native substance abuse (May 1994; Mancall 1995). Despite any biogenetic predispositions, however, the amount of substance abuse within a given population, much like the rate of Type II diabetes mellitus, is a reflection of social and economic conditions, not a sign of inferior racial biology. The health status of Native Americans and Alaska Natives, including substance abuse, is directly related to the socioeconomic conditions that exist in indigenous communities. Health levels, therefore, are directly linked to extant social, political, and economic forces.

THE SOCIOECONOMIC CAUSES OF SUBSTANCE ABUSE

Substance abuse and other afflictions are directly related to an array of socioeconomic conditions affecting indigenous communities. According to U.S. 2000 census data, 25.7 percent of American Indians and Alaska Natives live in poverty—twice the national average. Among selected tribes, poverty rates range from 18 percent to 38.9 percent. Paralleling poverty rates, the labor-force participation rate for American Indians and Alaska Natives is lower than among the general U.S. population. In addition, earnings among full-time, year-round Native workers are substantially lower than the earnings of all U.S. workers. This is particularly true for indigenous men, who also experience higher unemployment and underemployment rates.

Sheriff Discusses Efforts to Reduce DUI Arrests on the Flathead Indian Reservation, Montana, 2005. *Substance abuse among Native Americans continues to be a persistent issue.* **AP IMAGES.**

Level of education is clearly associated with labor-force participation and earnings. According to the Census Bureau, "the educational levels of American Indians and Alaska Natives were below those of the total population in 2000." In particular, 71 percent "had at least a high school education, compared with 80 percent of the total population" (U.S. Census Bureau 2006). As a result of this educational disparity the distribution of employment for Native peoples is heavily concentrated in the non-managerial positions and professions, clustering them in a particular class and economic sector.

American Indians and Alaska Natives have a higher percentage of single-parent homes than the total population. According to Census 2000, slightly more than 28 percent of Native households are single-parent homes, compared to 15.5 percent of total U.S. households. The vast majority of these households are headed by a woman with no husband present (20.7% of Native households). This percentage increases by 4.1 percent if the household is located on reservation lands, trust lands, or other tribally designated lands. Moreover, the average household size is 22.6 percent larger on tribally designated lands than among the total U.S. population.

It is estimated that Native Americans have six times the number of substandard homes as the rest of the United States. Many homes do not have water or adequate sewage systems. More than 30 percent of low-income American Indians live in overcrowded homes, as there is at least a 200,000 unit housing shortage across Indian country. Moreover, the construction of cluster housing on many reservations has created a particular type of residential segregation that contributes to elevated risks of violence, substance abuse, and other community health problems.

Finally, no other U.S. ethnic group has the lives of its people, including their health care, so heavily dictated by federal laws, policies, and treaties. As early as 1820, Western medical services became an integral component of U.S. Indian policy. As of 2007, the Indian Health Service (IHS), located within the Department of Health and Human Services, administers primary and preventive care to eligible Native peoples within their established service areas. The IHS largely operates on annual congressional appropriations, but the per capita expenditure for indigenous patients is only 61.3 percent of the per capita personal healthcare expenditures for the total U.S. population. This results in a rationing of health care, an inequitable distribution of healthcare resources, and limited primary treatment and prevention services. The U.S. Congress Office of Technology Assessment reports that these disparities pose significant risks for the development of health problems, particularly behavioral health issues such as substance abuse.

THE IMPACT OF SUBSTANCE ABUSE

Substance abuse mortality rates continue to exceed the rates for the general U.S. population. In 1995, the age-adjusted drug-related death rate for American Indians and Alaskan Natives was 65 percent higher than for the total population. In addition, the National Institute of Drug Abuse (NIDA) reported in 2003 that American Indians and Alaska Natives exhibit the highest estimated prevalence of past-month tobacco smoking and heavy alcohol consumption of any recognized racial/ethnic minority population. Age-adjusted lung cancer rates among this population increased 184 percent between 1973 and 2006.

Between 1985 and 2000, age-adjusted alcohol death rates among the Native population increased 28 percent, seven times the rate for the total population. The IHS reported in 1998–1999 that first diagnosis of alcoholic psychosis, alcoholism, alcohol-related chronic liver disease, and cirrhosis was 1.6 times higher in IHS and tribal hospitals than in U.S. general short-stay hospitals.

In addition to alcohol and cigarette abuse, illicit drug use and nonmedical prescription drug abuse is also becoming a plague among American Indian and Alaskan Native communities. A 2003 NIDA survey measuring prevalence of past-month drug use revealed that indigenous peoples consume illicit drugs, marijuana, and cocaine at significantly higher rates than any other racial/ethnic population. This data is corroborated by the 2003 National Household Survey on Drug Abuse Report, which recorded that American Indians or Alaska Natives aged twelve or older had a higher rate of past-year substance dependence or abuse than any other racial/ethnic population.

Mortality attributed to drug use is also increasing at a steady pace among Native peoples. Drug-related death rates for this population increased 164 percent between 1979 and 1998, when it was 1.8 times higher the U.S. all-races rate. Within the Native population, there is a large disparity in drug-related deaths between males and females. For the 1996–1998 period, the peak male age-specific drug-related death rate was 111 percent higher than the peak female rate, according to the IHS's report *Trends in Indian Health, 2000–2001.*

Methamphetamine (meth) abuse is causing havoc among Native Americans and Alaska Native communities. According to IHS data, the number of recorded patient services related to meth use rose 2.5 times from 2000 until 2005. Robert McSwain, the deputy director of the IHS reported to Congress in 2006 that the age cohort most affected by the use of this drug is age 15 to age 44. The social effects of methamphetamine addiction reach beyond the individual user. Addicted parents neglect their children, leading to child abuse, a rise in child placements, and more broken homes. The use and selling of this drug also fuels increases in homicides, aggravated assaults, rape, domestic violence, and possibly suicides. Statistics from a southwestern reservation indicate the extent of the crisis. In 2004 there were 101 suicide attempts on the reservation, with eight out of ten involving methamphetamine. That same year, 64 out of 256 babies born on the reservation were born to addicted mothers. Kathleen Kitcheyan, the chairwoman of the San Carlos Apache Tribe, has testified that of the child neglect and abuse cases reported in 2005 to Tribal Child Protective Services, 80 percent involved illicit drug use, alcohol use, or both.

Methamphetamine also is straining tribal law enforcement, health-care resources, and funding for tribal housing. For example, it is estimated that the elimination of hazardous material from a home used as a meth laboratory can cost $10,000. With IHS and tribal health programs funded at less than 60 percent of the level necessary to meet adequate levels of care, methamphetamine abuse is crippling an already overtaxed healthcare system.

SUBSTANCE ABUSE AND CRIME

There is an intimate and growing relationship between violent crimes and substance abuse. In 2004, the U.S. Department of Justice reported that American Indians experience a per capita rate of violence twice that of the U.S. resident population, with an average of one violent crime per ten residents aged twelve or older. Seventy-five percent of all investigations in Indian country by the Federal Justice system involve violent crimes. Significantly, indigenous victims of violence report that 62 percent of offenders were under the influence of alcohol at the time of the attack, with drugs being involved about 9 percent of the time. Fourteen percent of victims report that the offender was using both alcohol and drugs.

Similar to the introduction of alcohol centuries ago, methamphetamine is being injected into native communities by non-native drug cartels. On a Great Plains reservation, for example, a Mexican meth cartel attempted to introduce the drug to the reservation. In an Oklahoma Native community, the Satan's Disciples, a violent Chicago street gang, organized a methamphetamine trafficking operation targeting indigenous peoples.

Paralleling the rise in drug use and drug trafficking is a rise in youth gang activities. The onset of gang activity is associated with a variety of factors, including the frequency with which families move off and onto the reservation; poverty, substance abuse, and family dysfunction; the development of reservation cluster housing; and a waning connection to tribal cultural traditions. According to a 2004 report titled "Youth Gangs in Indian Country," drug sales account for 22 percent of criminal offenses by gang members, with aggravated assault accounting for 15 percent of offenses. Communities surveyed cited substance abuse, particularly alcohol (96%) and drugs (88%), as a significant problem contributing to antisocial behavior among youth and adults.

As a result of high levels of substance abuse, many racial minorities, including Native Americans, are disproportionately imprisoned for numerous offenses. According to data for 1999–2000, American Indians and Alaska Natives are incarcerated at a higher rate than any other racial/ethnic minority, except African Americans. Despite being the smallest racial/ethnic population, more than 4 percent of Native peoples are under correctional supervision, and this percentage is rising, due in large part to an increase in different forms of illicit substance abuse. The 2001 alcohol-related arrest rate for the American Indian and Alaska Native population was higher than the rate for all races. Indigenous peoples experience significantly higher rates of violent crime. Between 1992 and 2002, "among American Indians age 25 to 34, the rate of violent crime victimizations was more than 2½ times the rate for all persons the same age" (U.S. Department of Justice 2004). In 2001, 54.9 percent of American Indians entering the federal prison system had been convicted of violent crimes, while only 4.1 percent of whites and 13.3 percent of African Americans in prison had committed violent crimes. The Justice Department notes, however, that "approximately 60% of American Indian victims of violence, about the same percentage as of all victims of violence, described the offender as white" (U.S. Department of Justice 2004). Arrests for drug offenses accounted for 12.1 percent of American Indians entering the prison system.

Substance abuse, like other health challenges faced by American Indian and Native Alaska communities, is rooted in political economic conditions. Social and economic conditions that are prevalent in many indigenous communities provide fertile ground not only for the initiation of substance abuse, but also for its perpetuation. Substance abuse is only one component of the larger spectrum of health disparities that reflect race and class. Native peoples share the same racial and class landscape as other racial minorities and poor people.

BIBLIOGRAPHY

Agency for Healthcare Research and Quality. 2005. *2004 National Healthcare Disparities Report.* Rockville, MD: U.S. Department of Health and Human Services.

Berkhofer, Robert. 1979. *The White Man's Indian: Images of the American Indian from Columbus to the Present.* New York: Vintage Press.

Enoch, Mary-Anne, and David Goldman. 1999. "Genetics of Alcoholism and Substance Abuse." *Psychiatric Clinics of North America* 22 (2): 289–299.

Indian Health Service. 2000. *Trends in Indian Health, 1998–1999.* Rockville, MD: U.S. Department of Health and Human Services. Available from http://www.ihs.gov/PublicInfo/Publications.

———. 2002. *Trends in Indian Health, 2000–2001.* Rockville, MD: U.S. Department of Health and Human Services. Available from http://www.ihs.gov/NonMedicalPrograms/IHS_Stats/Trends00.asp.

———. 2007. *Year 2006 Profile.* Rockville, MD: U.S. Department of Health and Human Services. Available from http://info.ihs.gov/Files/ProfileSheet-June2006.pdf.

Keel, Jefferson. 2006. "Testimony of Jefferson Keel, First Vice President, National Congress of American Indians, before the United States Senate Committee on Indian Affairs: Oversight Hearing on the Problem of Methamphetamine in Indian Country, April 25, 2006." Washington DC: National Congress of American Indians. Available from http://www.ncai.org/Methamphetamine_Resources.195.0.html.

Kitcheyan, Kathleen. 2006. "Testimony of Chairwoman Kathleen Kitcheyan of the San Carlos Apache Tribe before the United States Senate Committee on Indian Affairs:

Oversight Hearing on the Problem of Methamphetamine in Indian Country, April 25, 2006." Washington DC: National Congress of American Indians. Available from http://www.ncai.org/Methamphetamine_Resources.195.0.html.

Major, Aline K., et al. 2004. "Youth Gangs in Indian Country." *Juvenile Justice Bulletin*. Washington DC: U.S. Department of Justice, Office of Juvenile Justice and Delinquency Prevention. http://www.ncjrs.gov/pdffiles1/ojjdp/202714.pdf.

Mancall, Peter. 1995. *Deadly Medicine: Indians and Alcohol in Early America*. Ithaca, NY: Cornell University Press.

May, Phillip. 1994. "The Epidemiology of Alcohol Abuse among American Indians." *American Indian Culture and Research Journal* 18 (2): 121–143.

McSwain, Robert. 2006. "Statement of Robert McSwain, Deputy Director, Indian Health Service, before the Senate Committee on Indian Affairs: Oversight Hearing on the Problem of Methamphetamine in Indian Country, April 25, 2006." Washington DC: National Congress of American Indians. Available from http://www.ncai.org/Methamphetamine_Resources.195.0.html.

Li, Ming D. "The Genetics of Smoking-Related Behavior." *American Journal of the Medical Sciences*. 326 (4): 168–217.

National Institute of Drug Abuse. 2003. *Drug Use among Racial/Ethnic Minorities*. Rev. ed. Bethesda, MD: U.S. Department of Health and Human Services.

Office of Applied Studies. 2003. *The NHSDA Report: Substance Abuse among American Indians or Alaskan Natives*. Rockville, MD: U.S. Department of Health and Human Services. Available from http://www.oas.samhsa.gov/2k3/AmIndians/AmIndians.cfm.

———. 2005. *Substance Abuse Treatment Admissions among American Indians and Alaska Natives: 2002*. Rockville, MD: U.S. Department of Health and Human Services.

Quintero, Gilbert. 2001. "Making the Indian: Colonial Knowledge, Alcohol, and Native Americans." *American Indian Culture and Research Journal* 25 (4): 57–71.

U.S. Census Bureau. 2006. *We the People: American Indians and Alaska Natives in the United States*. Washington DC: U.S. Department of Commerce. Available from http://www.census.gov/prod/2006pubs/censr-28.pdf.

U.S. Congress, Office of Technology Assessment. 1986. *Indian Health Care*. Washington DC: Government Printing Office.

U.S. Department of Justice. 2004. *American Indians and Crime: A BJS Statistical Profile, 1992–2002*. Washington DC: U.S. Department of Justice. Available from http://www.ojp.usdoj.gov/bjs/pub/pdf/aic02.pdf.

Gregory R. Campbell

SWEATSHOPS

Among the definitions the *Oxford English Dictionary* gives for *sweating* are: "the practice of doing piecework overtime," and "the practice of exacting hard work from employees for low wages, especially under a middleman by sub-contract." These features—piecework and working for a contractor—continue to define contemporary usage of the term and betray its origins in the garment and shoemaking industries of the mid-nineteenth century. Then, as in the early twenty-first century, it was the most vulnerable workers who were "sweated." That is, it is ethnic, "racial," or minority immigrants, and mostly women and children, who have worked under these conditions.

THE SWEATSHOP'S BEGINNINGS

The garment industry of the nineteenth century was ideally suited to this organization of production, because the labor-intensive and unskilled sewing work could be subcontracted by manufacturers to an "outside shop." This might entail scattering the work to several domestic outworkers, or else to small workshops that could be attached to the subcontractor's tenement housing. The skilled work of cutting and designing continued to be done in the "inside shop" of the manufacturer. In this type of system, the contractor competes for the work by providing the lowest, most competitive bid. Hence, the sole source of profit for contractors stems from the margin between the contracted price and the cost of hiring labor. In other words, the product is "sweated" out of the workers.

The new technologies of production that enabled the mechanization of clothing production in the 1860s also accelerated the process of sweated work. These technologies, including the band-saw cutting machine that cut multiple layers of cloth simultaneously and the sewing machine that replaced hand sewing, led to the creation of ready-to-wear garments and the replacement of skilled male tailors and seamstresses by semiskilled sewing-machine operators working as outworkers. Increasing urbanization expanded the market for ready-made goods and clothing at the same time that the pool of available labor for the industry was growing. Immigrant Jews fleeing eastern Europe, for example, made up large segments of the workforce in both Britain and America. Mechanization also led to the creation of large inside shops with centralized factory production. The historians Ava Baron and Susan Klepp have shown how centralized production in inside shops and decentralized production in outside shops coexisted in various segments of the American garment industry during the nineteenth century. They argue that the terms *inside* and *outside* describe processes rather than shops, because even large firms centralized only certain work processes, such as sewing, while others were conducted outside the shops. Thus, both the contracting system and manufacturing flourished under sweating conditions at the end of the century.

EARLY OPPOSITION AND REGULATION

This period also saw the rise of workers' organizing. In 1900, garment workers in New York City formed the International Ladies' Garment Workers' Union (ILGWU) to protest poor working conditions in the industry. The union's first strike was staged in 1909 by 20,000 shirtwaist makers, who were mostly women and children. Another strike, by 50,000 male cloak-makers, took place the following year. Along with a public outcry against sweatshops, these strikes ushered in a new era of industrial democracy. State regulations protecting workers were progressively strengthened, culminating in guarantees of workers' right to organize in 1935 and the passage of the Fair Labor Standards Act (FLSA), guaranteeing a minimum hourly wage, in 1938.

In the decades that followed, strong union membership and government enforcement of garment industry regulations seemed to have led to the abatement of sweatshops. But in reality garment manufacturers had begun relocating from New York to the nonunionized South as early as the 1920s and 1930s. In the 1970s the job loss was precipitous, as runaway shops continued to move south and southwest, to California, and finally offshore. At the same time, low-cost imports from newly industrializing East Asian countries hurt domestic producers, and in the 1980s the trend by manufacturers and retailers to source production globally continued, with apparel imports surpassing domestic production by the mid-1990s. Special trade regulations have enabled U.S. manufacturers to utilize offshore plants as assembly subcontractors ("outside shops") in Mexico. Under these regulations, manufacturers are allowed to reimport the goods assembled in Mexico, with a tariff charged only on the cost of labor inputs. These offshore assembly plants, or *maquiladoras,* sew the cut cloth that is provided by U.S. manufacturers and retailers. Cheap labor by young women is abundant in Mexico, and this model of *maquila* production has spread from apparel to the assembly of shoes, electronics, auto parts, white goods (major household appliances), data processing, and many other products and services.

The globalization of production has led to what sweatshop critics call a "race to the bottom," as big retailers such as Wal-Mart, and brand labels such as Nike and Old Navy, source manufacturing from cheaper and cheaper locations, pressuring others to follow suit. It also exerts downward pressure on wages in the United States, where the sweatshop has reemerged with a vengeance since the early 1980s. One solution is to raise wage levels to a living wage, which would result in only a minimal additional cost to consumers because apparel workers in developing countries earn only 1 to 2 percent of the retail cost of what they produce. Sweatshop advocates, on the other hand, argue that these jobs offer an improvement over alternative work opportunities for Third World workers.

RACE AND ETHNICITY

As in the past, immigrants and women are regarded as the cheapest and most exploitable workers, and they continue to make up the bulk of the garment workforce in the United States. The ethnic composition of the workforce in sweatshops varies by location: in Los Angeles, Latino immigrants outnumber Asian immigrants, such as the Koreans, Vietnamese and Chinese; whereas in San Francisco it is the Chinese who predominate, and in New York Mexican and Equadorian immigrants have now joined Chinese to form the vast majority of garment sweatshop workers. These patterns have shifted over time to reflect the changing profile of immigrants in the country. In the early twentieth century, it was Jewish and Italian immigrants who worked in the sweatshops of New York and Los Angeles, and in the 1990s, Mexicans and Chinese replaced the Puerto Ricans and Dominicans who worked in New York's sweatshops in the 1980s. In the face of increased global competitiveness, runaway shops from the unionized Northeast sought new sources of cheap non-union labor in the South. As a result, black garment workers, who had been incorporated into the southern apparel industry in the 1970s, have seen their work opportunities diminish. According to scholars Evelyn Blumenberg and Paul Ong, although blacks made up about 28 percent of the garment labor force in 1990 in North Carolina, then the epicenter of the industry in the South, and were an important source of employment for black workers, the large-scale garment production that was typical in the area has rapidly been diminished by capital flight to offshore production sites. Because of import competition, even brand-name manufacturers who had previously sourced to inside shops with union labor began outsourcing to small shops within the United States. This has led to a dramatic rise of employment in small shops in urban cities, where labor violations are more common and regulations are harder for the government to monitor. Workers dispersed into small workplaces are also harder to organize, and hence less likely to unionize.

For recent immigrants, language barriers, varying educational backgrounds, and a lack of knowledge regarding employment opportunities and job application procedures make working within what sociologists term "ethnic enclaves" (sections of the job market that are dominated by ethnic entrepreneurs and workers) more attractive. Scholars have pointed to the contradictory outcomes of being employed in such enclaves for workers' perceptions of class. When contractors are immigrants who employ workers from their own ethnic groups, this can lead to super-exploitative conditions of employment, in which

Women Work at Sewing Machines, El Salvador. *The globalization of production has led to what sweatshop critics call a "race to the bottom" as big retailers source from cheaper and cheaper locations.* AP IMAGES.

potential class conflicts are displaced by a shared ethnic identity or ethnic solidarity. For example, providing employment in ethnic and linguistic enclaves to recent migrants with little prior work experience, allowing workers' children into the workplace, advancing workers personal loans, and invoking personal ties with workers through shared ties to their place of origin enables employers to get such workers to work longer hours for less than minimum wages but still be viewed as benevolent benefactors by these workers. In other instances, when hierarchies between ethnic groups exist, such as those between Korean sweatshop owners and Latino garment workers in Los Angeles, class conflicts are permeated by, and expressed through, racial stereotypes. Notwithstanding the importance of race and ethnicity to the sweatshop economy, the problem with viewing sweatshops as ethnic enclaves is that the class relations between contractors and their workers are erroneously analyzed in isolation from the brand-name manufacturers and retailers that drive this mode of employment.

WOMEN OF COLOR

Historically, because it occurred in largely unregulated settings, sweated work was more accessible than factory labor to married women. Factory work demanded a full workday and a long-term commitment to work free of absenteeism or temporary withdrawals from the workforce, especially in the era before legislative provisions for maternity leave were put in place. Sweated outwork, on the other hand, required little training, could be taken up periodically, and did not have to be full-time work because it was paid by piece wages. Moreover, domestic outwork enabled poor and working-class wives and mothers to weave industrial work into their domestic reproductive routines.

The gendered division of domestic labor helps explain why industrial homework has been predominantly undertaken by women, but it does not explain why sweatshop workers, most of whom work overtime instead of part-time, are principally women, and especially women of color. For an explanation of this phenomenon, one must look instead to the ideological constructions of race and gender. The view of women's work as exceptional and temporary—and hence as supplemental to a male breadwinner's "family wage"—is a pervasive ideology that validates it as cheaper than male labor. Sweatshop jobs are feminized because they pay less than a living wage, and this sex-typing works alongside the naturalization of the actual skills required for work—such as the notion that women have naturally nimble fingers suited to sewing. Racial stereotypes of Latinos and Asians as hard and docile workers, and of immigrants (many of whom come from ex-colonial countries) as economically desperate with a history of manual and or agricultural labor, also justify their suitability for low-paid and low-skilled work. The precarious social location of immigrants, especially of undocumented workers, combined with their relative lack of knowledge regarding alternative work opportunities, translates into their weaker bargaining power in the labor market.

BACK TO THE FUTURE?

On May 10, 1993, a fire at the Kader toy factory on the outskirts of Bangkok, Thailand, killed 188 workers (174 of whom were women) and seriously injured 494 others. It has been described as the worst industrial fire in the history of capitalism, and certainly in the history of the textile, clothing, and footwear industries. The workers—some as young as thirteen—were assembling toys for familiar American brands such as Fisher-Price and Tyco, and for retailers such as Wal-Mart and Toys 'R' Us. Observers have been naturally drawn to comparisons with the previous fire that held this distinction for over eighty years: the 1911 Triangle Shirtwaist Factory fire in New York City that killed 146 garment workers, most of whom were immigrant women. Despite the eighty-two years separating these disasters, there are eerie similarities between them. In both cases, workers were unable to exit through doors that were either blocked by flammable work materials or locked by management to deter theft. In Thailand, as in New York, women workers were trapped by the fire and jumped out of windows several stories high to escape the flames. The 1911 disaster impelled consumers to unite with the cause of immigrant women workers, resulting in new workplace health and safety legislation. In 1998, however, the death and maiming of Third World women workers toiling in outsourced sweatshops overseas barely captured the attention of the U.S. media or consumers. The fate of the global sweatshop may rest on conscientious consumption by citizens who want to be more than just price-conscious consumers and who choose instead to pay for workers' dignity and respect.

SEE ALSO *Puerto Ricans.*

BIBLIOGRAPHY

Bao, Xiaolan. 2001. *Holding Up More than Half the Sky: Chinese Women Garment Workers in New York City, 1948–92.* Urbana: University of Illinois Press.

Baron, Ava, and Susan E. Klepp. 1984. "'If I Didn't Have My Sewing Machine ...': Women and Sewing Machine Technology." In *A Needle, A Bobbin, A Strike: Women Needleworkers in America*, edited by Joan M. Jensen and Sue Davidson, 20–59. Philadelphia, PA: Temple University Press.

Blumenberg, Evelyn, and Paul Ong. 1994. "Labor Squeeze and Ethnic/Racial Composition in the U.S. Apparel Industry." In *Global Production: The Apparel Industry in the Pacific Rim*, edited by Edna Bonacich, Lucie Cheng, Norma Chinchilla, Nora Hamilton, and Paul Ong, 309–327. Philadelphia: Temple University Press.

Bonacich, Edna. 1994. "Asians in the Los Angeles Garment Industry." In *The New Asian Immigration in Los Angeles and Global Restructuring*, edited by Paul Ong, Edna Bonacich, and Lucie Cheng, 137–163. Philadelphia: Temple University Press.

Esbenshade, Jill. 2004. *Monitoring Sweatshops: Workers, Consumers, and the Global Apparel Industry.* Philadelphia, PA: Temple University Press.

Louie, Miriam Ching Yoon. 2001. *Sweatshop Warriors: Immigrant Women Workers Take on the Global Factory.* Cambridge, MA: South End Press.

Pessar, Patricia. 1994. "Sweatshop Workers and Domestic Ideologies: Dominican Women in New York's Apparel Industry." *International Journal of Urban and Regional Research* 18 (1): 127–142.

Ross, Andrew, ed. 1997. *No Sweat: Fashion, Free Trade, and the Rights of Garment Workers.* New York: Verso.

Ross, Robert J. S. 2004. *Slaves to Fashion: Poverty and Abuse in the New Sweatshops.* Ann Arbor: University of Michigan Press.

U.S. General Accounting Office. 1988. "Sweatshops in the U.S." Washington, DC: U.S. Government Printing Office. Available from http://archive.gao.gov/d17t6/136973.pdf.

Jayati Lal

SWIFT, WESLEY

1913–1970

Wesley Swift was born in New Jersey in 1913, the son of a Methodist minister. He himself became a Methodist clergyman by the age of eighteen, but he abandoned his faith and adopted Christian Identity theology after moving to California to attend the Kingdom Bible College in Los Angeles in the early 1930s. Smith traveled and preached throughout Southern California before eventually settling in the Antelope Valley outside Los Angeles. By 1944, Smith had left his job as an auto-supply salesman to become politically active, and he began organizing for the Ku Klux Klan the following year.

Between 1946 and 1948 Swift established two organizations, the Great Pyramid Club and the Anglo-Saxon Christian Congregation. The name of the former group was derived from his belief that mathematical calculations could be used to correlate measurements of the Egyptian pyramids with biblical texts. According to Swift, the pyramids had been constructed by "Aryan" descendants of Adam. Swift used the Pyramid Club to identify individuals with strong anti-Semitic beliefs who could then be recruited into the Klan, while the chief goal of his Anglo-Saxon Christian Congregation was to build support for the Christian Identity movement. Although Swift's congregation first began meeting in 1945, it was not formerly incorporated until August 1948, and eight years later he changed the name to the Church of Jesus Christ, Christian.

Consistent with his Christian Identity beliefs, Swift denounced Jews, railed against "racial mongrelization," and alleged that "motion-picture heroes and heroines are not only dope fiends and sex perverts, but are conscious agents of the Soviet Union." While his sermons and speeches were vigorously criticized by Jewish groups, Swift benefited from high levels of anti-Jewish attitudes among the general public. By 1944, for example, 24 percent of Americans saw Jews as a "menace" to the country—up from 15 percent only two years earlier. By 1945, 58 percent of all Americans said Jews "had too much power," compared to 36 percent in 1938 (Dinnerstein 1994, Ch. 7).

Swift capitalized on these sentiments by preaching regularly to Identity groups and other gatherings of self-described "Christian Nationalists" throughout California, including approximately 200 of his own followers who were meeting weekly in Los Angeles by 1948. In an effort to further broaden his audience, Swift also launched a regular ten-minute morning radio broadcast called "America's Destiny." Swift's message was extended even further through numerous recordings of hundreds of his sermons and speeches, which were printed and distributed in tabloid newsletters and pamphlets across the United States.

Swift's prominence in right-wing political and religious circles was enhanced by his close personal and professional relationship with Gerald L. K. Smith, the leader of the Detroit-based Christian Nationalist Crusade. The two first met in 1945, when Smith visited California to preach and recruit supporters. For the next twenty years, Swift helped to raise money and organize meetings for the Crusade, and he even acted as Smith's personal bodyguard when Smith visited California. Along with other major Christian Nationalists of the World War II period, including Father Charles Coughlin, the Rev. Gerald Winrod, and William Dudley Pelley, Swift was instrumental in spreading anti-Semitism through the ranks of ultraconservative and anticommunist organizations. Swift's leadership of the California Anti-Communist League in the early 1950s provided him with yet another vehicle through which to gain political legitimacy as an anticommunist, while disseminating anti-Semitic beliefs and conspiracy theories.

Swift's influence also was heightened by those he converted to Identity theology, especially Richard Girnt Butler, a World War II veteran and the future founder of the neo-Nazi group Aryan Nations. Butler was personally introduced to Swift by William Potter Gale around 1962, when Butler was working as an aeronautical engineer and living in Whittier, California. Although Gale's father was Jewish, he had embraced Identity and was ordained by Swift in 1956. He parted ways with his theological mentor on bitter terms, however, some ten years later. A retired U.S. Army lieutenant colonel, Gale went on to found the right-wing paramilitary group, the Posse Comitatus in 1971.

Other notable followers and associates who helped connect and promote Swift to an array of right-wing groups include San Jacinto Capt, James K. Warner, and Bertrand L. Comparet, an Identity preacher and Stanford-educated lawyer with an undistinguished former career as a San Diego assistant city attorney. Comparet also helped manage Swift's legal affairs. Capt, former Klansman and devoted pyramidologist, converted William Potter Gale to Christian Identity. Warner later assumed control of the Christian Defense League (CDL), an Identity group, and founded the New Christian Crusade Church of Metairie, Louisiana. He considered himself to be Swift's spiritual heir and was responsible for reprinting many of Swift's sermons and speeches.

Swift died on October 8, 1970, at the age of fifty-seven, after collapsing in the waiting room of a Mexican clinic while awaiting treatment for kidney disease and diabetes. Four years after Swift's death, Butler relocated what remained of Swift's congregation to Idaho, where he constructed a chapel large enough to seat 100 people and began holding regular church services. The group later evolved into The Church of Jesus Christ Christian, Aryan Nations.

SEE ALSO *Christian Identity; Ku Klux Klan; Neo-Nazis.*

BIBLIOGRAPHY

Barkun, Michael. 1994. *Religion and the Racist Right: The Origins of the Christian Identity Movement.* Chapel Hill: University of North Carolina Press.

Dinnerstein, Leonard, 1994. "Anti-semitism at High Tide: World War II (1939–1945)." Chapter 7. In *Antisemitism in America.* Oxford: Oxford University Press.

Levitas, Daniel. 2002. *The Terrorist Next Door: The Militia Movement and the Radical Right.* New York: Thomas Dunne.

Urban Archives Center, Oviatt Library, California State University, Northridge. 2007. "Jewish Federation Council of Greater Los Angeles, Community Relations Committee Collection." Available from http://library.csun.edu/spcoll/.

Daniel Levitas

SYMBOLIC AND MODERN RACISM

Symbolic racism, also known as modern racism, is as of the early 2000s a new expression of prejudice that has developed in the United States. It is based on the belief that blacks violate key American values, particularly the idea of individualism, the belief in working hard to get ahead in life. Perceptions that blacks violate other values (including, for example, morality, self-restraint, and family traditionalism) have been less studied, but they may be important for understanding the range of values invoked in symbolic racism beliefs. The term *racism* is applicable because the belief that blacks violate cherished values is often strongly associated with negative feelings or antipathy toward blacks, while *symbolic* highlights the fact that the roots of the symbolic racism belief system are in these abstract, moral values, rather than in concrete self-interest or personal experiences, and because blacks are targeted as an abstract collectivity rather than as specific individuals.

Figure 1 represents the symbolic racism model and demonstrates what are considered the basic antecedents to and consequences of endorsing symbolic racism beliefs. The way symbolic racism is openly expressed is characterized by four specific themes or beliefs: (1) that blacks no longer face much prejudice or discrimination, (2) that the failure of blacks to progress results from their unwillingness

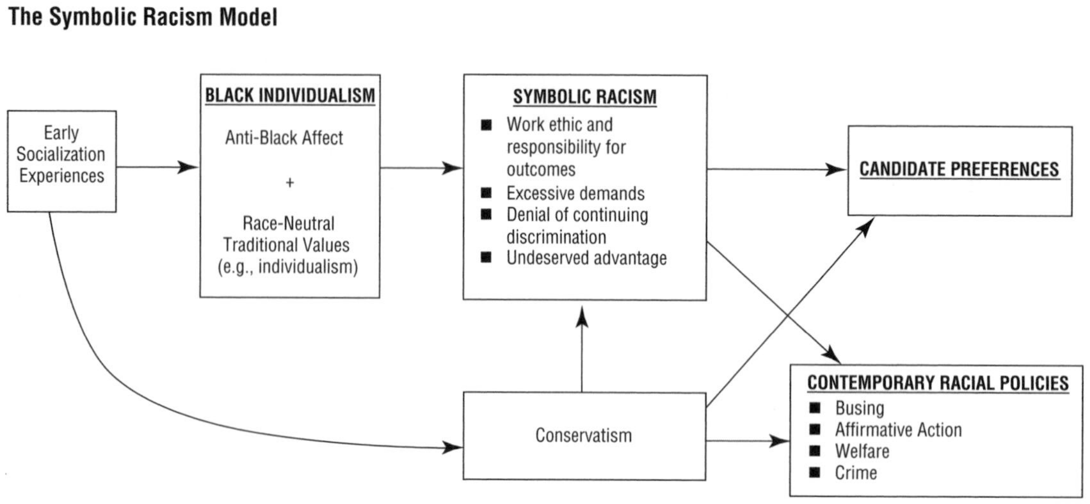

SOURCE: Reprinted from Sears, David O., and P. J. Henry. (2005). "Over Thirty Years Later: A Contemporary Look at Symbolic Racism." *Advances in Experimental Social Psychology*, 37: 95.

Figure 1.

to work hard enough, (3) that blacks are demanding too much too fast, and (4) that blacks have gotten more than they deserve. Endorsement of these beliefs is taken to reflect an endorsement of symbolic racism.

Symbolic racism became a widespread expression of discontent toward blacks by many white Americans after the civil rights era of the 1950s and 1960s. It is thought to have largely replaced previous forms of prejudice, commonly known as "old fashioned," "redneck," or "Jim Crow" racism, which are characterized by beliefs in the biological inferiority of blacks, support for segregation of the races, and formal racial discrimination. Symbolic racism replaced these old-fashioned racist beliefs in the sense that old-fashioned racism is no longer very popular and has very little influence in ordinary politics. Although examples of old-fashioned prejudice continue to arise in twenty-first century society (e.g., hate crimes committed against blacks, companies using blatant discriminatory practices), this kind of prejudice is rare compared to the more widespread beliefs found in symbolic racism.

SYMBOLIC RACISM INFLUENCES POLITICAL ATTITUDES

Symbolic racism has a powerful influence on American attitudes toward race-based politics. In particular, research has shown it to be a stronger predictor of racial policy preferences than other constructs. An impressive range of political attitudes are thought to be influenced by symbolic racism, including opposition to liberal racial policies such as affirmative action (programs designed to favor blacks in hiring, promotion, college admission, etc.), busing (the transportation of blacks to wealthier, white communities for racial integration in education), and attitudes toward less explicitly race-based policies that have a disproportionate effect on blacks such as stricter welfare regulations and punitive crime policies.

Symbolic racism also has an important influence on political campaigns, including opposition to black candidates such as Jesse Jackson; support for white candidates perceived as being unsympathetic to blacks, such as George H. W. Bush; or even support for more explicitly racist candidates such as the ethnocentrically oriented Pat Buchanan or the former Ku Klux Klan leader David Duke. When subtle racial appeals are used in campaigns, such as the infamous invocation of the black murderer and rapist Willie Horton during the 1988 presidential campaign, the political force of symbolic racism becomes even stronger.

Symbolic racism may also have played a strong influence on the general political shift from a nation governed by liberal Democrats at the end of World War II to one in which conservative Republicans seemed to have a consistent edge. A central factor in this shift is the conversion of the once Democratic "solid South" of white voters to a predominantly Republican white South. Symbolic racism remains stronger in the white South than elsewhere in the nation, and it has played a stronger role in white Southerners' voting than elsewhere. It is thus a major factor in causing the South's political realignment.

Willie Horton Jr. *In the 1988 presidential campaign, Vice President George Bush used the example of Willie Horton, a convicted rapist and murderer who raped a woman while on furlough from prison, to depict his opponent as soft on crime. When subtle racial appeals are used in campaigns, the political force of symbolic racism becomes even stronger.* AP IMAGES.

SEPARATING SYMBOLIC RACISM FROM OTHER INTERESTS

It is clear that symbolic racism has a major influence in politics, and its influences are thought to be independent of other political constructs, such as personal interests, group interests, and nonracial ideological conservatism. A great deal of research has been devoted to separating symbolic racism from these other constructs.

One key feature of the symbolic racism belief system that distinguishes it from personal interests is that it is rooted in abstract beliefs about groups violating important values that are socialized through one's parents, peers, and the media. For example, news media depictions of blacks cheating the welfare system are thought to reinforce symbolic racism beliefs that blacks violate the value of individualism or that they do not put forth the necessary efforts to get ahead in life. Emerging research demonstrates that the socialization of symbolic racism beliefs begins as early as adolescence, which is earlier than other political beliefs, and that it continues through the lifespan.

This idea that early-socialized, abstract beliefs influence attitudes toward racial policies is contrary to other theories that suggest attitudes toward race-based policies are driven by personal interests. For example, personal interests would theoretically influence a white individual's opposition to affirmative action if that person believed that affirmative action interferes with his or her ability to get a job or promotion, or it might influence a white citizen living near a black ghetto to vote for a white political candidate rather than a black one. Symbolic racism is thought to influence attitudes toward race-based political attitudes regardless of a person's personal interests.

In fact, the consensus of most research is that personal interests or self-interest plays little role in influencing people's attitudes toward race-based policies (Sears and Funk 1991). But group-based interests are another matter. It could be that American whites may oppose race-based policies such as affirmative action in an effort to protect the interest of whites as a group, even if they do not try to protect personal interests threatened by such programs. Indeed, it has been argued that even symbolic racism derives from these group-interested motivations. However, research has shown that symbolic racism still strongly predicts whites' racial policy preferences beyond indicators of any attachment to whites as a group. Strong white group identity, perceived common fate with other whites about valued resources, a perceived threat or competition for scarce resources between blacks and whites, and a perceived collective threat to whites' well-being from black people all tend to have weak effects. Symbolic racism beliefs seem to be quite separate from desires to protect the group-based interests of whites.

Symbolic racism can also be distinguished from conservative ideology. Although symbolic racism is related to conservatism, and both conservative beliefs and symbolic racism contribute to opposition to race-based policies like affirmative action, the two constructs also operate independently. Symbolic racism strongly predicts racial policy preferences among both ideological liberals and conservatives. Also, symbolic racism theory suggests that symbolic racism determines racial policy attitudes, rather than that opposition to race-based programs determines symbolic racism. Of course some conservatives oppose race-based policies without being racist, but racism is thought to be the more important determinant of such opposition. This remains an important controversy, however.

The Symbolic Racism 2000 Scale

1. It's really a matter of some people not trying hard enough; if blacks would only try harder they could be just as well off as whites.
   1 Strongly agree
   2 Somewhat agree
   3 Somewhat disagree
   4 Strongly disagree
2. Irish, Italian, Jewish and many other minorities overcame prejudice and worked their way up. Blacks should do the same.
   1 Strongly agree
   2 Somewhat agree
   3 Somewhat disagree
   4 Strongly disagree
3. Some say that black leaders have been trying to push too fast. Others feel that they haven't pushed fast enough. What do you think?
   1 Trying to push very much too fast
   2 Going too slowly
   3 Moving at about the right speed
4. How much of the racial tension that exists in the United States today do you think blacks are responsible for creating?
   1 All of it
   2 Most
   3 Some
   4 Not much at all
5. How much discrimination against blacks do you feel there is in the United States today, limiting their chances to get ahead?
   1 A lot
   2 Some
   3 Just a little
   4 None at all
6. Generations of slavery and discrimination have created conditions that make it difficult for blacks to work their way out of the lower class.
   1 Strongly agree
   2 Somewhat agree
   3 Somewhat disagree
   4 Strongly disagree
7. Over the past few years, blacks have gotten less than they deserve.
   1 Strongly agree
   2 Somewhat agree
   3 Somewhat disagree
   4 Strongly disagree
8. Over the past few years, blacks have gotten more economically than they deserve.
   1 Strongly agree
   2 Somewhat agree
   3 Somewhat disagree
   4 Strongly disagree

Note: The following is the standard procedure for combining the items into a scale: After collecting the data, items 1, 2, 4, and 8 need to be recoded so that a 1 = 4, 2 = 3, 3 = 2, and 4 = 1. Item 3 needs to be recoded so that 1 = 3, 2 = 1, and 3 = 2. For combining the items into a scale, there are several options, ranging from the simplest to the most precise: (1) One could simply add the raw scores together for each item, so that each individual has a score that could range from 8 to 31. (2) To compensate for any missing data, one could average the raw scores. (3) To compensate for the differences in the number of response alternatives, one could recode each of the items on a 0 to 1 scale, so for item #3, a 1 = 1, 2 = 0, and 3 = .50, and for the other items the high response is a 1, the next a .66, the next a .33, and the low response is a 0. (This third technique is the one used in Henry & Sears, 2002.) (4) To equate the variability across items, one could create standardized (z) scores for each of the items in the scale, then average the responses.

SOURCE: Reprinted from Henry, P. J., and David O. Sears. (2002). "The Symbolic Racism 2000 Scale." *Political Psychology*, 23: 3.

Symbolic Racism Scale.

MEASURING SYMBOLIC RACISM

Symbolic racism is typically measured with sample surveys of the general public. Typically, respondents complete a computer-based or paper-and-pencil questionnaire, or they are interviewed over the telephone or in person. Good measures of symbolic racism include items representing the four themes discussed earlier. These different themes all have the same effects on determining policy attitudes, and they can be seen as variants of the underlying perception that blacks violate cherished American values.

Items in any such scale of prejudice morph over time, just as language in a society morphs. For example, one item from the commonly used Modern Racism Scale (McConahay 1986), which asks whether the respondent believes that "blacks have more influence on school desegregation plans than they ought to have," is not as relevant in the early twenty-first century as it was in the 1970s, when court-ordered school desegregation plans were the focal points of much political controversy. Consequently, this type of item is not typically used any more in capturing symbolic racism attitudes.

SYMBOLIC RACISM AND SIMILAR CONSTRUCTS

Symbolic racism is similar to some other constructs that also reflect the nature of modern prejudice. It is essentially the same as "modern racism" or "racial resentment," both in concept and in the items used. Its underlying psychology is similar to other theories that also assume that a "new racism" became politically potent after the civil rights movement of the 1960s, embodying both negative feelings toward blacks and conservative non-racial values, including *subtle prejudice,* which reflects a defense of traditional values, an exaggeration of cultural differences, and a denial of positive emotions toward blacks; *racial ambivalence,* which describes many whites as vacillating between "problack" attitudes rooted in humanitarianism and egalitarianism and "antiblack" attitudes based in such traditional values as the Protestant ethic; or *laissez-faire racism,* which combines perceptions of little continuing racial discrimination with blacks' own lack of sufficient effort in a market-driven society.

Symbolic racism is also related to *aversive racism,* which is characterized by the paradox that many white Americans feel favorable attitudes toward blacks but engage in subtle behaviors that discriminate against blacks, such as negative or avoidant nonverbal behavior or failing to help blacks in distress. Aversive racism is particularly likely when alternative explanations for behaviors do not imply negative racial attitudes. For example, even a white person who expresses favorable attitudes toward blacks may be less likely to help a black person than a white person when there is the easy, nonracial excuse to avoid help (for example, the presence of others available who could help). Aversive racism focuses on the paradoxical behaviors of those who hold positive attitudes toward blacks, while symbolic racism focuses on the range of racial attitudes from positive to negative.

SEPARATING SYMBOLIC RACISM FROM AUTOMATIC PREJUDICES

Symbolic racism is often distinguished from implicit prejudice, which is thought to be rooted in unconscious, automatic, or uncontrollable mental processes. It was first identified with reaction-time measures, which are difficult to control. For example, one might measure how quickly a participant associates negative words with photos of blacks, and the strength of this association has been considered by some to be a kind of negative racial attitude. Evidence on the relationship of implicit measures of prejudice to measures of symbolic racism is mixed; sometimes there is little evidence of a relationship between the two, other times the relationship is meaningful (for example, when the attitudes involved are particularly important to an individual). Some evidence suggests that symbolic racism predicts deliberate responses such as policy and voting preferences, whereas implicit prejudice predicts more automatic responses, such as nonverbal interactions and subtle behaviors toward blacks. There is much debate about whether survey measures of prejudice such as symbolic racism and implicit measures of prejudice found in reaction-time studies capture different dimensions of racism, or whether one is a more "real" measure of racism than the other.

CRITICISMS OF SYMBOLIC RACISM

A number of criticisms have arisen concerning symbolic racism. Conservatives have suggested that symbolic racism is not racism, just a proxy for nonracial conservative beliefs, and that prejudice is really only a minor political force. On the other end of the political spectrum, social structuralists, who see society as strongly stratified along a racial hierarchy, with competition among racial groups to move up and avoid moving down, have suggested that symbolic racism is just a proxy for group-based interests. Their perspective posits that symbolic racism is merely a tool used by the dominant whites in society as a means of maintaining their privileged position.

These controversies are particularly important in light of race relations in the early 2000s. If the symbolic racism claim about early-socialized prejudice against blacks is correct, much remedial work needs to be done on the education of whites concerning racial inequities in society. If it is wrong, and conservative views that politics have been freed from racial prejudice is correct, then pressure would be placed upon blacks to adapt to a society in which they are no longer being treated unfairly by other Americans. Alternatively, if social structuralists are correct in stating that whites are primarily motivated by a defense of their privileged position, then a different strategy is called for, perhaps one that calls for more direct exercise of whatever powers minorities may have.

Another set of criticisms concerns the conceptualization and measurement of symbolic racism. The symbolic racism construct began as a largely intuitive account of the most politically potent form of racism outside the South in the post–civil rights era. It is not surprising that the construct was not initially sharply and consistently conceptualized. Symbolic racism was also originally described as a single construct, but it was later described as having a variety of subdimensions. In the early twenty-first century it is consistently described as having four themes. Perceived value violations are thought to be the underlying thread that all four expressions of symbolic racism have in common. They represent simply different ways one can express negative attitudes toward blacks in terms of this perception of value violations.

A second question arises about the contention that symbolic racism is a "blend" of early-acquired antiblack feelings and conservative traditional values that have no intrinsic link to race, such as individualism. Defining that blend as a fusion of the two elements in a single attitude is more in harmony both with the original theorizing and with current empirical evidence about the origins of symbolic racism. Research shows that symbolic racism is first acquired in late adolescence and becomes stronger as individuals progress through their lives.

A third critique arises from the fact that some early measures of symbolic racism included direct measures of opposition to race-based policies. Consequently, the criticism arose that the relationship between symbolic racism and racial policy preferences was circular, that symbolic racism was being captured by the measures it was intended to predict, even though those studies focused on candidate choice rather than policy preferences. For clarity, current measures of symbolic racism no longer refer to government action or involvement.

A fourth concern has been that people may hide their true prejudices when responding to symbolic racism items. Ironically, symbolic racism was initially thought to be an indirect measure of racism that avoided these kinds of response biases, in contrast to measures of old-fashioned racism that were too readily interpreted by respondents as measuring racism, and so underestimated prejudice. Symbolic racism, too, may be susceptible to respondent dissembling; some research shows lower levels of symbolic racism reported by whites when the scale is administered by a black interviewer. However, symbolic racism has stronger predictive power over voting preferences than other racial constructs such as old-fashioned racism, stereotypes, and antiblack feelings, which also are thought to suffer from similar social-desirability response biases. This finding suggests that social-desirability biases cannot adequately explain symbolic racism effects. Other evidence shows that implicit measures of prejudice may not be free from social and contextual influences either.

THE FUTURE OF SYMBOLIC RACISM

The theory of symbolic racism has been largely confined to the study of negative attitudes toward blacks in the contemporary United States. Scientific advancements have extended this research to identify other types of symbolic prejudices, or they have otherwise identified the importance of recognizing the power of perceiving other groups as violating cherished values. This research has been extended to include the study of symbolic racism toward Latino and Asian immigrants in the United States, modern sexism attitudes, modern anti-fat attitudes, modern heterosexism, and other forms of prejudice. The study of the perception of value violations as an important factor in determining general group-based attitudes is a growing line of research.

Americans continue to live in a society that seems unable to put race aside or deal with racism openly. Racial inequality continues to pervade most areas of social and economic life in the United States, and it does not seem to be diminishing rapidly. Nor is it clear how this situation can be rectified. The perspective from symbolic racism is that the future may be optimistic, but that a great deal of work is necessary to rectify negative attitudes toward blacks in the United States. White America seems to have developed a case of collective amnesia that allows it to treat racism as an ugly chapter in American history, a chapter that was closed for good with the passage of civil rights legislation in the 1960s. But neither people nor societies change that quickly. There is much data that testify to the continuing political power of racism. It may be that antiblack racism in the United States, like German anti-Semitism, cannot be put aside without a strong majority demonstrating and acknowledging the continuing role of racial prejudice and discrimination in society.

SEE ALSO *Affirmative Action; Aversive Racism; Mental Health and Racism.*

BIBLIOGRAPHY

Dovidio, John F., Kerry Kawakami, and Samuel L. Gaertner. 2002. "Implicit and Explicit Prejudice and Interracial Interaction." *Journal of Personality and Social Psychology* 82 (1): 62–68.

Henry, P. J., and David O. Sears. 2002. "The Symbolic Racism 2000 Scale." *Political Psychology* 23 (3): 253–283.

Kinder, Donald R., and Lynn M. Sanders. 1996. *Divided by Color: Racial Politics and Democratic Ideals.* Chicago: University of Chicago Press.

McConahay, John B. 1986. "Modern Racism, Ambivalence, and the Modern Racism Scale." In *Prejudice, Discrimination, and Racism*, edited by John Dovidio and Samuel Gaertner, 91–126. Orlando, FL: Academic Press.

Myrdal, Gunnar. 1944. *An American Dilemma: The Negro Problem and Modern Democracy.* New York: Harper & Row.

Reyna, Christine, P. J. Henry, W. Korfmacher, and A. Tucker. 2005. "Examining the Principles in Principled Conservatism: The Role of Responsibility Stereotypes as Cues for Deservingness in Racial Policy Decisions." *Journal of Personality and Social Psychology* 90 (1): 109–128.

Sears, David O., and Carolyn L. Funk 1991. "The Role of Self-Interest in Social and Political Attitudes." In *Advances in Experimental Social Psychology*, edited by Mark P. Zanna, vol. 24, pp. 2–91. New York: Academic Press.

Sears, David O., and P. J. Henry. 2005. "Over Thirty Years Later: A Contemporary Look at Symbolic Racism." *Advances in Experimental Social Psychology* 37: 95–150.

Sears, David O., Jim Sidanius, and Lawrence Bobo, eds. 2000. *Racialized Politics: The Debate about Racism in America.* Chicago: University of Chicago Press.

Sidanius, Jim, Shana Levin, Joshua L. Rabinowitz, and Christopher M. Federico. 1999. "Peering into the Jaws of the Beast: The Integrative Dynamics of Social Identity, Symbolic Racism, and Social Dominance." In *Cultural Divides: Understanding and Overcoming Group Conflict,* edited by Deborah A. Prentice and Dale T. Miller, 80–132. New York: Russell Sage.

Sniderman, Paul M., and Philip E. Tetlock. 1986. "Symbolic Racism: Problems of Motive Attributions in Political Analysis." *Journal of Social Issues* 42: 129–150.

Swim, Janet K., Kathryn J. Aikin, Wayne S. Hall, and Barbara A. Hunter. 1995. "Sexism and Racism: Old-Fashioned and Modern Prejudices." *Journal of Personality & Social Psychology* 68: 199–214.

Valentino, Nicholas A., and David O. Sears. 2005. "Old Times There Are Not Forgotten: Race and Partisan Realignment in the Contemporary South." *American Journal of Political Science* 49 (3): 672–688.

P.J. Henry
David O. Sears

SYMBOLIC ETHNICITY

The concept of symbolic ethnicity is most closely associated with the pioneering work of the sociologist Herbert Gans, who attempted to account for the simultaneous decline and resurgence of ethnic identification in the United States after World War II. Gans defined symbolic ethnicity as "a nostalgic allegiance to the culture of the immigrant generation, or that of the old country; a love for and a pride in a tradition that can be felt without having to be incorporated in everyday behavior" (1979, p. 9).

THE GROWTH OF SYMBOLIC ETHNICITY

In the postwar decades, researchers documented ethnic assimilation among whites, measured by increases in rates of intermarriage and decreases in non-English language usage and religious observance. Jews and Christians were marrying one another, and second-generation immigrants were speaking only English and not going to church or temple.

Despite these trends toward what was presumed to be an "American" identity—at the expense of a Jewish or Catholic or Irish or Hungarian or other national origin identity—there also appeared to be a rise in ethnic identification during the 1970s. White Americans were reclaiming ethnic affiliations, joining ethnic clubs and organizations, celebrating ethnic holidays, and researching their ethnic ancestries. For instance, many Americans whose parents had been, for instance, Jews or Poles, but who previously had thought of themselves simply as Americans were becoming "Jewish-Americans" and "Polish-Americans." There was a resurgence, and sometimes an emergence, of ethnic-American identity claims for the first time in many individuals' biographies.

BUILDING AN ETHNIC IDENTITY

How could people behave in ways that disregarded traditional ethnic boundaries while at the same time asserting an ethnic affiliation? Many scholars attempted to solve this puzzle of waning and waxing ethnicity by examining the symbolic aspects of ethnicity and the extent to which ethnic identification is volitional. It appeared that individuals were choosing to emphasize some aspects of their ethnic ancestry and ignoring others. This suggested that an individual's ethnicity is at least partly the result of individual choice and that ethnicity is not primordial or fixed. Rather, ethnic identification can be thought of as an ingoing process that uses material from the past and the present to build new or revitalized ethnic identities and groups. In some cases, history seems to be a relatively weak ingredient in the ethnic reconstruction project. For instance, in her discussion of Armenian-American ethnicity, Anny Bakalian shows how the symbolic aspects of ethnicity become disconnected from many traditional markers of ethnic group boundaries, such as language, religion, culture, community:

> For American-born generations, Armenian identity is a preference and Armenianness is a *state of mind* ... One can say he or she is an Armenian without speaking Armenian, marrying an Armenian, doing business with Armenians, belonging to an Armenian church, joining Armenian voluntary associations, or participating in the events and activities sponsored by such organizations (Bakalian 1993, p. 13).

The renowned sociologist Joshua Fishman documented a similar symbolic "revival of ethnicity," and Richard Alba, a distinguished professor of Race and Ethnicity at the State University of New York at Albany, has emphasized the transformation of ethnic identity among white ethnics from a set of cohesive nationality-based ethnic groups to a more general racial category marked by few, if any, constraints on behavior. For late twentieth-century white Americans, ethnicity had increasingly become what the Harvard professor Mary Waters terms an "ethnic option"—a choice to be or not to be ethnic. According to this view, once the decision is made in favor of an ethnic identity, whites have a wide variety of ancestral strains to select from, and few limitations in determining the content of their chosen ethnicities.

The notion that ethnicity can be chosen or not, changed or maintained, and excavated or invented, was first systematically articulated by the Norwegian anthropologist Fredrik Barth, who argued that ethnicity is less about a fixed historical culture and more the result of human action:

> Ethnic categories provide an organizational vessel that may be given varying amounts and forms of content in different socio-cultural systems.... The critical focus of investigation from this point of view becomes the ethnic boundary that defines the group, not the cultural stuff that it encloses (Barth 1969, p. 14–15).

Barth's notion of ethnicity is that it resembles a vessel that gets filled with meaning. A more contemporary device for imagining the construction of ethnic culture is the shopping cart. An ethnic group boundary may be thought of as the *shape* of the shopping cart (size, number of wheels, composition, etc.). Ethnic culture, then, is the *contents* of the cart, or all of the things an individual puts into ethnicity to give it meaning, such as art, music, dress, religion, norms, food, beliefs, symbols, myths, and customs (Nagel 1994). Ethnicity is not simply a historical legacy, just as culture is not a "shopping cart" that comes already loaded with a set of historical cultural goods. Rather, people construct both culture and ethnicity by picking and choosing items from the shelves of the past and the present. In other words, cultures change; they are borrowed, blended, rediscovered, and reinterpreted. In this way, ethnicity is symbolically modified and deployed in one's ethnic construction projects.

VOLUNTARY VERSUS INVOLUNTARY ETHNICITY

The idea of symbolic ethnicity has provided valuable insights into white Americans' relationship to ethnicity. It has also led to some distortions. The emphasis on the voluntary dimensions of ethnic identification, the choices involved in deciding which features of ethnicity individuals will embrace and which they will discard, and the enriching aspects of ethnic "feeling" and "playing" overstates the extent to which ethnicity is under one's control (Deloria 1999). For many individuals, ethnicity is not an option, and it is not free. Symbolic ethnicity stresses the internal dimensions of ethnic identity and emphasizes the agency of ethnic actors: Individuals have the power to define ethnicity or to deny ethnicity in favor of a national or "American" identity. What is obscured in the symbolic ethnicity model is the powerful external machinery of ethnic ascription and the capacity of observers to determine one's ethnicity. We are not always who or what we think we are. We are, ethnically, what others, especially others with power, define us to be—no matter what ethnicity we try to assert.

In order to understand the limits of symbolic ethnicity as a model for understanding ethnic identification, persistence, and violence in the contemporary world, it is useful to think of ethnicity as the result of a dialectical process that emerges from the interaction between individuals and those whom they meet as they pass through daily life. An individual's ethnicity is a negotiated social fact—what individuals think is their ethnicity versus what others think is their ethnicity. Individuals carry a portfolio of ethnic identities, some of which are more or less salient in various situations and among various audiences. As settings and spectators change, the socially defined array of ethnic options open changes: white, Irish, Catholic, black, Jamaican, Navajo, Muslim, American Indian.

A person's ethnicity is, then, a matter of structure and power: Which ethnic categories are available in a society for one to be sorted into, and who gets to do the sorting. The symbolic ethnicity model emphasizes the emotional and volitional dimensions of ethnic identification, but it does not address the political and dialectical aspects of ethnic categorization.

There is another important consequence of embracing fully the notion that symbolic ethnicity: It is primarily a matter of individual choice. Ethnic options are much more available to white Americans than to individuals of color, and they can thus be understood as a manifestation of white privilege. Whether or not to have an ethnicity is something over which nonwhites have much less control. As Waters notes, the result is that having ethnic options tends to reinforce whites' view of nonwhites as resisting assimilation, rejecting a color-blind society, and clinging to racial difference: If whites can choose not to have an ethnicity, can blacks choose not to have a race?

Despite the limitations and critiques of the symbolic ethnicity model of contemporary ethnic identification in the West, researchers continue to note the power and allure of the symbolic aspects of ethnicity. In *Ethnicity and Race* (1998), Steven Cornell and Douglas Hartmann discuss "thick" and "thin" ethnicity to distinguish between aspects of ethnicity that have a significant impact on individuals' lives and behaviors ("thick") and the more symbolic, optional ("thin") form of ethnicity. Christopher Fries, a professor of sociology at the University of Calgary, argues that ethnicity can be seen as a repository of symbolic capital, or personal social worth, where cultural meanings are symbolically negotiated and where individuals can emphasize ethnicity to obtain a sense of belonging while downplaying inconvenient ethnic traditions. Research shows that ethnic symbols can be imbued with great meaning and link individuals to their ethnic community and that social ties with families or other ethnic networks reinforce the importance of ethnicity in adding meaning and solidarity to social relationships. The Indian journalist Syed Ali notes that while symbolic ethnicity is elective, it often occurs in a collective framework, and that it sometimes has the capacity to subvert or challenge stereotypical views of outsiders.

Symbolic ethnicity is both ubiquitous and dynamic. Ethnic identities can change over time, depending on geographical considerations, residential patterns, political opportunities, and economic resources. As Mary Kelly points out in her 2000 article "Ethnic Pilgrimages," patterns of ethnic identification can also be affected by events in ancestral homelands and can take the form of ethnic pilgrimages. Instead of being passively influenced by events that they read about in newspapers, ethnic pilgrims decide to experience the "authentic" life of their ancestors by visiting their ancestral homelands, and sometimes by participating in redevelopment projects. Ethnic pilgrims often develop ties with relatives who never immigrated, start businesses in their homeland, or simply take a vacation in a country that has symbolic meaning for them. Although such pilgrimages can reinforce or strengthen ethnic identity, they also can weaken ethnic identity if previously held ideal expectations about the ancestral homeland are violated. In fact, a common complaint of ethnic pilgrims is that the food they eat in their homeland is not "authentic" because it does not taste like the Americanized version of the food. Sometimes the reality confronted in ethnic homelands can overwhelm symbolic ethnic identities. But it can also strengthen them or make them more "authentic." In fact, upon their return, ethnic pilgrims are often regarded as "experts" by their co-ethnics.

Symbolic ethnicity emphasizes the immigrant experience in the United States, and for that reason, the model has been taken to task by scholars who insist that researchers need to take into account the importance of ethnicity to people in postcolonial settings as well as those facing the fragmentation and refragmentation of industrial societies. Ethnic resurgences, symbolic or otherwise, can lead to increased conflict over ethnicity, particularly in postcolonial societies such as India, the Philippines, or Nigeria. Because of the role of migration in the production of new ethnic groups and identities, transnationalism and globalization promise a continuing place for symbolic ethnicity in contemporary states.

BIBLIOGRAPHY

Alba, Richard. 1992. *Ethnic Identity: The Transformation of White America.* New Haven, CT: Yale University Press.

Ali, Syed. 2002. "Collective and Elective Ethnicity: Caste among Urban Muslims in India." *Sociological Forum* 17 (4): 593–620.

Bakalian, Anny. 1993. *Armenian-Americans: From Being to Feeling Armenian.* New Brunswick, NY: Transaction Books.

Barth, Fredrik. 1969. *Ethnic Groups and Boundaries.* Boston: Little, Brown.

Cornell, Stephen, and Douglas Hartmann. 1998. *Ethnicity and Race: Making Identities in a Changing World.* Thousand Oaks, CA: Pine Forge Press.

Deloria, Philip J. 1999. *Playing Indian.* New Haven, CT: Yale University Press.

Erdmans, Mary. 1998. *Opposite Poles: Immigrants and Ethnics in Polish Chicago, 1976–1990.* University Park: Pennsylvania State University Press.

Fishman, Joshua. 1985. *The Rise and Fall of the Ethnic Revival.* Berlin: Mouton.

Fries, Christopher. 2005. "Ethnocultural Space and the Symbolic Negotiation of Alternative as 'Cure.'" *Canadian Ethnic Studies Journal* 37: 87–100.

Gans, Herbert. 1979. "Symbolic Ethnicity: The Future of Ethnic Groups and Cultures in America." *Ethnic and Racial Studies* 2 (1): 1–20.

Kelly, Mary E. 2000. "Ethnic Pilgrimages: People of Lithuanian Descent in Lithuania." *Sociological Spectrum* 20 (1): 65–91.

Kivisto, Peter, and Ben Nefzger. 1993. "Symbolic Ethnicity and American Jews: The Relationship of Ethnic Identity and Group Affiliation." *Social Science Journal* 30: 1–12.

Nagel, Joane. 1994. "Constructing Ethnicity: Creating and Recreating Ethnic Identity and Culture." *Social Problems* 41 (1): 152–176.

Waters, Mary. 1990. *Ethnic Options: Choosing Identities in America.* Berkeley: University of California Press.

Yancey, William, Eugene Erickson, and Richard Juliani. 1976. "Emergent Ethnicity: A Review and Reformulation." *American Sociological Review* 41 (3): 391–403.

Mary E. Kelly
Joane Nagel

T

TAY-SACHS AND "JEWISH" DISEASES

Tay-Sachs disease (TSD) is a rare metabolic disorder prevalent in, but not exclusive to, Jews of Eastern European, or *Ashkenazi,* descent. Though most commonly associated with Ashkenazi Jews, TSD has also been found in some French-Canadian communities in eastern Quebec, among the French-Americans of southwestern Louisiana, and, to a lesser extent, in the general population. TSD has several forms, including the juvenile and late-onset adult variations, but the most frequently occurring (though still rare) form is the classic and fatal infantile Tay-Sachs. (Other so-called Jewish diseases include Niemann-Pick, Canavan's, and Gaucher's disease.)

TSD is caused by a genetic mutation that affects the body's manufacturing of the Hex A enzyme, which functions to regulate the level of lipids (fat) in the brain and nervous system. When this enzyme is deficient, an excess of fat accumulates, leading to profound neurological deterioration. In Infantile TSD, early signs include red spots on the retinas, enlargement of the head due to the increase of water around the brain, an alteration in muscle tone, hyperacusis (extreme sensitivity to sound), mental retardation, and social withdrawal. In time the vision becomes completely impaired and the child becomes paralyzed, with death usually occurring by the age of four or five. Infantile Tay-Sachs is considered the most severe of childhood lipid-storage disorders.

As one of the first of a series of genetic diseases identified at the molecular level using recombinant DNA technology, TSD has become widely understood in Mendelian terms to be an autosomal recessive disorder. The child of two genetic carriers or *heterozygotes* has a one-in-four chance of inheriting the allele for TSD from both parents and subsequently developing the disease. The chromosomal connection was determined in 1969 by the American neuroscientist John O'Brien, and screening technology for the disease was subsequently developed in the early 1970s. Since that time, Jewish individuals have participated in Tay-Sachs blood screening programs throughout the world, and along with the use of pedigrees and genetically strategic mate selection, such widespread genetic screening has led to the virtual eradication of this disease, at least among the world's Jewish communities.

TSD is one of many diseases that are more common in an ethno-racial group and have been labeled as ethno-racial diseases. In reality, however, it is not possible to identify pure races based on gene frequencies, so there is really no such thing as a "Jewish disease" per se (nor a black, Italian, Aboriginal, or other racial or ethnic disease.) As Robert Pollack argues, "Jews are not in fact a single biological family; there are no DNA sequences common to all Jews and present only in Jews." Thus, so-called Jewish diseases, such as TSD, are evidence rather of a shared ancestry, including "periodic massacres of such ferocity that only a small number of families were able to survive." That a proportion of Jews possesses similar genetic mutations "suggests that the Jews whose ancestors came from the Pale—about nine of every ten Jews alive today—are the descendants of a small remnant of a few thousand families who survived a particularly devastating pogrom in the Pale of the mid-1600s" (Pollack 1999, p. 194). In other words, there are a number of single-gene traits (Tay-Sachs being one of them) that, if used as loci to regroup populations, would not yield the racial groups assigned by classical physical anthropologists.

Nevertheless, the construction of racial disease categories has long been a means of demarcating human groups. Sickle-cell anemia, for example, has been classified as a "black disease," or a disease of "negro blood," since it was first diagnosed in 1910 (Tapper 1999). Though it begins several decades earlier, the history of Tay-Sachs disease takes a similarly racialist trajectory, insofar as it has, since the outset of its history in the late nineteenth century, always been seen as a "Jewish disease," despite evidence that it occurs in other populations.

The remainder of this entry will consider this perception in its historical and sociological context. In particular, it will describe the early discovery and medical racialization of TSD (its construction as a racial disease) in terms of anti-immigrationism directed at Jews, especially in the United States in the 1910s and 1920s, when both Jewish immigration and the discourse of eugenics were on the rise.

EARLY DISCOVERY AND RACIALIZATION

The symptoms of TSD were first described in 1881 by the British ophthalmologist and surgeon Warren Tay (1843–1927). At a meeting of the Opthalmological Society of the United Kingdom (recorded in the first volume of its *Transactions*), he reported that, upon examination of his patient's eyes with an ophthalmoscope, he had observed an inexplicable "brownish-red, fairly circular spot" at the center of the optic discs. In the society's *Transactions* of 1884, Tay published a similar description—the third instance of the disorder in the same family.

A few years later, in 1887, the American neurologist Bernard Sachs (1858-1944) made a similar report, though he had not yet heard of Tay's discoveries. Sachs began his medical career in New York, where he had a private practice for the treatment of mental and nervous diseases. By 1887 Sachs was widely regarded as one of America's leading clinical neurologists and had been appointed as an instructor at the New York Polyclinic Hospital. It was there that he reported on his first case of "arrested cerebral development" (as he described it), which he presented before the American Neurological Association and then reported in *The Journal of Nervous and Mental Disease*. Sachs also described a red spot in the eyes of his two-year-old patient, a little girl he referred to as "S."

In 1896, in a report in the same journal, Sachs named the condition "Amaurotic Family Idiocy" (though it would not be long before doctors began to refer to the disease as Tay-Sachs). Still unaware of Tay's earlier reports, the fact that Sachs chose to include "familial" in the disease name is significant, because it reflected the growing practice of tracing patients' lineage as part of the diagnosis of TSD. In other words, it was already becoming apparent to doctors that the disease was hereditary. What was less clear to them, however, was how inheritance worked exactly. (Although Mendel had already published his work on pea plants, it would be decades before his findings were formally taken up.)

The emergent nature of the understanding of heredity led physicians to entertain various causation theories, including the possibility that TSD was transmitted through breast milk. This theory was rejected because, as Dr. Sachs observed (in *Osler's Modern Medicine,* 1910), several of his young patients had not been "nursed by their own mothers, but by wet-nurses of a different race and different nationality."

With this observation, Sachs introduced a key element of TSD, namely the perception that it was exclusive to the apparently overly inbred "Hebrews," especially those from Russia. In fact, it was not long after Sachs's first case report in 1887 that TSD was declared a Jewish disease. Indeed, by 1895, Dr. Sachs had reported in *A Treatise on the Nervous Diseases of Children for Physicians and Students* that of the cases known so far, the condition had been observed almost entirely among Jews.

Many doctors agreed that "genuine TSD" was exclusive to the Jews. In 1910 the physicians Hildred B. Carlyll and F. Mott recorded in the *Proceedings of the Royal Society of Medicine* that the Jews possessed an "inborn lack of specific vital energy of the nerve-cells, due to a racial inherited failure of the germinal determinants of the nervous system." In contrast, the cases with special features of interest were those in children who, according to the physician R. Sattler, "can not like all others reported be said to have a Jewish parentage" (Sattler 1914). These remarks suggest that the Jewish heritage of patients with Tay-Sachs was the defining feature of the disease. Thus, evidence of TSD in Gentile patients was met with skepticism, especially if the doctor believed that there was Jewish blood in the patient's history.

However, not all doctors were prepared to accept the classification of TSD as exclusively Jewish, nor the notion that Jews were biologically inferior, and to this end they adapted the discourse of race science in ways that served their own interests (Rafael Falk, 1998; Eric L. Goldstein, 1997; and Mitchell Hart, 2001). For some, such as the British Jewish biologist and physician Redcliffe N. Salaman (1874–1955), the goal was to counter anti-Semitism by advocating Zionism. Salaman used the tools and language of genetics and inheritance to show that the Jews were distinct and in need of their own Jewish state. Amaurotic Family Idiocy was, for him, a key indicator of Jewish raciality: As he wrote in a 1911 article titled "Heredity and the Jew," published in the *Journal of*

Genetics, according to "all the authorities" TSD was "probably unknown outside the Jewish people." Salaman later argued before the 1921 Second International Congress of Eugenics (published as *Eugenics in Race and State: Second International Congress of Eugenics, 1921,* Vol. 2, edited by Charles B. Davenport) that Jewish Tay-Sachs was evidence in favor of the Jews' "ethnic differentiation."

For others, such as Dr. Maurice Fishberg, race science provided a means of advocating for Jewish assimilation into U.S. society. As an anthropologist, the medical examiner for the United Hebrew Charities, and himself a Russian Jewish immigrant to New York, Fishberg was a strong opponent of Zionism and in his 1911 treatise *The Jews: A Study of Race and Environment* he used race science to show that Jews were no more diseased than or inferior to other inhabitants of New York.

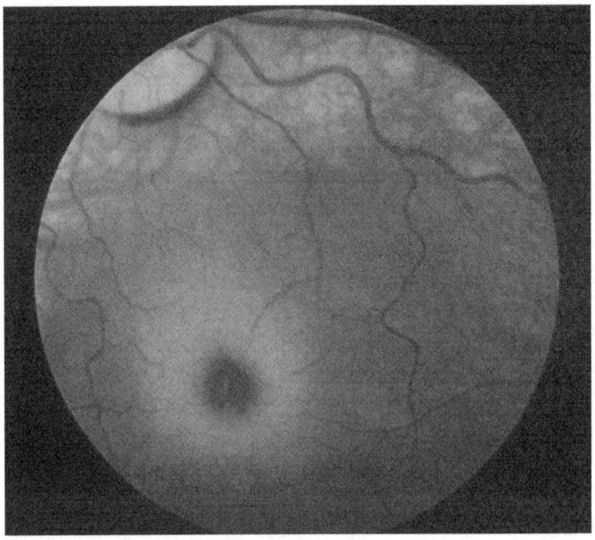

Effects of Tay-Sachs's Disease on the Eye. *Tay-Sachs disease (TSD) is a rare metabolic disorder prevalent in, but not exclusive to, Jews of eastern European, or Ashkenazi, descent.*
© DR. CHARLES J. BALL/CORBIS.

TAY-SACHS DISEASE AND ANTI-IMMIGRATIONISM

For those who saw the Jews as a problematic racial group—biological arguments served a different set of interests; specifically, they were used to argue against Jewish immigration to the United States from eastern Europe. Second only to Italians, eastern European Jews (of varying degrees of religiosity) were increasingly constructed as troublesome and problematic as their numbers grew (between 1881 and 1914, more than two million Jews entered the United States). Various articles on eugenics and public health that appeared in periodicals such as *Popular Science Monthly* (e.g., Alfred C. Reed's "Immigration and the Public Health" and J. G. Wilson's "The Crossing of the Races") typified the view that Jewish immigrants had undesirable habits—such as inbreeding or "racial incest" (Friedman, quoted in Reed 1913, p. 325)—and were inherently "clannish" (Wilson 1911, p. 494–495) because they continued to practice their distinct religion, speak their own language (Yiddish), and had a system of organization based on their communities of origin, newspapers, theater, and more (Waxman 1999). These perceived faults amplified the Jews' tendency to isolate themselves rather than assimilate American standards, as well as exacerbate their marginal status as "the Other." Central to their marginalization was their construction as a "community of the ill" and a "collective at risk"—a stereotype that reinforced a widely held perception that race and disease were linked (Gilman 2003) and reason enough to implement restrictive immigration policies. Reports of Tay-Sachs from this period suggested that the alleged link between race and disease was not limited to infectious conditions such as tuberculosis, typhus, and cholera, but came to include genetic disorders such as TSD as well (Kraut 1994; Markel 1997).

In fact, the organized eugenics movement that had emerged in the United States by 1910, with its belief that social ills were the result of defects in heredity, along with the anti-immigrationist opinion that "the gates [had been] left open too long" (as the well-known nativist Edward Alsworth Ross put it in his *Roads to Social Peace, The Weil Lectures on American Citizenship* [1924]), led to the growing view that America's immigration problem was "at heart a biological one" (Higham 1992, p. 151). Kenneth M. Ludmerer (1972) similarly describes the emergence of genetic theories that marked southern and eastern European immigrants as biologically inferior and warned that race-mixing would lead to the nation's overall decline. These sorts of arguments directly informed American policy to restrict immigration. With a growing resentment directed at Jews (and other immigrants) who were seen to be taking what few jobs were still available, initial temporary legislation to restrict immigration to certain quotas passed through Congress in 1921. By 1924 a more permanent piece of legislation, the Johnson-Reed Act, further restricted immigration.

It is not coincidental that the TSD cases reported in the years leading up to and following this legislation contained some of the most explicit racialist and nativist rhetoric, portraying "the Jew" as profoundly susceptible to nervous diseases (including Tay-Sachs) due to an inferior racial constitution. Consistent with this was the tendency for doctors to include in their reports of TSD specifics about their patients' foreign origins, often noting how long it had been since the patient's family had immigrated to the United States, or simply describing the patients, as Drs. Carlyll and Mott did in 1910, as being from "alien families." Some doctors emphasized that although there had been reports of the disease from eastern Europe, it was really a problem for immigrant families in America. What they were implying by this was that the foreign-born population was bringing their health problems with them to American soil. There is certainly no mistaking this sentiment in Dr. Earl Tarr's observation in a 1916 report in the *Louisville Monthly Journal of Medicine and Surgery* that his colleagues "frequently stated that the condition is rare in Russia and that it occurs in children [only] after they have emigrated to the United States." Not surprisingly, this was seen as burdensome to American society. In contrast, Gentile patients demonstrating symptoms of TSD were usually described simply as being of American extraction, and often as showing no evidence of consanguinity (i.e., of inbreeding).

Reading the early reports of TSD against the backdrop of racial and anti-immigration ideology makes it possible to see how this disease category was deployed and how medical discourses both shape and are shaped by cultural concerns. Tay-Sachs represented a threat that was not confined to the children in whose bodies it manifested in the immediate present; rather, it was seen as having the potential to be a permanent and damaging feature of American society as long as Jewish immigrants continued to have unfettered access to the nation. Thus, the early history of TSD was as much about foreignness and immigration as it was about health and disease.

SEE ALSO *Diseases, Racial; Sickle Cell Anemia.*

BIBLIOGRAPHY

Falk, Rafael. 1998. "Zionism and the Biology of the Jews." *Science in Context* 3–4: 587–607.

Fishberg, Maurice. 1911. *The Jews: A Study of Race and Environment.* New York: Charles Scribner's Sons.

Gilman, Sander. 2003. *Jewish Frontiers: Essays on Bodies, Histories, and Identities.* New York: Palgrave Macmillan.

Goldstein, Eric L. 1997. "'Different Blood Flows in Our Veins': Race and Jewish Self-Definition in Late Nineteenth Century America." *American Jewish History* 86 (1): 29–55.

Hart, Mitchell B. 2001. "Racial Science, Social Science, and the Politics of Jewish Assimilation." *Isis* 90: 268–297.

Higham, John. 1992 (1955). *Strangers in the Land: Patterns of American Nativism, 1860–1925.* New Brunswick, NJ: Rutgers University Press.

Kraut, Alan M. 1994. *Silent Travelers: Germs, Genes, and the "Immigrant Menace."* New York: Basic Books.

Ludmerer, Kenneth M. 1972. *Genetics and American Society: A Historical Appraisal.* Baltimore, MD: Johns Hopkins University Press.

Markel, Howard. 1997. *Quarantine! East European Jewish Immigrants and the New York City Epidemics of 1892.* Baltimore, MD: Johns Hopkins University Press.

Paul, Diane B. 1995. *Controlling Human Heredity: 1865 to the Present.* Atlantic Highlands, NJ: Humanities Press.

Pollack, Robert. 1999. *The Missing Moment: How the Unconscious Shapes Modern Science.* Boston: Houghton Mifflin.

Reed, Alfred C. 1913. "Immigration and the Public Health." *Popular Science Monthly* Vol. LXXXIII: 320–338.

Reuter, Shelley Z. 2006. "The Genuine Jewish Type: Racial Ideology and Anti-Immigrationism in Early Medical Writing about Tay-Sachs Disease." *Canadian Journal of Sociology* 34 (1): 291–323.

Ross, Edward Alsworth. 1924. *Roads to Social Peace. The Weil Lectures on American Citizenship.* Chapel Hill: University of North Carolina Press.

Salaman, Redcliffe N. 1921. *Eugenics in Race and State: Second International Congress of Eugenics.* Vol. 2, edited by Charles B. Davenport. *Journal of Heredity* 12: 219–223.

———. 1911. "Heredity and the Jew." *Journal of Genetics.*

Tapper, Melbourne. 1999. *In the Blood: Sickle Cell Anemia and the Politics of Race.* Philadelphia: University of Pennsylvania Press.

Waxman, Chaim I. 1999. "The Sociohistorical Background and Development of America's Jews." In *Jews in America: A Contemporary Reader*, edited by Roberta Rosenberg Farber and Chaim Waxman. Hanover, NH: Brandeis University Press.

Wilson, J. G. 1911. "The Crossing of the Races." *Popular Science Monthly* November, 79, 29: 486–495.

Shelley Z. Reuter

TELEVISION

In his book *Watching Race*, Herman Gray describes television as a medium used to "engage, understand, negotiate, and make sense of the material circumstances of [everyday life]" (Gray 1995, p. 43). A person's entire worldview is obviously influenced by many factors, but it remains evident that, in many parts of the world, television plays a significant role in shaping public perceptions of race and racial differences.

Racialized groups are relegated to the role of the "invisible other" in television programming in the United States. Viewers of most commercial programming are led to believe racial/ethnic groups are virtually nonexistent, and that those that do exist reside in racial worlds or on television channels of their own. Cultural programming is needed that expresses the range of experiences of African Americans, Native Americans, Asian Americans, and Latino Americans. In the early twenty-first century, however, the major television networks (CBS, NBC, ABC, and FOX) continue to marginalize and stigmatize racial minorities in their programming.

AFRICAN AMERICANS

In early television programming, African-American performers occupied stereotypical, unflattering roles. These actors gradually became a part of mainstream society at the expense of self-degradation, and the visual images of blacks on network television created a false portrayal of African-American identity. Such controlling images as the Jezebel, mammy, servant, matriarch, buffoon, minstrel, and slave presented a distorted reality of racial identity for African Americans. Shows such as *Amos and Andy* (1951–1953), *Beulah* (1950–1953), and *Jack Benny* (1950–1965) portrayed African Americans as lacking intellect and seemingly enjoying their subservient and less powerful positions in the world. As an example, the show *Beulah* typified the "good old-fashioned minstrel show" (Haggins 2001, p. 250). The lead character, Beulah, was the stereotypical domestic servant who was "happy" with her lot in life serving her boss. Similarly, her friend Oriole was her queen-sized "childlike idiot friend," perpetuating the "pickaninny" stereotype of the bulging-eyed child with thick lips, unkempt hair, and eating a slice of watermelon. The third character typified the "Uncle Tom" and "Coon" character. Beulah's boyfriend Bill embodied what it allegedly meant to be a black man. While in the presence of whites, Bill was hardworking, dependable, and content. In his "real" state, however, he was lazy and avoided the work and responsibilities he should have held as a man. Although more recent televisual depictions have not been as blatantly racist as this, shows such as *Beulah* paved the way for controlling images to be constructed, transformed, and perpetuated in all forms of media. Unfortunately, these images continue to create an illusion of African Americans as subservient and of less value, in addition to being criminal, predatory, and a threat to European Americans. These negative portrayals are a result of slavery and the objectification of African slaves as sexual creatures and servants to the whites who colonized North America, a stigma that remains in place in the twenty-first century.

Television portrayals have, to some degree, begun to challenge many of the long-standing controlling images associated with African Americans. Although they may not be as blatantly racist as they were in the past, networks, reporters, and television writers still perpetuate a subtle form of media racism that R. R. Means Coleman has dubbed "neominstrelsy." According to Coleman, neominstrelsy refers to contemporary versions of the minstrel images of African Americans that were pervasive in early television programming. The early images set the stage for current media images, which often still function to sustain the myth that African Americans are unscrupulous, lack morals, and are only capable of entertaining others through comedy. According to the media reasearcher Robert Entman, "images of Blacks are produced by network news [that] reinforce whites' antagonism toward Blacks," and these images perpetuate stereotypic depictions and contribute to this cycle of television racism (Entman 1994, p. 516). Because television is one of the most heavily used media for information and entertainment purposes, it is imperative that media outlets and creators begin to rethink how these distorted images create an unrealistic picture of African-American life.

Unlike other racial groups, African Americans have been depicted in many television shows in which they have made up the vast majority of the cast. These shows include, but are not limited to, *Good Times* (1974–1979), *The Cosby Show* (1984–1992), *A Different World* (1987–1993), *Moesha* (1996–2001), *Sister, Sister* (1994–1999), *Girlfriends* (2000–), *Half & Half* (2002–), and *Everybody Hates Chris* (2005–). These shows have portrayed the diversity that exists within the African-American community. Yet while different kinds of relationships and life experiences have been portrayed in these shows, the constant is that African Americans are generally confined to shows that have a neominstrelsy theme. The characters are comedic and, to varying degrees, embody the Jezebel, mammy, matriarch, buffoon, minstrel, and "Stepin Fetchit" stereotypes. These images sustain the myth that African Americans are unscrupulous, lack morals, and are only capable of entertaining others through comedy. *The Cosby Show* was an exception, however, for it attempted to debunk these stereotypes. Yet while the show was praised for communicating a positive image of African-American identity, it was also criticized for not being "black" enough.

In the 2006–2007 television season, there were fewer than seven programs with a predominately African-American cast. While this may be better than blacks

***Bill Cosby in* The Cosby Show.** The Cosby Show *was both praised for communicating a positive image African Americans and criticized for not being "black" enough.* AP IMAGES.

having no visibility at all, little is being done to deconstruct societal beliefs about Africans Americans. Sadly, the shows are rarely fully developed and confine blacks to the genre of comedy, making it difficult to counter long-standing controlling images that impact real world perceptions of the African-American community.

NATIVE AMERICANS

Native Americans are rarely portrayed in movies or on television, and when they are shown they are often wearing stereotypical attire (i.e., headdress) or armed with antiquated artillery (i.e., bow and arrow), ready to fulfill the all too familiar image of the "noble" savage. These images perpetuate a negative image of racial/ethnic identity for First Nations people and instill the belief that being Native American is a "thing of the past." Audiences are led to believe that Native Americans either do not exist or are too small in number to be fairly represented. No matter what period of time in which a story is being told, "contemporary portrayals [of First Nations persons] are typically presented in an historic context" (Merskin 1998, p. 335).

This depiction is a visual representation of a linguistic image accepted as an accurate symbol of First Nations people. They are restricted to an image of being a homogenous group of people lacking any distinctive qualities (e.g., tribes) or heterogeneity. The most pervasive and troubling image is the "conventionalized imagery [that] depicts Indians as wild, savage, heathen, silent, noble, childlike, uncivilized, premodern, immature, ignorant, bloodthirsty, and historical or timeless, all in juxtaposition to the white civilized, mature, modern (usually) Christian American man" (Meek 2006, p. 119). Other stereotypes include the portrayal of Native Americans as drunkards, gamblers, and wards of the government, and these images are too often perceived as accurate representations of the original inhabitants of North America. Television programs with a periodic or a recurring Native American character include, but are not limited to, *The Lone Ranger* (1949–1957), *Dr. Quinn, Medicine Woman* (1993–1998), *Walker, Texas Ranger* (1993–2001), *Northern Exposure* (1990–1995), *McGyver* (1985–1992), and *Quantum Leap* (1989–1993).

These shows portray First Nations people as either occupying a space on the Western frontier or being virtually invisible on television's racial landscape. This portrayal is attributed to movie and television "Westerns," which created the stereotypical genre of media representations. According to the sociologist Steve Mizrach, "Indians are shown as bloodthirsty savages, obstacles to progress, predators on peaceful settlers, enemy 'hostiles' of the U.S. Cavalry, etc.... the political context of the Indian Wars completely disappears" (Mizrach 1998). To this day, notes Duane Champagne of the Native Nations Law and Policy Center at the University of California, Los Angeles, "Hollywood prefers to isolate its Indians safely within the romantic past, rather than take a close look at Native American issues in the contemporary world" (Champagne 1994, p. 719). These archaic, inaccurate portrayals are further problematized by "images in which the linguistic behaviors of others are simplified and seen as deriving from those persons' essences" (Meek 2006, p. 95) and "remind us of an oppressive past" (Merskin 2001, p. 160). Through these depictions, First Nations people are presented as "nonnative, incompetent speaker[s] of English" (Meek 2006, p. 96). This is a strategy used to emphasize "Indian civilized otherness by having the character speak English in monosyllables" (Taylor 2000, p. 375).

U.S. companies have long used images of American Indians for product promotion, mainly to "build an association with an idealized and romanticized notion of the past" (Merskin 2001, p. 160). Products such as Land O' Lakes butter, Sue Bee honey, Big Chief sugar, and Crazy Horse malt liquor have stereotypic caricatures on their labels that are supposed to reflect Native American ethnicity, but which are actually "dehumanizing, one-dimensional images based on a tragic past" (Merskin 2000, p. 167).

ASIAN AMERICANS

Asian Americans are represented on television as a homogenous group of people whose ethnicity is Chinese, Korean, or Japanese. This worldview of a population that is in reality very ethnically diverse is both problematic and restricting. Stereotypes of Asian Americans emerged from efforts by whites to oppress racial groups deemed inferior, and from a nineteenth-century fear of an Asian expansion into white occupations and communities, often referred to as the "Yellow Peril." These controlling images emerged in order to reduce Asian-American men and women to caricatures based on how the dominant society perceived their racial and gendered identities.

There are both general cultural stereotypes and gender-specific stereotypes of Asian Americans disseminated in the media. General cultural stereotypes include assumptions that Asian Americans are: (1) the model minority, (2) perpetual foreigners, (3) inherently and passively predatory immigrants who never give back, (4) restricted to clichéd occupations (e.g., restaurant workers, laundry workers, martial artists), and (5) inherently comical or sinister. Controlling, gender-specific images of Asian-American identity include Charlie Chan, Fu Manchu, Dragon Lady, and China Doll. Charlie Chan and Fu Manchu are emasculated stereotypes of Asian men as eunuchs or asexual. Charlie Chan, a detective character, was "effeminate, wimpy," and "dainty," (Sun 2003, p. 658), as well as "a mysterious man, possessing awesome powers of deduction" (Shah 2003). He was also deferential to whites, "non-threatening, and revealed his 'Asian wisdom' in snippets of 'fortune-cookie' observations." Conversely, there is the Fu Manchu character, who is "a cruel, cunning, diabolical representative of the 'yellow peril'" (Sun 2003, p. 658).

Asian-American women are portrayed as being hypersexual–or as the opposite of "asexual" Asian men (Sun 2003). The Lotus Blossom (i.e., China Doll, Geisha Girl, shy Polynesian beauty) is "a sexual-romantic object," utterly feminine, delicate, and welcome respites from their often loud, independent American counterparts" (Sun 2003, p. 659). Dragon Lady is the direct opposite of the Lotus Blossom. She is "cunning, manipulative, and evil," "aggressive," and "exudes exotic danger" (Sun 2003, p. 659). There are also the "added characteristics of being sexually alluring and sophisticated and determined to seduce and corrupt white men" (Shah 2003).

Shows with at least one recurring character of Asian descent include: *The Courtship of Eddie's Father* (1969–1972), *Happy Days* (1974–1984), *Quincy, M.E.* (1976–1983), *All-American Girl* (1994–1995), *Ally McBeal* (1997–2002), *Mad TV* (1995–), *Half* & *Half* (2002–), *Lost* (2004–), and *Grey's Anatomy* (2005–). Examples of how long-held stereotypes of Asian-American women are perpetuated include the character Ling Woo on *Ally McBeal* and Miss Swan on *Mad TV*. Ling Woo was an attorney (portrayed by the Chinese actress Lucy Liu) who was "tough, rude, candid, aggressive, sharp tongued, and manipulative" and hypersexualized (Sun 2003, p. 661). She was also a feminist, in stark contrast with past portrayals of Asian women. While some Asian Americans believed Ling was a stereotype breaker, she still perpetuated the Dragon Lady stereotype, especially when she "growl[ed] like an animal, breathing fire at Ally, walking into the office to the music of Wicked Witch of the West from *The Wizard of Oz*" (Sun 2003, p. 661).

Miss Swan is an Asian-American character on FOX's sketch comedy show *Mad TV*. She is played by the Jewish comedian Alexandria Borstein and represents an example of "yellowface," which is the Asian equivalent of blackface and refers to a non-Asian person "performing" an Asian identity. Miss Swan is "a babbling nail salon owner with a weak grasp of the English language" (Armstrong 2000), and she is always depicted as the perpetual foreigner, inherently predatory and restricted to the occupation of nail salon owner. She is also a comic character who speaks broken, unintelligible English. Ms. Borstein is not Asian, which has appeared to be okay with the show's audience. This mixed casting of Asian characters was also a problem with the short-lived sitcom *All-American Girl*, which portrayed a Korean family but cast only one Korean actor (the comedian Margaret Cho). All the other actors were either Japanese American or Chinese American, thus perpetuating the assumption that Asians are interchangeable and must assimilate to mainstream (white) culture in order to "fit in."

The controlling images of Asian Americans distort what it means to belong to this very heterogeneous ethnic group. Attempts to diversify television programming were made with *All-American Girl*, but much more work is needed to accurately represent Asian Americans. Both *Lost* and *Grey's Anatomy* have strong and visible Asian-American actors as part of the regular cast. As the journalist Donal Brown notes, UCLA researchers believe these shows and characters are complex and have great appeal across racial and ethnic groups, but they are "concerned that the Asian American characters on television [are] portrayed in high status occupations perpetuating the 'model minority' stereotype" (Brown 2006).

LATINO AMERICANS

"Latino representation in Hollywood is not keeping pace with the explosion of the U.S. Hispanic population, and depictions of Latinos in television and film too often reinforce stereotypes" (Stevens 2004). Television shows purport to reflect reality in their programs, but they rarely, if ever, do so when casting characters. According to advocacy group Children Now, Latinos make up over 12.5 percent of the U.S. population, yet only 2 percent of characters on television are Latino (Stevens 2004), not including those Latinos who are portraying white (non-ethnic) characters.

Latino Americans have been subjugated and oppressed as immigrants "invading" U.S. culture. Contemporary immigration issues notwithstanding, the most prevailing stereotypes associated with Latino-American males are the glorified drug dealer, the "Latin lover," the "greaser," and the "bandito" (Márquez 2004). Latina women are depicted as deviant, "frilly señoritas" or as "volcanic temptresses," and Latino families, in general, are "unintelligent," "passive," "deviant," and "dependent" (Márquez 2004). These depictions may be rare, but they can undoubtedly have a significant impact on perceptions and attitudes people develop about individuals of Latin descent. Images of Latino Americans do not reflect the "Latino explosion" in U.S. culture, and they ultimately reinforce the stereotypes that should be countered. These images may not be fully positive or fully negative, but their rarity makes it more problematic that these images are so restricting.

Notable television programs featuring or including a Latino-American character include: *Chico and the Man* (1974–1978), *Luis* (2003), *The Ortegas* (2003), *NYPD Blue* (1993–2005), *Will* & *Grace* (1998–2006), *Popstar* (2001), *George Lopez* (2002–), *The West Wing* (1999–2006), *The Brothers Garcia* (2000–2003), *Taina* (2001–2002), *Dora the*

America Ferrera as Ugly Betty, 2006. *The popular series* Ugly Betty *features a Latino woman who aspires for success in the fashion industry, but is faced with opposition because she does not fit the industry standard of beauty.* ABC-TV/THE KOBAL COLLECTION/FELD, DANNY.

Explorer (2000–), *Desperate Housewives* (2004–), *CSI: Miami* (2002–), and *Ugly Betty* (2006–). Latino-American culture has had tremendous appeal in popular culture, yet members of the different ethnic groups within the Latino community remain marginalized in primetime television programming. One promising program that can potentially debunk these controlling images is *Ugly Betty*, starring the actress America Ferrera. Betty is aspiring for success in the fashion industry and is faced with opposition because she does not fit the industry (read mainstream) cultural standard of beauty. Despite much opposition, she refuses to succumb to societal expectations and remains committed to not compromising her character and integrity.

Ugly Betty is based on an incredibly popular Columbian telenovela (soap opera), *Yo soy Betty, la fea*, that was very successful in Mexico, India, Russia, and Germany. Although the lead character defies conventional wisdom regarding televisual success, the show may presage an era in which issues concerning racial representation in television are dealt with onscreen as well as off.

Television demographics in the United States should mirror the racial demographics of both the country and the cities within which the television programs take place, but many analyses suggest they do not (see Márquez 2004). This becomes particularly salient for individuals who have had limited interpersonal contact with people from other racial groups. Diversifying television production teams and actors is an effective strategy for eradicating subtle and blatant racism, or "symbolic annihilation" (Meek 1998). Community activism is also a powerful tool in this regard. Through research and the creation of "diversity development" programs at networks like FOX, the national Children Now organization offers practical approaches to addressing racial representation in the media. Efforts by Children Now and other organizations committed to addressing issues of fair racial and ethnic representation in the media are critical in bringing about such change. It is only through education and formal efforts that programmers, scriptwriters, and other pivotal players can be made aware of the exclusionary nature of television. Awareness of such racism will ideally prompt the television community to become proactive in redefining their role in perpetuating controlling images that continue to plague twenty-first-century portrayals of racial groups.

SEE ALSO *Cultural Racism; Film and Asian Americans; Social Psychology of Racism; Stereotype Threat and Racial Stigma; Symbolic and Modern Racism.*

BIBLIOGRAPHY

Armstrong, Mark. 2000. "Mr. Wong, Miss Swan: Asian Stereotypes Attacked." E!-Online News, August 11. Available from http://www.eonline.com/news.

Brown, Donal. 2006. "Asian Americans Go Missing When It Comes to TV." Available from http://news.pacificnews.org/news/view_article.html?article_id=2187822d260441c375f65241320819d0.

Champagne, Duane, ed. 1994. *Native America: Portrait of the Peoples*. Detroit, MI: Visible Ink.

Chihara, Michelle. 2000. "There's Something About Lucy." *Boston Phoenix*, February 28. Also available from http://www.alternet.org/story/290/.

Collins, Patricia Hill. 1990. *Black Feminist Thought: Knowledge, Consciousness, and the Politics of Empowerment*. Boston: Unwin Hyman.

Entman, Robert. 1994. "Representation and Reality in the Portrayal of Blacks on Network Television Shows." *Journalism Quarterly* 71 (3): 509–520.

Gray, Herman. 1995. *Watching Race: Television and the Struggle for "Blackness."* Minneapolis: University of Minnesota Press.

Haggins, B. L. 2001. "Why 'Beulah' and 'Andy' Still Play Today: Minstrelsy in the New Millennium." *Emergences: Journal for the Study of Media & Composite Cultures* 11 (2): 249–267.

Inniss, Leslie B., and Joe R. Feagin. 1995. "The Cosby Show: The View from the Black Middle Class." *Journal of Black Studies* 25 (6): 692–711.

Mayeda, Daniel. M. "EWP Working to Increase Diversity in Television." USAsians.net. Available from http://us_asians.tripod.com/articles-eastwest.html.

Means Coleman, R. R. 1998. *African American Viewers and the Black Situation Comedy: Situating Racial Humor*. New York: Garland.

Meek, B. A. 2006. "And the Injun Goes 'How!': Representations of American Indian English in White Public Space." *Language in Society* 35 (1): 93–128.

Méndez-Méndez, Serafín, and Diane Alverio. 2002. *Network Brownout 2003: The Portrayal of Latinos in Network Television News*. Report Prepared for the National Association of Hispanic Journalists. Available from http://www.maynardije.org/resources/industry_studies.

Merskin, Debra. 1998. "Sending up Signals: A Survey of Native American Media Use and Representation in the Mass Media." *Howard Journal of Communications* 9: 333–345.

———. 2001. "Winnebagos, Cherokees, Apaches and Dakotas: The Persistence of Stereotyping of American Indians in American Advertising Brands." *Howard Journal of Communications* 12: 159–169.

Mizrach, Steve. 1998. "Do Electronic Mass Media Have Negative Effects on Indigenous People?" Available from http://www.fiu.edu/mizrachs/media-effects-indians.html.

Rebensdorf, Alicia. 2001. "The Network Brown-Out." AlterNet. Available from http://www.alternet.org.

Shah, Hemant. 2003. "'Asian Culture' and Asian American Identities in the Television and Film Industries of the United States." *Studies in Media & Information Literacy Education* 3. Also available from http://www.utpjournals.com/simile/issue11/shahX1.html.

Stevens, S. 2004. "Reflecting Reality: A Fordham Professor Testifies before Congress about the Dearth of Latinos on Television and in Film." Available at http://www.fordham.edu/campus_resources/public_affairs/inside_fordham/inside_fordham_archi/october_2004/news/professor_discusses__16624.asp.

Sun, Chyng Feng. 2003. "Ling Woo in Historical Context: The New Face of Asian American Stereotypes on Television." In *Gender, Race, and Class in Media: A Text-Reader*, 2nd ed., edited by Gail Dines and Jean M. Humez. Thousand Oaks, CA: Sage.

Taylor, Rhonda H. 2000. "Indian in the Cupboard: A Case Study in Perspective. *International Journal of Qualitative Studies in Education* 13 (4): 371–384.

Tina M. Harris

TEXAS RANGERS

The Texas Rangers are a modern law enforcement agency that traces its origins to 1823, when Stephen F. Austin, the leader of the Anglo colonists in Texas, proposed the formation of a volunteer force to defend white settlements from Indian raids. Formally established twelve years later, the constabulary gradually evolved from a group of citizen soldiers into a professional, paramilitary organization that served the needs of the state's political and business leaders. After 1870 the Rangers were invested with the responsibilities typical of peace officers. For much of the nineteenth century, however, Texas authorities used the constabulary to promote the state's territorial and economic development. This mission involved the expulsion of Native peoples, the defense of cattle syndicates from aggrieved homesteaders, and the policing of industrial disputes. The force achieved its greatest notoriety, however, by subjugating ethnic Mexicans in South Texas between 1850 and 1920.

Ranger anti-Mexican vigilance must be understood in the context of intense white prejudice against Tejanos (Mexican Texans), which in the nineteenth century flowed from a host of sources. For one thing, notwithstanding the fact that a number of Mexicans had fought alongside Sam Houston and other white leaders during the struggle for Texas independence, bitter memories of the slaughters perpetrated by the Mexican Army in 1836 at the Alamo and Goliad, coupled with doubts about Tejano political loyalty to the new Republic of Texas, fostered a climate of white distrust. Moreover, the southern origins of most Anglo-Texans imbued many of them with the racist tenets of *herrenvolk* democracy, characterized by a low opinion of those not belonging to the supposed master race. Ranger atrocities committed against Mexicans during the Mexican-American War—actions for which they became known as *los diablos Tejanos* (the Texan devils)—deepened the animosity between whites and Mexicans during the late 1840s.

Conditions for Texas Mexicans deteriorated rapidly after 1848. Although guaranteed equal citizenship by the Treaty of Guadalupe Hidalgo, Tejanos who elected to remain in the United States following the war became second-class citizens and suffered dispossession at the hands of a small but powerful Anglo elite that included Mifflin Kenedy, Richard King, Stephen Powers, and Charles Stillman. Throughout the 1850s, Texas Mexicans lost much of their land in the Nueces Strip (the area between the Nueces River and the Rio Grande), a process facilitated by tight white control of the legal establishment. Such injustices led some South Texas Mexicans to take up arms in the fall of 1859 under the leadership of Juan Cortina, a wealthy landowner. Although the rebellion was crushed the following spring, Ranger excesses during the fighting, which included the lynching of an elderly Cortina lieutenant, once again worsened relations between white Texans and Mexicans.

While the Civil War caused a lull in such hostilities, the period immediately after the conflict witnessed a surge in racial violence in South Texas, which was the result of widespread cattle rustling. Anglos blamed Mexicans (including Juan Cortina, who had taken refuge across the

Rio Grande in the Mexican state of Tamaulipas), but the question of theft was thorny, for Tejanos insisted that they were merely reclaiming livestock that had been stolen from them by whites since 1848. Responding to the unrest, in 1874 the Texas legislature institutionalized two divisions of the Rangers, with one of them, the Special Force, charged with ending alleged Mexican depredations in the Nueces Strip.

Under the command of Leander McNelly, a Confederate veteran of the Civil War, the Special Force initiated a brutal campaign against Mexican "bandits" (a ubiquitous pejorative intended to discredit Tejano grievances). In June 1875, for instance, McNelly's squad encountered a party of Mexicans herding a large group of cattle allegedly stolen from white ranchers. Without warning, the Rangers attacked them, killing all twelve of the suspected raiders and stacking their bodies in the plaza at Brownsville as a warning to other prospective rustlers. Later that same year, McNelly and his men crossed the Rio Grande into Mexico, where they hoped to recover another herd of supposedly stolen livestock. Acting on a bad tip, they ambushed the wrong ranch, killing at least five (and perhaps as many as thirty) *vaqueros* (Mexican cowboys). Though the Rangers continued on to their intended destination, they were intercepted by several hundred Mexicans, who drove them back to the Rio Grande. Once at the river, the Rangers dug in to fight, but they eventually crossed back into Texas under cover provided by a U.S. Army detachment posted nearby. Incredibly, McNelly bluffed the Mexicans into returning sixty-five cattle.

The Rangers employed other strategies besides ambush and invasion to eradicate cattle theft by Mexicans in South Texas, including torture and extrajudicial killings. Some of the latter were performed under the auspices of *la ley fuga*, or the "fugitive law," by which an unarmed suspect (allegedly in the act of escape) was shot and killed. (The "fugitive law" provided for the shooting of a criminal suspect who attempted escape; the Rangers exploited this provision, murdering Mexicans in cold blood and then claiming the prisoner had tried to flee.) The force also used intimidation and the threat of violence to hold Tejanos in thrall, as recalled by one member of McNelly's squad, Ranger N.A. Jennings. In his memoir, *A Texas Ranger* (1899), Jennings wrote that members of the Special Force visited border towns in the 1870s in order "to carry out a set policy of terrorizing the residents at every opportunity." Describing police tactics, he explained that, "If we could find a *fandango*, or Mexican dance, going on, we would enter the dancing-hall and break up the festivities by shooting out the lights" (pp. 151–152). Such actions made the Rangers hated among Tejanos, who used the derogatory term *rinche* to describe members of the constabulary.

As the nineteenth century waned, the Rangers broadened their efforts to subdue Mexican unrest in the Lone Star State. In 1877, near the West Texas town of El Paso, an ad hoc Ranger detachment attempted to quell a disturbance arising from the privatization by a white entrepreneur of salt lakes used communally by the area's large Mexican population. When local residents killed the Anglo businessman, a local merchant, and one of the Rangers, the detachment (augmented by vigilantes from New Mexico) perpetrated a series of rapes and murders against Mexicans as retribution. Then, during the 1890s, the force helped the U.S. Army to defeat an insurrection led by the journalist Catarino Garza, and they also clashed with Mexican residents in the border town of Laredo when the police attempted to enforce an unpopular smallpox quarantine. Rangers also took part in the storied 1901 pursuit of Gregorio Cortez, a South Texas ranchero wanted by Anglo authorities for murder. Cortez was apprehended just as he was about to cross into Mexico.

The low point for Tejanos came in the summer of 1915. Earlier that year, a group of Mexicans from both sides of the border had fomented a rebellion aimed at creating an independent nation carved from lands seized by the United States after the Mexican-American War. Although the U.S. Army was on hand to protect Texas residents, the Rangers—whose ranks were swelled by "specials" sworn in to meet the perceived emergency—led a backlash directed against the rebels (and ethnic Mexicans more generally), killing at least 300 and perhaps as many as 5,000 people. Ranger atrocities committed during the so-called Plan de San Diego uprising led José Tomás Canales, the sole Tejano member of the state legislature, to launch a probe into the activities of the force in 1918. In the end, the constabulary was reduced in size for a variety of reasons, and in 1935 it was folded into the Texas Department of Public Safety, where it continues to serve as the primary investigative arm of the agency.

Although the Texas Rangers of the early twenty-first century have moved well beyond their reputation as oppressors of the state's Tejano population and now count many ethnic Mexicans among their number, the force remains a divisive symbol. For instance, some of the old animosities surfaced in the late 1960s during a bitter strike by agricultural workers in the Rio Grande Valley. The laborers were Mexican, and the Rangers seemed to favor the Anglo farm owners, leading some observers to conclude that race relations in South Texas had changed little since the days of the Canales investigation. Others accused the Rangers of intimidating Mexican political activists, such as those who agitated in 1963 and 1969 against corrupt Anglo rule in the town of Crystal City. While the Rangers continue to exert a cultural influence within and beyond the Lone Star State, a surge in recent scholarship on the force has opened new lines of debate about their role in enforcing exclusion in the Southwest.

SEE ALSO *Alamo; La Raza; Mexicans; Social Psychology of Racism; Treaty of Guadalupe Hidalgo; Zoot Suit Riots.*

BIBLIOGRAPHY

Graybill, Andrew R. 2007. *Policing the Great Plains: Rangers, Mounties, and the North American Frontier, 1875–1910.* Lincoln: University of Nebraska Press.

Harris, Charles H., III, and Louis R. Sadler. 2004. *The Texas Rangers and the Mexican Revolution: The Bloodiest Decade, 1910–1920.* Albuquerque: University of New Mexico Press.

Johnson, Benjamin H. 2003. *Revolution in Texas: How a Forgotten Rebellion and its Bloody Suppression Turned Mexicans into Americans.* New Haven, CT: Yale University Press.

Samora, Julian, Joe Bernal, and Albert Peña. 1979. *Gunpowder Justice: A Reassessment of the Texas Rangers.* Notre Dame, IN: University of Notre Dame Press.

Utley, Robert M. 2002. *Lone Star Justice: The First Century of the Texas Rangers.* New York: Oxford University Press.

Webb, Walter Prescott. 1935. *The Texas Rangers: A Century of Frontier Defense.* Boston: Houghton Mifflin.

Andrew R. Graybill

TILLMAN, BENJAMIN "PITCHFORK"

1847–1918

Benjamin Ryan ("Pitchfork Ben") Tillman was born into a wealthy slaveholding family in the plantation district of Edgefield, South Carolina, on August 11, 1847. He served with a murderous paramilitary unit, agitated for agricultural reform, and was elected to two terms as South Carolina's governor and four terms as a U.S. senator. Throughout that career, Tillman sought to reshape the post–Civil War nation by limiting the political and social freedoms of African Americans and those of any whites who challenged those limits.

An illness during the Civil War kept Tillman out of the Confederate military and cost him his left eye. After the war, he supervised former slaves as agricultural laborers in Florida and South Carolina. During Reconstruction, he joined former slaveholders and ex-Confederate officers and soldiers in the rifle club movement, which threatened and assaulted South Carolina's Republican officials and their black and white supporters. He took part in the Hamburg Massacre (July 8, 1876), in which rifle club members (known thereafter as "Red Shirts") besieged a black militia unit, took many prisoners, and selected several militia men and local black officials from among them. They shot these men in the head before telling the rest to flee and firing upon them as they did. Contrary to frequent depictions of such violence as spontaneous eruptions of white Southern men's rage, this was a premeditated slaughter. Tillman later explained that "the leading white men of Edgefield" had determined "to seize the first opportunity that the negroes might offer them to provoke a riot and teach the negroes a lesson ... [by] having the whites demonstrate their superiority by killing as many of them as was justifiable" (Kantrowitz 2000, p. 67).

Maintaining the "superiority" of whites remained Tillman's primary objective, but black aspirations were not the only threat to that superiority. Throughout the 1880s and 1890s, he worried that the dire state of the agricultural economy would persuade hard-pressed white farmers to renew the Reconstruction-era coalition between black and white voters. Supporters of movements such as Populism sometimes seemed willing to sacrifice white supremacy if doing so would help advance their economic and political programs. Tillman argued that the Populists' insistence on federal intervention in the economy, coupled with their intermittent appeals to black voters, augured a return to the political, economic, and racial evils of Reconstruction.

Tillman responded with a vision of agricultural renewal that focused explicitly and exclusively on the grievances of white farmers. Because Tillman's rejection of federal intervention made it impossible for him to address the large structural issues confronting postbellum agriculture, he focused his ire on the lawyers, politicians, merchants, "aristocrats," and "Bourbons" whom he claimed ran the state. He pursued this course in national politics as well: It was his threat to stick a pitchfork in Grover Cleveland, whom he depicted as the enemy of white farmers, that gained Tillman his nickname. He accused individuals of corruption and called for a "farmers college" for young white men. In the late 1880s he was able to ride the broad regional wave of political discontent into power. He so outraged elements of the Democratic establishment that when he won the party's nomination for governor, some disgruntled white elites bolted the party and appealed to black voters for support. Nevertheless, Tillman was overwhelmingly elected governor in 1890.

As governor, Tillman's commitment to white uplift and white liberty was generally trumped by his fear of a black political and social resurgence. He oversaw the establishment of Clemson College for white men and Winthrop College for white women, but he remained less committed to the practice of higher education than to the principle of white supremacy. In 1891 he refused to accept federal aid for Clemson if doing so would require him to accept a proportionate amount of aid for black higher education. Tillman was the prime mover behind the South Carolina Constitutional Convention of 1895, which achieved his goal of disfranchising most black voters without running afoul of the Fifteenth Amendment. His promise that no white man would lose his vote under the new constitution was greeted with skepticism, and the 1894 referendum on calling a convention was fiercely contested. In the end, pro-convention forces probably won their narrow victory through electoral fraud. Tillman then helped draft a constitution under which men had to own substantial taxable property, prove their literacy, or demonstrate an understanding of the Constitution in order to register to vote. As a result white eligibility and turnout fell dramatically, and black voting was virtually eliminated.

Tillman asserted that black men, freed from slavery's policing, presented a dire and constant sexual threat to white women. He condemned lynching as an assault on the authority of the state and sometimes called out militia units to protect prisoners, but he also publicly pledged that in cases where a black man was accused of raping a white woman, he would himself lead the lynch mob. Tillman never put his pledge into practice, but he did collude with lynch mobs. In one 1893 case, he sent a black rape suspect to face a crowd of many hundreds protected by only a single guard. The man was lynched. Tillman argued that white men's violence toward accused black rapists was a product of their instinct for "race preservation," a force so powerful that it could cause "the very highest and best men we have [to] lose all semblance of Christian beings" (Kantrowitz 2000, p. 260). As long as foolish or wicked men attempted to subvert "race preservation" by mandating racial equality, he asserted, white men would respond with violence.

Tillman voiced similar sentiments in the U.S. Senate and, as he became a popular speaker, on platforms throughout the nation. Most journalists and public officials depicted Tillman as a "wild man," an impression that drew credibility from many of his activities, including his frequent boasts about his own part in the Hamburg Massacre and his apparent embodiment of the "white savage" he described in his speeches. His nickname, "Pitchfork Ben," seemed to capture this image of violent (and agrarian) discontent. Tillman proved himself to be a skilled organizer and a competent legislator, but the nickname and reputation served him very well, for they supported his argument that white men opposed black freedom and equality instinctively and impulsively. The depiction of Tillman as the spokesman of the instinctively racist white southern man reinforced Tillman's argument that white supremacy was something bred in the bone, not a social and political program that required enforcement and reinforcement in order to succeed.

Tillman sought to prevent the federal government from making the "race problem" worse. He fervently opposed U.S. imperialism, fearing that the occupation of territories such as the Philippines would bring millions more nonwhite people into the American polity. From the Senate, especially during the administration of Democrat Woodrow Wilson, Tillman worked to segregate the federal bureaucracy, strip prominent black men of federal offices, and relegate black federal workers to the lowest rungs of the civil service. Ben Tillman died on July 3, 1918, near the end of his fourth term in the U.S. Senate.

SEE ALSO *Southern Politics, 1883–1915.*

BIBLIOGRAPHY

Burton, Orville Vernon. 1976. "Ungrateful Servants?: Edgefield's Black Reconstruction; Part 1 of the Total History of Edgefield County, South Carolina." Ph.D. diss., Princeton University.

Kantrowitz, Stephen. 2000. *Ben Tillman and the Reconstruction of White Supremacy.* Chapel Hill: University of North Carolina Press.

Simkins, Francis Butler. 2002 (1944). *Pitchfork Ben Tillman, South Carolinian.* Columbia: South Carolina University Press.

Williamson, Joel M. 1984. *The Crucible of Race.* New York: Oxford University Press.

Stephen Kantrowitz

TOKENISM

In response to a television reporter who stated that "racial progress takes time," James Baldwin offered this telling response: "It has taken my mother's time, my father's time, my brothers and my sisters' time, my nieces and my nephews' time. How much time do you want for your progress?"(McBride 1999, p. 8).

Tokenism is a problem that continues to pervade American culture. It refers to the practice or policy of admitting an extremely small number of members of racial (e.g., African American), ethnic (e.g., Latino) or gender (i.e., women) groups to work, educational, or social activities to give the impression of being inclusive, when in actuality these groups are not welcomed. In the workplace the practice has been relied on to show compliance with laws, rules, and regulations requiring institutions to hire people of color or women. This article addresses tokenism as it applies to African Americans in the workplace.

THE RISE OF TOKENISM

Racism and its protracted history in American society gave rise to the concept of tokenism. To the extent that employers, both private and public, could keep African Americans out of the workforce, they did so, and with impunity. Prior to Title VII of the Civil Rights Act of 1964, no federal laws compelled employers to refrain from discriminating against people on the basis of such characteristics of race, color, religion, national origin, or gender. Thus, African Americans and other groups were explicitly and intentionally excluded from participation in private- and public-sector workforces. Parenthetically, the Civil Rights Acts of 1866 and 1871, intended to enforce the Thirteenth and Fourteenth Amendments to the U.S. Constitution, were aimed at prohibiting discrimination in the workplace. However, as with other initiatives of the Reconstruction era, these laws were never enforced.

With enactment of the Civil Rights Act in 1964, private employers were no longer able explicitly to refuse to hire or promote African Americans. Of course, passage of the law did not result in the immediate end of discriminatory practices. On the contrary, employers developed ways to continue their exclusionary practices. One notable example can be found in the U.S. Supreme Court case *Griggs v. Duke Power* (1971). The Duke Power Company operated a power-generating facility in Draper, North Carolina. It was organized into five departments. The lowest-paying jobs were in the labor department, where even the highest-paying job paid less than the lowest-paying jobs in the other four departments. In 1964, there were sixteen African Americans working at the power plant, and they were all segregated into the labor department. In short, Duke Power openly discriminated on the basis of race in hiring and in job placement. On July 2, 1965, the day the Civil Rights Act took effect, the company instituted new requirements for getting jobs in all departments other than labor. A high school diploma was now required, which effectively kept all the African Americans in the labor department. Later the company required employees to pass two aptitude tests to transfer to any department outside labor. Willie Griggs filed a class-action lawsuit challenging the practices. The case reached the U.S. Supreme Court, which rendered a decision in favor of Griggs, stating that Title VII prohibits not only overt discrimination but also practices that may seem neutral but are discriminatory in operation.

The *Griggs* decision was landmark in that it proscribed not just overt discrimination but also subtle or covert practices that seem innocuous but are discriminatory in their impact. The fear of potential lawsuits—which can be very costly to employers—forced companies to begin hiring African Americans, albeit in small numbers. In turn, tokenism was spawned. Organizations at least in the private sector now had a legal imperative that made it necessary to demonstrate that they did not engage in discriminatory practices. Hiring one or even two African Americans would give the appearance of inclusion and hence compliance with antidiscrimination laws such as Title VII and later affirmative action polices. Tokenism, in effect, was symbolic and perfunctory. Government employers would follow suit in 1972, when Title VII was extended to public-sector workforces with passage of the Equal Employment Opportunity Act. Such agencies as police and fire departments, which continue to be dominated by white males even in the early twenty-first century, were forced to show at least a semblance of compliance with the law, and would hire the token African-American police officer or firefighter.

THE EFFECTS OF TOKENISM

Early on, some argued that tokenism was an important first step for African Americans to gain a foothold in the workplace. It would, it was maintained, open the doors for others, thus representing some progress. Many others, however, maintained that tokenism perpetuated the victim status of African Americans and represented an absolute failure of public policies and programs aimed at ending discriminatory practices.

Only a nominal few benefit from tokenism, and organizations hire the token not for what she or he can contribute to the institution but to give the outward appearance of inclusion. Malcolm X put it this way in a speech he delivered to the Afro-American Broadcasting Company in Detroit in 1965: "Tokenism benefits only a few. It never benefits the masses, and the masses are the ones who have the problem, not the few. That one who benefits from tokenism, he doesn't want to be around us anyway—that's why he picks up on the token" (Malcolm X 1965).

Tokenism has proven to be demeaning, demoralizing, and debilitating. Research has illustrated that it leads to a loss of black identity, multiple demands on being African American, a sense of isolation, and pressure to show greater competence (Jackson, Thoits, and Taylor 1995). Kanter (1977), who has written extensively about the effects of tokenism on women, points out that tokens are always under greater scrutiny than others and are forced constantly to prove themselves. They also internalize a sense of inferiority because they perceive their job evaluations as being based not on achievements but on their "blackness." Jackson, Thoits, and Taylor (1995) also point out that tokens are always reminded of their "differences" through jokes, banter, and "loyalty tests." While tokens feel pressure to blend in, they are invariably relegated to a degrading stereotyped, caricatured role.

In effect, tokens face increased vulnerability and stress, which ultimately diminish their work performance as well as their overall physical and psychological well-being (Morash, Haarr, and Kwak 2006). And, equally as devastating, is the myth that has arisen from tokenism: that standards are lowered when African Americans are hired. This perverse belief has no grounding in empirical reality. It is a falsehood that has been perpetuated by those who have opposed affirmative action and other efforts aimed at diversifying the workplace (Riccucci 2002). This duplicity, in turn, propagated the fallacious, incendiary concept of "reverse discrimination."

Tokenism can never be a viable policy or practice. It only compounds the problems of exclusion, marginalization, inferiority, and low morale. Yet, in various forms, it persists.

CONTEMPORARY TOKENISM

American society continues to be plagued by discriminatory practices. Although public and private institutions are more diverse in the twenty-first century than they were in the early 1960s, discrimination persists. It may be the case, however, that tokenism has become less of a problem at least in the lower echelons of private and government workforces, because to the extent progress has been made in diversifying the workplace, it has been at the lower levels. However, the upper levels of public- and private-sector workforces continue to be dominated by males who are white and of European ancestry. It is in these upper, higher-paying jobs that tokenism continues to exist. Organizations disingenuously dot the landscape of the highest rungs of hierarchical structures with African Americans to illustrate that they are making an effort to diversity the upper, more powerful levels of the organization.

Among the *Fortune* 500 companies—the top 500 public corporations in America as measured by gross revenue—African Americans continue to represent the token on corporate boards. A study by James and Wooten (2005) showed that only 8 percent of the total 5,572 board seats of *Fortune* 500 companies consist of African Americans. Moreover, as of 2007, there were only seven African-American chief executive officers among all the *Fortune* 500 companies.

Until every organization and corporate board structure is fully diversified at every level and layer, we can continue to ask, as James Baldwin did many years ago, "How much time do you want for your progress?"

SEE ALSO *Civil Rights Acts.*

BIBLIOGRAPHY

Griggs v. *Duke Power Company,* 401 U.S. 424 (1971).

Jackson, Pamela Braboy, Peggy A. Thoits, and Howard F. Taylor. 1995. "Composition of the Workplace and Psychological Well-Being: The Effects of Tokenism on America's Black Elite." *Social Forces* 74 (2): 543–557.

James, Erika Hayes, and Lynn Perry Wooten. 2005. The *2004 Census of African-Americans on Board of Directors of Fortune 500 Companies.* Washington, DC: Executive Leadership Council.

Kanter, Rosabeth M. 1977. *Men and Women of the Corporation.* New York: Basic Books.

McBride, Dwight, ed. 1999. *James Baldwin Now.* New York: New York Press.

Malcolm X. 1965. Speech. Delivered in Detroit, Michigan, February 14. Available from http://blackhistory.cmgworldwide.com/speeches/malcolm/speech1.htm

Morash, Merry, Robin Haarr, and Dae-Hoon Kwak. 2006. "Multilevel Influences on Police Stress." *Journal of Contemporary Criminal Justice* 22 (1): 26–43.

Riccucci, Norma M. 2002. *Managing Diversity in Public Sector Workforces.* Boulder, CO: Westview Press.

Norma M. Riccucci

TOURISM AND NATIONAL HERITAGE (U.S.)

Heritage tourism is a form of cultural tourism. According to Bob McKercher and Hilary du Cros (2002), cultural tourism builds on "a community or a nation's cultural heritage assets" (p. 7). According to the International Council on Monuments and Sites (ICOMOS), heritage includes both tangible and intangible assets, culturally significant places both built and natural, collections of papers and artifacts, and "past and continuous cultural practices, knowledge, and living experiences" (ICOMOS, 1999, p. 7). African American heritage tourism is therefore part of the cultural discourse of both communities and nations. In addition to a resurgence of interest in and development of heritage tourist sites in the United States, African American heritage travel includes travel to African nations such as Senegal and Ghana, nations of the Caribbean, as well as Europe, Latin America, and Canada.

African American heritage tourism raises issues of how history and heritage are spoken of, the interests of potential audiences and funders, and conflicting perspectives on the meaning of historical events, artifacts, personages, and sites. The inclusion of African American heritage and its movement from margin to center in U.S. history is itself a radical revisioning of national heritage.

The first Africans were brought to the New World in 1619 to the settlement of Jamestown, Virginia, one year before the Pilgrims landed at Plymouth Rock. According to Henry Chase in *In Their Footsteps: The American Visions Guide to African-American Heritage Sites* (1994), Africans were originally brought in as indentured servants. However, within one generation slavery had become a lifelong condition in custom, if not in law, as tobacco farming increased the demand for labor. Hence, from its very beginnings slavery, race, and place are essential components of any depiction of national heritage in the United States, and, as such, become sites of contested meanings. African American heritage tourism forces a revisiting of conflicting discourses about the meaning of African American experience in U.S. history, as well as the meaning of U.S. history itself. While African American heritage tourism comprises multiple eras and facets of African American history, the focus here is on the legacy of slavery.

Perhaps the most important feature of this continuing cultural discourse is the fact that the stories of African Americans have been marginalized and erased from the national heritage of the United States. African American heritage tourism changes this and provides economic incentive for a variety of communities to recognize the role of

African Americans in their history. However, in significant ways this interest and development has had to be fought for, overcoming resistance to dominant discourses of the nation that have historically minimized and erased African American participation. At the same time, heritage tourism presents a commodified version of heritage framed to attract consumers. As McKercher and Du Cros (2002) point out, the interests of cultural heritage management are not identical to those involved in cultural tourism. Barbara Kirshenblatt-Gimblett (1995), however, sees commodification as essential to the heritage industry as part of heritage tourism: "Heritage is a value-added industry. … Heritage organizations ensure that places and practices in danger of disappearing because they are no longer occupied or functioning or valued will survive. It does this by adding the value of pastness, exhibition, difference, and where possible indigeneity" (p. 370). The heritage industry transports the tourist to the past, "from a now that signifies hereness to a then that signifies thereness" (p. 370). Tourism and heritage are complementary insofar as heritage marks a site as a potential destination and tourism makes the destination economically viable as a "representation" or "museum" of itself (p. 371).

INTERPRETATION

Interpretation is integral to the production of the sites of heritage tourism. It is provided by informative placards, by how things are named, by apparently neutral descriptions in guidebooks and guided tours, by the role-play of interpreters at recreations of life at historic sites, and by all sorts of systematic inclusions and exclusions. As Fath Davis Ruffins points out in "Mythos, Memory, and History" (1992), interpretation is an essential feature of any historical site, artifact, or story. Things do not speak for themselves. History is not equivalent to the unalienable facts, but is itself an interpretation of what should rightfully be termed "the past," the flow of "events and movements, debates and ideas, migrations and discoveries" that occur over time, not all of which become part of the historical record (p. 509).

Parker B. Potter Jr. and Mark Leone (1992) articulate this problematic. History museums and historical exhibitions reflect the interests and ideologies of their founders and clients, as well as curators' attempts to avoid controversy. As a result, although "it is impossible to judge the realism of a place such as Williamsburg," the depiction produces a kind of a sense of realism that matches visitors' preconceptions of eighteenth-century Virginia and produces a passivity in audiences toward historical questioning (p. 479). Potter and Leone advocate an interpretive practice that stimulates empowerment of the tourist by encouraging historical consciousness and questioning. The guides on their site tours in Annapolis are working archaeologists who expose their methodology and share tentative conclusions with visitors who are encouraged to see themselves as "participants in the creation of historical knowledge" (pp. 490–491).

Interpretations are essentially ideological; they are structured by discourses. A discourse is a structure of vocabulary, concepts, and assumptions that frame issues according to a particular perspective or argument that reflects a communal way of thinking and the interests of that group. Discourses are socially available through language and are often unconsciously adopted as depictions of the real and of how the world is. For example, Ruffins (1992) notes that government museums such as the Smithsonian have historically offered a narrative of U.S. history that marginalized the contributions of African Americans, and therefore curators did not collect artifacts of slavery (p. 593). Potter and Leone point out that when sites such as Williamsburg, Virginia, are recreated to reflect an image of the eighteenth century according to the understanding of its founding family, the Rockefellers, they reflect a discourse that is dominant both because it espouses a version of reality that reflects the assumptions of an elite group but also because those assumptions about reality make up the dominant discourse of the United States and its understanding of its history. Interpretations of African American heritage sites offer conflicting versions of reality by introducing an alternative discourse within which to frame events of the past as well as social relations of the present.

MYTHOS, MEMORY, AND HISTORY

Plantation Narratives and Dominant Discourses. The interpretation on plantations at public historical sites illustrate how discourses structure meaning according to the dominant mythos of the southern region of the United States. According to Ruffins in "Revisiting the Old Plantation: Reparations, Reconciliation, and Museumizing American Slavery" (2006), silence about slavery was the norm. Slavery was not mentioned at American museums before 1980 (p. 394). The interpretive canon at historic Williamsburg—home and, more importantly, workplace, for slaves who maintained the lifestyle of the elite who occupied the historic dwellings—did not mention the slavery system as underlying colonial society and the economic system depicted (p. 394). While there has been significant change since the 1980s, the same silence was common and remains in place at many plantation sites. Where there is not silence, there are depictions of slavery that conform to a dominant discourse, allowing tourists to enter into a version of the past that dwells on the richness of a lost, but attractive, social world without dwelling on the sordid underpinnings. These discourses invite white tourists to reimagine a world of gracious living.

This understanding of the discourse around southern plantations structures the analysis by Jessica Adams in "Local Color: The Southern Plantation in Popular Culture" (1999). Adams situates plantations narratives within struggle over issues of "collective identity" as marginalized groups and notions of multiculturalism are being incorporated into U.S. national heritage and identity (p. 164). Plantations are transformed from sites of slave labor to a "vision of the plantation as an 'antebellum home,' and elegant reminder of 'the way things were'" (p. 163). Slavery is essentially erased in these depictions and the plantation becomes "imbued with nostalgic possibility" (p. 164). In the plantation as tourist destination, "historical fantasies in which race and class are never points of contention" seek to "construct and perpetuate a myth of a white American subject who can be defined without reference to blackness" (p. 164). Ironically, the southern white planter "inhabits the place forcibly vacated by the slave, as blacks get effaced from plantation life; the planter becomes the real laborer, and the real victim, of slavery.. . .This reconceived white subject transcends Southernness to embody American identity" (p. 166). Adams sees this as a backlash or reaction to the burgeoning multiculturalism that is being incorporated into the U.S. mythos.

According to Adams, evidence of slavery is effaced from the material settings, as slave quarters are allowed to go to ruin or remain disguised as they are reconstructed as restrooms or tourist sleeping quarters. The plantation is "reinvented" as a place of leisure rather than work. White, female guides dressed in hoop skirts and resembling "house-proud mistresses, mothers, or daughters" show tourists around the plantation house presented as a "home" rather than a workplace. The erasure of slave labor achieves a "validation of a social order in which white privilege is both desirable and unquestioned" (pp. 170, 175). Similarly, gift shops become "feminized spaces," with female staff and stock based on decorative household items (p. 170). The rhetoric of brochures and guidebooks echo this discourse in which "slave masters are changed into passive recipients of the land's bounty" and slave work is "rhetorically disguised" by "describing the antebellum domestic staff as 'butlers,' 'skilled nannies,' and 'servant boys'" (pp. 171, 178). What is "mourned . . . is not the inhumanity of the slave system, but rather the loss of planters' quality of life that accompanied the end of the Civil War" (p. 172). In this discourse, the plantation has become an "important symbol in the nation's collective consciousness" where "African-Americans . . . exist simply as local color, while privileged whites assume the now reimagined position of 'other'" (p. 179).

According to Grant H. Cornwell and Eve W. Stoddard (2001), a similar erasure of slave labor occurs in the restoration of eighteenth-century sugar estates in the Caribbean, where ruins of plantation houses, sugar factories, and windmills are "prominent markers in island landscapes. . .being read, appropriated, and restored through a variety of discourses and codes" (p. 134). Their focus is on two sites, the Annaberg sugar mill in Virgin Islands National Park and the Duloo plantation, which has become the site for Caneel Bay Resort. Both are on the island of St. John, part of the U.S. Virgin Islands. Both restorations emerged out of the "vision" of Laurance Rockefeller, who donated the Annaberg site for the national park and constructed the resort. According to Cornwell and Stoddard, the windmill ruins "exist within a creolized space and a creole history," by which they mean a layered interpenetration of the cultures of the colonizers and the colonized (p. 137). The windmills show this hybridization. They were owned by European planters, adapted European technology to the conditions of sugar production in the New World, and built and worked by African-descended slaves for the profit of colonizing European planters and to enable the consumption of sugar by Old World Europeans (p. 137).

Rockefeller's vision for the luxury resort and national park was to recreate the "pristine condition" of the land when it was first discovered by Europeans (Cornwell and Stoddard, 2001, p. 140). This vision essentially erased both the history and the presence of the local community, including a slave rebellion in 1733 in which the slaves took over the island for six months (p. 142). According to Cornwell and Stoddard, the plantation with its historic cannons used to repel the Africans was "the last bastion of the whites during the uprising" and "has continued to play that role in the modern Virgin Islands. Caneel Bay Resort has continued to harbor a wealthy, mostly white clientele on an island populated by people of African descent" (p. 144).

The walking tour and interpretive placards provided by the U.S. Park Service uses neutral terms to describe the sugar-making process with "no explicit critique of the plantation system" (p. 147). Slave labor is "kept on the margins of the viewer's consciousness" and the word *slave* is barely used (p. 147). In a placard interpreting the ruins of some slave quarters, tourists are instructed that "workers," not slaves, and their "families lived mostly outdoors" (pp. 147–148) According to Cornwell and Stoddard, the fact that tourists are not moved to question the need for the plantation mansion or "great house" reflects the "continuing hegemony of the plantation system, now transmuted into the politics and economics of Caribbean tourism" (p. 148). The dominant discourse makes the social inequality between the "poverty of black and brown 'natives' in contrast to the wealth of white visitors" to appear natural and not in need of questioning. The resort, with its service workers of African descent "evokes for white tourists a nostalgia for the imagined luxury . . . of tropical plantation ownership, while simultaneously eliding the realities of slavery and . . . hinting at the way of life in which masters were dominant over a subordinate workforce of people at their beck and call" (p. 151).

Cornwell and Stoddard contrast the depiction of Caribbean slavery in Cuba, where the site of a major slave revolt on a sugar estate is commemorated with a museum devoted to the history of plantation slavery and where slaves are "honored as Cuba's first revolutionaries, bringing the historical narrative into the service of Cuba's national identity" (pp. 146–147).

Ruffins (2006) documents changes in attitudes about remembering slavery. National, state, and local museums (and of course, the more than 100 African American museums) had had exhibitions on African American achievements in art and science in the post-slavery period, as well as covering the history of the civil rights movement. Before 1980 there was "a virtual silence" about slavery on the national level (p. 394). Ruffins characterizes this change in openness to depictions and discussions of slavery as a "new moment in U.S. cultural history" (p. 395). What made this possible? The civil rights movement of the 1950s and 1960s paved the way by reopening questions of African Americans' place in U.S. society, and television programs such as *Roots,* which traced author Alex Haley's ancestors to Africa and the slave trade, brought African Americans to the center of national consciousness as the "first unified portrayal of the African and African American experience of slavery from the perspective of the enslaved" (p. 398). Films such as *Glory* (1989), *Amistad* (1997), and *Beloved* (1998) brought the "representation of slavery" to the general public (pp. 403–404). Major exhibitions at national museums such as the Smithsonian integrated materials on slavery for the first time. In 1991 the Museum of the Confederacy in Richmond, Virginia, mounted an exhibition on slavery that "challenged not only the nationwide silence about slavery but also the outright rejection of slavery as the crucial element of southern life for which the Confederates fought" (p. 405). In 1994 Colonial Williamsburg opened Carter's Grove, a plantation, and rebuilt the slave quarters. In 1999 African American interpreters developed a presentation of a slave auction as part of the living history programming, and by 2000 they had developed an "escaped slave" program in which visitors are confronted by a "runaway slave" and "surrounded by slave catchers" (pp. 406–407).

The work by Antoinette Jackson (2001) exemplifies a revisioning through critical examination of discourse that allows for a different understanding of the role of Africans in plantation life. According to Jackson, "to reduce the view of African association with plantations to 'slave' life portraits is to continue to perpetuate a narrow historical representation of Africans in American history" (p. 13) and to miss the fact that plantations were "essentially self-sustaining African communities and agricultural production centers" (pp. 21-22). Jackson's inquiry focused on Snee Farm, the country home of Charles Pinckney, a pro-slavery drafter of the U.S. Constitution. She points out that Africans made up "not only the majority of the population in antebellum plantation communities but typically were the only permanent year round residents" (p. 22). While the original rationale for Snee Farm plantation as a National Historic Site was "for interpreting and representing the life of Charles Pinckney, this was eventually "expanded to include an interpretation of the life of 'all' the site's inhabitants, free and 'slave' (Blythe 2000, p. 13).

Jackson advocates a critical reappraisal of the "continued use of the labels 'slave' and 'sharecropper' in public forum productions of American history (i.e., National Historic Site venues)" (2001, p. 20). The label tends to both "mask the diversity of African plantation experience and minimize the cultural contributions" (p. 21) as it squeezes a multifaceted community life and structure into "a single template—one defined by an imposed condition created by the institution of slavery" (p. 21). Jackson highlights the diversity of work on the plantation ranging from agricultural and domestic occupations to a variety of crafts such as basketmaking, brick masonry, gardening, and sewing. Her research methodology focused on interviewing residents of the contemporary African community who passed on narratives of their community history from their own and their ancestral perspective, including the post Emancipation community of families who "continued to live in slave cabin housing. . .and to follow their same occupations. . .[for] pay. . .." or who owned their own property and thus were misrepresented by the "sharecropper label [which] has been uniformly ascribed to descendants of enslaved Africans in. . .community history" (2003, p. 103). For Jackson, oral history data "underscore the need for utilizing more complex models of interaction—such as the heterarchical approach, which can elaborate, and not obscure, the variety and fluidity of roles that Africans and their descendants performed in plantation communities. . ." (p. 103). Jackson derived the concept of heterarchy from C. Crumley as a way of "avoiding either top-down or bottom-up approaches" to analyzing power relationships (p. 93). Instead, the inquirer analyzes "relationships between people when they are unranked, or when they possess the potential for being ranked in a number of different ways" (p. 93).

According to Jackson (2001), "the primary significance of the narratives collected is that they privilege

African agency. . . .[where] the subject is brought into the picture as a participant, as a creative force. . . . " (p. 20). Jackson discovered an image of community that ran counter to her expectations of a narrative composed of "sad stories, stories of pain" (p. 24). Instead, she found that her respondents offered her "a chance to return home, to find home . . . in the spirit of this community, a community that has managed to survive so I could survive" (p. 24).

An important influence was the success of the Holocaust Memorial Museum in Washington, D.C., which demonstrated that "negative history," the telling of a "horrific story with dignity," was a suitable charter for a museum (Ruffins 2006, p. 399). In addition, the Holocaust Museum had become a "symbolic archetype, architectural and exhibitionary, for expressing the sacrifices and tragedies of a people's collective identity," as well as for showing that such a specific story can have a "universal" meaning (p. 399). The challenges were greater, for whereas in the Holocaust narrative, the oppressors were Europeans, in the case of slavery, they were to be found on home soil.

Discussing Slavery as National Heritage. Ruffins (2006) concludes that there is "social and political space" now in the national consciousness to discuss slavery (p. 408). For African Americans two narrative interpretive possibilities have emerged for this incorporation of slavery into the dominant discourse. One emphasizes the "Black Holocaust" and African American suffering and calls for national apologies and reparations. This holocaust concept centers attention on a history of atrocities from the transatlantic passage through the period of enslavement, through lynchings and race riots from the 1880s, to the 1950s civil rights era (pp. 410–411). The second narrative possibility is to focus interpretive work in the direction of interracial reconciliation. In 1995, the National Park Service published a list of 400 stations of the Underground Railroad, which stimulated local development of interpretive tours and living history programs. This narrative, which allows for incorporating "white support for freedom from slavery," incorporates what was a "truly secretive and dangerous effort" on the part of African Americans into the dominant discourse of the nation (pp. 420–421). The interest in the Underground Railroad "represent[s] an attempt to include oneself, one's family, and one's locale into a more liberating narrative of the American past" (p. 421). As slavery becomes part of the national narrative, its interpretation remains contested. In 2003 a presidential commission called for an African American museum to be built on the Mall in Washington, D.C. (pp. 424–425). Ruffins reports that surveys of African Americans "do not want to rush toward reconciliation, but rather wish to have institutions squarely place the blame where it is deserved" (p. 423). In Richmond, Virginia, the plans for the Tredegar National Civil War Center propose to "present a unified history of the Civil War, incorporating the 'three views'—northern, southern, and African American" in the "former capital of the Confederacy" (p. 423). Ruffins suggests that it is a difficult task to fund new institutions devoted to depicting slavery as the "cultural construction . . . inevitably shaped by diametrically opposed ideas about the meaning of slavery (and race) in the American past" (p. 423).

Another ideologically contested site at the intersection of African American and national heritage is the Independence Mall and Liberty Bell Pavilion in Philadelphia, Pennsylvania. Mark Hutter (2007) has depicted how excavations for the new exhibition center revealed that the entrance was the site of former slave quarters for house and stable slaves brought by George Washington from Mount Vernon, his Virginia plantation, to serve him during his first term as president in the 1790s (p. 144). Slavery was illegal in Pennsylvania. According to Hutter, the U.S. Park Service decided "not to promote or even recognize the existence of slave buildings in Revolution-era Philadelphia," prompting criticism from the *Philadelphia Tribune*, an African American newspaper in Philadelphia, that the Park Service was effectively erasing American history (p. 144). A "public outcry at the blatant attempt to hide history led to an accommodation that will have slavery and the Liberty Bell in spatial juxtaposition" (p. 145). Hutter notes that despite its Revolution-era origins, the "Liberty Bell" was named by Civil War–era abolitionists, who used it as their symbol. Ironically, in the early twenty-first century the U.S. Park Service recognizes that maintaining the connection with slavery "may attract a much sought-after diverse tourist population" and is considering the development of a series of tours, educational programs, excavations of free African American housing sites from the eighteenth century, an Underground Railroad walking tour, a museum devoted to African American experience, and a Civil War museum (pp. 145–146). Hutter notes that "the economic benefits to the city are not being ignored. It is estimated that about a third of the visitors to Philadelphia are nonwhite. That translates into tourist dollars of about $1 billion in annual revenue" (p. 146). Philadelphia is projected to become "a destination of choice for tourists of color" (p. 146). Hutter notes that local officials recognize an "emerging new collective memory of Philadelphia," as further archaeological digs produce evidence of the existence of a vibrant eighteenth- and nineteenth-century free African American community in the city (p. 147).

This revaluation of "negative history" is occurring nationally, recapturing the history of slavery and commemorating it for historical and tourist purposes. As slavery enters the national conversation, it is perhaps most prominently seen in Colonial Williamsburg, on some plantations, particularly on those of presidents, Mount Vernon, home of George Washington, the Monticello home of

National Underground Railroad Freedom Center, Cincinnati, Ohio. *The revaluation of "negative history" is occurring nationally, recapturing the history of slavery and commemorating it for historical and touristic purposes.* MIKE SIMONS/GETTY IMAGES.

Thomas Jefferson, the 400 official stops of the Underground Railroad certified by the U.S. Park Service, numerous sites of slave auctions, runaway slaves, and slave rebellions, as well as former slave quarters in cities and small towns across the country with any history of slave labor to reclaim as part of their history, in the South, Midwest, West, and Northeast. Potential tourists for African American heritage sites can get information from guidebooks specifically directed to African American heritage, such as *In Their Footsteps* (1994) by Henry Chase and *Black Heritage Sites: An African American Odyssey and Finder's Guide* (1996) by Nancy C. Curtis. Both include more than capsule summaries of available historical information on each site and point out the existence of slave quarters as the point of interest in a plantation visit. Chase attempts to enumerate the population of slaves at any plantation site, as well as describe what is known of the conditions of their work and lives.

The explosion of interest in African American heritage means that tourists also have access to pamphlets from the National Park Service and tourist brochures published by municipal and state governments devoted to their local African American heritage, as well as those published by tourist attractions themselves. Tour companies often include an "African American tour" and companies have emerged who specialize in African American travel. Of course, much of this content is available on the internet. The National Park Service has embraced African American heritage on an extensive Web site with listings of park sites related to African American history, short historical essays, resources for education, and site brochures and information. The tourist brochure for the Kingsley Plantation in Florida emphasizes the slave quarters and explicitly describes sites of slave labor at stops one through six of its walking tour, while the waterfront and master's home are mentioned at stop seven.

While the focus here has been on slavery, popular tour destinations include the sites of the great events of the Civil Rights struggle in the 1950s and 1960s, including homes, churches, and educational institutions associated with civil rights leaders such as the Reverend Martin Luther King Jr., or in neighborhoods deemed historically significant that have been historically connected with African American populations and great African American achievements in science, the arts, education, politics, and sports. *The African American Travel Guide* by Wayne C. Robinson directs tourists to historical landmarks, museums, and colleges, as well as to restaurants, travel agents and tours, entertainment, and lodging in seventeen United States cities and two Canadian provinces.

What had previously been left to African Americans to document as their own heritage has become part of a national conversation and a burgeoning tourist industry. This means that the narrative of African American heritage is subject to the pressures of being part of an industry devoted to both a market niche and a broader national market. The reclamation of this "negative history" depends on the availability of historical records and collections of artifacts to document any historical revisiting and revisioning of the past. And it depends on the perspective or motivation of the person interpreting the documents.

DOCUMENTING THE PAST TO CONSTRUCT HERITAGE

The dominant national or external mythos of the nineteenth century was not interested in African American materials because of its orientation, which came to be organized around the notion of a "theoretical racism" that defined African Americans as "outside. . .the national character," as "primitive, childlike, violent, musical, sexually voracious, and superstitious.. . .Cultural forms that differed from mainstream European American forms. . . [were seen]. . .as evidence that confirmed an inferior or primitive past" (Ruffins, 1992, p. 521). Social Darwinism proclaimed that "Africans. . .inhabited a lower rung on the ladder of evolution" (p. 522).

This dominant ideology pervaded the culture of the curators and scholars who headed the development of the major national museums, including the Smithsonian and major natural history museums. As a result, there are few pre-Civil War objects of African Americans in the major national museums (p. 523). Whereas Native American artifacts became a focus for collecting, "no object was collected specifically because it reflected African American culture" (p. 523). However, some artifacts and papers were "inadvertently collected" as parts of collections of abolitionist materials or connected to plantations such as Mount Vernon and Monticello, homes of Presidents George Washington and Thomas Jefferson, with their legacy of slavery (p. 523). Collections of papers and artifacts have an important role in documenting and thereby substantiating the historical record as authoritative records become gatekeepers as well as inspiration for national memory.

Libraries of African American papers are better served because of the employment of an African American, Daniel Alexander Payne Murray, at the Library of Congress, who was allowed to embark on an ambitious campaign of collecting documents, manuscripts, books, and letters. The Smithsonian, however, missed a chance to create an important collection of materials. A longtime African American employee, Solomon Brown, was not empowered to collect on behalf of the museum. He did become a "leading preservationist" in the African American community of Washington, D.C., and was "renowned in the 1880s and 1890s for organizing annual trips to Harpers Ferry on the anniversary of John Brown's 1859 raid" (p. 526). This might be the first recorded instance of African American heritage tourism.

Collecting of artifacts and literary materials primarily went on in African American institutions and organizations, primarily churches, colleges, literary and historical societies, and civic organizations. The internal mythos of African Americans in the nineteenth century was of their special destiny and role as truth tellers. African Americans connected their history of enslavement and deliverance with the ancient Hebrews and with the suffering of Christ (pp. 514–515). Narratives of former slaves' memories of slavery "intersected with this larger mythos" and were published by abolitionist presses (p. 515). Frederick Douglass's life and memoir were seen as "emblematic of this larger mythos" (p. 516). At his death in 1896, his home, Cedar Hill, in Washington, D.C., became the first African American historic house, maintained for seventy years by African American civic organizations such as the National Association of Colored Women's Clubs and the National Council of Negro Women (pp. 516–517). In 1963 it became the first African American property acquired by the United States Park Service and thereafter maintained by the national government and entering into the dominant discourse as part of the commemoration of the Civil War (p. 517).

Ruffins (1992) documents the changing attitudes and mythos of African Americans toward Africa, as well as toward slavery. While in the eighteenth century organizations mentioned African heritage, the nineteenth century marked a shift away from identification with Africa (p. 518), perhaps affected by the dominant racist discourse about primitivity. William H. Sheppard, a missionary among the Kuba tribe in the Belgian Congo, became a collector who argued for the sophistication of African society. His collection of artifacts were donated to Hampton Institute in Virginia and marked a change in attitude toward collecting African objects.

Twentieth-century African American movements were to be more embracing of African heritage. Black Victorians, as Ruffins calls the educated nineteenth-century African Americans, who founded the main cultural institutions, were also uninterested in collecting the material culture of enslaved or even rural African Americans and there are few extant examples of eighteenth-century artifacts: quilts, clothing, musical instruments, basketry, and other household items. They are mostly recovered from southern plantations that have become museums (pp. 519–520). The Black Victorian mythos embraced a notion of the "heroism of everyday life," where those who "founded businesses, practiced professions…, taught school, or led congregations were seen not only as model citizens but as living proof that Black people could and did achieve middle-class respectability" (p. 517). Educated African Americans collected the artifacts of their own achievements, but distanced themselves from slavery and rural populations, reflecting the dominant discourse of the nineteenth century. These artifacts became the basis for collections, as well as documents of churches, businesses, and newspapers. The homes and businesses of these nineteenth-century professionals are themselves tourist destinations for heritage travel. According to Judith Wellman, their documents, as well as those of nineteenth-century white abolitionists, became the historical evidence that allowed sites to be certified by the U.S. Park Service as official sites of the Underground Railroad and thereby enter into the dominant discourse (pp. 11–29).

HERITAGE TRAVEL

Heritage travel for African Americans includes a variety of United States destinations. Every major city across the United States and every rural town in the south and other regions have rediscovered their African American roots and compete with each other for the tourist dollar. Whereas Europe, the Caribbean, Latin America, and Canada have also constructed African American tourist destinations, arguably the most moving destination is to journey back to the continent of origin—heritage travel to Africa. African nations such as Senegal and Ghana have responded to this interest of the African diaspora in returning to its roots.

According to Edward M. Bruner, the West African nation of Ghana is attempting to develop its tourist industry around the "star features" of the "historic castles of Elmira and Cape Coast, which were used as staging areas for the mid-Atlantic slave trade" (1996, p. 290). Elmira Castle, built in 1482, has received designation as a World Heritage Monument from UNESCO. Of 17,091 visitors in 1992, 12.3 percent were from North America, including African Americans. According to Bruner, these represented a "class-privileged and more educated segment of the larger African American population" (p. 290). The interests of Ghanaians is economic development of their country and they see tourism as an important vehicle. The interest of African Americans is on the historic significance of the dungeons at Elmira Castle as an opportunity "to experience one of the very sites from which their ancestors may have begun the torturous journey to the New World" (p. 291). Elmira represents "sacred ground not to be desecrated" and a "return to the slave forts for diaspora blacks has been called a 'necessary act of self-realization'" (p. 291).

The Ghanaians' focus on Elmira is not primarily on slavery. Elmira's 500-year history represents a series of foreign occupations, as well as their own independence in 1957 (Bruner 1996, p. 292). Restoring the castle has raised issues of interpretation: whose story should be told? One Africa Productions, an organization founded by the Robinsons, an African American couple living in Ghana, is "dedicated to the reuniting of Africans from the diaspora with Africans from the continent, and, for a fee, they also conduct performances in the dungeons, primarily for African American tourists" (p. 294). Because of the European history of Elmira and the presence of European tourists, tours of the castle shift emphasis depending on who is visiting. One concern of a meeting of the African Travel Association in 1994 was whether to focus marketing strategies of Elmira to African Americans or to a broader tourist market. The recommendation that emerged from the conference was that "the cultural heritage of all the different epochs and powers should be presented, but also that the area symbolizing the slave trade be given reverential treatment" (Bruner 1996, p. 294).

Controversies have emerged over whitewashing Elmira to maintain it and the closing of a restaurant-bar as inappropriate to its location over the men's dungeons at Cape Coast Castle. Ghanaians saw the restaurant as a means to keep tourists in the area and stimulate the economy. Legitimate tourist attractions would include programs of music and religious services (Bruner 1996, p. 294). Bruner highlights a further disparity between the expectations of Ghanaians and African American tourists. The Ghanaians calls them "obruni" which means "'whiteman," but "the term is extended to Europeans, Americans, and Asians regardless of skin color, so it has a meaning of foreigner. This second meaning is also ironic, since the diaspora blacks see themselves as returning 'home'" (p. 295).

The Robinsons' performance for African American tourists at the Elmira dungeon site is a participatory reenactment of the slaves' passing "Through the Door of No Return–The Return," where "the tourist group assembles in the dungeon, where they hold hands, light candles, pray together, usually weep together, pour libation as a homage to the ancestors, and then pass through the door that the slaves went through to the slave ships taking them to the Americas" (Bruner 1996, p. 296). In the tourist reenactment, the tour group sings "We Shall Overcome" and the Negro National Anthem, then return to the castle singing and dancing to African music to "celebrate their joyous return to mother Africa" (p. 296). Bruner describes another "Through the Door of No Return" tour that is geared to the native Ghanaian market, produced by a tour operator from Accra, where "the performance ends after going through the door, and there is no reentry to the castle, or symbolically no return to Africa" (p. 296). For Bruner these differences reflect "different versions of black history and dramatically reveal the disparate understandings of African Americans and Ghanaians" (p. 296).

Other areas of contradiction surround the role of African participation in the slave trade that is not addressed and some Ghanaian feelings about the obvious economic advantages of diaspora blacks and how that may represent a "fortunate" impact of slavery (Bruner 1996, p. 296). Bruner remarks that the castles have been segregated from native Ghanaians for the sake of preservation. They are more available to tourists than to the local population, and the elimination of local markets and the restaurant has meant less opportunity for locals to benefit from the tourist trade (pp. 298-299).

Paulla A. Ebron describes a similar tour when she accompanied a group under the sponsorship of the McDonald's Corporation. The tour guides reminded the tourists that they were on a "pilgrimage, not a safari" (1999, p. 916). She experienced the tour as a "deliberately designed" ritual that "resolved at the end of the trip to create a sense of transformation and reintegration" (p. 916). The phrase, "pilgrimage, not a safari" was offered "first [as] a subtle suggestion; as it was repeated throughout the course of the trip, it became like an advertising jingle, a collective prayer, as well as our hosts' desperate plea that we remember the distinction between this tour and an ordinary tourist jaunt.... Even in the moment of becoming tourists with our bodies and baggage, we were called upon to be more than tourists; we were to be pilgrims" (p. 918).

The trip to the slave fort on Goree Island in Senegal effected the change from tourist to pilgrim. Although it played only a "minor role in the slave trade," it has become "symbolically significant for African Americans as well as tour company ventures" (Ebron 1999, p. 920). For Ebron, the ferry ride and walk to the fort created the sense of "homecoming," as well as "apprehensive moments and perhaps even a sense of awe brought about by the meeting of the myths of our African home with the material site, the slave fort, the place where it all began" (p. 921). Touring the narrow slave quarters a second time after the curator's dramatic narrative of the capture and deportation of the slaves, which "confirmed a sense of collective history," the group became sober and there was a "hush." A prayer and libations were offered and the group entered a room with walls of chain irons and log books of slaving records. Ebron notes that "certificates—written verification of our visit to Goree—were available for purchase" (p. 292).

The group stayed on the island for four hours, bonding with each other and producing a "potent ... deeper connection" (Ebron 1999, p. 922). Ebron notes that this "pensive and reflective period was disrupted by the swarm of peddlers that surrounded the group once we were no longer protected by the walls of the fort. The historical return met present time, and we were urged back into our tourist status" (p. 292). Ebron highlights the counter-narratives of tourists and natives as they interact with different interests. These disjunctures—between identity as pilgrim or tourist, as coming home or foreign—occurred throughout the journey, which continued to Gambia, but the group had taken its "first step in the collective experience of regenerating an emotional connection to what had only previously been a more distant set of fragmentary semblances. Images of ship hulls packed with Africans are African American memories. ..." (p. 922).

Christine Mullen Kreamer also describes the contradictory interests of Africans and African Americans as she describes the creation of the museum exhibition space at Cape Coast Castle in Ghana and the debates that ensued from the multiple perspectives of those who "to varying degrees, claimed ownership of the use and interpretation of Ghana's historic forts and castles" (2006, p. 437). She likens the process to Ebron's analysis of the globalized context of her 1994 tour experience, where "transnational trends and ideas about culture and identity converged with the strategies of multinational capitalists, the dreams of diasporic communities, and the income-generating plans of African national governments to produce Africa as a commodified cultural object of global significance" (p. 439). The conflict concerned how narratives would be prioritized in a limited exhibition space. The Ghanaian narrative topicalized Ghana's "five hundred year history" of "interactions with European economic and political interests," its "struggle for ... independence from colonial domination," and a celebration of contemporary culture. The second narrative described the transatlantic slave trade and the "struggle for freedom and equality of peoples of African descent in the Americas" (p. 438). Kreamer points out that the controversy over the role of Ghanaian ancestors in the slave trade provides a "subtext" to the conflicts over the museum space and the desire on the part of African Americans to "educate" Ghanaians about the slave trade, including African complicity (p. 456).

The disparity in incomes and the need for the tourist dollar adds fuel to the conflicts. Tours run by "outside tour groups" such as the Nation of Islam and the Robinsons' One Africa Productions bypassed the official museum guides. These tourist ventures "generated considerable fees, only a fraction of which were shared with the museum to help it with its operating funds" (p. 456). An "atonement ceremony ... performed for visiting African Americans ... by some local Ghanaian chiefs ... was received with mixed reviews by Ghanaians, some of whom felt offended and coerced to participate in the ceremony or to admit that their ancestors played a role in the trade" (Kreamer 2006, p. 457).

The controversy highlights "an increasing sense of ownership among people of African descent for sites in Africa associated with the transatlantic slave trade (Kreamer 2006, p. 460). As designated UNESCO World Heritage sites, the forts and castles of Senegal and Ghana take on the identity of world heritage sites and the claims of a global constituency to share in their meaning (pp. 438, 450). These sites are "akin to shrines where people of African descent come to mourn their enslaved ancestors, to question the culpability of Africans during nearly four centuries of the trade, and to create mechanisms that allow for reconciliation" (p. 460). At the same time, for the Africans who are custodians of these sites, other stories are equally important to tell. Kreamer concludes that "the voices of the African diaspora have diminished the voices of the Ghanaians in the representation" of these sites (p. 462).

DISCOURSE, POWER, AND COMMODIFICATION IN HERITAGE TOURISM

Stories that get told, retold, revised, and revised again reflect more than the collective memories of communities and nations or the outcome of objective historical research. They reflect the power of those who sponsor and fund museums, historical monuments, and the refurbishing of tourist destinations. As a potential market, African Americans are enjoying an upsurge in the development of tourist destinations focused on a part of history that has been underrepresented in the dominant discourse that the United States has historically erased: the history of slavery. The stories of African Americans, more specifically the discourses in which African Americans draw strategies of narration, develop different emphases from the dominant discourse; the trip to the plantation focuses on the slave quarters, rather than the big house. As African Americans claim a central place in the national narrative, their power as tourists involves them in the transnational discourse of global tourism and the narration of the national heritage of African nations.

BIBLIOGRAPHY

Adams, Jessica. 1999. "Local Color: The Southern Plantation in Popular Culture." *Cultural Critique* 42: 163–187. Available from http://links.jstor.org

Adler, Margot. 2007. "Douglass Memorial Sparks Debate on Art vs. History." *All Things Considered*, National Public Radio, March 5. Available from http://www.npr.org.

Arnoldi, Mary Jo. 1992. "A Distorted Mirror: The Exhibition of the Herbert Ward Collection of Africana." In *Museums and Communities: The Politics of Public Culture*, edited by Ivan Karp, Christine Mullen Kreamer, and Steven D. Lavine. Washington, DC: Smithsonian Institution Press.

Austen, Ralph A. 2001. "The Slave Trade as History and Memory: Confrontations of Slaving Voyage Documents and Communal Traditions." *William and Mary Quarterly*, 3rd Series 58 (1): 229–244.

Baram, Uzi, and Yorke Rowan. 2004. "Archaeology after Nationalism: Globalization and the Consumption of the Past." In *Marketing Heritage: Archaeology and the Consumption of the Past*, edited by Yorke Rowan and Uzi Baram. Walnut Creek, CA: Altamira Press.

Blythe, R. 2000. *Charles Pinckney National Historic Site Historic Resource Study*. Atlanta, GA: National Park Service, U.S. Department of the Interior.

Bordewich, Fergus M. 2007. "History's Tangled Threads." *New York Times* February 2.

Bruner, Edward M. 1996. "Tourism in Ghana: The Representation of Slavery and the Return of the Black Diaspara." *American Anthropologist*, New Series 98 (2): 290–304.

Chase, Henry. 1994. *In Their Footsteps: The American Visions Guide to African-American Heritage Sites*. New York: Henry Holt.

Cline, Francis X. 2006. "The City Life; Summoning Frederick Douglass." *New York Times* November 3.

Cohen, Noam. 2007. "In Frederick Douglass Tribute, Slave Folklore and Fact Collide." *New York Times* January 23.

Cornwell, Grant H., and Eve W. Stoddard. 2001. "Reading Sugar Mill Ruins: 'The Island Nobody Spoiled' and Other Fantasies of Colonial Desire." *South Atlantic Review* 6 (2): 133–157.

Crew, Spencer R., and James E. Sims. 1991. "Locating Authenticity: Fragments of a Dialogue." In *Exhibiting Cultures: The Poetics and Politics of Museum Display*. Washington, DC: Smithsonian Institution Press.

Crumley, C. 1995. "Heterarchy and the Analysis of Complex Societies." In *Heterarchy and the Analysis of Complex Societies*, edited by R. Ehrenreich, C. Crumley, and J. Levy, 1-5. Arlington, VA: American Anthropological Association.

Curtis, Nancy C. 1996. *Black Heritage Sites: An African American Odyssey and Finder's Guide*. Chicago: American Library Association.

Dann, Graham M. S., and Robert B. Potter. 2001. "Supplanting the Planters: Hawking Heritage in Barbados." In *Slavery, Contested Heritage and Thanatourism*, edited by Graham M. S. Dann and A. V. Seaton. New York: Haworth Press.

Dann, Graham M. S., and A. V. Seaton, eds. 2001. *Slavery, Contested Heritage and Thanatourism*. New York: Haworth Press.

Ebron, Paulla A. 1999. "Tourists as Pilgrims: Commercial Fashioning of Transatlantic Politics." *American Ethnologist* 26 (4): 910–932.

Gaither, Edmund Barry. 1992. "'Hey! That's Mine': Thoughts on Pluralism and American Museums." In *Museums and Communities: The Politics of Public Culture*, edited by Ivan Karp, Christine Mullen Kreamer, and Steven D. Lavine. Washington, DC: Smithsonian Institution Press.

Gery, Michael E. C. 2003. "Follow the Flying Geese: How a Secret Code of Quilt Patterns Displayed a Map to Freedom Along the Underground Railroad." *Carolina Country*, February. Available from http://www.carolinacountry.com.

Handler, Richard, and Eric Gable. 1997. *The New History in an Old Museum: Creating the Past at Colonial Williamsburg*. Durham, NC: Duke University Press.

Hutter, Mark. 2007. *Experiencing Cities*. Boston: Pearson.

ICOMOS. 1999. Cultural Tourism Charter. ICOMOS, Paris. Available from http://www.icomos.org.

Jackson, Antoinette. 2001. "Heritage Tourism and the Historical Present: Africans at Snee Farm Plantation." *Southern Anthropologist* 28 (1): 12–27.

———. 2003. "Africans at Snee Farm Plantation: Informing Representations of Plantation Life at a National Heritage Site." In *Signifying Serpents and Mardi Gras Runners: Representing Identity in Selected Souths*, edited by Celeste Ray and Luke Eric Lassiter. (Southern Anthropological Society Proceedings, No. 36, Michael V. Angrosino, Series Editor.) Athens: The University of Georgia Press.

Jacobs, Claude F. 2001. "Folk for Whom? Tourist Guidebooks, Local Color, and the Spiritual Churches of New Orleans." *The Journal of American Folklore* 114 (453): 309–330. Available from http://links.jstor.org.

Kingsley Plantation Grounds Tour Brochure [Text Only Version]. National Park Service: Timucuan Ecological and Historic Preserve. Available from http://www.nps.gov/.

Kirshenblatt-Gimblett, Barbara. 1995. "Theorizing Heritage." *Ethnomusicology* 39 (3): 367–380.

———. 2006. "World Heritage and Cultural Economics." In *Museum Frictions: Public Cultures/Global Transformations*, edited by Ivan Karp, Corinne A. Kratz, Lynn Szwaja, and Tomas Ybarra-Frausto. Durham, NC: Duke University Press.

Kraemer, Christine Mullen. 2006. "Shared Heritage, Contested Terrain: Cultural Negotiation and Ghana's Cape Coast Castle Museum Exhibition 'Crossroads of People, Crossroads of Trade.'" In *Museum Frictions: Public Cultures/Global Transformations*, edited by Ivan Karp, Corinne A. Kratz, Lynn Szwaja, and Tomas Ybarra-Frausto. Durham, NC: Duke University Press.

Little, Barbara J. "Is the Medium the Message? The Art of Interpreting Archaeology in U.S. National Parks." In *Marketing Heritage: Archaeology and the Consumption of the Past*, edited by Yorke Rowan and Uzi Baram. Walnut Creek, CA: Altamira Press.

McKercher, Bob, and Hilary du Cros. 2002. *Cultural Tourism: The Partnership between Tourism and Cultural Heritage Management*. New York: Haworth Hospitality Press.

Munjeri, Dawson. 1991. "Refocusing or Reorientation? The Exhibit or the Populace: Zimbabwe on the Threshold." In *Exhibiting Cultures: The Poetics and Politics of Museum Display*. Washington, DC: Smithsonian Institution Press.

Norkunas, Martha. 1999. "The New History in an Old Museum: Creating the Past at Colonial Williamsburg by Richard Handler and Eric Gable." *Journal of American Folklore* 112 (444): 215–217.

Potter, Parker B., Jr., and Mark P. Leone. 1992. "Establishing the Roots of Historical Consciousness in Modern Annapolis, Maryland." In *Museums and Communities: The Politics of Public Culture*, edited by Ivan Karp, Christine Mullen Kreamer, and Steven D. Lavine. Washington, DC: Smithsonian Institution Press.

Robinson, Wayne C. 1997. *The African-American Travel Guide*. Edison, NJ: Hunter.

Ruffins, Fath Davis. 1992. "Mythos, Memory, and History: African American Preservation Efforts, 1820–1990." In *Museums and Communities: The Politics of Public Culture*, edited by Ivan Karp, Christine Mullen Kreamer, and Steven D. Lavine. Washington, DC: Smithsonian Institution Press.

———. 2006. "Revisiting the Old Plantation: Reparations, Reconciliation, and Museumizing American Slavery." In *Museum Frictions: Public Cultures/Global Transformations*, edited by Ivan Karp, Corinne A. Kratz, Lynn Szwaja, and Tomas Ybarra-Frausto. Durham, NC: Duke University Press.

Wellman, Judith. 2002. "The Underground Railroad and the National Register of Historic Places: Historical Importance vs. Architectural Integrity." *The Public Historian* 24, no.1 (Winter): 11–29.

Allison Carter

TRACK AND FIELD

Track and field athletic events had their origins in the Olympic Games of ancient Greece about 2,500 years ago. Track and field consists of a variety of running, walking, jumping, hurdling, and throwing events that take place between competing individuals or teams. The running and hurdling events range in length from the 50-meter sprint to the marathon (26 miles, 385 yards long). These events require different combinations of strength, speed, stamina, and agility.

The idea that any particular group of people, a race or national group, should dominate track and field as a whole is absurd. However, at various times in the history of European society, this view has been propagated (e.g., the superiority of the Aryan athlete on the verge of the 1936 Olympic Games). Today's theories of racial supremacy in track and field revolve around the claim that various races differ in specific athletic abilities, predisposing them for dominance in a particular series of events. These include claims that North American blacks are superior sprinters and jumpers, hybrid "races" such as North Africans are superior middle-distance runners, and East African blacks are superior long-distance runners.

Northern Europeans are claimed to be superior in events related to upper-body strength.

Much of the modern racial theory of track and field has been summarized by popular journalist Jon Entine in *Taboo: Why Black Athletes Dominate Sports and Why We Are Afraid to Talk About It*, first published in 2000. Entine claims that human races can be defined, if loosely, and that genetically determined features of these races can be used to predict individual predispositions for success in world-class athletics. He points to the dominance of western African (black) sprinters and jumpers, eastern African (black) long-distance runners, and northern Europeans in strength events. East Asians reputedly excel in flexibility and thus dominate such sports as gymnastics and diving. These claims are made by using patterns in male athletics. Entine recognizes that profound social forces (in particular the denial of athletic opportunities for female athletes) often skew the results of women's track and field to favor European nations.

The core claims of racial superiority with regard to track and field performances are: (1) that biologically definable races differ in physiology relative to performance in various track and field events; (2) that these biological differences are causal factors producing the patterns of elite performance in track and field; and (3) that there is racial clustering in elite performance in track and field.

SPRINTING, JUMPING, AND RACIAL BIOLOGY

Proponents of the alleged West African black advantage in sprinting and jumping often point to muscle physiology, hormone levels, and skeletal advantages. The relationship between running and jumping ability and the genetic differences in muscle-fiber types between "blacks" and "whites" has been linked to supposed differences in sprinting and endurance. Proponents argue that fast-twitch (type IIa and IIx) fibers are good for power and speed, while slow-twitch (type I) fibers are best for endurance. Empirical studies suggest that the legs of a world-class sprinter would have about 80 percent fast-twitch fibers and 20 percent slow-twitch, while the average active person would be expected to have about 50 percent of each. As of 2007, there have been no systematic analyses of muscle-fiber-type distributions in untrained persons around the world.

However, much has been made of the few studies that have examined differences between "racial" groups. For example, a 1986 study examined fast- and slow-twitch muscle types between West African "blacks" and French Canadian "whites." The authors found that the blacks were 67.5 percent fast muscle, but whites were only 59 percent. Using these averages, and applying a normal curve based on the variability in the data, the researchers concluded that the black curve would have a greater probability of producing fast-muscle percentages consistent with what would be expected in world-class sprinters (they estimated world-class sprinters should have more than 90 percent fast-twitch fibers). Because they believed that the differences in muscle-fiber proportion were genetically determined, and therefore immutable, they claimed blacks were naturally more likely to produce world-class sprinters rather than long-distance runners. However, without a worldwide large-scale sampling of untrained individuals, there is no real way to interpret any differences in muscle-fiber composition among athletes or to make any legitimate comparisons of genetic predispositions for long-distance running. The differences may be a matter of training rather than genetic inheritance.

Wilson Kipketer of Denmark Competes in the 800 Meter Race, Athens Olympics, 2004. *Racial typologists claim that Northern and Eastern Africans are genetically predisposed for middle- and long-distance running, a claim supported on the surface by the success of Wilson Kipketer, a runner of Kenyan descent.* ANDY LYONS/GETTY IMAGES.

Even factors as subtle as differences in diet or conditions faced during gestation could influence the expression of various genes, and hence produce a physical difference. Diet influences hormone levels, which can, in turn, influence the proportion of muscle-fiber types in animals. Testosterone level is responsible for the different muscle-fiber percentages between male and female mice (females have more type I fibers). Given that no large-scale studies of muscle-fiber percentage throughout the world have been conducted and that the few existing studies never controlled for dietary factors, claiming that the differences in muscle-fiber percentages result from differences in underlying genes is simply not credible (Graves 2005).

In addition, there are no systematic studies of candidate genes for any features associated with any sort of athletic performance. For example, two studies of American blacks and whites, which examined both inactive college-age men and college football players, show no significant differences in muscle-fiber proportions and muscle architecture (Abe, Brown, and Brechue 1999; Duey et al. 1997). These studies did show, however, that the black athletes had significantly greater quadriceps, hamstring, and bicep muscle thickness compared to the whites, though any number of social or environmental factors could explain these results (such as a longer history of strenuous exercise in the blacks examined).

Intrinsic racial difference in muscle-fiber percentages does not explain the differences currently observed between the number of world-class sprinters of African American and European American origins. The racial typologists claim that there is a greater percentage of blacks whose range of type II muscle fibers is suitable for producing world-class sprinters. Yet even if this greater percentage were ten times more likely to produce world-class sprinters, it would still not explain the observed differences in world-class sprinter distribution. The actual number of world-class sprinters originating from a racial group would depend on the size of the population in question. Using the total population size and the relative proportions of whites and blacks in the United States, one would expect to find 303,118 blacks and 206,672 whites with the genetic architecture required to be world-class sprinters. Proportionately, there should be only 1.46 times more blacks than whites with the proper genetics to be world-class sprinters (Graves 2005). Yet African Americans have dominated sprinting in America in the late-twentieth and early-twenty-first century in numbers greater than predicted by this theoretical distribution of genotypes. It must be remembered that this scenario assumes that blacks are ten times more likely than whites to have the proper muscle distributions, which data during this stretch of time show is highly unlikely. Therefore, other reasons must be found to explain why whites have not excelled in sprinting.

Genetic differences controlling muscle-fiber types between blacks and whites have been linked to supposed differences in endurance. Generally, long-distance runners are small, light-framed, and have high endurance, which may be linked to the percentage of endurance muscle-fiber types found in an individual. Empirical studies suggest that the legs of a world-class marathon runner have 80 percent slow-twitch and 20 percent fast-twitch muscles. It has been assumed that genetic factors fix the proportion of fiber types, so that training cannot drastically alter their ratio. However, research shows that endurance training can change type IIa fibers into type I fibers and that super-fast-twitch (type IIb) fibers can be changed into type IIa. Strength training, however, does not convert type I into type II fibers (Anderson, Scherling, and Saltin 2000).

Research on the heritability of muscle-fiber determination using monozygotic and dizygotic twins suggests that muscle-fiber distribution is about 45 percent genetic and 40 percent environmental, with about 15 percent of the variance in muscle type explained by sampling and technical error (Simoneau and Bouchard 1995). This means that if all technical error were removed, muscle-fiber distribution could be at most 60 percent genetic. This hardly provides strong support for the idea that running ability is genetically determined, which also means that a biologically racial theory of track and field performance cannot be tenable.

Furthermore, human groups that have been described as "races" are highly variable genetically. A study of Kenyan and Scandinavian long-distance runners showed no differences between their muscle-fiber proportions. In both groups studied, 60 to 70 percent of the muscle fibers were type I (Saltin 1995). A 2004 study that examined untrained individuals and national-class runners in Poland found 41.7 percent of the muscle fibers in the former were type I, while in the latter 64.3 percent were type I. However, without worldwide large-scale sampling of untrained individuals, it is difficult to interpret any differences in muscle-fiber composition among athletes or to make any legitimate comparisons of genetic predispositions for long-distance running.

HORMONES AND ATHLETICISM

Another consistent theme used to explain the superior performance of black male athletes is that of their supposedly greater hormone levels. Black males are said to have higher levels of circulating sex hormones called androgens than do whites and Asians. It is further argued that these differences make blacks more aggressive, violent, and lawless. In the early 1990s, a study of racial hormone levels examined males discharged from the U.S. Army between 1965 and 1971. The study examined more than 4,000 non-Hispanic whites, blacks, Hispanics, Asian and Pacific Islanders, and Native Americans in their late thirties. It was found that the amount of testosterone in the blood was greatest in Asian and Pacific Islanders, followed by blacks, whites, Hispanics, and then Native Americans. After the samples were adjusted for both the age and the weight of the individuals in the groups, the order of the groups changed to blacks, Asian and Pacific Islanders, Native Americans, whites, and then Hispanics. There were a number of problems with how these data were obtained, but even if one accepts these results, they do not match the predictions of those who claim that socially defined race determines athletic performance. For example, the study predicts that Asian and American Indian men should be more aggressive than white or Hispanic men. Yet American society sees Asian Americans as the model minority group and not as likely to be superstars in aggressive and violent sports such as football or boxing.

Finally, while it is widely known that testosterone levels influence sex drive and aggression in male primates, it is also known that learning strongly modifies the influence of sex hormones. When additional testosterone is given to males, it does not increase their sex drive above normal levels, and testosterone levels are strongly influenced by daily and seasonal rhythms. There is also an extensive literature that shows strong environmental influences on hormone levels. In addition, transient aggression influences testosterone levels in human males. Such factors as tennis matches, stress, collegiate exams, or army basic training can decrease testosterone levels. Studies that have used psychological rating scales to quantify levels of aggression and hostility in human males have found no relationship between aggression and androgen levels (Graves 2005).

Even more revealing is that studies of hormone levels have not found any difference between the testosterone levels of African-American and European-American men. One study found that male testosterone level was correlated with age, body mass index (BMI), and waist circumference (Gapstur 2002). When black and white males were compared for testosterone level with only age and BMI being controlled for, black males had about a 3 percent higher testosterone level. However, once waist circumference was included in this analysis, there was no difference between the groups. (The 1992 study of men discharged from the army did not control for BMI or waist circumference.) Furthermore, research concerning the genetic controls of testosterone level show that it is a complex trait. A genome-wide linkage scan for genes controlling steroid hormones found that more than sixteen different genes were involved in the process. The loci were not the same in the black and white families examined in this study, providing strong evidence that many environmental influences alter sex hormone levels.

Once again, the same underlying problem exists in all the biological comparisons of socially constructed races: Unless all the subjects in these testosterone measurements experienced the same environments and the same social conditions, and displayed the same psychological responses to them, such studies are literally meaningless. American society certainly does not treat African American and European-American males equally, so measurements of hormone levels in these groups cannot be correlated to any supposed genetic differences between them, nor can it be posited that hormonal levels determine success in any specific sport.

RACE AND THE PHYSIOLOGY OF ATHLETIC PERFORMANCE

Environmental and genetic explanations for racial domination in sports ability are difficult, if not impossible, to disentangle. The first obstacle is that human genetic variation cannot be unambiguously partitioned into races (Graves 2005). The second problem is that environmental influences that might impact physiological performance are not consistently associated with any particular population (however defined). Finally, any investigation of athletic performance must take into account social, cultural, and economic factors that influence who is likely to have the opportunity to achieve in a given sport at the highest levels.

It is true that general physiological rules control the evolution of human body types—for example, Bergman's rule, which relates body size to average environmental temperature. This principle states that within the same species, body sizes that evolve in cooler climates will be larger than those in warmer climates. This results because large bodies retain heat better in cooler climates because of smaller surface area to volume ratio. An extension of Bergman's rule is Allen's rule, which states that protruding body parts, such as arms and legs, are generally shorter in cooler climates. These rules could be used to explain the differences in body features between Eskimos and northeastern Africans. The former tend to be shorter, have thicker chests, and are short limbed, while the latter are taller, leaner, and long limbed.

Between these extremes, however, many body types exist in human populations. This is particularly true on continents that span great extremes of geography and of climate. China, for example, is nearly 2,200 miles long from north to south. It contains altitudes that include the Tibetan plateau (Mt. Everest, at 29,035 feet) all the way down to sea level. The body proportions exhibited by northern Chinese tend to be different from those found among southern Chinese. Just as well, one would expect different body traits in Tibetans as compared to Chinese from the region around Guangzhou. Yet anthropologists and geneticists almost never think of classifying these groups as different races. In theory, indigenous Tibetans should have some of the best high-altitude physiological adaptations in the world, but these cultures do not produce many world-class distance runners.

While the biomechanical features of individual athletes influence their potential for success in a specific sport, in most portions of the world there is great variation in body types. Africa, for example, exhibits populations as diverse as the Mbuti Pygmies of Central Africa and the Watusi of Kenya. As a group, the Pygmies are very short, while the Watusi are very tall. These groups differ in the frequency of genes that affect height, and most likely have lost sufficient amounts of genetic variation at these loci. However, in large populations, there is more genetic variation within groups than there is between them. This means that in populations of sufficient size, one should observe virtually all body types within any chosen group, even if the average of the body-type features between arbitrarily constructed groups were different. If one accepts the principle that world-class athletes should be rare, then one predicts that a nation's population size should be an important factor in determining its production of athletes in any sport. What this means is that individuals with both the genetic predisposition for great performance and the environmental circumstances that allow the expression of these genes will be rare, without regard to the racial composition of the country.

Men's Top Times in the Mile, as of September 2005

Nation	Number of Top Times	Number of Runners Responsible	Individual With Best Time
Morroco	16	2	El Guerrouj, 3:43.13*
Kenya	20	12	Ngeny, 3:43.40
Algeria	12	2	Morceli, 3:44.39
Great Britain	18	5	Cram, 3:46.32
United States	14	5	Scott, 3:47.69
Spain	5	5	Gonzalez, 3:47.79
Burundi	3	1	Niyangabo, 3:46.70
Qatar	1	1	Bashir, 3:47.97
Australia	1	1	Moltram, 3:48.98
New Zealand	5	1	Walker, 3:48.08
Germany	1	1	Herold, 3:49.22
Somalia	1	1	Bile, 3:49.40
Russia	0	0	
Romania	0	0	
Ireland	1	1	Flynn, 3:49.77
Bulgaria	0	0	
Uzbekistan	0	0	
Portugal	1	1	Silva, 3:49.50
Switzerland	0	0	
Poland	0	0	

*World Record Holder

Note: The number of top 100 performances posted by a nation are given in column two; column three lists the number of individuals from that nation who are responsible for the top performances; column four names the individual from that nation with the top performance and lists his time.

SOURCE: Adapted from the Track and Field All-Time Performances Homepage, http://www.alltime-athletics.com (Accessed April 24, 2007).

Table 1.

SUCCESS IN WORLD-CLASS TRACK AND FIELD

If race as a biological grouping is a legitimate factor in determining an individual's ability to perform at the highest levels in track and field, there should be evidence for it. Much is made of African domination in sprinting events. As of 2006, persons of African descent hold the male and female world records in the 100-meter sprint (Assafa Powell, Jamaica, 9.77 seconds, and Florence Griffith Joyner, United States, 10.49 seconds), and the 200-meter sprint (Michael Johnson, 19.32 seconds, and Florence Griffith Joyner, 21.34 seconds, both from the United States). However, in the 400 meters, a West German woman, Marita Koch, holds the world record at 47.60 seconds; the male record holder is Michael Johnson of the United States, at 43.18 seconds. The world record in the high jump is held by Javier Sotomayor, a Cuban of some African ancestry, while the woman's record is held by Stefka Kostadinova of Bulgaria. The long-jump records are held by Mike Powell, an African American, and Galina Chistyakova of the Soviet Union. The triple-jump world records belong to Jonathon Edwards of the United Kingdom, who does not appear to be of African ancestry, and Inessa Kravets of the Ukraine. The 110-meter-hurdle record for men is shared by Xiang Liu of China and Colin Jackson of the United Kingdom (and of African descent). The women's record holder in the 100-meter hurdles is Yordanka Donkova of Bulgaria. Thus, an examination of the world record holders in various events shows that African Americans are well represented but that Europeans and East Asians are also present. This is a weak case for supporting the idea that blacks are inherently faster sprinters and better jumpers than members of other races.

The claim that "hybrid" races dominate middle-distances is weakly supported by the superiority of male Kenyan and Moroccan runners in the 800 meters, 1,500 meters, and mile events during the late twentieth and the early twenty-first centuries (see Tables 1 and 2). These runners include Wilson Kipketer, a Kenyan who set the world record in the 800 meters in 1997 while running for Denmark, in a time of 1:41.11; and Hicham El

Men's Top Times in the 1500 Meters (Metric Mile), as of September 2005

Nation	Number of Top Times	Number of Runners Responsible	Individual With Best Time
Morroco	40	2	El Guerrouj, 3:26.00*
Kenya	20	10	Lagat, 3:26.34
Algeria	10	2	Morceli, 3:27.37
Great Britain	3	2	Cram, 3:29.67 United
States	1	1	Maree, 3:29.77
Spain	1	1	Cacho, 3:28.95
Burundi	3	1	Niyangabo, 3:29.18
France	1	1	Baala, 3:28.98
Bahrain	1	1	Ramzi, 3:30.00
Ukraine	1	1	Hesko, 3:30.33
Germany	0	0	
Somalia	0	0	
Russia	0	0	
Romania	0	0	
China	0	0	
Turkey	0	0	
Bulgaria	0	0	
Uzbekistan	0	0	
Portugal	1	1	Silva, 3:30.07
Switzerland	0	0	
Ethiopia	0	0	

*World Record Holder

Note: The number of top 100 performances posted by a nation are given in column two; column three lists the number of individuals from that nation who are responsible for the top performances; column four names the individual from that nation with the top performance and lists his time.

SOURCE: Adapted from the Track and Field All-Time Performances Homepage, http://www.alltime-athletics.com (Accessed April 24, 2007).

Table 2.

Women's Top Times in the Mile, as of September 2005

Nation	Number of Top Times	Number of Runners Responsible	Individual With Best Time
Morroco	0	0	
Kenya	1	1	Marenga, 4:24
Algeria	2	1	Boulmerka, 4:20.79
Great Britain	8	4	Pieterse, 4:17.57
United States	20	5	Slaney, 4:16.71
Spain	0	0	
Burundi	0	0	
Qatar	0	0	
Australia	0	0	
New Zealand	0	0	
Germany	2	2	Bruns, 4:21.59
Somalia	0	0	
Russia	19	12	Masterkova, 4:12.56*
Romania	25	8	Ivan, 4:15.61
Ireland	5	1	O'Sullivan, 4:17.25
Bulgaria	2	2	Yatzinska, 4:21.52
Uzbekistan	2	1	Zaytseva, 4:22.50
Portugal	3	1	Sacramento, 4:23.41
Switzerland	1	1	Weyermann, 4:23.92
Poland	1	1	Brzezinska, 4:22.96

*World Record Holder

Note: The number of top 100 performances posted by a nation are given in column two; column three lists the number of individuals from that nation who are responsible for the top performances; column four names the individual from that nation with the top performance and lists her time.

SOURCE: Adapted from the Track and Field All-Time Performances Homepage, http://www.alltime-athletics.com (Accessed April 24, 2007).

Table 3.

Guerrouj of Morocco, the world record holder in the 1,500 meters (3:26.00, set in 1998) and in the mile (3:43.13, set in 1999). However, viewing the entire top 100 times posted in these events, by both men and women, vitiates any racial view of success in middle-distance running. For example, while Moroccan and Algerian males have posted 28 of the top 100 performances in the mile (as of 2005), these times were run by only four individuals. Similarly, twelve Kenyan males have posted 20 of the top 100 times.

Other countries of note on this list are Great Britain and the United States, which have cultural ties to the mile race (English measurement). Thirty-two of the top 100, times in the mile were posted by ten runners (not of West or North African descent) from these two nations.

The fallacy of a genetic explanation for racial prominence is further illustrated when the distribution of the top 100 times in the mile by female runners is examined (see Table 3). In 2005, the three nations that dominate male long-distance running (Kenya, Morocco, and Algeria) produced only two women who accounted for three of the top 100 times. Thus, Morocco, which had two males with times in the top 100, produced no women runners who posted times in the top 100. The vast majority of top-100 times have now been run by women from Russia and eastern Europe (these countries have no male runners in the top 100). Russia, Romania, Bulgaria, Uzbekistan, and Poland account for 49 of the top 100. Svetlana Masterkova of Russia set the world record of 4:12.56 in 1996. The fastest time by a North African woman is 4:20.79, run by Hassiba Boulmerka of Algeria in 1991.

The contribution of cultural factors that contribute to success in middle-distance running is further illustrated by an examination of performances in the 1,500 meters. As with the mile, North African and Kenyan male runners have come to dominate at this distance. In 2005, El Guerrouj held the world record and 16 of the top 100 times at this distance, though only one other

Women's Top Times in the 1500 Meters (Metric Mile), as of September 2005

Nation	Number of Top Times	Number of Runners Responsible	Individual With Best Time
Morocco	0	0	
Kenya	2	2	Marenga, 3:57.41
Algeria	1	1	Boulmerka, 3:55.30
Great Britain	2	1	Holmes, 3:57.90
United States	2	2	Slaney, 3:57.24
Spain	0	0	
Burundi	0	0	
France	0	0	
Bahrain	0	0	
Ukraine	6	4	Pozdnyakova, 3:56.50
Germany	2	2	Wartenburg, 3:57.71
Somalia	0	0	
Russia	23	12	Kazankina, 3:52.47
Romania	14	8	Ivan, 3:53.96
China	23	12	Qu, 3:50.46*
Turkey	2	2	Ayhan-Top, 3:55.33
Bulgaria	1	1	Petrova, 3:57.40
Uzbekistan	1	1	Zaytseva, 3:56.14
Portugal	1	1	Sacramento, 3:57.71
Switzerland	1	1	Weyermann, 3:58.20
Ethiopia	1	1	Dulecha, 3:58.38

*World Record Holder

Note: The number of top 100 performances posted by a nation are given in column two; column three lists the number of individuals from that nation who are responsible for the top performances; column four names the individual from that nation with the top performance and lists her time.

SOURCE: Adapted from the Track and Field All-Time Performances Homepage, http://www.alltime-athletics.com (Accessed April 24, 2007).

Table 4.

Leading Nations for Track and Field Medals 2004 Summer Olympics

Nation	Gold	Silver	Bronze	Total
USA	36	39	27	102
Russia	27	27	38	92
China	32	17	14	63
Australia	17	16	16	49
Germany	13	16	20	49

SOURCE: Adapted from the International Olympic Committee website. Olympic Results: Medals by Country. http://www.olympic.org/uk/games/past/index_uk.asp?OLGT=1&OLGY=2004 (accessed April 24, 2007).

Table 5.

Moroccan runner was in the top 100. Bernard Lagat was the fastest Kenyan at this distance in 2005, holding 20 of the top 100 times (ten other Kenyan athletes were in the top 100). However, runners from Great Britain and the United States, which are based largely on the English rather than the metric system (though Great Britain is scheduled to fully convert to the metric system by 2009), posted only four top-100 times (by three athletes) in the 1,500 meters as of 2005. As previously mentioned, runners from these two nations have fared much better in the mile, which is equivalent to 1,607 meters and is thus a slightly longer race than the 1,500 meters. The 107-meter difference does seem to have an impact on how an athlete trains for the event or for strategies employed in running it. Thus, one cannot infer that an excellent miler will necessarily be an excellent 1,500-meter performer, and vice versa.

The previous point is also supported by the pattern shown in women's 1,500-meter times (see Table 4). Here is seen the emergence of Chinese women as the top performers in the world, a result not predicted by any of the racial typology theories of track and field. The world's top time at this distance was turned in by Qu Yunxia of China, who posted a time of 3:50.46 in 1993. China accounts for 23 of the top 100 at this distance, with twelve athletes on the list. Russia, meanwhile, also accounts for 23 of the top 100 (with twelve athletes), and Romania has 14 of the top 100 (with eight athletes). Again, the United States and Britain have had much less success in recent years, with only four top-100 times, posted by three athletes. Kenya and Algeria are also similarly reduced with three top-100 times, turned in by the same two athletes as in the mile event.

If the racial characteristics of nations do not predict their success in world track and field, what does? The evidence suggests that since world-class performance is rare and that it requires significant cultural and economic inputs to maintain, then population size and financial means should explain an individual's chance of becoming a world-class track and field athlete. For example, Table 5 supports this notion. The nations that won the most track and field medals at the 2004 Summer Olympics were nations that had both large populations and high gross domestic products. To test this idea for track and field in the aggregate, a multivariate analysis of variance was performed on the total track and field medal count from the 2004 Summer Olympics (see Table 6). Analysis of variance is a statistical technique that looks at the variance between groups and compares it to the variance within groups. If the variation within groups is greater than the variance between groups, then one concludes that the groups being compared are not statistically different from each other. If the opposite is true, then one concludes that the groups are statistically different from each other. The variables examined were gross domestic product (GDP), population size, and ethnicity/race. Countries were divided into eight categories by gross domestic product (GDP), eight categories by population size, and six categories by race/ethnicity. Five of the race/ethnicity categories were derived from nineteenth-century classification and geographical location: Negroid (sub-Saharan Africa), Caucasoid (northern/western European), Mongoloid (East Asian), Amerindian (Latin American nations), Australoid/Micronesians (nations with indigenous populations that were Australoid), and multiracial nations (nations such as the United States and the Republic of South Africa). The use of the GDP variable was to test the idea that the production of world-class track and field athletes is not influenced by the wealth of the nation.

As seen in Table 6, the results of the analysis support this last notion; GDP was not a statistically significant factor in medals awarded in track and field at the 2004 Olympic Games. Neither was the race/ethnicity of the nation statistically significant. The only statistically significant variable in this analysis was population size. However, the entire model, using GDP, population size, and race/ethnicity together, was significant. This results from the overwhelming impact of population size in determining the nation's ability to produce track and field medal winners at the 2004 Olympic Games. GDP and race/ethnicity alone were not significant; neither was their interaction significant in this model. These results support the hypothesis that the most reliable indicator of a nation's ability to produce world-class athletes is not its race/ethnicity but its population size.

An analysis of swimming medals awarded at the 2004 Olympic Games showed that GDP, population size, and race/ethnicity were all significant variables. Of the ninety-two medals in swimming at the 2004 games, only eleven were awarded to individuals not of European ancestry (Japan 8, China 2, and Trinidad Tobago 1). The three medals awarded to the Republic of South Africa went to swimmers of European descent. These results do not support the notion that only northern Europeans can swim; rather, it suggests that world-class swimming competition is still dominated by large, wealthy nations whose participant populations are mainly of European origin (United States, Australia, Germany, and Russia).

Those who wish to champion racial determination of track and field ability might raise the criticism that the racial identification of the nations in the analysis was not correct. The assignment of nations and their athletes followed the standard racial conventions used by the racialists. This argument, however, only strengthens the criticism of biological race as an ambiguous category, thus vitiating their objection. They might point to the fact that this analysis is general and therefore ignores the accomplishments of purported races in specific events. However, the analysis of specific events in this article undermine this claim. The burden of proof is with the racialists. They must demonstrate a pattern of racial achievement in track and field, which does not exist. Or they must propose a credible mechanism to explain the genetic basis of the racial differences. Scientifically valid evidence for these mechanisms at present does not exist. Thus, the racial explanation of track and field performance fails under the light of even elementary scrutiny of its core claims: Races exist, races differ in genes associated with athletic ability, and racially differentiated genes contribute to world-class track and field excellence.

Analysis of Variance: Track and Field Medal Count 2004

Tests of Between-Subjects Effects

Dependent Variable: Track

Source	Type III Sum of Squares	df	Mean Square	F	Sig.
Corrected Model	1067.0013[a]	57	18.720	7.825	.000
Intercept	264.263	1	264.263	110.471	.000
RankGDP	12.026	7	1.718	.718	.658
RankPop	180.984	8	22.623	9.457	.000
Ethnic	6.585	6	1.098	.459	.829
RankGDP * RankPop	12.574	2	6.287	2.628	.101
RankGDP * Ethnic	5.286	4	1.322	.552	.700
RankGDP * Ethnic	5.407	4	1.352	.565	.691
RankGDP * RankPop *Ethnic	0.000	0	.	.	.
Error	40.667	17	2.392		
Total	1340.000	75			
Corrected Total	1107.680	74			

[a]R Squared = .963 (Adjusted R Squared = .840)

SOURCE: Table by Dr. Joseph L. Graves

Table 6.

SEE ALSO *Genetic Variation Among Populations; Genetics and Athletic Performance; Olympic Games of 1904; Olympic Games of 1936.*

BIBLIOGRAPHY

Abe, Takashi, James B. Brown, and William F. Brechue. 1999. "Architectural Characteristics of Muscle in Black and White College Football Players." *Medicine and Sports Exercise* 31 (10): 1448–1452.

Ama, P. F., J. A. Simoneau, M. R. Boulay et al. 1986. "Skeletal Muscle Characteristics in Sedentary Black and Caucasian Males." *Journal of Applied Physiology* 61 (5): 1758–1761.

Anderson, J. L., P. Scherling, and B. Saltin. 2000. "Muscle, Genes, and Athletic Performance." *Scientific American* (September): 48–55.

Bale, John, and Joe Sang. 1996. *Kenyan Running: Movement Culture, Geography, and Global Change.* London and Portland, OR: Frank Cass.

Bramble, Dennis M., and Daniel E. Lieberman. 2004. "Endurance Running in the Evolution of *Homo*." *Nature* 432: 345–352.

Carrier, David R. 1984. "The Energetic Paradox of Human Running and Hominid Evolution." *Current Anthropology* 25 (4): 483–495.

Duey, William J., D. R. Bassett, D. J. Torok et al. 1997. "Skeletal Muscle Fiber Type and Capillary Density in College-Aged Blacks and Whites." *Annals of Human Biology* 24 (4): 323–331.

Ellis, Lee, and Helmuth Nyborg. 1992. "Racial/Ethnic Variations in Male Testosterone Levels: A Probable Contributor to Group Differences in Health." *Steroids* 57: 72–75.

Entine, J. 2000. *Taboo: Why Black Athletes Dominate Sports and Why We're Afraid to Talk About It.* New York: Public Affairs.

Gapstur, Susan M., Peter H. Gann, Peter Kopp et al. 2002. "Serum Androgen Concentrations in Young Men: A Longitudinal Analysis of Associations with Age, Obesity, and Race: The CARDIA Male Hormone Study." *Cancer Epidemiological Biomarkers and Prevention* 11: 1041–1047.

Graves, Joseph L. 2005. *The Race Myth: Why We Pretend Race Exists in America.* New York: Dutton.

Holden, Constance. 2004. "Peering Under the Hood of Africa's Runners." *Science* 305: 637–639.

Hugman, Barry, and Peter Arnold. 1988. *The Olympic Games: Complete Track and Field Results, 1896–1988.* New York: Facts on File.

Larsson, Peter. 2007. Track and Field All-Time Performances Home Page. http://www.alltime-athletics.com.

"Olympic Results: Medals by Country." International Olympic Committee. Available from http://www.olympic.org.

Saltin, Bengt, C. K. Kim, N. Terrados et al. 1995. "Morphology, Enzyme Activities and Buffer Capacity in Leg Muscles of Kenyan and Scandinavian Runners." *Scandinavian Journal of Medical Science and Sports* 5 (4): 222–230.

Simoneau, Jean-Aime, and Claude Bouchard. 1995. "Genetic Determinism of Fiber Type Proportion in Human Skeletal Muscle." *FASEB Journal* 9 (11): 1091–1095.

Willmer, Pat, Graham Stone, and Ian Johnston. 2004. *Environmental Physiology of Animals,* 2nd ed. Malden, MA: Blackwell.

Zawadowska, Bożena, J. Majerczak, D. Semik et al. 2004. "Characteristics of Myosin Profile in Human Vastus Lateralis Muscle in Relation to Training Background." *Folia Histochemica et Cytobiologica* 42 (3): 181–190.

Joseph L. Graves Jr.

TRANSNATIONAL LABOR ORGANIZING

Transnational labor organizing is the act of organizing workers in two or more nations into the same labor union affiliation or activist network. Labor unions historically have provided skilled and unskilled workers with better working conditions and higher wages. Although union leadership, organizers, and members in the United States have generally exhibited racist and sexist attitudes over the years, unions have nevertheless been valuable for people of color by protecting and furthering their labor rights. However, globalization has challenged the power of unions in industrialized nations. People of color and women employed in manufacturing are particularly vulnerable to the loss of unionized jobs. Unionized manufacturing industries offer relatively high wages and generous benefit packages. Unfortunately, these industries have been experiencing most of the job losses due to globalization. When unskilled workers lose these jobs, they generally tend to find employment in the predominantly nonunion service sector, where wages are significantly lower and benefits, especially health care, are often minimal or nonexistent.

THE IMPACT OF GLOBALIZATION

Modern technologies in transportation and telecommunications, coupled with an increase in free trade agreements (FTAs) and the activities of the World Trade Organization (WTO), have made it cost-effective for corporations to locate production in developing regions such as China. Two main reasons for such shifts are the extremely low labor costs and the authoritarian political systems found in these nations. For example, average labor costs in China are approximately 20 to 30 times lower than in the United States or Germany. In addition, the authoritarian governments and business culture of developing nations offer corporations a legal environment with little to no labor or environmental protections, which further reduces production costs. Such governments also often control and discipline their workforces through the use of police and military forces, in part to prevent autonomous worker organizing. Usually these developing nations establish what are commonly known as export processing zones (EPZs) to attract foreign companies. These are special industrial parks, such as the *maquiladoras* along the Mexican side of the U.S.-Mexico border. The working conditions within EPZs have been documented by activist and labor groups, including the New York–based National Labor Committee (NLC), as sweatshop conditions lacking basic human rights. Child labor, sexual favors as a condition for continued employment, retaliation against union organizers, and violations of labor laws are common. All these factors artificially prohibit labor costs from rising to the levels predicted by free market economics.

Corporations in high-wage regions of the world have been transferring production to developing nations—a practice commonly referred to as "outsourcing"—to take advantage of lower labor costs. As a consequence, unions in developed nations experience job losses and reduced negotiating power. Another common trend is for corporations to threaten relocation in order to extract concessions from their employees in high-wage nations. This has resulted in stagnant real wages, benefit reductions, and a disciplined contingent labor force in the United States and other industrialized nations.

This corporate strategy is similar to that used by businesses in the United States from the 1800s to the mid-1900s. Specifically, employers would use race to divide worker solidarity and prevent the formation of stronger, racially integrated unions. For example, white workers would be disciplined with threats of losing their jobs to blacks, and vice versa, pitting worker against worker. Globalization still includes racial elements that pit workers in high-wage regions, typically whites, against those in low-wage regions, typically Latinos, Africans, and Asians.

Labor scholars and union leaders argue that all workers in an enterprise need to be organized, regardless of geographic locale. This requires union members of advanced nations to develop a class-consciousness inclusive of race, gender, religion, culture, and geographic location, which can lead to transnational labor organizing. Although states openly sanction what is commonly referred to by activists as "corporate globalization," including FTAs, they do little to facilitate or encourage transnational labor organizing. A major reason for this is that governments of capitalist nations traditionally tend to be dominated by, and therefore express, upper-class and business interests. This also explains the historically hostile attitude of U.S. political and legal institutions toward organized labor. Consequently, workers have had to engage in transnational labor organizing largely on their own.

WHY ORGANIZE TRANSNATIONALLY?

The logic behind transnational organizing is that by organizing all the workers of a corporation, regardless of locale, it becomes harder for the company to shift production from facilities experiencing labor actions, such as a strike, to others that are not. It also prohibits the company from pitting its unionized high-cost employees against its nonunionized low-cost workers, who are typically in poor nations and are often nonwhites and women. In addition, unionizing workers in poor nations has the effect of raising their wages and benefits and creating a better balance with those in richer nations. In the long run, this reduces the competitive advantage of outsourcing and pitting developed-nation workers against those in developing regions. It also has the positive effect of improving the quality of work life and the standard of living for employees in poor nations.

EXAMPLES OF TRANSNATIONAL LABOR ORGANIZING

Although efforts to engage in transnational labor organizing are still rare, there are some prominent examples. One is the International Trade Union Confederation (ITUC), which is based in Brussels and has more than 300 affiliates representing more than 160 million workers in more than 150 nations. The ITUC was formed in 2006 from the merger of the World Confederation of Labour (WCL), the International Confederation of Free Trade Unions (ICFTU), and the Argentine Workers' Center (CTA). Older and more radical examples include the Industrial Workers of the World (IWW), popularly known as the "Wobblies." Formed in Chicago 1905 by anarchists and socialists, the IWW was suppressed by employers and the government alike, and its membership dropped dramatically from its 1923 highpoint of 100,000 members to about 2,000 members at the beginning of the twenty-first century.

In addition to the work of traditional labor unions, there are also examples of transborder organizing performed by indigenous people and activists. One example is Via Campesina, a transnational movement of small- to medium-scale farmers, landless peasants, indigenous communities, and rural women. Formed in 1992, Via Campesina operates in Europe, the Americas, Asia, and Africa. Its goals include providing access to land for local people, instead of basing land acquisition on free market forces as provided by the WTO and FTAs. Another goal includes food sovereignty, the ability to be self-reliant for food production rather than depending on international trade for food access. Finally, the movement also supports sustainable methods of agriculture based on local traditions and farming techniques.

Another example of activist transnational organizing is the Transnationals Information Exchange (TIE), formed in 1978. TIE is a decentralized nonprofit network that practices social movement unionism. Its goals include promoting social rights for women, immigrant workers, and people of color, as well as the development of democratic institutions where they do not exist. It also seeks to link economic rights with political rights, especially the freedom of association and the freedom to form a union in nations where such freedoms are still suppressed. The network opposes corporate globalization centered on FTAs that represent neoliberal policies, lean production, and casual employment, which are seen as privileging capital at the expense of labor, indigenous people, and local communities. The network includes workers that are both organized and unorganized in the informal, agricultural, and industrial sectors. The TIE especially targets industries dominated by transnational corporations (TNCs) in export-oriented sectors such as textiles. It encourages self-organizing and a variety of other activist strategies ranging from the local to the international level. Finally, the network attempts to promote solidarity between workers of developed and developing nations. It operates in most parts of the world, including Asia, the Americas, and Europe.

CHALLENGES TO TRANSNATIONAL ORGANIZING

There are a number of formidable obstacles to transnational labor organizing. For one, most labor legislation is nationally based. Given national sovereignty, corporations operating in different countries often have to comply with local labor laws, which tend to be much weaker than those of developed nations. In addition, many developing nations prohibit the very existence of independent labor unions. For example, many Mexican and Chinese labor unions are government controlled, often to the detriment of the workers. In fact, there are many cases where corporations have colluded with host developing nations to prevent the formation of unions. This is typically the case in EPZs. National labor laws are often suspended in these special zones in an effort to attract foreign investment. There are, however, examples of successful organizing in EPZs, such as in the Dominican Republic.

Another obstacle to transnational labor organizing is that even if a collective agreement is signed with workers in developing nations, corporations can easily relocate production to other EPZs around the world to evade higher labor costs. In such a case, the corporation effectively pits a national labor force in one developing country against that of another, and the workers willing to accept the least in terms of wages and benefits will win out. This also relates to the problem of divergent national interests. For example, workers in a poor nation may wish to focus on human rights issues, whereas those in developed nations may want to focus on improved benefit packages.

Finally, a major obstacle to transnational labor organizing is the existence of free trade institutions themselves. Specifically, most free trade rules mandate that participating nations conform to legal standards at the lowest common denominator. This significantly reduces the power of labor overall. However, there have been cases where labor organizers have used free trade rules to the advantage of workers—on the grounds of human rights, for example.

Globalization based on neoliberal principles presents a significant challenge to labor and political rights throughout the world. Nationally based organizing has been ineffective at addressing these issues, leading to the need for transnationally based organizing, particularly in light of the evolution of the globalized production process. In order to be effective, organizers are focusing on the importance of new ideologies that challenge the dominant ideology, which they believe privileges capital over labor and citizen rights. This includes developing transnational solidarity inclusive of geography, race, ethnicity, and gender. Evidence indicates that such an approach to worker rights is promising. However, globalization is a significant and ongoing process that is unlikely to reverse course. For this reason, the reaction from labor is also ongoing and solidifying into transnational alliances between unions, independent workers movements, activists, and many other groups.

Interestingly, the same telecommunication technologies that have made globalization possible are also enabling transnational organizing. For example, the Internet has proven to be an important tool for uniting diverse groups worldwide, helping them spread their message and coordinate their efforts. Groups such as the indigenous *Zapatistas* in Chiapas, Mexico, have used the Internet to recruit supporters and disseminate their message internationally. TIE is another example of activism based on Internet communications.

SEE ALSO *Labor Market; Transnationalism.*

BIBLIOGRAPHY

Armbruster-Sandoval, Ralph. 2003. "Globalization and Transnational Labor Organizing: The Honduran Maquiladora Industry and the Kimi Campaign." *Social Science History* 27 (4): 551–576.

———. 2004. *Globalization and Cross-Border Labor Solidarity in the Americas: The Anti-Sweatshop Movement and the Struggle for Social Justice.* New York: Routledge.

Brooks, Ethel. 2002. "The Ideal Sweatshop? Gender and Transnational Protest." *International Labor and Working-Class History* 61: 91–111. Available online from Cambridge University Press.

Domhoff, William G. 2006. *Who Rules America? Power, Politics, and Social Change*, 5th ed. Boston: McGraw Hill.

Gordon, Michael E., and Lowell Turner, eds. 2000. *Transnational Cooperation among Labor Unions.* Ithaca, NY: ILR Press.

Hurd, Richard W., Lowell Turner, and Harry C. Katz, eds. 2001. *Rekindling the Movement: Labor's Quest for Relevance in the Twenty-First Century.* Ithaca, NY: ILR Press.

Kay, Tamara. 2005. "Labor Transnationalism and Global Governance: The Impact of NAFTA on Transnational Labor Relationships in North America." *American Journal of Sociology* 111 (3): 715–756. Available from http://www.tamarakay.com.

Khagram, Sanjeev, Kathryn Sikkink, and James V. Riker, eds. 2002. *Restructuring World Politics: Transnational Social Movements, Networks, and Norms.* Minneapolis: University of Minnesota Press.

McMichael, Philip. 2004. *Development and Social Change: A Global Perspective*, 3rd ed. Thousand Oaks, CA: Pine Forge Press.

John Asimakopoulos

TRANSNATIONALISM

Transnationalism refers to the movement of ideas, people, and capital across national borders in the modern global era. The term emerged and became popular in the 1990s (though it had been in use before that), particularly in academic circles, as a way to describe and theorize the intercontinental displacements, economic relations, cultural forms, identities, and communities that characterize the contemporary era. As a concept, its emergence goes hand in hand with the ideologies of globalization and the technologies, processes, and networks that constitute an increasingly interdependent and connected world.

Transnationalism signals a different kind of analytical lens that emphasizes the connections and flows between different nation-states, territories, and regions in the world. It expands on and departs from older notions of identity that were based on national borders and allows a focus on subjectivity—or ways that identities are always in process, and constantly being inflected by different political, cultural, economic, and social factors. One key critique of the usage of the term *transnational* is that it tends to flatten out asymmetries of power between different regions of the world, nations, classes, and modes of displacement: There is a world of difference between the transnational capitalist class (a businessperson flying first-class, for example), an overseas contract worker whose mobility is regulated by the sending state, and an undocumented migrant whose mode of travel is highly perilous, and even fatal. As Caren Kaplan puts it in her 1996 examination of different metaphors of travel, "All displacements are not the same" (p. 2). Nevertheless, one way in which transnationalism remains such a key mode of analysis is the way it can bring the aforementioned businessperson, contract worker, and undocumented migrant together into one conceptual field, where the social, economic, cultural, and political forces that connect them can be analyzed, along with the kinds of effects they might have on each other's lives. In that sense, transnationalism encourages a connective but not necessarily flattening way to understand the world and its inhabitants.

THE SLAVE TRADE AND ITS LEGACIES

Although the term is relatively new, transnationalism itself is certainly not a new phenomenon: Even before the emergence and rise of the nation-state as a modern form of governance and identity (that is, before national boundaries existed), ideas, people, and goods traveled across other kinds of borders. The Atlantic slave trade (which took place between the fifteenth and nineteenth centuries) is one example of a transnational phenomenon that has had major repercussions on the condition of African, American, and European nation-states and peoples into the twenty-first century. The institutionalization of racism through the trafficking and enslavement of peoples of African descent had transnational effects that profoundly shape present-day economic and political development in Africa. Most historians estimate the total number of people trafficked at between nine and twelve million. As a result, the African continent suffered a tremendous loss of its human labor, the breaking up of family and tribal ties, and the devastation of ways of life. In contrast, the massive profits from the Atlantic slave trade fueled the continued development in Europe of architecture, the arts, and science, setting up a radically skewed transnational relationship that continues into the early twenty-first century.

As a transnational phenomenon, slavery laid the economic groundwork for the concept of race to emerge as an organizing mechanism of American society. Southern planters and slave traders needed to rationalize the dehumanization of a whole people in order to systematically exploit them as chattel, as property. As W. E. B. Du Bois stated almost four decades after the abolition of slavery in the United States in 1865, "the problem of the Twentieth Century is the problem of the color-line" (1996 [1903], p. 1).

The anticolonial poet and scholar Aimé Césaire, reflecting on the colonization that followed the abolition of the slave trade, writes about how these transnational historical processes shaped black life, identity, and consciousness in the New World. In his 1969 play, *Une tempête*, a rewriting of William Shakespeare's *The Tempest,* that elucidates the work that racism does in the relationship between colonizer and colonized, Césaire argues:

> you have ended by imposing on me
> an image of myself.
> underdeveloped, you brand me, inferior,
> That is the way you have forced me to see
> myself
> I detest that image! What's more, it's a lie!
> But now I know you, you old cancer,
> and I know myself as well.

Césaire and later his student, Franz Fanon, write about lives and cultures that have been profoundly shaped by the transnational processes of slavery and colonialism. Just as significantly, however, they write about a process of anticolonialism that was similarly transnational, much like the abolition movement that preceded it. Fanon's *Wretched of the Earth* (1965), a searing critique of European colonialism and racism in Africa (specifically the French in Algeria), influenced other anticolonial and liberation movements around the world, including the Black Power and black liberation movements in the United States. Recent scholarship, such as Paul Gilroy's 1993 examination of the transatlantic cultures of black music, shed light on the complex networks of creativity and survival in the African diaspora, in milieus shaped by the oppression of slavery and capital. In the early twenty-first century, the African continent continues to be marked by economic and political turmoil and communal violence that stems from these early transnational processes.

The AIDS crisis, which is a global crisis, is one example of how certain transnational phenomena, such as epidemics, natural disasters, and nuclear fallout, pay no attention to national borders. That nearly two-thirds of all the world's HIV-positive people live in sub-Saharan Africa, however, speaks to the continuing disparities that exist between Africa and its former colonizers. Old patterns of poverty, continuing social and political instability, and rapid urbanization and modernization have all contributed to Africa's disproportionate rate of infection and continuing inability to address the urgent needs of its HIV-positive citizens. In addition, AIDS continues to play a role in Africa's lagging economic development because of its impact on the labor force and households, yet treatment options and global aid for this problem fall short of the great need. Black Americans in the United States have been disproportionately affected by the AIDS epidemic, according to the U.S. Centers for Disease Control and Prevention, making up nearly half of all HIV/AIDS diagnoses. A related statistic, that one in every four black people in the United States lives in poverty, indicates the racialized and classed ways in which transnational phenomena such as epidemics continue to link the lives of African peoples long after the abolishment of slavery.

In the early twenty-first century, cross-border activities epitomized by the trafficking of women and girls continue old patterns of sexual, labor, and racial exploitation. Trafficking refers to the illegal and highly profitable trade in human beings that uses coercive tactics, violence, and debt bondage to control its victims. There are many parallels to the African slave trade here, and the usual victims come from countries in the global South, such as Thailand, the Philippines, and Indonesia, as well as from places that have undergone social, political, and economic turmoil, such as Bosnia and Herzegovina, the Soviet Union, and parts of Africa.

TRANSNATIONALISM AND LABOR MIGRATION

The construction of race and racism is deeply tied to the migration of labor. In his 1994 examination of race relations in nineteenth-century California, Tomás Almaguer argues that labor and its status as "free" or "unfree" became highly racialized, with the latter term becoming associated with people of color, who were seen as posing a threat to immigrant and "native" white labor. White labor unions successfully agitated for limitations on Asian immigration, and the Chinese Exclusion Act of 1882 was the first law that barred immigration on the basis of race.

One of the ways in which transnationalism is invoked in the early twenty-first century is in discussions of migration and the conditions that produce migration. In turn, such transnational processes of migration have a profound effect on processes of racial formation in different locales. As Michael Omi and Howard Winant suggest, racial formation is "the sociohistorical process by which racial categories are created, inhabited, transformed and destroyed" (1994, p. 55). Race, as generally construed, is the product of a social process marked by conflict, where meanings are assigned to different types of human bodies. Nowhere is this more evident than at one of the sites emblematic of transnational processes: the national border. At the U.S.–Mexico border, for instance, many institutional mechanisms work to help produce meanings about race and citizenship, and they do this by managing transnational flows of people, capital, and ideas.

When the United States closed off Chinese immigration in the late nineteenth century, one of the replacement sources for cheap labor came from Mexico, and Mexican workers were soon established as farm workers, miners, and railroad workers in the Far West. American labor shortages during World Wars I and II institutionalized a binational temporary contract labor program, the Bracero Program, between the United States and Mexico. With the permeability of the border, however, came anxiety about who could live in, work in, and claim the United States as their home. The establishment of the U.S. Border Patrol in 1924 to police the border also heralded institutionalization of the concept of "illegal alien," and the racial stereotyping of Mexican laborers began in earnest. This process of racial formation, with its creation and solidification of identities, is a transnational process, one that is highly dependent on an imbalance of political and economic power between the United States and Mexico. It is important to note the shifting perception of this population in U.S. culture. During times of labor shortage, the availability of the Mexican labor pool is viewed as an advantage. During economic downturns, however, this labor pool is portrayed as endangering the access that citizens have to the benefits of the American welfare state, and unfairly tapping the kinds of the entitlements that the state provides for working-class Americans.

The border issue is a highly volatile problem in the early twenty-first century, with illegal immigration cited as a top national priority and increasing militarization at the U.S.–Mexico border (along with a new fifteen-foot-high wall and night-vision scopes) cited as the solution. Larger transnational forces that affect migration, such as free trade agreements that established factories on the southern side of the U.S.–Mexico border to take advantage of looser environmental protection and tax laws as well as cheap labor, are also factors, as sociologist Saskia Sassen points out in "Regulating Immigration in a Global Age" (2005). Indeed, the continuing disparity of economic opportunities between the United States and Mexico has not been addressed by transnational mechanisms of trade, such as the North American Free Trade Agreement (1994), which has taken down trade barriers such as tariffs, while migrant workers continue to risk life and limb in crossing the border. At the same time, the evacuation of traditional industrial centers in the United States to the global South has resulted in increasing unemployment for Americans, setting up conflicts over resources and jobs, and putting into play anti-immigrant measures such as California's Proposition 187 of 1994.

SOCIAL AND CULTURAL FORMATIONS

This economic migration of people also sets up new patterns of kinship and affiliation that build on and extend old models of family and nation. In a transnational setting, new family forms are negotiated, and community affiliations are both strengthened and changed. Identity becomes understood as being a process that is marked by different, and perhaps contradictory, loyalties and identifications. Linda Basch, Nina Glick Schiller, and Cristina Szanton Blanc (1993) describe the multiple identifications of migrants, and the ways in which they maintain simultaneous identities linked to different nations over the process of migration and settling. The multiple loyalties are a result of these transnational processes and have an effect on how people negotiate notions of citizenship that are normally tied to the institution of the nation-state.

The cultural realm is often seen as a stage where transnational processes and identifications take shape that involve syncretic practices that fuse different cultural traditions, languages, and genres. Among transnational youth, who learn to be fluent in many different heritages and cultures, this mode of hybridity is a way of constructing what Stuart Hall has called "new ethnicities" (1996). In New York City, where the largest Indian-American population in the United States resides, Sunaina Marr Maira (2002) has observed the cultural fusions and identity negotiations of second-generation South Asian youth that take place in dance clubs, college campuses, and other urban spaces. Often savvier with Internet media and other communications technologies, transnational youth are often at the vanguard of new cultural productions and political mobilization.

In addition, new networks built around ethnic identity, social and cultural survival, and political mobilization form as a result of different kinds of displacements. Ties to nation and national identity do not necessarily disappear in a "borderless world" aided by technology. Nevertheless, identity and ways of understanding identity are increasingly complicated by other competing demands that are highlighted by transnational processes. Notions of race are bound less by national boundaries, enabling political activists and communities to make connections across national borders using a lens of race and racism—connections about structures of power, media and representation, the allocation of resources, militarization, and war.

SEE ALSO *African Economic Development; Border Patrol; Braceros, Repatriation, and Seasonal Workers; HIV and AIDS; Illegal Alien; Racial Formations; Social Welfare States.*

BIBLIOGRAPHY

Almaguer, Tomás. 1994. *Racial Fault Lines: The Historical Origins of White Supremacy in California.* Berkeley: University of California Press.

Basch, Linda, Nina Glick Schiller, and Cristina Szanton Blanc. 1993. *Nations Unbound: Transnational Projects, Postcolonial Predicaments, and Deterritorialized Nation-States.* New York: Routledge.

Césaire, Aimé. 1969. *Une tempête.* Paris: Éditions du Seuil.

Du Bois, W. E. B. 1996 (1903). *The Souls of Black Folk.* New York: Penguin.

Fanon, Franz. 1965. *The Wretched of the Earth.* Translated by Constance Farrington. New York: Grove Press.

Gilroy, Paul. 1993. *The Black Atlantic: Modernity and Double Consciousness.* Cambridge, MA: Harvard University Press.

Grewal, Inderpal, and Caren Kaplan. 2001. "Global Identities: Theorizing Transnational Studies of Sexuality." *GLQ: A Journal of Lesbian and Gay Studies* 7 (4): 663–679.

Hall, Stuart. 1996. "New Ethnicities." In *Stuart Hall: Critical Dialogues in Cultural Studies,* edited by David Morley and Kuan-Hsing Chen, 441–449. London: Routledge.

Kaplan, Caren. 1996. *Questions of Travel: Postmodern Discourses of Displacement.* Durham, NC: Duke University Press.

Maira, Sunaina Marr. 2002. *Desis in the House: Indian American Youth Culture in New York City.* Philadelphia: Temple University Press.

Omi, Michael, and Howard Winant. 1994. *Racial Formation in the United States: From the 1960s to the 1990s,* 2nd ed. New York: Routledge.

Ong, Aihwa, and Donald M. Nonini, eds. 1997. *Ungrounded Empires: The Cultural Politics of Modern Chinese Transnationalism.* New York: Routledge.

Sassen, Saskia. 2005. "Regulating Immigration in a Global Age: A New Policy Landscape." *Parallax* 11 (1): 35–45.

Wilson, Rob, and Wimal Dissanayake, eds. 1996. *Global/Local: Cultural Production and the Transnational Imaginary.* Durham, NC: Duke University Press.

Vernadette V. Gonzalez

TREATY OF GUADALUPE HIDALGO

On February 2, 1848, Nicholas Trist, a representative of the United States government, signed a treaty ending the Mexican-American War. This conflict had claimed more than forty thousand lives, most of them civilians, and arose out of an American desire to acquire more territory westward to the Pacific Ocean. The expansionism that caused the war was described by the phrase "Manifest Destiny," which highlighted the belief that God had given the white Anglo-Saxon American the mission to "civilize" all of the "lesser peoples" of North America, to bring them the benefits of Protestant Christianity and democracy, and in the process to take over their lands.

As a result of the war, the United States forced Mexico to cede about half of its territory, or more than 500,000 square miles. In particular, the Mexican Cession included the territories of California and New Mexico. In return, the United States agreed to pay Mexico fifteen million dollars. The treaty set new boundaries between the two countries, which created geographic ambiguities that necessitated the renegotiation of the international boundary a few years later in the Gadsden Treaty of 1853. Most significantly, Articles VIII and IX of the Treaty of Guadalupe Hidalgo, which Trist had signed, set the terms by which residents of the newly acquired territories would retain their property and be incorporated politically into the United States. The treaty stipulated that absentee Mexican landholders would have their property "inviolably respected," and that it would "be maintained and protected in the free enjoyment of their liberty and property." The treaty affected some 100,000 Mexicans in the new territories, including a large number of Hispanicized as well as free-ranging Indians.

As provided by Article VIII, a person had one year to "elect" his or her preference for Mexican citizenship. If this were not done, it was stipulated that they had elected, by default, to become United States citizens, and that they would be granted citizenship by Congress at some future

The Bandits Bride. *Mexicans who opposed the terms of the Treaty of Guadalupe Hidalgo were portrayed as bandits, as in this 1847 political cartoon.* THE LIBRARY OF CONGRESS.

time. As early as 1849, the nature of the citizenship rights of these Mexicans became the subject of controversy. In California, the delegates to the state constitutional convention wrestled with the problems of race, rights of citizenship, and the Treaty of Guadalupe Hidalgo. Six of the delegates were native Californios who were aware that Mexicans who looked like Indians faced the prospect of racial discrimination. Ultimately, they argued for the protection of Mexican Californians, even if it meant endorsing the racist views of their Anglo colleagues toward Indians and blacks.

There was some concern over whether the Mexicans remaining in the territories were in fact citizens of the United States. The delegates finally agreed that "it would seem that they are not in fact American citizens, but require some further action of Congress to make them citizens of the United States." The ambiguous citizenship of the Californios meant that they could not expect the full protection of the laws during this stressful and violent period in California's history. It was not until 1870, with the California Supreme Court case of *People v. de la Guerra,* that the status of the former Mexican citizens finally was resolved when the court ruled that Mexicans had become citizens in 1850.

The formal recognition of the rights of U.S. citizenship were somewhat abstract blessings for Mexican Americans, considering that most Anglo-Americans treated them as foreigners, regardless of their legal status. A more tangible promise offered by the Treaty of Guadalupe Hidalgo, included in Articles VIII and IX and the Protocol of Queretaro, was the promise of protection for private property. And it was in the realm of property rights promised by the treaty that the greatest controversies erupted.

LANDS AND THE TREATY: CALIFORNIA

In California, thousands of gold-rush migrants encroached on the original Mexican land grants and demanded that something be done to "liberate" the land. The result was the passage in Congress of the Land Act of 1851. This law set up a Board of Land Commissioners to adjudicate the validity of Mexican land grants in California. Every grantee was required to present evidence supporting title within two years. Those failing to do so would have their property pass to the public domain. The land commissioners were instructed by law to govern their decisions according to the Treaty of Guadalupe Hidalgo, the law of nations, Spanish and Mexican laws, and previous decisions of the U.S. Supreme Court.

Although the Board of Land Commissioners eventually approved many of the Mexican grants, most Californio holders lost their title due to legal expenses. Other individuals held perfect titles to their land and were able to survive economically, but then lost their holdings because they had not fulfilled the terms of the 1851 land law. A number of court cases involving Mexican and Spanish land grants emerged in regard to this issue, but the most famous one pertaining to the Treaty of Guadalupe Hidalgo was *Botiller et al. v. Dominguez* (1889). In that case the U.S. Supreme Court ruled that the laws of Congress (in the form of the Land Act) took precedence over the Treaty of Guadalupe Hidalgo, and that the court had no power to enforce the treaty. Thus, although Dominga Dominguez had a "perfect title" to her land, in the form of a grant from the government of Mexico dated August 28, 1835, she lost her title because she did not bring her papers before the Court of Land Claims within the specified time provided for in the 1851 law. *Botiller et al. v. Dominguez* was an important precedent, guiding the court in its future interpretation of conflicts between treaty obligations and domestic laws. In this case, the protection of private property ostensibly guaranteed by the Treaty of Guadalupe Hidaglo was essentially invalidated.

NEW MEXICAN LANDS AND THE TREATY

In the territory of New Mexico, federally appointed officials had to have their decisions approved by Congress, a lengthy and often politicized process. Ironically, New Mexico's more direct link to the national government meant that the property-rights guarantees under the Treaty of Guadalupe Hidalgo would be even less secure. In 1848, private and communal land grants in New Mexico covered about fifteen million square miles. In order to determine the federal domain, Congress established the office of Surveyor General, who was given broad powers to "issue notices, summon witnesses, administer oaths, etc.," and to report to the Secretary of Interior and, ultimately, Congress regarding the status of New Mexico land grants. Until Congress acted to confirm the findings of the Surveyor General, all lands were to be withheld from sale. By 1880, one thousand claims had been filed by the Surveyor General but only 150 had been acted upon by the federal government.

On March 3, 1891, Congress passed a law to establish a Court of Private Land Claims. The court was made up of five judges plus an attorney representing the interests of the U.S. government. Unlike the California Land Commission, the New Mexico Court of Land Claims did not require those holding perfect titles to apply to the court for confirmation; only those who had not fulfilled all the regulations of the Spanish and Mexican laws had to do so. Those not presenting their claims within two years would be considered to have abandoned their grant. But as a result of politically tainted maneuvers, the New Mexico court rejected two-thirds of the claims presented before it.

Ultimately, only eighty-two grants received congressional confirmation. This represented only 6 percent of the total area sought by land claimants. Thus, through the Court of Private Land Claims, the U.S. government enlarged the national domain at the expense of hundreds of *Hispano* villages, leaving a bitter legacy that would fester through the next century.

In the first half-century after ratification of the Treaty of Guadalupe Hidalgo, hundreds of state, territorial, and federal legal bodies produced a complex tapestry of conflicting opinions and decisions. What was clear was that the citizenship rights seemingly guaranteed by the treaty were not all that they seemed. The property rights for former Mexican citizens in California and New Mexico proved to be quite fragile. Within a generation, the Mexican Americans who had been under the ostensible protections of the treaty became a disenfranchised, poverty-stricken minority, as the promises of the treaty remained only promises.

SEE ALSO *Alamo; La Raza; Mexicans; Texas Rangers; Zoot Suit Riots.*

BIBLIOGRAPHY

Drexler, Robert W. 1991. *Guilty of Making Peace: A Biography of Nicholas P. Trist.* Lanham, MD: University Press of America.

Griswold del Castillo, Richard. 1990. *The Treaty of Guadalupe Hidalgo: A Legacy of Conflict.* Norman: University of Oklahoma Press.

Mahin, Dean B. 1997. *Olive Branch and Sword: The United States and Mexico, 1845–1848.* Jefferson, NC: McFarland.

Miller, Hunter, ed. 1931–1948. *Treaties and Other International Acts of the United States of America.* 8 vols. Washington, DC: Government Printing Office.

Pletcher, David M. 1973. *The Diplomacy of Annexation: Texas, Oregon, and the Mexican War.* Columbia: University of Missouri Press.

Rives, George Lockhart. 1913. *The United States and Mexico, 1821–1848.* 2 vols. New York: Charles Scribner's Sons.

Richard Griswold del Castillo

TRIANGULAR SLAVE TRADE

In the fifteenth century, Western Europe's sphere of influence began to expand. The opening of the Atlantic Ocean to world trade, specifically to trade within the confines of the Atlantic itself, played a major part in this growth. Portuguese adventurers navigated the coast of West Africa in search of gold and spices, capitalizing on technological advancements in shipping and developing new products for trade, with sugar being one of the most important. Over the centuries, sugar cultivation spread from India to the islands off the coast of West Africa and then to the Caribbean and Brazil in the sixteenth century. This expansion involved the employment of enslaved Africans to work the plantations. The combination of the three geographical regions (Europe, Africa, and the Americas) into a pattern of trade that involved the movement of labor from Africa to the Americas to produce goods for European markets has sometimes been referred to as a "triangular trade."

THE PRODUCTS OF TRIANGULAR TRADE

While sugar production was the cornerstone of this system, other commodities, such as tobacco, rice, cotton, coffee, and indigo, also fit the same pattern of using enslaved African labor on fertile land in the Americas to supply markets in Europe. Spain and Portugal both developed sugar production in the New World, extending production that had previously been located in the Mediterranean, the Canaries, Madeira, and the island of São Tomé. Environmental conditions made the Caribbean and Brazil ideal for the cultivation of sugar. However, Spanish interest in sugar diminished with the discovery of silver and gold in the territories of modern Mexico, Peru, and Bolivia. In contrast, the Portuguese monarchy invested in sugar production along the coast of modern Brazil, which led to the flooding of the European market with sugar.

In response to demand, France, England, and the Netherlands developed their own sugar colonies in the Americas, and they also introduced other crops into the plantation regime. As a result, they invested heavily in the purchase of enslaved African labor. These countries established trading posts in Africa for the purchase of slaves, and they then, in turn, founded their own colonies in the Americas, such as the English colonies established on Barbados in 1625, Jamaica in 1665, and the Gold Coast in 1661.

The Atlantic trading system appeared to operate in a triangular pattern, with European manufactured goods taken to Africa in exchange for slaves; enslaved Africans taken to the Americas to work; and the production of the Americas returned to Europe. An estimated 12 million Africans were forcibly moved to the Americas, especially to the Caribbean and Brazil, where many died under terrible working conditions. Their descendants suffered bondage until slavery was abolished in the late nineteenth century. The patterns of transatlantic trade and intercontinental exchange were far more complex than a simple triangle, however. The major components of the system united the Atlantic into a global phenomenon. European economic development was based on slave labor and benefited Europe and European colonies. The triangular

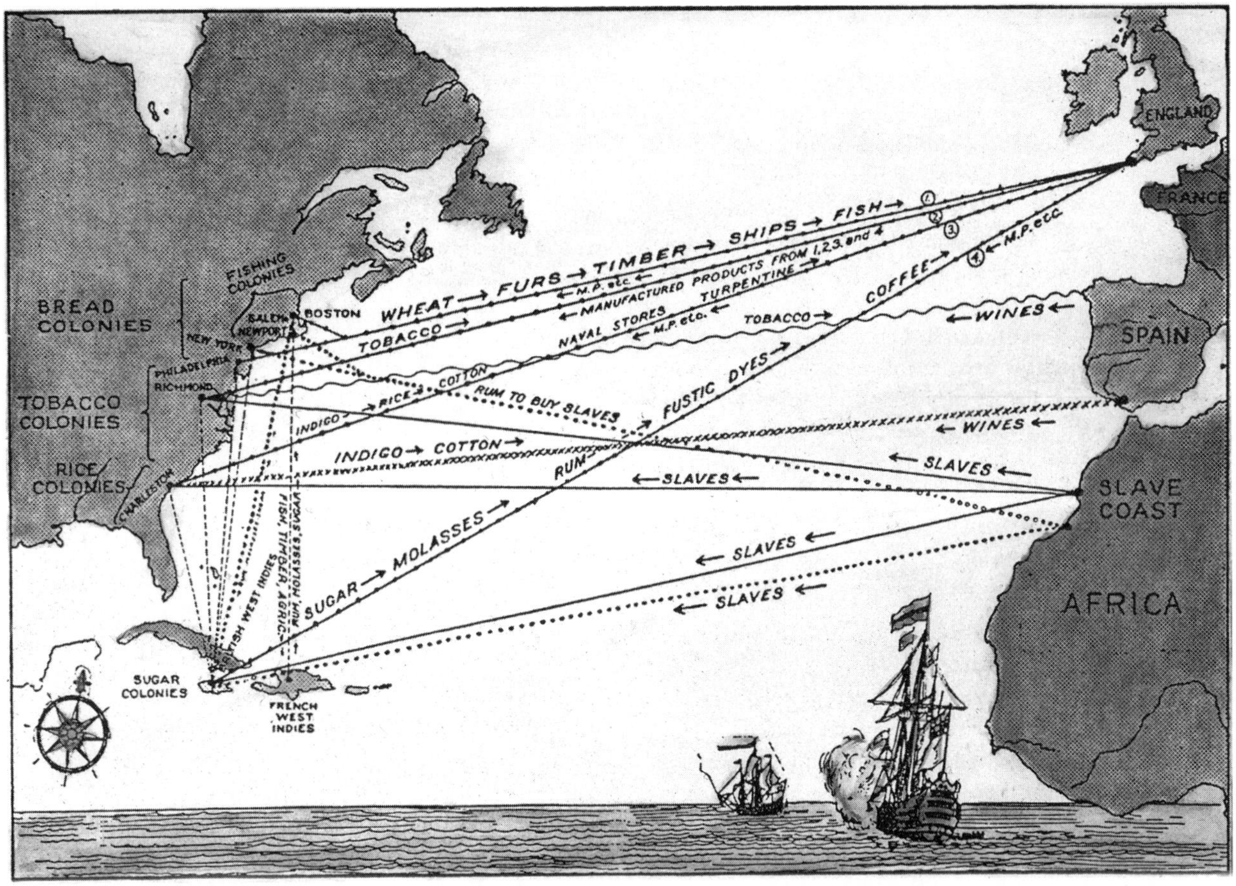

Map of the Triangular Slave Trade. *The pattern of trade that involved the movement of labor from Africa to the Americas to produce goods for European markets is known as a triangular trade.* THE GRANGER COLLECTION, NEW YORK.

trade was a circuit that relied on enslaved African labor, and it was an important factor in the emergence of the modern world economy.

Economic specialization and political factors complicated the picture, creating a far more complex network of production and trade than a simple triangular pattern. European countries often wanted to restrict trade to maximize profits within their own networks, once again suggesting a triangle across the Atlantic, but even these efforts, known as mercantilism, failed. Instead, trade flowed where it was profitable, at least in the long run, and entrepreneurs and adventurers tried different products and techniques in seeking profits from the trade across the Atlantic.

An examination of the goods and manufactures that were important in the trade with Africa, and which made the purchase of slaves possible, demonstrates the complexity of the system. Many of the items sold to Africa were objects used for money, such as cowrie shells (which came from the Maldive Islands in the Indian Ocean), strips of textiles that were produced in India, or objects of European iron and brass that were used as coins. Indeed, silver dollars were also used. The importance of these pieces of money in the trade with Africa demonstrates a level of economic development within Africa, one consequence of the triangular trade concept that is usually overlooked. Other trade commodities included weapons, particularly guns and ammunition, which had the effect of increasing the intensity of warfare in western Africa, and thereby increasing the number of enslaved Africans available for sale across the Atlantic. Increased warfare also led to further exploitation within Africa. Many other consumer goods—such as alcohol, tobacco, and sundry items of hardware, textiles, and jewelry—were also important, reflecting the buying power of elites in Africa. Again, these goods were often associated with the procurement of slaves. But the metals, alcohol, and tobacco came from the Americas, reflecting a bilateral trade, not a triangular one.

TRADE AND THE NATIVE POPULATION

Similarly, a singular focus on the triangular dimension of the Atlantic world that emerged with the spread of sugar overlooks the interaction with the indigenous population of the Americas. With the arrival of Europeans the Amerindian societies suffered near genocidal population losses as a result of enslavement, forced labor, spread of disease, poverty, and simply being murdered. Without this catastrophic destruction of the native inhabitants, there would have been little free, unoccupied land for exploitation, and there would not have been the demand for the importation of workers, whether they were indentured Europeans or enslaved Africans. In the sixteen century, Bishop Bartolomé de La Casas complained of the social impact of the European presence on the Amerindians, but only in the last decades of the twentieth century did scholars attempt to connect the plight of the Native Americans to the practices of land expropriation and slavery.

Scholars discovered that when Europeans arrived in the Americas, they encountered a variety of Amerindian populations, which were sustained by different levels of economic development. In some places, such as Central America, the concentration of the Amerindian population was relatively large. However, the introduction of smallpox, the common cold, and other infectious diseases by Europeans led to the rapid decrease of the local populations. In addition, the European use of forced Amerindians labor in the mining industry, under heavy workloads contributed to their decimation and a resulting labor shortage. Lacking cheap labor to work the vast amount of land at their disposal, Europeans turned to Africa to resolve their labor shortage. The large-scale forced migration of Africans resulted in the growth of tropical production and increased shipments to Europe. In the Americas, European countries sought to protect their respective monopolies by forcing their colonies to trade exclusively with the metropolis. Colonial planters were obliged to sell their products to the "mother country." Because it was forbidden to produce anything in the colonies that competed with homeland products, items such as textiles, tools, hats, food, books, clothing, and weapons had to be imported. These requirements stifled the development of local industries and the accumulation of capital in the Americas. European states also enacted navigation laws and created chartered companies to maintain economic monopolies in competition with one another. However, many ambitious traders operated illegally to evade these prohibitions to profit.

THE GROWTH OF EUROPEAN TRADE

In the late sixteenth century, the visibly increasing wealth from the overseas holdings of the Portuguese monarchy drew the attention of the British, Dutch, and French. By the mid-seventeenth century, Dutch traders in particular were participating actively in the trade through the Dutch West India Company. The Dutch were present in different regions of the Americas, from New Amsterdam to Guiana, and including Caribbean islands such as Curacao and Aruba. In 1630 the Dutch captured Pernambuco in northeast Brazil, obtaining control over sugar production there. In 1641 the Dutch also seized Portuguese holdings in Africa, such as the ports of Elmina, Luanda, Benguela, and the island of São Tomé. The Dutch West India Company monopolized the slave trade from African ports to Dutch and Spanish possessions in the Americas from 1621 through 1737. In 1648, Portuguese and Luso-Brazilian troops expelled Dutch merchants from Luanda and the northeast of Brazil. Still, the Dutch crown remained present in Netherlands Antilles, Suriname and Guiana, which enabled the slave trade to be one of the major economic activities in Holland until the end of the eighteenth century.

While the Dutch were expanding their empire, the French settled in Guadeloupe and Martinique in 1635, and they initiated trading contacts with Senegal in the 1670s. This was the beginning of the French Atlantic empire. The capture of St. Domingue (now Haiti) in 1697 increased the demand for African slaves. Slave traders sailed from France with their ships loaded with an assortment of trade goods, including metal tools and utensils (hoes, axes, buckets), textiles (European and Indian), alcohol (wine and brandy), tools (knives, swords, and machetes), and luxury items (porcelain, corral, mirrors, pearls, and decorated knives). In certain ports of West Africa, such as Saint Louis (at the mouth of the Senegal River), Elmina, and Ouidah, traders exchanged these goods for slaves. Ships sometimes transported more than 500 people at a time. In the "Middle Passage," slaves were fed products brought from Europe or acquired in Africa, such as dried fish and manioc flour.

In the eighteenth century, British traders established themselves at Calabar and Bonny in West Africa, where they traded metal products such as buckets and agricultural tools in exchange for African slaves. British slave traders transported slaves to Barbados, Jamaica, and Antigua, but also to mainland North America, particularly Virginia and the Carolinas to produce cotton, indigo, rice, ginger, and tobacco. The profitable production of these items depended on the importation of masses of African slave laborers. While the colonial mercantile system benefited Britain, North American and Caribbean colonies depended on Britain manufactures, creating a constant demand for British imports.

SLAVERY, TRADE, AND THE INDUSTRIAL REVOLUTION

In the 1940s, the distinguished historian Eric Williams proposed that the triangular trade stimulated the development of capitalism in Britain. According to Williams, African slaves acquired British goods, which helped the expansion of local industry in Britain. Meanwhile, African slaves produced valuable tropical products whose profits reverted to the development of industries in England, ultimately leading to the accumulation of capital and financing the Industrial Revolution. African slave labor was the foundation of the triangular trade and, ultimately, of British industrialization and development. According to Williams's critics, however, the slave trade and the plantation system were only one part of a complex British economy that expanded in many directions at once. Nonetheless, capital and expertise in finance and management were essential to the Industrial Revolution, and slavery and the slave trade played their part.

The trade across the South Atlantic between Africa and Brazil was in many ways bilateral and did involve Europe as much as trade with the Caribbean and North America did. Geographical conditions facilitated a direct link across the Atlantic, for winds and ocean currents forced ships sailing from Portugal to navigate to Recife or Salvador, Brazil, before changing the trajectory to disembark at Elmina in West Africa or in Luanda, south of the River Congo. Consequently, ship captains also had to stop at islands or ports in the New World to restock their food and water supply and to buy New World trade goods to be sold in Africa. This trade allowed New World merchants to accumulate capital through the sale of tropical products, including tobacco and alcohol. These merchants invested their profits in the slave trade. After 1700, Brazilian traders displaced Portuguese merchants, becoming the major slave traders supplying Rio de Janeiro and Bahian markets. Thus, in addition to a triangular trade, there was also a direct two-way trade between Africa and the Americas.

The Atlantic basin became a cohesive entity during the era of transatlantic slavery, with seaport cities arising on both sides of the ocean. The displacement of the approximately 12 million Africans who were forcibly moved to the Americas was a major demographic change in the Atlantic world. The profits generated by slavery increased the wealth of the Europeans involved, but it had negative effects on African economies. Scholars debate the number of victims because it is difficult to determine the number of people who died during the wars and crises in Africa that resulted in enslavement or during the long journeys to the coast from the interior and during the Atlantic crossing. African societies sold their enemies to Europeans in exchange for alcohol, guns, and textiles, among other foreign goods. However, textiles did not last, alcohol was consumed, and guns increased the production of captives. At the same time, Africans and their descendents were forced to work on plantations, in mines, and in urban centers in the Americas, producing wealth they were unable to acquire, and which was later used to purchase more African slaves.

BIBLIOGRAPHY

Boxer, Charles. 1962. *The Golden Age of Brazil, 1695–1750: Growing Pains of a Colonial Society.* Berkeley: University of California Press.

Dunn, Richard. 1972. *Sugar and Slaves: The Rise of the Planter Class in the English West Indies, 1624–1713.* Chapel Hill: University of North Carolina Press.

Eltis, David. 1987. *Economic Growth and the Ending of the Transatlantic Slave Trade.* New York: Oxford University Press.

———. 2000. *The Rise of African Slavery in the Americas.* Cambridge, U.K.: Cambridge University Press.

Florentino, Manolo. 2003. "Slave Trading and Slave Traders at Rio de Janeiro, 1790–1830." In *Enslaving Connections: Changing Cultures of Africa and Brazil during the Era of Slaving,* edited by José C. Curto and Paul E. Lovejoy, 57–79. Amherst, NY: Humanity Books.

Lovejoy, Paul E. 2000. *Transformations in Slavery: A History of Slavery in Africa,* 2nd ed. Cambridge, U.K.: Cambridge University Press.

Manning, Patrick. 2000. "Migrations of Africans to the Americas: The Impact on Africans, Africa, and the New World." In *The New World History: A Teacher's Companion,* edited by Ross E. Dunn, 206–221. Boston: St. Martin's Press.

Mintz, Sydney W. 1985. *Sweetness and Power: The Place of Sugar in Modern History.* New York: Viking.

Pritchard, James. 2004. *In Search of Empire: The French in the Americas, 1670–1830.* Cambridge, U.K.: Cambridge University Press.

Sollow, Barbara, and Stanley Engerman, eds. 1987. *British Capitalism and Caribbean Slavery: The Legacy of Eric Williams.* Cambridge, U.K.: Cambridge University Press.

Williams, Eric. 1944. *Capitalism and Slavery.* New York: Russell & Russell.

Paul E. Lovejoy

TRIRACIAL ISOLATES

Scattered throughout the eastern United States, particularly in the Southeast, there have been some 200 or more communities known as triracial isolates, which comprise individuals of mixed (blended) European-American, African-American, and Native American descent. Pluralistic in nature, triracial communities have historically lived apart from blacks and whites in isolated rural enclaves. In the early twenty-first century, large numbers of individuals remain in these rural communities as unskilled laborers or agricultural workers. However, some triracial communities boast of prosperous farmers, college graduates, and professionals. Since the mid-twentieth century, many individuals from these communities have migrated to the cities. This trend, along with increased intermarriage (generally with European Americans), has led to the extinction of many communities and the loss of collective identity.

Triracial isolate communities have historically straddled the racial divide. Some communities have identified with one particular group, usually white or Native American. Other communities have attempted to forge a new multiracial identity, refusing to deny their various ancestral backgrounds.

GROUP NAMES

Although these communities have been designated by social scientists as triracial isolates, many vehemently reject any such labeling. In fact, it would be wrong to think of them as one identifiable group. Commonalties among these groups have less to do with actual cultural bonds than with similarities in experiences, particularly their refusal to accept the "one-drop rule," through which individuals suspected of having any African ancestry are considered black.

Documentary evidence is scanty, and the exact origins of these groups are unknown. Furthermore, at different times in the antebellum period, depending on the determination of the census enumerator, the same families in some communities were listed variously as white, mulatto, and free people of color. To complicate matters further, the term "free people of color" did not become interchangeable with the categories of "free mulatto" and "free black" until the mid-nineteenth century. Up to that time, it had been an elusive term that included Native American reservations, Native American rural communities, multiracial populations of European-American and African-American descent, triracial populations, and free blacks. The communities probably evolved from frontier settlements that attracted runaway slaves, trappers, homesteaders, adventurers, deserters, outlaws, outcasts, and nonconformists of all racial backgrounds.

Triracial isolates have been known by a variety of names. New York has been the home of the Van Guilders, the Clappers, the Shinnecock, the Poospatuck, the Montauk, and the Mantinecock. New Jersey (and New York) is the residence of the Ramapo (or Ramapough) Mountain People (commonly referred to as "Jackson Whites"). In Pennsylvania, they have been called Pools; in Delaware, Nanticokes; in Rhode Island, Narragansetts; in Massachusetts, Gay Heads and Mashpees; and in Ohio, Carmelites. Maryland has its Wesorts; West Virginia, its Guineas; and Tennessee and Kentucky, the Melungeons. There are the Ramps, Issues, and Chickahominy in Virginia; the Lumbees, Haliwas, Waccamaws, and Smilings in North Carolina; and the Chavises, Creels, Brass Ankles, Redbones, Redlegs, Buckheads, and Yellowhammers in South Carolina. Louisiana has also been home to many triracial communities.

Appellations such as Chavis and Creel are family names, although many others, such as Brass Ankle, Redbone, and Jackson Whites were externally imposed and clearly meant to be insults. As such, those who bear these names have often rejected them, although many groups now embrace the names with pride. Names such as Chickahominy and Nanticoke, which suggest Native American derivation, have always been borne with pride. Some individuals in these communities would readily be taken as Native American. Others are indistinguishable from whites. However, many clearly show varying degrees of African ancestry in combination with European and/or Native American descent.

ANYTHING BUT BLACK

In the U.S. South, any term describing a racially blended background has generally not only included African ancestry, but also been equated with Mulatto and translated as "black." Consequently, Brewton Berry has argued that most triracial communities have historically tended to deny any African ancestry. They have prized indigenous origins, despite having retained little or no knowledge of either Native American culture or tribal affiliations, and despite being culturally indistinguishable from local whites. Thus, most of these communities have affirmed only two components—Native American and European American—if they acknowledged their multiracial ancestry at all. In this sense, the triracial isolate quest for identity appears to be more reactionary than radical. Yet these communities have manipulated the historical U.S. binary racial construction (i.e., black and white) to their advantage, forging instead a ternary racial construction that has destabilized binary racial thinking.

While racial composition and ancestry have always been fundamental to determining who is defined as African American, there is no universally accepted definition of Native American. The definitions employed by the U.S. Census Bureau and the Bureau of Indian Affairs (BIA) have often been at odds with each other, and both have changed over time. The BIA includes on its rolls only those individuals entitled to BIA services. Acceptance by a tribe in conjunction with proof of at least one-quarter degree of indigenous ancestry is generally required. For census purposes, self-definition has been the prevailing policy for all racial and ethnic groups since 1970. In the past, however, enumerators were instructed to record as Native American only those individuals enrolled on reservations or listed in agency rolls, persons of one-fourth or more indigenous ancestry, or individuals regarded as Native Americans by their communities.

FORGING A NATIVE AMERICAN IDENTITY

Historical accounts and oral traditions reveal that the indigenous ancestors of the contemporary Lumbees were composed largely of Cheraw Native Americans and related Siouan-speaking people known to have inhabited the area in present day Robeson County, North Carolina. They were first observed in 1724 on Drowning Creek (now known as the Lumber River), when the first European settlers arrived in the area.

North Carolina has recognized the Lumbee as a Native American tribe since 1885. With this recognition, the state provided educational assistance and other services. In 1887, the state established a Native American teachers-training school for the Lumbees, which grew into the nation's first state-supported school offering higher education to Native Americans. In the early twenty-first century it is known as the University of North Carolina at Pembroke and boasts of an enrollment of approximately 3,000 students. The school is part of the University of North Carolina system, which gives credence to Lumbee assertions that they have produced more doctors, lawyers, and Ph.D.s than any other Native American community in the United States.

According to the 2000 census, 51,913 Native Americans in the United States identified their tribe as Lumbee, making them the second largest tribe east of the Mississippi River. The Lumbee are the largest nonreservation tribe in the United States, and the largest not recognized by the federal government. It was not until 1956, however, that the United States Congress passed the Lumbee Act, which officially recognized the Lumbee Indians of North Carolina. Unfortunately, the bill contained language that made them ineligible for financial assistance and program services administered by the BIA.

Many Lumbees have held local elective office, and a Lumbee has represented Robeson County in the North Carolina legislature. Also, Lumbee tribal members are active in Native American affairs at the state and national levels and are still fighting for federal recognition as a tribe. (An attempt in 1992, failed by only two votes in the United States Senate.) Some say that other Native American tribes have not supported recognition of the Lumbee because it would decrease their share of government funds. Other critics point out that the Lumbee do not live on a reservation, have never signed a treaty with the U.S. government, and cannot prove they are all members of the same tribe. To the Lumbee, however, being Native American has nothing to with such criteria, but is a matter of how they are perceived and whether they are respected. By 1980, the Nanticoke of Delaware, the Houma in western Louisiana, and the Poospatuck of Long Island, New York, following in the footsteps of the Lumbee, succeeded in officially changing their earlier classification as mulattoes to nontreaty Native Americans. By 1990 this was also true of the Jackson Whites, who were recognized as the Ramapo Mountain Native Americans. Although this status excludes these groups from most federal government benefits, it does place them squarely on the indigenous side of the racial divide. However, their claims to indigenous status have been met with reluctance, if not resistance, from treaty or reservation groups (e.g., the Cherokee, Comanche, and Choctaw) that qualify for federal subsidies.

Although some African Americans have accused the triracial isolate communities of claiming Native American status to escape the stigma of being black, various triracial groups have cast their lot with African Americans. Most, however, have historically maintained a strong antiblack prejudice that has, in no small part, helped bolster support for their own identity by whites. The clearest example of this was during the era of segregation. Denied entry into white schools, numerous communities not only refused to attend schools and use public facilities for African Americans, but they gained support for establishing their own public restrooms and education facilities, as well as separate sections in churches and theaters.

FORGING A MULTIRACIAL IDENTITY

By the 1990s, groups such as the Issues and Melungeons succeeded in negotiating federally recognized identities as "other" nonwhites. Although some individuals have always passed for white, groups such as the Melungeons have fought for legal status as white—and succeeded in this in their local communities. However, these and other triracial communities have enjoyed a status just below that of whites, while elsewhere their status has been hardly distinguishable from that of blacks. This has often led to the denial of African ancestry, the avoidance of every suspicion of association with blacks, and at times to the casting off of darker relatives. Indeed, many contemporary triracial groups are now largely phenotypically indistinguishable from the surrounding European-American community. Over time, racial blending and the movement of many darker individuals into other communities of color, has diminished the earlier presence of more African and Native American phenotypical traits.

Since the 1990s, there has been a change in attitudes among some triracial communities such as the Redbones and Melungeons. Melungeon identity, after almost becoming extinct, is experiencing a resurgence. There has also been a surge of research that culminated in a gathering of Melungeons, called the "First Union," held in July 2005 at Clinch Valley College in Wise, Virginia. Since the "Second Union," held in 1998, these conferences have become yearly events. The Redbones held a similar event in June 2005, in Alexandria, Louisiana, titled "Taking Pride in Who We Are." This "new" triracial identity displayed by the Melungeons and Redbones differs from the "old" triracial identity in that it seeks to deconstruct the elitist and hierarchical premises upon which the previous identity was based by acknowledging and embracing the African and other ancestries.

This about-face in identification is best expressed by Brent Kennedy, a Melungeon who sees in the faces of his living relatives a panorama of all of those who have gone before. In a moment of eloquent prose, Kennedy writes:

> When I watch my own summer skin turn with lightning speed too reddish-brown for a blue-eyed Scotsman, and struggle to tame the steel-like waves in my graying Black hair, I smile at the living traces of unknown Mediterranean, African, and Native American ancestors whose ancient precious lives still express themselves in my countenance... And in my mind's eye, I can see those ancestors smiling back, wondering why it took the children of their children's children so long to rediscover the truth (Kennedy 1997, p. xiii).

SEE ALSO *Biracialism.*

BIBLIOGRAPHY

Berry, Brewton. 1963. *Almost White: A Study of Certain Racial Hybrids in the Eastern United States.* New York: Macmillan.

———. 1972. "America's Mestizos." In *The Blending of Races: Marginality and Identity in World Perspective,* edited by Noel P. Gist and Anthony Gary Dworkin. New York: Wiley-Interscience.

Blu, Karen. 1980. *The Lumbee Problem: The Making of an American Indian People.* New York: Cambridge University Press.

Bordewich, Fergus M. 1996. *Killing the White Man's Indian: Reinventing Native Americans at the End of the Twentieth Century.* New York: Doubleday.

Cohen, David Steven. 1986. *The Ramapo Mountain People.* New Brunswick, NJ: Rutgers University Press.

Daniel, G. Reginald. 2002. *More Than Black? Multiracial Identity and the New Racial Order.* Philadelphia: Temple University Press.

Kennedy, N. Brent, and Robyn Vaughan Kennedy. 1997. *The Melungeons: The Resurrection of a Proud People—An Untold Story of Ethnic Cleansing in America,* 2nd ed. Macon, GA: Mercer University Press.

Lumbee Tribe of North Carolina. Available from http://www.lumbeetribe.com/lumbee.

Marler, Don C. 2003. *Redbones of Louisiana.* Hemphill, TX: Dogwood Publishing Company.

Melungeon Heritage Foundation. Available from http://www.melungeon.org.

Nassau, Mike (McGlothlen). 1994. *Melungeons and Other Mestee Groups.* Gainesville, FL: McGlothlen Publishers. Available from http://www.geocities.com/melungeonorigin.

Official Ramapough Lenape Nation Web site. Available from http://www.ramapoughlenapenation.org.

Redbone Heritage Association. Available from http://www.redboneheritagefoundation.com.

Sider, Gerald. 1993. *Lumbee Indian Histories.* New York: Cambridge University Press.

Thornton, Russell. 1987. *American Indian Holocaust and Survival: A Population History since 1492.* Norman: University of Oklahoma Press.

Waak, Patricia Ann. 2005. *My Bones Are Red: A Spiritual Journey with a Triracial People in the Americas.* Macon, Georgia: Mercer University Press.

Winkler, Wayne. 2005. *Walking Toward the Sunset: The Melungeons of Appalachia.* Macon, GA: Mercer University Press.

G. Reginald Daniel
Christopher Bickel

TROTTER, WILLIAM MONROE
1872–1934

William Monroe Trotter was born on April 7, 1872 in Chillicothe, Ohio; he died on April 7, 1934, from a fall from the third floor of his Boston home on his sixty-second birthday, though he may have jumped. Trotter was a militant black activist whose instinctive desire for his race to improve meant doing so unassisted by whites. His key role model was his father, James, a Mississippi native who decided to settle in Boston for its amenities: the right to vote, hold public office, sit on juries, testify in court, intermarry, and attend integrated schools. Moreover, prohibited were racial discrimination on public transportation and at inns, public meetings, and public amusement places.

Living in a white neighborhood, James was a respected citizen; nevertheless, he suffered from racial discrimination. He worked entirely surrounded by whites at the Boston Post Office, a Republican domain, when in 1882 a white man was promoted to a chief clerkship over James. Acutely insulted, he resigned in protest. His greatest interest, however, was politics. Republican president Rutherford B. Hayes caused him to become a Democrat when he withdrew the last federal troops from the South in 1877; James considered this too soon and a betrayal of his race. Stressing the importance of the ballot and of political independence, he urged blacks to pursue more education as a means of exercising all their rights. He also exhorted his son to excel, setting high standards.

Monroe was not only a good student but also was elected president of his high school class, where he was the only black. On scholarships, he entered Harvard College in 1891 and in his junior year was elected to Phi Beta Kappa, the first black at Harvard to gain that honor. Harvard had an enormous influence on Trotter, as he felt inspired by friendships with white students from Europe and America, recognizing the democracy there that tangibly affirmed the possibilities for racial justice in the country. After earning his bachelor's degree magna cum laude in 1895, he received his master's degree the following year.

Trotter found his racial awareness deepening, as he experienced racial discrimination blocking his way for the first time. He had intended to enter international banking but instead worked as a clerk in four companies. Then he became a real estate agent for a Boston firm. In 1899, he founded his own company, dealing with insurance and mortgages, mostly for white clients. That same year, he married Geraldine Louise Pindell, daughter of an ex-slave, and they moved into a house in Dorchester. She died during the influenza epidemic of 1918, leaving no progeny.

The African American condition in America after Reconstruction had deteriorated steadily: Southern legislators instituted segregation and black disfranchisement, while lynching became accepted as southern justice. Booker T. Washington, the accommodationist, urged African Americans to find ways to get along with their white oppressors. In his "compromise speech" in Atlanta in 1895, Washington advocated maintaining the status quo for blacks. Washington, always subservient to white people, felt that Americans had to be in a frame of mind to listen to him, while blacks should wait to be given the vote until after they had proved they were law-abiding, productive citizens, and after they had acquired property and education. Substantive differences between the two men occurred on questions of accepting segregation, choosing education, agitating for rights, and engaging in politics. Washington represented the black masses, but Trotter, from a privileged, almost white background, seemed to personify more pride in his color and in his people.

Trotter became actively involved in racial matters. He founded or joined various associations that became militant forums for Boston's black elite, and through them, mounted an attack on Washington's servility. Such platforms proved insufficient, so Trotter and a librarian, George W. Forbes, started an outspokenly militant weekly newspaper, *The Guardian*, published first on November 9, 1901. Trotter, heir to a fortune amounting to around $20,000, provided the money, whereas Forbes provided the technical expertise. Appearing every Saturday, it typified black newspapers then, with eight pages of local and national news about African Americans. The new publication vehemently denounced discrimination and Washington; Trotter decried black people's treatment by white Americans, denouncing the culture from the very foundation of the Republic that produced the ruthless domination of blacks. He raged against Washington's timidity and deference to whites and called for aggressive protest and resistance, because compromise had failed. The newspaper became a national institution.

To Trotter, the North's relative freedom enabled him to battle for justice for all black Americans. Washington pushed to win short-term goals; Trotter stressed the long term. As Washington saw the right to vote as unnecessary, an eventual luxury, Trotter argued that intelligent political activity would force progress in other areas. For Trotter, the ballot was an important, perhaps the main, source of power, and he also urged independence in voting.

Moreover, Washington advocated vocational training because most blacks remained in the South working as farmers. Trotter opposed industrial education because it relegated blacks to what he called serfdom, as blacks would be considered innately inferior mentally. Trotter thought it necessary to prove the quality of black men's brains. He wanted blacks to seek and succeed at higher education, as he had.

Ever forceful, Trotter insisted on and never deviated from his racial militancy. The very name of his newspaper, *The Guardian*, suggests an ever vigilant watchdog. He wrote like the radical he was, allowing no compromise of human rights. His protests in person in various venues, ranging from churches to the White House, led to arrests. In 1904, Trotter split with Forbes, who could not abide the continuing fight against Washington. Additionally, Forbes was almost fired from his job because of The *Guardian*'s spirit of protest. Trotter decided to leave the real estate business and devote himself full-time to his paper.

In 1905, W. E. B. Du Bois, Trotter, and other blacks organized the Niagara Movement to renounce Washington's policies; it was a forerunner of the National Association for the Advancement of Colored People (NAACP). Trotter derided the NAACP because it had white leaders, with its only black officer, Du Bois, in charge of communications. Consequently, Trotter established his own organization, the National Equal Rights League (NERL). The NERL was organized by and for and was led by blacks only. He firmly believed that only blacks should lead and finance a movement for their own freedom. It became another platform for Trotter, who, as corresponding secretary, made statements in the NERL name as if it were the group's position. Thus, three factions vied for representation of blacks in America—Washington, the NAACP, and Trotter—all fighting for the same ends.

In 1913 Trotter led two African American delegations to the White House to protest segregation in the federal government, which was launched by President Woodrow

Wilson, a Georgia native. Trotter tangled with Wilson in a toe-to-toe, forty-five-minute argument, resulting in an offended Wilson banning Trotter from the White House.

Trotter continued to speak out against racism in all its forms. He advocated better treatment for World War I black solders and protested the Marcus Garvey back-to-Africa movement. Another important concern was D. W. Griffith's 1915 film, *The Birth of a Nation,* which received ecstatic critical acclaim among whites everywhere but fierce opposition from blacks in a dozen different cities. Trotter led a demonstration and went to court to protest the film's opening in Boston, and even began a fist fight resulting in hospitalization of both blacks and whites. The frustrated black community seemed to explode, yet even attempts to have a new censorship law passed banning the film failed.

The political activist Trotter protested segregation wherever he saw it, and he organized demonstrations successfully, one against Thomas Dixon's African-American-baiting play *The Clansman,* upon which *Birth of a Nation* was based. In the 1930s he defended the nine Scottsboro, Alabama, youths condemned to die on false charges of rape. His letters and visits to various presidents produced no apparent changes. He lost the battle to represent blacks to the NAACP. *The Guardian* was vitriolic, uncompromising. Yet most blacks, including intellectuals, supported Washington and his program. Trotter sought to change their attitude from acceptance to challenges, resulting in greater accomplishments for his race. *The Guardian* stopped publishing in 1957. The William Monroe Trotter Institute of the University of Massachusetts at Boston was founded in 1984 to address the needs and concerns of the black community.

SEE ALSO *Washington, Booker T.*

BIBLIOGRAPHY

Fox, Stephen. 1970. *The Guardian of Boston: William Monroe Trotter.* New York: Atheneum.

Logan, Rayford. 1965. *The Betrayal of the Negro, from Rutherford B. Hayes to Woodrow Wilson.* New York: Collier.

Meier, August. 1968. *Negro Protest Thought in America, 1880–1915.* Ann Arbor: University of Michigan Press.

Rudwick, Eliot. 1968. *W. E. B. Du Bois: Propagandist of the Negro Protest.* New York: Atheneum.

Barbara Reed

TRUTH, SOJOURNER
c. 1797–1883

Owing to her powerful and compelling personality and her forceful speaking for abolitionism and women's rights, Sojourner Truth is likely the best-known black woman of the U.S. antebellum period. Born to enslaved parents in upstate New York, Truth left a story presenting two sides of the racially charged debate about the mental capacities and judgement of black persons. The most substantial written records of Truth's life—an autobiography narrated by her to a transcriber, an account of her renowned "Ain't I a Woman" speech, and newspaper reports of her speeches and activity—were recorded predominantly by white writers. Yet these records present two representations of the same person.

On one hand, there is the stereotyped eighteenth-century black woman speaking broken English in a Southern dialect. On the other hand, there is the self-assured, self-aware person who walked away from bondage, preached against enslavement, and provided important support for abolitionism and women's rights. Truth often appears to have been conscious of dispelling notions that the historical accident of her illiterate and formerly enslaved black female body meant she lacked intellect, power, and ingenuity. The historian Nell Irvin Painter originally observed the role of stereotypes in Truth's life in *Sojourner Truth: A Life, A Symbol* (1996). Painter notes Truth's first language and first owners were Dutch, and that she spent her life in the northern United States. These two facts alone cast Truth outside images of enslaved black women typically populating the colonial imagination.

Sojourner Truth was originally named Isabella Baumfree, taking her surname from her first owner. Along with approximately ten siblings, she was sold away from her parents at age nine. Accounts of her early life also include memories of mother Elizabeth's moral and religious instruction and prayers with Isabella and her younger brother Peter, and of Elizabeth's death shortly after Isabella and Peter's sale.

Echoing the era's Protestant evangelicalism and traditions of black religiosity, Truth credited some of her most bold and independent actions and views to divine support. Isabella saw her father, James, only twice after Elizabeth's death. One visit occurred when she was around thirteen, a time when Isabella felt especially burdened by abusive slavers, the Nealys, who repeatedly whipped her for speaking only Dutch. She attributes James's role in her subsequent purchase by John J. Dumont to divine intervention. Isabella stayed with Dumont for about sixteen years—the majority of her enslaved adult life. While with Dumont, Isabella married a fellow bondsman named Thomas and bore five children. During this period, as Truth told her biographer, young Isabella created a sanctuary in a wooded area near a small stream, where she regularly meditated.

In late 1826 (six months before the state of New York's emancipation statute), Isabella prayed for divine guidance and left enslavement one morning before daybreak, taking her infant daughter along with her. Sheltered by Isaac Van Wagener, who paid twenty-five dollars for her and her daughter, Isabella soon began taking charge of her life. This was most apparent in her bold socioreligious activism. Though her religiosity generally was hybridized, while living with the Van Wageners Isabella practiced Methodist "holiness," including simple living, abstaining from alcohol, and avoiding anger. During this period she had a conversion experience that, consistent with such accounts by other enslaved persons, seems to mark a significant turning point in Isabella's sense of empowerment. When her son (also named Peter) was sold to slavers in Alabama, Isabella determined to have him returned. Sure that "God would help me get him" (1968 [1878], p. 45) she entered a complaint with a grand jury, sought assistance from Quakers, raised funds, and hired an attorney. She prevailed in her efforts, and Peter was returned to her custody.

Shortly after this incident, Isabella left her familiar surroundings and went to New York City with son Peter, who eventually took a career at sea. For the next sixteen years, she worked as a house servant to support herself. She attended services at the famous John Street Methodist Church, then moved to the all-black Zion Church, and eventually joined the extremist Robert Matthias's sect, a commune that practiced a more intense form of holiness. The Matthias group eventually collapsed, however, both fiscally and socially.

On June 1, 1843, Isabella changed her name to Sojourner and left New York City, saying she was following divine direction to go east and preach against enslavement. She joined the millenialist Millerite sect and became known for inspiring and cogent speaking. Sojourner honed her socioreligious rhetoric through a relationship with the cooperative Northampton (Massachusetts) Association for Education and Industry, an egalitarian commune that advocated free expression and supported women's rights, abolition, temperance, and vegetarianism. Uniting with the group in the fall of 1843, and remaining with them over the next several years, Sojourner had access to abolitionist and suffragist lecturers, including Frederick Douglass.

At Northampton, Sojourner began to express her religious piety in a decidedly social manner, as she began to speak more forcefully against slavery and to advocate women's suffrage. It was during this period that she took the surname Truth. When the association dissolved in 1846, she followed Douglass's example and published the narrative of her life. Income from the project allowed her to purchase her first home.

Sojourner Truth began giving antislavery speeches in 1844, first at Northampton and subsequently in New York. Invited by William Lloyd Garrison, she later joined the antislavery lecture circuit, speaking and selling her narrative. Her reputation as a compelling lecturer grew, and by 1846 Truth regularly addressed antislavery and women's rights gatherings, making frequent use of the Bible to argue for both. Truth delivered her famous and oft repeated "Ain't I a Woman" speech at the 1851 Akron, Ohio, women's rights convention. In the speech, recorded from observers' memories, Truth rebutted social and religious objections to women's rights. Pointing out the hard work and difficulties of her life as a woman, and observing that Christ came "from God and a woman," Truth countered arguments against female suffrage based on women's fragility and Christ's maleness. Celebrated for its powerful response to hecklers and incisive critique of a narrowly defined womanhood, this speech sealed Truth's reputation. Although she was illiterate, Truth demonstrated intellectual independence. She had scriptures read to her by children whom, she said, did not seek to interpret what they read. In a prescient 1853 speech, Truth included racial and gender analysis of the character Esther from Christian and Hebrew scripture to argue for full citizenship of white women and all black persons.

With outbreak of the Civil War, Truth moved to Washington, D.C., where she assisted blacks fleeing to the nation's capitol. In 1867, Truth began an effort to match newly freed persons with potential employers in New York and Michigan. She also initiated a petition drive calling on Congress to settle freed people on western lands. Congress never acted on the petition, however. Truth died at her home in Battle Creek, Michigan, in 1883.

SEE ALSO *Black Feminism in the United States.*

BIBLIOGRAPHY

Gilbert, Olive, and Frances W. Titus. 1968 (1878). *The Narrative of Sojourner Truth.* New York: Arno Press.

Painter, Nell Irvin. 1993. "Sojourner Truth." In *Black Women in America: An Historical Encyclopedia.* Vol. 2, edited by Darlene Clark Hine. New York: Carlson.

———. 1996. *Sojourner Truth: A Life, A Symbol.* New York: W. W. Norton.

Stanton, Elizabeth Cady, Susan B. Anthony, and Matilda Joslyn Gage, eds. 1881. *History of Woman Suffrage.* Vol. 1. New York: Fowler and Wells.

Rosetta E. Ross

TURNER, HENRY McNEAL
1834 –1915

Henry McNeal Turner was a major late nineteenth- and early twentieth-century African-American religious leader. In a long and varied career, he was a Civil War soldier, recruiter, and chaplain; a Freedmen's Bureau official; a spellbinding orator; a political organizer; an editor; and a bishop in the African Methodist Episcopal (AME)

Church. He also became one of the most outspoken advocates of reparations-funded African-American emigration to the African continent as a solution to the problem of racial justice in the United States.

Henry McNeal Turner was born on February 1, 1834, in antebellum South Carolina to Sarah Greer and Hardy Turner. Because both of his parents were born free, Turner was never enslaved. As a teenager he worked as a messenger and janitor in an Abbeville, South Carolina, law office. His white employers illegally and secretly taught him to read and write when they realized that his uncanny ability to recall a large amount of information perfectly could be useful to them. He thus became a secret legal courier. Known to outsiders only as a janitor, he was in reality conveying memorized documents for the firm.

Turner was permitted to sit in the rear of a white Methodist church on Sundays, but in 1858, at the age of twenty-four, Turner felt "called" to preach to black Methodists in Baltimore, Maryland, and Washington, D.C. He became a protégé of Bishop Daniel Payne, a highly educated black churchman. Payne's colleagues introduced Turner to theology and the Hebrew, Latin, and Greek languages, which were then associated with advanced Bible study.

Nowhere in the slave-holding South did Turner's photographic memory and extraordinary education shield him from the daily racism faced by all blacks. Embittered by the racial situation prior to the outbreak of the Civil War in 1861, Turner had become convinced that America would never do full justice to its African-derived population. However, his vigorous recruiting of free blacks for the Union earned him a commissioned army chaplaincy, a first for a person of color. When the war ended Turner joined the Freedmen's Bureau as an organizer, but quit his post because of the appalling racism of the bureau's field leadership. He quickly formed scores of Equal Rights Leagues, building up a political base that elected him to the Georgia state legislature in 1868, along with twenty-two other blacks. However, the white Democratic Party majority interpreted the Fifteenth Amendment as giving blacks only the right to vote and not to hold office, and they removed Turner and his fellow African Americans from their seats the following year. In Turner's last speech in office he asserted full equality in public and private life for blacks, stating "I claim the honor of having been the instrument of convincing hundreds—yea thousands—of white men that to reconstruct [Georgia] under the measures of the United States Congress was the safest and best course for the interest state." One of these measures, of course, was the Fourteenth Amendment, which made blacks citizens and guaranteed equal protection of the laws. The expulsion of Turner and his colleagues did accelerate the adoption of the Fifteenth Amendment, which prohibits state action in denying anyone the right to vote on account of "race, color, or previous condition of servitude." Because of his rather bold views on racial inequality, Turner received death threats from groups such as the Ku Klux Klan, which at the time was headed by Georgia's governor.

Through his remaining Republican Party connections, Turner became the postmaster in Macon, Georgia, in 1869, but resigned under the cloud of politically inspired allegations of sexual improprieties. He then received an appointment as Collector of Customs in Savannah. His religious activities, meanwhile, elevated him to he office of bishop in the AME Church in 1880. He ordained a woman as a deacon in 1885 (a first), and that same year he wrote *The Genius and Theory of Methodist Polity,* which contains some of his progressive views of religion and race.

In 1883 Turner became one of the first black leaders to raise the issue of enslavement reparations. He argued that America's blacks should collectively ask the government for $100 million to facilitate their relocation to the African continent. In *The Civil Rights Cases* (1883), the U.S. Supreme Court held that the Civil Rights Act of 1875, which protected individuals from discrimination and violence based on race, applied only to state action and not to acts of private individuals, such as Ku Klux Klan members. This decision reinforced Turner's belief that emigration was the only chance blacks had to live free of white racism.

Between 1891 and 1898, Turner visited Africa no fewer than four times, beginning with an organizing conference promoting Methodism in Sierra Leone. He saw Africa as a land of economic opportunity for black émigrés from a nation slowly eroding their citizenship rights. In 1892 he launched *Voice of Missions,* a monthly newspaper that promoted black migration. He assured his 4,000 readers that "I will keep you informed about the improvements being made in Africa, such as building railroads. ... I will tell you about mines of silver, gold and diamonds that have been ... and are being discovered and what the nations of the earth doing in parceling out the domain of the great continent regardless of the right or wrong involved in the case" (Redkey 1969, pp. 177–178). He also warned of the increased European presence in Africa, saying "it means the capture of the only spot on the globe the black man can ever hope to be in power and demonstrate the ability of self-government" (Redkey 1969, p. 180).

In addition to *Voice of Missions,* Turner was the editor of the AME *Christian Recorder,* which also promoted the idea of emigration. In 1894 Turner helped to organize the International Migration Society, which raised sufficient funds to charter two vessels to carry blacks to Africa. The *Horsa* departed for Liberia on March 19, 1895, and the *Laurada* left on March 2, 1896. The ships carried a total of 500 individuals. Turner then began promoting his denomination among blacks in Cuba and Central and South America, hoping that a common Protestant activist regional movement would promote ideas of pan-African independence and freedom in that part of the black diaspora. His advocacy of African Americans migrating to Africa anticipated Marcus Garvey's United Negro Improvement Association, which promoted a Back-to-Africa movement in the 1920s. Always in search of a better place to live, Turner died on May 8, 1915, while traveling in Toronto, Canada.

SEE ALSO *Black Reconstruction.*

BIBLIOGRAPHY

Hood, James W. 1895. *One Hundred Years of the African Methodist Episcopal Zion Church.* New York: A.M.E. Zion Book Concern.

Jackson, John G. 1970. *Introduction to African Civilizations.* Secaucus, NJ: Citadel Press.

McPherson, James M. 1964. *The Struggle for Equality: Abolitionists and the Negro in the Civil War and Reconstruction.* Princeton, NJ: Princeton University Press.

Mitchell, Michele. 2004. *Righteous Propagation: African Americans and the Politics of Racial Destiny after Reconstruction.* Chapel Hill: University of North Carolina Press.

Redkey, Edwin S. 1969. *Black Exodus: Black Nationalist and Back-to-Africa Movements, 1890–1910.* New Haven, CT: Yale University Press.

Wilmore, Gayraud. 1986. *Black Religion and Black Radicalism,* 2nd ed. Maryknoll, NY: Orbis Books.

Morris G. Henderson

TURNER, NAT

1800–1831

Nat Turner was born on October 2, 1800, in Southampton County, Virginia. After living as a slave for thirty-one years, he led the most significant rebellion in the history of American slavery. Nat Turner's Revolt, launched in southern Virginia in August 1831, attempted to overthrow the slave regime that had dominated Chesapeake society for more than 150 years. Local militia crushed the uprising, and violent reprisals spread across the region, resulting in the massacre of hundreds of enslaved Africans. For southern whites, Turner's Revolt underscored the high costs and constant risks of preserving race slavery indefinitely. For black and white abolitionists in the North, the rebellion reinforced the idea, later espoused by John Brown, that enslaved southerners were willing and able to rebel, needing only weapons and outside support. For black Virginians, "Nat Turner's War" was seen as the first major armed conflict in the long struggle to end slavery.

Five days after Turner was born, Virginia authorities executed Gabriel Prosser, a slave blacksmith who had plotted an uprising in nearby Richmond. As a boy, Nat must have heard stories about this legendary rebel. Turner's African-born mother, it is believed, saw her intelligent son as "intended for some great purpose." She noted "certain marks" on his head and chest, and she marveled when he related events that had occurred before his birth. The precocious boy built up a strong faith, combining African beliefs from his mother's world with the Christian faith of his first master, Benjamin Turner. He learned to read, memorized passages of scripture, and felt that he was specially chosen to destroy the oppressive slave system.

As a young man, Nat Turner took a wife, though evidence regarding Cherry Turner remains sketchy. More certain is the fact that he began to experience personal spiritual revelations. He claimed that once, while plowing in a field with his mind wandering in prayer, he was addressed by the same "Spirit" that "spoke to the prophets in former days" (Greenberg 2003, p. 46). In a powerful vision, Turner "saw white spirits and black spirits engaged in battle, and the sun was darkened—the thunder rolled in the Heavens, and blood flowed in streams." Other visions suggested that it was time for Nat to take up that yoke himself "and fight against the Serpent" (Greenberg 2003, pp. 46–48).

By the time he reached his mid-twenties, Turner had belonged to three masters. When his latest owner, Thomas Moore, died in 1828, Nat became the property of the man's nine-year-old son, Putnam Moore. In 1830, Putnam Moore's widowed mother married a local carriage maker named Joseph Travis.

When a solar eclipse occurred in February 1831, Nat interpreted the dramatic event as a sign that he must commence his work. He laid plans with others to act on the holiday of July 4, but when he fell ill the date was allowed to pass. Then, on August 13, when a summer haze changed the color of the sun, Turner took this as an additional sign. He notified a handful of trusted slave collaborators to join him for a meeting on August 21, a Sunday.

The conspirators gathered in the woods near the Travis homestead, and within hours they moved through the vicinity, killing white inhabitants regardless of age or sex. After securing more horses and weapons, they planned to march on Jerusalem, the county seat, and take the arsenal, which would give them a substantial beachhead. According to the *Richmond Enquirer,* Turner made it clear that "indiscriminate slaughter was not their intention after they obtained a foothold, and was resorted to in the first instance to strike terror and alarm. Women and children would afterwards have been spared, and men too who ceased to resist" (Higginson 1861, p. 177).

Several hours after midnight, Turner and five others launched their violent offensive, attacking the home of Turner's master and killing the Travis household, then proceeding on to other farmsteads to wreak similar vengeance. By Monday night, sixty or seventy African Americans had joined the cause, and on Tuesday morning Turner's army set out for Jerusalem. Behind them at least fifty-seven whites of all ages had been killed over a stretch of twenty miles.

When some rebels stopped to refresh themselves at a farm three miles from Jerusalem, the pause proved fatal. The militia managed to attack the insurgents, who were off guard and poorly armed. Turner never regained the initiative, and with his supporters killed or dispersed, he went into hiding. By midweek, the militia had received reinforcements from Richmond; frightened and vindictive white soldiers and volunteers launched a harsh and indiscriminate offensive throughout the region. One cavalry company slaughtered forty blacks in two days, and they mounted more than a dozen severed heads atop poles as public warnings. But Turner himself evaded authorities for six weeks.

After an enormous manhunt, authorities captured the rebel leader in a local swamp on October 30. Turner was tried on November 5 and executed on November 11, 1831. Days before the public hanging, a young lawyer named Thomas Ruffin Gray managed to interview the insurgent in his jail cell, and he later published the account as *The Confessions of Nat Turner*. The text has a ring of truth and provides much of what is known about Turner and his motives.

Turner's uprising forced Virginia's legislature to consider openly, if briefly, a proposal for gradual emancipation. It revived the colonization movement, which many whites saw as a way to remove dangerous bondsmen and reduce the free black community. The uprising also prompted tighter restrictions on black preaching and greater caution regarding slave access to the Gospel. Among African Americans, Turner became, and has remained, both a martyr and a folk hero.

BIBLIOGRAPHY

Davis, Mary Kemp. 1999. *Nat Turner before the Bar of Judgment: Fictional Treatments of the Southampton Insurrection.* Baton Rouge: Louisiana State University Press.

Greenberg, Kenneth S. 1996. *The Confessions of Nat Turner and Related Documents.* Boston: Bedford Books.

———, ed. 2003. *Nat Turner: A Slave Rebellion in History and Memory.* New York: Oxford University Press.

Higginson, T. W. "Nat Turner's Insurrection." *The Atlantic Monthly* 8: 46 (August 1861): 173–187.

Oates, Stephen B. 1975. *The Fires of Jubilee: Nat Turner's Fierce Rebellion.* New York: Harper and Row.

Tragle, Henry Irving. 1971. *The Southampton Slave Revolt of 1831: A Compilation of Source Material, Including the Full Text of "The Confessions of Nat Turner."* Amherst: University of Massachusetts Press.

Wood, Peter H. 1988. "Nat Turner: The Unknown Slave as Visionary Leader." In *Black Leaders of the Nineteenth Century,* edited by Leon Litwack and August Meier, 21–40. Urbana: University of Illinois Press.

Peter H. Wood

U

UNDEREMPLOYMENT

It is difficult to estimate the percentage of the world population that is jobless. Unemployment, underemployment, informal employment, and the ratio of employment to the total population are all indicators that measure employment instability. Because the use of such measures varies across countries and organizations, it is important to provide information on a number of key labor market indicators to better assess global joblessness (International Labour Organization 2007a).

To illustrate, the adult unemployment rate captures the proportion of the labor force that is not working but is looking for work (ages twenty-five and older). The "youth unemployment rate" applies to those unemployed persons between the ages of fifteen and twenty-four. Although unemployment is a commonly used indicator of joblessness, a large proportion of the non-working population is not captured with this measure. For example, the unemployment rate does not count "discouraged workers." Discouraged workers are those persons who are no longer included in the labor force, as they have essentially given up trying to find work. Nor does the unemployment rate represent the proportion of the labor force that is underemployed. According to the International Labour Organization (ILO) (2007b), the underemployed represent those "whose hours of work are insufficient in relation to an alternative employment situation in which the person is willing and available to engage." Finally, another key labor market indicator, the ratio of employment to the total population, is often used to assess employment opportunities at the global level and is thought to provide a better estimate of joblessness than that measured by the unemployment rate alone. This measure, however, also fails to capture the underemployed. Hence, to adequately capture global joblessness, employment opportunities and trends, it is important to provide information on unemployment, underemployment, and the ratio of employment to the total population.

ECONOMIC GLOBALIZATION AND UNDEREMPLOYMENT

Economic globalization constitutes the process of increasing economic interdependence across borders. With greater economic integration comes the potential for greater market productivity and efficiency. The process of globalization is observed in the growth of international trade, the rise in transnational corporations and investments, and in the unrestrained cross-border movement of capital and goods. As predicted by economists and other policy analysts, globalization has contributed to worldwide economic gains. Yet a closer look at the social dimension of globalization reveals an unequal distribution of these benefits within and across countries.

Although international economic growth and development have the potential to promote employment and decrease poverty and exclusion around the world, the evidence to date suggests that the opposite has occurred. Macroeconomic policies that enhanced global economic integration failed to sufficiently consider the national and international implications for countries with an unequal distribution of wealth. Moreover, global economic policy did not address how to increase or improve employment for the majority of workers, nor did such policies seek to remedy gender- or birth-ascribed labor market inequality. Consequently, world economic growth has been realized through globalization; however, inter- and intra-country inequality persists among the core and periphery, developed, transitioning, and underdeveloped countries, and across distinct social groups. In other words, a strong global gross domestic product (GDP) did not correspond to a reduction in global joblessness or poverty. Persistent and increasing unemployment, underemployment, informal employment, and poverty are observed in all countries, regardless of development. Moreover, such employment uncertainty associated with the global economy is further stratified by gender (Heintz 2006) and by birth-ascribed characteristics and features associated with subgroup membership (including race, ethnicity, nativity, caste, legal status).

HOW GLOBALIZATION AFFECTS EMPLOYMENT AND POVERTY

With growing interdependence comes greater vulnerability across borders. The SARS outbreak in Asia, the spread of HIV/AIDS in sub-Saharan Africa, Russia, and the Ukraine, the impact of 9/11 in the United States, the Iraq War and other armed conflicts and violence, have all had a negative, if temporary, effect on regional economies (Harasty and Schmidt 2004). In the global economy, regional events affect the global marketplace. For example, the volatility of markets in Latin America and Asia have slowed global economic growth, and the global tourism and travel industry has been negatively impacted by 9/11 and the subsequent War on Terror. Thus, global economic stability is correlated with national economic and non-economic crises and events.

In contrast, macroeconomic policies favoring globalization, such as freer trade and markets, government deregulation, and the emphasis on private over public sector oversight, have succeeded in increasing global productivity and efficiency. In 2006, International Monetary Fund (IMF) estimates report a slow but steady growth in global output and global labor productivity. For example, global output grew by 5.2 percent and global labor productivity grew by 3.4 percent (International Labour Office 2007b). It appears, then, that globalization benefits the economy by promoting strong worldwide economic development. Yet macroeconomic policies geared toward globalization have emphasized the unrestrained flow of capital and goods. Hence, global economic policies with a social dimension, such as increasing the cross-border flow of labor, enhancing or improving employment opportunities, or policies that attempt to reduce inter- and intra-national poverty or inequality across race, class, and gender, have not been pursued. Although it is reasonable to expect that global economic growth would likely enhance employment opportunities and reduce poverty around the world, the lack of macroeconomic policies that address these specific concerns has resulted in an increase in joblessness around the world. Employment trends between 1996 and 2006 suggest that on the whole, globalization has had a negative impact on employment outcomes and has increased poverty.

Day Laborers Await the Announcement of Day Jobs, San Francisco, 2002. *Informal employment is on the increase. Here potential workers wait to hear if there is a job available for that day.* AP IMAGES.

JOBLESSNESS

In 2006, global unemployment reached an all-time high of 195.2 million persons (6.3%), and world underemployment was estimated at between 25 and 30 percent (Köhler 2004; ILO 2007). Correspondingly, the world's employment-to-population ratio declined between 1993 and 2006 (to 61.4%, down from 62.6% in 1996 and 63.3% in 1993). The persistent decline in the employment-to-population ratio coupled with the rise in unemployment and underemployment suggests that the demand for jobs in the global economy has outstripped the supply of jobs that are available (Heintz 2006; ILO 2007b). Furthermore, the employment-to-population ratio and the unemployment and underemployment rate are stratified within and across countries. Poorer, underdeveloped countries face greater unemployment and underemployment than richer, developed countries. Moreover, underemployment is a far more prevalent and pressing problem than unemployment in underdeveloped countries (Köhler 2004). In particular, North Africa and the Middle East report the highest unemployment rate and the lowest employment-to-population ratio (12.2% and 47.3%, respectively) (ILO 2007b). Such findings reflect the limited employment options for women in these countries, the prominence of and dependence on the production of oil in the region (and which generates relatively few jobs), and population growth (ILO 2007b). In the United States, underemployment is associated with "the underclass," typified by U.S.-born black men who experience extreme and concentrated poverty and joblessness in America's inner-city neighborhoods. Observers note that underemployment in the United States is more likely to occur among women than men, ethnic and racial minorities than non-Hispanic whites, and immigrants than the U.S.-born (De Jong and Madamba 2001).

POVERTY

Nations experience poverty differently. For example, Latin America has experienced the largest gap between the rich and the poor in the less developed world. In particular, indigenous people in Latin America are disproportionately more likely to experience extreme poverty, as they make up only 10 percent of the population of Latin America but constitute the majority of the poor. In the developed world, the gap between the rich and poor is greatest in the United States. In the United States, the wealthiest 1 percent of the population is richer than the combined bottom 40 percent. The inequality gap between these two groups is widening rather than narrowing over time. Moreover, although global poverty is on the decrease, from 15.1 percent in 1993 to 12.7 percent in 2004, regional disparities remain. For example, rapid growth in China and East Asia have led to poverty reduction, but similar changes have not been realized in sub-Saharan Africa or the transition economies of Central Asia and Europe. Additionally, poverty is stratified by gender, race and ethnicity, and nativity. For example, female-headed households experience poverty at a greater rate than their male counterparts. Racial or ethnic minority status intersects with gender to heighten inequality. For example, approximately 40 percent of black and Latino female-headed households experience poverty in the United States. Moreover, immigrants are more likely to live in poverty than U.S.-born residents (17.1% compared to 11.8%, respectively).

Global poverty is difficult to measure. Rough estimates suggest that extreme poverty, the number of people worldwide who live on less than two dollars a day, has approached 1.4 billion persons, or about one-fifth of the world's population (ILO 2007b). Other estimates put this number at closer to 3 billion people. Children make up a third of this total population. According to figures generated by UNICEF, approximately 30,000 children die each day due to extreme poverty, about 11 million children under five years of age each year (Shah 2006). They "die quietly in some of the poorest villages on earth, far removed from the scrutiny and the conscience of the world. Being meek and weak in life makes these dying multitudes even more invisible in death" (UNICEF 2005). Notably, these staggering numbers actually reflect a decline in poverty that has occurred in the early years of the twenty-first century. This is due, in part, to the concerted effort by the United Nations and other international organizations to highlight and combat global poverty. Additionally, the proportion of the global labor force that is female is on the rise, which further contributes to the decline in poverty. Women are more likely to experience poverty because their work is generally low-skilled, low-wage, and insecure; however, at the level of the household, women's wages make a positive contribution to total income. The wages women contribute to the household often alleviate the risk of extreme poverty, especially in countries where women's work compensates for the increase in male unemployment (Heintz 2006).

Poverty is related to employment outcomes; therefore, an increase in unemployment or underemployment is often associated with an increase in poverty. Since unemployment and underemployment are on the rise, a substantial segment of the global population is vulnerable to falling below the poverty line. Growing joblessness coupled with a lack of productive and decent work in the formal sector of the global economy has led to a rise in informal employment. Informal work is generally low-skilled and low-wage, often located in the service sector, agriculture, or the non-durable manufacturing industry (Heintz 2006).

LABOR MARKET SEGMENTATION

National labor markets are stratified by gender and one or more birth-ascribed characteristics rooted in race, caste, ethnicity, nativity, or indigenous status, among others. The international labor market is a macrocosm of such structural inequality. For example, in the United States, globalization has ushered in a restructuring of the economy that is characterized by a decline in good-paying jobs in durable goods manufacturing and the aerospace and defense industries. At the same time, there has been a rise in low-wage, low-skilled jobs in non-durable goods manufacturing, such as in the garment or electronics industry, and the service industry. Hence, although jobs at the bottom and at the top of this "hourglass economy" remain plentiful, the "narrowing middle" forces occupational segregation and constrains intergenerational mobility, especially among racial and ethnic minority groups. Additionally, recent immigration policy reforms, such as the Hart-Cellar Act of 1965, the Immigration Reform and Control Act of 1986, and the Immigration Act of 1990, have dramatically increased legal immigration to the United States. Alongside legal immigration, illegal immigration by Mexican and Central American migrants continues unabated (Valdez 2005). Such economic and demographic changes have spurned a wage and work gap between non-Hispanic whites and ethnic and racial minorities that persists into the twenty-first century. For example, native-born ethnic and racial minorities are more likely to be unemployed and underemployed; native-born and foreign-born Latinos, regardless of legal status, are concentrated among the working poor. For men, such occupations include labor-intensive work in the construction or service industries. For women, occupations include domestic work or factory work in sweatshop-like conditions in the garment industry. Other industrialized nations face similar patterns of stratification across subgroups. In Japan, for instance, foreign-born men from Brazil and Pakistan work in occupations characterized as "dirty, dangerous, and difficult," while Filipinas are relegated to work in hostess bars and other occupations in the "entertainment" industry.

INFORMAL EMPLOYMENT

Informal employment in developed and underdeveloped countries and in rural and urban settings is on the increase for men and women, as "lean" and "just in time" production techniques decrease the number of jobs that are available in formal employment. Informal employment constitutes non-standard work that is low-skilled and low-wage, often requires excessive hours of work, is generally inflexible and insecure, and lacks protections, regulations, and benefits that more formal employment guarantees. Women engage in informal employment to a greater degree than men. In less developed countries, the majority of non-agricultural women's labor takes place in the informal sector. In developed countries, the highest percentage of informally employed women occurs in sub-Saharan Africa (84%).

The disproportionate number of women working in the informal sector relative to men is due, in large part, to gender inequality in developed and especially underdeveloped countries. For example, women in underdeveloped nations may work for subcontractors assembling work at home for a fixed price or work as unpaid family workers in family-owned enterprises. In developed nations, women's informal employment includes domestic work, work in the entertainment industry, factory work, "home work," and unpaid family work. Because such informal labor market practices lack the protections found in more formal employment such as childcare support or sick leave, and because women are more likely to engage in this type of work, women are more likely to experience poverty than men; this has been termed the "feminization of poverty."

Additionally, women's non-market work—unpaid labor that contributes to the maintenance of the household—is crucial for its socioeconomic stability. The time expended in non-market unpaid work is largely non-negotiable, however, and the hours left available for paid market work are compromised by such household responsibilities. The combination of unpaid non-market work and the fewer hours left available for wage-work, and the likelihood that such work will be located in the informal sector, results in the devaluation of women's work. This "feminization of labor" characterizes the majority of women's work in developed and developing nations (Heintz 2006).

Finally, in underdeveloped, post-colonial countries, the exploitation of children, women, and indigenous workers occurs at the national and international level. Outsourcing by developed countries leads to increased employment opportunities in less developed countries, but the factory or service jobs that are generated are labor intensive and low paying. In 2004, the ILO reported that one in six of the world's children (ages five to seventeen) engages in child labor, which may include forced labor, prostitution, or work that is hazardous and dangerous (Harasty and Schmidt 2004). Moreover, sex tourism in Southeast Asia, the Dominican Republic, and the Caribbean promotes the exploitation of women and children from underdeveloped countries by Westerners. For example, Thailand's sex tourism industry generates 4.3 billion U.S. dollars annually, which accounts for 3 percent of Thailand's GDP.

FAIR GLOBALIZATION

Research on globalization has emphasized the possibility of "fair globalization" (Halonen 2005). Fair globalization seeks to promote economic growth and development while at the same time improving employment opportunities and reducing poverty. Rather than suggesting that a fair globalization is ethical, moral, or idealistic, scholars, activists, and organizations argue that the observed economic growth that has been attributed to globalization cannot be sustained without a population of decently employed workers. In other words, macroeconomic policies that facilitate economic internationalization need to expand beyond policies that promote the unrestrained cross-border flow of capital and goods. Additional policies are required that would ensure decent and productive work. The ILO (2007) defines "decent and productive work" as "opportunities for women and men to obtain decent and productive employment in conditions of freedom, equity, security and human dignity." Such work is not produced in the informal sector but must be created in the formal sector. Policies in the early twenty-first century that target the social dimension of globalization are taking root, such as the United Nation's Millennium Declaration, which seeks to halve world poverty and achieve universal primary education by 2015, and the ILO's commitment to worldwide decent and productive employment as well as their strategic and aggressive policy to end child labor.

The attention being paid to the contradictions of globalization and global economic growth on the one hand and rising joblessness and poverty on the other, may have the desired effect. Macroeconomic policies may begin to address the unequal distribution of resources across developed and underdeveloped countries, if only to sustain future global economic growth. Whether such policy changes at the international (or national) level can address socioeconomic stratification at the national level is less clear, since gender and birth-ascribed stratification appears to be an endemic, structural feature of labor markets.

SEE ALSO *Poverty; Social Problems; Undocumented Workers.*

BIBLIOGRAPHY

De Jong, Gordon F., and Anna B. Madamba. 2001. "A Double Disadvantage? Minority Group, Immigrant Status, and Underemployment in the United States." *Social Science Quarterly* 82 (1): 117–130.

Halonen, H. E. Tarja. 2005. "A Fair Globalization." *Globalizations* 2 (2): 250–253.

Harasty, Claire, and Dorothea Schmidt. 2004. *Global Employment Trends.* Geneva: International Labour Organization. Available from http://www.ilo.org.

Heintz, James. 2006. "Globalization, Economic Policy and Employment: Poverty and Gender Implications." Employment Strategy Papers, Employment Policy Unit, International Labour Office. Available from http://www.ilo.org/publns.

International Labour Organization. 2007a. *Key Labor Market Indicators.* Geneva: Author. Available from http://www.ilo.org.

———. 2007b. *Global Employment Trends,* updated. Geneva: Author. Available from http://www.ilo.org.

Köhler, Gernot. 2004. "The Global Stratification of Unemployment and Underemployment." *Centro Argentino de Estudios Internacionales, Programa Teoria de las Relaciones Internationales.* Available from http://www.caei.com.ar/es/programas/teoria/t12.pdf.

Shah, Anup. 2006. "Global Issues: Social, Political, Economic and Environmental Issues that Affect Us All." Available from http://www.globalissues.org.

UNICEF. 2005. *The State of the World's Children.* Available from http://www.unicef.org/sowc05/english/index.html.

Valdez, Zulema. 2005. "Two Sides of the Same Coin? The Relationship Between Socioeconomic Assimilation and Entrepreneurship Among Mexicans in Los Angeles." In *Latino Los Angeles: Transformations, Communities, and Activism,* edited by Enrique C. Ochoa and Gilda L. Ochoa. Tucson: University of Arizona Press.

Zulema Valdez

UNDOCUMENTED WORKERS

Undocumented workers are foreign-born workers who lack the legal documentation required to work in the country in which they live. As outlined by Charles Kelly in a 1977 article, these individuals may have crossed a national border without going through the required inspection process, they may have entered with counterfeit documents, or they may have overstayed legitimate tourist or working visas. In the United States, an undocumented worker is someone who is foreign born, is not a permanent resident, and is not a U.S. citizen. An undocumented worker can be deported for being in violation of U.S. migration and naturalization law and for not possessing permission to work in the United States. These workers, like others in a country illegally, are often referred to as "illegal aliens," or "illegal immigrants."

TRACKING UNDOCUMENTED WORKERS

Because of their clandestine status, it is usually difficult to know exactly how many undocumented immigrants there are in a specific country or region. Demographers have created statistical methods to estimate how many undocumented immigrants exist in a population. According to estimates made by Jeffrey Passel, a researcher with the Pew Hispanic Center in Washington D.C., there were 11.1 million undocumented immigrants living in the United States in 2005. Of these, 7.2 million were unauthorized migrants employed in March 2005, accounting for about 4.9 percent of the civilian labor force. The other 3.9 million were home-stay woman and children. The same report showed that undocumented workers made up a larger share of the workers in certain occupational categories, including 24 percent of all workers employed in farming occupations, 17 percent in cleaning (or janitorial occupations), 14 percent in construction, and 12 percent in food preparation (Passel 2005, p.1). Passel also found that in 2005 undocumented immigrants made up 30 percent of the foreign-born population in the United States and were largely from Latin America, with most unauthorized migrants coming from Mexico.

In 2005 there were 6.2 million undocumented immigrants from Mexico in the United States. Passel's study found that between 60 and 75 percent of the more than 11.1 million undocumented immigrants in the United States entered the country illegally and without inspection, in most cases entering across the 2,000 mile U.S.-Mexican border. The other 25 to 40 percent entered legally and subsequently overstayed visas or violated the terms of their admission. If a foreign national enters a country legally and then overstays a visa or violates the terms of admission, he or she automatically becomes an undocumented immigrant. If the same person gets a job, then he or she becomes an undocumented worker.

GLOBALIZATION AND WORKER PATTERNS

The forces of globalization and market competition have encouraged the hiring of undocumented workers worldwide. By employing such workers, companies can compete more easily in the global market economy and make more profits. Increased profits are made by paying low wages to undocumented workers (in many cases under the minimum wage); by not investing in safety measures or appropriate working equipment, which can be very expensive, and therefore forcing the undocumented workers to labor under dangerous conditions; by not paying overtime; by denying workers benefits such as health insurance; and by paying them under the table.

For these reasons, such employers generally avoid investigating whether documents presented at the time of hiring are authentic. Workers are supposed to be asked by employers at the time of hire to provide proof that they are allowed to work in the United States. Foreign workers can present a Permanent Resident Card (also called a Green Card) or a working permit (or working visa), as well as a Social Security card. Some employers, however, just take a copy of the Permanent Resident Card and the social security card from the prospective worker and file it in their records, just in case they are investigated by immigration authorities. They can then demonstrate that they were given documentation, and that this documentation suggested that the worker was authorized to work in the United States.

Most undocumented workers, however, can buy fake documentation from counterfeiters in the informal markets of global cities for just a few hundred dollars. In most cases, Social Security numbers are made-up numbers, but in other instances they match the numbers of real citizens. According to a 2005 *New York Times* article by Eduardo Porter, as many as three quarters of the undocumented workers in the United States pay payroll taxes, contributing between $6 billion and $7 billion in Social Security funds that they will be unable to claim later in life.

IMMIGRATION LAW

In an attempt to control undocumented immigration, the U.S. Congress passed the 1986 Immigration Reform and Control Art (IRCA), which awarded amnesty to and legalized the status of more than three million undocumented immigrants. At the same time, a new federal law, known as the Employers Sanctions Provisions of IRCA, Immigration and Nationality Act, Section 274a, prohibited employers from hiring undocumented workers and threatened them with large fines if they did so. As a result, many companies changed their strategies of hiring undocumented workers directly, and instead subcontracted out the work. Thus, the employer could not be blamed for having undocumented workers on their premises. If they are caught, the company could (and still can) argue that they had merely hired the subcontractor and that they were not aware of the legal status of the workers.

In 2005 several Wal-Mart stores were accused of hiring undocumented workers. Wal-Mart authorities were not able to argue lack of knowledge of the problem because federal agents had taped a conversation that showed that Wal-Mart executives knew that the subcontractors they used had hired illegal immigrants. Moreover, an article carried by the Associated Press and other sources revealed the conditions that undocumented workers faced at Wal-Mart: "Many of the janitors—from Mexico, Russia, Mongolia, Poland and a host of other nations—worked seven days or nights a week without overtime pay or injury compensation, said attorney James L. Linsey. Those who worked nights were often locked in the store until the morning, Linsey said" (Associated Press 2005, p. 1). This is a damning illustration of the conditions faced by undocumented workers in America.

U.S. immigration law has opened the doors for numerous immigrants to enter the country, but this door is mainly open to skilled workers. Unskilled workers have very few options when applying for a visa, with the result that most such workers have to enter the country illegally. According to Rob Paral, a Research Fellow with the Immigration Policy Center, only one category of visas in U.S. immigration and naturalization policy is targeted to low-skilled workers, and only 5,000 of these are issued per year. Most visas are reserved for high-skilled occupations, and 130,000 of these are allowed per year. According to Timothy Hatton and Jeffrey Williamson, the authors of *Global Migration and the World Economy* (2005), high-skilled workers find it much harder to mask an illegal status and secure illegal employment that fully exploits their skills. Low-skilled jobs, however, are less likely to

Rebuilding New Orleans, 2006. *Following Hurricane Katrina, large numbers of undocumented workers, such as this laborer from Mexico, came to the region and performed much of the clean-up work.* MARIO TAMA/GETTY IMAGES.

require the licenses, certifications, and other documentation that might reveal legal status. They also point out that the wage differential between the countries of origin and destination is much larger for low-skilled work than for high-skilled work. It does not come as a surprise, therefore, that undocumented low-skilled workers are disproportionately represented in current immigration flows.

Undocumented workers are protected by labor rights in the United States and several other countries around the world. According to the *Workers' Rights Handbook*, examples of the kind of labor rights that undocumented workers may be awarded include the right to get paid at least the minimum wage, to get paid overtime, to receive workmen's compensation insurance, and the right to organize. Unfortunately, in most cases, undocumented workers do not fight for their labor rights even when they are violated due to the fear of losing their job or getting deported if they complain.

UNDOCUMENTED WORKERS WORLDWIDE

The phenomenon of undocumented migration and undocumented workers is not unique to the United States. Globalization and the demand for cheap labor in the global market economy have created an underground demand for undocumented workers all around the world, especially in the most developed nations. Structural adjustment programs in developing nations and the expansion of free trade have caused thousands of workers around the world to be displaced from their jobs, leading to very high rates of unemployment. Sometimes referred to as a new form of slave labor, undocumented workers in developed nations are paid low wages for doing jobs in which they work under unsafe conditions, are not given any labor-related benefits, and are often forced to work for long hours without being paid overtime, among other abuses. Even conservative estimates claim that the number of undocumented immigrants around the world is about 10 million (see Skeldon 2000). Nation-states all around the world are currently fighting the problem of undocumented workers, who some claim displace citizens from jobs and lower wages in the country of destination.

The majority of undocumented immigrants around the world enter the country of destination illegally through the use of a smuggler, who either smuggles the person into the country or finances the cost of undocumented entry. The cost of smuggling can range from a few hundred dollars to several thousand dollars depending on the place of origin of the migrant, method of smuggling (by earth, by air, or by sea), and how strict the border enforcement has become at the port of entry. In 2007, smuggler costs to get into the United States were on average between $1,500 to $3,000 for Mexicans and $5,000 to $10,000 for Central Americans (Flores, 2007). According to Ko-Lin Chin (1999), author of *Smuggled Chinese: Clandestine Immigration to the United States*, the fees paid by the Chinese range from $30,000 to $60,000. Family and friends often cover the cost of the smuggling fees at the time of arrival to the United States. In other instances, the debt the worker incurs is taken out of the wages earned when the immigrant begins to work in some kind of shop or restaurant that is owned by intermediaries of the smuggler. If the money was provided by family and friends, very rarely the debt is forgiven. In most instances, undocumented workers spend large amounts of time (several months or years) after their arrival trying to pay back their debt for smuggling fees.

Undocumented workers are less likely to bring family members with them because of the dangerous circumstances under which they are smuggled, and because they are more likely to get caught if they travel with family members. Thus, undocumented workers with family members in the country of origin are more likely to move more frequently back and forth between the two countries. In the case of the United States, tighter border enforcement has not helped to reduce the flow of undocumented immigrants, but it has increased the rates charged by smugglers and redirected illegal crossings to nontraditional ports of entry. These changes have resulted in a death toll of about 400 deaths per year since the border was militarized in 1993 (see Massey et al. 2002). Tighter border enforcement has also helped to increase the number of undocumented workers who stay longer in the United States, because it is more difficult for undocumented workers to continue with their traditional circulatory flow. Despite internal immigration enforcement laws, such as those enacted by the U.S. Congress, governments tend to poorly enforce their immigration laws due to political and economic factors. Moreover, the demand for workers to fill jobs not easily filled by native-born or documented workers only reinforces the dynamics of undocumented immigration, despite border enforcement.

IMMIGRANT WORKERS AND RACISM

In addition to high levels of exploitation, undocumented workers face high levels of racial discrimination. In most nations around the world, undocumented workers tend to be members of racial minorities. As in the case of the United States, where numerous undocumented workers look Hispanic or Latino, in other places around the world undocumented workers are easy to spot, and they can then be subjected to racial profiling and discrimination. In Germany, Turkish undocumented workers are often visually distinctive, and African undocumented workers are easily spotted in Spain because of their physical features and the color of their skin. Racial discrimination associated with undocumented migration status is considered a new form of racism, especially in the United States.

Anti-immigrant sentiment in the United States reached new heights during 2006, leading to millions of undocumented immigrants marching in the streets of major U.S. cities and protesting immigration laws that threatened to convert those who offer help to undocumented immigrants into felons. As a result of the nationwide protests, hundreds of new immigration laws curtailed the ability of employers to hire undocumented workers, forcing the police to inquire about the legal status of those who they detain, and allowing landlords to deny renting to undocumented immigrants. In most instances, these local laws have been revoked in federal courts given that such laws have been declared to be unconstitutional and according to federal law, only the federal government and not the local government can inquire about immigration status of any person (Rubinkam 2007). In addition, a 700-mile-long fence along the U.S.-Mexican border was approved by the Congress and signed by President George W. Bush. Other bills have been debated in Congress, including one that would award amnesty to millions of undocumented immigrants. A backlash against illegal immigration all over the United States has caused thousands of workers to be deported, so that families have been suddenly separated and children terrorized when they returned home from school to find that their parents had been taken away. Despite the deportations and the new laws, there is no sign that the flow of undocumented workers to the United States and other developed countries will come to an end any time soon.

SEE ALSO *Underemployment.*

BIBLIOGRAPHY

Associated Press. "Wal-Mart Mops Up Immigrant Flap." 2005. Washington, DC: CBS News, March 18. Available from http://www.cbsnews.com.

Baumer, Bennett. 2006. "Far-Right Bill Targets Immigrants, Punishes Helpers." *Newstandard News*, March 8. Available from http://newstandardnews.net/content.

Capps, Randolph, and Michael E. Fix. 2005. "Undocumented Immigrants: Myths and Reality." Washington, DC: Urban Institute. Available from http://www.urban.org/.

Chin, Ko-Lin. 1999. *Smuggled Chinese: Clandestine Immigration to the United States*. Philadelphia: Temple University Press.

Flores, Nadia Y. 2007. "International Migration from El Salvador." Texas A&M University, Department of Sociology, College Station, Texas. Working Paper.

Friebel, Guido, and Sergei Guriev. 2004. *Smuggling Humans: A Theory of Debt-financed Migration*. Bonn, Germany: Institute for the Study of Labor. Available from http://www.iza.org.

Friends of Farmworkers. "Workers' Rights Handbook." Available from http://friendsfw.org/Undocumented_Rights.

Hatton, Timothy J., and Jeffrey G. Williamson. 2005. *Global Migration and the World Economy: Two Centuries of Policy and Performance*. Cambridge, MA: MIT Press.

International Organization for Migration. 2003. *World Migration Report: Managing Migration; Challenges and Responses for People on the Move*. Geneva: International Organization for Migration.

Kelly, Charles B. 1977. "Counting the Uncountable: Estimates of Undocumented Aliens in the United States." *Population and Development Review* 3 (4): 473–481.

Massey, Douglas S., Jorge Durand, and Nolan J. Malone. 2002. *Beyond Smoke and Mirrors: Mexican Immigration in an Era of Economic Integration*. New York: Russell Sage Foundation.

Paral, Rob. 2006. "No Way In: U.S. Immigration Policy Leaves Few Legal Options for Mexican Workers." *Immigration Policy in Focus* 4 (5). Available from http://www.ailf.org/ipc/nowayin.asp.

Passel, Jeffrey. 2005. "Size and Characteristics of the Unauthorized Migrant Population in the U.S." Washington, DC: Pew Hispanic Center. Available from http://pewhispanic.org/reports.

Porter, Eduardo. 2005. "Illegal Immigrants Are Bolstering Social Security with Billions." *New York Times*, April 5.

Rubinkam, Michael. 2007. "PA. Immigrant Law Voided: Judge Strikes Down Hazleton's Tough New Anti-Illegal Immigration Law." *The Associated Press*, July 26, 2007. Available from http://biz.yahoo.com/ap/070726/illegal_immigrants_crackdown.html?.v=1.

Skeldon, Ronald. 2000. *Myths and Realities of Chinese Irregular Migration*. Migration Research Series 1. Geneva: International Office of Migration.

Nadia Y. Flores

UNESCO STATEMENTS ON RACE

The establishment of the United Nations (UN) following World War II led to a surge in declarations, conventions, and organizations aimed at promoting human rights and equality. The legacy of Nazism and the failure of the League of Nations galvanized the UN to formulate two critical postwar documents: the Universal Declaration of Human Rights (1948), and the Genocide Convention (1948). The United Nations Educational, Scientific and Cultural Organization (UNESCO) was established in 1945 to "embody a genuine culture of peace." It was within this international atmosphere that UNESCO, as one of its early public acts, issued a Statement on Race in 1950.

Racism was the essence of Nazism, and the defeat of that regime provided an opportunity to pursue an egalitarian agenda. Despite the defeat of Nazism, racism in the late 1940s remained a powerful ideology. Segregation in the United States was in full force, and southern racism was yet to be challenged politically. UNESCO took up the challenge and established a committee of experts that published the 1950 Statement on Race, which declared that there was no scientific basis or justification for racial bias (*The New York Times,* July 18, 1950). The publication created a controversy that, in various forms, has lasted ever since. Nevertheless, the publication of the statement marked the emergence of a new scientific orthodoxy that continues into the twenty-first century. This persistence is most remarkable given the ongoing changes in the study of the life sciences. But perhaps as noteworthy is how the specific makeup of the committee fanned the controversy, for while the subject matter reputedly dealt with issues of physical anthropology and biology, the scientists on the UNESCO committee were largely social scientists. The question of whether race is a biological phenomena or a social construct was, and remains, controversial.

The 1950 UNESCO statement was revolutionary. Although during the previous two decades significant shifts had taken place in scientific perspectives concerning the biology of race, the claim of biological equality advanced in the statement was unprecedented as a declaration by an official public body. The committee asserted human equality based on four premises: (1) the mental capacities of all races are similar, (2) no evidence exists for biological deterioration as a result of hybridization, (3) there is no correlation between national or religious groups and any particular race, and (4) "race was less a biological fact than a social myth," and that biology proved the "universal brotherhood of man." The first three, viewed from the perspective of half a century later, have become part of the mainstream, or at least part of liberal orthodoxy. But the fourth claim presented an epistemologically radical position. The "brotherhood of man" had a subversive ring to it at the beginning of the cold war, and the positive assertion about equality based on science remains controversial today. In 1950, many viewed this claim to be the weaker point of the statement, and it was subject to widespread criticism.

During the prewar years, the scientific community had moved from racist positions to a primarily agnostic understanding of the relation between racial biology and social manifestations. Biologists, anthropologists, and psychologists all contributed to a critique that delegitimized previously held racist theories, especially those associated with eugenics in the first quarter of the century. Among the prominent scientists who shaped this antiracist shift were Franz Boas (1858–1942) and his students, including Ruth Benedict and Margaret Mead in the United States, and biologists such as J. B. S. Haldane, Julian Huxley, Lancelot Hogben, and Lionel Penrose in England. It was Penrose who played a major role in undermining the positivists' claims regarding racial differences, by showing that in many cases mental ability resulted from a combination of biology-genetics and environment, including pathological causes. Penrose showed that the idea that there was an explicit clear correlation between genetics and IQ could not be proven. The critics, with some exceptions, tended to be outsiders or socially marginal to the scientific community because of their ethnicity, gender, or politics. Even those who were at the heart of the British elite, such as Huxley and Haldane, were outsiders by their professional position or politics. In other words, it was Jews, women, and leftists who predominated in the ranks of those critical of racist viewpoints. From the vantage point of early twenty-first century, the substance of the critics writing on race would be considered to fall among those who believe in deep and biological racial divides. In other words, the theories supported by anti-racist scientists in the 1940s would be considered now by many to be racist. What made them "critics" was that their relative position opposed the conventions of their time. The whole spectrum of scientific understanding of racial differentiation has shifted.

Among this group was Ashley Montagu (1905–1999), who was born to a Jewish immigrant family in London and later migrated to the United States. Informally part of the Boasian network in New York during the thirties, Montagu never achieved the academic prestige to which he aspired. As an outsider, however, he was to play a major role in the public understanding of the science of race. His most famous book, *Man's Most Dangerous Myth: The Fallacy of Race* was first published in 1942.

UNESCO's expert committee on race was created by the UNESCO Fourth General Conference, which called for the collection of scientific data on race problems and for an educational campaign to disseminate scientific knowledge of race. UNESCO's Director-General at the time was Julian Huxley, who had criticized unfounded racist claims for fifteen years and was the coauthor of the book *We Europeans,* probably the first book to argue for the use of the term *ethnic* as a replacement for *race*. This change in terminology was seen as a way to counter scientific and, in particular, Nazi racism. Perhaps even more important to the formation of the committee was the Brazilian anthropologist Arthur Ramos, who headed the Social Sciences Department of UNESCO. He determined the composition of the committee, which reflected his interest in the social sciences and thus challenged the more conventional view of race as a biological category. Montagu turned out to be the only committee member who was a physical anthropologist and had biological expertise. He was therefore chosen to be the rapporteur. In hindsight, it is clear that this choice increased the likelihood of a controversial statement. Montagu was more of an outspoken critic than a consensus builder, and his personal social qualities were not universally admired. His clear and often outspoken position on race was not unknown to the committee, so it would be wrong to assume that their findings were not embraced by the committee as a whole.

In the following decades, Montagu would publish extensively on numerous aspects of social relations, arguing against racism and other forms of discrimination and in favor of egalitarianism. At times, however, he took his analysis and claims further than his peers felt comfortable supporting. In 1950, neither the scientific community nor the public were ready to treat race as a social construction, but UNESCO's statement was destined to redraw the lines of the debate.

The draft statement of the expert committee was sent out to various international scientists, most of whom were sympathetic to its antiracist viewpoint and had participated in previous public declarations. Their replies underscore both the scientific and political concerns of what can be said about race scientifically, as well as what ought to be said politically. The internal concerns regarding the composition of the committee led UNESCO primarily to solicit the opinion of biologists. The prevailing responses to the draft criticized the positivist view put forth in the statement about the "universal brotherhood of man." Despite behind-the-scenes politicking, Montagu, as rapporteur, was able to keep this phrase in the final text. Once the statement was published, the result, as expected, was widespread criticism. Among the critics were prominent conservative and racist scientists such as Cyril Darlington, Ronald Fisher, and Ruggles Gates, but also less vehement sympathizers. In general, the debate was largely confined to small scientific circles, but the statement's effectiveness was damaged by exaggerated assertions that lacked scientific backing.

The press coverage was not extensive, but the scientific turmoil troubled UNESCO at a time when it was struggling to establish political and professional credentials. Consequently, it was pressured to establish a second committee comprising geneticists and physical anthropologists. In an effort to keep a façade of continuity, the new expert committee also included Montagu, and the new statement was presented as an explication of the first statement, not as revision. The new rapporteur was Leslie Clarence Dunn, one of the foremost developmental geneticists, who also published popular text book on biology, and wrote on race, and the focus shifted to biology and physical anthropology. Several of the new members were among the commentators on the draft of the first statement whose opinions were not incorporated into that statement. Among the prominent new members were John Burton Sanderson Haldane, and Solly Zuckerman. Haldane was a Communist who formulated his antiracism as an anti-Nazi stand. While not always sensitive to racial offense, his egalitarianism was explicit and political. Zuckerman's Jewishness made his position on race more egalitarian than might have been expected from his centrist political position. The committee was far from monolithic, yet it had a strong antiracist and egalitarian commitment. It published its "Statement on the Nature of Race and Race Differences" in June 1951, with its authors highlighted as being "Physical Anthropologists and Geneticists." It was sent to ninety-six scientists for comments before publication. In addition to the statement, UNESCO printed eight booklets on various aspects of race, and these served as more detailed mini-statements. The industry of scientific antiracism was thus beginning to take shape, moving beyond individual efforts and becoming institutionalized.

An examination of the differences between the first and the second statements displays a wide spectrum of attitudes on the concept of race among scientists in the early 1950s. While most commentators refrained from negating the biological basis for intelligence outright, they became comfortable assigning racial differences to social factors. Race was losing its scientific (i.e., biological) credibility, but it remained a powerful force in popular culture and society. The confusion among these categories has never really been resolved in the public discourse. Although the 1950 statement was primarily sociological, it offered an explanation of the mechanism of racial differentiation through evolution, denied "race" had any concrete meaning, and advocated replacing the concept of race with an "ethnic" framework. The 1951 statement was more tentative, recognized that race mixture (the term at the time for the population descended from recognizable two races) existed "for an indefinite but a considerable time," and argued that while the process of racial differentiation is unknown, many populations could be classified anthropologically in racial terms. The controversial declaration of the first statement on the biological evidence for universal brotherhood was ignored in the second statement.

The two statements contributed to a new dogma and to confusion about race. They emphasized what is unknown by science about race and pointed to the lack of positivist knowledge of what race is. By asserting that many populations can be classified racially, but then being unable to say much about such a classification, these statements were bound to lead to public confusion. So while the impact of the statements on policy has been questioned by historians, their influence has been significant, if indirect. They were part of a trend by scientists to renounce racial prejudices as lacking a scientific basis. UNESCO continued to fight racism and publish periodically on race, while scientists by and large switched their focus to environmentalism. Over the years, different organizations have pronounced on race, including the American Anthropological Association (AAA), the American Association of Physical Anthropologists (AAPA), and the American Sociological Association.

The 1998 statement on race by the AAA for example, illustrates how little had changed since 1950. The AAA statement (which followed the AAPA's statement) hardly differed in substance from the early UNESCO statements. The focus of the critique of the claims of racial differentiation remained on intragroup variability—differences within the group as opposed to between the group and any group it borders—which has been the main argument against racism since the 1930s. For example, if skin color is the variable to be examined, whites are more different among themselves than from the nearest non whites. The difference between Nordic and any darker skin whites is bigger than between the latter ones and light skin blacks. The principle distinction is true, regardless where one choose to draw the boundaries. It similarly applies to other characteristics. This viewpoint advocates that intragroup differences are far wider than intergroup distinctions. This has been recognized by writers since the 1920s, yet it was presented by the AAA as the central claim for a denial of the significance of race. Beyond this observation, the statement focused on the history of race as a reflection on the science of race. This particular history by the AAA amounted to a sharp criticism of race thinking over time, coupled with an inability to describe any "correct" aspects of race that would explain racial differences.

Another angle to view the transformation of scientific thinking can perhaps be viewed from those who were perceived as right wing conservatives. It is their ongoing explication of racial differences as an explanation of human behavior that provided the motivation for the more recent statements on race. Each of these anti-racist statements aimed to slay the dragon of racism once and for all. Among these scientists, even the hereditarians and racialists, who since the late sixties and early seventies reasserted themselves in claims about the correlation of race and science, followed by the debate over sociobiology, were far less deterministic than even the egalitarians of the earlier period. Their scientific claims were dismissed, but it is historically instructive to see how much the whole spectrum shifted against an epistemology of stable or identifiable races.

UNESCO published additional statements on race over the years, authored by leading scientific figures who pronounced on various questions with the persistent goal of advocating human equality. The dissonance between popular views that race matters in a certain biological sense and the scientific inability to clarify what these differences might be has left scientists criticizing misconceptions without being able to offer an alternative sets of positivistic beliefs. Thus, scientific dissonance is the dominant aspect of the debate. This is illustrated by the National Cancer Institute (NCI) statement, which posits that "race is not a biologically determined classification. Race is a product of our social and political history." This dissonance leads to explicit confusion within the NCI statement itself, which also states that "Despite the fact that race is not a tenable biological classification, there are valid reasons to retain it as an indicator of health outcomes" (1997).

Race persist in popular representations, but cannot be clearly captured by scientific definitions and studies. The need to name a race and to have a clear demarcation of the group conflicts with the wide human diversity that does not avail itself for such clear demarcations. The dissonance is a subject of popular and academic confusion, as the word race conveys different things in distinct discourses and in specific contexts. UNESCO's efforts to clarify it has done much to articulate an official anti-racist position, but did not succeeded in bringing the debate to an end.

SEE ALSO *Montagu, Ashley.*

BIBLIOGRAPHY

American Anthropological Association. "American Anthropological Association Statement on 'Race.'" Available from http://www.aaanet.org/stmts/racepp.htm.

American Association of Physical Anthropologists. 1996. "AAPA Statement on Biological Aspects of Race." Available from http://www.physanth.org/positions/race.html.

Barkan, Elazar. 1992. *The Retreat of Scientific Racism.* Cambridge, U.K.: Cambridge University Press.

Barkan, Elazar. 1996. "The Politics of the Science of Race: Ashley Montagu and UNESCO's Anti-Racist Declarations."

In *Race and Other Misadventures,* edited by Larry T. Raynolds and Leonard Lieberman, 96–105. Dix Hills, NY: General Hall.

Metraux, Alfred. 1950. "UNESCO and the Racial Problem." *International Social Science Bulletin* 2: 384–390.

Montagu, F. M. Ashley. 1942. *Man's Most Dangerous Myth: The Fallacy of Race.* New York: Columbia University Press.

———. 1972 (1951). *Statement on Race,* 3rd ed. London: Oxford University Press.

National Cancer Institute. 1997. "The Meaning of Race in Science—Considerations for Cancer Research." Available from http://deainfo.nci.nih.gov/advisory/pcp/09apr97.htm.

UNESCO. 1952. *The Race Concept; Results of an Inquiry.* Paris: UNESCO.

UNESCO. 1961. *Race and Science: The Race Question in Modern Science.* New York: Columbia University.

Elazar Barkan

UNITED FARM WORKERS UNION

The United Farm Workers of America (UFW) is a predominantly Mexican farm labor union operating primarily in California, but also in Arizona, Texas, Washington, and Florida. The organization first emerged in 1965 under the leadership of César Chávez. During the height of its activities in the 1960s and 1970s, the UFW was able to improve working conditions for farmworkers and was part of a broader movement for the social and political inclusion of people of Mexican origin into American society.

During the 1960s, a plethora of political advocacy organizations emerged in the United States pressing for social and political change. This time period is most often associated with the civil rights and antiwar movements, but women, gay and lesbian persons, Native Americans, and Latinos were also active in pressing for change throughout the country. The UFW was part of this social-movement cycle.

The emergence of the UFW in the 1960s was predicated on a long history of Mexican American political mobilizations, dating to the early part of the twentieth century. During the 1930s there were significant instances of farm labor insurgency throughout California (Daniel 1981, González 1999, L. Majka 1992). However, despite widespread labor mobilization, labor unions were unable to significantly alter their situation due to their extreme political and social marginalization.

A major obstacle to farm-labor mobilization during the 1940s and 1950s was the Bracero Program. From 1942 to 1964, the United States imported Mexican guest workers, referred to as "*braceros,*" to work in agriculture. Originally conceived in response to domestic labor shortages during World War II, the Bracero Program proved highly profitable, and growers successfully lobbied to have the program extended after the war. Because braceros were neither permanent nor American, they were a highly malleable low-wage labor force. Their widespread use throughout the industry depressed wages for domestic workers and made labor organizing exceedingly difficult. Farm-labor advocacy during this period was aimed at government legislation to terminate the program. Ernesto Galarza and the National Farm Workers Union worked closely with a wide variety of urban liberals, churches, and other progressive organizations to repeal Public Law 78, which authorized the program, and in 1964 Congress rescinded authorization to renew the program. The end of the Bracero Program initiated a new era in farm labor mobilization.

César Chávez started the National Farm Workers Association (NFWA), the organizational precursor of the UFW, in Delano, California, in 1962. The organization was originally intended to be a farm-labor-based social services and advocacy group with a broad range of goals for political and economic justice. It was only in 1965, when it joined forces with the AFL-CIO–affiliated Filipino Agricultural Workers Organizing Committee (AWOC) that the organization explicitly became as a farm labor union.

In 1965 the AWOC, led by Larry Itliong, demanded Coachella Valley grape growers in Southern California increase their wages. After a strike, growers agreed to the increase. Later in the growing season, AWOC workers demanded similar wage increases from growers in Delano. When growers began using Mexican scab labor, AWOC approached the NFWA for support. Although Chávez was initially reluctant, the organizations agreed to work together to better the lives of farmworkers. By 1970 the UFW was able to sign 150 contracts with growers producing 85 percent of California's grapes. The campaign was successful because of an effective public boycott, and because of links the UFW was able to build to a variety of progressive organizations and elites sympathetic to the farmworker cause.

In 1966 the AWOC and the NFWA officially merged to form the UFW. The new organization affiliated with the AFL-CIO. This relationship proved to be beneficial, as labor groups throughout the country and abroad provided financial support to the UFW. The union also forged links with clerics, church groups, students, civil rights activists, and political figures such as Robert Kennedy. During this period, Chávez began the first of several fasts, inspired by the non-violent tactics of the Indian nationalist leader Mahatma Gandhi. The UFW also participated in marches to the state capital, which were influenced by civil rights marches in the South. The public support received by these widely publicized events helped the UFW to counter the

United Farm Workers Rally, 2002. *The United Farm Workers of America (UFW) works to improve working conditions for farm laborers.* AP IMAGES.

efforts of California agribusiness and their political allies, and they eventually won favorable contracts with grape growers.

The use of Mexican cultural symbols has been central to UFW organization and strategy. It is notable that the grape boycott was started on September 16, 1965, Mexican Independence Day. The UFW emblem, a black eagle on the middle of a red background, is a reference to the eagle found on the Mexican flag. During strikes, marches, and other public events, images of Our Lady of Guadalupe, the patron saint of Mexico, and Emiliano Zapata, a revolutionary war hero who fought for peasant land rights, are prominently displayed. After the death of Chávez in 1993, he too has become a symbol for the movement.

In 1979 the union moved its headquarters from Delano to La Paz, a small town in the Tehachapi Mountains of California. The union suffered internal strife during this period, and several high-ranking officers left the organization. In the decade that followed, the UFW retreated from the fields and began to focus its efforts on direct-mailing techniques to call attention to the plight of farmworkers, especially the negative effects of pesticides. Scholars have pointed to a hostile political environment, and the increasingly effective anti-union strategies of agribusiness to account for the decreased activities of the union during this time period (Mooney and Majka 1995, Majka and Majka 1992).

When César Chávez died in 1993, his son-in-law, Arturo Rodriguez, took over as head of the organization. With Rodriguez at the helm, the UFW started to organize in the fields again. This effort began in 1996 with a campaign to organize strawberry workers on California's Central Coast, an enterprise that met with mixed results. The UFW has also moved into urban areas, organizing factories and buying low-income housing. The organization has also continued its political advocacy work, leading some critics to charge that it is neglecting its farmworker roots. While the UFW no longer has as many workers under contract as it did it the late 1970s, its work to increase the social and political well-being of farmworkers continues to be substantial. It is a major political advocacy organization, not only for farmworkers but for all Mexican Americans.

SEE ALSO *Chávez, César Estrada; Day Laborers, Latino; Farmworkers; Galarza, Ernesto; Immigrant Domestic Workers; Labor Market, Informal; Undocumented Workers.*

BIBLIOGRAPHY

Daniel, Clete. 1981. *Bitter Harvest: A History of California Farmworkers 1870–1941.* Ithaca, NY: Cornell University Press.

González, Gilbert G. 1999. *Mexican Consuls and Labor Organizing: Imperial Politics in the American Southwest.* Austin: University of Texas Press.

Levy, Jacques. 1975. *César Chávez: Autobiography of La Causa.* New York: W.W Norton.

London, Joan, and Henry Anderson. 1970. *So Ye Shall Reap: The Story of César Chávez and the Farm Workers' Movement.* New York: Apollo Editions.

Majka, Theo J., and Linda C. Majka. 1992. "Decline of the Farm Labor Movement in California: Organizational Crisis and Political Change." *Critical Sociology* 19: 3–36.

Martin, Philip L. 2003. *Promise Unfulfilled: Unions, Immigration, and the Farm Workers.* Ithaca, NY: Cornell University Press.

Mooney, Patrick H., and Theo J. Majka. 1995. *Farmers' and Farm Workers' Movements: Social Protest in American Agriculture.* New York: Twayne.

Gilbert Felipe Mireles Jr.

UNITED KINGDOM RACIAL FORMATIONS

The United Kingdom comprises the historic kingdoms of England and Scotland, the principality of Wales, and the province of Northern Ireland. The United Kingdom is also known as Great Britain, or simply as Britain. In 2006, for the first time in British history, the total population of the United Kingdom surpassed 60 million. In terms of contemporary ethnic affiliation, according to the National Statistics Office, Table 1 indicates the various nomenclatures that served to categorize the British population for the 2001 Census. The table shows that

Population of the United Kingdom: By Ethnic Group, April 2001

United Kingdom

	Total population (Numbers)	Total population (Percentages)	Non-White population (Percentages)
White	**54,153,898**	**92.1**	-
Mixed	**677,117**	**1.2**	**14.6**
Indian	1,053,411	1.8	-
Pakistani	747,285	1.3	16.1
Bangladeshi	283,063	0.5	6.1
Other Asian	247,664	0.4	5.3
All Asian or Asian British	**2,331,423**	**4.0**	**50.3**
Black Caribbean	565,876	1.0	12.2
Black African	485,277	0.8	10.5
Black Other	97,585	0.2	2.1
All Black or Black British	**1,148,738**	**2.0**	**24.8**
Chinese	**247,403**	**0.4**	**5.3**
Other ethnic groups	**230,615**	**0.4**	**5.0**
All minority ethnic population	**4,635,296**	**7.9**	**100.0**
All population	**58,789,194**	**100**	-

SOURCE: National Statistics website: www.statistics.gov.uk. Crown copyright material is reproduced with permission of the Controller of HMSO.

Table 1.

people of color made up 7.9 percent of the population at the beginning of the twenty-first century.

The story of "ethnic diversity" in the United Kingdom is not completely told by census figures, however, as they give a rather static or homogenous view of white ethnicity. Since the earliest times, many peoples with varied histories, beliefs, languages, and cultures have settled in Britain, from the Neolithic, Bronze, and Iron Ages (5000 BC–100 BC), to the Roman Britain era (55 BC–410 AD). In short, Picts, Celts, Romans, Saxons, Angles, Danes, Jutes, Vikings, and Normans are key historical cultural groups that led to the "normative" white ethnic categories now known as the English, Scottish, Welsh, and Irish. Thus, the ethnic heritage of the United Kingdom is one of deep-rooted cultural mixture. In modern times, contemporary white British ethnicities have continued to blend with the arrival of eastern European migrants after the break-up of the Soviet Union. Crucially, from a white ethnic historical perspective alone, racial formation in the United Kingdom is complex, fluid, and deeply mongrelized.

PEOPLES OF AFRICAN DESCENT AND BRITAIN

The British Empire, in both its colonial and postcolonial histories, has arguably the most responsibility for the majority of settlement by people of African heritage in Britain. After all, it was this colonial presence that pushed millions of Africans into what is now referred to as the African Diaspora.

However, there is evidence of an African presence in Britain during the Roman era. Noted British historians, such as James Walvin, have found archeological evidence for a legion of African soldiers. These were not enslaved individuals, and some were high-ranking officers within the Roman army. Coming up the centuries, we find that in 1596 Queen Elizabeth I was "discontented" with there being "too many negars and blackamoores in the realm" (Bygott 1992, p. 18).

Therefore, African descent has longevity on mainland Britain, yet it can be deemed a contentious presence in the minds of certain social forces in the power structure from the sixteenth century onward. But it is in the era of Empire, enslavement, and colonialism that people of African descent arrived from the North American continent after the American War of Independence. These were the African Americans that fought with the British and then emigrated to England and its Caribbean colonies.

Cities like Bristol, Cardiff, and Liverpool were built mostly with the profits of the transatlantic slave trade. Slavery in the British colonies was formally abolished in 1833, but the sea routes of the "Black Atlantic" continued to bring peoples of African heritage to the mother country. The numbers were not large, but there is evidence of black communities in London, Bristol, and Liverpool from the mid-1800s onward. These communities developed in a time of overt racism, for the proliferation of a popular culture that celebrated the British Empire also deemed subjected peoples to be inferior. This is the backdrop to black presence in Britain in the twentieth century.

THE WORLD WARS AND THE POSTWAR ERA

The United Kingdom looked to its colonies for funding, munitions workers, and soldiers during both world wars. West African, African Caribbean, and Indian volunteers worked for the British war effort in various capacities. India alone had almost four million individuals enrolled in all services. During World War II, two and a half million Indians, the largest volunteer army in history, put their lives at risk for the British Empire.

Once World War II ended, there was a need for labor in the United Kingdom to help rebuild the economy. It was mostly African Caribbean workers that were recruited to fill the jobs that most whites would not do. After World War II came the "laissez-faire" era of migration to Britain. Due to the need for labor, racism was not as prevalent in the late 1940s and early 1950s. A booming economy also made it a less discriminatory environment for black workers. However, this was not to last. By the late 1950s, political forces were to emerge to curtail the African Caribbean and Asian migration to Britain. African Caribbeans were often deemed the "reserve army of labor," and they were thought to be only a transient, not a permanent, working group. However, many thousands of African Caribbean migrants decided to stay and raise families in Britain. By the end of the 1950s, the black presence in Britain was largely defined as a social problem, though the issue of white racism was rarely raised in mainstream circles.

In terms of the contemporary generation of peoples of African descent in the United Kingdom, the majority of social indicators point to there being major disparities between them and their white counterparts in terms of education and employment opportunities. Whites are twice as likely to gain employment, and young black men are more likely to be excluded from schools. Moreover, Home Office figures for 2003 reveal, in terms of the criminal justice system, that young black men in England and Wales represented about 12 percent of the total prison population, while black women represented a staggering 19 percent of the total prison population. Given the fact that peoples of African descent are only 2 percent of the overall British population, there is some way to go to achieve racial equity in prison confinement.

ASIANS IN BRITAIN

The label "Asian," in relation to the United Kingdom context, most often refers to migrants and their children from the South Asian countries of Bangladesh, India, Pakistan, and Sri Lanka. However, the term also includes those peoples of Asian descent who previously resided in the African nations of Kenya, Tanzania, and Uganda. Asians came to the United Kingdom mainly in two periods: During the 1950s they came from their original homelands, and in the 1970s they came as refugees from these African nations. Finally, there are approximately 250,000 Chinese in the United Kingdom, though they are not usually considered in the same cultural reference as South Asians.

COLOR-CODED IMMIGRATION LEGISLATION

By 1960, with the threat of immigration legislation becoming more severe—in the form of laws that prevented black migrants from entering Britain—migration from the Caribbean, Pakistan, and India rose sharply. This ushered in the 1962 Commonwealth Immigrants Act. Basically, this immigration legislation meant that British colonial subjects were no longer "free" to enter Britain, that there was now no automatic right of entry. A system of employment vouchers was introduced, whereby migrants were "ranked" by skill and usefulness to the nation. Further immigration legislation in 1965, 1968, 1971, and 1981 effectively determined entry and the right to stay in Britain on racial grounds. Immigration policy was basically "color-coded," and only migrants from former colonial territories such as Australia, New Zealand, or Gibraltar—or those colonies that happened to be mainly white in ethnic terms—were secure in their rights to entry and stay in Britain. Throughout the 1980s, immigration legislation became more stringent for people of color, but evermore lax for white migrants.

Recorded "Race" Riots in the United Kingdom

1919	Liverpool and Cardiff experience anti-Black riots
1948	Liverpool anti-Black riots
1958	London, Nottting Hill anti-Black riots
1972	Liverpool anti-Black riots
1981	Bristol, Liverpool, Manchester, Birmingham, and other cities experience urban rioting, mainly among young Blacks and the Police
1985	Liverpool experience sporadic urban rioting in Toxteth/Liverpool 8
2001	Asians revolt in Bradford, Oldham, and Leeds

Figure 1.

ANTIRACIST AND ANTIDISCRIMINATION LAWS

During this period, antiracist and antidiscrimination laws focusing on "race" also emerged to offset prejudice and racism toward people of color in the United Kingdom. Arguably, the most pertinent of these laws are the 1976 Race Relations Act and the 2000 Race Relations Amendment Act. Basically, under the Race Relations Act, it is unlawful to discriminate against a person on the grounds of "race, colour, nationality (including citizenship), or ethnic or national origin" (Commission for Racial Equality). The key areas in which the legislation applies are the fields of employment, housing, health, education, and other public authorities associated with social welfare provision. Public authorities now have a statutory obligation to eradicate unlawful discriminatory practices. It is difficult to gauge the effectiveness of such laws in British society, and most social indicators in the mid-2000s show a rise, not a decline, in prejudice and racism, according to the Commission for Racial Equality. Moreover, commentators have long argued that these antiracist laws are generally "toothless" in terms of bringing to justice the perpetuators of racialized discriminatory practices. Finally, for the United Kingdom to have the Race Relations Act, which deems racial discrimination illegal, at the same time that there are overtly racist British immigration and

Neville Lawrence Speaks at a News Conference, 1997. *After the death of teen Stephen Lawrence at the hands of racist youths, there was a public inquiry that led to the Macpherson Report, which concluded that there was institutionalized racism throughout the British police force, and in other public institutions.* AP IMAGES.

asylum policies is somewhat contradictory. At the very least, it sends conflicting messages to the British public.

STEPHEN LAWRENCE AND THE MACPHERSON REPORT

The murder of Stephen Lawrence in April 1993 is seen as a watershed in dealing with the problem of race in Britain. Stephen Lawrence was an 18-year-old middle-class black man when he was killed by five white racist youths. He was stabbed to death at a London bus stop, and it was later found that the police failed to adequately deal with the murder scene in a professional manner. For instance, they let Lawrence die in a pool of blood without giving him immediate medical assistance, and they also let vital clues about the identity of his killers slip by. Stephen's parents, Doreen and Neville Lawrence, campaigned vigorously for social justice, and in 1997 there was a public inquiry that led to the Macpherson Report, released in 1999. In the report, Sir William Macpherson acknowledged that there was "institutionalized racism" throughout the British police force and in other public institutions. His recommendations for the prevention of racism led to a call for greater multicultural education. This would include the following: a value for cultural diversity would be put into the National Curriculum; Local Educational Authorities (LEAs) would need to promote antiracist strategies; LEAs would be inspected and monitored to see how antiracist policy was being implemented; both the police and local governments would promote cultural diversity initiatives. These recommendations had widespread publicity, and numerous "targets" for improving cultural diversity were established in these institutions. Only time will tell, however, if significant improvement occurs.

NEW IMMIGRANTS AND ASYLUM SEEKERS, 1990s–2000s

By the 1990s, immigration policy was turned more toward the asylum seeker, particularly those associated with the wars in Somalia and Sierra Leone and the breakup of the old Yugoslavia. Increasingly, the British public was bombarded by the right-wing press with the idea of "asylum seeking spongers" who were out to exploit the welfare state. This created a "moral panic" against asylum seekers not seen since the days of the anti-immigrationist Enoch Powell in the late 1960s. The era of Prime Minister Margaret Thatcher (1979–1990) and her successor John Major (1990–1997) created what could be deemed a "xenophobic Britain," particularly by the 1990s. The 1993 Asylum and Immigration Appeals Act established the right of asylum seekers to appeal a denial of asylum, but it also gave the Home Office stronger powers to deport those seeking asylum. Many thousands have not been allowed into Britain under this law. Under Prime Minister Tony Blair's tenure (1997–2007), a continued regression regarding asylum seekers occurred. The Home Office revealed in 2003 that the majority of applications for asylum come from Somalia, Iraq, Zimbabwe, Iran, and Afghanistan. In 2005, the Commission for Racial Equality in the United Kingdom stated that applications had reached a thirteen-year low, indicating the increasing difficulty such individuals have in entering Britain. Finally, Home Office figures reveal that around 375,000 people from eastern Europe came to work in the United Kingdom between 2004 and 2007, and the number of foreign workers in the United Kingdom stood at 1.5 million in 2007, or one in every twenty-five workers. This represents the largest group of migrants to the United Kingdom since the 1950s and 1960s.

Overall, in the context of black and Asian minorities in Britain, there is a definite difference in the experiences of these groups in British society. For example, Indians tend to be more affluent than Bangladeshi and Pakistani settlers. Asians also fair better in British schools compared to African Caribbean pupils and, in some instances, white ethnic groups. With these racial nuances becoming more and more clear in social analysis, racial formation in the United Kingdom will continue to offer both complexity and enduring racialized inequalities. Crucially, although people of color represent about 8 percent of the British population, their collective impact has had a tremendous impact on how the United Kingdom, in keeping with its past, continues to develop via both migrant and indigenous peoples. British racism is part of the experience that people of color have contended with and continue to contend with.

SEE ALSO *Africa: British Colonies; Colonialism, Internal; Racial Demographics in the Western Hemisphere; Racial Formations; Social Welfare States; White Racial Identity.*

BIBLIOGRAPHY

British Government Home Office. http://www.homeoffice.gov.uk/.

Bygott, David. 1992. *Black and British.* Oxford, U.K.: Oxford University Press.

Christian, Mark. 2005. "The Politics of Black Presence in Britain and Black Male Exclusion in the British Education System." *Journal of Black Studies* 35 (3): 327–346.

Commission for Racial Equality (UK). http://www.cre.gov.uk/.

Fryer, Peter. 1984. *Staying Power: The History of Black Peoples in Britain.* London: Pluto Press.

Modood, Tariq, et al. 1997. *Ethnic Minorities in Britain: Diversity and Disadvantage—Fourth National Survey of Ethnic Minorities.* London: Policy Studies Institute.

National Office for Statistics (UK). http://www.statistics.gov.uk/focuson/migration/.

Mark Christian

UNITED STATES CONSTITUTION

A constitution is a formal statement of the central governing principles of a nation. Generally, a constitution will set forth the structure, powers and duties of the government and state the rights of the government's citizens. The United States Constitution is considered the first modern constitution produced by the European Enlightenment and a model for virtually all subsequently written constitutions. However, the Constitution was written by men who were deeply influenced by the racial ideology of the day and who were also committed to protecting the significant economic benefits that were provided by the enslavement of African people. As a result, the United States inherited a political system that, due to its compromises over slavery, would allow race to remain a divisive political issue for much of the country's existence.

THE FRAMERS AND THEIR TIMES

In the seventeenth and eighteenth centuries, when the American colonies were established and a new nation was beginning to develop, notions of white supremacy and the inherent inferiority of Africans were widely held. The framers of the Constitution were no different in this respect from their fellow colonists. Thomas Jefferson, in his *Notes on the State of Virginia* (1787), mused that blacks "are inferior to whites in the endowments of both body and mind," and viewed Africans as less capable than whites in reason, imagination, and emotional capacity. Benjamin Franklin, admitting in *Observations Concerning the Increase of Mankind* (1755) that he was "partial to the Complexion" of his own race, wondered, "Why increase the Sons of Africa, by Planting them in America, where we have so fair an Opportunity, by excluding all Blacks and Tawneys [by which he meant Indians], of increasing the lovely White and Red [by which he meant only "Saxons" and "English"]?"

The United States Constitution, as originally framed and ratified, made no overt textual reference to race. Several provisions had direct or indirect racial significance, however, insofar as they accommodated the institution of slavery. The Constitutional Convention in 1787 represented an effort to overcome the perceived shortcomings of the earlier Articles of Confederation and form a more viable union. The primary impediment to this process was slavery. In his notes, James Madison described slavery as the principal source of division at the convention, eclipsing even the conflict between large and small states over political representation.

Although the slavery question was not part of the Convention's agenda, it lurked in the background of almost every major issue decided at the Convention and occasionally burst out into the open. The desire on the part of large states to replace the uniform representation of the Confederation Congress with proportional representation could not be resolved without considering the slavery issue. Although the enslaved could not vote, Southerners viewed them as a kind of property that deserved protection in the allocation of government power. Furthermore, the sparsely populated South was reluctant to join a governmental scheme that would leave them as the junior partner to the more populated North. Slavery also figured largely in the debate over Congress's power to tax and regulate commerce. Southern delegates sought to protect slavery by restricting Congress's ability to use its commerce and taxing powers to eliminate slavery or make it less profitable.

The interest in a more viable political and economic union was dispensable to some Southern delegates if it did not accommodate slavery. Opposition to slavery among Northern delegates melted when confronted with the intensity of this agenda. As Thurgood Marshall put it in a 1987 speech: "The record of the framers' debates on the slave question is especially clear: the Southern states acceded to the demands of New England states for giving Congress broad power to regulate commerce, in exchange for the right to continue the slave trade" (1987, p. 2).

ACCOMMODATIONS OF SLAVERY

The new union was predicated on federal acquiescence in slavery and the reservation of self-determination for each state. The document itself was drafted in terms that did not use the words *slavery* or *Negroes* or *Africans*, whether out of embarrassment or political expediency. But the concerns of the slaveholding regions were addressed in various ways. Proportionate representation in the House of Representatives and factoring of direct taxes was based on a population count that recognized a slave as three-fifths of a person. Congressional regulation of American participation in the international slave trade was prohibited until 1808. A fugitive slave clause was adopted as the basis for federal legislation that enabled slave owners to recapture runaway slaves without any legal process.

Other provisions in the Constitution accommodated slavery indirectly. Sections of the Constitution requiring the federal government to put down rebellions or to protect states from "domestic violence" clearly contemplated federal aid in event of a slave rebellion. Article I, Section 9, prohibiting federal taxes on exports, prevented an indirect tax on slavery through the taxation of exports produced by slaves. Article I, Section 10, likewise prevented states from taxing exports or imports. The establishment of an electoral college incorporating the slave-state weighted scheme of proportional representation in Congress meant that Southern states had greater influence on the selection of a president than they would have had with direct popular elections. Finally, the amendment process was cast in the South's favor. The three-fourths majority requirement for amendments made it difficult to amend the constitution without the agreement of slaveholding states, and those provisions of the Constitution permitting the slave trade and requiring direct taxes on slaves at a reduced three-fifths rate could not be amended at all until 1808.

The accommodation of slavery was a key to brokering the union's founding. It was a model of political resolution that continued through the first half of the nineteenth century, but with diminishing returns. Northern concessions to the slavery agenda were inspired in part by Southern acquiescence in the nation's first stage of territorial expansion. The Northwest Ordinance, which created the territories of Illinois, Indiana, Michigan, and Ohio, explicitly prohibited slavery. Southern delegates also fostered the sense that slavery was a dying system.

Far from being terminal, slavery grew during the nation's early years. Congress in 1808 prohibited American participation in the international slave trade. The impact of this action was limited by the federal government's inability to patrol the nation's shores effectively and the continuing demand for slaves. Territorial expansion and fugitive slave controversies ultimately undid original expectations that the union could accommodate slave and nonslave states. The creation of each new territory and admission of each new state generated increasingly acrimonious debate and sectional antagonism. Congress responded to these episodes by recycling the methods of resolution first used by the nation's founders. Among the most notable of these efforts was the Missouri Compromise, which in 1820 established a permanent geographical boundary between slave and nonslave states and territories.

Each new resolution of the slavery issue, however, merely prefaced an escalation of the controversy.

Westward expansion increased each side's fear that the other would gain the upper hand. Adding to the volatile mix was the abolitionist movement, which emerged in the 1830s and antagonized the South to the point that the movement was criminalized.

THE CIVIL WAR

By the 1840s the failure to address slavery at the founding was bearing threatening consequences. In *Prigg v. Pennsylvania* (1842), the Court invalidated a state enactment that prohibited a slave owner from capturing a fugitive slave without due process of law. It found specifically that the antikidnapping law conflicted with federal law permitting slave owners to enter a free state, capture, and remove runaway slaves. This decision sensitized the North to its complicity in slavery. For the South, the federal government's exclusive interest in fugitive slave matters suggested the potential for slavery to become a matter of national rather than state resolution.

As sectional antagonism and distrust mounted, the political system became increasingly challenged in its ability to manage the slavery issue. The creation of new territories and states by the 1850s had become a particularly high-stakes venture, as evidenced by the chicanery and violence in connection with the admissions of Kansas and Nebraska into the union. With the political process gridlocked on the issue of slavery, it eventually turned to the Supreme Court for a resolution. The Court responded with a decision that proved to be disastrous.

In *Dred Scott v. Sandford* (1856), the Court found that no person of African descent (slave or otherwise) could be a citizen of the United States or the beneficiary of rights under the federal Constitution. This determination was grounded in the notion that African Americans were inferior, had "no rights that white men are bound to respect," and could be justly and lawfully reduced to slavery. Chief Justice Roger B. Taney maintained further that Congress had no power to regulate slavery in the territories and that the right to own slaves was constitutionally protected.

Northern reaction to the Court's ruling was profoundly negative but generally did not reflect any premise of racial equality. To the contrary, racial segregation and discrimination were common aspects of the Northern cultural landscape. These sentiments were shared by President Lincoln, who observed that "when you cease to be slaves, you are far removed from being placed on an equality with the white man. . . . I cannot alter it if I could. It is a fact" (quoted in Fehrenbacher 1978, Introduction).

Lincoln ignored the Court's decision and midway through the Civil War issued the Emancipation Proclamation. Congress repealed fugitive slave legislation in 1862, and the Thirteenth Amendment (1865) formally prohibited slavery. The scholar Derrick Bell describes *Dred Scott* as "the most frequently overturned decision in history" (1973, p. 21). This observation reflects the reality that, although repudiating the *Dred Scott* ruling, the Thirteenth Amendment did not foreclose racist ideology as a driver of policy. Slavery, once outlawed, was superseded by the Black Codes, which established a comprehensive set of race-based burdens on opportunity, residence, travel, assembly, voting, and other activities.

EARLY CIVIL RIGHTS LEGISLATION

With the end of the Civil War, the issues dividing North and South returned to the political process. President Andrew Johnson, who took office upon Lincoln's assassination, adopted the position that the Thirteenth Amendment only abolished slavery. Despite Johnson's narrow view of the Thirteenth Amendment, Congress used it as authority to adopt the nation's first civil rights legislation. The Civil Rights Act of 1866 prohibited racial discrimination in civil rights or immunities and guaranteed that all persons, regardless of race, would have the same rights to make and enforce contracts, sue or be sued, inherit, purchase, lease, sell, and hold property, and be subject to like punishment.

President Johnson's veto of the law was overridden but evidenced the legislation's fragile foundation. To secure the enactment's long-term vitality, and consistent with concern that the Thirteenth Amendment was a limited source of authority, the Reconstruction Congress framed the Fourteenth Amendment, proposed in 1866 and ratified in 1868. This provision established that state citizenship derives from federal citizenship, not the reverse as the *Dred Scott* Court had indicated. It provided that the states could not abridge the privileges and immunities of federal citizenship, deprive a person of life, liberty, or property without due process of law, or deny a person equal protection of the laws. The amendment also empowered Congress to enforce its terms by appropriate legislation.

Missing from the Fourteenth Amendment, as initially framed, was any protection for the right to vote. Despite initial resistance to including this right in its postwar agenda, Congress eventually saw it as a means of accelerating movement toward reconstruction. The Fifteenth Amendment thus was framed and ratified, in 1870, with the expectation that the right to vote would provide the ultimate protection against political hostility toward former slaves.

The Court's ruling in *Strauder v. West Virginia* (1879) represented the first use of the Fourteenth Amendment to invalidate a racially discriminatory state law. The Court in this case found the exclusion of

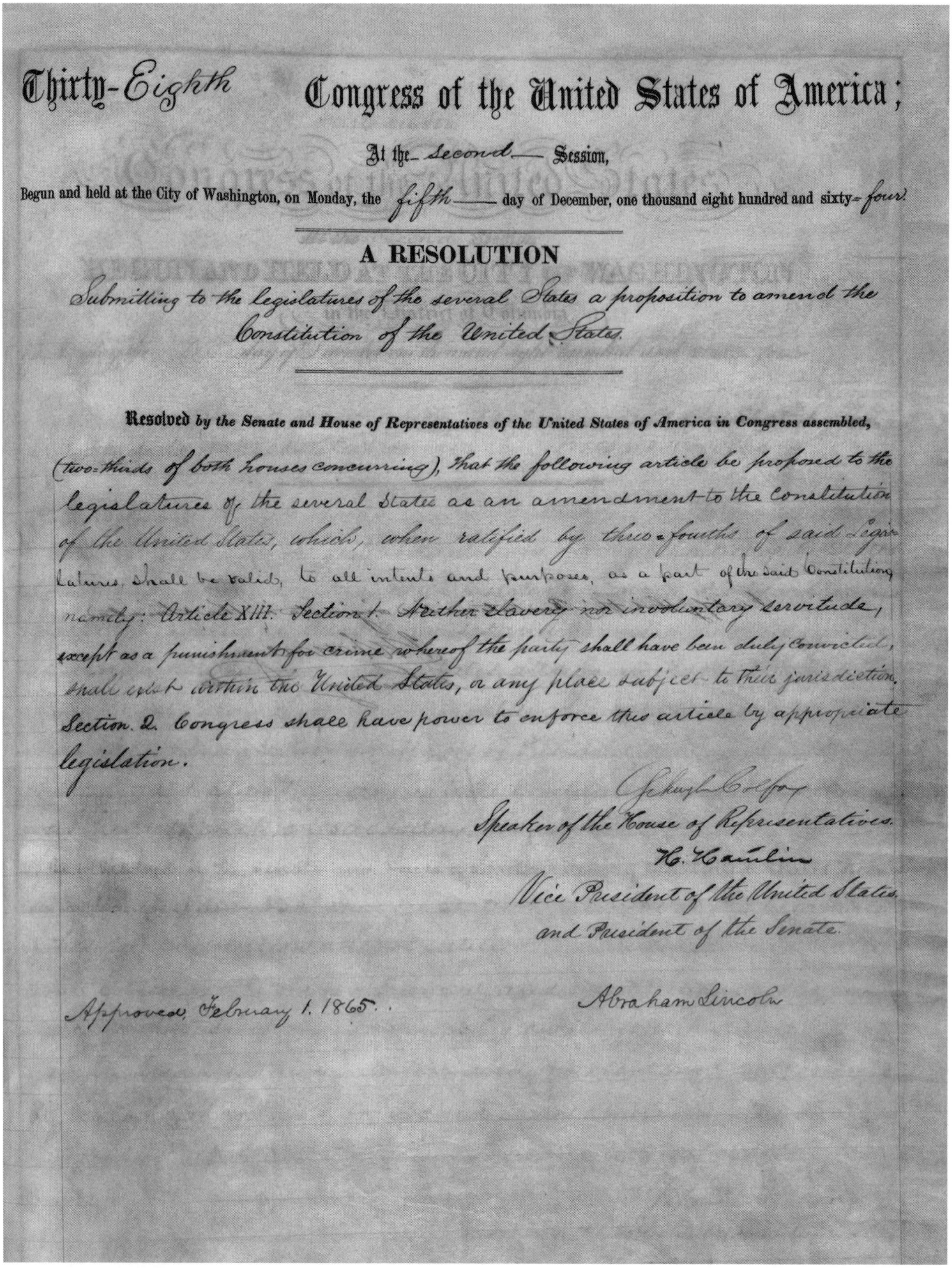
Thirty-Eighth Congress of the United States of America;

At the Second Session,

Begun and held at the City of Washington, on Monday, the fifth day of December, one thousand eight hundred and sixty-four.

A RESOLUTION

Submitting to the legislatures of the several States a proposition to amend the Constitution of the United States.

Resolved by the Senate and House of Representatives of the United States of America in Congress assembled, (two-thirds of both houses concurring), that the following article be proposed to the legislatures of the several States as an amendment to the Constitution of the United States, which, when ratified by three-fourths of said Legislatures, shall be valid, to all intents and purposes, as a part of the said Constitution, namely: Article XIII. Section 1. Neither slavery nor involuntary servitude, except as a punishment for crime whereof the party shall have been duly convicted, shall exist within the United States, or any place subject to their jurisdiction. Section 2. Congress shall have power to enforce this article by appropriate legislation.

Schuyler Colfax
Speaker of the House of Representatives.

H. Hamlin
Vice President of the United States, and President of the Senate.

Approved, February 1. 1865.

Abraham Lincoln

Thirteenth Amendment to the U.S. Constitution. *The Thirteenth Amendment formally prohibited slavery. The Black Codes, however, established a comprehensive set of race-based burdens on opportunity, residence, travel, assembly, voting, and other activities.* NATIONAL ARCHIVES & RECORDS ADMINISTRATION.

African Americans from juries unconstitutional. In striking down the enactment, the Court described the Fourteenth Amendment as prohibiting laws that singled out a group for legal discrimination, implied inferiority in civil society, lessened their enjoyment of rights others enjoy, or reduced persons to the condition of a subject race. The equal protection clause, as the Court saw it, ensured that state law would be the same for all persons regardless of their race. But the Court quickly narrowed this expansive view of the Fourteenth Amendment's scope.

Four years later, in the *Civil Rights Cases* (1883), the Court invalidated the Civil Rights Act of 1875 on grounds it exceeded Congress's regulatory authority under the Fourteenth Amendment. This legislation prohibited discrimination in public accommodations. The Court, however, determined that racial distinctions in this context were customary, and the legal system could not be used to reach "mere discriminations."

The *Civil Rights Cases* and the Supreme Court's subsequent jurisprudence created a constitutional environment accommodating toward racial discrimination. The key to enacting laws that differentiated on the basis of race was to present them (and have them accepted) as enactments that did not imply inferiority and were consistent with societal norms. Laws designed to establish and maintain separation on the basis of race emerged throughout the South in the late 1880s. These enactments candidly aimed to segregate, protect racial integrity, preserve white supremacy, and minimize cross-racial interaction. Such legislation actually was modeled on enactments in the North that traditionally had mandated racial segregation in education and other contexts. In *Plessy v. Ferguson* (1896), the Court noted these historical realities in determining that prescriptive racial segregation was constitutional.

The *Plessy* decision concerned a state law mandating separate but equal accommodations on passenger trains. Although acknowledging that the Fourteenth Amendment established absolute equality of the races under the law, the Court found that the amendment did not eliminate distinctions on the basis of color, enforce social (as opposed to political) equality, or require commingling of the races on terms that were unsatisfactory to either. It viewed official segregation as a reasonable exercise of the state's police power that accounted for the public's comfort, peace, and good order. The Court also determined that segregation did not constitute oppression of a particular group but an accommodation of custom and tradition. Responding to arguments that segregation implied inferiority in civil society, the Court attributed any such understanding to a misplaced interpretation by "the colored race." Justice Marshall Harlan, in a dissenting opinion, criticized the Court for denying segregation's true nature. He maintained that the Constitution forbids any "caste" system and is "color-blind."

A SYSTEM OF RACIAL ADVANTAGE

Prescriptive segregation became a dominant system of racial management that defined opportunity and advantage comprehensively on the basis of group status. For several decades after *Plessy,* the separate but equal doctrine maintained a formal concern for equality but in reality drove a system of racial advantage (and disadvantage). In *Cumming v. Richmond County Board of Education* (1899), the Court upheld a school board's closure of an all-black high school on grounds its financial resources were limited. This outcome previewed a legacy of extreme funding disparities in public education. South Carolina in 1915, for instance, spent ten times more money on educating white students than black students. In *Gong Lum v. Lee* (1927), the Court rejected arguments that a child of Chinese descent could attend a school reserved for whites.

During the 1930s, federal and state courts began to take a harder look at segregation. This development arose out of the litigation strategy of the National Association for the Advancement of Colored People (NAACP), which challenged obvious inequalities such as funding or lack of higher education opportunities altogether. In these cases, states operating single-race graduate and professional schools typically were given the choice of establishing parallel institutions for nonwhites or allowing nonwhites to matriculate.

The constitutional foundation for segregation also was weakened by evolving standards of judicial review. The Court in *United States v. Carolene Products Co.* (1938) found that prejudice against discrete and insular minorities impaired the political system's ability to protect minorities from hostile legislation. It thus signaled a readiness to evaluate laws enacted against groups that were excluded from the political process. In *Korematsu v. United States* (1944), the Court officially embraced a strict standard of review for laws that differentiated on the basis of race. The *Korematsu* case concerned the relocation of persons of Japanese descent from the West Coast during World War II. In the face of scant evidence of Japanese-American disloyalty, the Court deferred to alleged national security concerns in upholding the federal government's action. It observed, however, that any legal restriction burdening the civil rights of a particular racial group are "immediately suspect" and must be subjected "to the most rigid scrutiny." The *Korematsu* case was sharply criticized after the war and led to an official apology and reparations for internment camp survivors and their families in 1988.

In the years between the *Korematsu* ruling and the invalidation of segregated public education in *Brown v. Board of Education* (1954), states operating racially identifiable schools poured substantial resources into equalization. Even if equality of funding could be hypothetically demonstrated, however, the Court was willing to identify inequality with respect to intangible factors such as a school's reputation. In *Sweatt v. Painter* (1950), it determined that segregated legal education would remain unequal even if tangible differences were eliminated. The Court accordingly ordered desegregation of the University of Texas School of Law. It reached a similar conclusion in *McLaurin v. Oklahoma State Regents for Higher Education* (1950), when it found degrading restrictions on an African American admitted to an all-white graduate program—such as being forced to observe lectures from the hallway—unacceptable.

BROWN V. BOARD AND ITS AFTERMATH

The constitutional death knell for racially segregated schools was struck in *Brown v. Board of Education* (1954). Key to the outcome in this case was the Court's sense that it could not correlate modern law or understandings to the period in which the Fourteenth Amendment was adopted or segregation initially was upheld. It noted that public education had become a primary determinant of personal development and success and referenced psychological data showing that segregation had a detrimental effect on African-American children. The Court concluded that racial segregation in public education inherently was unequal.

Because the equal protection guarantee by its terms applied to the states but did not apply to the federal government itself, the Court turned to the Fifth Amendment due process clause as the basis for invalidating segregated schools in the District of Columbia. In *Bolling v. Sharpe* (1954) the Court determined that school segregation had no reasonable relationship to a legitimate government objective and thus constituted an arbitrary deprivation of liberty under the due process clause.

Having declared segregation unconstitutional, the Court faced the challenge of framing a remedy that would dismantle it. Knowing that resistance was likely, the Court in *Brown v. Board of Education II* (1955) announced that desegregation should take place "with all deliberate speed." This Court solicited input from the states that would be most affected by this ruling. Reaction to the desegregation mandate, however, generally was characterized as resistance, delay, evasion, and hostility.

Although the *Brown* decision technically governed segregation in public education, its logic extended to the entire public sector. In short order, segregation was invalidated in a variety of public settings. Even as desegregation became the law of the land, many states maintained their laws prohibiting interracial marriage. In *Loving v. Virginia* (1967), the Court reviewed an antimiscegenation law that the state justified on the grounds of applying it even-handedly. Despite this purported symmetry, the Court concluded that the law was grounded in racist ideology that conflicted with the central meaning of the Fourteenth Amendment.

The elimination of laws that formally classified on the basis of race did not account for all causes or conditions of racial disadvantage. Against this backdrop, a key issue of the 1970s was whether an equal protection claim could be established on the basis of disparate impact alone. In *Washington v. Davis*, the Court determined that a plaintiff must provide evidence of discriminatory purpose to establish an equal protection claim. This requirement reflected the Court's concern that a focus on effect alone would put a broad range of legitimate laws at risk.

Discerning a discriminatory purpose was simple when racial segregation was officially prescribed. When not manifest, illegal motive is difficult to prove. Dating back to *Yick Wo v. Hopkins* (1887), the Court has recognized that laws that are racially neutral on their face also must be assessed with respect to their application. In *Arlington Heights v. Metropolitan Housing Development Corp* (1978) the Court identified several other factors that may be relevant to determining discriminatory motive. Potential cues include statistical disparities, patterns, or effects that are inexplicable except on grounds of race, legislative history, and departures from normal procedures.

The Court seldom has found discriminatory purpose on the basis of circumstantial evidence. In *McCleskey v. Kemp* (1987) the Court upheld the Georgia death penalty despite a showing of significant disparities in its application to whites and nonwhites. This case arose against the backdrop of a dual system of criminal justice in Georgia. As Justice Brennan noted in a dissenting opinion, defense lawyers invariably would factor race into the advice they gave clients with respect to accepting or rejecting a plea agreement. The Court was unmoved by statistical disparities that, in its words, "[appear] to correlate to race." However, in a voting rights case, *Shaw v. Reno* (1993), the Court found that an oddly configured congressional district could not be understood as anything but racially motivated. The white plaintiffs in *Shaw* had alleged that the majority black district had been created in violation of the equal protection rights of white voters.

The Court's embrace of a discriminatory motive requirement represented a critical juncture in equal protection doctrine. Discriminatory intent is difficult to prove when not evidenced on the face of the law. The net result is that judicial relief other than for the most egregious forms of racial discrimination is difficult to find, and racial discrimination motivated by unconscious racism cannot be remedied at all.

AFFIRMATIVE ACTION

The Court's first substantive ruling on affirmative action, *Regents of the University of California v. Bakke* (1978), concerned a preferential admissions program at the University of California at Davis Medical School that set aside sixteen of one hundred spots for minority applicants. There was no majority opinion in the case and the justices split on whether the admissions plan passed constitutional muster. Justice Powell provided the deciding vote. He found that the program violated Title VI of the Civil Rights Act of 1964, but maintained that race could be a limited factor in the admission process.

Powell's opinion proved to be particularly influential on the eventual contours of affirmative action jurisprudence. Key points that he articulated, and that the Court eventually embraced, were that racial preferences should be strictly scrutinized and cannot be justified on the basis of societal (as opposed to particularized and proven) discrimination. Powell introduced the notions that affirmative action must be scrutinized for its potential to stereotype or stigmatize, and quotas are impermissible except in extraordinary circumstances. He also maintained that diversification of a student body represents a compelling interest that may justify the factoring of race as one of several considerations in the admission process.

A decade after *Bakke,* the Court remained divided on affirmative action and, in particular, the standard of review that should govern its analysis. A strict scrutiny standard measures whether the government regulatory interest is "compelling" and the regulatory means are "narrowly tailored" toward the regulatory objective. An intermediate standard of review assesses whether the regulatory interest is "important" and the regulatory means are "substantially related" to the regulatory objective. In *Richmond v. J. A. Croson Co.* a majority of the Court for the first time embraced strict scrutiny as the appropriate standard of review. At issue in *Croson* was a municipal program that set aside 30 percent of construction contracts to minority business enterprises. Justice Sandra Day O'Connor, writing for a plurality of four justices, maintained that "searching inquiry" was necessary to determine the true purpose of a racial classification and "smoke out" illegitimate uses of race. Strict scrutiny further ensured that the regulatory means closely fit the regulatory goal and guarded against motives based on illegitimate prejudice or stereotype.

Even if a government's intentions were good, O'Connor contended, racial classifications carried the risk of stigmatic harm and potential for promoting notions of racial inferiority and racial politics. Although acknowledging the nation's history of discrimination, she saw a greater risk in maintaining the relevance of race and opportunity for competing and immeasurable claims to relief from every disadvantaged group. Justice Antonin Scalia, in a concurring opinion, provided the fifth vote for strict scrutiny. He urged an even more rigorous analytical model that would allow race to be factored only when necessary to eliminate systems of unlawful discrimination.

The strict scrutiny standard announced in *Croson* applied to affirmative action programs adopted by states. Left open was the possibility that, given Congress's power to enforce the Fourteenth Amendment through appropriate legislation, a different standard might govern federal affirmative action programs. Despite some conflicting cases before and after *Croson,* the Court in *Adarand Constructors, Inc. v. Pena* (1995) concluded that federal affirmative action programs should be reviewed pursuant to the same strict scrutiny criterion governing state programs. The federal government, like the states, must demonstrate some instance of racial discrimination (for which it is responsible) as a basis for race-conscious remedial action.

The uniform application of strict scrutiny to governmental actions, whether they were intended to improve the condition of historically subjugated groups (and thus incidentally harmed the white majority), or intended to subjugate a particular group, is referred to as "formal equality" or "colorblindness." Following *Croson* and *Adarand,* colorblindness has become the centerpiece of the Supreme Court's constitutional jurisprudence of race. Using colorblind analysis, federal courts treat all governmental racial classifications in the same way—courts will evaluate a rule attempting to integrate a housing project in the same manner that they would a rule seeking housing segregation. On the surface, this even-handedness appears fair. However, critics of color-blindness have pointed out that failing to distinguish between oppressive acts and remedial ones when applying strict scrutiny makes it difficult for governments to take affirmative steps to advance racial justice. Consequently, existing racial disparities become locked in as the constitutional status quo. Critics of color-blindness seek to erode this roadblock, as they see it, in constitutional development by focusing judicial attention on result-determined measures of equality and away from process-based ones like formal equality. Other scholars have expressed interest in moving away from the Fourteenth Amendment as a measure of constitutionality and reinvigorating the Thirteenth Amendment's prohibition against the "badges and incidents of slavery" as a way to legitimate a government's efforts at racial remediation.

SEE ALSO *Affirmative Action; Brown v. Board of Education; Civil Rights Acts; Color-Blind Racism; Dred Scott v. Sandford; Peonage Cases; Voting Rights Act of 1965.*

BIBLIOGRAPHY

Bell, Derrick. 1973. *Race, Racism, and American Law.* Boston: Little Brown.

———. 1987. *And We Are Not Saved: The Elusive Quest for Racial Justice.* New York: Basic Books.

Branch, Taylor. 1988. *Parting the Waters: America in the King Years, 1954–63.* New York: Simon and Schuster.

Carter, Stephen L. 1991. *Reflections of an Affirmative Action Baby.* New York: Basic Books.

Delgado, Richard. 1996. *The Coming Race War?: And Other Apocalyptic Tales of America after Affirmative Action and Welfare.* New York: New York University Press.

Fairman, Charles. 1987. *History of the Supreme Court of the United States,* Vols. 6–7: *Reconstruction and Reunion, 1864–88.* New York: Macmillan.

Farrand, Max, ed. 1966. *The Records of the Federal Convention of 1787,* rev. ed. New Haven, CT: Yale University Press.

Fehrenbacher, Don E. 1978. *The Dred Scott Case: Its Significance in American Law and Politics.* New York: Oxford University Press.

Finkelman, Paul. 1981. *An Imperfect Union: Slavery, Federalism, and Comity.* Chapel Hill: University of North Carolina Press.

Hyman, Harold M. 1973. *A More Perfect Union: The Impact of the Civil War and Reconstruction on the Constitution.* New York: Knopf.

———, and William M. Wiecek. 1982. *Equal Justice under Law: Constitutional Development, 1835–1875.* New York: Harper and Row.

Jordan, Winthrop D. 1968. *White over Black: American Attitudes toward the Negro, 1550–1812.* Chapel Hill: University of North Carolina Press.

Kaczorowski, Robert J. 2005. *The Politics of Judicial Interpretation: The Federal Courts, Department of Justice, and Civil Rights, 1866-1876.* New York: Fordham University Press.

Kluger, Richard. 2004. *Simple Justice: The History of* Brown v. Board of Education *and Black America's Struggle for Equality,* rev. ed. New York: Knopf.

Lawrence III, Charles R., and Mari J. Matsuda. 1997. *We Won't Go Back: Making the Case for Affirmative Action.* Boston: Houghton Mifflin.

Lively, Donald E. 1992. *The Constitution and Race.* New York: Praeger.

Marshall, Thurgood. 1987. "Reflections on the Bicentennial of the United States Constitution." *Harvard Law Review* 101 (1): 1–5.

Sowell, Thomas. 1984. *Civil Rights: Rhetoric or Reality?* New York: Morrow.

Taylor, Jared. 1992. *Paved with Good Intentions: The Failure of Race Relations in Contemporary America.* New York: Carroll and Graf.

Donald E. Lively

URBAN LEAGUE

The National Urban League is a Progressive Era organization formed in New York City in 1911. It grew out of the cooperative efforts of black and white social reformers, who founded the organization and its precursors to confront the economic and social problems of African Americans, particularly those in the nation's northern cities. Many observers have noted that the Urban League and the National Association for the Advancement of Colored People (NAACP) essentially divided up the task of advancing the interests of African Americans, with the NAACP fighting for legal rights and the Urban League focusing on providing blacks with a stake in the American economy. Colloquially, the Urban League was often called the "State Department" of African-American affairs, while the NAACP was known as the "War Department."

ECONOMIC CONDITIONS

The Urban League emerged as a response to the lack of economic opportunity for African-American men in U.S. cities. New York City became the focal point for this effort because it had the largest population of African Americans of any city outside of the South. During the first decade of the twentieth century, the city's black population increased by 50 percent, and by 1910 there were about 75,000 blacks living there. This pattern of growth in the black population would be repeated in New York and other major cities as well during the Great Migration of the 1910s and 1920s. By 1930, for example, the black population of Harlem, New York, had grown to 165,000. In Chicago, the black population grew from 44,000 in 1910 to 110,000 in 1920. Cities such as Cleveland and Detroit saw similar growth rates. Most of those moving to these northern cities came in search of economic opportunity and to try to escape the blatant and legal racism of the Jim Crow South. With the growth of the black population in these cities, the Urban League grew to twenty-seven affiliates by 1919, all but one (in St. Louis, Missouri) east of the Mississippi River. While most were in the Northeast industrial corridor, a few appeared in cities in the South, such as Atlanta. In the first decade of the twenty-first century, the Urban League has 115 affiliates in thirty-four states and the District of Columbia, with 50,000 members and an annual budget of $45 million.

One of the major problems this burgeoning black population experienced was a lack of jobs, particularly in the professions and the industrial sector. Black men were often unable to find work because they lacked job training and skills, and because of entrenched discrimination in the labor force. Because they were unable to find work, their wives were often forced into the labor market, for women were able to find employment in domestic service and similar sectors. During this period it is estimated that 59 percent of black women in New York held jobs outside the home (in contrast to white women, whose labor participation rate was 24.6 percent, and foreign-born women at 27.2 percent). Additionally, blacks had the lowest percentage of home ownership of any U.S. city with a black population of 2,500 or more, a death rate one and a half times that of whites, and an illiteracy rate twelve times that of whites (Weiss 1974, p. 12). Meanwhile, the increased mechanization of labor often forced black men out of those jobs they were able to secure, while the labor unions, eager to protect the jobs of white men against both blacks and new waves of foreign immigrants, remained resistant to admitting African-American members.

EARLY HISTORY

The Urban League was formed from the consolidation of a number of organizations, including the Committee for Improving the Industrial Condition of Negroes in New York (CIICN), founded in 1906; the National League for the Protection of Colored Women (NLPCW), formed in 1905; and the Committee on Urban Conditions Among Negroes, formed in 1910. The chief goals of the CIICN, reflecting the ideology of Booker T. Washington, were to provide blacks with industrial and commercial training and then provide them access to jobs. For instance, it persuaded the New York Board of Education to offer evening programs in vocational education in black neighborhoods.

The NLPCW, with chapters in New York, Baltimore, Chicago, Philadelphia, and Washington, D.C., was particularly concerned about the large proportion of black women in domestic service—in New York City, some 90 percent of working black women—who typically labored long hours for low and sometimes uncertain pay. Many of these women had been lured North by unscrupulous labor agents in the South, who preyed on them by offering them hopes of prosperity that almost always went unfulfilled. They arrived in the cities with no place to stay, no money, and no job. Members of the NLPCW met these women at train stations, provided them with lodging, and developed a network of social agencies that provided them with help and information.

Although the Urban League was formally founded in 1911, its members often trace its founding to 1910 and the formation of the Committee on Urban Conditions, the Urban League's most immediate precursor. That year, the leaders of the three leading organizations met with the goal of joining forces and consolidating their efforts. After some initial resistance from the Committee on Urban Conditions, the organizations agreed to join, and on October 16, 1911, the National League on Urban Conditions Among Negroes was born. The organization took its current name, the National Urban League, in 1920. The NLPCW and the Committee on Urban Conditions remained as standing subagencies of the Urban League.

The principal goals of the Urban League were to provide employment opportunities in the private sector, break down the color line in organized labor, and promote vocational and occupational education. For the first two decades of its existence, its focus remained primarily on the private sector. The organization struggled financially, and not all of its programs, such as scholarships for undergraduates to study social work at black colleges, were entirely successful. The league did, however, succeed in persuading colleges and universities to include economics, sociology, and urban studies in their curricula, and it was able to place a large number of black social workers in social service agencies. Additionally, the league promoted such welfare services as charitable agencies, settlement houses, and immigrant-aid societies. It also promoted such values as proper dress, sanitation, personal hygiene, health, punctuality, and homemaking skills, and it sponsored summer camps, daycare centers, kindergartens, community centers, and the like.

Reliable data about the number of job placements attributable to the Urban League are hard to find. Some African-American men obtained industrial jobs because of labor shortages during World War I, while others obtained jobs without the help of the Urban League. Nevertheless, the organization did succeed in finding decent jobs for thousands of workers, particularly during the boom years of the 1920s. It was also successful in opening up industrial plants that had previously been closed to African Americans. The organization claimed, for example, to have placed some 15,000 workers in Chicago in 1920. In connection with these efforts, the league stressed the scientific investigation of the conditions of urban blacks, much of it reported in its journal, *Opportunity: Journal of Negro Life,* which was published from 1923 until 1949. This focus on investigation has continued in the league's current flagship publication, *Opportunity Journal*; an annual report titled *The State of Black America*, published since 1976; and the organization's twenty-year retrospective volumes, the last published in 1990.

NEW GOALS

With the coming of the Great Depression in the 1930s, the Urban League turned more of its attention to the public sector. It sought to have blacks included in the federal recovery and relief programs of the New Deal. By the 1940s and 1950s it was successfully attacking segregation in the defense industries and the military, though its primary mission remained education rather than civil rights. The civil rights movement of the 1950s and 1960s, however, led to calls for a change in the Urban League's mission. Under the leadership of Whitney Young, the league shifted its focus to civil rights and played an integral part in organizing the 1963 March on Washington and the 1968 Poor People's Campaign. The league called for a domestic "Marshall Plan" (the plan for financing the reconstruction of Europe after World War II), and it sponsored voter registration drives, help for black veterans, open-housing campaigns, adoption programs for hard-to-place black children, and similar projects. Young also initiated such programs as the Street Academy, which helped prepare high school dropouts for college, and New Thrust, a program that developed the leadership skills of urban blacks with a view to identifying and solving urban social problems.

This emphasis on a more activist approach continued into the 1970s, under the leadership of Vernon Jordan, and beyond. In the 1970s the federal government contracted with the Urban League to provide social welfare programs and government employment. The organization continues to work closely with Congress and other federal agencies to address such social problems as poverty, failing schools, teenage pregnancy, crime, gun violence, and households headed by single women. Affiliated organizations such as the Urban League of Young Professionals of Pittsburgh tap the leadership skills of African-American professionals to solve urban problems.

SEE ALSO *Civil Rights Movement; Labor Market; NAACP; Poverty; Social Problems; Washington, Booker T.*

BIBLIOGRAPHY

Hamilton, Charles V. 1976. *The Struggle for Political Equality.* New York: National Urban League.

Moore, Jesse Thomas, Jr. 1981. *A Search for Equality: The National Urban League, 1910–1961.* University Park: Pennsylvania State University Press.

Parris, Guichard, and Lester Brooks. 1971. *Blacks in the City: A History of the National Urban League.* Boston: Little Brown.

Weiss, Nancy J. 1974. *The National Urban League: 1910–1960.* New York: Oxford University Press.

Michael J. O'Neal

V

VESEY, DENMARK

c. 1767–1822

The man later known as Denmark Vesey was born around 1767, probably on the Caribbean island of St. Thomas. Captain Joseph Vesey, a Carolina-based slaver, purchased the boy in September or October of 1781 as part of a cargo of 390 bondpeople. During the passage to the French colony of Saint Domingue (present-day Haiti), Vesey noticed the child's "beauty, alertness and intelligence" and employed him as a cabin boy. But when his ship, the *Prospect,* reached Cap François, the captain decided he "had no use for the boy" and turned him over to his colonial agents. Either traumatized by his new life in Saint Domingue or feigning illness, the child began to display "epileptic fits." As a result, Vesey was forced to take the child back when he returned to Cap François on April 23, 1782. The fits promptly ceased, and Vesey decided to keep him as a servant.

Charleston authorities later described the child as a person of "superior power of mind & the more dangerous for it." Vesey, however, saw only the value of a tall, muscular boy already conversant in two languages. He gave the boy a new name, Telemaque, who in Homer's tale was the wandering son of Odysseus; over time, Carolina bondmen either punned or corrupted the name into "Denmak," which then became "Denmark."

In the spring of 1783, following the British evacuation of South Carolina, Vesey settled into Charleston as a ship chandler. At some point during this period, Denmark married his first wife, an enslaved woman named Beck. She may have been Denmark's senior, because she already had a daughter, Sarah, from a previous relationship. Beck had several masters over the course of her life, but she remained married to Denmark long enough to give birth to at least three of his children. Toward the end of his life, Vesey married again. His last wife, Susan, was born a slave around 1795 but was free by 1821, when tax collectors listed her under the name of "Susan Vesey" and characterized her as a "free negro." She was the only woman to carry his surname. Some historians have speculated that Vesey practiced polygamy, although no evidence exists to support the theory. In a time of high female mortality, especially among urban bondwomen, Vesey could easily have united with the several women his friend Monday Gell later spoke of and yet remain monogamous.

On September 30, 1799, Denmark happened upon a handbill announcing the "East-Bay Lottery." He bought a ticket and won the top prize of $1,500, a princely sum at the time, particularly for a slave. Joseph Vesey and his wife, Mary Clodner, agreed to sell him his freedom for $600, and on December 31, 1799, the thirty-three year old Denmark was at last free.

Chained to the South by family ties, Denmark remained in the city and apprenticed himself to a carpenter, an easy trade to learn and a lucrative business in Charleston, which was expanding up the peninsula. At the same time, he adopted "Vesey" as a surname, probably as a linguistic tie to an established businessman. He threw his enormous energies into his business, and, according to one former slave, labored "every day at de trade of carpenter" and "soon became much [re]spected" and "esteem[ed] by de white folks." But because of competition from white carpenters, free Mulattoes (whose fathers provided business contacts) and enslaved craftsmen (who lived with their masters and paid no rent), Vesey barely maintained a modest income. Despite published claims made in 1822 that he died a rich man worth nearly $8,000, there is no evidence that Vesey ever owned a single piece of property. His rented home, at 20 Bull Street, was owned by Benjamin Ireland, a white carpenter.

Although Vesey was briefly a practicing Presbyterian, around 1818 he joined the city's new African Methodist Episcopal congregation. Formed when 4,376 slaves and free blacks resigned from the Methodist fold because church authorities voted to construct a hearse house above a black cemetery, the African Church, as both whites and blacks called it, quickly became the center of Charleston's enslaved community. Sandy Vesey also joined, as did four of Vesey's closest friends—Peter Poyas, a literate ship carpenter; Monday Gell, an African-born Ibo who labored as a harness maker; Rolla Bennett, the manservant of Governor Thomas Bennett; and Jack Pritchard, a fellow carpenter. The temporary closure of the church by city authorities in June 1818, and the arrest of 140 congregants, one of them presumably Vesey himself, only reinforced the determination of black Carolinians to maintain a place of independent worship. In 1820 several "Negroes was taken up" for holding a late-night service at the church, and city authorities warned Reverend Morris Brown that they would not tolerate class leaders conducting instructional "schools for slaves," as "the education of such persons was forbidden by law." The "African Church was the people," Monday Gell replied. He and Pritchard had considered insurrection in 1818, "and now they had begun again to try it."

At the age of fifty-one, Vesey briefly thought about emigrating to the English colony of Sierra Leone. But as Beck's children remained slaves, Vesey resolved instead to orchestrate a rebellion, followed by a mass exodus from Charleston to Haiti, where President Jean-Pierre Boyer had recently encouraged black Americans to bring their skills and capital to his beleaguered republic. Vesey did not intend to tarry in Charleston long enough for white military power to present an effective counterassault. "As soon as they could get the money from the Banks, and the goods from the stores," Rolla insisted, "they should hoist sail" for Saint Domingue and live as free men. Vesey planned the escape for nearly four years. His chief lieutenants included Poyas, Gell, and Rolla Bennett. Vesey's inner circle also included "Gullah" Jack Pritchard, an East African priest purchased in Zinguebar in 1806. Although there are no reliable figures for the number of recruits, Charleston alone was home to 12,652 slaves in 1820, along with 10,653 whites and 1,475 free blacks (Wade 1964). Pritchard, probably with some exaggeration, boasted that he had 6,600 recruits on the plantations across the Cooper and Ashley Rivers. The plan called for Vesey's followers to rise at midnight on Sunday, July 14 (Bastille Day), slay their masters, and sail for Haiti and freedom. As one southern editor later conceded: "The plot seems to have been well devised, and its operation was extensive."

The plot unraveled in June 1822 when two slaves, including Rolla's friend George Wilson revealed the plan to their owners. Mayor James Hamilton called up the city militia and convened a special court to try the captured insurgents. Vesey was captured at the home of Beck, his first wife, on June 21, and he was hanged on the morning of Tuesday, July 2, together with Rolla, Poyas, and three other rebels. In all, thirty-five slaves were executed. Forty-two others, including Sandy Vesey, were sold outside the United States; some, if not all, became slaves in Spanish Cuba. Denmark Vesey's son Robert lived to rebuild the African Church in the fall of 1865.

BIBLIOGRAPHY

Egerton, Douglas R. 1999. *He Shall Go Out Free: The Lives of Denmark Vesey*. Madison, WI: Madison House Publishers.

Freehling, William W. 1994. *The Reintegration of American History: Slavery and the Civil War*. New York: Oxford University Press.

Lofton, John. 1964. *Insurrection in South Carolina: The Turbulent World of Denmark Vesey*. Yellow Springs, OH: Antioch Press.

Paquette, Robert L. 2002. "Jacobins of the Lowcountry: The Vesey Plot on Trial." *William and Mary Quarterly* 59 (1): 185–192.

Wade, Richard C. 1964. *Slavery in the Cities: The South 1820–1860*. New York: Oxford University Press.

Douglas R. Egerton

VIOLENCE AGAINST INDIGENOUS PEOPLE, LATIN AMERICA

> "You nobles are greatly burdened; the story of your hardships is no joke. It is a tale of partings, of endless deprivations, and of people being left by the roadside because there they had been knifed—as it was at Balcab, where you runners were cut up while on foot on the road, and as it was in the scrub forest, where the runners went along afraid of being raped, of being forced to assume a shameful burden by the foreigners, the abuse of all the foreign dogs together empowered by the possession of steel to lift skirts."
>
> "You! Man! Your clothes to the dogs!"
>
> The *cah* residents were lifted up and hung like pigs; they suspended them like swine.
>
> "Your clothes, man!"

> They had also abused the women in this way: "Woman! Your clothes! Off with your petticoat!" This was the nature of the burden.
>
> What has been told here happened not once, nor twice, but many times; on countless occasions these things were done to our lords here on the road to Calkini" (Restall 1998, p. 91–92).

This account of the experiences endured by the mid-sixteenth-century Yucatec Maya nobility, given in 1541 by the fifteen-year-old Alonso Canche, does not test modern expectations of what is meant by the term *violence*, which is generally conceived of in terms of physical acts. Yet a charting of such physical violence over the past 500 years would, for one thing, take volumes, and, as Michael Taussig provides a reminder, it would also be insufficient, for words on a page can never transmit adequately the experiences engendered by violence. What is more, any attempt to make the violence in Canche's account more familiar by noting the parallels between the rapes of men and women in his times and those that occur in modern cultures would fail to capture the racial character of the centuries of violence against indigenous people.

There is, however, a second level of the meaning of violence. That is, one can consider the types of conceptual or ideological violence that make physical violence acceptable or even advocated in the first place. Here, one confronts the way in which the violator justifies and legitimizes his act, the process by which violence becomes possible to begin with. This rationale will not, however, be found in the writings of indigenous authors, for such records were not widely circulated and so did not have an impact on the overall sensitivity toward indigenous people. One must therefore turn to those records that did get widely read and replicated by secondary authors, and thus contributed to an overall "outside" perspective of indigenous people. From this perspective, the main contributions to the racialization of indigenous people since the time of European contact can be recognized. Specifically, one can then confront an external ideological definition of racial difference coupled with the potential for substantial external economic gain that has enabled physical violence against indigenous people.

Such interplay is illustrated by Hernán Cortés's sixteenth-century letters to Charles V, the Holy Roman Emperor. Concerning his activities in the Aztec capital, Tenochtitlan, Cortés gave a conflicted description of local folk: "I will say only that these people live almost like those in Spain, and in as much harmony and order as there, and considering that they are barbarous and so far from the knowledge of God and cut off from all civilized nations, it is truly remarkable to see what they have achieved in all things" (Pagden 1986, p. 108). Much as, his companion in arms, Bernal Díaz del Castillo marveled at his first view of Tenochtitlan, comparing it to a dream, Cortés appreciated much of what he encountered. Yet his sixteenth-century Spanish sensibilities, anchored to Christian and Aristotelian ideologies, forced him to downplay an observationally derived appreciation in favor of ideological deprecation.

Indeed, the extent to which Christian and Greek philosophies justified racial violence (and from which Cortés consciously and subconsciously drew) took center stage in the Great Debate at Valladolid between Juan Ginés de Sepúlveda and Bartolomé de las Casas in 1551. Sepúlveda argued that indigenous people were to be considered natural slaves who would benefit from conquest, irrespective of whether or not they were first evangelized. Las Casas, on the other hand, championed the idea that the role of the Spaniards was to convert indigenous people to Christianity—that political or economic interests should take a back seat to spiritual demands. The fact that Las Casas enjoyed favorable royal appointments after the debate, along with the decree of Charles V's successor regarding forced labor in the Peruvian silver mines, might be interpreted retrospectively as signs that the concerns of indigenous people had been vindicated. A written diplomacy that took shape within the post-debate period, evidenced in Philip II's decree concerning the racialized maintenance of the Potosi mines' economic salience, also supports this view:

> "Given that the mines of Peru cannot be exploited using Spanish laborers, since those who are there will not work in them, and as it is said that slaves cannot withstand the work, owing to the nature and coldness of the land, it appears necessary to employ Indians. Though these are not to be forced or compelled, as has already been ordered, they must be attracted with all just and reasonable means, so that there will be the required number of laborers for the mines. To this end, it seems that great care must be given to the settlement of large numbers of Indians in nearby towns and estates, so that they might more easily apply themselves to the work involved" (Cole 1985, p. 5).

Whereas there is a hint here as to the unenviable position of being subject to "settlement," it would appear that indigenous Andeans were not only to be respected, but that they also might stand to gain financially from the mining operations.

This statement, however, serves to demonstrate the complexity of the continued racialization process of indigenous people, which cannot entirely be traced back to a hierarchically driven ideology. On the contrary, ideology and local sensibilities were amalgamated into local variants that produced strikingly similar experiences for the indigenous people subject to them, regardless of the degree to which they saw themselves as diverse in culture or identity. That such an amalgam existed in the

Peruvian mines during the late sixteenth and entire seventeenth centuries is readily attested, for example, by eyewitness accounts. At the close of the sixteenth century, Fray José de Acosta wrote:

> "They labor in these mines in perpetual darkness, not knowing day from night. And since the sun never penetrates to these places, they are not only always dark but very cold, and the air is very thick and alien to the nature of men; so that those who enter for the first time get as sick as at sea—which happened to me in one of these mines, where I felt a pain at the heart and a churning in the stomach. The [laborers] always carry candles to light their way, and they divide their labor in such a way that some work by day and rest by night, and others work by night and rest by day. The ore is generally hard as flint, and they break it up with iron bars. They carry the ore on their backs up ladders made of . . . twisted rawhide joined by pieces of wood . . . so that one man may climb up and another down at the same time. These ladders are twenty meters long, and at the top and bottom of each is a wooden platform where the men may rest. . . Each man usually carries on his back a load of twenty-five kilograms of silver ore tied in a cloth, knapsack fashion; thus they ascend, three at a time. The one who goes first carries a candle tied to his thumb, . . . thus, holding on with both hands, they climb that great distance, often more than 300 meters—a fearful thing, the mere thought of which inspires dread" (Cole 1985, p. 24).

The climbing of fifteen sequential six-story buildings with a fifty-pound load on one's back in the conditions described by Acosta may in itself constitute a type of violence, but the treatment of indigenous Andeans beyond the job description resolves any ambiguity. Engaging in a continued textual diplomacy, Viceroy Francisco de Toledo dictated at the time that mine laborers should be restricted to making two trips per day, but by the 1580s they were making more than ten times that. Moreover, indigenous laborers were "whipped, beaten, [and] struck with rocks" on their way to completing their individual daily quotas of nineteen loads, "despite the fact that quotas themselves had been prohibited by the viceroy" (Cole 1985, p. 24).

So the words spoken in Europe, even the decrees sent from Spain, would not overturn or unmake the stereotyping of racialized indigenous people or the persistent racialization (and its effects) in the Western Hemisphere en route to economic gain. The triumvirate of physical violence, racialized ideology, and economic gain worked together to engender violence, even after such governmental mandates as the post-debate upholding of the New Laws of 1542. Las Casas advocated for the new laws, which notably prohibited enslavement and mistreatment of indigenous peoples. These laws spurred a revolt that led to most of them being revoked on October 20, 1545.

The violence extended to indigenous families as well as entire communities. Jeffrey Cole gives an account of the degree of exploitation suffered by the mine laborers' families: "If a [laborer] died in the hospital . . . his wife and children were forced to hire a . . . substitute to serve in his stead. Hospitalized [laborers] and their families were further preyed upon by priests, who charged exorbitant sums for religious services and demanded devastating compensation for funerals" (Cole 1985, p. 31). The number of young men leaving their hometowns in order to avoid conscriptions further disturbed community life. The fact that indigenous voices were not heard in the "Great Debate," and that they played no positive role in shaping local sensibilities in Potosi regardless of purported royal sentiment, thus facilitated their continued racialization.

The discord between official declaration and local adaptation played out along racial lines as clearly in nineteenth- and early twentieth-century Colombia as in seventeenth- and eighteenth-century Peru. For example, Michael Taussig notes that, in reference to the extraction of rubber, authorities balked at the local use of the word *conquistar* to describe the interactions between representatives of the British Rubber Company and indigenous Amazonians. Joaquin Rocha, though, sent a ready response in his report of 1905:

> "When a tribe of savages is encountered which nobody knew about or which has never had contact with whites, then it is said that they have been conquered by the person who manages to trade with them so that they will work rubber, will plant food, and will build a house for him to live in their midst. Thus entering into the great and common labor of the whites, these Indians are brought into civilization" (Taussig 1987, pp. 24–25).

With the exception of substituting "whites" for "Spaniards," the reader will be challenged to find any way in which this statement differs from the underlying assumptions, motivations, expectations, or racializations of Europeans seeking financial gain from the Western Hemisphere during prior centuries. Moreover, the masking of indigenous experiences with euphemisms belies the eyewitness account provided by Roger Casement in 1912:

> "The number of Indians killed either by starvation—often purposely brought about by the destruction of crops over whole districts or inflicted as a form of death penalty on individuals who failed to bring in their quota of rubber—or by deliberate murder by bullet, fire, beheading, or flogging to death, and accompanied by a variety of atrocious tortures, during the course of these 12 years, in order to extort these 4,000 tons of rubber cannot have been less than

30,000, and possibly came to many more" (Taussig 1987, p. 20).

Again, racialization is a tool of foreign economic venture, and the same rhetoric is marshaled, leading to the same methods of physical violence. Indeed, there may be few master narratives still recognized by the postmodern academy, but one would be hard pressed to find anything so coherent or enduring as the story of violence against indigenous people in the Western Hemisphere.

Yet caution is needed here so as not to take this as a demonstration that to be indigenous is to be violated, or to be violated uniformly. Rather, it shows that among the countless indigenous experiences, those that have included encounters with colonialism, statehood, or globalization have been accompanied by a process of racialization that incorporates a propensity for violence.

On the other hand, to be indigenous is, in many ways, to recognize the groundedness of meaning in a community's locale. The very approach of European and European-derivative cultures to indigeneity, however, has explicitly violated this groundedness. The setting has not mattered, nor has the difference in goods, whether it be fabled gold, silver ore, or rubber trees. The racialization process has resulted in indigenous experiences that are independent of location, which is perhaps the greatest violence committed against them. The very fact that Aymara speakers from the Andes, Maya speakers of the Yucatan Peninsula, and Chumash speakers of the California Pacific Coast were all referred to in official documents simply as *indios* lays bare the role of indigenous peoples in European economic and religious ventures.

Taking violence now can thus be seen as a forced infringement on an individual's or a community's sovereignty. In this case, it becomes apparent that the racialization of indigenous peoples, through economic pressure and ideological irresponsibility, has been facilitated by a violence of representation. Namely, indigenous people have had no voice in representations of themselves, either as individuals or as a culture. These representations have consistently come from others, either in "travelers' tales," in records of the Inquisition that found their way into general histories, or in the tales of anthropologists from the nineteenth-century through the present day. The percentage of media representations of indigenous culture by indigenous people most likely does not register as a whole number. Are these not forced impositions on indigenous communities? And have they not facilitated the construction of racial images?

The issue of violence, thus defined is among the most important confronting indigenous attempts at cultural revival, of sovereignty and of the redress of human rights violations. Numerous coalitions have attempted to overcome this predicament for centuries (several by taking up arms), but the latest such attempt, that of the *Ejército Zapatista de Liberación Nacional* (EZLN, or Zapatista Army of National Liberation) in Chiapas, Mexico, carries with it an opportunity unavailable to previous groups relative to the factors discussed here. Namely, the indigenous Maya of the EZLN have used radio and the Internet to create their own voices and create representations of themselves. The degree to which this effort is successful may well impact the potential for future indigenous attempts at cultural revival, political representation, and civil rights advances.

SEE ALSO *Blackness in Latin America; Indigenismo in Mexico; Indigenous; Latin American Racial Transformations; Mexicans; Occupational Segregation; Zapatista Rebellion.*

BIBLIOGRAPHY

Cole, Jeffrey A. 1985. *The Potosí Mita 1573–1700: Compulsory Indian Labor in the Andes.* Stanford, CA: Stanford University Press.

Pagden, Anthony. 1986. *Hernan Cortés: Letters from Mexico.* New Haven, CT: Yale University Press.

Restall, Matthew. 1998. *Maya Conquistador.* Boston: Beacon Press.

Taussig, Michael. 1987. *Shamanism, Colonialism, and the Wild Man: A Study in Terror and Healing.* Chicago: University of Chicago Press.

Gerardo V. Aldana

VIOLENCE AGAINST WOMEN AND GIRLS

Violence against women and girls has come to be recognized as a major social problem with serious consequences for individuals, their families, communities, and society as a whole. Commonly understood to include sexual assaults, stalking, sexual harassment, and abuse by intimate partners and household members, the forms of violence that women and girls experience have particular dynamics that make the impact particularly profound.

According to the National Institute for Justice, 25 percent of women in the United States will experience abuse by their husbands or live-in intimate partners in their lifetimes, at a rate of approximately 1.5 million per year (Tjaden and Theonnes 2000). In terms of sexual assault, one in six women are raped each year, more than 86,000 children are molested, and anywhere from 30 to 70 percent of women experience sexual harassment that includes physical threats of abuse (Tjaden and Theonnes 1998). Studies of women in dating relationships, including same-sex relationships, reveal similar rates of violence, both physical and sexual in nature. Even in situations where the intimate relationship has ended, the abuse often continues, as in the case of women who are stalked by people they had a previous relationship with (Broaddus and Merrill 1998, Butler 1999).

When talking about these forms of abuse against women and girls, researchers and advocates are referring to situations that are far more menacing than simple arguments or fights between partners or annoying unwanted physical or sexual encounters. The kind of violence that is captured in the aforementioned statistics is profoundly serious, for the problems are not merely a series of isolated incidents, but rather a pattern of aggressive behavior that tends to escalate over time, leaving women in serious peril. For example, nearly one-third of all women murdered in the United States are murdered by current or former intimate partners; violence is the leading cause of death for women in some age groups; sexual assault is a major reason that adult women give for attempting suicide; child sexual abuse is a strong precursor to later problems with truancy, drugs; and alcohol; and stalking and sexual harassment cost women millions of dollars each year as they attempt to flee dangerous living and work situations (Cecil and Matson 2001, Baynard et al. 2002, Violence Policy Center 2004).

It is also important to recognize that the types of violence discussed here are decidedly gendered; the victims are overwhelmingly women and those who inflict intimate partner violence, those who rape, and those who are engaged in extreme forms of stalking are typically men (Bachman 1994). There are some exceptions to this, however, including same-sex violence and the abuse of frail elderly men by women who are their caretakers. The overall pattern, however, is one that firmly establishes women and girls as the primary targets of these forms of violence.

Emotional and psychological abuse reinforces physical and sexual assaults. Women who are physically assaulted are often made to feel like the abuse is their fault; children who are molested are isolated from other people as a way to increase the terror they feel; rape victims suffer greatly from the insults and the shame that accompany the physical aspect of the assault; and the general denial and minimization that enables abuse to continue is particularly painful for those who experience it over time.

Paradoxically, despite these serious consequences, violence against women is still casually accepted in some social spheres. The physical abuse of women that is normalized in mainstream movies, images of rape, and other forms of degradation of women can easily be found in popular music, and jokes about wife abuse and incest can be overheard in everyday conversations. This social acceptance of violence against women and girls is linked to their relative diminished social status (in terms of economic and cultural power). This explains why institutions have been slow to respond to these problems, why communities have not held accountable those who use violence, and why so many of the women and girls who experience violence have been forced or coerced into silence and submission.

Since the 1980s, however, great strides have been made to give voice to these problems. Advocates and activists have challenged the underlying gender dynamics that give rise to violence against women and girls, and they have attempted to change those institutions that are obligated to protect vulnerable members of society. In the early twenty-first century, there are shelters for battered women, rape crisis centers, prevention programs for children, and a range of other services designed to provide services and support to victims. Legal and legislative changes have heightened sanctions for those who use violence, and a growing body of research has established prevalence rates, the consequences of abuse, and the best practices to respond to these problems. Elected officials, well-known celebrities, and everyday citizens take a stand against violence against women, and both public and private donors support the work. Due in great part to grassroots feminist activism, the problem of violence against women is understood differently than it once was, and it is safe to say that hundreds of thousands of women and girls are safer in the early 2000s than they were before the advent of the social movement that responded to the problems of violence against women.

Race and racism have also figured into the understanding of and responses to the problem of violence against women in important ways. The rate of violence against women and girls reported in most communities of color is higher than the national average (Buchanan and Ormerod 1992, McNutt et al. 1999). A closer analysis of this statistic reveals that this difference is linked to variables such as income, age, employment status, the presence of children in the household, and social factors such as the presence of weapons, the use of drugs and alcohol, the availability of services, and the effectiveness of prevention messages (Honeycutt, Marshall, and Weston 2001; Taylor 2002). That is, the rates of violence against women of color might actually not differ that much from those of white women if other variables are controlled.

Furthermore, when violence occurs, institutions do not respond to needs of women of color as readily, resources are not sufficiently allocated to communities of color to ensure women's safety, and law enforcement agencies have not necessarily proven themselves to be agents of assistance in disadvantaged neighborhoods. Without opportunities for safe housing, good health care, or employment, women of color who experience violence are often left with few options but to remain in dangerous relationships and situations (Donovan and Williams 2002).

Many scholars and activists point to these and other social factors to explain why women of color are at particular risk, and they have challenged the antiviolence movement and related institutions dedicated to justice and safety to expand their attention to look at violence against women of color. In so doing, women of color, with support from male allies, have made significant contributions to the work to end violence against all women by challenging racial and patriarchal privilege and promoting the kind of broad-based social changes that ending violence against all women and children will require.

SEE ALSO *Feminism and Race; Pornography; Rape; Social Problems.*

BIBLIOGRAPHY

Bachman, Ronet. 1994. *Violence against Women: A National Crime Victimization Survey Report.* Washington, DC: U.S. Department of Justice, Bureau of Justice Statistics.

Banyard, Victoria, Linda M. Williams, Jane A. Siegal and Carolyn M. West. 2002. "Childhood Sexual Abuse in the Lives of Black Women: Risks and Resilience in a Longitudinal Study." *Women & Therapy* 25 (3/4): 45–58.

Broaddus, Toni, and Gregory Merrill. 1998. *Annual Report on Lesbian, Gay, Bisexual Transgender Domestic Violence.* San Francisco: National Coalition on Anti-Violence Programs.

Buchanan, Nicole T., and Alayne J. Ormerod. 2002. "Racialized Sexual Harassment in the Lives of African American Women." *Women & Therapy* 25 (3/4): 105–121.

Butler, Lola. 1999. "African American Lesbians Experiencing Partner Violence." In *A Professional's Guide to Understanding Gay and Lesbian Domestic Violence: Understanding Practice Interventions,* edited by Joan C. McClennen and John Gunther, 50–57. Lewiston, NY: Edwin Mellen Press.

Cecil, Heather, and Steven C. Matson. 2001. "Psychological Functioning and Family Discord among African American Adolescent Females with and without a History of Childhood Sexual Abuse." *Child Abuse and Neglect* 25: 973–988.

Donovan, Roxanne, and Michelle Williams. 2002. "Living at the Intersection: The Effects of Racism and Sexism on Black Rape Survivors." *Women & Therapy* 25 (3/4): 95–105.

Honeycutt, Todd C., Linda L. Marshall, and Rebecca Weston. 2001. "Towards Ethnically Specific Models of Employment, Public Assistance, and Victimization." *Violence Against Women* 7 (2): 126–140.

McNutt, Louise-Anne, Michelle van Ryn, Carla Clark, and Idelle Fraiser. 1999. "Partner Violence and Medical Encounters: African-American Women's Perspectives." *American Journal of Preventive Medicine* 19 (4): 264–269.

Richie, Beth. 1996. *Compelled to Crime: The Gender Entrapment of Black Battered Women.* New York: Routledge.

Taylor, Janette Y. 2002. "The Straw that Broke the Camel's Back: African American Women's Strategies for Disengaging from Abusive Relationships." *Women & Therapy* (3/4): 79–94.

Tjaden, Patricia, and Nancy Theonnes. 1998. "Stalking in America: Findings from the National Violence Against Women's Survey, Research in Brief." (NCJ 169592). Washington DC: U.S. Department of Justice, National Institute of Justice.

———. 2000. *Extent, Nature, and Consequences of Intimate Partner Violence: Findings for the National Violence against Women Survey.* (NCJ 181867). Washington, DC: U.S. Government Printing Office.

Violence Policy Center. 2004. *When Men Murdered Women: An Analysis of 2002 Homicide Data: Females Murdered by Males in Single Victim/Single Offender Incidents.* Washington, DC: Violence Policy Center. Available from http://www.vpc.org/studies/dv4cont.htm.

Beth E. Richie

VOTING RIGHTS ACT OF 1965

The Voting Rights Act of 1965 is generally considered to be one of the most significant pieces of federal civil rights legislation ever passed by the United States Congress. The Act has helped African Americans to exercise their right to vote and engage in political participation, overcoming almost a century of poll taxes, literacy tests, intimidation, and violence that served as obstacles to the Fifteenth Amendment's guarantee of a right to vote throughout the South. Though still contested on various fronts, the legislation has changed the American political landscape in significant ways, affecting small town and city governments as well as Congress.

Many historians and political scientists view the vote as the most important form of conventional political participation, and American civil rights leaders thought that the franchise was the most accessible and effective means of advancing the struggle for racial equality. According to James Button, in *Blacks and Social Change: Impact of the Civil Rights Movement in Southern Communities* (1989), "the assumption was that voting rights would pave the way for all other changes, since the franchise is the normal method by which demands of citizens are fulfilled" (p. 5). Many expected that through electing blacks and moderate whites to office, progress in the political realm would also enable African Americans to make important gains in areas such as education, employment, housing, and public services. Moreover, it was believed that the vote would have both a symbolic and practical effect on democratic practices, because it would provide a sense of viable citizenship and improved self-esteem. Finally, a reliance on federal rights and intervention would not only provide leverage to bargain over state and local resources, it would also insulate blacks from state-sanctioned or condoned violence and terror.

HISTORICAL BACKGROUND OF THE STRUGGLE TO VOTE

Passed as one of the Reconstruction amendments following the Civil War, the Fifteenth Amendment provides that "the right of citizens of the United States to vote shall not be denied or abridged by the United States or by any State on account of race, color, or previous condition of servitude." Each of these amendments also granted Congress the power to enforce the amendments by appropriate legislation. However, after the Hayes-Tilden Compromise of 1877, blacks were effectively disenfranchised through an interlocking system of discriminatory laws and widespread violence. In 1890, for example, Mississippi held a convention to write a new constitution. The spirit of the convention was captured by one white leader, who exclaimed, "We came here to exclude the Negro, from voting."

Under this new constitution, voters in Mississippi had to pay a poll tax two years before an election. Blacks at the bottom of the socioeconomic scale rarely had the funds to pay the tax, however. In addition, the state required all voters to pass a literacy test, though 60 percent of black men could not read at the time. What is worse, clerks, who were always white, would require blacks to interpret the most difficult passages of the test, while whites were routinely tested on uncomplicated passages. In 1898, Louisiana introduced a new device into its constitution, the "grandfather clause," which allowed anyone to register whose "grandfather" was qualified to vote before the Civil War. This benefited only whites, of course, because only white citizens could vote before the Civil War. In 1902, Mississippi passed a law that made political parties private organizations outside the authority of the Fifteenth Amendment. Because whoever won the Democratic primary almost always won the general election, this permitted Democratic parties in Southern states to openly exclude blacks from membership in the only party that mattered in the South. This voting regime was referred to as the white primary. Another method used to prevent African-Americans from voting was felony disenfranchisement, or withholding the right to vote from persons convicted of felony offenses. Several Southern states enacted felon disenfranchisement laws and carefully selected "disenfranchising crimes" to disqualify a disproportionate number of black voters.

The white primary, the grandfather clause, the poll tax, the literacy test, and felon disenfranchisement are simply the most well-known methods of disenfranchisement. Other inventive methods included transferring the power to determine voter qualifications to "private," all-white political clubs, giving newly enfranchised blacks only two weeks to register, and property ownership requirements. As late as 1940, as a direct result of these interlocking discriminatory laws and schemes, only 35 percent of blacks were registered to vote in the confederate states, with only 1 percent being registered in Mississippi. It was not until 1944, in the Supreme Court case of *Smith v. Allwright*, that the "white primary" was effectively struck down. The poll tax was not struck down until 1966, in *Harper v. Virginia Board of Elections.*

THE IMPORTANCE OF DIRECT-ACTION PROTEST IN THE 1960s

The activism of the civil rights movement was of central importance in assuring the right to vote. During the 1960s, direct action protests, marches, and sit-ins emerged as major instruments of political change. Indeed, during the summer of 1964, known as "Freedom Summer," thousands of civil rights activists conducted an intensive voter-registration campaign in the Southern states. The activists focused on Mississippi, because in 1962 only 6.7 percent of African Americans in the state were registered voters, the lowest percentage in the nation.

The activities of the civil rights workers were met with threats, protests, and brutal violence. In June 1965, for example, three young civil rights workers—James Chaney (an African American) and two white co-workers, Andrew Goodman and Michael Schwerner—were murdered near Philadelphia, Mississippi. Earlier, in March 1965, more than 600 peaceful civil rights marchers were beaten by Alabama state troopers and local sheriff's officers as they crossed the Edmund Pettus Bridge in Selma on their way to Montgomery. These incidents and others sparked national outrage and helped generate support for voting-rights enforcement. The national attention helped to spur President Lyndon B. Johnson to urge Congress to pass strong voting-rights legislation, which became the Voting Rights Act that was signed by President Johnson on August 6, 1965.

CONTESTED INTERPRETATIONS OF THE VOTING ACT

The Voting Rights Act generally prohibits the denial or abridgement of the right to vote because of one's race or color through the imposition of voting qualifications or prerequisites. Sections 5 and 2 of the act have generated the most controversy. Section 5 provides for extensive federal oversight and intervention to assure compliance, requiring federal approval, or "preclearance," of changes in voting procedures in areas with a history of discrimination (primarily, but not exclusively, Southern states and subdivisions). Section 2 prohibits any "voting qualification . . . which results in a denial . . . of the right . . . to vote on account of race or color." It assures that minority votes will not be diluted, or submerged within majority white districts, in ways that deny minority voters "an equal opportunity to participate in the electoral

Voting Rights Act of 1965. *President Lyndon Johnson gives Martin Luther King Jr. one of the pens used to sign the Voting Rights Act of 1965. The Act is generally considered to be one of the most significant pieces of federal civil rights legislation ever passed by the United States Congress.* THE LIBRARY OF CONGRESS.

process and to elect representatives of their choice" (*Thornburg v. Gingles*, 478 U.S. 30 [1986]).

Additionally, the Act was amended in 1975 to prohibit voting qualifications that would deny the right of any citizen to vote because he or she is a member of a language minority. As a result, covered states and political subdivisions must now supply bilingual or multilingual assistance or other materials or information relating to the electoral process. Importantly, the preclearance provisions of Section 5 and the protections for language minorities must be renewed periodically by Congress. Civil rights groups expect opponents will vigorously contest renewal when the issue is next before Congress in 2007.

COURTS AND THE VOTING RIGHTS ACT

In interpreting the Voting Rights Acts, courts have focused predominately on two issues: whether various voting procedures deny minority voters access to the ballot, and whether various political representation plans dilute minority votes to the point that members of minority groups cannot elect the candidate of their choice.

In 1980, in *City of Mobile v. Bolden*, a challenge to the city's at-large voting scheme, the Supreme Court held that Section 2 of the act would not afford relief in vote-dilution cases unless there was proof of intentional discrimination. But it was virtually impossible to provide such proof, and vote-dilution claims came to a virtual standstill after this decision. However, in 1982 Congress not only extended Section 5 for twenty-five years, it also amended Section 2 to prohibit discriminatory effects even in the absence of intent.

In 1986, in *Thornburg v. Gingles*, the Supreme Court construed the amended Section 2 for the first time. In a case involving a legislative redistricting plan of multimember districts in North Carolina, the Court held that minority plaintiffs can successfully establish a vote-dilution claim if they show that their community is sufficiently large and geographically compact enough to make up a majority in a single member district, that the group is politically cohesive, and that the white majority's bloc voting will defeat the minority candidate. After *Thornburg* v. *Gingles*, and throughout the 1980s, black voters were able to press for black majority districts, and, candidates of their choice, who were usually black, were consequently voted into office.

However, with the decision in *Shaw* v. *Reno* (1993), the Supreme Court announced a new voting rights jurisprudence based on color-blindness. In the case, white plaintiffs challenged a North Carolina redistricting plan on the grounds that majority-black district lines deliberately segregated voters into separate districts on the basis of race, violating their constitutional right to participate in a "color-blind" electoral process. Justice Sandra Day O'Connor, writing for the 5-4 majority, found that the district was so bizarrely drawn that it could not be understood as anything other than an effort to separate voters into different districts on the basis of race. Such a district, according to O'Connor, reinforced racial stereotypes and threatened to undermine the U.S. system of representational democracy by signaling to elected officials that they represented a particular racial group rather than their constituency as a whole. *Shaw* broke new ground, evidencing a judicial hostility to race based districting to empower blacks and to protect them from illegal gerrymandering and vote dilution.

Yet in spite of these cases, race conscious redistricting *per se* is not unconstitutional, although it is now weighed against the normative interests of rights that inhere in individuals. The Supreme Court thus set the stage for individualized color blindness to triumph over group-based race consciousness. In the context of vote dilution, this is a peculiar jurisprudence because, as Chandler Davidson (1984) observes, vote dilution is a racialized group phenomenon: "It occurs because the propensity of an identifiable group to vote as a bloc waters down the voting strength of another identifiable group.... [O]ne individual acting alone could not dilute the vote of another individual or of a group of individuals."

After the *Shaw* line of cases, increased attention has been paid to alternatives such as influence districts, cumulative voting, and proportional representation. Out of necessity, perhaps, the next chapters in the struggle for political participation by African Americans and other ethnic minorities may focus on these approaches.

SEE ALSO *Civil Rights Acts; Civil Rights Movement; Language; Social Psychology of Racism.*

BIBLIOGRAPHY

Bell, Derrick. 2004. *Race, Racism and American Law*, 5th ed. New York: Aspen Publishers.

Button, James W. 1989. *Blacks and Social Change: Impact of the Civil Rights Movement in Southern Communities*. Princeton, NJ: Princeton University Press.

Davidson, Chandler, ed. 1984. *Minority Vote Dilution*. Washington, DC: Howard University Press.

Grofman, Bernard, ed. 1998. *Race and Redistricting in the 1990s*. New York: Agathon Press.

Issacharoff, Samuel, Pamela S. Karlan, and Richard H. Pildes. 2001. *The Law of Democracy: Legal Structure of the Political Process*, 2nd ed. Westbury, NY: Foundation Press.

Keyssar, Alexander. 2000. *The Right to Vote: The Contested History of Democracy in the United States*. NY: Basic Books.

John O. Calmore

W

WAGNERIAN MUSIC

Taken solely as a musician, Richard Wagner (1813–1883) must be placed in the most elite rank of Western composers, alongside Bach, Mozart, and Beethoven. Nonetheless, his politics, philosophy, and theory of history are inseparable from nineteenth-century anti-Semitism. Identifying the exact nature and extent of Wagner's hostility to Jewish people, and the effects of this hostility on his art, is complicated by the fact that bigotry is always irrational. Moreover, anti-Semitism has cultural, religious, and pseudoracial manifestations. It is undeniable that each of these forms of anti-Semitism is reprehensibly present in Wagner's writings, but there is no consensus as to whether they are detectable in any of his operas.

In Wagner's theory of the musical stage was that all components of an opera must express an aesthetic system and a political and cultural philosophy. He believed that by writing his own texts, designing his own scenarios, and dictating elaborate stage directions, he could impose eternal control over the meanings that he considered essential to his works of art. Yet despite all his efforts, Wagner's works, no less than those of less deliberate composers, have been subjected to the subsequent interpretations of producers, audiences, and critics. It requires no particular inventiveness to discover anti-Semitism in Wagner's public and private utterances, but it is a more difficult matter to pinpoint precise expressions of anti-Semitism in the music or texts of his operas.

Wagner shamelessly expressed anti-Semitism in his infamous essay, *Das Judentum in der Musik* (1850). The common translation of this work, "Judaism in Music," seems to imply a religious element, but Wagner's purposes were more sweeping than that, and a more accurate translation might be "Jewishness in Music." Wagner was hostile towards all aspects of Jewish heritage, which he viewed as an alien and destructive force in German culture, and indeed in all European civilization. Wagner's anti-Semitism was not so much religious as racial and ethnic. Although he was contemptuous of bourgeois Christianity, he nonetheless accepted the traditional Christian view of the Jewish people as hoarders of money that was "slimy with the blood of countless generations." He confessed to an "involuntary repellance" for the "nature and personality of the Jews," who, he insisted, were responsible for a corruption of the public taste in the arts.

But if it was Wagner's intention to communicate anti-Semitism by strictly musical devices he seems to have failed in the meritless task. For while it is certain that the texts of his operas communicated idiosyncratic philosophical messages, the most careful searchers have failed to detect specific anti-Semitic references in his lyrics. Scholars debate whether certain of his characters were intended to personify any of the pejorative Jewish racial or cultural stereotypes that were all too prevalent in nineteenth century Europe, but they have offered little specific direct evidence of any such characterization. Finally, while Wagner, especially in *Die Meistersinger,* clearly contributed to a theory of what the Nazis later called *entartete musik* (degenerate music), it is unclear whether he attempted to incorporate his theoretical anti-Semitism into any of his musical compositions. His works do not contain travesties or pejorative depictions of Jewish liturgical music, which he disparages in *Das Judentum.* Although Wagner expressed patronizing or hostile attitudes towards Jewish composers such as Felix

Mendelssohn and Giacomo Meyerbeer, his attacks never took the form of a cheap musical parody.

Wagner desired that his music should express not only emotions, but complicated philosophical principles as well, and particularly the revolutionary ideals, radical moral values, and spiritual strivings that he associated with the German race. Like the classical Aristotlean critics and his contemporary composers of "tone poems," Wagner believed that music imitated emotional states, and he believed that he could communicate precise spiritual messages by assigning them to specific musical phrases, which he called "leitmotifs."

Musical notes, like words, can be used as symbols and arbitrarily assigned to specific referents, and a musical phrase, like a word phrase, can symbolize anything one chooses to attribute to it. A *Hakenkreutz* (swastika), for example, may have entirely different meanings to a Navaho, a Hindu, or a Jew. Likewise, pictures on canvas or actions on stage may have equivocal references. Wagner sought to exert maximum control over how the symbolic elements of his art would be perceived by reinforcing the occurrences on stage with words and music, imagining that he could prevent any distortion of his meanings. It is from his predictable failure to triumph over ambiguity that the greatest strength and beauty of Wagner's art, as well as its evil misuses, have arisen. Wagner's romanticized historiography included three mythical Germanic worlds. The first of these, comprising his four-opera cycle *Der Ring des Nibelungen,* had its sources in ancient pagan myths, including the Norse *Volsunga Saga* and the medieval German epic *Das Nibelungenlied,* from which he freely adapted his texts. The mythical sources of the operas *Tannhäuser, Parsifal,* and *Lohengrin* were in the Grail myths of late medieval Christianity. A third source, reflected most prominently in the setting of *Die Meistersinger,* was Wagner's idealized view of the organic German town, the *Burgertum* of the late Middle Ages and early renaissance. Each of these worlds clearly offers a setting to display grandiose conceptions of Germanic identity, and each of them is readily employable to racist, ethnocentric or anti-Semitic ends.

The mythology of the Ring Cycle presents a world in opposition to both Old and New Testament traditions. It is an attempted revitalization of pagan Germanic myth and an attempt to discover in it the uncompromised barbarian vigor and primitive virtues praised by the Roman historian Tacitus in his depiction of Germanic tribes. These virtues, which Wagner expressed through the eponymous hero of his opera *Siegfried,* included fearlessness in battle, the sanctity of oaths, and an absolute loyalty to the king.

In addition to its savage heroes, the world of *Der Ring* is populated by gods, giants, and dwarfs. Some people have seen in Wagner's dwarfs the embodiment of a vicious stereotype of the Jewish people as hoarders and manipulators of wealth. In *Das Judentum in der Musik,* Wagner wrote negatively about Jewish bankers, then proceeded to describe Jewish musicians with the same scurrilous imagery that he assigns to the subterranean dwarfs of *Das Rheingold.* He described the work of Jewish composers, for example, as a "worm-befretted carcass." Two years earlier, in an 1848 prospectus for *Der Ring des Nibelungen,* he had similarly characterized the gold-hoarding dwarfs as being "like worms in the dead body" of German art.

Wagner's chosen people, the Wälsungs, are a race with no perceptible virtue other than the warrior trait of physical courage, loyalty to their chief, and a somewhat ambiguous reverence for women (clouded by an extreme possessiveness and a tendency to regard women as trophies). Wagner's superman, Siegfried, is not a noble savage, but a virile barbarian who, like his father, is beyond Christian notions of good and evil. He shares these traits, presumably, with the *Übermensch* of Friedrich Willhelm Nietzsche, and one can see in him the precursor of the Hitler youth—tall, blonde, handsome, rash, unreflective, and controlled by forces he is incapable of contemplating.

Wagner's racial attitudes are often confused with those of Nietzsche, who, like Wagner, heralded the coming of a new "superman," unconstrained by the supposedly tender-hearted values of bourgeois Christianity. But where Nietzsche's philosophy placed supreme value on the individual will, Wagner celebrated the collective German *Volksgeist,* or "national character." Nietzsche expressed an admiration for certain cultural values that he associated with Jewish people, and he was equally hostile to the Jewish and the Christian religious heritage. Wagner's racial nationalism viewed the Jews as an inferior, unredeemable race who could play no role in the German nationalism he celebrated. But Nietzsche opposed racial anti-Semitism and the herd mentality of vulgar German nationalism. Thus, Wagner found himself in the contradictory position of trying to reconcile barbarian lawlessness with nationalistic communalism. The supermen of the Ring cycle—Siegmund and his son Siegfried—are antisocial outlaws as well as symbols of ethnic purity, tribal loyalty, and racial spirit.

Wagner's use of Grail mythology is more notable for its sexism than for its anti-Semitism. It centers on chaste knights whose holiness is often proven by their renunciation of sensual females, as in the examples of Parsifal and Tannhäuser. The opera *Lohengrin* combines familiar elements of classical, Germanic, and Hebraic mythology. A young woman is commanded by her husband and champion that she must never ask his name. When natural curiosity finally overcomes her, he reveals that he is Lohengrin, son of Parsifal, and a keeper of the Grail.

Adolf Hilter Unveils a Monument to Richard Wagner, 1934. *Nineteenth-century composer Richard Wagner's musical treatment of alleged Germanic folklore fanned the flames of racism in Germany and contributed to the success of the Nazi movement.*
© HULTON-DEUTSCH COLLECTION/CORBIS.

He then leaves her, returning to his sacred vigil at Mounserat, and she dies of grief. There is nothing anti-Semitic about this, unless one accepts the proposition that there is no place for Jews within the mythology of medieval Christianity, other than that of the Wandering Jew. But the only person in any of Wagner's operas with the name "Wanderer" is Wotan, the king of the gods and the progenitor of the Germanic master race, the Wälsung.

Die Meistersinger is the only Wagner opera that is not dominated by supernatural forces. Set in the sixteenth century, it involves a songfest and two competitions, one for a musical prize, the other for the hand of a beautiful young woman. There are two heroes, one of them the historical Hans Sachs, a shoemaker and poet. The other is Walther, a young knight who, somewhat incongruously, is not associated with any sort of practical hand trade, but who demonstrates his craftsmanship by composing a masterful song. Reminiscent of Marxism in its conception, the opera envisions a world before the rise of industrial capitalism and a time before workers were alienated from their labor. The villain of the opera is the unattractive character of Beckmesser, in whom some critics have seen a caricature of the Jewish bourgeoisie. There is no internal evidence for this interpretation, although in his blind attempts to adhere to rules that he does not understand, he resembles the fabrications of *Das Judenthum*. Some critics have seen in Beckmesser's unimaginative interpretation of the guild's formal rules, and in the horrid cacophonies he produces, an intentionally grotesque travesty on Jewish religious music.

The hostility of many audiences, Jewish and non-Jewish, to Wagner stems largely from the fact that he was much admired by Hitler. Indeed, his operas came to symbolize German racial and artistic supremacy to the

Nazis. Since the destruction of the Third Reich, Wagner's music has been associated in the popular mind with both fascism and Western imperialism. During the 1970s, for example, the most familiar of his musical themes, *The Ride of the Walküres,* accompanied the depiction of a helicopter attack on a Vietnamese village in Francis Ford Coppola's film *Apocalypse Now.*

Wagner did not publicly disclose his anti-Semitism in the first anonymously published edition of *Das Judentum,* which was released in 1850, but in the 1869 edition he restated his views shamelessly. It would seem, therefore, that if he had intended to portray the Dwarf Nibelungs as symbols of a supposedly Jewish capitalism, or Beckmesser as a symbol of decadent Jewish art, he could have done so openly and without any qualms. Yet when one compares Wagner's abstract anti-Semitic blathering to his formulations of German myth in the prospectus for *Der Ring,* and then compare those to the texts of his operas, it is easy enough to find continuities. It is thus perfectly understandable that, given Wagner's unsavory anti-Semitic attitudes and the deployment of them by the Nazi generation, there is a continuing hostility to any performance of his works in Israel. Despite the fact that some Jewish musicians and conductors insist that there are no specific expressions of anti-Semitism in his music, there are many persons, both Jewish and non-Jewish, whose appreciation of his music will always be diminished by the composer's avowed anti-Semitism.

SEE ALSO *Anti-Semitism.*

BIBLIOGRAPHY

Katz, Jacob. 1986. *The Darker Side of the Genius.* Hanover, NH: Published for Brandeis University Press by University Press of New England.

Meyer, Michael. 1991. *The Politics of Music in the Third Reich.* New York: Peter Lang.

Rose, Paul Lawrence. 1992. *Wagner: Race and Revolution.* New Haven: Yale University Press.

Weiner, Marc A. 1995. *Richard Wagner and the Anti-Semitic Imagination.* Lincoln, NE: University of Nebraska Press.

Wilson J. Moses

WALKER, DAVID
c. 1796–1830

David Walker was born free in Wilmington, New Hanover County, North Carolina, to a free black woman and an enslaved man. Walker was one of fewer than two dozen free blacks in the city, most of whom labored side by side with the enslaved in the city's port economy. Accounting for nearly 60 percent of New Hanover County's total population, African Americans on the Lower Cape Fear were dominant as workers in the maritime trades, into which they infused their specialized knowledge and cultural heritage. Highly concentrated in the population, they also shaped institutions such as the church. Walker likely encountered the Methodist faith here, which was strong in Wilmington. Church membership offered Wilmington African Americans—particularly free blacks such as Walker—opportunities to gain leadership skills, discuss troubles confronting them, and learn of the situations of blacks in other locations. This was particularly true of enslaved blacks working with seamen, whose vessels traveled up and down the Atlantic coastline and abroad.

LIFE IN CHARLESTON

Moving to another seaport city—Charleston, South Carolina—sometime in the 1810s, Walker found a much larger black population, numbering more than 3,600 in 1820 and constituting almost three-quarters of the city's residents, and a complex urban economy. Established a century earlier by English slaveholders from Barbados, Charleston had an almost Caribbean pattern of racial relations, featuring important social distinctions between Caucasians, white-appearing free black elites, and dark free African American and enslaved black masses. A product of complex racial histories that privileged the descendants of mixed-race unions, this multi-tiered racial caste system (whites, free black elites, nonelite free blacks, and the enslaved) at times fostered class divisions among African Americans that likely informed Walker's concern with black disunity.

Charleston also offered a rich institutional life for the city's large free black population, which numbered nearly 1,400 in 1820. In 1817 the city became home to a congregation of the newly founded African Methodist Episcopal (AME) Church, the first independent black church in the nation. Walker was clearly influenced by, and likely participated in, this rare autonomous black institution in the heart of the plantocracy. Another institution, the Brown Fellowship Society, likely imparted a subtler but just as critical influence on Walker. Begun in 1790 as a burial society, the institution catered only to Charleston's free mulatto ("colored" or "brown") elite. Inspired by these experiences, Walker later wrote clearly about the class and status divisions that undermined the unity of African-descended people in America.

During his time in Charleston, Walker could not have been unaffected by the prosecution of African Americans involved in Denmark Vesey's alleged plot to lead a slave revolt involving thousands. Vesey, a free black man, conspired with enslaved African Americans and other free blacks to rise up on July 14, 1822—a date commemorating the French Revolution's Bastille Day—and take over the city before fleeing to the black Caribbean nation of Haiti. Betrayed by two slaves, the plan never came to fruition. White authorities responded with a brutal campaign of repression, during which forty-three of Vesey's followers were deported and thirty-five hanged, including Vesey himself. In the wake of this repression, Walker may have decided to move north.

LIFE IN BOSTON

After moving to Boston by 1825, Walker encountered a community of African Americans numbering around 1,000, most of whom were economically and socially depressed. On Brattle Street, Walker opened a clothing business, which became a locus of black organizing, and married Eliza Butler, a member of Boston's African American middle class. As his business grew, he took on roles of community leadership. He became a Prince Hall Mason, a member of Samuel Snowden's Union United Methodist Episcopal Church, and an agent for *Freedom's Journal*, the first black newspaper in America. Walker was also a cofounder of the Massachusetts General Colored Association (MGCA), a pioneer black antislavery and racial uplift group established in 1826.

In meetings of the MGCA, often in his store, Walker developed the ideas that would coalesce into his most significant historical contribution, a revolutionary seventy-six-page pamphlet titled *David Walker's Appeal, in Four Articles, Together with a Preamble, to the Coloured Citizens of the World, but in Particular, and Very Expressly, to Those of the United States of America*. First published in late 1829 by a sympathetic Boston printer, the *Appeal* went through three quick editions, each featuring minor changes, the last being published in June 1830. Understanding the incendiary nature of his work, Walker relied on friends and sympathizers in the shipping trades to distribute the *Appeal* to southern ports, going so far as to smuggle copies in the lining of sailors' clothing.

Four themes dominated Walker's concerns in the *Appeal*. The first was that American slavery constituted the gravest moral violation in the history of the world, a crime that demanded immediate abolition. "We, (coloured people of these United States) are the most degraded, wretched, and abject set of beings that ever lived since the world began," Walker charged. Following this, he asserted that God's judgment would fall upon the country for slavery unless the institution was immediately abolished. God would redeem the nation once slavery and prejudice were extirpated. Relying on a long tradition of American jeremiad, Walker admonished the nation about the consequences of countenancing slavery. "Americans!!," he railed, "I warn you in the name of the Lord . . . to repent and reform, or you are ruined!!!"

Walker declared that African Americans had a duty to awaken themselves politically. Primarily, this meant conscious efforts to forge a much needed unity, defined by the goal of self-liberation, among scattered black populations. Walker repeatedly stressed the importance of unity among African Americans. "Remember that unless you are united," he wrote, "keeping your tongues within your teeth, you will be afraid to trust your secrets to each other, and thus perpetuate our miseries under the Christians!!!!!" Walker thus called upon black people themselves to play the foremost role in dismantling the mechanisms of their oppression. While violence served as one possible means, more important was the effort to uplift the black population through a rigorous campaign of self-education. This promised not simply to combat the ignorance caused by slavery and racism but also to expose the long history of wrongs done to blacks. "For colored people to acquire learning in this country, makes tyrants quake and tremble on their sandy foundation," Walker believed; the words of educated African Americans would make blacks' oppressors "know that their infernal deeds of cruelty will be made known to the world."

Contemporary black thinkers such as William J. Watkins of Baltimore and Samuel Cornish of New York and *Freedom's Journal*, had expounded on themes similar to those Walker expressed in the *Appeal*. Unlike earlier black expressions of discontent, the pamphlet was revolutionary because of its uncompromising rhetoric and strident tone. Walker replaced the supplication characteristic of an earlier phase of black protest with a new militancy. In considering the prospect of revolt against slaveholders, for example, Walker cautioned his black readers, "Do not trifle, for they will not trifle with you. . . . If there is an attempt made by us, kill or be killed." Thus, employing a strident rhetorical style, more common to street-corner exhortation than learned discourse, Walker sought above all to energize his listeners. He clearly accomplished this among the southern white authorities who sought to suppress the work—by seizing copies of it when they could, initiating laws banning distribution of antislavery literature, and offering rewards for its author's apprehension. Walker's untimely death in 1830 was rumored to have been caused by these forces of reaction, though it is also likely that he fell victim to consumption.

While the *Appeal* helped inspire the conservative defense of slavery, it played an even more important role in the history of radical antislavery thought. Walker's pamphlet helped drive white reformers such as William Lloyd Garrison to espouse the immediate abolition of slavery, though most white abolitionists distanced themselves from Walker's militancy. Black activists such as Henry Highland Garnet consciously incorporated Walker's themes into their own radicalism. The *Appeal* thus served as a comprehensive model for much later black protest thought, both modeling a tradition of black self-help designed to command whites' respect and serving as a form of pragmatic black nationalism built on the political unity of all people of African descent. In the end, David Walker's life and thought heralded the birth of a militant tradition of racial politics, in which a marginalized people sought to sway the "public mind" through the use of the printed word.

SEE ALSO *Vesey, Denmark.*

BIBLIOGRAPHY

PRIMARY WORKS

Walker, David. 1965 (1829). *David Walker's Appeal, in Four Articles, Together with a Preamble, to the Coloured Citizens of the World, but in Particular, and Very Expressly, to Those of the United States of America.* Edited by Charles M. Wiltse. New York: Hill and Wang.

———. 2000. *David Walker's Appeal to the Coloured Citizens of the World.* Edited by Peter P. Hinks. University Park: Pennsylvania State University Press.

SECONDARY WORKS

Aptheker, Herbert. 1965. *One Continual Cry: David Walker's Appeal to the Colored Citizens of the World, 1829–1830, Its Setting & its Meaning, Together with the Full Text of the Third, and Last, Edition of the Appeal.* New York: Humanities Press.

Garnet, Henry Highland. 1848. *Walker's Appeal, With a Brief Sketch of His Life. By Henry Highland Garnet. And Also Garnet's Address to the Slaves of the United States of America.* New York: J.H. Tobitt.

Hinks, Peter P. 1997. *To Awaken My Afflicted Brethren: David Walker and the Problem of Antebellum Slave Resistance.* University Park: Pennsylvania State University Press.

Horton, James Oliver, and Lois E. Horton. 1979. *Black Bostonians: Family Life and Community Struggle in the Antebellum North.* New York: Holmes and Meier.

Patrick Rael

WASHINGTON, BOOKER T.
1856–1915

Booker Taliafero Washington, a black educator, orator, and leader, was born a slave in Franklin County, Virginia, on April 5, 1856. His mother, Jane, was a cook, and his father was a white man who has remained unidentified. After emancipation in 1865, Booker, his mother, and his brother moved to Malden, West Virginia, where, with his stepfather, he worked in salt and coal mines and as a houseboy for the mine owners, General Lewis Ruffner and his wife Viola. In 1872, after acquiring a rudimentary education at public schools and from Mrs. Ruffner, Washington enrolled in the Hampton Normal and Agricultural Institute, in Virginia. Founded to educate former slaves, the school taught habits of rectitude, hard work, and service along with industrial and liberal arts. Washington flourished at what was essentially a high school, and after graduation he was invited to teach at his alma mater.

In 1881, Washington accepted a position as principal for a new state-funded school for blacks in Tuskegee, Alabama. Modeling the school after Hampton, Washington built Tuskegee into a showcase of industrial education and black self-help. Although the idea of industrial education was not original with Washington, he became its most ardent and noted black advocate. By century's end, Tuskegee boasted an endowment of nearly two million dollars, more than one hundred buildings, a faculty of nearly two hundred black men and women, and an international student body.

In 1895, Washington was catapulted to national prominence when he delivered a five-minute speech at the Atlanta Cotton States and International Exposition. His "Atlanta Compromise" speech summarized the program of education, self-help, and racial cooperation that he had pursued at Tuskegee. Whites concluded that Washington offered a palatable resolution of the nation's "Negro problem," namely black acquiescence to white supremacy in social, political, and economic matters. Washington himself believed that he was striking a bargain with whites, not surrendering to them. In return for white aid for greater educational and economic opportunity, he set aside black claims for civil and political equality in the South. Accommodating to, but not endorsing, racial segregation, Washington proposed, "In all things that are purely social, we can be as separate as the fingers, yet one as the hand in all things essential to mutual progress."

His widely published speech caught the attention of white philanthropists, who selected Washington to serve as the conduit through which charitable donations reached black institutions across the nation. His influence soon extended to national politics, and two U.S. presidents, Theodore Roosevelt and William Howard Taft, discussed race relations with him and solicited his advice regarding patronage appointments. Washington simultaneously extended his influence over black institutions by founding the National Negro Business League in 1900 to foster black entrepreneurship, by subsidizing newspapers and organizations, and by undermining groups that were hostile to him. By the turn of the century, no meeting or discussion on racial topics was complete without an appearance or a comment by Washington.

Washington's rise to leadership was symptomatic of the deteriorating status of African Americans at the end of the nineteenth century. Increasingly denied meaningful political participation in the South, blacks had few mechanisms to select black leaders who could be assured of recognition

Booker T. Washington and President Theodore Roosevelt, 1901. *Both presidents Theodore Roosevelt and William Howard Taft discussed race relations with Washington and sought his advice on patronage appointments.* © CORBIS.

by whites. Whites, not blacks, effectively selected the leaders who spoke on behalf of blacks. In Washington's case, connections, ambition, and circumstances, rather than a democratic process, anointed him a race leader. Yet his power remained tenuous because it derived from white patronage, which could never be taken for granted.

Constrained by the source of his power, Washington elected to use furtive means to challenge white supremacy. While voicing only tepid opposition to the disenfranchisement of southern blacks, he secretly funded legal challenges to constitutions in Louisiana and Alabama that restricted black voting. His private behavior, including a controversial meal with Theodore Roosevelt in the White House in 1901, also periodically breeched racial conventions, demonstrating that, despite his talk about the races being as distinct as fingers on a hand, he acceded to segregation only out of expediency.

Washington's power over black institutions inevitably bred resentment among African Americans, however. As early as 1892, Washington alienated black clergy by suggesting that they were unfit to lead the black community, and his emphasis on industrial education irked black proponents of liberal arts education. In addition, his dismissal of electoral politics outraged black politicians who were struggling to retain their offices and influence in the face of disenfranchisement. In 1903, Washington's perceived persecution of William Monroe Trotter, a black editor and civil rights activist in Boston, drew out other critics, including Ida B. Wells-Barnett, who fumed about his restrained denunciations of lynching; W. Calvin Chase, a Washington D.C. editor, who criticized Washington's alleged "political dictatorship"; and W. E. B. Du Bois, who offered a comprehensive criticism of Tuskegee and its creator. A year later, Du Bois and other militants gathered at Niagara Falls, Canada, where they founded the so-called Niagara Movement. By 1909 they had forged a coalition of white racial liberals, reform-minded social workers, socialist radicals, and black militants into the National Association for the Advancement of Colored People (NAACP).

Washington eyed the NAACP warily, and his relationship with the organization soon deteriorated into open and permanent competition. An even greater threat to Washington's power was the election of Woodrow Wilson, a southern-born Democrat, who rapidly expanded the segregation of federal offices. No longer able to use his influence in the nation's capitol to reward allies and punish critics, and no longer able to control the black press as he once had, Washington was dismayed in 1913 when the NAACP turned to the issue of black education and organized an association of black industrial and secondary schools.

In the final years of his life, despite his deteriorating health, Washington maintained a punishing regimen of speaking engagements, meetings, and fund-raising tours. He seemingly became impatient with the obstacles that impeded his program and became more outspoken in his condemnation of lynching, segregation, and disenfranchisement. By 1912, Washington's increasingly strident denunciations of racial injustice surprised even his blacks critics. The optimism that had made his earlier pronouncements seem far too optimistic was replaced by a new urgency. Finally, on November 14, 1915, his body gave out and he died of "nervous exhaustion and arteriosclerosis." Appropriately, he was buried in a cemetery on the grounds of Tuskegee, the institution and cause to which he had devoted his life.

Washington was married three times. He married his first wife, Fannie N. Smith, in 1882. They had one child, Portia M. Washington, before Fannie's death in 1884. A year later, Washington married Olivia A. Davidson, a teacher at Tuskegee who subsequently served as assistant principal at Tuskegee. Before her death in 1889, she and Washington had two sons, Booker T. Washington Jr. and Ernest Davidson Washington. In 1893, Washington married Margaret James Murray. As Washington achieved international prominence, Murray likewise emerged as a leading figure in various women's organizations. They had no children together. Murray died in 1925.

BIBLIOGRAPHY

Brundage, W. Fitzhugh. 2003. *Booker T. Washington and Black Progress: "Up from Slavery" 100 Years Later.* Gainesville: University Press of Florida.

Denton, Virginia Lantz. 1993. *Booker T. Washington and the Adult Education Movement.* Gainesville: University Press of Florida.

Harlan, Louis R. 1972. *Booker T. Washington: The Making of a Black Leader, 1856–1901.* New York: Oxford University Press.

———. 1983. *Booker T. Washington: The Wizard of Tuskegee, 1901–1915.* New York: Oxford University Press.

———, ed. 1972–1983. *The Booker T. Washington Papers.* 14 vols. Urbana: University of Illinois Press.

Washington, Booker T. 1901. *Up from Slavery: An Autobiography,* New York: Doubleday.

W. Fitzhugh Brundage

WATSON, THOMAS E.
1856–1922

Thomas E. Watson was a southern politician who rose to fame on the intersecting paths of class and race. In his early years he was a powerful spokesman for populism and the poor; later he combined economic radicalism with extreme Negro-, Jew-, and Catholic-baiting. His career carried him from Thomson, Georgia, where he was born on September 5, 1856, to the Georgia State Legislature, the U.S. House of Representatives, and the U.S. Senate.

In his youth Watson attended local schools, then a small Baptist college. He began studying law while teaching school, was admitted to the bar in 1875, and became a success as a trial lawyer. He was elected to the Georgia State Legislature in 1882, where he supported public education for children of both races and opposed the convict lease system. As the agrarian rebellion of the mid-1880s spread, he adopted as his own the platform of the Farmers' Alliance, which included abolition of national banks and opposition to the crop-lien system. He was elected to Congress in 1890 as a Democrat from Georgia's Tenth District, but upon entering Congress he shifted his allegiance to the new People's (Populist) Party then emerging on a program of nationalization of transportation and communication, a graduated income tax, direct election of senators, the eight-hour workday, free coinage of silver, and other reforms. In Georgia, he led the fight for an interracial movement of the poor: At one point during the election campaign of 1892, when a black Populist campaigner was threatened with lynching, Watson called upon Populists to rally to the man's defense. Two thousand white farmers marched to the Thomson village courthouse under arms, where they heard speeches by the black Populists and by Watson, who declared, "We are determined in this free country that the humblest white or black man that wants to talk our doctrine shall do it." As one historian put it, "The spectacle of white farmers riding all night to save a Negro from lynchers was rather rare in Georgia." "Watson has gone mad," howled the conservative press (Woodward 1963, p. 240).

Watson's call for unity of black and white poor was widely perceived as the most subversive aspect of his teachings. In an article in *Arena,* he wrote: "Now the People's Party says to these two men, 'You are kept apart that you may be separately fleeced of your earnings. You are made to hate each other because upon that hatred is rested the keystone of the arch of financial despotism which enslaves you both'" (Woodward 1963, p. 220). One editor wrote, "The South and especially the tenth district is threatened with anarchy and communism" because of "the direful teachings of Thomas E. Watson" (Woodward 1963, p. 223). At the same time, there were fissures in the coalition, due in part to the differences in standing between black wage laborers and white farm owners. When the Colored Farmers' Alliance proposed to call a strike of black cotton pickers, the president of the (white) alliance denounced it as an effort "to better their condition at the expense of their white brethren" (Woodward 1963, p. 219).

Watson ran for reelection in 1892 and again in 1894 but was defeated both times because of fraud and violence; in one election his opponent received a majority of 13,780 votes in a county with only 11,240 eligible voters. Nevertheless, the Populists made gains nationally, polling 1,471,000 votes in the congressional elections of 1894 and gaining several governorships. The party gained support in urban areas, where radical sentiments increased in the wake of the depression of 1893 and the 1894 Pullman strike, and hoped to replace the Democrats as one of the two national parties.

In 1896, the national Democratic Party, feeling the heat of Populism, nominated William Jennings Bryan for president on a platform of free coinage of silver. Whereas free silver had always been a Populist demand, it had been only one of many; now the party was confronted with a dilemma—to go with Bryan or hold out for the complete platform. At its St. Louis convention the party split, some voting to support Bryan ("fusion"), others to remain independent ("mid-road"). Watson resisted fusion, but as a compromise he agreed to accept the Populist nomination for vice president on a ticket headed by Bryan.

The election, won by Republican William McKinley, was a debacle for Populism, leaving its supporters embittered and leading to the party's demise. Watson withdrew from politics, turning his attention to writing histories, biographies, and a novel. In 1904 he returned to politics with a new idea: The so-called Negro Question had always been his nemesis. If, he reasoned, the black vote could be eliminated as a factor in elections, poor whites would no longer be afraid to vote their interests and the banker-industrialists dominating the New South could be overturned. Hence, he endorsed the disfranchisement of black voters by any means necessary. In 1905 Watson asked in a widely distributed statement, "What does Civilization owe to the Negro? Nothing!! NOTHING!!! (Woodward 1963, p. 380). By 1913 when blacks were lynched at a rate of one per week, he wrote that "Lynch law is a good thing; it showed that a sense of justice yet lives among the people"

(Woodward 1963, p. 432). The violence of his language propelled him to the front ranks of southern white-supremacist demagogues. He also launched attacks against the Catholic Church, which he accused of serving a foreign power, and against Jews, whom he saw as representatives of northern capitalist interests. His stirring up popular resentment of Jews led to the 1915 lynching of Leo Frank in Atlanta.

For fifteen years after his return he dominated Georgia politics, continuing to present himself as a champion of poor whites. He opposed U.S. entry into World War I, declaring it a war fought to safeguard Morgan's loans to Britain: "Where Morgan's money went, your boy's blood must go" (Woodward 1963, p. 455). In 1920 he got himself elected to the U.S. Senate, where he supported the Bolshevik Revolution and opposed U.S. intervention in Russia. He denounced the League of Nations as an imperialist alliance and fought against increased military appropriations. To the supporters of a standing army, he asked, "Whom, then, do you fear? You are afraid of your own proletariat. . . . Such men as Mellon, and Hoover, and Elbert Gary, and J. P. Morgan . . . these vast combinations of capital want a standing army in order to beat down the dissatisfied" (Woodward 1963, p. 480).

Watson died on September 26, 1922. "Between seven and ten thousand people were said to have attended the funeral services at [his home in Georgia]. . . . Most conspicuous among the floral tributes was a cross of roses eight feet high, sent by the Ku Klux Klan" (Woodward 1963, p. 486).

SEE ALSO *Southern Politics, 1883-1915.*

BIBLIOGRAPHY

Adam, Anthony, and Gerald Gaither. 2004. *Black Populism in the United States: An Annotated Bibliography*. Westport, CT: Praeger.

Gaither, Gerald. 1977. *Blacks and the Populist Revolt: Ballots and Bigotry in the "New South."* Tuscaloosa: University of Alabama Press.

McMath, Robert C. 1993. *American Populism: A Social History, 1877–1898*. New York: Hill and Wang.

Perman, Michael. 2001. *Struggle for Mastery: Disfranchisement in the South, 1888–1908*. Chapel Hill: University of North Carolina Press.

Woodward, C. Vann. 1963 (1938). *Tom Watson: Agrarian Rebel*. New York: Oxford University Press.

Noel Ignatiev

WELLS-BARNETT, IDA B.
1862–1931

Ida Bell Wells-Barnett, a journalist, suffragist, and civil rights activist, was best known for launching the nation's first anti-lynching campaign in 1892. Born on July 16, 1862, in Holly Springs, Mississippi, Wells began her activist career in 1883 when she sued the Chesapeake, Ohio and Southwestern Railway in Memphis, after being refused a first-class seat in a ladies' car. Although Wells ultimately lost the case in 1887, she was the first black plaintiff to challenge a separate coach case before a state supreme court after the U.S. Supreme Court invalidated the civil rights act of 1875.

On March 9, 1892, the lynching of three black men in Memphis, including Thomas Moss—a close friend of Wells and the president of a co-op grocery that successfully competed with a white-owned store—was the catalyst for Wells's life-long career as an anti-lynching activist. Her efforts began with a boycott of the city's streetcars and calls for blacks to leave Memphis for new territories then opening up for settlement in Oklahoma. Whereas she was not the first to protest lynchings, conservatively estimated to number nearly five thousand between 1880 and 1930, Wells was the first to grasp its full significance in a period that saw the emergence of the New South and the anxieties that accompanied rapid industrial growth and urbanization. This period witnessed challenges to traditional gender roles, the assertiveness and economic success of the post-slavery generation of African-Americans, and the popular dissemination of "scientific" texts that posited that peoples of African descent were biologically predetermined to regress into primitivism and hypersexual behavior. Allegations that black men were raping white women allowed lynchings to be carried out with impunity. Wells, using the methods of investigative journalism, statistics on lynching published annually by the *Chicago Tribune*, and, on occasion, detective agencies, provided evidence that the charge of rape was primarily used as a pretext to lynch either defiant blacks or those, such as Thomas Moss, who challenged the economic status quo.

The most provocative aspect of Wells's campaign, however, was her insistence that many of the accusations of rape were actually consensual sexual relationships between black men and white women. After she published an editorial on May 21, 1892, reflecting this view in the *Memphis Free Speech*—a militant weekly she co-owned—white Mempians destroyed her newspaper and forced Wells into exile. From New York, she continued to write anti-lynching editorials for the *New York Age*, published by T. Thomas Fortune. These became the basis for her 1892 pamphlet, *Southern Horrors,* which was the first comprehensive analysis of lynching. It documented the fact that only about a third of black victims were actually accused of rape, much less guilty of it.

An analog to Wells's findings was the continued sexual coercion of black women by white men of all social strata. In sum, her conclusions critiqued the congealing late-nineteenth-century ideology of white supremacy by challenging the myth of (sexually) pure white womanhood, the hypersexuality of black women and men, the integrity of the "best white men," and the pseudoscience of social Darwinism, which was used to confirm the superiority of white civilization.

Wells's anti-lynching discourse also challenged the conservative ideology of elite African-American leaders who believed that racial violence was spurred by lower-class whites against criminally prone blacks. These leaders believed that racism would cease with evidence of increasing black economic and social progress, rather than militant protest. *Southern Horrors,* on the other hand, called for armed self-defense, civil disobedience, and an insurgent black laboring class. Wells's activist strategy also included appeals to progressives, both black and white, to mobilize against lynching and pass a federal anti-lynching law.

In 1893 and 1894, Wells took her campaign to the British Isles, where she was able to rally the support of prominent journalists and denominational church leaders, as well as members of Parliament, anti-imperialist organizations, and feminist groups. A number of these individuals formed the London Anti-Lynching Society, which was headed by John Douglas Sutherland Campbell, the Duke of Argyll. Their criticism of lynching practices was instrumental in making racial violence an issue in the United States that could no longer be ignored.

When Wells returned to America, she attempted to foment an interracial, nationwide movement against lynching. Anti-lynching committees were formed in numerous cities, and Wells received important endorsements from numerous organizations and religious bodies. But Wells, a polarizing figure whose views were too radical for many reformers, both white and black, failed to get the economic support to sustain an independent movement. Nevertheless, after 1892 the number of lynchings never again reached the high of 241 that was recorded that year, and her campaign can be credited for the passage of anti-lynching laws in southern states, including Georgia, Texas and South Carolina, between 1893 and 1897. Wells's activism was also a catalyst for the formation of the National Association of Colored Women (NACW) in 1896: the first secular, nationwide organization of African-American women. Its motto, "lifting as we climb," informed its activities, which included community betterment, suffrage, and anti-lynching work.

In 1895, Wells married Ferdinand L. Barnett, a like-minded militant lawyer in Chicago, and four children were born to the couple between 1896 and 1904. In a chapter of her autobiography, *Crusade for Justice,* Wells-Barnett wrote of her "divided duty" between motherhood and activism, but she continued to campaign against racial violence and to establish important institutions and organizations to empower black men and women, both in Illinois and nationally. Wells-Barnett founded the Ida B. Wells Club, the first women's club in Chicago to become a part of the NACW; the Alpha Suffrage Club, the first black women's suffrage club in Chicago; and the Negro Fellowship League, a settlement house. In 1909 she was among the "founding forty" of the organization that later became known as the National Association for the Advancement of Colored People (NAACP).

However, Wells-Barnett's militant strategies were more in tune with the nationalism of Marcus Garvey and the militancy of the Boston editor Monroe Trotter—both of whom she allied with—than with the NAACP. Nevertheless, she provided the model for the organization's own belated campaign against lynching and it was the NAACP's public lobbying effort to pass a federal anti-lynching law in 1922 that established it as the premiere civil rights organization in the country. During the mid-1920s, Wells-Barnett was instrumental in the successful campaign to mobilize black support in Chicago to establish a branch of the Brotherhood of Sleeping Car Porters and Maids in the city. In 1930, a year before her death, Wells-Barnett became the first black woman to run for an Illinois state senate seat. Both in theory and practice, Wells-Barnett's campaign against lynching and activism for black empowerment were harbingers for the late twentieth-century movements against racism and sexism. She died in Chicago on March 25, 1931, at the age of sixty-eight.

BIBLIOGRAPHY

Bates, Beth Tomkins. 2001. *Pullman Porters and the Rise of Protest Politics in Black America, 1925–1945.* Chapel Hill: University of North Carolina Press.

Bruce, Philip A. 1889. *The Plantation Negro as a Freeman.* New York: G.P. Putnam's Sons.

Brundage, W. Fitzhugh. 1993. *Lynching in the New South: Georgia and Virginia, 1880–1930.* Urbana: University of Illinois Press.

Giddings, Paula J. 1984. *When and Where I Enter: The Impact of Black Women on Race and Sex in America.* New York: William Morrow.

McMurry, Linda O. 1998. *To Keep the Waters Troubled: The Life of Ida B. Wells.* New York: Oxford University Press.

Salem, Dorothy. 1990. *To Better Our World: Black Women in Organized Reform.* Brooklyn, NY: Carlson.

Schecter, Patricia A. 2001. *Ida B. Wells-Barnett and American Reform, 1880–1930.* Chapel Hill: University of North Carolina Press.

Shaler, Nathaniel S. 1884. "The Negro Problem." *Atlantic Monthly* (November): 696–709.

Wells, Ida B. 1969. *Southern Horrors* (1892) and *The Red Record* (1894). Reprinted in *On Lynchings: Southern Horrors, A Red Record, Mob Rule in New Orleans.* New York: Arno Press.

———. 1970. *Crusade for Justice: The Autobiography of Ida B. Wells*, edited by Alfreda M. Duster. Chicago: University of Chicago Press.

———. 1990 (1893). "Lynch Law in All Its Phases." Reprinted in *Ida B. Wells-Barnett: An Exploratory Study of An American Black Woman,* 1893–1930, edited by Mildred I. Thompson, pp. 171–187. Brooklyn, NY: Carlson.

Zangrando, Robert L. 1980. *The NAACP Crusade against Lynching, 1909–1950.* Philadelphia: Temple University Press.

Paula J. Giddings

WHITE, WALTER FRANCIS
1893–1955

Walter Francis White, born on July 1, 1893, in Atlanta, Georgia, was at the critical age of sixteen when the National Association for the Advancement of Colored People (NAACP) was founded in 1909. He was positioned to play a vital role in its future. He grew up in a middle-class family; his father, George, a postman, and his mother, Madeline, a school teacher, were both so light in complexion they could pass for white. Walter himself had blue eyes and blond hair, which sometimes belied his African-American ancestry.

His family complexion offered him little comfort: It was considered "too light" by blacks and "suspiciously too dark" by whites. The family often walked rather than ride in public transportation—if they rode in the black conveyances, blacks would mistake them for white, and vice versa. But there was one major advantage for a political activist: White was the perfect person to infiltrate and investigate the atrocities of the Ku Klux Klan (KKK).

Walter White learned about the violence of racism at an early age. At thirteen, he found himself standing in front of his home with his father, with guns cocked trying to protect their property from a white mob intent on burning all the homes in black neighborhoods. This was the Atlanta race riot of 1906.

With no high schools for blacks in Atlanta at the time, Walter attended the private high school established within the campus of Atlanta University. When he graduated from Atlanta University in 1916, his first job out of college was selling life insurance for Standard Life, a major African-American company in Atlanta. He organized the first chapter of the NAACP in Atlanta and used its leverage to force the city of Atlanta to improve public facilities for African Americans. Because of the effectiveness of his efforts in Atlanta, James Weldon Johnson, the first African-American general secretary of the NAACP and author of the song "Lift Every Voice and Sing," secured a position for White as assistant to the organization's chief administrative officer in 1918.

White came to the NAACP with some knowledge and experience of the social situation of blacks in the Deep South. In 1919 White was sent to investigate what was known as the Elaine race riot in Phillips County, Arkansas. White published his undercover findings about the riot in the *Daily News*, the *Chicago Defender,* the *Nation*, and the NAACP's *Crisis* magazine. He went on to investigate more than forty-one lynchings, eight race riots, and dozens of KKK cross burnings, posing as a white reporter who wanted to give the South's side of the story. At one point he was even invited to join the Ku Klux Klan. One southern sheriff gave him a badge and a gun and took him along on hunts for blacks. As the NAACP executive secretary, White tried relentlessly—and unsuccessfully—to persuade congressmen to pass an anti-lynching law. Anti-lynching laws that were proposed in the House of Representatives were reported out of committee, passed by the full House, and ultimately defeated via filibusters in the Senate. Southern senators, in particular, argued that anti-lynching laws violated state's rights.

In Helena, Arkansas, while White was on his way to interview Negroes jailed for joining a sharecroppers' union, he learned that a mob planned to ambush and lynch him. The white conductor of the northbound train wondered why White (who was now desperate to get out of town) would leave and thus miss the execution of plans to lynch a Negro passing through town. This episode formed the basis for his book *Rope and Faggot: A Biography of Judge Lynch*, published in 1929. In 1926 White had published *The Fire in the Flint* and *Flight*, and later he wrote *What Caused the Detroit Riot?* (1943), *A Rising Wind* (1945), an autobiography, *A Man Called White* (1948), *Civil Rights: Fifty Years of Fighting* (1950), and *How Far the Promised Land?* (1955).

In addition to pushing for anti-lynching measures and writing books, White was involved in various initiatives throughout his tenure as head of the NAACP. He met many of the influential writers of the Harlem Renaissance and assisted in breaking down barriers for them. White also worked tirelessly to bring about civil rights legislation. When President Herbert Hoover nominated John P. Parker, who had publicly renounced voting rights for blacks, to the Supreme Court, White testified before the Senate Judicial Committee and launched a letter-writing campaign against his nomination. Parker's nomination was defeated in the Senate; Hoover, however, refused to remove Parker from consideration and consequently alienated many blacks. His action contributed to the Democrat Franklin D. Roosevelt's winning the nomination for president in 1932. White developed a strategy to attack racial discrimination at its roots when he started to fight for blacks' right to vote and to be admitted to professional and graduate schools in state universities, and for equal pay for black teachers in public schools.

White urged President Roosevelt to extend Social Security benefits to agricultural and domestic workers and to amend the National Labor Relations Act to prohibit union discrimination. He supported A. Philip Randolph's March on Washington campaign in 1940 and 1941. He took on racial stereotypes in the entertainment industry and helped to quell race riots in Detroit and Harlem. In the last ten years of his life, White witnessed the outlawing of restrictive covenants in real estate deeds—for which the NAACP had fought for more than thirty years—and the landmark *Brown v. Board of Education* case, which desegregated public schools on May 17, 1954.

His accomplishments notwithstanding, White was not without his critics. He clashed with W. E. B. Du Bois because, like other leading black intellectuals, some of whom were critical of the NAACP, he opposed his notion of "black economic self-determination," believing it was contrary to the integrationist aims of the NAACP. Other critics argued that White was too close to FDR's New Deal and was not able to parlay his support for FDR's initiatives into tangible gains for the NAACP. There were also those who believed White's autocratic leadership style caused him not to recognize other organizations and leaders as potential allies. However, White's body of work shows a man dedicated and committed to bringing all blacks fully into the mainstream of American life. Where his efforts failed, it was not because of lack of commitment to his causes but because the obstacles were insurmountable at the time. Congress never had any intention to pass a federal law against lynching, for example, despite the moral clarity of White's position.

White was the recipient of several awards and honors throughout his long tenure at the NAACP, including a Guggenheim Fellowship early in his career and the 1937 Spingarn Medal. And because of his indefatigable work against lynching, *Time* magazine named him its "man of the year" in 1938. White died of a heart attack on March 21, 1955, in New York at the age of sixty-two.

SEE ALSO *Ku Klux Klan; NAACP.*

BIBLIOGRAPHY

Black, Allida M. 1996. *Casting Her Own Shadow: Eleanor Roosevelt and the Shaping of Postwar Liberalism*. New York: Columbia University Press.

Cortner, Richard C. 1988. *A Mob Intent on Death: The NAACP and the Arkansas Riot Cases*. Middleton, CT: Wesleyan University Press.

Fleming, Robert. 2007. "A Heinous Act: Lynching Is America's Dirty Secret of Racial Injustice and Hatred." *Black Issues* 9 (1).

Waldron, Edward E. 1978. *Walter White and the Harlem Renaissance*. Port Washington, NY: Kennikat Press.

White, Walter Francis. [1948] 1995. *A Man Called White: The Autobiography of Walter White*. Athens: University of Georgia Press.

Russell Mootry Jr.

WHITE CITIZENS' COUNCIL AND THE COUNCIL OF CONSERVATIVE CITIZENS

The first White Citizens' Council (officially known as the Citizens' Council or, as a group, the Citizens' Councils of America) was formed in Indianola, Mississippi, in July 1954 following the *Brown v. Board of Education* Supreme Court decision that initiated school desegregation. Branches of this white supremacist organization soon formed in other states. Most active in Alabama, Louisiana, South Carolina, and Mississippi, where Robert Patterson emerged as a leading figure, Citizens' Councils were established throughout southern states, in most major U.S. cities, and in many northern states. Membership peaked at around 250,000 in 1957. Citizens' Councils often became the focal points for the massive resistance to desegregation, and organizing rallies were held to protest against university integration.

Participants claimed that they were not extremists, and they distanced themselves from groups like the Ku Klux Klan. Indeed, Councils generally pursued the maintenance of racial segregation through courts and legislatures. Active in state and local elected offices, Citizens' Council members were often perceived to be the "uptown Klan," or a white supremacist organization populated by supposedly respectable members of society (e.g., scholars, doctors, politicians) who sought measures sustaining racial segregation through legal means. A newspaper, *The Citizens' Council*, was regularly produced, containing articles that reiterated racist stereotypes and depicted African Americans as innately inferior. Contributors asserted the need for states' rights, segregated schools, and bans on interracial marriage to maintain racial integrity. By the mid-1960s, with desegregation progressing under federal authority, Citizens' Councils lost support and influence, and they were all but moribund by the 1970s.

The Council of Conservative Citizens (CCC) was founded in 1985 from the remnants of the Citizens' Councils, and many members of the earlier groups joined, most notably Robert Patterson. Headquartered in Missouri, the CCC opposes school desegregation, interracial marriage and race mixing, affirmative action, welfare programs, and immigration. It advocates states' rights and

Confederate heritage. One consistent theme in CCC publications, Web sites, and its *Citizens' Informer* newsletter is the gruesome description of interracial crime, particularly that committed by blacks against whites in the United States and elsewhere.

The CCC argues that race is a fundamental aspect of the human condition and that blacks and whites have innate differences in physical and mental abilities. These differences are supposedly irreconcilable—whites are intelligent, for example, while blacks are predisposed to violent behavior. In every instance, white supremacy is affirmed by CCC studies and affiliated scholars who use pseudo-scientific and statistical evidence to prove black inferiority. CCC leaders include Gordon Lee Baum, a former Citizens' Council organizer, and syndicated columnist Samuel Francis. Some high-ranking Republican Party members—such as Senator Trent Lott of Mississippi (1988–), Representative Robert L. Barr of Georgia (1995–2003), and Governor Kirk Fordice of Mississippi (1992–2000) had connections to the CCC. These politicians typically expressed solidarity with the organization before bad publicity forced them to apologize. Others, such as Governor Haley Barbour of Mississippi (2004–), attended CCC events but did not subsequently retract their association. In addition to its positions on race, the CCC professes patriotism; Christianity; the centrality of people of European descent to the foundation, future, and identity of the United States; opposition to international treaties and bodies such as the United Nations and North American Free Trade Agreement (NAFTA); and animosity toward homosexuality.

BIBLIOGRAPHY

Bartley, Numan V. 1969. *The Rise of Massive Resistance: Race and Politics in the South during the 1950's*. Baton Rouge: Louisiana State University Press.

McMillen, Neil R. 1971. *The Citizens' Council: Organized Resistance to the Second Reconstruction, 1954–1964*. Urbana: University of Illinois Press.

Potok, Mark. 1999. "Sharks in the Mainstream: Racism Underlies Influential 'Conservative' Group." *Southern Poverty Law Center Intelligence Report* 93: 16–21. Available from http://www.splcenter.org/intel/intelreport/article.jsp?aid=360.

Euan Hague

WHITE RACIAL IDENTITY

White racial outlook (WRO) theories are considered some of the most influential psychological variables when studying whites' views of self and of persons of color. They offer a framework from which to understand views of race and ethnicity in a racialized society. These theories grew from previous research on black racial identity models, and they provide ways of assessing and predicting white racial attitudes. They are important because racial information may interfere with or enhance cross-racial interactions. Further refinements in an understanding of racial attitudes can help modify these attitudes. In essence, instead of stating that a white individual is racist or not, white racial outlook theories suggest that attitudes that whites have cannot be so simply categorized, although these attitudes may have components of racism embedded within them.

These theories also enhance some of the social-psychological literature, including theories of symbolic or modern racism. The majority of whites in the United States are less likely to behave in the overtly racist ways that whites did prior to the civil rights movement, though traces of such racism may be present covertly. Rather than measure racism as a unidimensional, bipolar construct (i.e., racist or not racist), WROs can delineate nuances of racial attitudes. These WRO theories offer a means to determine whether whites understand the sociopolitical realities of race, and they help explain why a person may behave in a racist fashion in one setting but not in another. They have been examined to determine how whites cognitively and behaviorally structure racial information across a wide range of situations, such as consultation environments, counseling dyads, and multicultural competence training. This brief introduction includes two major theories of white racial outlook, their assumptions, their instruments used to measure them, and their relationships to racism.

THE DEVELOPMENT OF WRO THEORY

A brief introduction to the origin of WROs as an offshoot of black racial identity theory can help one to understand their development. In the late 1960s and early 1970s, William Cross Jr. and others developed stage models of black racial identity (understanding self-concept as both a black individual and as part of the black community) as a means of understanding the development blacks go through to live within a white-dominated society. This was an era in which a variety of historically oppressed groups became more vocal politically and socially, including the gay community, the American Indian community, and the black community. Pride movements, including Black Pride, were becoming prominent. From this era, more psychological research into black attitudes developed, with Cross developing his "Nigrescence" model. In this model, levels of black racial identity were presented that highlighted attitudes toward both the in-group (other black Americans) and out-groups (predominantly white Americans). The model has since been updated, and other prominent researchers, such as Janet Helms (1995), have presented their own models of black racial identity. Helms devised her model of black racial identity in the early 1980s, and she later formulated white racial identity models from that original black identity model.

TYPES OF WROs

There are a few white racial outlook models but the psychological literature focuses primarily on two, the White Racial Identity (WRI) model and the White Racial Consciousness (WRC) model. The two are built on different theoretical philosophies, have different assumptions, and have different means of measuring and understanding racial attitudes. Helms's WRI model rests on the assumption that whites are aware of what being white means to them and that they move through a series of developmental ego statuses (or stages)—from being oblivious to racial issues to becoming comfortable with whiteness—while simultaneously accepting other racial groups. Whites grow up privileged in society and learn to recognize themselves as privileged, though often unconsciously. In order to protect this privilege, whites distort race-related reality, which contributes to racism. Helms indicated that in order for whites to not be racist, their two primary developmental issues are to abandon the entitlement and privileges they receive from society and adopt to a nonracist white identity. In fact, in part because of her work in this area, there has been new psychological research literature focusing on white privilege.

Essentially, whites must begin to understand that they are given benefits in society simply because they are white, while also recognizing that persons of color are not afforded those same benefits. After recognizing these benefits, they can begin to achieve a nonracist identity. Helms's white racial identity theory states that racial identity develops through a sequential process in which more mature ego differentiations occur as statuses mature. The differentiation occurs through various information processing strategies, which are used to incorporate racial information and can be either dominant or nondominant. Helms highlighted that because of the dominant-nondominant theoretical component, whites generally do not fit into only one status prior to moving into another status. In essence, when a white individual comes across racial information the ego selects the status that is dominant depending on the situation and environment.

The White Racial Identity (WRI) Model. The WRI comprises six statuses, with the first three (Contact, Disintegration, Reintegration) reflecting movement toward the abandonment of a racist identity, while the last three (Pseudo-independence, Immersion/Emersion, and Autonomy) are reflective of movement and acceptance of a nonracist identity. Abandoning racist ideology begins with the Contact status, in which whites are unaware of societal or individual racism and are satisfied with the racial status quo. The Disintegration status arises because of racial anxiety and ambivalence, often resulting from an event that causes a person to question previous views of race. During this status, people must reconsider their racial viewpoints, and they can either eventually maintain the status quo or move toward greater involvement with persons of other races and racial information in general. Movement into the Reintegration status is underscored by denigrating other racial groups and idealizing one's own racial group.

Accepting a nonracist ideology begins with Pseudo-independence, which is highlighted by an intellectualized approval of other racial groups, although full acceptance is not accomplished. Those moving into the Immersion/Emersion status begin to understand the benefits and privileges that have impacted and influenced them simply for being white. At this status, some people begin to join activist groups against oppression; at the very least they begin to understand their role living in a racist society. Finally, those that attain the Autonomy status have an appreciation for other racial groups, understand the sociopolitical realities within society, but also have an appreciation for being white. Their racial worldview is more complex and they are willing to renounce racial privileges.

In order to assess WRI, the White Racial Identity Attitude Scale (WRIAS, or RIAS-W) was developed. While there appears to be some psychometric evidence validating the WRI theory, John Behrens (1997), Jane Swanson and colleagues (1994), and others have found that the WRIAS does not seem to measure the WRI model well. They argue that the instrument is merely a unidimensional, bipolar racism scale that simply measures the racist and nonracist attitudes of white Americans toward black Americans. It is still used by WRI researchers, however.

The White Racial Consciousness (WRC) Model. An alternative model was developed in the early 1990s by Wayne Rowe and colleagues (1994, 2002) as a reaction to the WRI model, called the White Racial Consciousness (WRC) model. Readers will notice both similarities and differences with the WRI, as both present views of "whiteness." The WRC framers believed that whites do not move through the identity developmental statuses devised by Helms, instead arguing that whites learn racial information in the same manner as other information. The theoretical and functional structure is embedded with a sociocognitive approach, is theoretically simpler, and conforms more to the racial attitude research historically highlighted by social-psychological researchers. Essentially, the WRI discusses white identity while the WRC discusses white attitudes. The WRC focuses on the present attitude type determined through attitude formation, and it presumes that racial attitudes are learned in much the same way as other attitudes. It does not focus on the underlying psychological mechanisms that drive the attitude types.

The model is measured by the Oklahoma Racial Attitude Scale (ORAS) and includes four attitude types: Dominative, Integrative, Conflictive, and Reactive. Briefly, the Dominative attitude is reflected in ethnocentric attitudes, with individuals believing that the white race is either superior or rationalizing the oppression of groups of color. Integrative types feel comfortable with racial issues and recognize white privilege and racial oppression. Conflictive types are opposed to overt racism and discrimination yet have difficulty with programs designed to assist those who have been historically oppressed. Finally, Reactive individuals are aware of white privilege yet hold onto white guilt over past and current oppression, taking on a parental attitude toward groups of color. Thus, the Dominative and Conflictive attitude types are considered racist, whereas the Integrative and Reactive types are considered nonracist.

WRO theories have relevance toward racial issues within the therapeutic relationships, business relationships, or various trust issues within a community, among others. Researchers working in this area can explore multiple possibilities that can yield fruitful rewards. Whether at the individual level or the group level, there are many racial concerns within the United States and other countries, and more study of WROs can help individuals in politics, business, education, and therapy appreciate the racial barriers and racial assets needed to understand racial identities.

SEE ALSO *Aversive Racism; Symbolic and Modern Racism.*

BIBLIOGRAPHY

Behrens, John T. 1997. "Does the White Racial Identity Attitude Scale Measure Racial Identity?" *Journal of Counseling Psychology* 44: 3–12.

Cross, William, E., Jr. 1971. "The Negro-to-Black Conversion Experience." *Black World* 20 (9): 13–27.

———, and Beverly J.V. Vandiver. 2001. "Nigrescence Theory and Measurement: Introducing the Cross Racial Identity Scale (CRIS)." In *Handbook of Multicultural Counseling,* 2nd ed., edited by Joseph G. Ponterotto, et al., 371–393. Thousand Oaks, CA: Sage.

Helms, Janet E. 1995. "Update on Helms's Racial Identity Models." In *Handbook of Multicultural Counseling,* 2nd ed., edited by Joseph G. Ponterotto, et al., 181–198. Thousand Oaks, CA: Sage.

LaFleur, N. Kenneth, Wayne Rowe, and Mark M. Leach. 2002. "Reconceptualizing White Racial Consciousness." *Journal of Multicultural Counseling & Development* 30 (3): 148–152.

Leach, Mark M., John T. Behrens, and N. Kenneth LaFleur. 2002. "White Racial Identity and White Racial Consciousness: Similarities, Differences, and Recommendations." *Journal of Multicultural Counseling and Development* 30 (2): 66–80.

Rowe, Wayne, Sandra K. Bennett, and Donald R. Atkinson. 1994. "White Racial Identity Models: A Critique and Alternative Proposal." *The Counseling Psychologist* 22 (1): 129–146.

Rowe, Wayne, John. T. Behrens, and Mark M. Leach. 1995. "Racial/Ethnic Identity and Racial Consciousness: Looking Back and Looking Forward." In *Handbook of Multicultural Counseling,* 2nd ed., edited by Joseph G. Ponterotto, et al., 218–235. Thousand Oaks, CA: Sage.

Swanson, Jane L., David M. Tokar, and Lori E. Davis. 1994. "Content and Construct Validity of the White Racial Identity Attitude Scale." *Journal of Vocational Behavior* 44: 198–217.

Mark M. Leach

WHITE SETTLER SOCIETY

The term *white settler society* refers to a group of societies that sprang up as a result of the great European expansion into other regions of the globe from the late fifteenth century onward. The white settler societies established by the British, French, Portuguese, Spanish, German, and Dutch conquerors in the Americas, Africa, and Australasia all established forms of white racial dominance in the course of their development. They also provided important incubators for the development of theories and practices of racism, sometimes producing their own racial theorists and theories, as occurred in the United States. Examples of the latter would include the scientist and physical anthropologist Dr. Samuel George Morton (1799–1851) who wrote the influential book *Crania Americana* (1839), arguing that Negroes belonged to a separate species, and his disciples Josiah C. Nott and George Glidden, who championed polygenism in their book *Types of Mankind* (1854). In the middle of the nineteenth century, experiences of colonization in Australia, including attempts to "civilize" Australian Aborigines, contributed to the development of theories of "polygenism"—the belief in separate origins for different groups of people, and thus the inherent separation of human "races"—as news from the Australian colonies filtered back to racial theorists like Robert Knox at the imperial center.

White settler societies were different from other types of colonies. D. K. (David Kenneth) Fieldhouse, in his classic study *The Colonial Empires* (1965), classified the varying colonial situations found across the globe under four major categories: occupation, mixed settlement, plantation, and pure settlement. During the Age of Expansion, European colonizers exploited the more densely populated and organized societies of Africa and Southeast Asia for labor and material goods and then used them as a market for surplus European goods. In these colonies of occupation, the primary aim (and opportunity) was not to settle European populations (though this usually occurred to some extent), nor was it to impose a European political and legal framework over the territory and its indigenous populations (though, again, this happened to a lesser or greater extent). As George M. Fredrickson, the comparative historian of racism, points out, "the new European overlords could profit most handily by skimming a surplus 'off the top' without systematically destroying the traditional cultures, modes of production, or forms of local governance." As a consequence these colonies "did not undergo a radical and thoroughgoing social reorganization to reflect the hegemony of a substantial and permanent white status group" (1988, p. 219). In the era of decolonization after World War II, these societies, including important examples such as India and Indonesia, threw off their colonial shackles and reinvented themselves as independent nations.

However, social reorganization, as well as the establishment of permanent white status groups, was exactly what happened in the colonies of settlement (the other three categories). Here, European colonizers primarily sought the land itself, and not indigenous labor or goods, both for exploitation and to provide space for an expansion of the European population. In societies such as South Africa and America (hybrids of the plantation and mixed settlement types), the Latin American countries (mixed settlement), the sugar islands of the West Indies (plantation), and Australia (pure settlement), the goal was to set up European-style societies in new lands, under the assumption that this represented the spread of civilization.

The term *white settler society* covers a diverse range of societies and racial formations. South Africa has a minority white population and a much larger black African population. This was an important factor in the setting up of the racist apartheid system in the second half of the twentieth century. As in other parts of southern Africa including Rhodesia (later Zimbabwe) and Kenya, these white settler societies were structured in particular ways because they formed small white enclaves administering and dominating much larger black African populations. Whites in these situations developed strict regimes of racial separation and segregation. As the twentieth century wore on they became increasingly fearful of what their long suppressed black populations might have in store for them, should they ever achieve equality and democratic rights. They also tended to develop rigid and conservative colonial cultures, determined not to let themselves be "contaminated" by the indigenous African populations that lived alongside them, or by the environment, which was often seen as a potential source of degeneration to Europeans.

White settler societies were also shaped by the different types of terrain and people they encountered. For example, they would be influenced by the lifestyle of the original inhabitants. Confronting largely nomadic peoples in sparsely settled lands (rather than settled agriculturists), colonists in Australia and Canada developed large white-majority societies with small indigenous populations, which were supplanted and peripheral to the emerging capitalist mode of production. After World War II, however, as a result of mass immigration, these societies increasingly became ethnically diverse, and in the early twenty-first century they have significant nonwhite immigrant populations along with the white majority population.

The United States also supplanted indigenous populations and developed into a large white-majority society, but one with a large minority black population as a result of the slave trade, in addition to a large mixed Hispanic population as a result of the annexation of territory that formerly belonged to Mexico and both legal and illegal immigration. Like Canada and Australia, the United States is ethnically diverse, and it is often referred to as the world's largest multicultural society.

Brazil, Argentina, and Mexico, as a result of the circumstances of their colonization—including their use of both local labor and imported slaves, as well as their adoption of Spanish and Portuguese attitudes and laws about intermarriage—developed large mixed, or mestizo, populations alongside their white populations. This had significant implications for their particular racial formations. Race boundaries tended to be less rigid than they were in South Africa or the United States, for example. Brazil, which had imported millions of slaves up until the nineteenth century, developed a large black African immigrant population and an elaborate racial classification system. This provided ample opportunities for racial "passing," which allowed lighter-colored people to move up the racial hierarchy in ways less possible in the United States, with its "one-drop rule." Here, after emancipation and the erection of Jim Crow laws, the one-drop rule meant that having even one drop of African blood classified a person as black.

As racist theories consolidated during the nineteenth century, white settler societies found a compelling justification for maintaining white rule. Many racial myths that have since been discredited found a powerful resonance in these societies. In the white settler colonies of the British Empire, the myth of Anglo-Saxon superiority among the hierarchy of races was used to justify or explain the continuing domination of white over black in the United States, Australia, Canada, Kenya, and Rhodesia. Immigration policies aimed at keeping nonwhite peoples out of white settler societies were also established. During the gold rushes of the nineteenth century, California and some Australian colonies enacted restrictions on Chinese immigration. Australia's immigration restriction of all nonwhites, commonly known as the "White Australia" policy, lasted from the beginning of the twentieth century until the early 1970s.

It is sometimes argued that the white settler societies arising from Spanish and Portuguese colonization—such as Brazil, Argentina, and Mexico—were less concerned with race and a racial hierarchy. Rules regarding intermarriage between the "races" were either lax or absent, resulting in large mixed-race populations. Some authors, however, have questioned this view, suggesting that Brazil, Mexico, and Argentina were in fact deeply racialized societies in which an intricate color coding structured social relations, privilege, and status (see Menchaca 2001, Wolfe 2001). White racial myths were also prevalent in these societies.

White settler societies had mixed fortunes as they moved beyond explicitly racist and discriminatory social formations in the second half of the twentieth century. The nightmares that some white South Africans had regarding how those they had tortured and suppressed might exact their revenge has not played out in the post-apartheid era. Since the 1990s, however, many whites have left South Africa. At the same time, the plight of white farmers in Zimbabwe became increasingly untenable under the repressive Mugabe regime from the late 1990s onwards, also leading to whites leaving the country. The fate of such white colonial enclaves was to largely disappear or find reduced significance as the societies reverted to black majority rule.

The United States had long struggles with racial segregation during the twentieth century, and the nation still bears the scars of its turbulent racial history. However, as a majority white society, it survived and prospered (unlike Rhodesia and Kenya) in the same era that saw the collapse of scientific racism and the delegitimization of various forms of racial discrimination. Australia, which still called itself White Australia at the end of the 1960s, has been peacefully transformed into a relatively harmonious multicultural society, as has Canada. In the last decades of the twentieth century, both Canada and Australia sought accommodations with the indigenous peoples they had supplanted, granting them rights they had previously been denied. These nations also removed the last vestiges of official racial discrimination. The white settler societies of Mexico, Argentina, and Brazil have had far more turbulent histories following decolonization, including military coups, revolutions, and economic instability.

BIBLIOGRAPHY

Crapanzano, Vincent. 1985. *Waiting: The Whites of South Africa.* New York: Random House.

Denoon, Donald. 1983. *Settler Capitalism: The Dynamics of Development in the Southern Hemisphere.* Oxford: Clarendon Press.

Fieldhouse, D. K. 1982. *The Colonial Empires: A Comparative Survey from the Eighteenth Century*, 2nd ed. London: Macmillan.

Fredrickson, George M. 1988. "Colonialism and Racism." In *The Arrogance of Race: Historical Perspectives on Slavery, Racism, and Social Inequality*, edited by George M. Fredrickson, 216–235. Middleton, CT: Wesleyan University Press.

———. 1997. *The Comparative Imagination: On the History of Racism, Nationalism, and Social Movements.* Berkeley: University of California Press.

Gossett, Thomas. 1997 (1963). *Race: The History of an Idea in America.* New York: Oxford University Press.

Hartz, Louis. 1964. *The Founding of New Societies: Studies in the History of the United States, Latin America, South Africa, Canada, and Australia.* New York: Harcourt, Brace & World.

Horsman, Reginald. 1981. *Race and Manifest Destiny: The Origins of American Racial Anglo-Saxonism.* Cambridge, MA: Harvard University Press.

Jordan, Winthrop D. 1968. *White over Black: American Attitudes toward the Negro, 1550–1812.* Chapel Hill: University of North Carolina Press.

Kennedy, Dane. 1987. *Islands of White: Settler Society and Culture in Kenya and Southern Rhodesia, 1890–1939.* Durham, NC: Duke University Press.

Markus, Andrew. 1979. *Fear and Hatred: Purifying Australia and California, 1850–1901.* Sydney: Hale & Iremonger.

Menchaca, Martha. 2001. *Recovering History, Constructing Race: The Indian, Black, and White Roots of Mexican Americans.* Austin: University of Texas Press.

Wolfe, Patrick. 2001. "Land, Labor, and Difference: Elementary Structures of Race." *The American Historical Review* 106 (3): 866–905.

Anthony Moran

WILKINS, ROY
1901–1981

The grandson of former slaves from Holly Springs, Mississippi, Roy Ottoway Wilkins was born August 30, 1901, in St. Louis, Missouri. As soon as he learned how to write, he dropped his middle name, the name of the doctor who delivered him. His mother died from tuberculosis when he was four years old; a brother and sister died from the same disease. After the death of his mother, Wilkins's father, who worked in a brick kiln, could not care for him and his siblings. As a result, they went to live with his maternal aunt Elizabeth and uncle Sam Williams in a lower income, integrated neighborhood in St. Paul, Minnesota. He was generally spared the blatant racism often encountered by African Americans in the southern states.

After graduating from Mechanic Arts High School, Wilkins entered the University of Minnesota. He worked his way through college by taking jobs as a stockyard worker and Pullman car waiter. He also worked as a journalist and night editor with the *Minnesota Daily* and became editor of the *St. Paul Appeal,* an African American weekly newspaper. He was a member of the local branch of the National Association for the Advancement of Colored People (NAACP). After graduating from the University of Minnesota in 1923 with a degree in sociology and a minor in journalism, Wilkins became editor of the *Kansas City Call,* another African American weekly. He married social worker Aminda "Minnie" Badeau in 1929; they had no children.

In Kansas City he first came face-to-face with racism. There he discovered that even having good manners was a crime for black men. Wilkins recounted a story of an incident when he offered his seat on a streetcar to an elderly white woman. Her response to another white passenger was that she was not so old that she would take a seat from a "nigger." Wilkins indicated that he quickly changed from a "soft shell boy to a well-armored Kansas City slicker." He began to use the pages of the *Call* to attack white racism. For example, he used the paper to wage a campaign against racist Missouri senator Henry J. Allen, who was subsequently defeated. When he moved the paper from simply generating sensational stories to bringing attention to segregation issues, circulation went from 4,000 to 20,000. This made the *Call* the second largest African American weekly in the country, after the *Chicago Defender.*

Wilkins continued to be actively involved in the local NAACP, serving as secretary of the Kansas City branch. Those activities and Wilkins's work on the newspaper exposing segregation brought him to the attention of Walter White, executive director of the NAACP. In 1931, White recruited Wilkins to serve as assistant secretary of the organization in New York.

One of Wilkins's first assignments was to investigate lynching and African American working conditions in the South. In 1932 he traveled incognito to the river camps set up along the Mississippi River to investigate the slave-labor-like conditions facing black convicts on federally controlled flood projects. His report, *Mississippi Slave Labor,* led to Congress enacting reform measures that improved the working conditions in levee labor camps. From that point forward, Wilkins was at the forefront of the NAACP's efforts at addressing lynching, fair housing, equal employment opportunity, and integration. When W. E. B. Du Bois left the NAACP in 1934, Wilkins became editor of *The Crisis,* the official magazine of the organization. He served in that role until 1949.

After White's death in 1955, Wilkins became executive secretary of the NAACP. By this time he was known to have an excellent reputation as an articulate advocate for civil rights. One of his first actions was to assist activists in Mississippi who were facing a credit squeeze by the racist White Citizens' Council. Dr. T. R. M. Howard, a physician and local race relations activist, was the head of the Regional Council of Negro Leadership in Mound Bayou, Mississippi. He proposed to Wilkins that black businesses and organizations should move their accounts to a black-owned bank. Wilkins backed the proposal. By the end of 1955, approximately $280,000 had been deposited in Tri-State Bank of Memphis, Tennessee. The bank then made loans to African Americans who had been turned down by white banks. The venture proved to be successful.

Wilkins's leadership coincided with the beginnings of the civil rights movement. One year after the organization's victory in the landmark 1954 Supreme Court case *Brown v. Board of Education,* Rosa Parks, a member and former secretary of the Montgomery, Alabama, branch of the NAACP, refused to yield her seat on a segregated bus to a white rider. As a result, a one-day boycott against the transit system was initiated. The boycott lasted a year and catapulted to fame Dr. Martin Luther King Jr. King, then pastor of the Dexter Avenue Baptist Church, spearheaded the Montgomery movement. Shortly after the Supreme Court ruled in *Gayle v. Browder* (1956) that segregation on city buses was unconstitutional, King founded the Southern Christian Leadership Conference (SCLC), an association of scores of black churches. This organization became a competitor to the NAACP, its membership consisting of groups of churchgoers, whereas NAACP membership was individual, reflecting the NAACP's legalist approach to racial issues. Wilkins had to contend with King's belief that change would occur mainly through direct community action. Wilkins continued to promote the NAACP's mission to fight segregation through legal challenges and legislation. However, he did work hand-in-hand with the SCLC on all major civil rights activities.

Wilkins participated in all the major events during the turbulent years of the 1960s. He helped to organize the 1963 March on Washington and appeared on the cover of *Time* magazine on August 30, 1963, just two days after the momentous march. He participated in the Selma to Montgomery march in 1965 and the March Against Fear in 1966. He led the NAACP in its efforts to secure support for and passage of the 1964 Civil Rights Act and the 1965 Voting Rights Act. In his role as executive director (the title changed from secretary to director in 1964), Wilkins was the individual who testified on behalf of the organization before Congress and consulted with presidents.

Wilkins not only directly consulted with all presidents from John F. Kennedy to Jimmy Carter but also had knowledge of the actions of presidents going back to Franklin Roosevelt. He analyzed the role that presidents played in responding to the NAACP's agenda. He felt that Roosevelt was overrated, pointing to the fact that the New Deal's social security program excluded farmers and domestics, the two areas of employment in which African Americans were most heavily represented. He gave more credit to Harry Truman, who, he felt, risked his reelection by throwing the full authority of the federal government behind a call for civil rights for all American citizens. Wilkins felt that Dwight Eisenhower was guilty of moral abdication in his tardy intervention in the Little Rock, Arkansas, Central High School desegregation case. Wilkins acknowledged that while John Kennedy improved the moral climate, he was evasive when it came to action. In his view, Lyndon Johnson was the most sincere and passionate advocate of civil rights. Richard Nixon was indifferent and set back the cause of civil rights, despite having introduced the concept of affirmative action.

As the civil rights movement gave way to the militancy of the Black Power movement, Wilkins was often criticized by black militants as leading an organization that was antiquated. Stokely Carmichael of the Student Nonviolent Coordinating Committee (SNCC) was especially critical of Wilkins and the NAACP. He and others saw Wilkins as a "knee-bowing supplicant" who was out of touch with the needs of the community. Wilkins saw the militants as young firebrands whose defiance in white America was "desperate lunacy." He continued to appeal to the conscience of America, stating that America was as much the land of African Americans as of any other group. He held that African Americans help build and defend the nation and had every right to participate in society on all levels. The NAACP under his leadership provided financial and legal support for community-action programs in urban areas that were sponsored by the very organizations that criticized his leadership.

In addition to his NAACP duties, Wilkins was an adviser to the War Department during World War II. He chaired the American delegation to the International Conference on Human Rights in Teheran and was president of the Leadership Conference on Civil Rights. For his work in civil rights Wilkins was awarded the Spingarn Medal by the NAACP in 1964, and he received the coveted Presidential Medal of Freedom in 1967 from President Johnson.

Wilkins retired from the NAACP at age seventy-six in 1977. He was succeeded by Benjamin Hooks. Wilkins died September 8, 1981, in New York. His autobiography, *Standing Fast: The Autobiography of Roy Wilkins*, was published posthumously in 1982. In 1986, on behalf of Congress, President Ronald Reagan presented his widow, Aminda Wilkins, the Congressional Gold Medal to commemorate Wilkins's contributions to the cause of human liberty. He was also the twenty-fourth African American honored with a commemorative stamp as part of the U.S. Postal Service's Black Heritage series. The stamp was unveiled January 24, 2001, in Minneapolis.

SEE ALSO *NAACP*.

BIBLIOGRAPHY

"The Awful Roar." 1963. *Time*. August 30. Available from http://www.time.com/time/magazine/article/0,9171,940696,00.html

Minnesota Historical Society. 2007. "Roy Wilkins." Available from www.mnhs.org/library/tips/history_topics/129wilkins.htm.

Reagan, Ronald. 1986. "Remarks at the Presentation Ceremony for the Congressional Gold Medal Honoring Roy Wilkins." Available from www.reagan.utexas.edu/archives/speeches/1986/11686d.htm.

Wilkins, Roy, and Tom Mathews. 1982. *Standing Fast: The Autobiography of Roy Wilkins*. New York: Viking.

Williams, Juan. 1987. *Eyes on the Prize: America's Civil Rights Years, 1954–1965*. New York: Viking Penguin.

Mamie E. Locke

WOMANISM

One of the most destructive manifestations of racism is the erasure of the cultures and experiences of people of color and the presumption that whiteness is dominant and normative. In the United States, the experiences of black people have been the particular targets of such erasures. In the aftermath of the civil rights movement, white women activists, including some who participated in the civil rights movement, sparked a feminist movement that challenged patriarchy and generated new modes of thinking about gender and women's experience. In the words of one black feminist critique, however, "all the women are white." Consistent with American racial hierarchies, white women's experiences provided the foundation for feminist thought; the problem of racism was presumed to be subsumed within the problem of patriarchy.

A NEW WORD FROM ALICE WALKER

The term *womanist* was created in 1981 by novelist, poet, essayist, critic, and feminist Alice Walker. The term provided the foundations for a theory of black women's history and experience that highlighted their significant roles in community and society. Heavily appropriated by black women scholars in religious studies, ethics, and theology, womanist became an important tool for approaching black women's perspectives and experiences from a standpoint that was self-defined and that resisted the cultural erasure that was and still is such a destructive component of American racism.

Critical of the ways in which white feminists used their own experiences to interpret black women's experiences, Walker first used the term in a review of Jean Humez's book, *Gifts of Power: The Writings of Rebecca Jackson, Black Visionary, Shaker Eldress*. Shakers built a religious movement that required its members to be celibate. On becoming a Shaker, Rebecca Cox Jackson left her husband and assumed a life of celibacy. Because Jackson traveled with a woman partner, similar to many black women missionaries and evangelists of the nineteenth and early twentieth centuries, Humez chose to call Jackson's lifestyle "lesbian."

Walker objected to Humez's imposition of a term that was not grounded in Jackson's definition of the situation. Walker questioned "a non-black scholar's attempt to label something lesbian that the black woman in question has not" (p. 81). Within the essay, Walker laid the foundations of her definition by rejecting a term for women's culture based on an island (Lesbos) and insisting that black women, regardless of how they were erotically bound, would choose a term "consistent with black cultural values" that "affirmed connectedness to the entire community and the world, rather than separation, *regardless* of who worked and slept with whom" (pp. 82–83).

A CONCEPT GROUNDED IN BLACK WOMEN'S EXPERIENCE

Humez's choice of labels was an example of the ways white feminists perpetuated an intellectual colonialism. This intellectual colonialism reflected the differences in power and privilege that characterized the relationships between black and white women. The term *womanist* was Walker's attempt to provide a word, a concept, and a way of thinking that allowed black women to name and label their own experiences. For Walker, the invention of the term was an act of empowerment and resistance, thus addressing and challenging the dehumanizing erasure that is a perpetual problem in a racist society.

In 1983, Walker provided an elaborate, dictionary-style definition of the term in her collection of essays, *In Search of Our Mothers' Gardens: Womanist Prose* (pp. xi–xii). This book of essays, which included her review of *Gifts of Power*, provided a more extensive view of her understandings of the experiences and history of black women as a distinctive dimension of human experience and a powerful cultural force. Her definition can be viewed as a philosophical overview of her work in novels, short stories, essays, and poetry.

First, Walker defines a "womanist" as a "black feminist or feminist of color." Clearly Walker includes the liberationist project of feminism in her definition. However, that liberationist project, as her definition goes on to demonstrate, should be grounded in the history and culture of the black women's experience.

Walker gives the term an etymology rooted in the African American folk term *womanish*, a term African American mothers often used to criticize their daughters' behavior. "Womanish" meant that girls were acting too old and engaging in behavior that could be sexually risky and invite attention that was harmful. Walker, however, subverts "womanish" and uses it to highlight the adult responsibilities that black girls often assumed in order to help their families and liberate their communities. Jackson lost her mother at age thirteen and helped raise her brothers and sisters along with one of her brother's children. As a civil rights worker in Mississippi Freedom Schools, Walker taught women whose childhoods ended early, limiting their educations. Walker also observed the participation of young people in civil rights demonstrations and was aware of the massive resistance of children in such places as Birmingham and Selma, Alabama. Walker describes the term "womanish" as an opposite of "girlish," subtly hinting that the pressures of accelerated development are facts of black female life not apprehended by white women's experiences. "Womanist" implied a desire to be "Responsible. In charge. *Serious*" (p. xi).

A womanist, according to Walker, loves other women and prefers women's culture, a very antipatriarchal orientation. However, womanists evince a commitment "to survival and wholeness of entire people, male *and* female." A womanist is "not a separatist, except periodically, for health" and, as a "universalist," she transcends sources of division, especially those dictated by color and class (p. xi). Walker subverts the antagonisms of class and color, often overemphasized by black nationalists, as differences among family members. A womanist also evinces a determination to act authoritatively on behalf of her community. Walker evokes very specific black women role models such as Mary Church Terrell, a clubwoman whose politics transcended color and class, and Harriet Tubman, famous for her exploits on the Underground Railroad and Civil War battlefields.

Finally, Walker offers a description of black women's culture that is at odds with some major emphases in white culture. Walker's key word is "love," and she links it to spirituality, creative expression, and political activism. Her definition includes a love of "food and roundness" that stands in stark contrast to the body images and gender norms of the dominant culture, a culture that celebrates pathologically thin white women and socially produces eating disorders. Walker emphasizes self-love, "Loves herself, *regardless*," a direct challenge to the self-hatred that is a consequence of racism (p. xi).

FROM WOMANIST TO WOMANISM

Although *womanist* has not displaced the terms *feminist* and *feminism*, the womanist idea resonated with many black women as a grounded and culturally specific tool to analyze black women's experiences in community and society. Walker's idea was particularly useful for black women in religious studies and theology, where the confrontation between black and white theologies, in the context of liberation theologies, was particularly vibrant and direct. In normative disciplines such as ethics, theology, and biblical studies, the idealism and values in Walker's idea were especially helpful. Katie Geneva Cannon, author of *Black Womanist Ethics* (1988), Jacqueline Grant, author of *White Women's Christ and Black Women's Jesus: Feminist Christology and Womanist Response* (1989), and Renita Weems, author of *Just a Sister Away: A Womanist Vision of Women's Relationships in the Bible* (1988), utilized Walker's perspective to explore the relationship of African American women's experiences to the construction of ethics, to theological and christological ideas, and to the meaning and importance of biblical stories about women. Their work laid a foundation for an explosion of womanist analysis in religious studies and elsewhere.

Scholars using womanist analysis challenged not only black male theologians to expand their analysis of gender but also pushed white female theologians to expand their analysis of race. Walker's idea also inspired other culturally specific forms of analysis such as "Mujerista theology" among Latina theologians. In a "roundtable" among feminist scholars in 1989, Cheryl Sanders questioned the usefulness of Walker's idea, because she gave "scant attention to the sacred." The points and counterpoints in that roundtable emphasized the wide-ranging invitation to analysis and criticism contained in Walker's idea.

Although bell hooks in *Talking Back: Thinking Feminist, Thinking Black* (1989) suggested that some women use the term "womanist" to avoid asserting they are "feminist," the issue is more complex. For many black women who were self-identified as feminists, the emphases of late-twentieth-century white feminists did not match their own concerns and experiences. Feminist ethicist Barbara Andolsen offered an analysis of racism in the feminist movement. In *Daughters of Jefferson, Daughters of Bootblacks: Racism in American Feminism* (1986), she pointed to areas of disagreement between black women who identified specifically as black feminists and white feminists. She identified work, rape, beauty, and gender separatism as sources of conflict between black and white feminists. Walker's definition of *womanist* and her larger body of writings directly engage all of these issues.

Although Walker did not indicate a desire to create a womanist movement, the term *womanism* was a natural extension of *womanist*. Walker's writings and ideas, however, emphasized black women's creativity, enterprise, and community commitment, and "womanist" links these specifically to feminism. Womanism is identified as both the activism consistent with the ideals embedded in Walker's definition and the womanist scholarly traditions that have grown up in various disciplines, especially religious studies. "Womanism is," as Stacey Floyd Thomas (2006) points out, "revolutionary. Womanism is a paradigm shift wherein Black women no longer look to others for their liberation" (p. 1).

SEE ALSO *African Diaspora; Black Consciousness; Black Feminism in Brazil; Black Feminism in the United Kingdom; Black Feminism in the United States; Feminism and Race; Pan-Africanism.*

BIBLIOGRAPHY

Andolsen, Barbara Hilkert. 1986. *"Daughters of Jefferson, Daughters of Bootblacks": Racism and American Feminism.* Macon, GA: Mercer University Press.

Cannon, Katie Geneva. 1988. *Black Womanist Ethics.* Atlanta, GA: Scholars Press.

Floyd-Thomas, Stacey, ed. 2006. *Deeper Shades of Purple: Womanism in Religion and Society.* New York: New York University Press.

Grant, Jacquelyn. 1989. *White Women's Christ and Black Women's Jesus: Feminist Christology and Womanist Response.* Atlanta, GA: Scholars Press.

hooks, bell. 1989. *Talking Back: Thinking Feminist, Thinking Black.* Boston: South End Press.

Mitchem, Stephanie. 2002. *Introducing Womanist Theology.* Maryknoll, NY: Orbis Books.

Sanders, Cheryl. 1989. "Roundtable Discussion: Christian Ethics and Theology in Womanist Perspective." *Journal of Feminist Studies in Religion* 5 (2): 83–112.

Walker, Alice. 1983. *In Search of Our Mothers' Gardens: Womanist Prose.* San Diego, CA: Harcourt Brace Jovanovich.

Weems, Renita J. 1988. *Just a Sister Away: A Womanist Vision of Women's Relationships in the Bible.* San Diego, CA: LuraMedia.

Cheryl Townsend Gilkes

WOODSON, CARTER G.

SEE *Association for the Study of Negro Life and History.*

WORKFARE AND WELFARE

Workfare in its narrowest definition is mandatory "work for benefits"—for government cash and services. In its strongest and broadest applications it is part of a larger array of means-tested benefits that are prominent in the Anglo-American democracies but most developed in the United States. The American welfare system consists of inadequate benefits and income for poor families, significant inequities in the flow of cash and services, heavy reliance on means testing, and extensive monitoring for welfare fraud, which inspires an expensive, time-consuming apparatus of investigation and surveillance—a bewildering array of programs and agencies that recipients must negotiate when they need help. Although much exaggerated, some work disincentives are part of the welfare system, especially America's unique avoidance of national health insurance (welfare recipients who receive Medicaid targeted to the poor eventually lose coverage if they go to work). Added to inadequacy, inequity, punitiveness, and inefficiency is an unfortunate lack of fiscal and policy control. All this constitutes a welfare mess that makes the nonworking, nonaged, nondisabled poor highly visible and unpopular, easy targets for scapegoating (Wilensky 2002, ch. 10). The mobilization of fear and resentment, in turn, provokes mass backlash against "welfare" and recurrent attempts to reform public assistance under such tough-sounding slogans as "workfare" and "end welfare as we know it." It also blocks the formation of a stable congressional coalition to fund the alternative policies most rich democracies have adopted, especially family policies and active labor-market policies.

For several centuries of modernization every generation has discovered its own undeserving poor or "dangerous classes." Modern debates about the causes of poverty—personal moral failure or lack of opportunity—are as old as the English Poor Laws of the sixteenth century. The welfare reform bill of 1996 ("Temporary Assistance for Needy Families") is merely one more episode in a long cycle of crackdowns on the poor followed by reforms to ease up a bit. Even the harshest of them all, the British Poor Law of 1834, was quickly followed by strong criticism. The critics noted that it did not distinguish between the non-working poor who receive poor relief and the more deserving poor who did not; or that it undermined incentives to obey the work ethic; or that it lumped together the worthy and unworthy in a miserable poorhouse, where criminals, alcoholics, women, mothers, children, infants, the aged, and the sick were jammed together and where brutality and corruption were common. Serving later as Conservative prime minister from 1874 to 1880, Benjamin Disraeli complained that the Poor Law Reform Bill of 1834 made it "a crime to be poor"—an idea echoed by today's liberals who are repelled by the "conservative" urge to punish the poor for their poverty. The principles of Elizabethan poor law—direct aid for the unemployed, work (or the workhouse or almshouse, or prison) for the able bodied, and local administration that would keep welfare benefits below the lowest wage and thus provide incentives to work—persist to this day in the United States (Handler 1995, pp. 12 ff.).

This never-ending cycle is most prominent in the Anglo-American democracies, which rely most heavily on means-tested benefits targeted to the poor (Wilensky 2002, Table 8.3). The cycle occurs around a long-term upward trend toward more cash and services for the poor as modern democracies became quite rich, but there is no doubt that since the mid-1990s the United States has been in a phase of getting tough on welfare. The welfare reforms of 1996 and 2006, accenting workfare, are the latest expression of that mood.

In the intensity of political fuss about it, the welfare mess is peculiarly American, but in its broad outlines it is shared by several other countries that rely heavily on means-tested programs and have high rates of poverty (United Kingdom, Canada, Ireland, and Switzerland). The American welfare mess is perpetuated first by politicians who use welfare mothers (in the public image they are racial minorities) as convenient scapegoats who are somehow responsible for problems of racial conflict, crime, family breakup, illegitimacy, budget deficits, and moral rot; and second, by the limited political capacity to reduce poverty by other more universal means—by education, active labor-market and family policies, and fiscal policy. It will last as long as the United States maintains a high rate of poverty and inequality and succumbs to polarized politics in government.

For decades workfare advocates have marketed a misleading stereotype of an epidemic of teenage sexuality, pregnancy, and parenthood—a picture of very young, black, never-married mothers, living in an inner-city ghetto, who are permanently welfare dependent and receive generous benefits, an incentive to have many children who will perpetuate welfare dependency across generations. This picture has been widely circulated in a spate of books sponsored by neoconservative think tanks (e.g., Charles Murray's 1984 *Losing Ground*). Research, however, has shown that welfare benefits in the United States are anything but generous; on average they have eroded while eligibility rules tightened. Neither the level nor the trend of welfare benefits has any relation to fertility rates. In fact, in size and fertility trend welfare families are like nonwelfare families. In attitudes, welfare mothers embrace the work ethic as much as the nonwelfare population. The welfare population is heterogeneous in race and ethnicity, physical and mental health, and the number and age of children. About half of welfare mothers are white, about a third are black, a fifth Hispanic.

Very few are teenagers, though most are young. Poor single mothers with enormous deficits in human capital are over-represented among welfare recipients. What welfare parents frequently pass on to their children is not welfare status but poverty and all its pathologies.

DOES WORKFARE WORK?

Because work-for-benefits—the core of 1996 welfare reform—has a long history and in one form or another has been evaluated systematically since the late 1970s (e.g., Friedlander and Gueron 1992, Table 4.1), it is possible to summarize what has become a consensus of the experts. By the single criterion of cutting the rolls, workfare with strong sanctions—certain time limits for all welfare benefits if work is not obtained—can be effective. For instance, if the sole concern is removing people from the rolls under a deadline, considerable success can be achieved with a week or two of orientation, followed by sanctions if any job at all is refused. A credible threat to cut off welfare will also encourage a substantial percentage of welfare recipients who already work off the books to disappear from the rolls. If at the same time the country is blessed with an economy that is booming (as it was in the 1993–1999 period), the result is a fine cost/benefit ratio for such tough workfare rules—so long as one does not follow the people who have moved from welfare to work too long or worry about how much they earn. But if the aim is to prepare the typical welfare family (a mother with young children, little education, little job experience, and other handicaps) for stable employment in the real world of work and not merely perpetuate the longstanding pattern of alternating or simultaneous low-wage temporary work and welfare, policy-makers must get serious about expensive education and training, placement, wage subsidies, job creation, counseling, child care, housing, transportation, rehabilitation of those on drugs or alcohol or who are mentally ill, and more.

Some of the most sophisticated evaluation research ever done has been focused on these programs. Using a variety of methods and research designs, mostly social experiments where a group exposed to a particular workfare program is compared to a randomly selected control group, an army of researchers has descended upon these welfare clients to assess outcomes. (See especially the reports, summaries, and critical assessments by the Manpower Demonstration Research Corporation and academic researchers: Gueron and Pauly 1991; Handler and Hasenfeld 1991, chapter 5; Burghardt et al. 1992; Friedlander and Gueron 1992; Greenberg and Wiseman 1992; Bane and Ellwood 1994; Riccio, Friedlander, and Freedman 1994; Friedlander and Burtless 1995; *Cong. Rec.* 1995; Nightingale, Smith, and Haveman 1995; Harris 1996; Besharov, Germanis, and Rossi, 1997; Miller et al. 1997; Blank 2006; and Jencks 2005.)

Here is a brief summary of findings on which almost all researchers agree:

1. In implementing work-focused mandates, states show substantial variation in their degree and kind of success.
2. If researchers compare welfare recipients who are subjected to (varied) welfare-to-work mandates with control groups who are not and measure the respective earnings gains over anywhere from a few months to five years, the workfare programs on average do show modest relative earnings gains for the workfare participants.
3. Obviously, different program packages have different outcomes. Especially effective in decreasing welfare spending are short-term measures. Job clubs, a week or two of charm school (how to dress, how to show deference and enthusiasm in an interview, etc.), and a little help in job search can move many people into jobs quickly (on average raising the percentage of people who find a job by a modest five percentage points); it can also save taxpayers money. But such quick solutions do not improve job quality and job stability, nor succeed with the more disadvantaged. In varying amounts, some workfare programs add more expensive skills training, basic education, counseling, job creation, and other work supports. These appear to produce better jobs for some people and probably make a greater long-term difference in earnings. Workfare does not work on the cheap.
4. The population targeted by welfare-to-work programs has many unfavorable characteristics for steady long-term employment. Nationally and for the past twenty-five years of study, most who get jobs do not keep them. There are four major sources of this instability: (1) The job pays close to the minimum wage—and the former or current welfare recipient cannot support a family on it. (2) Jobs are dead end because most welfare recipients lack education, basic literacy and numeracy, and skills necessary for moving up. Gary Burtless (1995, pp. 77–78) found that among twenty-five-year-old respondents to the National Longitudinal Survey of Youth who had received welfare in all of the previous twelve months, 72 percent scored in the bottom quarter of the Armed Forces Qualification Test. Judith Gueron (1995, p. 5) notes that a survey of people who were targeted for the JOBS program "shows that between a quarter and half lacked prior work experience, at least a third had extremely low literacy skills, and more than a quarter said they could not participate ... because they or their child had a health or emotional problem." The survey excludes AFDC recipients who were not currently subject to the

New York Workfare Program, 1995. *New York has the largest workfare program in the United States. Instead of a paycheck workers receive welfare benefits.* AP IMAGES.

JOBS work mandate because of still worse handicaps. (3) There are well-known disincentives built into the system—the welfare recipients typically lose Medicaid and related benefits when they leave welfare, and their low-wage, high-turnover jobs seldom provide any or adequate benefits. (4) Labor markets turn down in an industry, area, or national slump. Workfare programs do almost nothing about (1), (2), and (4), and the resources are seldom available to do much about (3)—anything beyond limited assistance for child care and health care for a transition period only. Researchers agree that a substantial portion of the welfare population is simply unemployable without very expensive, long-term help, if then.

If one examines the characteristics of the minority who exit from welfare, stay off welfare, and hold stable jobs for as long as a few years, one can see why it is so hard to break the revolving-door pattern of welfare dependency. In these successful cases, the best evidence shows an interaction of education, marriage opportunity and stability, and stability of employment (Harris 1996; Wilson 1996; Jencks 2005; and Duncan, Huston, and Weisner 2007). Even a modest amount of education improves the welfare mother's chances of securing stable work. Both education and work increase her chances of marrying or cohabiting with a partner who works. Education and partnering to a stable worker, in turn, improve the mother's chances to stay off welfare, gain additional education, and maintain employment. The combined income and mutual help under these unfortunately rare circumstances often moves the family above the poverty line. Such transitions from welfare to relatively stable work are rare because only a small minority of welfare recipients combine the necessary education, job opportunity, and the opportunity to marry a working partner (Harris 1996, pp. 420–423).

5. The final conclusion from the workfare evaluations is that staffing is weak for the purpose of training, job development, placement, and work support. At the root of the problems is America's lack of an active labor-market policy—for example, training and rehabilitation, placement, counseling, work-study programs, mobility incentives, wage subsidies, and job creation (Wilensky 2002, pp. 100–108, 706–707).

Almost all welfare-to-work programs in the past twenty-five years have had conflicting goals. It is misleading to declare victory when the welfare rolls have declined. Consider these obvious conflicts: The number of families on welfare can be reduced at the same time that total welfare costs increase if the reduction is achieved by providing the necessary apparatus of support. Both the costs and the rolls can be decreased by further impoverishing poor children and their parents while increasing the long-run costs of foster care, homelessness, malnutrition, family violence, crime, the criminal-justice system, and prisons (see Wilensky 2002, ch. 14, for evidence of these connections). Some women who have competitive advantages can be forced to take minimum-wage jobs without the necessary support and thereby increase child neglect. In short, the goals of reducing the rolls and cost cutting, dominant in "welfare reform" since the mid-1990s, conflict with the goals of reducing child poverty, moving welfare recipients into stable jobs with above-poverty earnings and prospects for advancement, and improving the economic base for stable family life and even marriage.

THE POLITICS OF MEANS-TESTED POLICIES

What explains the limited funding and impact of workfare is the politics of American "welfare" in particular and of means-tested programs in general. For understanding national differences in poverty reduction and the politics of the welfare state, Wilensky has found that a gross distinction between complex, most-visible means tests and simple, least-visible income tests is most useful. Means testing refers to (1) noncategorical benefits targeted to the poor via a stiff income and/or assets test; (2) applied by welfare administrators with substantial discretion; (3) with a high probability of stigma. "Income-testing" is the opposite. It is categorical as a social right with copayments graded by income bracket and, because it is private and invisible, has no stigma.

Means testing is characteristic of the United States, Britain, and other fragmented and decentralized democracies (Canada, Ireland, Switzerland). In contrast are most "corporatist" democracies of continental Europe with more centralized, consensual bargaining arrangements among government, labor, management, and strong political parties, especially those with cumulative labor-left power. They avoid overreliance on means tests and instead accent universalistic social policies and simpler income tests. They implement the two policy packages that are most effective in avoiding the welfare mess—family policies and active labor-market policies targeted to everyone. They have long maintained high standards for primary and secondary schools and have paid attention to the connections between education, work, low-income housing, transportation, and other infrastructure problems. They all have national health insurance. Almost all have family policies that help all working parents to balance the demands of the labor market and parenting (e.g., child care, including universal preschool and day-care centers, before- and after-school leisure centers; short workdays for parents, parental leave, home help or long-term care for the frail elderly, pensions with flexible retirement). In other words, these countries have recognized that the long list of measures needed to move people from welfare out of poverty, and, where possible, to work, is the same as the list of policies needed to improve the lives of the nonwelfare population—the working poor and the celebrated "middle class." The benevolent side-effect of universal social policies has been to prevent the political mobilization of the middle class white voters with high school or part-college education against the poor (see Wilensky 2002, pp. 375–378).

The alternative, aggressively pursued by the United States, is to accent stiff means tests for scores of separate, uncoordinated programs; to develop a large, expensive, intrusive apparatus of surveillance and harassment of the poor; and to make the welfare poor dramatically visible, the target of mass resentment and political scapegoating, and thereby make certain that funding for welfare reform will be meager and the maze of programs, ineffective.

NATIVISM AND TAX-WELFARE BACKLASH

In a systematic study of tax revolts in nineteen rich democracies, it proved impossible to separate antitax, anti–social spending, antibureaucratic protest movements and parties from nativist, xenophobic, or racist protests; these two themes appear together in all the high-scoring countries (Wilensky 2002, pp. 373–378). When Hollywood actor Ronald Reagan swept California in the 1966 gubernatorial election, he sounded not only the familiar antitax, anti–social spending, antibureaucratic themes but at the same time baited welfare mothers. He brought the house down when he asserted that welfare recipients are on a "prepaid lifetime vacation plan." (A careful survey experiment shows that voters hear these as code words for black welfare poor; see Gilens 1996.) In 1970, after four years in office, Governor Reagan ran and won on the same slogans: "We are fighting the big-spending politicians who advocate a welfare state, the welfare bureaucrats whose jobs depend on expanding the welfare system, and the cadres of professional poor who have adopted welfare as a way of life" (*The Wall Street Journal*, October 9, 1970). As president, Reagan repeatedly referred to mythical "welfare queens" as symbols of welfare fraud and abuse. That movement culminated in eight years of the Reagan presidency and ultimately a Republican takeover of Congress in 1994 with identical campaign themes—antitax, antispend, antibureaucracy combined with the complaint that immigrants and other poor racial and linguistic minorities were creating immense burdens of welfare and crime. Populist right politicians in the United States and abroad have sounded these themes for decades.

SUMMARY AND CONCLUSION

The history of welfare reform in the United States since the 1960s is one of increasingly tough talk about the evils of welfare dependency or the need to "make the tough decisions" to save money combined with strident demands that states and localities put huge numbers of welfare recipients to work. The reform of 1996 cut the rolls in half by 2000. But it was not typically accompanied by the upfront money and staff to make work mandates even modestly effective in improving the lives of welfare mothers and their children. Only in a few states or urban areas with booming economies that have greatly increased spending and support services are there hints of success in both reducing poverty and expanding job opportunity for welfare recipients.

Neither welfare nor workfare can be done on the cheap. The outcome of "welfare-to-workfare" policies for those who entered the programs since 1996 is typically a move from welfare poverty to unstable working poverty. The politics of welfare reform continues to block adequate funding of support services for both workfare and welfare, although workfare has for a time reduced grand-scale scapegoating of racial minorities in congressional debate.

This article is based, in part, on Wilensky, 2002, chapters 8, 10, 14, and 18.

SEE ALSO *Education, Racial Disparities; Labor Market; Nativism; Social Welfare States; Underemployment.*

BIBLIOGRAPHY

Bane, Mary Jo, and David Ellwood. 1994. *Welfare Realities: From Rhetoric to Reform*. Cambridge, MA: Harvard University Press.

Besharov, Douglas J., Peter Germanis, and Peter H. Rossi. 1997. *Evaluating Welfare Reform: A Guide for Scholars and Practitioners*. College Park, MD: School of Public Affairs, University of Maryland.

Blank, Rebecca M. 2006. "What Did the 1990s Welfare Reform Accomplish?" In *Poverty, the Distribution of Income and Public Policy*, edited by Alan J. Auerbach, David Card, and John M. Quigley. New York: Russell Sage Foundation.

Burghardt, John, Anu Rangarajan, Anne Gordon, and Ellen Kisker. 1992. *Evaluation of the Minority Female Single Parent Demonstration*. Summary Report. Vol. 1. Princeton, NJ: Mathematica Policy Research.

Burtless, Gary. 1995. "Employment Prospects of Welfare Recipients." In *The Work Alternative: Welfare Reform and the Realities of the Job Market*, edited by Demetra Smith Nightingale and Robert H. Haveman, 71–106. Washington DC: Urban Institute Press.

Duncan, Greg J., Aletha C. Huston, and Thomas S. Weisner. 2007. *Higher Ground: New Hope for the Working Poor and Their Children*. New York: Russell Sage Foundation.

Friedlander, Daniel, and Gary Burtless. 1995. *Five Years After: The Long-Term Effects of Welfare-to-Work Programs*. New York: Russell Sage Foundation.

Friedlander, Daniel, and Judith M. Gueron. 1992. "Are High-Cost Services More Effective than Low-Cost Services?" In *Evaluating Welfare and Training Programs*, edited by Charles F. Manski and Irwin Garfinkel, 143–198. Cambridge, MA: Harvard University Press.

Gilens, Martin. 1996. "'Race Coding' and White Opposition to Welfare." *American Political Science Review* 90 (3): 593–604.

Greenberg David, and Michael Wiseman. 1992. *What Did the Work-Welfare Demonstrations Do?* Discussion Paper #969-92. Institute for Research on Poverty, University of Wisconsin–Madison.

Gueron, Judith M., and Edward Pauly. 1991. *From Welfare to Work*. New York: Russell Sage Foundation.

Handler, Joel F. 1995. *The Poverty of Welfare Reform*. New Haven, CT: Yale University Press.

———, and Yeheskel Hasenfeld. 1991. *The Moral Construction of Poverty: Welfare Reform in America*. Newbury Park, CA: Sage.

Harris, Kathleen Mullan. 1996. "Life After Welfare: Women, Work, and Repeat Dependency." *American Sociological Review* 61 (3): 407–426.

Jencks, Christopher. 2005. "What Happened to Welfare?" *New York Review of Books* December 15: 76–81, 86.

Miller, Cynthia, Virginia Knox, Patricia Auspos, et al. 1997. *Making Welfare Work and Work Pay: Implementation and 18-Month Impacts of the Minnesota Family Investment Program*. Manpower Demonstration Research Corporation, State of Minnesota, Department of Human Services.

Murray, Charles A. 1984. *Losing Ground: American Social Policy, 1950–1980*. New York: Basic Books.

Nightingale, Demetra Smith, and Robert H. Haveman, eds. 1995. *The Work Alternative: Welfare Reform and the Realities of the Job Market*. Washington, DC: Urban Institute.

Riccio, James, Daniel Friedlander, and Stephen Freedman. 1994. *GAIN: Benefits, Costs, and Three-Year Impacts of a Welfare-to-Work Program: California's Greater Avenues for Independence Program*. New York: Manpower Demonstration Research Corporation.

Testimony of Judith M. Gueron, president, Manpower Demonstration Research Corporation, before the U.S. Senate Committee on Finance. *Congressional Record*, 104th Cong., 1st sess., March 20. Washington, DC: U.S. Government Printing Office, 1995.

Wilensky, Harold L. 2002. *Rich Democracies: Political Economy, Public Policy, and Performance*. Berkeley: University of California Press.

Wilson, William J. 1996. *When Work Disappears: The World of the New Urban Poor*. New York: Knopf.

Harold L. Wilensky

Z

ZAPATISTA REBELLION

The Zapatista rebellion began on January 1, 1994, in the southern state of Chiapas, Mexico. Considered by many to be the first postmodern revolution, the Zapatista movement is a powerful example of the response capacity of indigenous peoples to racism and colonialist *indigenismo* in an era of neoliberalism and globalization. It is more than coincidence that the same day that the North American Free Trade Agreement (NAFTA) took effect between the United States of America, Canada, and Mexico, the Zapatista Army for National Liberation (*Ejército Zapatista de Liberación Nacional,* or EZLN) emerged on the national political scene with the shout "*Ya Basta!*" (Enough!). This cry served as a reminder that Mexico would not enter into the First World through NAFTA, as the Mexican government proposed, without first paying its historical debt to the indigenous peoples of the nation.

The answer of the Mexican state to the conflict that soon raged in Chiapas was a program of genocide against the EZLN, their communities, and their supporters, as well as the instigation of a low-intensity war in the Mexican indigenous regions, located mainly in the states of Guerrero, Oaxaca, Tabasco, and Chiapas. The main obstacle to solving the conflict in Chiapas has been the lack of commitment on the part of the Mexican State and the major Mexican political parties to accept the multiculturalism of Mexico. This has been evident in their reticence to implement the San Andrés Accords, a set of agreements signed by the EZLN and the federal government in 1996.

In 2001 the Mexican Congress enacted constitutional reforms addressing indigenous rights and culture. But because these reforms did not directly address issues important to the indigenous groups, such as autonomy and free determination, the indigenous peoples as subjects of public right, lands and territories, the use and enjoyment of natural resources, the election of municipal authorities and the right to regional association, they have been indicted by the EZLN as treason and a mockery of previous agreements. In 2005, in the Sixth Declaration of the Lacandon Jungle, the EZLN announced that it would begin a new stage in the history of the indigenous movement, in which a permanent dialogue with Mexican civil society would be sought.

THE ROOTS OF THE REBELLION

The Zapatista rebellion must be framed historically within the long and complex process of cultural resistance of the Mayan peoples, beginning with the European invasion in the sixteenth century. The deep causes of the rebellion are multiple and complex, but their deep roots undoubtedly lie in a long history of colonialism, social exclusion, and ethnic and racial discrimination.

Nevertheless, the postmodern conflict in Chiapas is closely related to the neoliberalism adopted by Mexico in the early 1980s, which brought about a social crisis and aggravated the difficult living conditions of the indigenous peoples in Mexico. The implemented neoliberal policies bet the Mexican future on an ambitious modernization project that included the thinning of the state, with minimal state intervention, a free market, and commercial openings through the signing of NAFTA. Nevertheless, the neoliberal policies applied by the government of Carlos Salinas de Gortari (1988–1994) did not include the

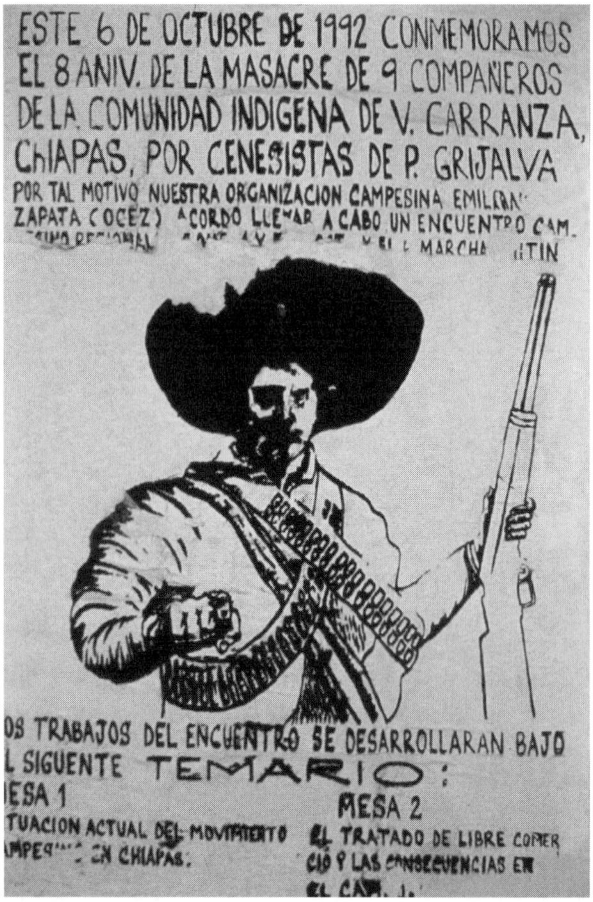

Zapatista Poster, 1992. *The causes of the Zapatista Rebellion are rooted in a long and complex process of cultural resistance of the Mayan peoples, beginning with the European invasion in the sixteenth century.* KARIM DAHER. LIASON AGENCY.

indigenous peoples of Mexico in this modernization. This ontological blindness showed the homogenizing and exclusionary face of Mexico, and it constituted a serious mistake that had enormous political, economic, and social costs for Mexican society as a whole.

The Zapatista rebellion displayed the country's amnesia about indigenous peoples, the flaws of the neoliberal modernization project, and the weaknesses of the Mexican financial system. The Mexican stock market's dependency on offshoring (the relocation of business processes from one country to another) and foreign financial investments was revealed, and the resultant political instability migrated to other countries, causing the Mexican peso crisis and the loss of confidence of foreign investors in a number of Central and South American countries (this spread of capital flight to other nations has been dubbed the "tequila effect").

Among the causes of the Zapatista rebellion, several specialists have pointed to the drop in coffee prices in 1989, the dismissal of public policies in education, health and food, the weakness of the benefactor state (Mexico), and the signing of NAFTA in 1993. The EZLN was founded on November 17, 1983, in the Lacandon jungle of Chiapas, by older militants of various political organizations in Mexico. It was the fidelity of the EZLN to the revolutionary political ideology of the legendary Emiliano Zapata, the *campesino* leader during the Mexican Revolution (1910–1920), that led the group to anoint themselves the "Zapatistas." But the Spanish writer Manuel Vázquez Montalván points out that there was apparently little receptivity and support for the EZLN in the Mayan towns at first.

THE "ENCOUNTER BETWEEN TWO WORLDS"

In 1992 the International Union for the Scientific Study of Population (IUSSP) sponsored a Conference on the Peopling of Americas in Veracruz, Mexico. Prior to this inquiry into the "Encounter between Two Worlds," the Mexican government considered it prudent to implement constitutional amendments with the implicit purpose of addressing the challenge of the Mexican indigenous movement. In 1991, President Salinas sent a legal initiative to the Mexican Congress, asking them to make an addition to Article 4 of the Political Constitution of Mexico. This constitutional addition, approved by the Mexican Congress in July 1991, defines Mexican nation as pluricultural and declares that Mexican law system will protect and promote indigenous peoples and cultures. The addition to Article 4 was approved by the Mexican Congress in July 1991. The government of Mexico also ratified the International Labour Organization (ILO) Convention 169 concerning Indigenous and Tribal Peoples in Independent Countries, the foremost international instrument dealing specifically with the rights of indigenous peoples. ILO Convention 169 took effect in September 1991.

These constitutional reforms and agreements did not stop the impetus of the indigenous movement, which was well organized and united around the "Campaign for 500 Years of Indigenous, Afro-American, and Popular Resistance." This campaign was proposed in the "Bogota Declaration," during the continental encounter for peasants-indigenous organizations, an important meeting that took place in Bogota, Colombia in October 1989. The Mexican Council for 500 Years of Indigenous Resistance organized many demonstrations around the country. On October 12, 1992, in San Cristobal de las Casas, Chiapas, leaders of the indigenous organizations demolished the sculpture of Diego de Mazariegos, the Spanish conqueror of Chiapas, because they considered it to be an offense against the dignity of their peoples.

The indigenous movement also declared that the reforms to Article 4 of the constitution were limited to recognizing the existence of the indigenous peoples in Mexico, but that their ethnic rights were still unrecognized (Ruiz 1999). The indigenous leaders felt that their indigenous laws were in essence reduced to mere "uses and customs," that their religious practices were equated with "witchcraft and beliefs," and that their *ejidos* (communal lands) were being sold off or transferred away due to the agrarian reforms. With respect to ILO Convention 169, the indigenous organizations declared their support for the ratification, though they considered the convention very limited with respect to the indigenous people's demands. According to the indigenous organizations, ILO Convention 169 puts many "padlocks" on the recognition of their political status and on their autonomy claims within international law.

ZAPATISTA REBELLION

On May 27, 1993, the Mexican army, while conducting a routine military exercise in Chiapas Jungle found, by chance, *Las Calabazas*, a military advance post of the EZLN. The EZLN had built several military posts around Chiapas Jungle in strategic geographic localizations, far away from the mayor cities. These military posts stored food and guns, and operated a training camp. The government of Mexico hid this information from the public in order to avoid risking negotiations for the NAFTA agreement. Thus, the Mexican army and its military intelligence were being reinforced in Chiapas, while the government was obtaining information about the organization of the EZLN, which had been founded in 1983.

The quietly organized EZLN, composed mainly of young people from various indigenous groups, including the Tzotzil, Tzeltal, Chol, and Tojolabal, staged their first armed action at 5 a.m. on January 1, 1994. Several hundred Zapatistas, many armed only with useless "guns of wood" or machetes, took control of five municipalities in the state of Chiapas: San Cristóbal de las Casas, Altamirano, Ocosingo, Chana, and Las Margaritas. They released about 200 prisoners and took Absalon Castellanos, the former governor of Chiapas, as a hostage. They also demanded the resignation of officials of the federal and state government and that democratic elections be held. The spokesman for the rebels was a shadowy figure nicknamed Subcomandante Marcos (all of the members of the EZLN wore masks during their military actions). Since the actions of 1992, Marcos has published numerous articles and books outlining his views.

The demands of the Zapatistas were outlined in the First Declaration of the Lacandon Jungle. Not only did

Subcomandante Marcos, leader of the Zapatista Army for National Liberation (Ejército Zapatista de Liberación Nacional, or EZLN), 2006. *Overall, nearly 20,000 indigenous people have been displaced by the conflict in Chiapas.* AP IMAGES.

they ask for indigenous peoples' rights to be respected, they also enumerated several demands regarding work, land, housing, food, health, education, independence, freedom, democracy, justice and peace (Collier 1999, p. 156). The Mexican government, in response to what they considered a conflict originated by a "group of 200 insurgents led by foreign professionals," launched a military campaign that lasted twelve days, during which the Mexican army recovered control of the city of San Cristobal de Las Casas and the rest of the municipalities. The fighting was fierce, however. In Ocosingo, the Mexican army killed hundreds of unarmed Zapatistas and civilians. The newspaper *La Jornada* denounced the discovery of five Zapatistas who had been murdered with their hands tied, the "disappearance" of communitarian leaders, and several attacks on journalists and members of the International Red Cross, all in violation of international law.

The Mexican army, in the subsequent months, increased their armed forces in the area to more than 17,000 soldiers, in order to encircle the region of the Lacandon jungle. The events in Chiapas grabbed attention in the national news, and many were surprised to learn that Chiapas had the worst Human Development Index in Mexico, despite producing 35 percent of the electrical energy of the country, possessing large fuel deposits, and providing the national market with precious wood, meat, coffee, flowers, fruits, vegetables, and other products. In general, Chiapas was one of the richest Mexican states in natural resources, but its people were among the poorest.

A LOW-INTENSITY CONFLICT

On January 16, 1994, just when the Zapatistas had diffused themselves into the Lacandon jungle, the Mexican government announced a general amnesty and cease-fire. President Salinas named Manuel Camacho Solis as the Commissioner for Peace and Reconciliation. The first peace dialogues took place in the Catholic diocese of San Cristóbal de las Casas, and Bishop Samuel Ruiz became a fundamental figure in this process because of the enormous respect he enjoyed as an advocate for indigenous rights. As a good-will gesture, the EZLN, with the intermediation of the International Red Cross, released Absalón Castellanos on February 17, 1994. The government released several Zapatistas in return.

The EZLN released the Second Declaration of the Lacandon Jungle on June 10, 1994. In this declaration they informed the people about the worsening of the conflict in Chiapas and called Mexicans "to a civic and peaceful effort. This was the National Democratic Convention, which was to achieve the profound changes that the nation demanded." The EZLN emphasized that its movement members were Mexicans and not aliens, and in its demonstrations they displayed the Mexican flag with pride and sang the national anthem.

On December 1, 1994, Ernesto Zedillo Ponce de León, a leader of the Institutional Revolutionary Party (PRI), became president of Mexico. The dialog between EZLN and the Mexican government with Bishop Ruiz as a negotiator was broken in July, when the EZLN rejected the government proposals. The new government launched a new military campaign in Chiapas and increased its military forces in the region. However, on December 19, 1994, the EZLN broke the military encirclement of thirty-eight independent municipalities. The new government then initiated a mass media campaign, declaring that the Zapatistas were terrorists. In addition, orders were given for the apprehension of Rafael Sebatián Guillén Vicente, who was believed to be subcommander Marcos.

The counterinsurgency effort now took the form of a permanent low-intensity conflict. Six paramilitary groups were created to help the Mexican army search for the insurgents' infrastructure and divide the EZLN from the indigenous communities. These paramilitary groups were located in strategic areas of the military encirclement, and their members were affiliated with the PRI and the Cardenista Front for the National Reconstruction (FCRN).

THE SAN ANDRÉS ACCORDS

At the beginning of 1995, the EZLN released the Third Declaration of the Lacandon Jungle, which summoned Mexican society to form a national liberation movement and "to install a transitional government, a new constitutional body, a new constitution, and the destruction of the system of the Party-State."

In March, the Mexican Congress approved the Law for the Dialogue, Reconciliation and Peace with Dignity in Chiapas. A cease-fire was ordered, as well as an end to military hostilities against the EZLN. Negotiations were then initiated, centered on indigenous rights and culture, democracy and justice, welfare and development, and women's rights. The meetings took place in the Municipality of San Andrés Larraínzar with the Commission for Agreement and Pacification of the Mexican Congress (COCOPA) and the National Mediation Intermediation Commission (CONAI) acting as intermediaries. The first meetings finished in September 1996. The EZLN then called for an international and national referendum, in which more than a million people participated. These developments led to the signing of the San Andrés Accords on February 16, 1996. These accords laid the groundwork for further negotiations on indigenous rights, conservation of natural resources on Native territories, political participation, and the autonomy of the indigenous communities. However, in September 1996, due to the lack of movement on these issues by the governmental delegation, the EZLN left the negotiations.

The Zapatistas, in an effort to pressure the government, organized the *Zapatour*, in which thousands of Zapatistas traveled from Chiapas to Mexico City. The purpose was to inform Mexican civil society and the international public of the human rights violations in Chiapas and the manipulation of media information. In February 2001, twenty-four ski-masked Zapatista leaders, including Subcomandante Marcos, left Chiapas, followed by a caravan of supporters. They arrived in Mexico City fifteen days later and were greeted by throngs of supporters.

The EZLN also organized the First Intercontinental Encounter for Humanity and Against Neo-liberalism, which took place in Chiapas in July 1996. Indigenous organization leaders from five continents were present, as well as diverse intellectuals, politicians, and civil society members.

In the Fourth Declaration of the Lacandon Jungle, released on January 1, 1996, the EZLN announced the creation of the Zapatista Front of National Liberation (FZLN) as their political organization. On December 22, 1997, a massacre was committed in Acteal, Chiapas, by PRI members and cardenistas. As reported by the Peace Brigades International and SIPAZ, a Web site created to monitor the conflict in Chiapas:

> On Monday, December 22, an armed group of supporters of the ruling PRI (Institutional Revolutionary Party) massacred 45 displaced indigenous persons who had sought refuge from earlier violence in Acteal in the county of Chenalho in the Chiapas highlands. The victims were Zapatista supporters or members of the peasant organization "the Bees" (Sociedad Civil Las Abejas, a group with politics similar to the Zapatistas but which does not support armed struggle). They were attending Mass in the Catholic church when the shooting started. ... [T]he attackers included at least 60 heavily armed men. ... The Mexican Red Cross reported 45 deaths, including nine men, 21 women, 14 children and one baby. Nineteen others were wounded. (Peace Brigades International 1996)

The following day, during a mass funeral, the community identified forty-three suspects and the police arrested them. In the aftermath of the massacre, President Zedillo affirmed in a national message that it was a deplorable act that undermined the unity of all Mexicans.

The Chiapas governor, Roberto Albores Guillén, was accused of giving little social and economic aid to the indigenous communities. In response, Governor Guillén proposed a law initiative on indigenous rights and culture. Meanwhile Protestant Christian groups started a defamation campaign against Samuel Ruiz. Though canon law required Ruiz to resign his position as bishop in 1999, when he turned seventy-five, he has continued to advocate for indigenous rights.

In July 1998, the EZLN published the Fifth Declaration of the Lacandon Jungle, which contained a summons to a "national consultation concerning the legal initiative on indigenous rights" of COCOPA. Moreover, they insisted that CONAI and Mexican civil society to take part in this process of consultation.

THE FALL OF THE PRI

The historical inability of the Mexican state to achieve a social consensus on indigenous rights only worsened the conflict in Chiapas, leading to the first electoral defeat of the PRI in the presidential elections since 1928. The EZLN stayed away from the 2000 electoral process, and they called for Mexican society to abstain from voting.

The new president, Vicente Fox of the National Action Party (PAN), had promised during his electoral campaign resolve the conflict in Chiapas in 15 minutes. EZLN demanded, before it would resume the peace process, the fulfillment of "three signals": the San Andrés accords, the freedom of EZLN prisoners, and the closure of the seven military posts. Luis H. Alvarez was appointed head of COCOPA, and Fox sent the Senate his proposed COCOPA Law, which recommended constitutional changes to address the demands for indigenous rights.

It was in this context that the Zapatour arrived in Mexico City, with the Zapatistas chanting the slogan "Never More a Mexico Without Us," a clear reference to the exclusionary policies and racism of the Mexican state. Nevertheless, the Mexican Congress made numerous changes to the COCOPA initiative, which became known as the Indigenous Rights Law, essentially removing many of the elements important to the indigenous community. The EZLN indicated their complete disapproval, arguing that the changes represented a treasonous action. On September 6, 2002, the Supreme Court of Justice rejected the complaints filed by various indigenous organizations against the Congress's actions on constitutional reform. As a result, the reforms were enacted. A possible explanation for the inability of the Mexican state to adequately address the calls for indigenous rights include the racism of the state in failing to recognize multiculturalism. It might also be related to the *Plan Puebla Panamá,* a large-scale development plan designed to promote regional integration in the nine southern states of Mexico. The plan has been criticized by indigenous groups because they feel it impels the United States, Mexico, and the Central American countries to obtain control of strategic natural resources in the Mesoamerican region. Any political and territorial autonomy of the indigenous peoples over these natural resources would therefore hinder this plan.

In the following months the conflict in Chiapas lost the attention of the public due to Zapatista silence caused by military harassment, and a governmental abandonment of this population in resistance. After a long silence, during which many political analysts speculated that Comandante Marcos had left the country, the EZLN again "took over" the city of San Cristóbal de las Casas on January 1, 2003. Following this demonstration of their continued determination and power, they left the city peacefully.

During 2004, in the Municipality of Zinacantan, the Zapatistas and members of the Democratic Revolution Party (PRD), which controls the municipality, came into conflict over access to water. Dozens of Zapatistas were hurt and 125 Zapatista families were displaced from the community of Jechvo as a consequence. Overall, nearly 20,000 indigenous people have been displaced by the conflict in Chiapas.

THE SIXTH DECLARATION OF THE LACANDON JUNGLE

In 2005, after a long consultation process, the EZLN distributed the Sixth Declaration of the Lacandon Jungle, in which they announced the decision of Zapatista communities to bet their future on the utopia of political participation with Mexican civil society. The EZLN decided to channel their efforts in alliance with other social movements, particularly with Mexican "workers, *campesinos* teachers, students, employees . . . the workers of the city and the countryside." Nevertheless, the EZLN has recently criticized certain political candidates and exhibited a loss of interest in the electoral process and a loss of confidence in Mexican civil society.

There are several possibilities for the future regarding this conflict. On one hand, it is evident that the EZLN will reinforce the "other campaign" that it launched as a new strategy based on listening in order to seek alliances with the Mexican civil society. The EZLN's role in Mexican politics during the electoral period has been cautious, though decisive in Chiapas. On the other hand, the Mexican government has again diminished the Chiapas conflict and the indigenous people's demands. It would not be a surprise to see new popular movements or rebellions occurring in Mexico in the near future.

SEE ALSO *Mayan Genocide in Guatemala; Violence against Indigenous People, Latin America.*

BIBLIOGRAPHY

Canal 6 de Julio. 1998. *Acteal Masacre de Muerte.* Documentary video. Mexico: Canal 6 de Julio

Collier, George. 1994. *Basta! Land and the Zapatista Rebellion in Chiapas.* Oakland, CA: Food First.

Ejército Zapatista de Liberación Nacional (EZLN). Available from http://www.ezln.org/. The texts of the six Declarations of the Lacandon Jungle can be found at http://www.ezln.org/documentos.

Holloway, John, and Eloína Peláez, eds. 1998. *Zapatista!: Reinventing Revolution in Mexico.* London: Pluto Press.

García de León, Antonio. 1989. *Resistencia y utopía. Memorial de agravios y crónica de revueltas y profecías acaecidas en la provincia de Chiapas durante los últimos 500 años de su historia.* Mexico City: Editorial ERA.

Muñoz Ramírez, Gloria. 2003. *EZLN: 20 y 10, el fuego y la palabra.* Mexico City: Desarrollo de Medios.

Ordóñez, Carlos Salvador. 1996. "Derechos humanos de los pueblos indios." In *Etnicidad y Derecho un diálogo postergado entre científicos sociales,* edited by José Ordóñez. Mexico City: Universidad Nacional Autónoma de México.

Peace Brigades International. 1996. "Massacre in Acteal (Chenalho), Chiapas—Paramilitary group kills 45 Tzozil Indians." Available from http://www.peacebrigades.org/ern/ernchiapas.html.

Ruiz Hernández, Margarito. 1999. "La Asamblea Nacional Indígena Plural por la Autonomía. (ANIPA) Proceso de construcción de una propuesta legislativa autonómica nacional." In *México Experiencias de Autonomía Indígena,* edited by Aracely Burguete Cal y Mayor. Copenhagen, Denmark: Grupo Internacional de Trabajo Sobre Asuntos Indígenas.

Servicio Internacional para la Paz (SIPAZ). "Brief History of the Conflict in Chiapas." Available from http://www.sipaz.org/fini_eng.htm.

Vázquez Montalván, Manuel. 2001. *Marcos: El señor de los espejos.* Madrid, Spain: Aguilar.

Womack, John, ed. 1999. *Rebellion in Chiapas: An Historical Reader.* New York: New Press.

Carlos Salvador Ordóñez

ZIONISM

Zionism is the political movement created to foster the establishment of a Jewish state. It is based on the idea that Jews, wherever they live, constitute a single people. It developed in Europe in the late nineteenth century against a backdrop of rising nationalism and anti-Jewish sentiment, especially in areas ruled by the czar, where the greatest number of Jews lived, but also in France, where the *Dreyfus* case revealed widespread resentment of Jews, even in a modern democracy where they were comparatively assimilated. Because it defines *Jew* not by religious observance, language, place of birth, or culture, but by descent, Zionism is an ideology of race.

To many early Zionists, the location of the future Jewish state was of no importance; among the areas contemplated were Argentina and Uganda. The first World Zionist Congress, organized by Theodore Herzl and held in Basel, Switzerland, in 1897, set its sights on Palestine in order to draw upon the religious tradition that holds that with the coming of the Messiah, Jews will be reunited there and the kingdom of God will be accomplished for the whole of humankind.

MODERN PALESTINE

In 1868 there were 13,000 Jews in Palestine, out of an estimated population of 400,000; the majority were religious pilgrims supported by charity from overseas. In 1882 the Frenchman Baron Edmond de Rothschild, combining philanthropy and investment, began to support Jewish settlers from eastern Europe who were brought to Palestine to build a plantation system along the model the French had set up in Algeria. By 1895 the number of Jews had grown to 50,000; they spoke Yiddish, Arabic, Persian, Georgian, and other languages. Hebrew was a liturgical language, spoken in daily life by no one. As late as 1907, Jews made up only 80,000 out of a population of 700,000.

In 1917, Lord Balfour, the British foreign minister, seeking support for Britain's efforts in World War I, issued a declaration expressing sympathy with efforts to establish a Jewish homeland in Palestine, then under British rule. He also vowed that such a homeland would not harm the interests of the Arab majority. The Zionists seized upon this statement, interpreting it to mean support for a Jewish state. At the time of the Balfour Declaration, Jews constituted less than 10 percent of the population and owned 2.5 percent of the land in Palestine.

The problem of building a Jewish society amid an overwhelmingly non-Jewish majority came to be known as the "conquest of land and labor." The Zionists formed a corporation, known as the Jewish National Fund (JNF), which acquired land in the name of the Jewish people. They leased this land only to Jews, who were not allowed to sublet it. Leases from the JNF specifically prohibited the employment of non-Jewish labor on JNF plots. In some cases, when land was bought from absentee landlords, the Arab peasants who resided on and worked the land were expelled. The effort to establish a Jewish monopoly extended to industry, and the Zionists formed an institution, the Histadrut, to organize Jewish workers and exclude Arabs from competing with them in the labor market.

Despite these policies, and the encouragement of the British government, in the thirty years following the Balfour Declaration the majority of the world's Jews showed no interest in settling in Palestine. In the years between 1920 and 1932, only 118,000 Jews moved to Palestine, less than 1 percent of world Jewry. Even after the rise of Hitler, Jews in Europe did not choose Palestine. Out of 2.5 million Jews who fled Europe between 1935 and 1943, scarcely 8.5 percent, about 200,000 persons, went to Palestine. Almost two million went to the Soviet Union, 182,000 to the United States, and 67,000 to Britain—in spite of strict quotas on admissions in the latter two countries.

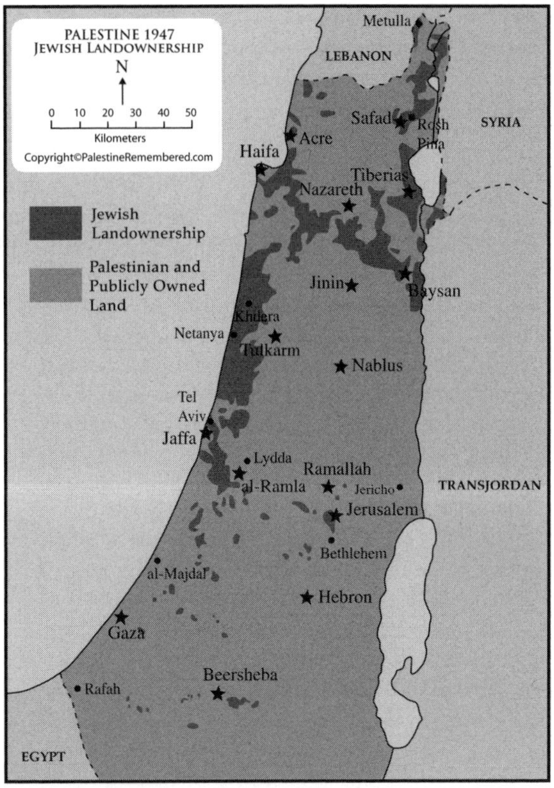

Jewish Landownership in Palestine, 1947.

U.S. and British limitations on the number of Jews admitted coincided with Zionist policy, as enunciated by David Ben-Gurion, the first prime minister of Israel: "If I knew that it would be possible to save all the children in Germany by bringing them over to England, and only half by transporting them to Eretz Yisrael [the Land of Israel], then I would opt for the second alternative. For we must weigh not only the life of these children, but also the history of the People of Israel" (Brenner 1983, pp. 149–150). The policy of attaching more importance to the establishment of Israel than to the survival of the Jews (which was consistent with the Zionist rejection of assimilation) led the Zionists to collaborate with the Nazis (with whom they shared the belief that Jews were a racial community based on blood) in promoting Jewish emigration to Palestine.

THE BIRTH OF ISRAEL

The triumph of Zionism was made possible by the millions left homeless in Europe at the end of World War II, the continued restrictions on immigration to the United States and Britain, and the sympathy Jews had won as victims of Nazi persecution. After Britain announced its intention in 1947 to relinquish its control over Palestine, the United Nations voted to divide Palestine into Arab and Jewish states—awarding the Jewish state 54 percent of the territory, notwithstanding the fact that Jews owned no more than 7 percent of the land. Although 75,000 Jews had moved to Israel between 1945 and 1948, Jews still were a minority in the country. Even before the proclamation of the State of Israel, the Zionists had begun driving out Arab residents. The attack on the Palestine village of Deir Yassin in April 1948, in which Zionist paramilitary forces under the command of the future prime minister Menachem Begin massacred more than 250 Palestinian civilians, thereby sending a message to others that they should depart, is the best-known example of how this population transfer was brought about. Some fled bombing attacks from British planes directly aiding the Israelis. In the war that ensued, the Zionist forces, trained and equipped by Britain and with additional arms from other countries, were easily able to defeat the outnumbered and outgunned forces of Jordan, Egypt and four other Arab states, whose rulers had already accepted the partition of Palestine.

The war ended with the Zionists in control of 80 percent of Palestine; more than 750,000 Arabs were driven from their homes. Some went to neighboring countries; others became refugees in their own country. These people and their descendants make up the Palestinian refugee problem—one fourth of the total number of refugees in the world. Although the United Nations has repeatedly demanded they be allowed to return, the Israeli government has refused.

The founding of the State of Israel meant the destruction by the Zionists of nearly 400 Arab villages. In a famous speech before students at the Israeli Institute of Technology in Haifa in 1969, Moshe Dayan, the Israeli defense minister from 1967 through 1974, stated:

> Jewish villages were built in place of Arab villages. You do not even know the names of these Arab villages, and I do not blame you because geography books no longer exist. Not only do the books not exist, the Arab villages are not there either. Nahial arose in the place of Mahlul; Kibbutz Gvat in the place of Jibta; Kibbutz Sarid in the place of Huneifis; and Kebar Yehusha in the place of Tal al-Shuman. There is not a single place built in this country that did not have a former Arab population (Davis 1987, p. 108).

The first census of the state of Israel, conducted in 1949, counted 650,000 Jews and 150,000 Arabs. The legal foundation for a *racial* state was laid down in two laws passed the following year. The first, the Law of Return, permitted any Jew, from anywhere in the world, the right to immigrate to Israel and acquire citizenship. The second was the Absentee Property Law, which confiscated the property of Arabs no longer residing on the land over which they held title. Arab refugees living inside Israel were termed "present absentees" and prohibited from returning to their property. Those who attempted to do so were termed "infiltrators," and some were shot in the attempt. Confiscated lands have since become Israel Lands, leased only to Jews and accounting for the vast majority of new Jewish settlements.

The state of Israel does not belong, even in theory, to those who reside on its territory, but has been held by Israeli courts to be the "sovereign state of the Jewish people," wherever they may exist. Consistent with this self-conception, the state has never defined its borders or even declared the existence of an Israeli nationality.

JEWISH PRIVILEGES IN ISRAEL

Under Israeli law, anyone born of a Jewish mother is Jewish, unless such a person converts to another religion. The rationale for this departure from the Judaic code is that such persons weaken Jewish national identity because of their tendency to intermarry. At the same time, the State of Israel, eager to increase the numbers of loyal residents, has extended the Right of Return to persons who lack a Jewish mother but have an affiliation with Jewish identity by marriage or inheritance through the male line. Such persons are registered as "under consideration." In addition, a few individuals have gained Jewish status by converting to Judaism and having their conversion officially approved.

Jew in Israel is an assigned identity. Among the privileges attached to it, in addition to immigration and land acquisition, are citizenship, housing preferences, education and employment opportunities, political participation, and preferred treatment within the justice system.

Citizenship. Jews who immigrate to Israel become citizens automatically. Arabs seeking citizenship must meet a series of requirements, with final discretion resting with the minister of the interior. This applies also to Arabs born in what is now Israel but who resided elsewhere for any period of time. Arab noncitizens who marry citizens receive only residency status, not citizenship. As one scholar has stated, "citizenship is almost never granted to non-Jews" (Adalah 1998, pp. 24–28).

Housing. The government of Israel openly discriminates in housing. The Supreme Court has ruled that an Arab seeking to buy a home in a Jewish district could legally be barred from doing so on the grounds that the apartments were intended to help Jews overcome the effects of discrimination under British rule. Rates for government-subsidized mortgages are at least one-third lower for Jews than for non-Jews. The authorities restrict the development of Arab towns by denying them expansion permits, while permits are granted to Jewish towns with smaller populations. Building licenses are routinely denied to Arabs, and obstacles are placed in the way of Arabs when they seek to build homes. Of 429 localities designated as National Priority A Areas under the National Planning and Building Law, only four are Arab. As a result, Arabs have been forced into overcrowded areas in mixed cities and into unrecognized towns lacking such basic services as running water, sewers, and electricity. Residents of these areas live under constant threat of being evicted and having their homes demolished.

Education and Family Policy. The country operates what is essentially a segregated school system. Significant gaps exist between Jewish and Arab schools at every level from early childhood to higher education. The Ministry of Education exercises control over the curriculum for Arab schools and secular Jewish schools, while granting autonomy to Jewish religious schools. The curriculum, even in Arab schools, stresses Jewish history and culture and ignores the history and culture of the indigenous Palestinians. Because Arabs do not serve in the armed forces, they are not eligible for financial benefits, including scholarships, loans, and child allowances available to those who serve. The Supreme Court has ruled, however, that paying subsidies to Jewish students who study in religious schools and are exempt from military service, while denying them to Arab students who do not serve, is not discriminatory.

Employment. The Histadrut was born as a combination labor union and cooperative society for Jewish workers. For many years it was the dominant institution in Israeli society and served as the mass base for the governing Labour Party. In recent years, as the Israeli economy has evolved, the Histadrut has faded in importance, but its legacy remains, as Jewish workers dominate the advanced sectors of the economy and Arab workers constitute a low caste. Further, Arab workers are increasingly being displaced by Thais and Filipinos, partly in response to the growth of the Palestinian resistance.

Political Participation. No party that denies the existence of Israel as a Jewish state is permitted to contest elections. It is against the law even to display symbols and sing anthems of anti-Zionist groups. Furthermore, the major parties have made it clear that no governing coalition can depend on the support of the Arab community (which makes up 20% of the population), and no important decision relating to the future of the Jewish state can be taken without a Jewish majority in parliament. Thus, the non-Jewish minority is prevented not merely from seeking to overturn its second-class status through parliamentary means, but even from throwing its weight on the scale when Jewish opinion is divided.

The Justice System. The state does not provide comparative information on sentencing of Jews and Arabs convicted of criminal offenses, but an examination of court records shows great disparities in sentencing as well as indictments. Israeli courts, up to the Supreme Court, have consistently ruled that discrimination between Arabs and Jews is legitimate given the founding of Israel as a state for Jews. In one representative case, a Jewish settler was convicted of shooting an Arab child. The judge sentenced him to a suspended jail term of six months plus community service. In response to critics, the judge declared, "It is wrong to demand in the name of equality, equal bearing and equal sentences to two offenders who have different nationalities who break the laws of the State. The sentence that deters the one and his audience, does not deter the other and his community" (Adalah 1998, pp. 17–21).

The types of discrimination noted above apply within the so-called "Green Line"—the area of the Israeli state as set up in 1948. In 1967, Israel occupied East Jerusalem, the West Bank of the Jordan River, the Sinai Peninsula, and the Gaza Strip, restoring the territorial integrity of Palestine, which had been an administrative unit for centuries, first under Ottoman and later under British rule, except for the two decades after 1948. After 1967 the system of military administration first established in 1948, which had been partially lifted within Israel in 1966, was imposed on the remainder of Palestine, and the area was opened for Jewish settlement, with state subsidies for settlers.

Palestinians Walk Past Israel's Controversial Separation Barrier in Jerusalem, 2007. *In 2002 the Israeli government, citing the need to maintain internal security, began building a thirty-foot-high concrete-and-barbed-wire Separation Barrier throughout historic Palestine.* AP IMAGES.

In the early twentieth century there are 500,000 Jews residing in the West Bank. They live in fortified towns surrounded by soldiers, are served by their own services and utilities, and are connected by a network of roads for Jews only. Arab cities and towns are isolated from each other by hundreds of checkpoints and motorways on which Arabs are forbidden to travel. In 2002, the Israeli government, citing the need to maintain internal security, began building a thirty-foot-high concrete-and-barbed-wire structure snaking through historic Palestine. Although the barrier was, in theory, to follow the Green Line (except for East Jerusalem, which was officially annexed to Israel), it became an opportunity for new Jewish expansion. In 2003, the military commander of the West Bank signed an order declaring all land between the Wall and the Green Line closed to all but Israeli citizens.

DEMOCRACY IN ISRAEL

Since the founding of the State of Israel, its defenders have had difficulty reconciling the reality of a Jewish state with a vision of democracy. Some have dealt with the matter by rejecting democracy as a goal for non-Jews. Among this number is Ariel Sharon, who became prime minister in 2001; Sharon stated, "Our grandparents did not come here to build a democratic state. They came to build a Jewish state." Others have denied any contradiction, insisting on both the Jewish and democratic character of the state. For these people, the occupation of the West Bank and Gaza has posed new ideological problems: If the Arabs living within the State of Israel, comprising one-fifth of the population of Israel, can be said to be second-class citizens, the 3.5 million Arabs residing in the territories occupied after 1967 must be regarded as stateless people with no representation or legal rights whatever. Under pressure from internal critics and international opinion, the Zionist authorities have accepted the principle of a separate state on some part of historic Palestine. The problem, then, has become how to maximize the area to become part of the Jewish state while minimizing the numbers of indigenous Palestinians within it. To this end, Zionist authorities have continued to expand the Jewish settlements (to strengthen their claims to additional land in anticipation of a settlement) while evicting indigenous Palestinians, destroying villages, and making life difficult for those who remain.

Zionist authorities have since withdrawn from Gaza, a six-by-twenty-eight mile strip of land that is home to 1.4 million indigenous Palestinians, mostly refugees from 1948 or 1967 and their descendants. They have removed 7,500 Jewish settlers (1.7 percent of the total number of settlers in the territories occupied by Israel after 1967), but have left the area surrounded by barbed-wire electric fences and guard towers. All traffic and commerce into and out of Gaza are controlled by Israel, as are the airspace and water resources. There are even plans for an offshore fence to provide Israel with full control of its coastal boundary.

Meanwhile, the expulsion of Palestinians from the West Bank continues without interruption. It appears that the dream of one of the principal architects of the Jewish state is close to being realized: As Joseph Weitz, former chairman of the Israel Land Authority, stated, "Among ourselves it must be clear that there is no place in our country for both peoples together. The only solution is Eretz Israel, or at least the western half of Eretz Israel, without Arabs, and there is no other way but to transfer the Arabs from here to the neighboring countries, transfer all of them, not one village or tribe should remain."

BIBLIOGRAPHY

Adalah: The Legal Center for Arab Minority Rights in Israel. 1998. *Equal Rights and Minority Rights for the Palestinian Arab Minority in Israel: A Report to the UN Human Rights Committee on Israel's Implementation of Articles 26 and 27 of the International Covenant on Civil and Political Rights.* Shfaram, Israel: Adalah. Available from http//www.arabhra.org/publications/reports/PDF/lccpr98.pdf/.

Al-Qawuqji, Fauzi. 1972."Memoirs, 1948 Part 1."*Journal of Palestine Studies* 1 (4): 27–58.

Brenner, Lenni. 1983. *Zionism in the Age of the Dictators.* Westport, CT: Lawrence Hill.

Davis, Uri. 1987. *Israel: An Apartheid State.* London: Zed Books.

Finkelstein, Norman. 2003. *Image and Reality of the Israel-Palestine Conflict*, 2nd ed. London: Verso.

Khalidi, Walid. 1988. "Plan Dalet: Master Plan for the Conquest of Palestine." *Journal of Palestine Studies* 18 (1): 4–33.

Menuhin, Moshe. 1965. *The Decadence of Judaism in Our Time.* New York: Exposition Press.

Morris, Benny. 1988. *The Birth of the Palestinian Refugee Problem, 1947–1949.* Cambridge, U.K.: Cambridge University Press.

Qumsiyeh, Mazin B. 2004. *Sharing the Land of Canaan: Human Rights and the Israeli-Palestinian Struggle.* London: Pluto Press.

Segev, Tom. 1999. *One Palestine, Complete: Jews and Arabs under the British Mandate.* Translated by Haim Watzman. New York: Henry Holt.

Shlaim, Avi. 1988. *Collusion across the Jordan: King Abdullah, the Zionist Movement and the Partition of Palestine.* Oxford: Clarendon Press.

———. 1995. "The Debate about 1948." *International Journal of Middle Eastern Studies* 27: 287–304.

van Creveld, Martin. 1998. *The Sword and the Olive: A Critical History of the Israeli Defense Force.* New York: Perseus.

Noel Ignatiev

ZOOT SUIT RIOTS

The "Zoot Suit Riots" occurred in Los Angeles from roughly June 3 to June 13, 1943. Although there were few reported serious injuries and property damage was minimal relative to other major twentieth-century civil disturbances, this event represents an especially violent episode in the history of race and racism in the United States.

During the Zoot Suit Riots, white servicemen, some of whom were accompanied by civilians, attacked "zooters," or youths wearing zoot suits. In particular, they targeted zoot-clad Mexican Americans, who were sometimes known as *pachucos* and *pachucas*. For at least ten days, servicemen from across Southern California, and some from as far away as Las Vegas, Nevada, poured into Los Angeles and roamed the streets of downtown, Chinatown, Chavez Ravine, East Los Angeles, and Watts in search of their prey. In some instances, they stopped and boarded streetcars, burst into movie houses and private homes, and set upon people of color regardless of

Servicemen During the Zoot Suit Riots. *During the Zoot Suit Riots in 1943, white servicemen attacked youths wearing zoot suits in Los Angeles.* © BETTMANN/CORBIS.

their attire. When they apprehended zooters, they sometimes sheared their hair and stripped them of their distinctive clothing. All the while, the police turned a blind eye to the rampaging servicemen but arrested zooters.

By 1943 the zoot suit had become a symbol of youthful rebellion, working-class style, racial difference, and even un-Americanism. With its excessive use of fabric, the masculine version of the zoot suit—which usually consisted of a long coat, billowing trousers that tapered at the ankle, a long watch chain that sometimes extended from the waist to the calves, a pair of thick-soled shoes, and in some instances, a broad-brimmed hat—represented an affront to wartime rationing measures. Female zooters often wore dark lipstick, a skirt that exposed the knees, and either a V-neck or cardigan sweater or a long coat similar to that of their male counterparts. Some wore the masculine version of the zoot suit. In addition, both female and male zooters wore their hair in a distinctive style. Many female zooters used foam inserts known as "rats" to lift their hair into a high bouffant, while their male counterparts often combed their hair in a pompadour on top and a ducktail in back. With his relatively long hair and flamboyant costume, the black or brown male zooter appeared to be the antithesis of the clean-cut and uniformed white serviceman. Female zooters, meanwhile, especially those who cross-dressed, defied conventional standards of feminine beauty and decency.

During World War II, the zoot look peaked in popularity in the United States among working-class youths of various races and ethnicities, many of whom were jazz and jitterbug aficionados. As they entered the wartime consumer-wage economy, these young men and women flaunted their new-found spending power on the street and in places of leisure, such as ballrooms, movie houses, and billiard halls. Across the Atlantic, French youths known as *les zazous* adopted a look similar to that of American zooters, and after World War II a variation of the zoot suit spread to youths in Britain.

Despite its widespread popularity, the zoot suit came to be associated in Los Angeles with racial minorities, especially Mexican Americans. Law enforcement and the mainstream press branded Mexican-American zooters juvenile delinquents in the wake of what became known as the Sleepy Lagoon incident. This event took place the night of August 1, 1942, and involved an alleged gang fight and murder at a swimming hole in Los Angeles. During the Grand Jury hearing that followed, Captain Edward Duran Ayres of the Los Angeles County Sheriff's Department argued that by virtue of their Aztec blood, Mexican Americans were intrinsically more violent than, and therefore biologically inferior to, white Americans. Ironically, as the United States combated Nazi eugenics and anti-Semitism abroad, the Ayres report blatantly espoused biological racism on the home front. Furthermore, it equated Mexicans with "Orientals" and, by extension, the Japanese enemy. Like Japanese Americans, Mexican Americans exceeded the putative black-white binary of American racial identity. Bilingual and bicultural, many of these racial and cultural hybrids embodied an alien ambiguity during a period of heightened jingoism, xenophobia, and paranoia.

During the Sleepy Lagoon investigation and trial, Los Angeles's dominant newspapers fomented anti-Mexican hysteria by publishing stories about violent, marijuana-addicted, sexually depraved, zoot-clad Mexican-American youths. In doing so, they rendered the zoot suit a hallmark of Mexican-American juvenile delinquency and sexual pathology. Angeleno newspapers continued to publish sensationalist stories about predatory *pachucos* and loose *pachucas* in the days and weeks prior to the Zoot Suit Riots. On the eve of the outbreak of violence, they reported that *pachucos* harassed and raped women, notably sailors' wives and girlfriends.

The Zoot Suit Riots were the culmination of a series of altercations between *pachucos*, *pachucas*, and servicemen, many of whom were stationed in neighborhoods with high concentrations of Mexican Americans. As a contest over public space, the riots revealed a latent anxiety concerning Mexican Americans' place on city streets and in the nation. Prior to World War II, Mexicans in the United States were a primarily immigrant, poor, rural, and relatively invisible population. However, the exigencies of war pulled them and their American-born children into a stratified urban proletariat. In their showy ensembles, second-generation *pachucas* and *pachucos* were especially conspicuous. Moreover, the riots expressed anxiety regarding the fluidity of gender and sexuality. As servicemen "depantsed" male zooters and cut their hair, they forced their victims to conform to a narrow definition of heterosexual and American manhood.

The Zoot Suit Riots ended after the Navy barred sailors from Los Angeles. Although city officials adamantly denied that the riots were racist, members of the committee convened by Governor Earl Warren to investigate the event maintained that "race prejudice" had been a factor. Across the United States, violence continued to erupt in urban centers with relatively high concentrations of African Americans, such as Detroit, New York, and Philadelphia, during the summer of 1943.

Within Chicano studies, the Zoot Suit Riots continue to receive considerable attention. Scholars, artists, and activists have looked to the riots as a turning point in Mexican-American history, and to the *pachuco* as an icon of Chicano resistance and style.

SEE ALSO *Chicano Movement; Mexicans.*

BIBLIOGRAPHY

Alvarez, Luis. 2005. "Zoot Violence on the Home Front: Race, Riots, and Youth Culture during World War II." In *Mexican Americans and World War II*, edited by Maggie Rivas-Rodríguez, 141–175. Austin: University of Texas Press.

Escobar, Edward J. 1999. *Race, Police, and the Making of a Political Identity: Mexican Americans and the Los Angeles Police Department, 1900–1945*. Berkeley: University of California Press.

Mazón, Mauricio. 1984. *The Zoot Suit Riots: The Psychology of Symbolic Annihilation*. Austin: University of Texas Press.

McWilliams, Carey. 1968 (1948). *North from Mexico: The Spanish-speaking People of the United States*. New York: Greenwood Press.

Pagán, Eduardo Obregón. 2003. *Murder at the Sleepy Lagoon: Zoot Suits, Race, and Riot in Wartime L.A.* Chapel Hill: University of North Carolina Press.

Ramírez, Catherine S. 2002. "Crimes of Fashion: The Pachuca and Chicana Style Politics." *Meridians: Feminism, Race, Transnationalism* 2 (2): 1–35.

Catherine S. Ramírez

Annotated Filmography

Compiled by Antoinette Jackson, Ph.D., University of South Florida. ***Note from author:*** *In addition to consulting with numerous friends and colleagues and perusing my own library of sources (as well as the Internet), I found the following sources very informative: California Newsreel, which produces and distributes cutting edge, social justice films that inspire, educate, and engage audiences (founded in 1968, California Newsreel is the oldest nonprofit, social issue documentary film center in the country); First Run/Icarus Films; The Black Film Center and Archive, Indiana University, Bloomington, Indiana; the* Journal of Chicano Studies; *the 1998 Aztlán Film Institute's list of top 100 films; Third World Newsreel; Women Make Movies, a multicultural, multiracial, nonprofit media arts organization that facilitates the production, promotion, distribution, and exhibition of independent films and videotapes by and about women; and the Independent Television Service (ITVS), which brings to local, national, and international audiences high-quality, content-rich programs created by a diverse body of independent producers. ITVS programs take creative risks, explore complex issues, and express points of view seldom seen on commercial or public television. ITVS programming reflects voices and visions of underrepresented communities and addresses the needs of underserved audiences, particularly minorities and children.*

FEATURE AND SHORT FILMS

Adanggaman (French and Bambara). 2000. Directed by Roger Gnoam M'bala. Abyssa Film. M'bala's film provides an African perspective of the seventeenth-century slave trade.

Avalon. 1990. Directed by Barry Levinson. Baltimore Pictures. An autobiographical story of a family of eastern European Jewish immigrants to the United States who settle in Baltimore, Maryland, at the beginning of the twentieth century. *Avalon* explores themes of assimilation, modernity, and the change faced by an immigrant family in America.

BabaKiueria. 1986. Directed by Don Featherstone. A satirical made-for-TV film made by the Australian Aboriginal community to commemorate the bicentennial of British rule. The 29-minute film is in fact a role-reversal study, presenting a fictional past in which indigenous Australians invade *BabaKiueria*, a land of stereotypical European Australians.

Bamboozled. 2000. Directed by Spike Lee. In this satire of the TV industry, a failing network hits the ratings jackpot by marketing an old-time black minstrel show, complete with reconstructed racist stereotypes.

The Battle of Algiers (French, Italian, English, and Arabic). 1967. Directed by Gillo Pontecorvo. Casbah Films. The story of the Algerian struggle to gain independence from French colonialism.

The Birth of a Nation. 1915. Directed by D. W. Griffith. David W. Griffith Corporation. A Civil War and Reconstruction era drama and an enormously popular film in its day, this controversial classic dramatizes the racial beliefs and fears of whites in America following the Civil War through the racist portrayals of stereotypes and caricatures of blacks (primarily played by white actors in blackface), framed against a backdrop of "white heroes" (i.e., the Ku Klux Klan).

Black and White in Color *(Noirs et blancs en couleur).* 1976. Directed by Jean-Jacques Annaud. France 3 Cinéma. A clever satire, this French film looks at World War I imperialism, the impact of colonialism, and the ideology of racial superiority through an array of characters stationed at an African trading post run by French colonials. It won an Academy Award for Best Foreign Picture.

Blood of the Condor (Quechua and Spanish). 1969. Directed by Jorge Sanjinés. Ukamau Group. The classic film *Blood of the Condor (Yawar mallku)* is set in Bolivia and focuses on actual events that occurred in a Quechua community in 1968. People who appear to be U.S. Peace Corps volunteers establish a medical and birth-control clinic in which women are sterilized without their knowledge or consent. Violence ensues, and viewers are taken from the highlands and the exploration of race relations within the village to urban La Paz, where the treatment of indigenous people seeking help is explored.

La Boca del Lobo. *(The Lion's Den).* 1988. Directed by Francisco J. Lombardi. Inca Film. Based on true incidents that took place in the mountain town of Chuspi, Peru, between 1980 and 1983, the film examines a violent struggle between the Peruvian military and the Shining Path guerrillas. A Quechua community in highland Peru is caught in the middle of the violence, graphically illustrating the conflation of "Indian" and "subversive" and the relationship between gender and racism. In Spanish.

The Brother from Another Planet. 1984. Directed by John Sayles. Anarchist's Convention Films. Sayles's satire literalizes race by presenting "the brother" as an alien who looks very much like a black man and has landed in Harlem, New York.

Brother to Brother. 2004. Directed by Rodney Evans. Miasma Films. This drama about famous faces from the Harlem Renaissance (e.g., Langston Hughes, Zora Neale Hurston) provides an inspiring story about racial politics and sexuality in twentieth-century urban America. The film won a Special Jury Prize at the Sundance Film Festival.

Chronicle of the Years of Embers *(Chronique des années de braise).* 1975. Directed by Mohamed Lakhdar-Hamina. Algeria's struggle for independence from French colonial rule is the subject of this Arabic-language film. The story follows a peasant's migration from his drought-stricken village to his eventual participation with the Algerian resistance movement, just prior to the outbreak of the Algerian War of Independence. The film won the prestigious Palme d'Or at Cannes in 1975.

The Colored Museum. 1991. Directed by Andrew Carl Wilk and George C. Wolfe. Public Broadcasting Service (PBS). A critical satire that addresses the impact of slavery on America from the perspective of African Americans impacted by the baggage, burden, and struggles that the legacy of slavery has brought to bear on issues of identity.

Crash. 2005. Directed by Paul Haggis. Bull's Eye Entertainment. Several stories interweave during two days in Los Angeles, as a collection of interrelated characters experience the impact of race and racial stereotypes on day-to-day relationships and encounters, sometimes with tragic results. The film won the Academy Award for Best Picture.

Cry Freedom. 1987. Directed by Richard Attenborough. Marble Arch Productions. Set in the late 1970s during the apartheid era in South Africa, *Cry Freedom* is based on the true story of newspaper editor David Woods's investigation into the death of nationalist leader Steve Biko, who was murdered while in police custody.

The Crying Game. 1992. Directed by Neil Jordon. British Screen Productions. Provides a look into colonial and postcolonial British subjectivity, including smart intersections with race, class, sexuality, and gender.

Daughters of the Dust. 1991. Directed by Julie Dash. American Playhouse. An excellent film that honors African ancestry and spirituality in America by telling the story of the Gullah people of the Sea Islands off the South Carolina and Georgia coast. Gullah culture is explored by focusing on one family's history and experiences.

A Day Without a Mexican. 2004. Directed by Sergio Arau. Eye on the Ball Films. A satirical look at what would happen if all the Latinos suddenly disappeared from California.

Days of Glory *(Indigènes).* French and Arabic. 2006. Directed by Richid Bouchareb. Tessalit Productions. During World War II, four North African men enlist in the French army to liberate that country from Nazi oppression and fight French discrimination.

Do the Right Thing. 1989. Directed by Spike Lee. 40 Acres & A Mule Filmworks. On a hot day in the predominantly black Bedford-Stuyvesant neighborhood of Brooklyn, New York, an eruption of racial tensions is prompted by a chain of interrelated events.

Driving Miss Daisy. 1989. Directed by Bruce Beresford. Majestic Films International. When an elderly Jewish widow living in Atlanta in the 1950s finds she can no longer drive, her son hires a black driver. Although she is highly resistant at first, the two slowly become friends. The film chronicles nearly twenty years of racial history in the U.S. South through their life experiences of traveling together. Based on Alfred Uhry's Pulitzer Prize–winning play, the film won the Academy Award for Best Picture.

The End of Violence (English and Spanish). 1997. Directed by Wim Wenders. Ciby Pictures. When a wealthy director is forced to go into hiding, his life becomes enmeshed with the lives of the workers he encounters and lives with for a time. The film deals with issues of race, class, and the invisibility of Mexican workers.

Final Solution. 2001. Directed by Cristóbal Krusen. Integrity Media. Based on the life of the Afrikaner racist named Gerrit Wolfaardt, *Final Solution* deals with the final days of apartheid in South Africa. The film has a religious message of redemption and a story line that appeals to a broad audience.

Forgiveness. 2004. Directed by Ian Gabriel. Giant Films. A complex film on the theme of truth and reconciliation. A former South African policeman seeks forgiveness from the family of an ANC activist that he tortured and killed.

Gandhi. 1982. Directed by Richard Attenborough. Carolina Bank. A chronicle of the life of Mohandas "Mahatma" Gandhi, from his beginnings as a South African–educated lawyer through his historic, galvanizing struggle to free India from British colonial rule.

God's Stepchildren. 1938. Written, produced, and directed by Oscar Micheaux. Micheaux Film Corporation. A look at issues of racial passing and other intraracial power dynamics.

Having Our Say: The Delany Sisters' First 100 Years. 1999. Directed by Lynne Littman. Columbia TriStar Television. A made-for-TV movie based on the true story of Sadie and Bessie Delany, who lived well beyond the age of 100 after having built successful careers at a time when most women—and most African Americans—were being denied opportunities in the United States due to segregation, racism, and sexism.

Hotel Rwanda (English and French). 2004. Directed by Terry George. Kigali Releasing Limited. A tragic accounting of the Rwanda genocide, which claimed an estimated 800,000 lives. The film tells the story of one man's courage in the face of ethnic violence when two arbitrarily defined ethnic groups, the Tutsis and Hutus, are pitted against one another.

Hush-a-Bye Baby. 1990. Directed by Margo Harkin. Channel 4 Television Corporation (Great Britain). The tale of a fifteen-year-old girl in Northern Ireland who discovers she is pregnant after her boyfriend is locked up in a British prison.

I Am Joaquin (English and Spanish). 1969. Directed by Luis Valdez. A graphic presentation of one of the most influential poems of the Chicano movement, this 20-minute film is a first-person narrative of independence that exposes viewers to leading figures and major events in Mexican and Chicano history.

Illusions. 1982. Written and directed by Julie Dash. Dash's short film explores the illusions perpetuated by the Hollywood studio system in terms of stereotypes of race, gender, and class. The story revolves around two women who pass for white in the film industry in the 1940s.

Imitation of Life. 1934. Directed by John M. Stahl. Universal. A tragic look into the social realities of race in America, focusing on the story of a mother and daughter engaged in the politics of "passing for white" and the toll it takes on their relationship. Nominated for three Academy Awards. The film was remade in 1959, when it was directed by Douglas Sirk.

Inch'Allah dimanche (French and Arabic). 2001. Directed by Yamina Benguigui. ARP Sélection. In the aftermath of World War II, France attempted to replenish its weakened work force by recruiting men from North Africa. In the mid-1970s, the French government relaxed its immigration policy to allow the families of the Algerian men to join them. This film is a moving story of Zouina, a woman who leaves her homeland with her three children to join her husband in France, where he's been living for the past ten years. It underscores the sense of isolation and vulnerability that the immigrant family experienced upon their arrival at a time when racial integration was virtually nonexistent.

Jungle Fever. 1991. Directed by Spike Lee. 40 Acres & A Mule Filmworks. A successful married African American architect begins an interracial romance with an Italian American woman who is hired as a temporary secretary by his firm. The lovers come under intense pressure from family and friends as a result of their relationship. The term *jungle fever* is used in the film to refer to the sexual attraction between two different races.

Killer of Sheep. 1977. Directed by Charles Burnett. An award-winning film shot in the Los Angeles neighborhood of Watts in the 1970s. It is a richly descriptive black-and-white art film about the lives of poor black people in America that reaches beyond stereotypical profiles.

Lagaan: Once Upon a Time in India. 2001. Directed by Ashutosh Gowariker. An examination of race and imperialism in colonial India. Set in the latter half of the nineteenth century, "Lagaan" looks at the adversities and injustice perpetrated by the British upon the innocent peasants who face extraordinary circumstances with fortitude and dignity.

Living in Paradise *(Vivre au paradis).* 1998. Directed by Bourlem Guerdjou. 3B Productions. Set in France in 1961–1962, this film depicts the conditions of life of Algerian immigrant workers in France during the last days of French colonial rule in Algeria. In French and Arabic.

Lone Star. 1996. Directed by John Sayles. Castle Rock. In the Texas border town of Frontera, people of differing ethnicities face difficult social problems as they grapple with questions of race, ethnicity, history, identity, economic and political power, education, and the future of the town. The plot is set in motion by the discovery of the remains of the town's former sheriff.

The Long Walk Home. 1990. Directed by Richard Pearce. New Vision Pictures. A dramatization of the events in Montgomery, Alabama, in 1955–1956, when blacks boycotted public transportation. It highlights the friendship, courage, and determination of two women (a maid and her employer) facing racial tensions in the American South.

The Lunch Date. 1989. Directed by Adam Davidson. In a cafe, a white woman walks away from her table to get silverware. When she returns, she sees a black man eating her lunch. What ensues in this classic short tells a simple but powerful story about race, racial stereotyping, and wrong assumptions.

Malcolm X. 1992. Directed by Spike Lee. 40 Acres & A Mule Filmworks. Award-winning biography of Malcolm X, documenting the numerous transformations the famous African American leader went through during his life. Beginning with his birth as Malcolm Little, the son of a minister killed by the Ku Klux Klan, the film explores his life as a gangster, his religious conversion to the Nation of Islam, and his pilgrimage to the city of Mecca. Malcolm's struggle to overcome the impact and challenges of racism in America, on both a personal and public leadership level, is explored.

Men With Guns. 1997. Directed by John Sayles. Anarchist's Convention Films. A retired physician seeks to learn the result of a health-care project in the provinces of a Spanish-speaking country where indigenous peoples live with the challenges of improper medical care. Issues of race, place, and class are examined through the life-and-death struggle between government and guerrilla forces.

Mississippi Masala. 1991. Directed by Mira Nair. Black River Productions. An Indian family, after being expelled from Uganda when Idi Amin takes power, moves to Mississippi, where an Indian daughter falls in love with a black man. Tensions erupt as everyone deals with issues of race, ethnicity, and the power of love.

Monster's Ball. 2001. Directed by Marc Forster. Lee Daniels Entertainment; Lionsgate Films. An intergenerational look at the toil racism, racist thinking, and hatred have on one family and those they encounter. An embittered prison guard, Hank, lives with his aging racist father and his own twenty-something son. Hank's interracial affair with the widow of an inmate he helped prepare for death in the electric chair forces him to reevaluate how deeply prison work and his father's hatred have affected his life.

Mother India (Hindi). 1957. Directed by Mehboob Khan. Mehboob Productions; British Film Institute. One of the first great epics of Indian cinema, *Mother India* has had a profound influence in Bollywood and beyond. The film is an epic drama of human struggle, including gendered dialogues on colonialism and nationalism in the early twentieth century.

My Family *(Mi Familia).* 1995. Directed by Gregory Nava. American Playhouse. A story about three generations of a Mexican American family that emigrated from Mexico to Los Angeles beginning in the 1930s. The family members face challenges of ethnic bigotry, assimilation, acculturation, and past family problems.

El Norte 1983. Directed by Gregory Nava. American Playhouse. This epic film tells the story of a Guatemalan brother and sister who fled persecution at home and journeyed north with dreams of finding a new home in the United States. They are treated as illegal aliens in a country whose economy functions on the cheap labor that they provide. *El Norte* explores the conflicting experiences, including racial and ethnic challenges, faced by people trying to achieve the "American Dream."

Once Upon a Time When We Were Colored. 1995. Directed by Tim Reid. BET Pictures. The lives and day-to-day experiences of an African American family are examined from the perspective of a young male member of a family growing up in the U.S. South during the period of racial segregation.

Pièces d'Identités *(Pieces of Identity).* French and Wolof. 1998. Produced and directed by Mweze Ngangura. Films Sud; California Newsreel. On the surface this is the timeless story of an old king, his beautiful daughter, and the Prince Charming who rescues them. At the same time, it raises the troubling issues of identity facing people of African descent in the diaspora during the late twentieth century. The film shows both the daily indignities Africans face at the hands of racist police and ordinary citizens as well as decent white citizens who help the king along his journey.

Please Don't Bury Me Alive (English and Spanish). 1976. Produced and directed by Efraín Gutiérrez. An important example of regional filmmaking, this bicultural and bilingual narrative expanded the way that films are made. It profiles barrio life in South Texas while dramatizing the challenges facing a young Chicano in the spring of 1972 during the Chicano movement. The film is described as being as significant to paradigm development as "race movies" were for black audiences from the 1920s to the 1940s.

Pride. 2007. Directed by Sunu Gonera. Lionsgate Films. Based on true events, the film, set in 1973, tells the story of Jim Ellis, a college-educated African American who lands a job with the Philadelphia Department of Parks and Recreation. Driven by his love of competitive swimming, he proceeds to restore the abandoned recreational pool hall in the poor Philadelphia neighborhood where he works to restore its former level of beauty and functionality. Jim fights city officials, who mark the facility for demolition, and racism within and outside the community to recruit and transform a motley team of novices into capable swimmers in time for the upcoming state championships.

Quilombo. 1986. Directed by Carlos Diegues. CDK; Embrafilme; Société des Etablissements L. Gaumont. Palmares is a seventeenth-century quilombo, a settlement of escaped slaves in northeast Brazil. In 1650, plantation slaves revolt and head for the mountains, where they find others led by the aged seer Acotirene. She anoints one of them, who becomes Ganga Zumba, a legendary king. For years, his warriors hold off Portuguese raiders.

Rabbit-Proof Fence. 2002. Directed by Phillip Noyce. Australian Film Commission. A tale of Aboriginal defiance in the face of racism and racist practices in Australia in the 1930s, told through the lives of three young girls.

A Raisin in the Sun. 1961. Directed by Daniel Petrie. This adaptation of Lorraine Hansberry's award-winning and highly acclaimed play examines African American life in the 1950s. It profiles the life of a black family in a Chicago South Side tenement, particularly their hopes of escaping the bigoted and oppressive environment in which they live.

Real Women Have Curves. 2002. Directed by Patricia Cardoso. HBO Independent Productions. Ana, a first generation Mexican American teenager on the verge of becoming a woman, lives in the predominately Latino community of East Los Angeles. Freshly graduated from high school, she receives a full scholarship to Columbia University and is torn between her mainstream ambitions and her cultural heritage. The film highlights issues of race, place, and ethnic identity in America.

Roots. 1977. Directed by Marvin J. Chomsky, John Erman, David Greene, and Gilbert Moses. David L. Wolper Productions. The famous TV miniseries is a saga of African American life based on the writer Alex Haley's family history. The story begins with the abduction of Kunta Kinte from his African village. He is then sold into slavery and taken to America. Throughout the series, notable events in U.S. history, such as the Revolutionary and Civil Wars, slave uprisings, and emancipation, serve as a background to the life experiences of Kunte Kinte's family.

Rosewood. 1997. Directed by John Singleton. New Deal Productions. The film depicts the horrific attack of a racist lynch mob on an African American community in the 1920s, when a black town in Florida was burned to the ground.

Ruby Bridges. 1998. Directed by Euzhan Palcy. Marian Rees Associates. The true story of Ruby Bridges, a six-year-old African American girl who helped to integrate the all-white schools of New Orleans in 1960.

Sankofa. 1993. Written, directed, and produced by Haile Gerima. Channel Four Films (U.K.). The legacy of slavery is revisited in the present by a black woman's visit to a slave castle as a tourist and model on a film shoot in Ghana, West Africa. This movie by the Ethiopian-born Gerima offers a powerful look at the brutality and cruelty of slavery in America and the role Africans in America played in working together to fight the conditions imposed upon them.

Schindler's List. 1993. Directed by Steven Spielberg. Amblin Entertainment; Universal Pictures. Spielberg's film is based on the true story of a Czech businessman, Oskar Schindler, who used Jewish labor to start a factory in Nazi-occupied Poland. As World War II progresses, and the fate of Jews under Hitler's regime becomes more and more clear, Schindler's motivations switch from profit to sympathy and he is able to save over 1,100 Jews from death in the gas chambers.

School Daze. 1988. Directed by Spike Lee. 40 Acres & A Mule Filmworks. A comedic look at black college life. Two groups clash over the Greek fraternity system and issues of self-identity and self-esteem.

Seguin. 1979. Directed by Jesús Salvador Treviño. KCET Los Angeles. A PBS American Playhouse drama that was broadcast nationally, this film tells the controversial story of Juan Seguín, who fought on the side of the Anglo-Americans against Mexican General Santa Ana at the battle of the Alamo. Seguín is portrayed as a hero of the revolution in Texas who later becomes a victim of racial and cultural prejudice.

Smoke Signals. 1998. Directed by Chris Eyre. Based on characters in Sherman Alexie's short story collection, *The Lone Ranger and Tonto Fistfight in Heaven*, the film tells the story of Victor Joseph and Thomas Builds-the-Fire, who live on an Indian reservation in Idaho. When Victor's father dies in Arizona, the two young men set out to retrieve his ashes and belongings. Along the way they do some soul searching regarding their identity as "Indians" in America.

Sunshine State. 2002. Directed by John Sayles. Anarchist's Convention Films. Explores the implications of corporations buying property in a Florida beach town. Race, gender, and class are major factors in the tensions that arise as local residents confront corporate real estate developers in an effort to preserve the rich history and heritage of the community.

To Kill a Mockingbird. 1962. Directed by Robert Mulligan. Brentwood Pictures. An award-winning film based on Harper Lee's Pulitzer Prize–winning book of 1960. Atticus Finch, a lawyer in a racially divided Alabama town in the 1930s, agrees to defend a young black man who is accused of raping a white woman.

Tsotsi (Zulu, Xhosa, Afrikaans, English). 2005. Directed by Gavin Hood. UK Film & TV Production Company PLC. Based on a novel by the South African writer Athol Fugard, *Tsotsi* is an extremely violent yet poignant look at one boy's life as a thug in a township in South Africa. It tells the story of a tiny fraction of township life in South Africa, contrasting the boy's life with that of an upper-middle-class family in South Africa.

Watermelon Woman. 1996. Directed by Cheryl Dunye. Dancing Girl; First Run Features. An exploration of cinematic representations of black women that refute racist stereotypes. The film provides a fresh, contemporary, and challenging look at issues of racism, sexism, gender, and sexuality by following the story of one woman's quest to trace the life and history of a fictional 1930s black woman film star. It won awards at the Berlin International Film Festival, the Cretiel International Festival of Women's Cinema, the New York International Lesbian and Gay Film Festival, and the Torino International Gay and Lesbian Film Festival, among others.

West Side Story. 1961. Directed by Jerome Robbins and Robert Wise. Mirisch Corporation; United Artists. An adaptation of the classic romantic tragedy *Romeo and Juliet*. The feuding families are transformed into two warring New York City gangs in the 1950s: the white Jets, led by Riff, and the Puerto Rican Sharks, led by Bernardo. Racial and ethnic tension escalates to a point where neither can coexist with any form of understanding, and violence ensues. Then Riff's best friend (and former Jet) Tony and Bernardo's younger sister Maria meet at a dance and fall in love, with tragic consequences. Like the Broadway musical on which it is based, the movie asks whether love can overcome racial and ethnic stereotypes.

DOCUMENTARIES

A. Philip Randolph: For Jobs and Freedom. 1996. Directed by Dante James. WETA Washington D.C. James's film takes viewers on a tour of twentieth-century civil rights and labor history in the United States as it chronicles Randolph's efforts to build a more equitable society. Randolph believed that economic rights were the key to advancing civil rights. In response to the race riots of 1919, Randolph helped formed the National Association for the Promotion of Labor Unionism among Negroes, and he was asked to help them organize the Brotherhood of Sleeping Car Porters. In 1963 Randolph participated in the March on Washington and introduced Dr. Martin Luther King Jr. at the rally that ended the march.

Afro-Punk: The "Rock n Roll Nigger" Experience. 2003. Directed by James Spooner. *Afro-Punk* explores racial identity within the punk scene and the experience of being a minority inside a minority community.

The Agronomist. 2003. Directed by Jonathan Demme. Clinica Extetico. An examination of the inspiring life and tragic death of the pioneering Haitian radio journalist and human-rights activist Jean Dominique.

American Red and Black: Stories of Afro-Native Identity. 2006. Directed by Alicia Woods. Native Voices. This 39-minute documentary follows a self-identified African American as she researches and reflects on her Native American heritage. Topics such as the relationship between art and ethnic identity and racism within communities of color are explored through discussions with Afro-Natives from around the United States.

Ancestors in the Americas: Coolies, Sailors, Settlers. 1996. Directed by Loni Ding. CET Productions. TV documentary. The untold story of how Asians (e.g., Filipinos, Chinese, Asian Indians) first arrived in the Americas. Film crosses centuries and oceans from the sixteenth-century Manila-Acapulco trade to the Opium Wars and nineteenth-century plantation coolie labor in South America and the Caribbean. Loni Ding's documentary looks at the enormous contributions made by Asian peoples in the development of North and South America, contributions that go beyond the stereotypical notions that the Asians were only laborers, launderers, and owners of exotic restaurants.

At the River I Stand. 1993. Directed by David Appleby, Allison Graham, and Steven Ross. California Newsreel. A documentary recounting the two months leading to Martin Luther King Jr.'s death in 1968, focusing on the 65-day strike of 1,300 Memphis sanitation workers. Issues of race, class, economic disparities, and civil rights in America are underscored.

Baadasssss Cinema. 2002. Directed by Isaac Julien. Independent Film Channel (IFC). An exploration of the "blaxploitation" genre, with film excerpts and interviews. This documentary is a good introduction to white-black relationships in the United States in the late 1960s.

Beah: A Black Woman Speaks. 2003. Directed by Lisa Gay Hamilton. Clinica Estetico. In 1999, the actress Lisa Gay Hamilton sat down with the activist, poet, and fellow actress Beah Richards for a series of frank, thought-provoking conversations. The resulting documentary film presents the hard-earned wisdom of a remarkable artist and activist who has confronted the challenges of race, class, gender, growing-up, and living in America. The film also explores the deep and tender relationship that developed between the two women. *Beah* won the Documentary Jury Prize at the 2003 American Film Institute (AFI) International Film Festival.

Beat of Distant Hearts: The Art of Revolution in Western Sahara (English and Arabic). 1999. Directed by Danielle Smith. Dakkuma Productions. *Beat of Distant Hearts* tells the story of the Saharawis, a formerly nomadic people who have been under Spanish colonial rule for ninety years. They were forced to flee their homeland when Morocco was invaded in 1975, but they have sought to keep their culture alive while carrying on their fight to gain the independence of Western Sahara, the last colony in Africa. The film explores their collective experience of exile, loss, and war, offering insights into how the work of poets, singers, and painters has played a role in the struggle for freedom by colonized people.

bell hooks: Cultural Criticism and Transformation. 1997. Directed by Sut Jhally. Media Education Foundation. This two-part video of a lecture by the writer and activist bell hooks challenges how people look at and interpret the various and varying forms and processes of representation of themselves and others as encountered in everyday life. The lecture is illustrated with clips from films and music videos.

Bethlehem Diary. 2001. Directed by Antonia Caccia. First Run Icarus Films. Bethlehem Diary was filmed during Christmas in Bethlehem in the year 2000. The town was expecting five million visitors to celebrate the end of the millennium, but the streets are deserted, the hotels shut, the shops empty. The Israeli army has closed off Bethlehem since the second Intifada began the previous September. The film looks at two middle-class Palestinian families and a human rights lawyer during this tumultuous period. It shows their struggles to live under curfew and closure, with their every move monitored by the Israeli army.

Beyond Freedom: The South African Journey. 2006. Directed by Jacquie Trowell. Big World Cinema. This short documentary creatively utilizes animation to profile a cross-section of South Africans talking about their struggles to modernize or just plain survive in their post-apartheid nation.

Black and Gold: The Latin King and Queen Nation. 2000. Directed by Richard Rowley and Jacqui Soohen. Big Noise Films. In 1994 the Latin Kings, a powerful street gang in New York City, became the Latin King and Queen Nation. This film documents the emergence of an important political voice as the group, which claims to have abandoned its criminal past, dedicates itself to working toward change in the community and in America.

Black Indians: An American Story 2000. Directed by Chip Richie. Rich-Heape Films. A documentary film that presents the rarely told story of the relationship between Native Americans and African Americans. It profiles how the histories of these two groups are intertwined and examines the challenges facing them at the beginning of the twenty-first century. This story literally begins with the birth of America, in the presence of the mixed-race Boston Massacre martyr Crispus Attucks, and it includes the tragic aspects of the nineteenth century, including through the Seminole Wars and the expulsion of the Cherokee nation on the infamous Trail of Tears.

Black Is, Black Ain't. 1994. Directed by Marlon Riggs. Independent Television Service (ITVS). An upfront examination of racism, sexism, and homophobia within the black community. The film challenges African Americans to define what is black, black enough, or too black.

The Black Press: Soldiers without Swords. 1998. Directed and produced by Stanley Nelson. California Newsreel. The first documentary to provide an in-depth examination of the history and contributions of African American newspapers, which have existed in almost every major U.S. city since the early 1800s.

Black Russians (English). 2001. Directed by Kara Lynch. Third World Newsreel. A look at the lives of contemporary Afro-Russians in Soviet Russia. The interplay of two ideological currents that shaped the twentieth-century world—race and communism—is explored.

Black Women in Brazil *(Mulheres Negras).* 1986. Directed by Silvana Afram. Women Make Movies. This film exposes viewers to a critical examination of the racially segregated caste system of Brazil, as seen from the perspective of black women in Brazil coping with the system through their music and religion.

Blind Spot: Hitler's Secretary (German). 2002. Directed by André Heller and Othmar Schmiderer. Dor Film Productions. In 1942, at the height of World War II,

Adolf Hitler hired the 22-year-old Traudl Junge as his private secretary. As the Nazi regime teetered on the brink of destruction, Junge became a firsthand witness to Hitler's plunge into delusion, apathy, and depression. After more than a half-century of silence, in this documentary film, Junge sheds new light on the private life of Adolf Hitler, underscoring the horror of racist policies and practices in Germany and throughout eastern Europe.

The Borinqueneers. 2007. Produced and directed by Noemi Figueroa Soulet. El Pozo Productions; Public Broadcasting Service. This PBS documentary tells the story of the Puerto Rican 65th Infantry Regiment, the only all-Hispanic unit in the history of the U.S. Army.

The Boys of Baraka. 1995. Directed by Heidi Ewing and Rachel Grady. Loki Films. A documentary about the lives of four boys who are transported from a crime-ridden Baltimore, Maryland, neighborhood to a boarding school in Kenya. Issues of race, place, and economic status are profiled and explored through the daily activities of these boys.

Brother Outsider: The Life of Bayard Rustin. 2003. Directed by Nancy Kates and Bennett Singer. California Newsreel. Rustin was there at most of the important events of the civil rights movement, but always in the background. This film examines why this was so in this vivid drama about one of the most enigmatic figures in twentieth-century American history. Rustin was one of the first "Freedom Riders," an adviser to Dr. Martin Luther King Jr. and A. Philip Randolph, and an organizer of the 1963 March on Washington. Intelligent, gregarious, and charismatic, Rustin was denied his rightful place in the limelight primarily because he was gay.

Brothers and Others. 2002. Directed by Nicolas Rossier. Baraka Productions. A documentary on the impact of the September 11th tragedy on Muslims and Arabs living in America. The film follows a number of immigrants and American families as they struggle in the heightened climate of hate, FBI and INS investigations, and economic hardships that erupted in America following the attacks on the World Trade Center and the Pentagon.

Chasing Daybreak. 2006. Directed by Justin Leroy. MAVIN Foundation. Five self-identified mixed-raced individuals take a road trip across America, intent on engaging people in discussions on the social realities of race and racism. The film raises questions about the role of a mixed-race movement and the eradication of racism in America.

Chicano! History of the Mexican-American Civil Rights Movement. 1996. Series produced by Hector Galán. NLCC Educational Media and Galán Productions. A four-part documentary series dealing with Mexican American struggles to achieve equality and full rights as citizens of the United States. It address issues concerning land, labor, education, and political empowerment that took place between 1965 and 1975, a pivotal period of the Mexican American civil rights movement.

Chicana. 1979. Directed by Sylvia Morales. Women Make Movies. The history of Chicana and Mexican women from pre-Columbian times to the present is chronicled in this 23-minute film. Women's role in Aztec society, their participation in the 1810 struggle for Mexican independence, their contributions to the 1910 Mexican revolution, and their leadership and activism in contemporary civil rights causes are all given attention.

The Chicano Collection. 2005. Directed by Tamara Hernandez. Produced to accompany "The Chicano Collection," an exhibition of Hispanic art, the film describes the personal journeys and viewpoints of the twenty-six featured artists and their struggle for acceptance by American art museums.

Chinatown. 1997. Directed by Felicia Lowe. PBS/KQED. Although it focuses on one neighborhood, this documentary is in many ways the story of all Chinese in America. For decades, San Francisco's Chinatown was the largest community of Chinese outside Asia, and yet it was a neighborhood that was forced to be independent, even isolated, from the rest of society. Its residents were barred from even the basic rights of citizenship. Even so, Chinatown's residents have managed to create a thriving community that is the second most popular destination for visitors to San Francisco (after the Golden Gate Bridge).

Chisholm '72: Unbought & Unbossed. 2004. Directed by Shola Lynch. Realside Productions. Shirley Chisholm's 1972 bid for the Democratic presidential nomination is chronicled in this film. Chisholm was the first black woman to run for president of the United States, and the politics of race, gender, class, and differential access to wealth and power in the United States are underscored in this film, which was nominated for the Grand Jury Prize at the Sundance Film Festival.

The Civil War. 1990. Directed by Ken Burns. American Documentaries, Inc.; Florentine Films; WETA Washington. This groundbreaking miniseries traces the course of the U.S. Civil War from the abolitionist movement through all the major battles to the death of President Abraham Lincoln and the beginnings of Reconstruction. A very vivid profile of American culture and of its bloodiest confrontations over issues of race, power, and place.

Classified People (French). 1987. Directed by Yolanda Zauberman. Obsession. By detailing the nature of racial classification and segregation in South Africa, *Classified People* provides a penetrating look at the arbitrary mechanics of apartheid.

Color Adjustment. 1992. Directed by Marlon Riggs. California Newsreel. An examination of the racist images perpetuated by the film industry, *Color Adjustment* provides an analysis of the evolution of television's earlier, unflattering portrayal of blacks from 1948 until 1988.

Color of Fear. 1994. Directed by Lee Mun Wah. StirFry Seminars. A small group of men from different ethnic groups come together to discuss issues of racism prevalent in American society.

Color of Fear 2: Walking Each Other Home. 1998. Directed by Lee Mun Wah. StirFry Seminars. In this sequel to *The Color of Fear*, a small group of men from different ethnic groups come together to talk about racism in American society. The film explores in greater depth the relationships among the men, as well as answering the question, "What can whites do to end racism?"

The Color of Honor. 1989. Directed by Loni Ding. Center for Educational Telecommunications (CET). Portrays the complex variety of responses of Japanese American men during World War II. While reviled and interned in their home country for their ethnic heritage, they were also confronted with the rise of fascism abroad. Some wanted to prove they were loyal Americans and fought bravely in the highly decorated Japanese American 442nd Regimental Combat Unit, which liberated European towns, while some felt they could not in good conscience serve in the U.S. Armed Forces as long as their families were "interned" in violation of the Constitution they were supposed to defend.

The Color of Olives (Arabic). 2006. Directed by Carolina Rivas; produced by Daoud Sarhandi. Arab Film Distribution. A chronicle of the life of a Palestinian family who live surrounded by the infamous West Bank Wall. Their daily lives are dominated by electrified fences, locks, and a constant swarm of armed soldiers. As their dramas unfold, one glimpses their constant struggles and the small, endearing details that sustain them: including olive trees, two small donkeys, and their many friendships. The film contemplates the effects of racial segregation, the meaning of borders, and the absurdity of war.

Community Voices: Exploring Cross-Cultural Care Through Cancer. 2001. Directed by Jeannie Greene and Kim Newell. Harvard Center for Cancer Prevention. An examination of how issues of race, class, and culture impact health, health-care delivery, and access to health care. The film asks how people can work together to provide high-quality care to diverse individuals and communities.

The Cry of Reason. 1987. Directed by Robert Bilheimer. Tracks the personal and social odyssey of the Reverend Beyers Naude as he moves from being a member of the Afrikaner secret society that invented apartheid to becoming a student of anti-apartheid activist Steve Biko. Naude commits himself to the liberation of South Africa's black population.

Cuban Roots/Bronx Stories. 2000. Directed by Pam Sporn. Third World Newsreel. An intimate portrayal of a black Cuban immigrant family living in the Bronx. Three siblings recount their family's reasons for leaving Cuba, yet they grow to appreciate some aspects of the revolution through their exploration of the radical black and Latino movements of the 1960s and 1970s in the United States.

Desire. 2005. Directed by Julie Gustafson. Women Make Movies. A diverse group of young women in New Orleans—two teenagers from the Desire housing projects, a single mother from the working-class suburb of Belle Chasse across the river, and two girls from the most prestigious private high school in New Orleans—made short films about their own desires for this documentary study of race and class. The intimate dramas of their changing lives are portrayed, as is the coming of age of the filmmaker, who is forced to rethink her role in the production of the film.

Divided We Fall: Americans in the Aftermath (English and Punjabi). 2006. Directed by Sharat Raju. New Moon Productions. Valarie Kaur, a college student, drove across America in the aftermath of the September 11, 2001, terrorist attacks, trying to discover stories that did not make the evening news. The resulting film documents hate crimes against Sikhs, Muslims, and others, and it examines how Americans react to the perceived "Other" in times of war.

The End of the Nightstick: Confronting Police Brutality in Chicago. 1993. Produced and directed by Peter Kuttner, Cyni Moran, and Eric Scholl. First Run/Icarus Films. Investigates and documents institutional racism, brutality, and cover-ups in Chicago's police department.

The Essential Blue-Eyed. 1999. Produced and directed by Bertram Verhaag. California Newsreel. Documents the experiments of the teacher and activist Jane Elliott, as she divides a multiracial group of Midwesterners on the basis of eye color and then subjects the blue-eyed members to a regime of humiliation and contempt.

In just a few hours into the experiment, a noticeable difference between the two groups appears. In particular, the blue-eyed members are clearly disoriented and unsure of themselves. Elliott's method is based on her belief that people can best be motivated to fight discrimination by experiencing it themselves, if only for a few hours in a controlled environment.

Ethnic Notions. 1986. Directed by Marlon Riggs. California Newsreel. An Emmy-winning documentary, *Ethnic Notions* traces the evolution of racial consciousness in America. It critically examines deep-rooted stereotypes in American history and dramatizes the impact that these ideas and imagery have had in terms of fueling antiblack prejudice.

The Eyes of the Rainbow. 1997. Directed by Gloria Rolando. A documentary by the independent video group Imágenes del Caribe, this film depicts the life of Assata Shakur, the Black Panther and Black Liberation Army leader who escaped from prison and was given political asylum in Cuba.

Eyes on the Prize. 1987. Directed by Henry Hampton. Blackside and the Public Broadcasting Service (PBS). This award-winning 14-hour television series covers all of the major events of the civil rights movement in the United States from 1954 to 1985.

Farm: Life Inside Angola Prison. 1998. Directed by Liz Garbus, Wilbert Rideau, and Jonathan Stack. Gabriel Films. A profile of life among inmates at Louisiana State Penitentiary, one of America's largest maximum security prisons. The film won numerous awards, including the Grand Jury Prize at the Sundance Film Festival.

Farmingville. 2004. Directed by Catherine Tambini and Carlos Sandoval. The story of the hate-based attempted murder of two Mexican day laborers in Farmingville, New York. Issues of racism, fear, and violence in an American community are explored.

February One: The Story of the Greensboro Four. 2003. Produced by Rebecca Cerese, with Steven Channing serving as executive producer. Video Dialog. A documentary about the day that four college freshmen changed the course of American history. The film tells the story of the 1960 Greensboro lunch counter sit-ins that revitalized the civil rights movement.

500 Dunam on the Moon (Arabic, French, and Hebrew). 2002. Directed by Rachel Leah Jones. RLJ Productions. The movie tells the story of Ayn Hawd, a Palestinian village that was converted into a Jewish artists' colony in 1953 with the help of Romanian artist Marcel Janco. The village, which was renamed Ein-Hod, had been destroyed during the 1948 war.

Forget Baghdad: Jews and Arabs—The Iraqi Connection (Arabic, English, and Hebrew). 2002. Directed by Samir Naqqash. Dschoint Ventschr Film-produktion AG. The forgotten story of four Baghdadi-Jews, all former members of the Iraqi Communist Party, who were forced to emigrate at Israel's founding. The four elderly protagonists were influenced in their youth by the internationalism of the Iraqi Communist Party, but in the early 1950s their Jewish identity put them at odds with rising Arab nationalism. The divided identities and confusion of these four men's lives tell a much larger tale of global, political, and cultural disorder. Winner of the 2002 Locarno Jury Prize.

4 Little Girls. 1997. Directed by Spike Lee. HBO Films. A historical documentary about the 1963 bombing of the 16th Street Baptist Church in Birmingham, Alabama. The film underscores the tragic result of race hatred in an American context.

Frantz Fanon: Black Skin, White Mask. 1996. Directed by Isaac Julien. Normal Films. A film biography that explores the life of Frantz Fanon, the preeminent theorist of anticolonial movements. Fanon's two major works, *Black Skin, White Masks* and *The Wretched of the Earth*, are pioneering studies of the psychological impact of racism on both the colonized and the colonizer.

Freedom Bags. 1990. Directed by Stanley Nelson. Abena Productions. The story of African American women who migrated from the rural South during the first three decades of the twentieth century. Trying to escape the racism and poverty of the post–Civil War South, they headed north, but because of their limited education, most could find jobs only as domestics.

Freedom on My Mind. 1994. Directed by Connie Field and Marilyn Mulford. Tara Releasing. This story about the Mississippi freedom movement in the early 1960s looks at how a small group of young activists changed history. The film was an Academy Award nominee for Best Documentary Feature, and it won the best documentary prize from both the American Historical Association and the Organization of American Historians.

From One Blood: The Story of Gerrit Wolfaardt. 2003. Directed by Cristóbal Krusen. Mix Holdings. A documentary about the life of Afrikaner Gerrit Wolfaardt and his transformation from a life of hate, in which he devised a plan to rid South Africa of "The Black Danger" during apartheid, to one of redemption, in which he preaches a message of racial reconciliation to audiences in South Africa and the United States. The film includes scenes from *Final Solution* (also profiled here), a feature film based on his life.

From Swastika to Jim Crow. 2000. Directed by Lori Cheatle and Martin D. Taub. Pacific Street Films. The period in American history from the 1930s to the rise of the civil rights and Black Power movements serves as the background to this previously untold story of the many German Jewish professors who, having been expelled from their homeland by the Nazis, found new lives and careers at all-black colleges and universities in the South.

Generations of Resistance. 1980. Directed by Peter Davis. Sveriges Radio. The history of black resistance to white rule in South Africa is chronicled, from its origins in the Bambata Rebellion of 1906 through the founding of the African National Congress to the ultimate abolition of apartheid.

Half of Anything. 2006. Directed by Jonathan S. Tomhave. Native Voices. Four interview subjects (Christina Entrekin, Deborah Bassett, John Trudell, and Sherman Alexie) share insights about American Indian identity in this 24-minute film.

Hands on the Verdict: The 1992 Los Angeles Uprising. 1992. Directed by Elizabeth Canner and Julia Meltzer. Los Angeles Video Activists. This short film probes the issues of racism, economic disparity, and police brutality surrounding the civil unrest that took place after the verdict in the Rodney King case. It opens with a collage of rough footage of the Rodney King beating, the 1992 Los Angeles riots, and the 1965 Watts riot.

The Hero *(O Herói).* Portuguese. 2005. Directed by Zézé Gamboa; Produced by Fernando Vendrell. David & Golias. The story of Angola, a nation torn apart by forty years of uninterrupted anticolonial and civil warfare, as it tries to reconstruct itself. The story is told from the perspective of the lives of a veteran who has lost his leg, a prostitute who has lost a child, and an orphaned boy. It takes place in the city of Luanda, which is trying to absorb the millions of people displaced by civil strife and global economic change. Winner of Grand Prize at the World Dramatic Competition during the 2005 Sundance Film Festival.

Hoop Dreams. 1994. Directed by Steve James. KTCA Minneapolis. Two African American students in Chicago have dreams of becoming professional basketball players and are recruited by a predominantly white high school with an outstanding basketball program. This chronicle of their experiences raises issues about race, class, economic divisions, educational opportunities, and values in American society.

Ida B. Wells: A Passion for Justice. 1989. Produced and directed by William Greaves. California Newsreel. The life and times of Ida B. Wells-Barnett are examined in this 53-minute film. Wells was an African American journalist, activist, and suffragist who fought against the plague of lynching in the post-Reconstruction period.

If You Only Understood (Spanish). 1998. Written and directed by Rolando Diaz. A Cuban film director's search for an actress to star in his new musical comedy exposes issues of racism and other conflicts in the Cuban society. (Spanish title: *Si me comprendieras.*)

In Search of History: The Night Tulsa Burned. 1999. Weller-Grossman Productions; The History Channel. A section of Tulsa, Oklahoma, known as Greenwood, was dubbed the "Black Wall Street" in 1920, but this upper-middle-class neighborhood was destroyed in 1921 by the worst racial uprising in the history of America. This film chronicles the complete destruction of Greenwood by an angry mob of white men.

In the White Man's Image. 1991. Directed by Christine Lesiak. Public Broadcasting Service ("American Experience" series). A chronicle of the efforts of Captain Richard Pratt to transform Native Americans into members of the mainstream white culture. Pratt began the Carlisle School for Indians in 1879, and it lasted into the late 1930s.

The Inner Tour (English, Arabic and Hebrew). 2001. Directed by Ra'anan Alexandrowicz. Zeitgeist Films. A documentary about a diverse group of Palestinians living in the West Bank. Through a quirk in the law, they are allowed to become tourists and visit their homeland for the first time since the occupation. They take a three-day bus tour in 2000 across the "Green Line" and go inside the heart of Israel. One of the men uses a map of Palestine to refresh his memory of where the Arab villages were in 1948 that have been replaced by Jewish settlements. *The Inner Tour* shows how differently both sides view the same thing, as one side calls the land Israel while the other calls it Palestine.

International Sweethearts of Rhythm. 1986. Produced and directed by Greta Schiller and Andrea Weiss. Jezebel Productions. This 30-minute film looks at issues of race and racism in America through the story of a multiracial all-women jazz band of the 1940s.

The Intolerable Burden. 2002. Directed by Chea Prince. Public Domain, Inc.; Center for the Study of Southern Culture. In Drew, Mississippi, in 1965, the sharecroppers Matthew and Mae Bertha Carter are committed to obtaining a quality education for their children. The film examines the conditions of segregation prior to 1965, the hardships the family faced during desegregation, and the massive white resistance to a plan to provide equality in education.

Iraq in Fragments (Kurdish and Arabic). 2006. Directed by James Longley. Daylight Factory. Ethnic tensions and issues of identity in Iraq are explored in Longley's film. The three principal groups in Iraq—Sunnis, Shiites, and Kurds—are profiled in this examination of the divisive forces that are tearing the country apart. Young Mohammed, a Sunni, works at an auto shop and drifts in and out of school; The Shiite leader Moqtada al-Sadr ruthlessly enforces Islamic Law in the country's southern region; and a family of Kurdish farmers struggles to survive.

James Baldwin: The Price of the Ticket. 1990. Directed by Karen Thorsen. Nobody Knows Productions; California Newsreel. James Baldwin (1924–1987) was a major twentieth-century American author, a civil rights activist, and a critical voice calling on Americans, black and white, to confront racism as a shared tragedy. Baldwin was black, gifted, and gay, which gave him a unique insight into American culture. The film chronicles his formative years and explores his retreats in Paris, the South of France, Istanbul, and Switzerland—places where Baldwin was able to write away from the racial tensions of America.

Japanese American Women: A Sense of Place. 1992. Directed by Rosanna Yamagiwa Alfano and Leita Hagemann. Women Make Movies. The stereotype of the polite, docile, exotic Asian woman is shattered in this 28-minute documentary, in which a dozen women speak about their experiences as part of the "model minority." The film explores the ambivalent feelings the women have toward both Japan and the United States.

Jazz. 2001. Directed by Ken Burns. British Broadcasting Corporation; Florentine Films; WETA Washington. This PBS film series explores the history of the major American musical form. It tracks its development in African American culture, its rise to prominence with its golden age of popularity spanning from the 1920s to the mid-1940s, and its popular decline and the rise of vital new subgenres.

Jefferson's Blood. 2000. Produced and directed by Thomas Lennon. WGBH Boston; Frontline. This PBS documentary examines the life of Thomas Jefferson and follows the descendants of Jefferson and his enslaved African mistress, Sally Hemings, as they undergo DNA testing, search out their family history, and try to sort out their place along America's blurred color line.

John Henrik Clarke: A Great and Mighty Walk. 1996. Directed by St. Clair Bourne. Black Dot Media. Documentary about the black scholar and activist John Henrik Clarke (1915–1998), who discusses representations of African and African-descendent people throughout history, using newsreel footage to highlight his views.

July '64. 2006. Directed by Carvin Eison. ImageWordSound; WXXI-TV. The night of Friday, July 24th, 1964, started off normally enough in Rochester, New York, but by the next morning the way that race relations in the North were looked at would never be the same again. *July '64* examines the underlying causes of the Rochester riots and the urban unrest that swept through black communities in America that summer and in the years that followed.

Last Chance for Eden. 2002. Directed by Lee Mun Wah. StirFry Seminars. This two-part documentary is about a small group of men and women who get together to have an open conversation about racism and sexism and its impact on their lives, especially with respect to the workplace.

Last Grave at Dimbaza. 1974. Directed by Chris Curling and Pasco Macfarlane. First Run/Icarus Films. A rare exposé of everyday life in South Africa during the period of apartheid. Filmed throughout South Africa, including the black townships and desolate bantustans, this film portrays the stark contrasts between living and working conditions for the majority populace of 18 million blacks and the 4 million whites who rule over them.

The Lemon Grove Incident. 1985. Directed by Frank Christopher. KPBS Television; California Council for the Humanities; Corporation for Public Broadcasting. This film focuses on one of the earliest cases of desegregation in U.S. history. It profiles the response of the Mexican American community in Lemon Grove, California, to a 1930 school board attempt to create a segregated school for Mexican Americans.

Life and Debt. 2001. Produced and directed by Stephanie Black. Tuff Gong Pictures. The stories of individual Jamaicans, whose strategies for survival and day-to-day existence are determined by the United States and other foreign economic agendas, are the subject of *Life and Debt.* Issues of race, place, class, and nationality are examined through a look into the complexity of international lending, structural adjustment policies, and free trade. The film utilizes excerpts from the writer Jamaica Kincaid's "A Small Place" (1987).

The Life and Times of Sara Baartman. 1998. Directed by Zola Maseko. First Run/Icarus Films. This documentary tells the story of a Khoi Khoi woman who was taken from South Africa, labeled the "Hottentot Venus," and exhibited as a freak across Britain.

A Litany for Survival: The Life and Work of Audre Lorde. 1995 Directed by Ada Gay Griffin and Michelle Parkerson. Independent Television Service. The film provides an examination of race, gender, class, sexism, and sexuality in America through a profile of the African American poet Audre Lorde.

Living in America: A Hundred Years of Ybor City. 1987. Directed by Gayla Jamison. The multicultural community of Ybor City, in Tampa, Florida, was founded in the 1880s when Cuban, Spanish, and Italian immigrants arrived to work in the area's thriving cigar factories. In this film, older residents reminisce about their vibrant ethnic enclaves, especially the lively social clubs that provided not only entertainment but medical care for their members. The film also highlights how life for black Cubans differed in terms of experiences and memories in Ybor.

Long Night's Journey into Day (English and Arfikaans). 2000. Directed by Deborah Hoffmann and Frances Reid. Reid-Hoffman Productions. Four stories of apartheid in South Africa are examined in the context of the post-apartheid Truth and Reconciliation Commission. The film asks if there can be forgiveness when the truth is finally known.

Looking for Langston. 1988. Directed by Isaac Julien. British Film Institute. A poetic look at high-society gay black men during the Harlem Renaissance in America. Issues of race, class, and sexuality are highlighted in this film meditation on the work and life of the poet Langston Hughes.

Lost Boys of Sudan (English, Arabic, Dinka, and Swahili). 2003. Directed by Megan Mylan and Jon Shenk. Actual Films. A comment on the myth of the American dream, the film follows the incredible journey that two teenage Sudanese refugees make from their African homeland to America. They confront extreme cultural differences, including issues of race, place, class, and ethnicity in American society. Winner of a 2004 Independent Spirit Award.

Lumumba. (French and Lingala). 2000. Directed by Raoul Peck. Canal+; Zeitgeist Films. This film tells the true story of the rise to power and brutal assassination of Patrice Lumumba, the formerly vilified and later esteemed leader of the independent Congo. It examines racism, colonialism, and the fight for political and economic power and control in Africa.

The Maids! 1985. Directed by Muriel Jackson. Women Make Movies. A short documentary film that looks at the division of labor from a race, gender, and class perspective through an exploration of the history of African American women's labor in domestic service.

Maids and Madams. 1986. Directed by Mira Hamermesh. Shot in South Africa, this powerful yet historic documentary examines complex relationships between black household workers and white employers during the apartheid era.

Mama, I'm Crying. 1987. Directed by Betty Wolpert and Joyce Seroke. The story of two women, one black, the other white, who grew up at the same time in South Africa and return home and grapple with the reason some blacks no longer think that nonviolence is the way to fight apartheid. Their differing perspectives on life make it seem as if they were brought up in two different countries.

Mandela. 1996. Directed by Angus Gibson and Jo Menell. Clinico Estetico; Island Pictures. A full-length documentary looking at the life of Nelson Mandela and his fight to end apartheid in his homeland of South Africa. Filmed during the seven months leading up to the historic 1994 presidential election in South Africa, the film features exclusive interviews and narration from Mandela himself.

Master Race. 1997. Directed by Jonathan Lewis. WGBH Boston; British Broadcasting Corporation. Part of the documentary TV film series "People's Century," the film chronicles the rise of Nazism in Germany and the persecution of those identified as being black, Jewish, Gypsy, or homosexual in Germany from the 1930s onward. The story is told through accounts of both those that were and were not part of the Final Solution instituted by Hitler as a strategy for creating and maintaining his vision of a master race.

Mayan Voices: American Lives. 1994. Directed by Olivia Carrescia. First Run/Icarus Films. Set in Indiantown, Florida, *Mayan Voices* profiles the lives and experiences of Mayan families (from Guatemala) in the United States and the impact of these new immigrants on a predominantly white community.

Mighty Times: The Legacy of Rosa Parks. 2002. Directed by Robert Houston. Tell the Truth Pictures. This Academy Award–nominated short revisits this familiar historical event of December 1, 1955, when Rosa Parks's act of defiance in refusing to give up her seat on a bus to a white person sparked the Montgomery Bus Boycott, while it also finds new stories that introduce new heroes of the civil rights era.

Mirrors of Privilege: Making White Visible. 2006. Produced and directed by Shakti Butler. World Trust Educational Services. Features the experiences of white women and men who have worked to gain insight into what it means to challenge notions of racism and white supremacy in the United States.

Mirrors of the Heart: Race and Identity. 1993. Produced and Directed by Lourdes Portillo. WGBH Boston. Part 4 of a 10-part PBS series examining the shifting social, political, and economic forces at work in South America, Central America, and the Caribbean. The film explores issues of race and ethnicity from the perspective of identity and social standing in Bolivia, Haiti, and the Dominican Republic.

Mississippi Triangle. 1984. Directed by Christine Choy, Worth Long, and Allan Siegel. Third World Newsreel. Explores the triracial configuration of black, white, and Chinese in the Mississippi Delta.

Mother Ireland. 1998. Directed by Anne Crilly. Derry Film and Video Collective. Leading Irish feminists trace the images of women in Irish history (e.g., "Mother Ireland," "The Old Woman") and their impact on women's lives. Particular focus is placed on aspirations for freedom, the revolutionary struggles for independence from England, and the movements for unification of the country.

Motherland: A Genetic Journey. 2003. Directed by Archie Baron. Takeaway Media Productions; British Broadcasting Corporation. A documentary on genetic testing and the meaning of genes, race, identity, and geography. Three black individuals reconnect with the precise population groups from which their ancestors were separated by slavery.

Mumia Abu-Jamal: A Case for Reasonable Doubt? 1997. Directed by John Edginton. Otmoor Productions. A documentary film about Mumia Abu-Jamal, a black nationalist and journalist in Philadelphia, Pennsylvania, who was convicted in 1982 of killing a Philadelphia police officer and sentenced to death. His trial was marked by controversial prosecution and defense tactics and charges of racism.

New Orleans. 2007. Directed by Stephen Ives. Insignia Films Production; American Experience; Louisiana Public Broadcasting. A portrait of one of America's most distinctive cities, a small French settlement surrounded by water that ultimately would become the home of America's biggest party, Mardi Gras, and its most original art form, jazz. The site of explosive struggles with both integration and segregation, New Orleans has been a proving ground for national ideas about race, class, and equality in America.

New Orleans Black Indians: A Case Study in the Arts. 1983. Insight Media. This documentary, part of the "Faces of Culture" film series, explores the Black Indian tribes of New Orleans as they carry out a century-old tradition of participation in the pre-Lenten Mardi Gras celebration.

Paris is Burning. 1991. Directed by Jennie Livingston. Off White Productions. An exploration of race, class, and gender in America, the film chronicles the ball culture of New York City and the poor, African American, and Latino gay and transgendered communities involved in it.

Paul Robeson: Here I Stand. 1999. Directed by St. Clair Bourne. Part of the "American Masters" television series, the film includes archival film footage (speeches, Broadway and musical concert performances) of the athlete, singer, scholar, and political activist Paul Robeson.

A Place of Rage. 1991. Directed by Pratibha Palmer. Women Make Movies. Prominent black women (such as June Jordon, Angela Davis, Alice Walker, and Trinh T. Minh-Ha) discuss issues of race and racial discrimination in American culture, including the impact of racial discrimination on American society. The film also includes historical footage of the 1960s civil rights movement.

Postville: When Cultures Collide. 2001. Iowa Public Television. When Hasidic Jews from New York establish a kosher slaughterhouse in predominantly Lutheran Postville, issues of diversity surface in the rural Iowa town. Eventually, more Jews, then Hispanics and eastern Europeans, make Postville their home. The film is an excellent study of racial, ethnic, cultural, and religious diversity, as profiled through the experiences of one small heterogeneous population.

A Question of Color. 1993. Directed by Kathe Sandler. Independent Television Service. This documentary confronts a subject considered taboo by many African Americans, namely the disturbing feelings many people harbor about themselves and their appearance. Sandler examines the often subconscious world of "color consciousness," a caste-like system based on how closely skin color, hair texture, and facial features conform to a European ideal.

Race: The Floating Signifier. 1997. Directed by Sut Jally. Media Education Fund. The film features the Jamaica-born sociologist and racial theorist Stuart Hall, who argues against the biological interpretation of racial difference and asks the viewer to consider the cultural processes by which visual differences in appearance are ascribed specific classifications that are considered natural.

Race: The Power of an Illusion. 2003. California Newsreel. A film series (three hour-long episodes) that questions the very idea of race as a biological fact, suggesting instead that a belief in race is a false paradigm, while acknowledging that race still matters. It illustrates that just because race does not exist in biology does not mean it is not a social reality that shapes life chances and opportunities.

Race Is the Place. 2005. Produced and directed by Raymond Telles and Rick Tejada-Flores. Paradigm Productions; KERA TV Dallas-Fort Worth; Independent Television Service. A visual and verbal critique on race in

America from a wide variety of artists, poets, rappers, performance artists and stand-up comics. The film combines racially charged clips from old movies with interviews and performances. ITVS Community hosted a national broadcast of *Race Is the Place* on the "Independent Lens" series on November 22, 2005.

The Return of Sarah Baartman. 2003. Produced and directed by Zola Maseko. First Run/Icarus Films. Looks at the tragic impact of racism and imperialism by chronicling the return of the remains of Sara Baartman, a black woman who had been exhibited as a freak in the early nineteenth-century Europe. Her remains were returned to South Africa from France, where they had been kept at the Museum of Man. Sara's repatriation involved years of lobbying by people in South Africa.

The Rise and Fall of Jim Crow. 2002. Series produced by Richard Wormser. WNET New York. This four-part film series offers a comprehensive look at race relations in America between the Civil War and the civil rights movement. It documents a brutal era in American history, marked by the growing refusal of many southern states to grant slaves freed in the Civil War equal rights with whites. Winner of the 2003 Peabody Award and the 2003 IDA Achievement Award.

The Road to Brown. 1990. Directed by William Elwood and Mykola Kulish. California Newsreel. Focuses on segregation and the brilliant legal campaigning against it that helped launched the civil rights movement in America. It is also a moving tribute to Charles Hamilton Houston, an avid and highly effective opponent of Jim Crow.

A Seat at the Table: Struggling for American Indian Religious Freedom. 2004. Directed by Gary Rhine. Kifaru Productions. Rhine's film consists of eight segments, each one dealing with an important obstacle to American Indian religious freedom. The film includes commentary from Native leaders, as well as sequences shot in threatened Indian sacred sites and scenes from the Third Parliament of the World's Religions in Cape Town, South Africa.

Shake Hands with the Devil: The Journey of Roméo Dallaire. 2005. Directed by Peter Raymont. White Pine Pictures (Canada). Over 800,000 men, women, and children were massacred in the small African country of Rwanda. The victims were mainly Tutsis, murdered by their Hutu neighbors. The UN peacekeeping mission was headed by the Canadian general Roméo Dallaire, who had only a handful of soldiers and was ordered not to use force to protect Rwandans from the mass slaughter. This documentary film is based on Dallaire's best-selling book, and it follows Dallaire as he comes to grips with the events that came to haunt him, including his struggles with top UN officials, expedient Belgian policymakers, and Clinton administration officials who ignored his pleas for reinforcements.

Shalom Y'all. 2003. Directed by Brian Bain. National Center for Jewish Film. This documentary chronicles Jewish life in the American South. It is a record of the travels of the filmmaker Brian Bain, a third generation Jew from New Orleans, who sets out on a 4,200-mile road trip though the American South in a vintage Cadillac.

Shattering the Silences: The Case for Minority Faculty. 1997. Directed by Stanley Nelson. California Newsreel. This film tells the stories of four pioneering scholars—an African American, a Latino, a Native American, and an Asian American—at predominantly white universities. It shows in concrete terms how a diverse faculty enriches and expands traditional disciplines and contributes to a more inclusive campus.

Skin Deep: Building Diverse Campus Communities. 1995. Directed by Francis Reid. Iris Films. The eye-opening journey of a diverse group of college students as they confront each other's racial prejudices.

Strange Fruit. 2002. Produced and directed by Joel Katz. Oniera Films. An exploration of the history and legacy of the Billie Holiday classic "Strange Fruit." The song's evolution tells a dramatic story of America's past, using one of the most influential protest songs ever written as its epicenter. The saga brings viewers face to face with the terror of lynching as it spotlights the courage and heroism of those who fought for racial justice, even though doing so meant risking ostracism or even death.

Still Black, at Yale. 2004. Produced by Monique Walton and Andia Winslow. Examines issues of race and racism at universities in America with a specific focus on critiquing what it means to be black at an Ivy League school. The filmmakers were inspired by the 1974 student-made documentary *Black at Yale*.

Stolen Ground. 1993. Directed by Lee Mun Wah. StirFry Seminars. Six Asian American men come together to talk about their struggles against racism in America. They also address the myth of the "model minority" and the pressures of blending into the American culture.

Struggles in Steel: A Story of African-American Steelworkers. 1996. Directed by Tony Buba and Raymond Henderson. Braddock Films; California Newsreel. The story of the African American struggle for equality in the U.S. steel industry, based in Pittsburgh, Pennsylvania. In a series of interviews intermixed with archival footage and stills, the film shows how these workers faced and overcame discrimination that came from white workers, the big steel companies, and even from their own unions.

Sun, Moon & Feather. 1989. Directed by Bob Rosen and Jane Zipp. A short musical comedy and documentary about three Native American sisters growing up in Brooklyn during the 1930s and 1940s.

Tales from Arab Detroit. 1995. Directed by Joan Mandell. Issues of race, place, and identity in America are underscored in this documentary on the Arab community in Detroit. The film concentrates primarily on the Muslim experience.

A Time for Burning. 1967. Directed by Bill Jersey and Barbara Connell. Quest Productions. Reverend William Youngdahl's move from an integrated Lutheran church in New Jersey to an all-white congregation in Omaha, Nebraska, in 1965 is the subject of this film. It uncovers quiet acts of racism and issues of institutionalized racism in America.

Todos Santos: The Survivors. 1989. Directed by Olivia Carrescia. First Run/Icarus Films. The film focuses on postwar Guatemala and the colonization projects of the highlands. It examines the civil war of the 1980s, as well as the subsequent establishment of civil patrols, giving a general portrait of racism in the country.

Tongues Untied. 1989. Directed by Marlon Riggs. CAC Productions; MTR Productions; Frameline. Riggs examines the black gay experience and looks at issues of racism and homophobia in America.

Transitions: Destruction of a Mother Tongue. 1991. Produced and directed by Darrell Kip and Joe Fisher. Native Voices Public Television Workshop. Explores the relationship between language, thought, and culture. The film chronicles the disappearance of the Blackfeet tribal language during the period fron 1890 to 1990 and analyzes the impact of the loss of culture and language on Native communities.

Trouble Behind. 1990. Produced and directed by Robbie Henson. California Newsreel. Henson's film examines the disturbingly common occurrence of racism in America today. The origins of today's racism are sought by looking into the history of a seemingly typical small town—Corbin, Kentucky, the home of Kentucky Fried Chicken.

Twelve Disciples of Mandela (Afrikaans and English). 2006. Directed by Thomas Allen Harris. Chimpanzee Productions. A look into the organizational and psychological dynamics of liberation movements in general, and of the African National Congress (ANC) in South Africa in particular. A concise overview of the ANC's struggle for an end to apartheid is set against the background of the pan-African movement, the rise of black nationalism in the United States, and the dream of a shared identity among all people of the African descent.

Two Towns of Jasper. 2002. Directed by Whitney Dow and Marco Williams. Independent Television Service; Two-Tone Productions. A feature-length documentary about the 1998 racially motivated murder of James Byrd Jr. in Jasper, Texas.

Unchained Memories: Readings from the Slave Narratives. 2003. Directed by Ed Bell. HBO. Selections from the extensive Federal Writers' Project Slave Narrative Collection are read by various actors, interspersed with archival photographs, music, films and period images.

Unforgivable Blackness: The Rise and Fall of Jack Johnson. 2004. Directed by Ken Burns. Florentine Films; WETA Washington. In this film Burns tells the story of Jack Johnson, the first African American heavyweight boxing champion of the world, whose dominance over his white opponents spurred furious debates and race riots in the early twentieth century.

W. E. B. Du Bois: A Biography in Four Voices. 1996. Directed by Louis J. Massiah. Scribe Video Center; California Newsreel. A portrait of an important African American sociologist, W. E. B. Du Bois, who grew up in America during the period of segregation. He went on to study at Harvard and wrote about the challenges black people faced inhabiting and navigating within spaces dominated by white cultural norms. The film demonstrates Du Bois's broad internationalist perspective and underscores why his thoughts about the future of race in America were considered ahead of his time.

Wall. 2004. Directed by Simone Bitton. Lifesize Entertainment. A cinematic meditation on the Israeli-Palestinian conflict, in which the filmmaker blurs the lines of hatred by asserting her double identity as both Jew and Arab. Bitton conducts interviews with those on both sides of the wall being built around the West Bank by Israel.

Watermarks. 2004. Directed by Yaron Zilberman. HBO. *Watermarks* is the story of the champion women swimmers of the legendary Jewish sports club, Hakoah Vienna. Hakoah ("The Strength") was founded in 1909 in response to the notorious Aryan Paragraph, which forbade Austrian sports clubs from accepting Jewish athletes. In 1938 the Nazis shut down the club, but the swimmers all managed to flee the country before the war. Sixty-five years later, Zilberman met the members of the swimming team and arranged for them to have a reunion in their old swimming pool in Vienna.

The Way Home: Race, Gender, and Class in America. 1998. Produced and directed by Shakti Butler. Over the course of eight months, sixty-four women from a cross-section of cultures (indigenous, African American, Arab, Asian, European American, Jewish, and Latina) and racial identifications share their experience of racism in America. The candid conversations in this documentary film are enriched by an abundance of photographs, dance, and music.

What's Race Got to Do With It? Social Disparities and Student Success. 2006. Written, produced, and directed by Jean Cheng. California Newsreel. This documentary film goes beyond identity politics, celebratory history, and interpersonal relations to consider social disparities and their impact on student success in today's post–civil rights world.

When the Levees Broke: A Requiem in Four Acts. 2007. Directed by Spike Lee. 40 Acres & A Mule Filmworks, in collaboration with HBO. A heart-rending portrait of New Orleans in the wake of the destruction of Hurricane Katrina, Lee's film tells the personal stories of those who endured this harrowing ordeal and survived to tell the tale of misery, despair and triumph. Issues of race, class, and place in America are illustrated via the stories people tell about this tragic experience.

Without Reservations: Notes on Racism in Montana. 1995. Native Voices Public Television. Racism against Native Americans is viewed through the eyes of an Indian teacher, a Native American man working in the police department, and an interracial couple.

Women of Islam: Veiling and Seclusion. 2004. Directed by Farheen Umar. While traveling through Pakistan, Iran, Turkey, and the United States, Farheen Umar talks with Muslim women and challenges the assumptions about the practice of wearing veils. This documentary explores the origins of certain stereotypes and confronts misconceptions about the tradition of covering in Muslim society.

Yo Soy Chicano (Spanish). 1972. Directed by Jesús Salvador Treviño. One of the first nationally broadcast documentaries profiling Mexican American history, from the time of the Spanish Conquest through the early 1970s, when critical Chicano social issues and struggles came to the fore.

Young Soul Rebels. 1991. Directed by Isaac Julien. British Film Institute. Issues of race, gender, sexuality, and nationality are explored in this profile of a black gay British male in London in 1977.

List of Primary Sources

Tears of the Indians

Tecumseh's Confrontation of Indiana Governor William Henry Harrison in August, 1810

"American Slavery As It Is"

Dred Scott v. Sandford *(excerpts)*

Black Codes of Mississippi

Geronimo's Defense of Himself and His Actions to U.S. Army General George Crook in 1886

Booker T. Washington's "Atlanta Compromise" Speech

Plessy v. Ferguson *(excerpts)*

"Lynch Law in America" (excerpt)

"Unity of the Human Race"

Protocols of the Elders of Zion

The Platform of the Niagara Movement

Statement of Mr. William Joseph Simmons, of Atlanta, Georgia

Correspondence Regarding the Tuskegee Syphilis Experiment

Regulation for the Elimination of the Jews from the Economic Life of Germany, November 12, 1938

"Concentration Camp: U.S. Style"

Executive Order 9981—Establishing the President's Committee on Equality of Treatment and Opportunity in the Armed Services

Universal Declaration of Human Rights, December 10, 1948

Brown v. Board of Education *(excerpt)*

The Long Shadow of Little Rock: A Memoir (excerpt)

The 1963 Inaugural Address of Governor George C. Wallace (excerpt)

Civil Rights Act of 1964 (excerpts)

Malcolm X's "The Ballot or the Bullet" Speech

Martin Luther King Jr.'s "The American Dream"

"Black Power—Its Relevance to the West Indies"

Lusaka Manifesto, 1969

Declaration of Sanctions against South Africa by the U.S. Congress

"The State of Native America"

"Growing Up in Mississippi"

Nelson Mandela's Address to the People of Cape Town, Grand Parade, on the Occasion of His Inauguration as State President

Report on Rwanda from Amnesty International

Report on Crimes against Humanity in Guatemala

"Darfur: A 'Plan B' to Stop Genocide?"

TEARS OF THE INDIANS

SOURCE *Public Domain.*

INTRODUCTION *The Spanish conquistadors were not known for their kind treatment of the natives they found in the Americas. Bartolome De Las Casas was a missionary priest who first went to Cuba in 1502 where his military services were rewarded with an* Encomienda, *or an estate complete with his own serfs—Native Cubans, or "Indians." In 1513 he was ordained a priest—claimed to be the first ordination in the Americas. The following year he renounced any claim he had over his serfs and began a series of voyages back and forth to Spain to seek out settlers who would come to Cuba to establish towns where Spaniard and Indian could live in harmony, as equals. He stirred up controversy with his* Brief Report on the Destruction of the Indians *(also known as* Tears of the Indians*) a passionate, and what some thought to be an exaggerated, report of Spanish atrocities against the natives. In 1523 he retreated from his public life into a Dominican monastery as a friar, but emerged again in Spain in 1540. At that time, he helped get laws passed that prohibited slavery among the natives of the Americas and help preserve their rights. He returned to Spain in 1547 where he would live out his life until his death in 1566. He spent those last years speaking and writing on behalf of the natives.*

OF THE ISLAND OF *CUBA*.

In the year 1511, they went over into the Island of *Cuba*, which extends as far in length as it is from *Valladolid* to *Rome*, in which there were many fair Provinces, inhabited with an infinite number of people, where the humanity and clemency of the *Spaniards* was not only as little as it had been in other places, but their cruelty and rage much greater. In this Island many things were done worthy of observation. A certain Lord of great power among them by name *Hathvey*, who had fled over to *Cuba*, that he might avoid either death or perpetual captivity, hearing by some of the *Indians* that the *Spaniards* were also come into this Island, having assembled the *Indians* together, he began as followeth:

Countreymen and Friends, you are not ignorant of the rumour by which we understand that the Spaniards *are come among us, neither am I now to tell you how they have used the inhabitants of* Hapti (so they call *Hispaniola*, in the Indian language) *you know it by a sad experience: nor can we hope to finde them more merciful then they did.* Then quoth he, *Countreymen do you know the Errand which brings them hither?* To whom they replyed, *that was unknown to them*, yet they further replyed, *that they were well assured of the cruel nature of the* Spaniard. Then quoth he, *Ile tell ye the cause of their coming. They do worship some covetous and unsatisfied Deity, and to content the greedy worship of that Celestial Power, they require many things from us, using all their endeavour to murther and enslave us.* Which having said, taking up a little Chest filled with Gold, he proceeded in these words: *Behold here the God of the* Spaniards; *and therefore if you think fitting, let us daunce and sing before this their God, Perhaps we may thereby appease his rage, and he will then command the* Spaniards *to let us alone:* Who with an unanimous shout cryed out all, *Well said, well said;* and so they went to dauncing round this box, not ceasing till they had sufficiently wearied themselves. Then the Lord *Hathvey* going on with his speech, quoth he, *If we do keep this God till he be taken from us, we shall be surely slain, and therefore I think it expedient for us to cast it into the River;* so his counsell being followed, the Chest was cast into the River.

When the *Spaniards* had landed in this Island, this Noble man that had sufficient Tryal of their manner, avoided them as much as he could, still flying from them and defending himself by force of armes upon all occasions. But at length being taken, for no other reason, but because he fled from those that sought his life, and defended himself that he might not be tormented to death, he was by the *Spaniards* burnt alive. While he was tyed to the stake, there came to him a Monk of the Order of St. *Francis*, who began to talk to him of God and of the Articles of our Faith, telling him, that the small respite which the Executioner gave him was sufficient for him to make sure his salvation if he believed. Upon which words after *Hathvey* had a little while paus'd, he asked the Monk if the door of heaven was open to the *Spaniards*, who answering, *Yes to the good Spaniards*. Then replyed the other, *Let me go to Hell that I may not come where they are.*

It happened once that the Citizens of a very fair City distant about twelve miles from the place where we were, came forth of the City to do us honour, and to submit themselves to the King of *Castile*, but they being returned home, the Governour of the *Spaniards* about the middle of the night as they were sleeping in their bed, and least suspecting any such thing, sent a company who came suddenly upon them, and set fire upon their houses, burning up both men, women and children, here some they murthered, others whom they spared, they tormented to make them tell where they had hid their Gold, after which they made them their slaves, having first marked them in the body: and immediately as soon as the fire was spent, they ran to finde out the Gold. At that time the

Spaniards got above ten hundred thousand Crowns of Gold, out of which the King, scarce had three hundred thousand sent him; there were slain in this place eight hundred thousand people; and those other Tyrants that came afterwards, emptied the Island of those that remained.

Among all the notorious enormities committed by the foresaid Governour, there is one not to be omitted: a certain noble *Indian* presenting him, perhaps more for fear then love, a present of above nine thousand Crowns, the *Spaniards* not content with this, tied him to a stake, and stretching out his Legs, put fire to them, requiring a greater sum of Gold, who not able to endure the torment sent home for three thousand more; notwithstanding the *Spaniards* with a fresh rage began to torment him again, but seeing that he was able to give them no more, they kept him so long over the fire till his marrow dropt from the soles of his feet, whereof he died. These were the torments wherewith they murthered not only the common People, but the Peers and Lords of those Nations.

Sometimes it would happen, that a Band of *Spaniards* ranging abroad would light upon a mountain where the *Indians* were fled for protection from their cruelty, where they immediately fell upon the *Indians*, killing the Men, and taking the Women and Virgins captive; & when a great company of the *Indians* pursued them with weapons for the recovery of their Wives and Children, they resolving not to let go their prey, when the *Indians* came near them, immediately with the points of their swords ran the poor Women and Children through the bodies. Upon which the wretched *Indians* beating their brests for grief would now and then burst forth in these words, *O perverse men, O cruel Spaniards, What will ye kill helplesse women?*

There was the house of a Noble man distant from *Panama* above 15 miles; he was by name called *Paris*, and he was very wealthy in Gold; to him the *Spaniards* came, and by him they were entertained like Brothers, he giving to the Captain, as a present, fifteen thousand Crowns; who by that perceiving that he must of necessity have a very great treasure, feigned a departure, but about the middle of the night returning, again entred the City, set it on fire, sacrificing the poor people to the flames. Hence they took away about fifty or sixty thousand Crowns. The Noble man escaping, gathered together what force he could and made after the *Spaniards*, who were gone away with no lesse than a hundred and forty thousand Crowns of his own Treasure; when he had overtaken them, he fell upon them, and having slain above fifty of the *Spaniards*, he recovered his Gold again. The rest saved themselves by flight. But not long after the *Spaniards* returned with greater force upon the Noble man and having routed him, made slaves of all his people.

TECUMSEH'S CONFRONTATION OF INDIANA GOVERNOR WILLIAM HENRY HARRISON IN AUGUST, 1810

SOURCE *Tecumseh, in a conversation with Governor W. H. Harrison in 1810, in* I Have Spoken: American History Through the Voices of the Indians. *Edited by Virginia Irving Armstrong. Swallow Press Inc., 1971. Copyright © 1971. Reproduced by permission.*

INTRODUCTION *Born around 1768, just a few years before Americans declared their independence from the British, Shawnee Indian chief Tecumseh learned to be a warrior at an early age. He treasured his native land of Ohio and what would become the state of Indiana. The loved the valleys of the Ohio, Allegheny, and Monongahela Rivers. As a young man he fought alongside the British in the Revolutionary War against the Americans. He mistrusted the Americans and despised their bid to take more and more land away from his tribe and other native tribes. He believed that the land belonged to all tribes. He was angry that the treaties individual tribes were making with the white people were not only a bid to steal their land but undermined what he believed should be a union of all Native Americans. When Harrison defeated him at Tippecanoe and more lands escaped into the hands of the Americans, Tecumseh would never forget or forgive them. He died during the War of 1812 at the Battle of Thames (near Detroit) fighting for the British.*

Houses are built for you to hold councils in; Indians hold theirs in the open air. I am a Shawnee. My forefathers were warriors. Their son is a warrior. From them I take my only existence. From my tribe I take nothing. I have made myself what I am. And I would that I could make the red people as great as the conceptions of my own mind, when I think of the Great Spirit that rules over us all.... I would not then come to Governor Harrison to ask him to tear up the treaty. But I would say to him, "Brother, you have the liberty to return to your own country."

You wish to prevent the Indians from doing as we wish them, to unite and let them consider their lands as the common property of the whole. You take the tribes aside and advise them not to come into this measure.... You want by your distinctions of Indian tribes, in allotting to each a particular, to make them war with each other. You never see an Indian endeavor to make the white people do this. You are continually driving the red people, when at last you will drive them onto the great lake, where they can neither stand nor work.

Since my residence at Tippecanoe, we have endeavored to level all distinctions, to destroy village chiefs, by whom all mischiefs are done. It is they who sell the land to the Americans. Brother, this land that was sold, and the goods that was given for it, was only done by a few.... In the future we are prepared to punish those who propose to sell land to the Americans. If you continue to purchase them, it will make war among the different tribes, and, at last I do not know what will be the consequences among the white people. Brother, I wish you would take pity on the red people and do as I have requested. If you will not give up the land and do cross the boundary of our present settlement, it will be very hard, and produce great trouble between us.

The way, the only way to stop this evil is for the red men to unite in claiming a common and equal right in the land, as it was at first, and should be now—for it was never divided, but belongs to all. No tribe has the right to sell, even to each other, much less to strangers.... Sell a country! Why not sell the air, the great sea, as well as the earth? Did not the Great Spirit make them all for the use of his children?

How can we have confidence in the white people?

When Jesus Christ came upon the earth you killed Him and nailed him to the cross. You thought he was dead, and you were mistaken. You have Shakers among you and you laugh and make light of their worship.

Everything I have told you is the truth. The Great Spirit has inspired me.

"AMERICAN SLAVERY AS IT IS"

SOURCE *Public Domain.*

INTRODUCTION *In 1839 Theodore D. Weld of New York, an ardent abolitionist, and The American Anti-Slavery Society wanted to stir up sentiments around the United States against what they considered the inhumane act of slavery. The group had been founded in Philadelphia in 1833 following the violent 1831 rebellion led by a slave named Nat Turner. That coupled with other slave uprisings and the policies of President Andrew Jackson, which southerners believed a threat to their way of life, created increasing anxiety among slaveholders. Though there were about 200 slave uprisings between 1776 and 1860, the year before the start of the Civil War, the Turner rebellion had been the one that brought fear into the lives of the southern slaveholders. With the bloody violence still fresh, the anti-abolitionist movement was pressed into arguing not simply the illegality of slavery. They wanted to appeal to people regarding the horrid conditions under which slaves were forced to live—from the unending brutal labor forced on them to the poor quality of life and sustenance they were known to endure. By personalizing the nature of the cause, just as a prosecutor might address a jury, this and other similar writings served to stir up widespread emotion. For those in the North, anti-slavery sentiment only grew. For those in the South, defending their way of life as slaveholders rose to a fevered pitch. Another 22 years would pass before the Civil War would begin. This "trial" places the burden on the readers to reach the only conclusion the abolitionists thought they could reach.*

READER, YOU are empaneled as a juror to try a plain case and bring in an honest verdict. The question at issue is not one of law, but of act—"What is the actual condition of slaves in the United States?"

A plainer case never went to jury. Look at it. TWENTY SEVEN HUNDRED THOUSAND PERSONS in this country, men, women, and children, are in SLAVERY. Is slavery, as a condition for human beings, good, bad, or indifferent?

We submit the question without argument. You have common sense, and conscience, and a human heart—pronounce upon it. You have a wife, or a husband, a child, a father, a mother, a brother or a sister—make the case your own, make it theirs, and bring in your verdict.

The case of Human Rights against Slavery has been adjudicated in the court of conscience times innumerable. The same verdict has always been rendered—"Guilty;" the same sentence has always been pronounced "Let it be accursed;" and human nature, with her million echoes, has rung it round the world in every language under heaven. "Let it be accursed...."

As slaveholders and their apologists are volunteer witnesses in their own cause, and are flooding the world with testimony that their slaves are kindly treated; that they are well fed, well clothed, well housed, well lodged, moderately worked, and bountifully provided with all things needful for their comfort, we propose—first, to disprove their assertions by the testimony of a multitude of impartial witnesses, and then to put slaveholders themselves through a course of cross-questioning which will draw their condemnation out of their own mouths.

We will prove that the slaves in the United States are treated with barbarous inhumanity; that they are overworked, underfed, wretchedly clad and lodged, and have insufficient sleep; that they are often made to wear round their necks iron collars armed with prongs, to drag heavy chains and weights at their feet while working in the field, and to wear yokes and bells, and iron horns; that they are often kept confined in the stocks day and night for weeks together, made to wear gags in their mouths for hours or days, have some of their front teeth torn out or broken off, that they may be easily detected when they run away; that they are frequently flogged with terrible severity, have red pepper rubbed into their lacerated flesh, and hot brine, spirits of turpentine etc., poured over the gashes to increase the torture; that they are often stripped naked, their backs and limbs cut with knives, bruised and mangled by scores and hundreds of blows with the paddle, and terribly torn by the claws of cats, drawn over them by their tormentors; that they are often hunted with blood-hounds and shot down like beasts, or torn in pieces by dogs; that they are often suspended by the arms and whipped and beaten till they faint, and when revived by restoratives, beaten again till they faint, and sometimes till they die; that their ears are often cut off, their eyes knocked out, their bones broken, their flesh branded with red hot irons; that they are maimed, mutilated and burned to death, over slow fires. All these things, and more, and worse, we shall *prove*. . . .

We shall show, not merely that such deeds are committed, but that they are frequent; not done in corners, but before the sun; not in one of the slave states, but in all of them; not perpetrated by brutal overseers and drivers merely, but by magistrates, by legislators, by professors of religion, by preachers of the gospel, by governors of states, by "gentlemen of property and standing," and by delicate females moving in the "highest circles of society."

We know, full well, the outcry that will be made by multitudes, at these declarations; the multiform cavils, the flat denials, the charges of "exaggeration" and "falsehood" so often bandied, the sneers of affected contempt at the credulity that can believe such things, and the rage and imprecations against those who give them currency. We know, too, the threadbare sophistries by which slaveholders and their apologists seek to evade such testimony. If they admit that such deeds are committed, they tell us that they are exceedingly rare, and therefore furnish no grounds for judging of the general treatment of slaves; that occasionally a brutal wretch in the *free* states barbarously butchers his wife, but that no one thinks of inferring from that, the general treatment of wives at the North and West.

They tell us, also, that the slaveholders of the South are proverbially hospitable, kind, and generous, and it is incredible that they can perpetrate such enormities upon human beings; further, that it is absurd to suppose that they would thus injure their own property, that self-interest would prompt them to treat their slaves with kindness, as none but fools and madmen wantonly destroy their own property; further, that Northern visitors at the South come back testifying to the kind treatment of the slaves, and that slaves themselves corroborate such representations. All these pleas, and scores of others, are build in every corner of the free States; and who that hath eyes to see, has not sickened at the blindness that saw not, at the palsy of heart that felt not, or at the cowardice and sycophancy that dared not expose such shallow fallacies. We are not to be turned from our purpose by such vapid babblings. In their appropriate places, we proposed to consider these objections and various others, and to show their emptiness and folly.

DRED SCOTT V. SANDFORD (EXCERPTS)

SOURCE *Public Domain.*

INTRODUCTION *Supreme Court Justice Roger Brooke Taney led his Court to a decision in 1856 that would become a final impetus in the movement toward the Civil War. Dred Scott was the slave of an Army surgeon, John Emerson, who had moved from Missouri, a slave state, to Illinois, a free state. Scott also moved with his owner into the Wisconsin Territory where slavery was prohibited by the Missouri Compromise. Three years after Emerson's death in 1843, Scott sued his widow for his freedom. His argument was that since he had lived in a free state and a free territory, he should be a free man. A Missouri state circuit court agreed with him. The Missouri Supreme Court reversed that decision. Because Scott was now the property of John F.A. Sandford of New York and did not live in Missouri, his lawyers successfully transferred the case to federal court. Both the lower federal court and the U.S. Supreme Court in an appeal decided against Scott's case. Not only did the decision deny that any African American could claim U.S. citizenship. It declared an act of Congress unconstitutional for only the second time in history. In 1868 when Congress adopted the Fourteenth Amendment to the Constitution extending citizenship to former slaves, the* Dred Scott *decision was overturned.*

In 1835, Dred Scott, born a slave in Virginia, became the property of John Emerson, an Army doctor, in the slave state of Missouri. From there, he was taken into the free state of Illinois and later to the free territory of Minnesota.

In 1847, Scott instituted suit in the circuit court of the St. Louis County, Missouri, arguing that he should be given his freedom by virtue of his having resided on free soil. After nine years, his case was certified to the

United States Supreme Court, where five of the nine justices, were Southerners.

In delivering his opinion, Chief Justice Roger Brooke Taney declared that, by virtue of both the Declaration of Independence and the Constitution, African Americans could not be regarded as citizens of the United States. Moreover, the Court could not deprive slaveholders of their right to take slaves into any part of the Union, North or South. In effect, therefore, the Missouri Compromise, as well as other antislavery legislation, was declared to be unconstitutional.

Under the terms of the Missouri Compromise, Missouri was allowed to join the Union with a slave population of almost 10,000; Maine was admitted as a free state. However, the compromise also prohibited the expansion of slavery into any part of the Louisiana Territory north of Latitude 36 degrees, 30 minutes N. It was here, into Illinois and the territory of Wisconsin, that Dred Scott's master brought him, and in 1846 Scott sued his master for his freedom.

After numerous delays, trials, and retrials, the case reached the United States Supreme Court in 1856. Hearing this case, the Court was not only faced with the question as to whether Scott was a free man, as a result of his sojourn in a free territory, but it also had to consider whether Congress had the authority under the Constitution to outlaw slavery in the territories. Although, each of the nine justices delivered a separate opinion, the opinion of Chief Justice Roger Brook Taney has been generally accepted as the Court's ruling on the matter.

The question is simply this: Can a negro, whose ancestors were imported into this country and sold as slaves, become a member of the political community formed and brought into existence by the constitution of the United States, and as such become entitled to all the rights, and privileges, and immunities, guaranteed by that instrument to the citizen?....

The words "people of the United States" and "citizens" are synonymous terms, and mean the same thing. They both describe the political body who, according to our republican institutions, form the sovereignty, and who hold the power and conduct the government through their representatives. They are what we familiarly call the "sovereign people," and every citizen is one of this people, and a constituent member of this sovereignty. The question before us is, whether the class of persons described in the plea in abatement compose a portion of this people, and are constituent members of this sovereignty? We think they are not, and that they are not included, and were not intended to be included, under the word "citizens" in the constitution, and can therefore claim none of the rights and privileges which that instrument provides for and secures to citizens of the United States. On the contrary, they were at that time considered as a subordinate and inferior class of beings, who had been subjugated by the dominant race, and, whether emancipated or not, yet remained subject to their authority, and had no rights or privileges....

It is not the province of the court to decide upon the justice or injustice, the policy or impolicy, of these laws. The decision of that question belonged to the political or law-making power; to those who formed the sovereignty and framed the constitution. The duty of the court is, to interpret the instrument they have framed, with the best lights we can obtain on the subject, and to administer it as we find it, according to its true intent and meaning when it was adopted.

In discussing this question, we must not confound the rights of citizenship which a State may confer within its own limits, and the rights of citizenship as member of the Union. It does not by any means follow, because he has all the rights and privileges of a citizen of a State, that he must be a citizen of the United States. He may have all of the rights and privileges of the citizen of a State, and yet not be entitled to the rights and privileges of a citizen in any other State. For, previous to the adoption of the Constitution of the United States, every State had the undoubted right to confer on whomsoever it pleased the character of citizen, and to endow him with all its rights. But this character of course was confined to the boundaries of the State, and gave him no rights or privileges in other States beyond those secured to him by the laws of nations and the comity of States. Nor have the several States surrendered the power of conferring these rights and privileges by adopting the constitution of United States....

It is very clear, therefore, that no State can, by any act or law of its own, passed since the adoption of the constitution, introduce a new member into the political community created by the constitution of the United States. It cannot make him a member of this community by making him a member of its own. And for the same reason it cannot introduce any person, or description of persons, who were not intended to be embraced in this new political family, which the constitution brought into existence, but were intended to be excluded from it.

The question then arises, whether the provisions of the constitution, in relation to the personal rights and privileges to which the citizen of a State should be entitled, embraced the negro African race, at that time in this country, or who might afterwards be imported, who had then or should afterwards be made free in any State; and to put it in the power of a single State to make him a citizen of the United States, and endue him with the full rights of citizenship in every other State without consent? Does the constitution of the United States act upon him whenever he shall be made free under the laws of a State, and raised there to the rank of a citizen, and immediately clothe him with all the privileges of a citizen in every other State, and in its own courts?

The court thinks the affirmative of these propositions cannot be maintained. And if it cannot, the plaintiff in error could not be a citizen of the State of Missouri, within the meaning of the constitution of the United States, and, consequently, was not entitled to sue in its courts.

It is true, every person, and every class and description of persons, who were at the time of the adoption of the constitution recognized as citizens in the several States, became also citizens of this new political body; but none other; it was formed by them, and for them and their posterity, but for no one else. And the personal rights and privileges guaranteed to citizens of this new sovereignty were intended to embrace those only who were then members of the several State communities, or who should afterwards by birthright or otherwise become members, according to the provisions of the constitution and the principles on which it was founded....

In the opinion of the court, the legislation and histories of the times, and the language used in the declaration of independence, show, that neither the class of persons who had been imported as slaves, nor their descendants, whether they had become free or not, were then acknowledged as a part of the people, nor intended to be included in the general words used in that memorable instrument....

... The government of the United States had no right to interfere for any other purpose but that protecting the rights of the owner, leaving it altogether with the several States to deal with this race, whether emancipated or not, as each State may think justice, humanity, and the interests and safety of society, require....

The act of Congress, upon which the plaintiff relies, declares that slavery and involuntary servitude, except as a punishment for crime, shall be forever prohibited in all that part of the territory ceded by France, under the name of Louisiana, which lies north of thirty-six degrees thirty minutes north latitude and not included within the limits of Missouri. And the difficulty which meets us at the threshold of this part of the inquiry is whether Congress was authorized to pass this law under any of the powers granted to it by the Constitution; for, if the authority is not given by that instrument, it is the duty of this Court to declare it void and inoperative and incapable of conferring freedom upon anyone who is held as a slave under the laws of any one of the states....

We do not mean ... to question the power of Congress in this respect. The power to expand the territory of the United States by the admission of new states is plainly given; and in the construction of this power by all the departments of the government, it has been held to authorize the acquisition of territory, not fit for admission at the time, but to be admitted as soon as its population and situation would entitle it to admission. It is acquired to become a state and not to be held as a colony and governed by Congress with absolute Authority; and, as the propriety of admitting a new state is committed to the sound discretion of Congress, the power to acquire territory for that purpose, to be held by the United States until it is in a suitable condition to become a state upon an equal footing with the other states, must rest upon the same discretional....

But the power of Congress over the person or property of a citizen can never be a mere discretionary power under our Constitution and form of government. The powers of the government and the rights and privileges of the citizen are regulated and plainly defined by the Constitution itself....

These powers, and others, in relation to rights of person, which it is not necessary here to enumerate, are, in express and positive terms, denied to the general government; and the rights of private property have been guarded with equal care. Thus the rights of property are united with the rights of person and placed on the same ground by the Fifth Amendment to the Constitution, which provides that no person shall be deprived of life, liberty, and property without due process of law. And an act of Congress which deprives a citizen of the United States of his liberty of property, without due process of law, merely because he came himself or brought his property into a particular territory of the United States, and who had committed no offense against the law, could hardly be dignified with the name of due process of law....

It seems, however, to be supposed that there is a difference between property in a slave and other property and that different rules may be applied to it in expounding Constitution of the United States. And the laws and usages of nations, and the writings of eminent jurists upon the relation of master and slave and their mutual rights and duties, and the powers which governments may exercise over it, have been dwelt upon in the argument.

But, in considering the question before us, it must be borne in mind that there is no law of nations standing between the people of the United States and their government and interfering with their relation to each other. The powers of the government and the rights of the citizen under it are positive and practical regulations plainly written down. The people of the United States have delegated to it certain enumerated powers and forbidden it to exercise others. It has no power over the person of property of a citizen but what the citizens of the United States have granted. And no laws or usages of other nations, or reasoning of statesmen of jurists upon the relations of master and slave, can enlarge the powers of the government or take from the citizens the rights they have reserved. And if the Constitution recognizes the right of property of the master in a slave, and makes no distinction between that description of property and other property owned by a citizen, no tribunal, acting under the authority of the United States, whether it be legislative, executive, or judicial, has a right to draw such a distinction or deny to it the benefit of the provisions and guaranties which have been provided for the protection of private property against the encroachments of the government.

Now, as we have already said in an earlier part of this opinion, upon a different point, the right of property in a slave is distinctly and expressly affirmed in the Constitution. The right to traffic in it, like an ordinary article of merchandise and property, was guaranteed to the citizens of the United States, in every state that might desire it, for twenty years. And the government in express terms is pledged to protect it in all future time if the slave escapes from his owner. That is done in plain words—too plain to be misunderstood. And no word can be found in the Constitution which gives Congress a greater power over slave property or which entitles property of that kind to less protection than property of any other description. The only power conferred is the power coupled with the duty of guarding and protecting the owner in his rights.

Upon these considerations it is the opinion of the court that the act of Congress which prohibited a citizen from holding and owning property of this kind in the territory of the United States north of the line therein mentioned is not warranted by the Constitution and is therefore void; and that neither Dred Scott himself, nor any of his family, were made free by being carried into this territory; even if they had been carried there by the owner with the intention of becoming a permanent resident. . . .

BLACK CODES OF MISSISSIPPI

SOURCE *Public Domain.*

INTRODUCTION *Following emancipation, and particularly after the end of the Civil War, many states, particularly those in the South, wanted to impose restrictions on the activities of the freed slaves. Many white people were uncomfortable with the new role of African Americans. They did not want them to find a place at the same social level as whites. Thus they created "codes" such as these imposed in Mississippi. What seemed to be recognition of these freed slaves' civil rights were in fact a way to achieve the goal of keeping African Americans socially and economically disadvantaged. The vagrancy laws were especially harsh. These were designed to make it easy to fine or arrest those African Americans who might not be used to their new lives or be gainfully employed—something that was not easy to achieve in the post–Civil War South, where feelings against freed slaves tended toward animosity.*

AN ACT TO CONFER CIVIL RIGHTS ON FREEDMEN, AND FOR OTHER PURPOSES

Section 1. All freedmen, free negroes and mulattoes may sue and be sued, implead and be impleaded, in all the courts of law and equity of this State, and may acquire personal property, and choses in action, by descent or purchase, and may dispose of the same in the same manner and to the same extent that white persons may: Provided, That the provisions of this section shall not be so construed as to allow any freedman, free negro or mulatto to rent or lease any lands or tenements except in incorporated cities or towns, in which places the corporate authorities shall control the same.

Section 2. All freedmen, free negroes and mulattoes may intermarry with each other, in the same manner and under the same regulations that are provided by law for white persons: Provided, that the clerk of probate shall keep separate records of the same.

Section 3. All freedmen, free negroes or mullatoes who do now and have herebefore lived and cohabited together as husband and wife shall be taken and held in law as legally married, and the issue shall be taken and held as legitimate for all purposes; and it shall not be lawful for any freedman, free negro or mulatto to intermarry with any white person; nor for any person to intermarry with any freedman, free negro or mulatto; and any person who shall so intermarry shall be deemed guilty of felony, and on conviction thereof shall be confined in the State penitentiary for life; and those shall be deemed freedmen, free negroes and mulattoes who are of pure negro blood, and those descended from a negro to the third generation, inclusive, though one ancestor in each generation may have been a white person.

Section 4. In addition to cases in which freedmen, free negroes and mulattoes are now by law competent witnesses, freedmen, free negroes or mulattoes shall be competent in civil cases, when a party or parties to the suit, either plaintiff or plaintiffs, defendant or defendants; also in cases where freedmen, free negroes and mulattoes is or are either plaintiff or plaintiffs, defendant or defendants. They shall also be competent witnesses in all criminal prosecutions where the crime charged is alleged to have been committed by a white person upon or against the person or property of a freedman, free negro or mulatto: Provided, that in all cases said witnesses shall be examined in open court, on the stand; except, however, they may be examined before the grand jury, and shall in all cases be subject to the rules and tests of the common law as to competency and credibility.

Section 5. Every freedman, free negro and mulatto shall, on the second Monday of January, one thousand eight hundred and sixty-six, and annually thereafter, have a lawful home or employment, and shall have written evidence thereof as follows, to wit: if living in any incorporated city, town, or village, a license from the mayor thereof; and if living outside of an incorporated city, town, or village, from the member of the board of police of his beat, authorizing him or her to do irregular and job work; or a written contract, as provided in Section 6 in this act; which license may be revoked for cause at any time by the authority granting the same.

Section 6. All contracts for labor made with freedmen, free negroes and mulattoes for a longer period than one month shall be in writing, and a duplicate, attested and read to said freedman, free negro or mulatto by a beat, city or county officer, or two disinterested white persons of the county in which the labor is to be performed, of which each party shall have one: and said contracts shall be taken and held as entire contracts, and if the laborer shall quit the service of the employer before the expiration of his term of service, without good cause, he shall forfeit his wages for that year up to the time of quitting.

Section 7. Every civil officer shall, and every person may, arrest and carry back to his or her legal employer any freedman, free negro, or mulatto who shall have quit the service of his or her employer before the expiration of his or her term of service without good cause; and said officer and person shall be entitled to receive for arresting and carrying back every deserting employee aforesaid the sum of five dollars, and ten cents per mile from the place of arrest to the place of delivery; and the same shall be paid by the employer, and held as a set off for so much against the wages of said deserting employee: Provided, that said arrested party, after being so returned, may appeal to the justice of the peace or member of the board of police of the county, who, on notice to the alleged employer, shall try summarily whether said appellant is legally employed by the alleged employer, and has good cause to quit said employer. Either party shall have the right of appeal to the county court, pending which the alleged deserter shall be remanded to the alleged employer or otherwise disposed of, as shall be right and just; and the decision of the county court shall be final.

Section 8. Upon affidavit made by the employer of any freedman, free negro or mulatto, or other credible person, before any justice of the peace or member of the board of police, that any freedman, free negro or mulatto legally employed by said employer has illegally deserted said employment, such justice of the peace or member of the board of police issue his warrant or warrants, returnable before himself or other such officer, to any sheriff, constable or special deputy, commanding him to arrest said deserter, and return him or her to said employer, and the like proceedings shall be had as provided in the preceding section; and it shall be lawful for any officer to whom such warrant shall be directed to execute said warrant in any county in this State; and that said warrant may be transmitted without endorsement to any like officer of another county, to be executed and returned as aforesaid; and the said employer shall pay the costs of said warrants and arrest and return, which shall be set off for so much against the wages of said deserter.

Section 9. If any person shall persuade or attempt to persuade, entice, or cause any freedman, free negro or mulatto to desert from the legal employment of any person before the expiration of his or her term of service, or shall knowingly employ any such deserting freedman, free negro or mulatto, or shall knowingly give or sell to any such deserting freedman, free negro or mulatto, any food, raiment, or other thing, he or she shall be guilty of a misdemeanor, and, upon conviction, shall be fined not less than twenty-five dollars and not more than two hundred dollars and costs; and if the said fine and costs shall not be immediately paid, the court shall sentence said convict to not exceeding two months imprisonment in the county jail, and he or she shall moreover be liable to the party injured in damages: Provided, if any person shall, or shall attempt to, persuade, entice, or cause any freedman, free negro or mulatto to desert from any legal employment of any person, with the view to employ said freedman, free negro or mullato without the limits of this State, such costs; and if said fine and costs shall not be immediately paid, the court shall sentence said convict to not exceeding six months imprisonment in the county jail.

Section 10. It shall be lawful for any freedman, free negro, or mulatto, to charge any white person, freedman, free negro or mulatto by affidavit, with any criminal offense against his or her person or property, and upon such affidavit the proper process shall be issued and executed as if said affidavit was made by a white person, and it shall be lawful for any freedman, free negro, or mulatto, in any action, suit or controversy pending, or about to be instituted in any court of law equity in this State, to make all needful and lawful affidavits as shall be necessary for the institution, prosecution or defense of such suit or controversy.

Section 11. The penal laws of this state, in all cases not otherwise specially provided for, shall apply and extend to all freedman, free negroes and mulattoes.. ...

AN ACT TO REGULATE THE RELATION OF MASTER AND APPRENTICE, AS RELATES TO FREEDMEN, FREE NEGROES, AND MULATTOES

Section 1. It shall be the duty of all sheriffs, justices of the peace, and other civil officers of the several counties in this State, to report to the probate courts of their respective counties semiannually, at the January and July terms of said courts, all freedmen, free negroes, and mulattoes, under the age of eighteen, in their respective counties, beats, or districts, who are orphans, or whose parent or parents have not the means or who refuse to provide for and support said minors; and thereupon it shall be the duty of said probate court to order the clerk of said court to apprentice said minors to some competent and suitable person on such terms as the court may direct, having a particular care to the interest of said minor: Provided, that the former owner of said minors shall have the preference when, in the opinion of the court, he or she shall be a suitable person for that purpose.

Section 2. The said court shall be fully satisfied that the person or persons to whom said minor shall be apprenticed shall be a suitable person to have the charge and care of said minor, and fully to protect the interest of said minor. The said court shall require the said master or mistress to execute bond and security, payable to the State of Mississippi, conditioned that he or she shall furnish said minor with sufficient food and clothing; to treat said minor humanely; furnish medical attention in case of sickness; teach, or cause to be taught, him or her to read and write, if under fifteen years old, and will conform to any law that may be hereafter passed for the regulation of the duties and relation of master and apprentice: Provided, that said apprentice shall be bound by indenture, in case of males, until they are twenty-one years old, and in case of females until they are eighteen years old.

Section 3. In the management and control of said apprentices, said master or mistress shall have the power to inflict such moderate corporeal chastisement as a father or guardian is allowed to infliction on his or her child or ward at common law: Provided, that in no case shall cruel or inhuman punishment be inflicted.

Section 4. If any apprentice shall leave the employment of his or her master or mistress, without his or her consent, said master or mistress may pursue and recapture said apprentice, and bring him or her before any justice of the peace of the county, whose duty it shall be to remand said apprentice to the service of his or her master or mistress; and in the event of a refusal on the part of said apprentice so to return, then said justice shall commit said apprentice to the jail of said county, on failure to give bond, to the next term of the county court; and it shall be the duty of said court at the first term thereafter to investigate said case, and if the court shall be of opinion that said apprentice left the employment of his or her master or mistress without good cause, to order him or her to be punished, as provided for the punishment of hired freedmen, as may be from time to time provided for by law for desertion, until he or she shall agree to return to the service of his or her master or mistress: Provided, that the court may grant continuances as in other cases: And provided further, that if the court shall believe that said apprentice had good cause to quit his said master or mistress, the court shall discharge said apprentice from said indenture, and also enter a judgment against the master or mistress for not more than one hundred dollars, for the use and benefit of said apprentice, to be collected on execution as in other cases.

Section 5. If any person entice away any apprentice from his or her master or mistress, or shall knowingly employ an apprentice, or furnish him or her food or clothing without the written consent of his or her master or mistress, or shall sell or give said apprentice spirits without such consent, said person so offending shall be guilty of a misdemeanor, and shall, upon conviction there of before the county court, be punished as provided for the punishment of persons enticing from their employer hired freedmen, free negroes or mulattoes.

Section 6. It shall be the duty of all civil officers of their respective counties to report any minors within their respective counties to said probate court who are subject to be apprenticed under the provisions of this act, from time to time as the facts may come to their knowledge, and it shall be the duty of said court from time to time as said minors shall be reported to them, or otherwise come to their knowledge, to apprentice said minors as hereinbefore provided.

Section 9. It shall be lawful for any freedman, free negro, or mulatto, having a minor child or children, to apprentice the said minor child or children, as provided for by this act.

Section 10. In all cases where the age of the freedman, free negro, or mulatto cannot be ascertained by record testimony, the judge of the county court shall fix the age.....

AN ACT TO AMEND THE VAGRANT LAWS OF THE STATE

Section 1. All rogues and vagabonds, idle and dissipated persons, beggars, jugglers, or persons practicing unlawful games or plays, runaways, common drunkards, common night-walkers, pilferers, lewd, wanton, or lascivious persons, in speech or behavior, common railers and brawlers, persons who neglect their calling or employment, misspend what they earn, or do not provide for the support of themselves or their families, or dependents, and all other idle and disorderly persons, including all who neglect all lawful business, habitually misspend their time by frequenting houses of ill-fame, gaming-houses, or tippling shops, shall be deemed and considered vagrants, under the provisions of this act, and upon conviction thereof shall be fined not exceeding one hundred dollars, with all accruing costs, and be imprisoned, at the discretion of the court, not exceeding ten days.

Section 2. All freedmen, free negroes and mulattoes in this State, over the age of eighteen years, found on the second Monday in January, 1866, or thereafter, with no lawful employment or business, or found unlawfully assembling themselves together, either in the day or night time, and all white persons assembling themselves with freedmen, free negroes or mulattoes, or usually associating with freedmen, free negroes or mulattoes, on terms of equality, or living in adultery or fornication with a freed woman, freed negro or mulatto, shall be deemed vagrants, and on conviction thereof shall be fined in a sum not exceeding, in the case of a freedman, free negro or mulatto, fifty dollars, and a white man two hundred dollars, and imprisonment at the discretion of the court, the free negro not exceeding ten days, and the white man not exceeding six months.

Section 3. All justices of the peace, mayors, and aldermen of incorporated towns, counties, and cities of the several counties in this State shall have jurisdiction to try all questions of vagrancy in their respective towns, counties, and cities, and it is hereby made their duty, whenever they shall ascertain that any person or persons in their respective towns, and counties and cities are violating any of the provisions of this act, to have said party or parties arrested, and brought before them, and immediately investigate said charge, and, on conviction, punish said party or parties, as provided for herein. And it is hereby made the duty of all sheriffs, constables, town constables, and all such like officers, and city marshals, to report to some officer having jurisdiction all violations of any of the provisions of this act, and in case any officer shall fail or neglect any duty herein it shall be the duty of the county court to fine said officer, upon conviction, not exceeding one hundred dollars, to be paid into the county treasury for county purposes.

Section 4. Keepers of gaming houses, houses of prostitution, prostitutes, public or private, and all persons who derive their chief support in the employments that militate against good morals, or against law, shall be deemed and held to be vagrants.

Section 5. All fines and forfeitures collected by the provisions of this act shall be paid into the county treasury for general county purposes, and in case of any freedman, free negro or mulatto shall fail for five days after the imposition of any or forfeiture upon him or her for violation of any of the provisions of this act to pay the same, that it shall be, and is hereby, made the duty of the sheriff of the proper county to hire out said freedman, free negro or mulatto, to any person who will, for the shortest period of service, pay said fine and forfeiture and all costs: Provided, a preference shall be given to the employer, if there be one, in which case the employer shall be entitled to deduct and retain the amount so paid from the wages of such freedman, free negro or mulatto, then due or to become due; and in case freedman, free negro or mulatto cannot hire out, he or she may be dealt with as a pauper.

Section 6. The same duties and liabilities existing among white persons of this State shall attach to freedmen, free negroes or mulattoes, to support their indigent families and all colored paupers; and that in order to secure a support for such indigent freedmen, free negroes, or mulattoes, it shall be lawful, and is hereby made the duty of the county police of each county in this State, to levy a poll or capitation tax on each and every freedman, free negro, or mulatto, between the ages of eighteen and sixty years, not to exceed the sum of one dollar annually to each person so taxed, which tax, when collected, shall be paid into the county treasurer's hands, and constitute a fund to be called the Freedman's Pauper Fund, which shall be applied by the commissioners of the poor for the maintenance of the poor of the freedmen, free negroes and mulattoes of this State, under such regulations as may be established by the boards of county police in the respective counties of this State.

Section 7. If any freedman, free negro, or mulatto shall fail or refuse to pay any tax levied according to the provisions of the sixth section of this act, it shall be *prima facie* evidence of vagrancy, and it shall be the duty of the sheriff to arrest such freedman, free negro, or mulatto, or such person refusing or neglecting to pay such tax, and proceed at once to hire for the shortest time such delinquent taxpayer to any one who will pay the said tax, with accruing costs, giving preference to the employer, if there be one.

Section 8. Any person feeling himself or herself aggrieved by judgment of any justice of the peace, mayor, or alderman in cases arising under this act, may within five days appeal to the next term of the county court of the proper county, upon giving bond and security in a sum not less than twenty-five dollars nor more than one hundred and fifty dollars, conditioned to appear and prosecute said appeal, and abide by the judgment of the county court; and said appeal shall be tried *de novo* in the county court, and the decision of the said court shall be final.. . . .

GERONIMO'S DEFENSE OF HIMSELF AND HIS ACTIONS TO U.S. ARMY GENERAL GEORGE CROOK IN 1886

SOURCE *Vanderwerth, W. C. From* Indian Oratory: Famous Speeches by Noted Indian Chieftains, *University of Oklahoma Press, 1971. Copyright © 1971 University of Oklahoma Press. Reproduced by permission.*

INTRODUCTION *Geronimo was born in 1829, near the headwaters of New Mexico's Gila River. The United States was a young nation whose western territories were still being settled. In the Apache homeland of the Chiricahua mountain range in what is now southwestern Arizona, the Native Americans were still engaged in a centuries' long struggle with the Spanish who had been there since the 1500s. By Geronimo's time, white settlers were also beginning to encroach upon his people's land. In 1858, Mexicans killed his mother, wife, and children. His pain and anger then led him into a series of raids against white settlers in the region. Geronimo then retreated peacefully into a reservation in Arizona. It was not until the U.S. government attempted to force the Chiricahua Apaches to move to a reservation in New Mexico that Geronimo's refusal took him into a ten-year guerrilla war against both the Mexicans and the Americans. More often than not, even after several captures he would head back into the safe hideout of the mountains with his followers, continually eluding capture. In 1886 he was finally cornered by U.S. troops and threatened with a move to a Florida reservation if the Apache raids did not stop. He delivered this defense to U.S. Army General George Crook when he met and realized that surrender might be the only option. Some thought this was his own version of the truth rather than the remarks of an innocent man. Regardless of the debate over the objectiveness of his point of view,, his speech worked. He lived out his life in peace, long enough to attend the presidential inauguration ceremonies of Theodore Roosevelt in 1905. He died in 1909 and is buried at Ft. Sill, Oklahoma.*

I want to talk first of the causes which led me to leave the reservation. I was living quietly and contented, doing and thinking of no harm, while at the Sierra Blanca. I don't know what harm I did to those three men, Chato, Mickey Free, and Lieutenant Davis. I was living peaceably and satisfied when people began to speak bad of me. I should be glad to know who started those stories. I was living peaceably with my family, having plenty to eat, sleeping well, taking care of my people, and perfectly contented. I don't know where those bad stories first came from. There we were doing well and my people well. I was behaving well. I hadn't killed a horse or man, American or Indian. I don't know what was the matter with the people in charge of us. They knew this to be so, and yet they said I was a bad man and the worst man there; but what harm had I done? I was living peaceably and well, but I did not leave on my own accord. Had I left it would have been right to blame me; but as it is, blame those men who started this talk about me.

Some time before I left an Indian named Wodiskay had a talk with me. He said, "They are going to arrest you," but I paid no attention to him, knowing that I had done no wrong; and the wife of Mangus, Huera, told me that they were going to seize me and put me and Mangus in the guardhouse, and I learned from the American and Apache soldiers, from Chato, and Mickey Free, that the Americans were going to arrest me and hang me, and so I left.

I would like to know now who it was that gave the order to arrest me and hang me. I was living peaceably there with my family under the shade of the trees, doing just what General Crook had told me I must do and trying to follow his advice. I want to know now who it was ordered me to be arrested. I was praying to the light and to the darkness, to God and to the sun, to let me live quietly with my family. I don't know what the reason was that people should speak badly of me. I don't want to be blamed. The fault was not mine. Blame those three men. With them is the fault, and find out who it was that began that bad talk about me.

I have several times asked for peace, but trouble has come from the agents and interpreters. I don't want what has passed to happen again. Now, I am going to tell you something else. The Earth-Mother is listening to me and I hope that all may be so arranged that from now on there shall be no trouble and that we shall always have peace. Whenever we see you coming to where we are, we think it is God—you must come always with God. From this on I do not want that anything shall be told you about me even in joke. Whenever I have broken out, it was always been on account of bad talk. From this on I hope that people will tell me nothing but the truth. From this on I want to do what is right and nothing else and I do not want you to believe any bad papers about me. I want the papers sent you to tell the truth about me, because I want to do what is right. Very often there are stories put in the newspapers that I am to be hanged. I don't want that any more. When a man tries to do right, such stories ought not to be put in the newspapers.

I don't know what the reason was that people should speak badly of me.... From this on I want to do what is right and nothing else.... There are very few of my men left now. They have done some bad things but I want them all rubbed out now and let us never speak of them again. There are very few of us left. We think of our relations, brothers, brothers-in-law, father-in-law, etc., over on the reservation, and from this on we want to live at peace just as they are doing, and to behave as they are behaving. Sometimes a man does something and men are sent out to bring in his head. I don't want such things to happen to us. I don't want that we should be killing each other.

What is the matter that you don't speak to me? It would be better if you would speak to me and look with a pleasant face. It would make better feeling. I would be glad if you did. I'd be better satisfied if you would talk to me once in a while. Why don't you look at me and smile at me? I am the same man; I have the same feet, legs, and hands, and the sun looks down on me a complete man. I want you to look and smile at me.

I have not forgotten what you told me, although a long time has passed. I keep it in my memory. I am a complete man. Nothing has gone from my body. From here on I want to live at peace. Don't believe any bad talk you hear about me. The agents and the interpreter hear that somebody has done wrong, and they blame it all on me. Don't believe what they say. I don't want any of this bad talk in the future. I don't want those men who talked this way about me to be my agents any more. I want good men to be my agents and interpreters; people who will talk right. I want this peace to be legal and good. Whenever I meet you I talk good to you, and you to me, and peace is soon established; but when you go to the reservation you put agents and interpreters over us who do bad things. Perhaps they don't mind what you tell them, because I do not believe you would tell them to do bad things to us. In the future we don't want these bad men to be allowed near where we are to live. We don't want any more of that kind of bad talk. I don't want any man who will talk bad about me, and tell lies, to be there, because I am going to try and live well and peaceably. I want to have a good man put over me.

While living I want to live well. I know I have to die sometime, but even if the heavens were to fall on me, I want to do what is right. I think I am a good man, but in the papers all over the world they say I am a bad man; but it is a bad thing to say so about me. I never do wrong without a cause. Every day I am thinking, how am I to talk to you to make you believe what I say; and, I think, too, that you are thinking of what you are to say to me. There is one God looking down on us all. We are all children of the one God. God is listening to me. The sun, the darkness, the winds, are all listening to what we now say.

To prove to you that I am telling you the truth, remember I sent you word that I would come from a place far away to speak to you here, and you see us now. Some have come on horseback and some on foot. If I were thinking bad, or if I had done bad, I would never have come here. If it has been my fault, would I have come so far to talk to you? I have told you all that has happened. I also had feared that I should never see Ka-e-te-na again, but here he is, and I want the past to be buried. I am glad to see Ka-e-te-na. I was afraid I should never see him again. That was one reason, too, why I left. I wish that Ka-e-te-na would be returned to us to live with his family. I now believe what I was told. Now I believe that all told me is true, because I see Ka-e-te-na again. I am glad to see him again, as I was told I should. We are all glad. My body feels good because I see Ka-e-te-na, and my breathing is good. Now I can eat well, drink well, sleep well, and be glad. I can go everywhere with good feeling. Now, what I want is peace in good faith. Both you and I think well and think alike.

Well, we have talked enough and set here long enough. I may have forgotten something, but if I remember it, I will tell you of it tonight, or tomorrow, or some other time. I have finished for today, but I'll have something more to say bye and bye.

BOOKER T. WASHINGTON'S "ATLANTA COMPROMISE" SPEECH

SOURCE *Public Domain.*

INTRODUCTION *Born into slavery and deprived of an education until after the Emancipation Proclamation, when he and his family were freed, Booker T. Washington understood the value of education. He would eventually rise to great prominence as an educator and play a key role in the founding of the*

Tuskegee Institute. Known for his genteel manner and criticized by many for being too accommodating, Washington still secretly funded anti-segrationist groups. In this speech, delivered at the Atlanta Exposition in 1895, Washington recognized that the early years of freedom for his people were a struggle without all of the chances the white Americans had at their disposal for climbing up out of poverty. He told the people that day that it would be in the South where these freed slaves should find their best opportunity and that the leaders in the South should recognize the remarkable resource of willing workers they had right in front of them. When the movie The Birth of a Nation *opened in 1915, he spoke out with many others who protested the stereotype of the African American that the movie portrayed. He died just a few months later.*

Mr. President and Gentlemen of the Board of Directors and Citizens:

One-third of the population of the South is of the Negro race. No enterprise seeking the material, civil, or moral welfare of this section can disregard this element of our population and reach the highest success. I but convey to you, Mr. President and Directors, the sentiment of the masses of my race when I say that in no way have the value and manhood of the American Negro been more fittingly and generously recognized than by the managers of this magnificent Exposition at every stage of its progress. It is a recognition that will do more to cement the friendship of the two races than any occurrence since the dawn of our freedom.

Not only this, but the opportunity here afforded will awaken among us a new era of industrial progress. Ignorant and inexperienced, it is not strange that in the first years of our new life we began at the top instead of at the bottom; that a seat in Congress or the State Legislature was more sought than real estate or industrial skill; that the political convention or stump speaking had more attractions than starting a dairy farm or truck garden.

A ship lost at sea for many days suddenly sighted a friendly vessel. From the mast of the unfortunate vessel was seen a signal: "Water, water; we die of thirst!" The answer from the friendly vessel at once came back: "Cast down your bucket where you are." A second time the signal, "Water, water; send us water!" ran up from the distressed vessel, and was answered: "Cast down your bucket where you are." And a third and fourth signal for water was answered: "Cast down your bucket where you are." The captain of the distressed vessel, at last heeding the injunction, cast down his bucket, and it came up full of fresh, sparkling water from the mouth of the Amazon River. To those of my race who depend on bettering their condition in a foreign land, or who underestimate the importance of cultivating friendly relations with the Southern white man, who is their next door neighbor, I would say: "Cast down your bucket where you are"—cast it down in making friends in every manly way of the people of all races by whom we are surrounded.

Cast it down in agriculture, mechanics, in commerce, in domestic service, and in the professions. And in this connection it is well to bear in mind that whatever other sins the South may be called to bear, when it comes to business, pure and simple, it is in the South that the Negro is given a man's chance in the commercial world, and in nothing is this Exposition more eloquent than in emphasizing this chance. Our greatest danger is, that in the great leap from slavery to freedom we may overlook the fact that the masses of us are to live by the productions of our hands, and fail to keep in mind that we shall prosper in proportion as we learn to dignify and glorify common labor, and put brains and skill into the common occupations of life; shall prosper in proportion as we learn to draw the line between the superficial and the substantial, the ornamental gewgaws of life and the useful. No race can prosper till it learns that there is as much dignity in tilling a field as in writing a poem. It is at the bottom of life we must begin, and not at the top. Nor should we permit our grievances to overshadow our opportunities.

To those of the white race who look to the incoming of those of foreign birth and strange tongue and habits for the prosperity of the South, were I permitted, I would repeat what I say to my own race, "Cast down your bucket where you are." Cast it down among the 8,000,000 Negroes whose habits you know, whose fidelity and love you have tested in days when to have proved treacherous meant the ruin of your firesides. Cast down your bucket among those people who have, without strikes and labor wars, tilled your fields, cleared your forests, builded your railroads and cities, and brought forth treasures from the bowels of the earth, and helped make possible this magnificent representation of the progress of the South. Casting down your bucket among my people, helping and encouraging them as you are doing on these grounds, and, with education of head, hand and heart, you will find that they will buy your surplus land, make blossom the waste place in your fields, and run your factories. While doing this, you can be sure in the future, as in the past, that you and your families will be surrounded by the most patient, faithful, law-abiding, and unresentful people that the world has seen. As we have proved our loyalty to you in the past, in nursing your children, watching by the sick bed of your mothers and fathers, and often following them with tear-dimmed eyes to their graves, so in the future, in our humble way, we shall stand by you with a devotion that no foreigner can approach, ready to lay down our lives, if need be, in defense of yours, interlacing our industrial, commercial, civil, and religious life with yours in a way that shall make the interests of both races one. In all things that are purely social we can be as separate as the fingers, yet one as the hand in all things essential to mutual progress.

There is no defense or security for any of us except in the highest intelligence and development of all. If anywhere there are efforts tending to curtail the fullest growth of the Negro, let these efforts be turned into stimulating, encouraging, and making him the most useful and intelligent citizen. Effort or means so invested will pay a thousand percent interest. These efforts will be twice blessed—'blessing him that gives and him that takes.'

There is no escape through law of man or God from the inevitable:

"The laws of changeless justice bind
Oppressor with oppressed;
And close as sin and suffering joined
We march to fate abreast."

Nearly sixteen millions of hands will aid you in pulling the load upwards, or they will pull against you the load downwards. We shall constitute one-third and more of the ignorance and crime of the South, or one-third its intelligence and progress; we shall contribute one-third to the business and industrial prosperity of the South, or we shall prove a veritable body of death, stagnating, depressing, retarding every effort to advance the body politic.

Gentlemen of the Exposition, as we present to you humble effort at an exhibition of our progress, you must not expect over much. Starting thirty years ago with ownership here and there in a few quilts and pumpkins and chickens (gathered from miscellaneous sources), remember the path that has led from these to the invention and production of agricultural implements, buggies, steam engines, newspapers, books, statuary, carving, paintings, the management of drug stores and banks, has not been trodden without contact with thorns and thistles. While we take pride in what we exhibit as a result of our independent efforts, we do not for a moment forget that our part in this exhibition would fall far short of your expectations but for the constant help that has come to our educational life, not only from the Southern States, but especially from Northern philanthropists, who have made their gifts a constant stream of blessing and encouragement.

The wisest among my race understand that the agitation of questions of social equality is the extremist folly, and that progress in the enjoyment of all the privileges that will come to us must be the result of severe and constant struggle rather than of artificial forcing. No race that has anything to contribute to the markets of the world is long in any degree ostracized. It is important and right that all privileges of the law be ours, but it is vastly more important that we be prepared for the exercise of those privileges. The opportunity to earn a dollar in a factory just now is worth infinitely more than the opportunity to spend a dollar in an opera house.

In conclusion, may I repeat that nothing in thirty years has given us more hope and encouragement, and drawn us so near to you of the white race, as this opportunity offered by the Exposition; and here bending, as it were, over the altar that represents the results of the struggle of your race and mine, both starting practically empty-handed three decades ago, I pledge that, in your effort to work out the great and intricate problem which God has laid at the doors of the South, you shall have at all time the patient, sympathetic help of my race; only let this be constantly in mind that, while from representations in these buildings of the product of field, of forest, of mine, of factory, letters, and art, much good will come, yet far above and beyond material benefits will be that higher good, that let us pray God will come, in a blotting out of sectional differences and racial animosities and suspicions, in a determination to administer absolute justice, in a willing obedience among all classes to the mandates of law. This, coupled with our material prosperity, will bring into our beloved South a new heaven and a new earth.

PLESSY V. FERGUSON (EXCERPTS)

SOURCE *Public Domain.*

INTRODUCTION *In 1878 the Supreme Court had ruled in* Hall v. DeCuir *that states could not outlaw segregation in transportation modes such as streetcars or railroads. In 1896, after an African American man named Homer Adolph Plessy was arrested for refusing to ride in the "colored" railroad coach while traveling from New Orleans to Covington, Louisiana, he challenged the arrest. Once again, "separate but equal" was claimed to be the law of the land when Justice Billings Brown ruled that it was a reasonable use of state power, and that in this case, the Fourteenth Amendment providing for equal protection was not meant to abolish social or racial distinctions to the point of forcing a mingling together of the races. Until*

1954 and the ruling of Brown v. Board of Education *racial discrimination would continue to find legal support in the highest court of the United States.*

Justice Brown delivered the opinion of the Court.

This case turns upon the constitutionality of an act of the General Assembly of the state of Louisiana, passed in 1890, providing for separate railway carriages for the white and colored races.....

The constitutionality of this act is attacked upon the ground that it conflicts both with the Thirteenth Amendment of the Constitution, abolishing slavery, and the Fourteenth Amendment, which prohibits certain restrictive legislation on the part of the states.

1. That it does not conflict with the Thirteenth Amendment, which abolished slavery and involuntary servitude, except as a punishment for crime, is too clear for argument. Slavery implies involuntary servitude—a state of bondage; the ownership of mankind as a chattel, or at least the control of the labor and services of one man for the benefit of another, and absence of a legal right to the disposal of his own person, property, and services.....

A statute which implies merely a legal distinction between the white and colored races—a distinction which is founded in the color of the two races, and which must always exist so long as white men are distinguished from the other race by color—has no tendency to destroy the legal equality of the two races, or reestablish a state of involuntary servitude. Indeed, we do not understand that the Thirteenth Amendment is strenuously relied upon by the plaintiff in error in this connection.

2. By the Fourteenth Amendment, all persons born or naturalized in the United States, and subject to the jurisdiction thereof, are made citizens of the United States and of the state wherein they reside; and the states are forbidden from making or enforcing any law which shall abridge the privileges or immunities of citizens of the United States, or shall deprive any person of life, liberty, or property without due process of law, or deny to any person within their jurisdiction the equal protection of the laws.....

The object of the amendment was undoubtedly to enforce the absolute equality of the two races before the law, but in the nature of things it could not have been intended to abolish distinctions based upon color, or to enforce social, as distinguished from political, equality, or a commingling of the two races upon terms unsatisfactory to either. Laws permitting, and even requiring, their separation in places where they are liable to be brought into contact do not necessarily imply the inferiority of either race to the other, and have been generally, if not universally, recognized as within the competency of the state legislatures in the exercise of their police power. The most common instance of this is connected with the establishment of separate schools for white and colored children, which has been held to be a valid exercise of the legislative power even by courts of states where the political rights of the colored race have been longest and most earnestly enforced.....

So far, then, as a conflict with the Fourteenth Amendment is concerned, the case reduces itself to the question whether the statute of Louisiana is a reasonable regulation, and with respect to this there must necessarily be a large discretion on the part of the legislature. In determining the question of reasonableness it is at liberty to act with reference to the established usages, customs, and traditions of the people, and with a view to the promotion of their comfort, and the preservation of the public peace and good order. Gauged by this standard, we cannot say that a law which authorizes or even requires the separation of the two races in public conveyances is unreasonable or more obnoxious to the Fourteenth Amendment than the acts of Congress requiring separate schools for colored children in the District of Columbia, the constitutionality of which does not seem to have been questioned, or the corresponding acts of state legislatures.

We consider the underlying fallacy of the plaintiff's argument to consist in the assumption that the enforced separation of the two races stamps the colored race with a badge of inferiority. If this be so, it is not by reason of anything found in the act, but solely the colored race chooses to put that construction upon it. The argument necessarily assumes that if, as has been more than once the case, and is not unlikely to be so again, the colored race should become the dominant power in the state legislature, and should enact a law in precisely similar terms, it would thereby relegate the white race to an inferior position. We imagine that the white race, at least, would not acquiesce in this assumption. The argument also assumes that social prejudices may be overcome by legislation and that equal rights cannot be secured to the Negro except by an enforced commingling of the two races. We cannot accept this proposition. If the two races are to meet upon terms of social equality, it must be the result of natural affinities, a mutual appreciation of each other's merits, and a voluntary consent of individuals..... Legislation is powerless to eradicate racial instincts or to abolish distinctions based upon physical differences, and the attempt to do so can only result in accentuating the difficulties of the present situation. If the civil and political rights of both races be equal, one cannot be inferior to the other civilly or politically. If one race be inferior to the other socially, the Constitution of the United States cannot put them upon the same plane.

It is true that the question of the proportion of colored blood necessary to constitute a colored person, as distinguished from a white person, is one upon with there is a difference of opinion in the different states, some holding that any visible admixture of black blood stamps the person as belonging to the colored race . . . others that it depends upon the preponderance of blood . . . and still others that the pre-dominance of white blood must only be in the proportion of three-fourths. . . . But these are questions to be determined under the laws of each state and are not properly put in issue in this case. Under the allegations of his petition it may undoubtedly become a question of importance whether, under the laws of Louisiana, the petitioner belongs to the white or colored race.

The judgment of the court below is therefore, *Affirmed.*

In respect of civil rights, common to all citizens, the Constitution of the United States does not, I think, permit any public authority to know the race of those entitled to be protected in the enjoyment of such rights. Every true man has pride of race, and under appropriate circumstances with the rights of others, his equals before the law, are not to be affected, it is his privilege to express such pride and to take such action based upon it as to him seems proper. But I deny that any legislative body or judicial tribunal may have regard to the race of citizens when the civil rights of those citizens are involved. Indeed, such legislation, as that here in question, is inconsistent not only with that equality of rights which pertains to citizenship, national and state, but with the personal liberty enjoyed by everyone within the United States.

The Thirteenth Amendment does not permit the withholding or the deprivation of any right necessarily inhering in freedom. It not only struck down the institution of slavery as previously existing in the United States, but it prevents the imposition of any burdens or disabilities that constitute badges of slavery or servitude. It decreed universal civil freedom in this country. This Court has so adjudged. But that amendment having been found inadequate to the protection of the rights of those who had been in slavery, it was followed by the Fourteenth Amendment, which added greatly to the dignity and glory of the American citizenship, and to the security of personal liberty, by declaring that "all persons born or naturalized in the United States, and subject to the jurisdiction thereof, are citizens of the United States and of the state wherein they reside," and that "no state shall make or enforce any law which shall abridge the privileges or immunities of citizens of the United States; nor shall any state deprive any person of life, liberty, or property without due process of law, nor deny to any person within its jurisdiction the equal protection of the laws." These two amendments, if enforced according to their true intent and meaning, will protect all the civil rights that pertains to freedom and citizenship. Finally, and to the end that no citizen should be denied, on account of his race, the privilege of participating in the political control of his country, it was declared by the Fifteenth Amendment that "the right of citizens of the United States to vote shall not be denied or abridged by the United States or by any state on account of race, color, or previous condition of servitude."

These notable additions to the fundamental law were welcomed by the friends of liberty throughout the world. They removed the race line from our governmental systems.

It was said in argument that the statute of Louisiana does not discriminate against either race but prescribes a rule applicable alike to white and colored citizens. But this argument does not meet the difficulty. Everyone knows that the statute in question had its origin in the purpose, not so much to exclude white persons from railroad cars occupied by blacks, as to exclude colored people from coaches occupied by or assigned to white persons. Railroad corporations of Louisiana did not make discrimination among whites in the matter of accommodation for travelers. The thing to accomplish was, under the guise of giving equal accommodation for whites and blacks, to compel the latter to keep to themselves while traveling in railroad passenger coaches. No one would be wanting in candor as to assert the contrary. The fundamental objections, therefore, to the statute is that it interferes with the personal freedom of citizens. If a white man and a black man choose to occupy the same public conveyance on a public highway, it is their right to do so, and no government, proceeding alone on grounds of race, can prevent it without infringing the personal liberty of each.

It is one thing for railroad carriers to furnish, or to be required by law to furnish, equal accommodations for all whom they are under a legal duty to carry. It is quite another thing for government to forbid citizens of the white and black races from traveling in the same public conveyance, and to punish officers of railroad companies for permitting persons of the two races to occupy the same passenger coach. If a state can prescribe, as a rule of civil conduct, that whites and blacks shall not travel as passengers in the same railroad coach, why may it not so regulate the use of the streets of its cities and towns as to compel white citizens to keep on one side of a street and black citizens to keep on the other? Why may it not, upon like grounds, punish whites and blacks who ride together in streetcars or in open vehicles on a public road or street? Why may it not require sheriffs to assign whites to one side of a courtroom and blacks to other? And why may it not also prohibit the commingling of the two races in the galleries of legislative halls or in public assemblages convened for the consideration of the political questions of the day? Further, if this statute of Louisiana is consistent with the personal liberty of citizens, why may not the state require the separation in railroad coaches of native and naturalized citizens of the United States, or of Protestants and Roman Catholics?

The answer given as the argument to these questions was that regulations of the kind they suggest would be unreasonable and could not, therefore, stand before the law. Is it meant that the determination of questions of legislative power depends upon the inquiry whether the statute whose validity is questioned is, in the judgment of the courts, a reasonable one, taking all the circumstances into consideration? A statute may be unreasonable merely because a sound public forbade its enactment. But I do not understand that the courts have anything to do with the policy or expediency of legislation. The white race deems itself to be the dominant race in this country. And so it is, in prestige, in achievements, in education, in wealth, and in power. So, I doubt not, it will continue to be for all time, if it remains true to its great heritage and holds fast to the principles of constitutional liberty. But in view of the Constitution, in the eye of the law, there is in this country no superior, dominant, ruling class of citizens. There is no caste here. Our Constitution is color-blind and neither knows nor tolerates classes among citizens. In respect of civil rights all citizens are equal before the law. The humblest is the peer of the most powerful. The law regards man as a man and takes no account of his surroundings or of his color when his civil rights, as guaranteed by the supreme law of the land, are involved. It is, therefore, to be regretted that this high tribunal, the final expositor of the fundamental law of the land, has reached the conclusion that it is competent for a state to regulate the enjoyment by citizens of their civil rights solely upon the basis of race.....

The sure guarantee of the peace and security of each is the clear, distinct, unconditional recognition by our governments, national and state, of every right that inheres in civil freedom, and of the equality before the law of all citizens of the United States without regard to race. State enactments, regulating the enjoyment of civil rights, upon the basis of race, and cunningly devised legitimate results of the war, under the pretense of recognizing equality of rights, can have no other result than to render permanent peace impossible, and to keep alive a conflict of races, the continuance of which must do harm to all concerned.....

The arbitrary separation of citizens, on the basis of race, while they are on a public highway, is a badge of servitude wholly inconsistent with the civil freedom and the equality before he law established by the Constitution. It cannot be justified upon any legal grounds.

If evils will result from the commingling of the two races upon public highways established for the benefit of all, they will be infinitely less than those that will surely come from state legislation regulating the enjoyment of civil rights upon the basis of race. We boast of the freedom enjoyed by our people above all other peoples. But it is difficult to reconcile that boast with a state of the law which, practically, puts the brand of servitude and degradation upon a large class of our fellow-citizens, our equals before the law. The thin disguise of "equal" accommodations for passengers in railroad coaches will not mislead anyone, nor atone of the wrong this day done.....

I am of opinion that the statute of Louisiana is inconsistent with the personal liberty of citizens, white and black, in that state, and hostile to both the spirit and letter of the Constitution of the United States. If laws of like character should be enacted in the several states of the Union, the effect would be in the highest degree mischievous. Slavery, as an institution tolerated by law, would, it is true, have disappeared from our country, but there would remain a power in the states, by sinister legislation, to interfere with the full enjoyment of the blessings of freedom; to regulate civil rights, common to all citizens, upon the basis of race, and to place in a condition of legal inferiority a large body of American citizens, now constituting a part of the political community called the People of the United States, for whom, and by whom through representatives, our government is administered. Such a system is inconsistent with the guarantee given by the Constitution to each state of a republican form of government, and may be stricken down by congressional action, constitutional or laws of any state to the contrary notwithstanding.

For the reasons stated, I am constrained to withhold my assent from the opinion and judgment of the majority.....

"LYNCH LAW IN AMERICA" (EXCERPT)

SOURCE *Public Domain.*

INTRODUCTION *In 1900 America, lynching seemed to be the law of the land, rather than the "national crime" as Ida B. Wells-Burnett announced in this article she published for a national audience. Because of legalized discrimination and segregation, violence toward African Americans seemed to flourish. Any number of excuses were made when groups of angry white men took it upon themselves to lynch an African American. One of them was a common claim of violence against white women—an accusation which was seldom met with any solid proof. As Wells-Burnett pointed out, the bulk of the crimes did not match the claims that were made as it was, let alone the number of those that were falsified. This woman, who became known as the most influential black female activist in the country, even petitioned President William McKinley in 1898 after an African American postmaster in South Carolina was lynched. As she also noted, lynching was not only a crime of the South. Lynchings were going on all over the country, and she provided statistics to back up her claims. The terrible reality was that in 1900, these crimes against African Americans would only begin to get worse before the struggle for civil rights was successful.*

Our country's national crime is *lynching*. It is not the creature of an hour, the sudden outburst of uncontrolled fury, or the unspeakable brutality of an insane mob. It represents the cool, calculating deliberation of intelligent people who openly avow that there is an "unwritten law" that justifies them in putting human beings to death without complaint under oath, without trial by jury, without opportunity to make defense, and without right of appeal. . . .

. . . These advocates of the "unwritten law" boldly avowed their purpose to intimidate, suppress, and nullify the negro's right to vote. In support of its plans the Ku-Klux Klans, the "red-shirt" and similar organizations proceeded to beat, exile, and kill negroes until the purpose of their organization was accomplished and the supremacy of the "unwritten law" was effected. Thus lynchings began in the South, rapidly spreading into the various States until the national law was nullified and the reign of the "unwritten law" was supreme. Men were taken from their homes by "red-shirt" bands and stripped, beaten, and exiled; others were assassinated when their political prominence made them obnoxious to their political opponents; while the Ku-Klux barbarism of election days, reveling in the butchery of thousands of colored voters, furnished records in Congressional investigations that are a disgrace to civilization.

The alleged menace of universal suffrage having been avoided by the absolute suppression of the negro vote, the spirit of mob murder should have been satisfied and the butchery of negroes should have ceased. But men, women, and children were the victims of murder by individuals and murder by mobs, just as they had been when killed at the demands of the "unwritten law" to prevent "negro domination." Negroes were killed for disputing over terms of contracts with their employers. If a few barns were burned some colored man was killed to stop it. If a colored man resented the imposition of a white man and the two came to blows, the colored man had to die, either at the hands of the white man then and there or later at the hands of a mob that speedily gathered. If he showed a spirit of courageous manhood he was hanged for his pains, and the killing was justified by the declaration that he was a "saucy nigger." Colored women have been murdered because they refused to tell the mobs where relatives could be found for "lynching bees." Boys of fourteen years have been lynched by white representatives of American civilization. In fact, for all kinds of offenses—and, for no offenses—from murders to misdemeanors, men and women are put to death without judge or jury; so that, although the political excuse was no longer necessary, the wholesale murder of human beings went on just the same. A new name was given to the killings and a new excuse was invented for so doing.

Again the aid of the "unwritten law" is invoked, and again it comes to the rescue. During the last ten years a new statute has been added to the "unwritten law." This statute proclaims that for certain crimes or alleged crimes no negro shall be allowed a trial; that no white woman shall be compelled to charge an assault under oath or to submit any such charge to the investigation of a court of law. The result is that many men have been out to death whose innocence was afterward established; and to-day, under this reign of the "unwritten law," no colored man, no matter what his reputation, is safe from lynching if a white woman, no matter what her standing or motive, cares to charge him with insult or assault.

It is considered a sufficient excuse and reasonable justification to put a prisoner to death under this "unwritten law" for the frequently repeated charge that these lynching horrors are necessary to prevent crimes against women. The sentiment of the country has been appealed to, in describing the isolated condition of white families in thickly populated negro districts; and the charge is made that these homes are in as great danger as if they were surrounded by wild beasts. And the world has accepted this theory without let or hindrance. In many cases there has been open expression that the fate meted out to the victim was only what he deserved. In many other instances there has been a silence that says more forcibly than words can proclaim it that it is right and proper that a human being should be seized by a mob and burned to death upon the unsworn and the uncorroborated charge of his accuser. No matter that our laws presume every man innocent until he is proved guilty; no matter that it leaves a certain class of individuals completely at the mercy of another class; no matter that it encourages those criminally disposed to blacken their faces and commit any crime in the calendar so long as they can throw suspicion on some negro, as is frequently done, and then lead a mob to take his life; no matter that mobs make a farce of the law and a mockery of justice; no matter that hundreds of boys are being hardened in crime and schooled in vice by the repetition of such scenes before their eyes—if a white woman declares herself insulted or assaulted, some life must pay the penalty, with all the horrors of the Spanish Inquisition and all the barbarism of the Middle Ages. The world looks on and says it is well.

Not only are two hundred men and women put to death annually, on the average, in this country by mobs, but these lives are taken with the greatest publicity. In many instances the leading citizens aid and abet by their presence when they do not participate, and the leading journals inflame the public mind to the lynching point with scare-head articles and offers of rewards. Whenever a burning is advertised to take place, the railroads run excursions, photographs are taken, and the same jubilee is indulged in that characterized the public hangings of one hundred years ago. There is, however, this difference: in those old days the multitude that stood by was permitted only to guy or jeer. The nineteenth century lynching mob cuts off ears, toes, and fingers, strips off flesh, and distributes portions of the body as souvenirs among the crowd. If the leaders of the mob are so minded, coal-oil is poured over the body and the victim is then roasted to death. This has been done in Texarkana and Paris, Tex., in Bardswell, Ky., and in Newman, Ga. In Paris the officers of the law delivered the prisoner to the mob. The mayor gave the school children a holiday and the railroads ran excursion trains so that the people might see a human being burned to death. In Texarkana, the year before, men and boys amused themselves by cutting off strips of flesh and thrusting knives into their helpless victim. At Newman, Ga., of the present year, the mob tried every conceivable torture to compel the victim to cry out and confess, before they set fire to the faggots that burned him. But their trouble was all in vain—he never uttered a cry, and they could not make him confess.

This condition of affairs were brutal enough and horrible enough if it were true that lynchings occurred only because of the commission of crimes against women—as is constantly declared by ministers, editors, lawyers, teachers, statesmen, and even by women themselves. It has been to the interest of those who did the lynching to blacken the good name of the helpless and defenseless victims of their hate. For this reason they publish at every possible opportunity this excuse for lynching, hoping thereby not only to palliate their own crime but at the same time to prove the negro a moral monster and unworthy of the respect and sympathy of the civilized world. But this alleged reason adds to the deliberate injustice of the mob's work. Instead of lynchings being caused by assaults upon women, the statistics show that not one-third of the victims of lynchings are even charged with such crimes. The Chicago *Tribune*, which publishes annually lynching statistics, is authority for the following:

In 1892, when lynching reached high-water mark, there were 241 persons lynched. . . .

Of this number, 160 were of negro descent. Four of them were lynched in New York, Ohio, and Kansas; the remainder were murdered in the South. Five of this number were females. The charges for which they were lynched cover a wide range. They are as follows:

Rape 46
Murder 58
Rioting 3
Race Prejudice 6
No cause given 4
Incendiarism 6
Robbery 6
Assault and battery 1
Attempted rape 11
Suspected robbery 4
Larceny 1
Self-defense 1
Insulting women 2
Desperadoes 6
Fraud 1
Attempted murder 2
No offense stated, boy and girl 2

In the case of the boy and girl above referred to, their father, named Hastings, was accused of the murder of a white man. His fourteen-year-old daughter and sixteen-year-old son were hanged and their bodies filled with bullets; then the father was also lynched. This occurred in November, 1892, at Jonesville, La.

Indeed, the record for the last twenty years shows exactly the same or a smaller proportion who have been charged with this horrible crime. Quite a number of the one-third alleged cases of assault that have been personally investigated by the writer have shown that there was no foundation in fact for the charges; yet the claim is not made that there were no real culprits among them. The negro has been too long associated with the white man not to have copied his vices as well as his virtues. But the negro resents and utterly repudiates the efforts to blacken his good name by asserting that assaults upon women are peculiar to his race. The negro has suffered far more from the commission of this crime against the women of his race by white men than the white race has ever suffered through *his* crimes. Very scant notice is taken of the matter when this is the condition of affairs. What becomes a crime deserving capital punishment when the tables are turned is a matter of small moment when the negro woman is the accusing party.

But since the world has accepted this false and unjust statement, and the burden of proof has been placed upon the negro to vindicate his race, he is taking steps to do so. The Anti-Lynching Bureau of the National Afro-American Council is arranging to have every lynching investigated and publish the facts to the world, as has been done in the case of Sam Hose, who was burned alive last April at Newman, Ga. The detective's report showed that Hose killed Cranford, his employer, in self-defense, and that, while a mob was organizing to hunt Hose to punish him for killing a white man, not till twenty-four hours after the murder was the charge of rape, embellished with psychological and physical impossibilities, circulated. That gave an impetus to the hunt, and the Atlanta *Constitution*'s reward of $500 keyed the mob to the necessary burning and roasting pitch. Of five hundred newspaper clippings of that horrible affair, nine-tenths of them assumed Hose's guilt—simply because his murderers said so, and because it is the fashion to believe the negro peculiarly addicted to this species of crime. All the negro asks is justice—a fair and impartial trial in the courts of the country. That given, he will abide the result.

But this question affects the entire American nation, and from several points of view: First, on the ground of consistency. Our watchword has been "the land of the free and the home of the brave." Brave men do not gather by thousands to torture and murder a single individual, so gagged and bound he cannot make even feeble resistance or defense. Neither do brave men or women stand by and see such things done without compunction of conscience, nor read of them without protest. Our nation has been active and outspoken in its endeavors to right the wrongs of the Armenian Christian, the Russian Jew, the Irish Home Ruler, the native women of India, the Siberian exile, and the Cuban patriot. Surely it should be the nation's duty to correct its own evils!

Second, on the ground of economy. To those who fail to be convinced from any other point of view touching this momentous question, a consideration of the economic phase might not be amiss. It is generally known that mobs in Louisiana, Colorado, Wyoming, and other States have lynched subjects of other countries. When their different governments demanded satisfaction, our country was forced to confess her inability to protect said subjects in the several States because of our State-rights doctrines, or in turn demand punishment of the lynchers. This confession, while humiliating in the extreme, was not satisfactory; and, while the United States cannot protect, she can pay. This she has done, and it is certain will have to do again in the case of the recent lynching of Italians in Louisiana. The United States already has paid in indemnities for lynching nearly a half million dollars....

Third, for the honor of Anglo-Saxon civilization. No scoffer at our boasted American civilization could say anything more harsh of it than does the American white man himself who says he is unable to protect the honor of his women without resort to such brutal, inhuman, and degrading exhibitions as characterize "lynching bees." The cannibals of the South Sea Islands roast human beings alive to satisfy hunger. The red Indian of the Western plains tied his prisoner to the stake, tortured him, and danced in fiendish glee while his victim writhed in the flames. His savage, untutored mind suggested no better way than that of wreaking vengeance upon those who had wronged him. These people knew nothing about Christianity and did not profess to follow its teachings; but such primary laws as they had they lived up to. No nation, savage or civilized, save only the United States of America, has confessed its inability to protect its women save by hanging, shooting, and burning alleged offenders.

Finally, for love of country. No American travels abroad without blushing for shame for his country on this subject. And whatever the excuse that passes current in the United States, it avails nothing abroad. With all the powers of government in control; with all laws made by white men, administered by white judges, jurors, prosecuting attorneys, and sheriffs; with every office of the executive department filled by white men—no excuse can be offered for exchanging the orderly administration of justice for barbarous lynchings and "unwritten laws." Our country should be placed speedily above the plane of confessing herself a failure at self-government. This cannot be until Americans of every section, of broadest patriotism and best and wisest citizenship, not only see the defect in our country's armor but take the necessary steps to remedy it.

"UNITY OF THE HUMAN RACE"

SOURCE *Public Domain.*

INTRODUCTION *This 1902 article, written by J. W. Sanders for the* African Methodist Episcopal Church Review, *and other articles like this were crucial to spreading the word to African Americans on key social and religious issues. The church itself had been founded in 1787 by a group of African American Methodists who were protesting racial segregation. During the Reconstruction period following the Civil War, from 1865 to 1867, this group's political involvement helped elect more than fifty church members to public office in the state legislatures of Alabama, Florida, Georgia, South Carolina, and other states. By the time Sanders addressed the key issue of racial division, unrest among African Americans was reaching another level. Frustration over segregation and discrimination based on racism grew as prejudice and and acts of violence against them increased. His argument was that a concept of unity among all people was at the heart of redemption for all—socially, politically, and morally.*

One might at first thought say, "What does it matter if a Chinaman disclaims any genetic connection with a Malay? or, if perchance, a Caucasian denies having any racial connection whatever with the Negro, as is often done?" It matters much every way. In the first place, we observe there are two forces playing ceaselessly on the hearts of the children. One, an internal force, we will call inspiration the second, the external power of friendly environment. Now, the proper conception of the truth of the "oneness of man" leads to the encouragement of peoples who are down, by causing the exercise of the brotherly instincts of the dominant race: the improper conception leads to the paralysis of every aspiration of the lower races to rise from a state of inferiority. It means either that I am to be recognized as a man and brother, and thus be offered every inducement and encouragement to scale the heights, or that by all the strength of a dominant race I am to be held in subjection and made subservient to those who rule.

Now, if you will for a moment consider, you will readily discover that the full acceptance of the "unity of man" does not obtain among the vanguard of the nations whose potent influence dominates the earth.

There are nine millions of Afro-Americans in this country, and they are popularly considered inferior to others in mental, moral and spiritual power. And this inferiority is not looked upon as an accident of birth, or as resulting, from a lack of opportunities, but is viewed as the unchangeable status of a race under the ban of God's displeasure. Nor should there arise in the souls of the sons of Ham thoughts and longings never so lofty, is it to be considered for a moment that the dark-skinned child of fate—who was to fair-skinned Israel, "but a hewer of wood and drawer of water"—should ever aspire, even after the year of jubilee, to purify himself and walk into the congregation and take his seat with others. They say God has set barriers in nature with a "Thus far shalt thou come, but no farther."

So that no Negro need expect to develop that culture, refinement, Christian grace and elegance necessary to exact from the proud Caucasian a hearty reception to places of honor. We are to inquire whether the color of a man's skin and the texture of his hair, which are the two chief marks of difference in a physiological sense, are the results of climatic influences, or are they indicative of a different order of being? I have heard it preached that Negroes have no brain to speak of, could only learn enough to serve their masters. They had no souls; Christ did not die for them; it was nonsense to talk of the stocky mothers with dark skins and thick lips having any racial connection with the white race. Dr. John Miley has given us the benefit of exhaustive research. He says, at some length. "Let us compare notes along two general lines. First—Physical; Second—Mental; and if we find that the differences along these lines are only superficial, and the result of environment or circumstances, then the objections raised against the doctrine of the unity of man will fall to the ground." This is largely a question of science, says he, or, at least, we must go to science for a knowledge of the facts. The unity of the human race is a question of the unity of species. Definitions setting forth the idea of species greatly differ, but the following will cover the idea we wish to convey approximately—"Species is a collection of individuals more or less resembling each other, which may be regarded as having descended from a single pair by an uninterrupted and natural succession of families." Herein is found two fundamental facts: First—Resemblance; Second—Genetic connection. The idea of genetic connection is the deeper idea.

There are wide variations, particularly in size, form and color. We are to inquire, whether these variations are consistent with a common parentage. While some hold four or five, up to sixty, different origins of the human family, the weight of scientific authority is for a unity of origin. This question of species is common to the manifold forms of vegetable and animal life. Fixation of racial types is no disproof of unity. There are numerous instances of physiological change as a result of new conditions. Let us cite a few: 200 years ago the Irish were driven from Armagh and the South of Down, and have become prognathous like the Australians. The Yankees are descendants of the English, and yet they have a type of their own. Certain tribes of Indians have permanently changed the shapes of their heads by bandaging them in infancy. The Jews are confessedly of one origin, and yet we have the Polish Jews who are light-haired, and the dark Jew of the Nile Valley. Again, the Portuguese, who settled in East India in the sixteenth century, are now as dark as the Hindus themselves. Also we find that Africans become lighter as they go up the Aluvial River banks to higher ground; and, on the contrary, the coast tribes, who drive out the Negroes of the interior and take their territory, end by becoming Negroes themselves. Hence, we argue that there is a oneness of races in physical characteristics. The distinctions are superficial and the result of local influences. The human body is one in chemical elements, one in anatomical structure, one in physiological construction, one in pathological susceptibilities, one in psychological endowment. Of course, you could set in wide contrast the barbaric Negro against the Christian Caucasian, but lo and behold! there are differences almost as great even among the same Caucasian race. But that is understood to be only accidental, or superficial. There are the same sensibilities, with their marvelous adjustments to manifold relations of mind in all; the same moral and religious nature. While it may sink to barbarism and idolatry in the white man, it may rise to the highest moral and Christian life in the Mongolian and the Negro. Here is a vast law of nature, that like shall produce like. Throughout the different orders of created beings this great law holds good; and nature sets bars in the way of the infraction of this law, both in animal and vegetable life. The law of hybridity contravenes when sacrilegious hands are laid on this law to disturb its orderly workings, so that strict sterility is seen when an attempt is made to bring together different species, as in the case of the horse and the mule. [Genesis] "And God said let the earth bring forth grass, the herb yielding seed, and the fruit tree yielding fruit after his kind whose seed is in itself upon the earth, and it was so." Now, if science speaks to me in her many toned and yet harmonious voices that in all essential physical points all races of men are one, if the voice of psychology tells me that all men, in mental endowments, are one, and if the voice of revelation tells me that there is no respect of persons with God, I have but to buckle on my armor and move up the line, in spite of all powers that oppose. But I have not introduced a witness in this case, which, perhaps, is the most convincing of all, for it is found in the chambers of one's own soul. It is that of consciousness. A voice within speaks to each man upon whom the light of God's truth has shone and tells him that the same God who circled the heavens upon which to sit, has made each man—all men—to work out for himself a glorious destiny; and this voice is so convincing that, though a dozen kings should meet a peasant and should decry the noble aspirations swelling his breast methinks the humble man would smile at the usurpers and would turn from them feeling that in true dignity and inherent worth he was on a par with the mightiest potentate beneath the sun. I must understand, however, if I am to achieve any noble results in life, it must be through earnest personal efforts. We must work, work, work as a race, and we shall gradually rise in the scale of being.

"The planets at their Maker's will
Move onward in their cars,
For Nature's wheel is never still:
Progressive as the stars,
The moments fly on lightning's wing:
And life's uncertainty, too—
We've none to waste on foolish things,
There's work enough to do."

PROTOCOLS OF THE ELDERS OF ZION

SOURCE *Segel, Binjamin W. From "Appendix: The First Protocol," in* A Lie and a Libel: The History of the Protocols of the Elders of Zion. *Edited and translated by Richard S. Levy. University of Nebraska Press, 1995.*

INTRODUCTION *The author of this text would have had people believe that Russian Jewish elders got together in a secret meeting in the late 1880s and produced these* Protocols. *They were the outline of how the Jews would take over the world—or at least how they would come into power to control the media and finance. Published in 1903 these principles were used to help spur on anti-Semitic sentiment and fuel all of the unfounded fears that the Jewish people were out to exploit and manipulate non-Jews. They would satisfy their own greed for wealth and power ultimately by playing on the greed and weaknesses of others. Some believe that this document was written by a Russian-French journalist named Matvei Golovinski in the 1890s. No one has ever found the irrefutable answer to the question. Refutations of the* Protocols *emerged early, though a series of articles in the the* Times *of London in 1921 offered the best case for fraud. Much of the document was shown to be plagiarized from a piece known as* The Dialogue in Hell Between Machiavelli and Montesquieu *that was a satire and was not meant to foster anti-Semitism. Despite the widespread knowledge that it was a fraud, it was circulated by those opposed to the Russian Revolution in 1905—believed to be circulated by the czar's army as a tool against the Jews. After 1920 it gained popularity in Germany with the rise of Nazism.*

THE FIRST PROTOCOL

I have framed the basic principles of our league, in general and in particular, without regard to scientific considerations. I describe our doctrines and our system as it appears to us and to non-Jews.

I assert that men with evil motives outnumber those with good character. In the administration of the state, therefore, more can be achieved by force and unscrupulousness than by scientific discussions. Every man strives for power; every individual wants to be master of his own decisions and deeds; each would be master of himself (a dictator), if only he could. This striving after power is so strong that there is scarcely a man who would not be ready to sacrifice the common good for his own personal advantage.

What instincts rule over the beasts of prey that feed upon the blood of men? What have been their actions and desires through all time? Since the rise of human society, beasts of prey in human form have seized raw, blind force for themselves. From this I conclude that *force* alone is the determining factor, no matter that it be veiled and disguised. Thus it follows that the basic law of existence rests wholly on the idea: Right is based on force, on strength.

The Idea of Freedom—Freethinking

Civil freedom is an idea, a concept, but not a fact. This idea transforms itself as soon as the power of a nation is suppressed and strangled, as soon as a party striving after dominance seeks to force its will upon the countermovement. This task becomes essentially easier when the opponent is himself contaminated with a false concept of "freedom" and yields his power on account of this incorrect notion. On this is based the victory of our doctrine: when the reins slide along the ground and leadership is lacking, the accomplished licentiousness ends quickly, for a new hand draws in the reins. A new domination steps into the place of the old, which was robbed of its power by freethinking.

Gold, Faith in God, Self-government

In our day, when the genuine freethinkers govern the state, the power of gold is the sole determining factor. There was a time when faith in God governed. The concept of freedom was still without system. No one understood how to exploit it for his purposes. No nation can exist for even the shortest time when it does not create a *rational* self-government, without which it sinks into licentiousness. From this moment there enters inner divisiveness, issuing in economic battles in the wake of which governments fall; gradually mob rule takes the rudder.

Domination of Money

A government finding itself under the influence of internal upheavals, or one that is at the mercy of external enemies because of the disordered conditions in its own land, must be undoubtedly consigned to oblivion. Then it is in our power. The dominance of money, over which we alone dispose, extends a straw to the government that it must grasp for good or ill if it wants to keep from sinking helplessly into the abyss.

To those freethinkers who believe such considerations to be immoral, I say: every realm has two enemies. If it is allowable to employ immoral methods in the struggle against the external enemy, for example, concealment of intentions or a sudden attack, attacking at night or with overwhelming superiority of forces, can one say it is morally impermissible to use such methods against the worst [internal] enemy, the destroyer of social harmony and economic well-being?

The Masses and Lawlessness

Can a man of sound and logical intelligence hope to rule the masses of a nation successfully if he merely employs rational principles and logical arguments when the possibility of contradiction exists in the people? Would an even half-way intelligent people be thereby easier to govern? If such a man relied exclusively on minor measures—on old customs, traditions, sentiments, and emotional dogmas, the masses would divide and reject such a government. For the masses have no sense for rational exhortation. Every action of the masses depends upon an accidental or artificially constructed majority. Ignorant of the artifices of statecraft, they are carried along into foolish decisions, and thus the seed of lawlessness is planted within the state.

Statecraft and the Moral Law

Statecraft and the moral law have not the slightest to do with one another. A ruler who wants to rule by the moral law understands nothing about statecraft and is never for a moment secure upon his throne. He who would rule must labor with slyness, cunning, evil, hypocrisy. High moral character—openness, honor, honesty—these are the reefs of statecraft upon which the best will founder because the enemy makes use of different and truly more effective measures. Let these character traits be the hallmarks and principles of non-Jewish realms. We can never under any condition labor with such wrong-headed principles.

Our right lies in strength. "Strength" is a limited expression, not a universally valid concept. The word in itself never signifies more than: "Give me what I want so that it may be clear and self-evident to all the world that I am stronger than you."

Where does right begin? Where does it end? In a state where power is badly managed and laws and governors are rendered impersonal by freethinking [civil] rights, I shall create a new right. [I shall] demolish all institutions according to the right of the stronger, lay hands upon the law, transform all governing bodies, and become master of them. The power of these rights shall voluntarily transfer to us—because of freethinking.

The Invulnerability of Jewish Freemasonry

While at present all the powers have begun to totter, ours will be more invulnerable than any of the others because it will be invisible. Thus it shall remain unshakable until that time when it has become so empowered that no act of violence can repress it.

Out of the transitory calamities that we must now cause, there will emerge the benefaction of an unshakable government that shall reestablish the regulated development of national existence, undisturbed by freethinking. The results justify the means. Thus we shall direct our plans less by attention to the good and moral than by the necessary and useful.

Before us lies a plan, the lines of which are drawn according to the rules of war. We cannot deviate from it without endangering the labor of many centuries.

The Masses Are Blind

To achieve the goal of common efforts, we must learn to grasp the worthlessness, inconstancy, and vacillation of the masses. We must realize their incapacity to understand the questions of state life and their own welfare. We must comprehend that the great masses of the people are blind and wholly without understanding and that they willy-nilly stagger from right to left, backward and forward. A blind man cannot lead the blind without leading them into the abyss. Consequently, even the "inquisitive" and creative among the masses can never perform as leaders in governing the states. Even when they supposedly possess some intelligence, they are still not fit to act as trailblazers and leaders of the masses. They will attain to no other goal than the ruin of the entire people.

Only a personality educated to self-mastery from youth can recognize and act upon the great tendencies and principles of statecraft.

Party Strife

A people that delivers itself to the upstarts from out of the masses destroys its own structure by party battles, by the struggle for the leading positions of power, by the hunting after honors and dignities, and by the disorders and movements arising from all this. Is it possible that the masses can judge without prejudice, peacefully and matter-of-factly, that they can guide the destiny of the land without regard to purely personal interests? Can they defend the realm against external foes? That is senseless, for to distribute governance of the state among so many personalities, so many heads from out of the masses, will sacrifice its unity and it will become nonviable and powerless.

Only under the leadership of a self-controlled personality can the state be directed in full clarity and good order; only thus can the whole body politic labor in peace. From this it follows that the most appropriate form of the state for a country is found when the direction lies in the hands of a single responsible personality. Without unqualified power, no state system can thrive upon a moral basis. This basis cannot rest upon the masses but rather on the competent leader, be he who he may. The masses consist of barbarians who bring their coarseness and barbarity to bear at every opportunity. As soon as the masses seize power for themselves, they fall into lawlessness, the highest degree of barbarity.

Alcohol, Humanism, Vice

Observe the drunkards, befogged by alcohol. They believe themselves to possess the right to unlimited pleasure, which they confuse with the concept of freedom. From that idea we take leave for all time. The non-Jewish peoples are befogged with alcohol; their youths are infatuated with humanism and premature vices. To these they have been led by our agents, administrators, teachers, servants, governesses to the rich, educational institutions, and so forth, as well as by our women in pleasure resorts and public houses. Among these I also count the so-called society ladies, who willfully ape the example of vice and ostentation.

Principles of the Jewish Freemason Lodges

Our slogan is *Power and Artifice*! Power alone wrests the victory in questions of state, that is, when it is in the possession of personalities who have something to say in the state. Force forms the basis, but cunning and fraud work as the means to power for such governments as are not willing to lay their crowns at the feet of the representatives of a new power. These are the only means to the goal that hovers before us. Therefore, we must not shrink from bribery, fraud, or treason if they serve for the attainment of our plans. In statecraft we must be clever enough not to shrink from uncanny methods, if power and subjection be achieved thereby.

Terror

Our realm, which is founded on the paths of peaceful conquest, will replace the terrors of war with less visible but all the more effective punishments. It must institute a reign of terror in order to compel blind, unconditional obedience. Stern, pitiless, and ruthless measures are the best props of state power. Not alone for advantage but above all in the name of duty and for the sake of victory, we must hold firmly to the employment of force and cunning. . . . It is not only in the scientific evaluation of means, but above all in their ruthless and merciless application that our predominance, our superiority, shall be secured. It shall suffice to know that we are merciless and that we understand how to compel obedience.

Liberty, Equality, Fraternity

Already in antiquity we allowed the call for Liberty, Equality, Fraternity to echo from the ranks of the peoples. Since that time, these words have been endlessly repeated in the most varied disturbances and upheavals. Sometimes the intentions have been honorable, to bring actual well-being and true freedom of the personality to the world; sometimes it has just been to satisfy the vanity of the masses. Not even the intelligent and clever non-Jews have recognized the inner contradictions in these words. They have not said that there can be no equality, no freedom in nature. All of nature rests upon the inequality of forces, characteristics, peculiarities. Nature is subject to eternal laws. It is clear that the masses are a blind force, and the chosen upstarts are as blind as the masses themselves. The initiated, even if he is a fool, can govern, while the uninitiated, even when he is high-minded, can understand nothing about statecraft. All these things are forgotten by the non-Jews.

Principle of Princely Government

[On the non-Jews] depended the principle of princely government. The father bequeathed his knowledge of statecraft to the son, so that it was known only to members of the dynasty and none could betray the secrets to the peoples ruled over. In time the sense of the true content of statecraft was lost in the transmission, and this contributed to the success of our cause.

Abolishing the Privileges of the Non-Jewish Nobility

In all the corners of the world, with the help of our secret societies, the slogan Liberty, Equality, Fraternity led gigantic crowds to our ranks and carried our banners to victory. Those words were the worms that gnawed at the welfare of non-Jews, everywhere undermining peace, calm, community, common values, and thereby destroying the foundation of their domination. Gentlemen, you see the consequences that have served the triumph of our cause. *They gave us the possibility of playing out the highest trump: the annihilation of noble privilege, or, better said, the actual system of non-Jewish noble dominance, which has been the only means of defense of the non-Jewish peoples and states against us.*

The New Nobility

On the ruins of the old blood and family nobility we have set the nobility of our educated and at its tip, the money nobility. The standard of this new nobility lies in wealth, which depends upon us, and in the teachings disseminated by our secret associations.

Calculating Human Weaknesses

Our triumph was made all the easier in that we could exploit people useful to us by working on the most impressionable side of human intelligence: with consideration to money, greed, and the insatiable desire for gain. If we seize upon the right moment, all the extraordinarily numerous human weaknesses are suited to paralyze the powers of decision making. Those who best understand how to exploit human weaknesses are thus enabled to enslave the wills of men.

The concept of freedom made it possible to convince the masses that the government was nothing more than the deputies for those who possessed the land, that is, the people. The people therefore felt competent to change [governments] as one would change gloves.

Changes in the parliament delivered it into our power. It is elected or not, at our discretion.

THE PLATFORM OF THE NIAGARA MOVEMENT

SOURCE *Public Domain.*

INTRODUCTION *Not all African Americans were as willing to compromise on the issue of race relations as was Booker T. Washington—the person many considered a traitor to his race, even if he did eventually become more militant. In 1904, one group of African Americans got together behind closed doors at Carnegie Hall in New York to develop the Committee of Twelve for the Advancement of the interest of the Negro Race, but it soon fell apart due to the conflicts among themselves. The next year W. E. B. Du Bois and William M. Trotter brought together another group that included Frederick L. McGhee and C.E. Bentley, and 59 well-known business men. They gathered in western New York. Then 29 of them went to the Canadian side of Niagara Falls and joined together in what they would call the* Niagara Movement. *Because of Washington's opposition and the support he had from so many African Americans, this organization did not last long. By 1910, Du Bois turned his energies to the new organization, the National Association for the Advancement of Colored People (NAACP). The platform of the Niagara Movement was an expression of the frustration and anger of African Americans who wanted to end Jim Crow and other acts of discrimination and inequality.*

"THE PLATFORM OF THE NIAGARA MOVEMENT"

The second annual meeting of the so-called Niagara Movement was held recently at Harper's Ferry. This is a movement of negroes for negro rights. It represents the more political and the more assertive spirit in the negro race, under the leadership of Dr. Du Bois, as the Tuskegee Movement under the leadership of Dr. Washington represents the more industrial and the more pacific spirit. It is probably not unjust to say that something of the quality of the Niagara Movement is indicated by the fact that its leaders chose this year Harper's Ferry for its place of assemblage, and in its closing utterance the assembly declared, "Here, on the scene of John Brown's Martyrdom, we reconsecrate ourselves, our honor, our property, to the final emancipation of the race which John Brown died to make free." Its adopted platform comprises five principles: (1) The right to vote: "We want full manhood suffrage, and we want it now, henceforth, and forever." (2) Condemnation of all race discrimination in public accommodations: "Separation in railway and street cars, based simply on race and color, is un-American, undemocratic, and silly." (3) Freedom of social intercourse: "We claim the right of freemen to walk, talk, and be with them that wish to be with us. No man has a right to choose another man's friends, and to attempt to do so is an impudent interference with the most fundamental human privilege." (4) Equality in the enforcement of laws: "Justice even for criminals and outlaws;" "Congress to take charge of Congressional elections;" "the Fourteenth and Fifteenth Amendments enforced." (5) "The National Government to step in and wipe out illiteracy in the South;" an undying hostility to "any proposal to educate black boys and girls simply as servants and underlings, or simply for the use of other people."

"THE PLATFORM OF THE OUTLOOK"

We can best state our views respecting these demands by putting with them what appear to us to be the just and reasonable bases for the settlement of the so-called race issue. Those bases we should state somewhat as follows: (1) Manhood suffrage, provided the manhood comes first and the suffrage afterwards. The ballot is not a natural right, like the right to the protection of person and property; it is a prerogative to be given only to those, black or white, who have furnished some evidence that they possess the intellectual and moral qualifications to use the ballot for the benefit of the community. But it should be based on personal qualifications, not on race or color. (2) It is better for both races that they have their separate schools and separate churches. It is no more an injustice to the black race than to the white race to provide separate cars for them, if the accommodations are equally good for both races. (3) Social fellowship cannot be restrained by law, neither can it be claimed as a right. In general, the way to secure social recognition is not to demand it. (4) The demand for the equality of law enforcement is wholly just. The demand for Congressional charge of Congressional elections is wholly unnecessary. Congress has already charge of Congressional elections. It has the right to reject any Representative on evidence that his election has been accomplished by corruption, fraud, violence, or threatening of any description, and it ought to exercise this right far more vigorously than it has been accustomed to do. (5) We want the National Government to "wipe out illiteracy in the South," and we protest against any "proposal to educate black boys and girls simply as servants and underlings;" but we also affirm as a truth of universal applicability that the end of all education should be to fit the pupil for the work which it is probable he will have to do, for the service which he will probably have to render. We add the demand for the open door of industrial opportunity to all men, black and white, and insistence upon the principle that every man shall fit himself, as his first duty to the community, to render the best service of which, taking account of his training and his inheritance, he is capable. On the whole, we think the Niagara Movement would be more useful if it demanded more of the negro race and put less emphasis on its demands for the negro race.

"THE NEGRO PROBLEM: BOOKER WASHINGTON'S PLATFORM"

In The Outlook of last week we gave a summary of the platform adopted at the second annual meeting of the so-called Niagara Movement held at Harper's Ferry under the special leadership of Dr. Du Bois. It is instructive to compare with this platform the address by Dr. Booker Washington before the meeting of the National Negro Business League, of which he is President, held last week at Atlanta, Georgia. This address may fairly be regarded as embodying the platform of this League; and just as the Niagara Movement stands for the more political and assertive spirit in the negro race, so the National Business League, as represented in Dr. Washington's address, stands for the industrial and pacific spirit. Dr. Washington expressed this tersely when he said, "Let constructive progress be the dominant note among us in every section of America: an inch of progress is worth more than a yard of faultfinding." He declared that "while the world may pity a crying, whining race, it seldom respects it." As to the progress actually made, he pointed out that in Georgia alone the negroes own $20,000,000 worth of taxable property, and that in the whole country, at a conservative estimate, the negro is now paying taxes upon over $300,000,000 worth of property, while in the Southern States negroes are conducting thirty-three banks. In fact, Dr. Washington believes that there is practically no section of the South where encouragement cannot be found for the negro farmer, mechanic, merchant, and even banker, with reasonable opportunity for prosperity, and he reaffirms his formerly expressed opinion that the Southern States offer the best permanent abode for the negro. He would welcome immigration, for he believes that healthy competition is much needed in the South, and that the salvation of his race is to be found "not in our ability to keep another race out of the territory, but in our learning to get as much out of the soil, out of our occupations or business, as any other race can get out of theirs." Dr. Washington spoke strongly and plainly as to crime on the part of the negro; he admitted the seriousness of the problem, did not hesitate to say that the large number of crimes committed by members of his race was deplorable, but challenged his hearers to show instances of crime committed by graduates of the educational institutions, or, with rare exceptions, by negroes who own their homes, are taxpayers, have regular occupation, and have received education. From these facts he argued that "ignorance will always mean crime, and crime will mean an unwieldy burden fastened about the neck of the South." The crime of lynching was equally denounced. Dr. Washington said: "Let us bear in mind that every man, white or black, who takes the law into his hands to lynch or burn or shoot human beings supposed to be or guilty of crime is insulting the executive, judicial, and lawmaking bodies of the State in which he resides. Lawlessness in one direction will inevitably lead to lawlessness in other directions. This is the experience of the whole civilized world." The trend and force of Dr. Washington's address might almost be summed up in this sentence: "The more I study our conditions and needs, the more I am convinced that there is no surer road by which we can reach civic, moral, educational, and religious development than by laying the foundation in the ownership and cultivation of the soil, the saving of money, commercial growth, and the skillful and conscientious performance of any duty with which we are intrusted." Comparing this utterance with the platform quoted last week, it will be seen that they are not antagonistic, but that they differ in spirit. One makes demands for the negroes, the other lays its demands upon the negro; one emphasizes his rights, the other his duties; one complains of the wrongs the white inflicts upon the negro, the other asks for co-operation between the white and the negro. We see far more hope for the negro in the spirit of the Business Men's League than in that of the Niagara Movement.

STATEMENT OF MR. WILLIAM JOSEPH SIMMONS, OF ATLANTA, GEORGIA

SOURCE *Public Domain.*

INTRODUCTION *The original Ku Klux Klan was born in the South during the humiliating period of Reconstruction following defeat in the South's bid to secede. It was first created as a social club in Tennessee in 1865 but quickly became an organization that set out to intimidate patrolling Union soldiers and newly freed African Americans who might intend to act as free men with the same rights as white men. Already by 1871, the U.S. Congress grew concerned about their activities and held hearings that led to passage of anti-Klan legislation. President Ulysses S. Grant even dispatched troops to the areas where Klan activity was rampant. These measures were apparently successful and the original organization faded into distant memory. In 1915, with increasingly tense social, political, and cultural relations, and with the premiere of D.W. Griffith's movie* The Birth of a Nation, *and its cultural stereotypes, a new Ku Klux Klan arose. A Georgia veteran of the Spanish-American War named William Joseph Simmons, known as the "Colonel," though only a self-proclaimed one, gained inspiration at the movie's Atlanta premiere. He decided the time was right to begin another Klan movement. This time the group not only targeted African Americans but other groups such as Catholics, Jews, and other recent immigrants. Once again, as in 1871, Congress took notice and held hearings to determine what dangers this new Klan posed. Simmons' testimony offers insight to the organization.*

My name is William Joseph Simmons, residing in Atlanta, Ga. They call me "Colonel," largely out of respect. Every lawyer in Georgia is called "Colonel," so they thought that I was as good as a lawyer, so they call me that. However, since that matter has been called into question. I am a veteran of the Spanish-American War. I am a past commander of my Spanish-American war veterans' post. I am a past national aid-de-camp of the Spanish-American War Veterans' Association and also a past provisional division commander. I was at one time the senior colonel in command of five regiments and colonel of my own regiment of the uniform rank of the Woodmen of the World, and I was known as "Colonel." I have used that title on certain literature of the klan for the reason that there are three other "W.J. Simmonses" in Atlanta, and for some time our mail got confused. It is merely a designation. They accord it to me as an honor and I appreciated it, but at no time and in no place have I arrogated to myself the fact that I was a colonel of the Army. I served there, but I was under a colonel and I found out how the colonels do. . . .

Twenty years ago I received the inspiration to establish a fraternal, patriotic, secret order for the purpose of memorializing the great heroes of our national history, inculcating and teaching practical fraternity among men, to teach and encourage a fervent, practical patriotism toward our country, and to destroy from the hearts of men the Mason and Dixon line and build thereupon a great American solidarity and a distinctive national conscience which our country sorely stands in need of.

At that time I was a mere young man and knew that my youth and immature thought would not permit me to successfully launch the movement, so I kept my own counsel all through 15 subsequent years, working, thinking, and preparing my head and heart for the task of creating this institution for the interest of our common country and for the promotion of real brotherhood among men. To this work and to this end I dedicated my life and all my energies, after being thoroughly convinced that there was a place for such a fraternal order and that the order could and would fill that place.

It was in the month of October, 1915, that I decided to launch the movement. . . .

Through the dark hours of struggle and bitter sacrifice incident to the launching of this movement, for over nine long months I had an average of one meal a day. I have fought a good fight. I have truly kept the faith, and God permitting me, Mr. Chairman, I shall finish my course, with love toward all, with malice toward none. I shall pursue the right as God shall give me a vision of the right.

If the Knights of the Ku-Klux Klan has been a lawless organization, as has been charged, it would not have shown the remarkable growth it has, for in the klan is as fine a body of representative citizens as there is in the United States. In each community where there is a klan will be found members from the lending citizens, men who stand at the forefront in their cities. These men would not stand for lawlessness.

It has been charged that the klan is a gigantic swindle, run solely to enrich a few of the inside ring. I, as the executive head of the klan, have received during the past six years altogether approximately $12,000, an average of $2,000 per year. I can not be in any wise accurate in these figures, because I have not run it up, but I may state just here that for two or three years I received not a penny, only what I could get out and do myself. I have also a home, purchased by klan members, but not by the klan, but by voluntary subscriptions of 25 cents and 50 cents and a dollar. This home is not completely paid for, and I knew nothing of this until it was given to me as a complete surprise as a birthday remembrance on the 6th day of last May by members of the klan from every section of the country.

And I may add just here, from what has been presented for my information regarding the home in which I now reside, that property is in the hands of a board of trustees who are looking after it; and they told me, "When we get the home paid for then the deed will be made to you; but we do not want you to bother with that until it is all paid for." A board of trustees is handling that home.

The secretary, treasurer, and other officials of the klan receive salaries lower than they would receive from business institutions for their ability and for the work that each of them does. I introduce here, marked "Exhibit B," the pay roll and salaries paid and the expenses of the klan.

If the klan was seeking to enrich a few insiders the money would go into our pockets. Instead, we are spending the surplus money of the klan in the education of young men and women who are the very foundation of the Nation. . . .

The charge has been made that the klan takes the law into its own hands; that it terrorizes private citizens in many communities by lawless acts against person and property. These charges are untrue. I state, Mr. Chairman, that klans can not take action on anything outside of their lodge rooms or ceremonial duties unless they have an order, so to speak, written and signed by myself. That is a law in the klan to keep anyone within our membership from doing things—in other words, holding them in control—that contravene the law. Before God and this honorable committee, I have never authorized nor signed any kind of instructions that could in any way be construed as a violation of the law or to be carried out in violation of the law of my country.

There have been only a few instances where lawless acts have been alleged against individual members of the klan. You will notice I say "alleged," and there is a possibility that if individual members of the klan have committed acts of lawlessness that those same men were members of other fraternal orders, and should the other fraternal orders be condemned? No. In these instances the charter in that community was revoked or suspended, although the acts of the individual members were not the acts of the klan as a body and were condemned by all those disbanded klan members. The charter was revoked or suspended, as we have no room in our organization for those who take the law into their own hands, because to do so violates a most solemn oath. Individual members of other organizations have committed and been charged with outrages and crimes, but that does not condemn the whole order, as an order, of lawlessness....

The klan does not countenance nor will it tolerate any lawless acts by its members. Instead we teach respect for the law, love of country, and a closer fellowship of service. I here introduce, marked Exhibit G, and will read later, the ritual, oath, and other secret books and works of the klan. In the oath attention is called to the section where all klan members swear to uphold and respect the law of the United States, the State, county, and city where the members live. No man who would break his solemn oath by taking the law into his own hands is worthy of membership in any organization or worthy to be a citizen of our glorious country.

The charge has also been made that the klan as an organization gives an opportunity for evil-minded persons to threaten others, to satisfy their private grudges, and to commit outrages, using the klan as a cloak. This charge is absurd on its face when an examination of the records for the past 10 years will show that there were as many of these so-called outrages committed before the klan was organized as since its organization....

I noticed some time ago that the klan was charged with outrages, or, rather, an outrage against a Negro in Arkansas, and I state to you as an honorable man that that particular outrage occurred in Arkansas 18 months before we had one member in Arkansas.

It has been charged that this organization incites to riot. Can that charge be substantiated? No; because no man can place his finger on any spot on the map of the United States in which a klan has been organized and well established where there has ever been a riot, racial or otherwise, and in every town where riots have occurred there is no klan there or was not there at the time of the riots.

The charge has also been made that the klan is organized for the purpose of assisting the enforcement of the law. Nothing to substantiate this charge has been produced, and there is no room in the United States for any organization organized for any such purpose. The law is supreme, and if we were organized for any such absurd purpose the klan would not have lived a year and could not have grown as it has.

The charge is made that we are organized to preach and teach religious intolerance, and especially that we are anti-Roman Catholic, anti-Jew, and anti-Negro. The conduct of the klan proves this absolutely untrue. Many alleged outrages have been attributed to the klan, but none of these were against Roman Catholics, Jews, and Negroes per se, and none were committed by the klan. It is indeed strange that if we organized to persecute the Roman Catholics, Jews, and Negroes that nothing has been done against them. In the United States the question is not and should never be whether a citizen is a Protestant, a Roman Catholic, a Jew, or a Negro, but whether he is a loyal American.

Since the fight against the klan we have been offered and urged to use, by those who are anti-Roman Catholic and not members of the klan, possibly the greatest existing mass of data and material against the Roman Catholics and Knights of Columbus. In this material, so we are told, there are affidavits and other personal testimony attributing to the Roman Catholics and Knights of Columbus in American more outrages and crimes than the klan has ever been charged with. Included in these charges against the Roman Catholics and Knights of Columbus are murder, whipping, tar and feathers, and crimes of all natures.

If the klan was anti-Roman Catholic we would have certainly used the material offered us, but the offer was received, although those making it are anxious that this evidence be presented to Congress. If the klan is to secure members on an anti-Roman Catholic, anti-Jew, and anti-Negro appeal, we do not want such members, and have never secured them in this way. Discussions involving any man's religious beliefs are never allowed in a meeting of the klan. If it ever occurs and the fact is made known to the proper officials of the klan, those who indulge in it, even the presiding officers who permit it, are rigidly penalized.

CORRESPONDENCE REGARDING THE TUSKEGEE SYPHILIS EXPERIMENT

SOURCE Journal of Chronic Disease, *v. 26, 1973. Copyright © 1973 Elsevier Inc. Reproduced with permission from Elsevier. http://www.sciencedirect.com/science/journal/00219681.*

INTRODUCTION *When this experiment was begun in the early 1930s, African American males were recruited from Macon County, Alabama, because that county had the highest rate of untreated syphilis in a multi-county area that was being studied by the United States Public Health Service. Penicillin was not yet available. Doctors at the time noted that these men with syphilis might seek treatment in the primary stage of the disease but did not return until they were in stage three of the disease when symptoms were apparent. The racial stereotype was that African American males were genetically endowed with a greater sex drive than males of other races. And because of the high rates of the disease, the scientific community held the widespread belief that the disease was different in African Americans and treatment was not effective. When the experiment was exposed in the early 1970s, outrage prevailed among the public. Once pencillin was available after World War II, the Tuskeegee subjects did not receive it when it was known that it was effective in treating the disease. Hugh S. Cumming, a doctor from Virginia, and later a part of the Public Health Service was ultimately responsible for this study going forward. Both racism and the refusal to admit a mistaken hypothesis—likely due to that racism—compromised the health and cost the lives of many African Americans.*

August 29, 1932

Doctor J. N. Baker

State Health Officer

Montgomery, Alabama

Dear Doctor Baker:

I have for some time wished to talk over with you a piece of research work that might be carried out on syphilitic Negroes in Macon County, the expense of which is to be bourne by the Public Health Service. If you are likely to be in Montgomery about the middle of September I should like to arrange to leave Washington on the afternoon of September 12th en route for Montgomery to talk this matter over with you in person and then proceed to Tuskegee with a view of securing the cooperation of the Andrews Memorial Hospital of Tuskegee Institute.

In working up the data for the final report to the Julius Rosenwald Fund I was particularly impressed with the fact that a negligible number, something less than 35, of the Negroes under treatment in Macon County during the period of the demonstration had ever had any previous treatment. It seems to me that this situation in a very heavily infected population group affords an unparalleled opportunity of studying the effect of untreated syphilis on the human economy. If you think you will be interested in this subject, but nevertheless cannot arrange to be in Montgomery on the date or dates specified above, I shall arrange to visit you on any date that may be mutually satisfactory.

Very Sincerely Yours,

Taliaferro Clark

Assistant Surgeon General

Division of Venereal Diseases

September 20, 1932

Doctor R. R. Moton

Tuskegee Institute

Alabama

Dear Doctor Moton:

I regret your unavoidable absence from Tuskegee that prevented your meeting Assistant Surgeon General Taliaferro Clark at the time of his recent visit to Tuskegee because I wanted him to explain to you at firsthand the proposed study of the effects of untreated syphilis on the human economy with the cooperation of your hospital. It is expected the results of this study may have a marked bearing on the treatment, or conversely the non-necessity for treatment, of cases of latent syphilis. For this reason I shall be grateful if you shall be able to extend the splendid cooperation offered by Doctor Dibble contingent on your approval.

The recent syphilis control demonstration carried out in Macon County, with the financial assistance of the Julius Rosenwald Fund, revealed the presence of an unusually high prevalence rate in this county and, what is still more remarkable, the fact that approximately 99 per cent of this population group was entirely without previous treatment. This combination, together with the expected cooperation of your hospital, offers an unparalleled opportunity for carrying on this piece of scientific research which probably cannot be duplicated anywhere else in the world. No doubt Doctor Dibble has explained our plan of procedure to you that contemplates, among other things, an intensive physical and serological examination of untreated cases having positive Wassermann, which may not be carried out in the necessary scientific detail except in a hospital. You can readily see, therefore, that the success of this important study really hinges on your cooperation.

Sincerely,

H. S. Cumming

Surgeon General

REGULATION FOR THE ELIMINATION OF THE JEWS FROM THE ECONOMIC LIFE OF GERMANY, NOVEMBER 12, 1938

SOURCE *Regulation for the Elimination of the Jews from the Economic Life of Germany (1938): Goring, Hermann. From "Regulation for the Elimination of the Jews from the Economic Life of Germany, November 12, 1938," in* Documents on the Holocaust. *Edited by Yitzhak Arad, Israel Gutman, and Abraham Margaliot. Ktav Publishers House, 1982, in association with Yad Vashem. Reproduced by permission of Yad Vashem.*

INTRODUCTION *Only three days before the issuance of this* regulation *one of the most horrific events of Nazi terror occurred: On November 9, 1938, a night that would come to be known as* Kristallnacht, *or more commonly in English as, "Night of Broken Glass," brought widespread rioting throughout Germany against the Jewish communities. A Jewish student named Herschel Grynszpan living in Paris had asked and received an audience by a diplomat at the German embassy there. The diplomat was Ernst vom Rath. When he came in to receive Grynszpan, the student shot him, and vom Rath died two days later. Grynszpan was angered by the knowledge that the Nazis had ordered the expulsion of the approximately 18,000 Polish Jews from Germany, on October 27, his family among them—even though his father had lived in Hanover since 1911. These Jews had been taken back to the Poland in railway cattle cars and were forced to exist in appalling conditions, according to a postcard Grynszpan's father had sent to him. This incident was used as the justification for the riots against the Jews, the removal of the economic capabilities of the German Jews, and eventually, their elimination from life there altogether.*

On the basis of the regulation for the implementation of the Four Year Plan of October 18, 1936 (*Reichsgesetzblatt*, I, p. 887), the following is decreed:

§ 1

1) From January 1, 1939, Jews (§ 5 of the First Regulation to the Reich Citizenship Law of November 14, 1935, *Reichsgesetzblatt*, I, p. 1333) are forbidden to operate retail stores, mail-order houses, or sales agencies, or to carry on a trade [craft] independently.

2) They are further forbidden, from the same day on, to offer for sale goods or services, to advertise these, or to accept orders at markets of all sorts, fairs or exhibitions.

3) Jewish trade enterprises (Third Regulation to the Reich Citizenship Law of June 14, 1938—*Reichsgesetzblatt*, I, p. 627) which violate this decree will be closed by police.

§ 2

1) From January 1, 1939, a Jew can no longer be the head of an enterprise within the meaning of the Law of January 20, 1934, for the Regulation of National Work (*Reichsgesetzblatt*, I, p. 45).

2) Where a Jew is employed in an executive position in a commercial enterprise he may be given notice to leave in six weeks. At the expiration of the term of the notice all claims of the employee based on his contract, especially those concerning pension and compensation rights, become invalid.

§ 3

1) A Jew cannot be a member of a cooperative.

2) The membership of Jews in cooperatives expires on December 31, 1938. No special notice is required.

§ 4

The Reich Minister of Economy, in coordination with the ministers concerned, is empowered to publish regulations for the implementation of this decree. He may permit exceptions under the Law if these are required as the result of the transfer of a Jewish enterprise to non-Jewish ownership, for the liquidation of a Jewish enterprise or, in special cases, to ensure essential supplies.

Berlin, November 12, 1938

Plenipotentiary for the Four Year Plan

GÖRING

Field Marshal General

"CONCENTRATION CAMP: U.S. STYLE"

SOURCE *Public Domain.*

INTRODUCTION *Designated as a measure for national security, President Franklin Roosevelt signed Executive Order 9066 on February 19, 1942, about two months following the Japanese attack at Pearl Harbor. Over the next several months, more than 110,000 people of Japanese ancestry, many of them American citizens or native-born Americans were removed from their homes by force and relocated to camps further inland, from the western mountain states to Arkansas. By June of 1942 these Japanese Americans were being housed in camps where conditions were less than adequate and sometimes squalid. Ted Nakashima, who wrote this article for* The New Republic *on June 15, 1942, alerted all of America to the plight of these loyal American citizens.*

Unfortunately in this land of liberty, I was born of Japanese parents; born in Seattle of a mother and father who have been in this country since 1901. Fine parents, who brought up their children in the best American way of life. My mother served with the Volunteer Red Cross Service in the last war my father, an editor, has spoken and written Americanism for forty years.

Our family is almost typical of the other unfortunates here at the camp. The oldest son, a licensed architect, was educated at the University of Washington, has a master's degree from the Massachusetts Institute of Technology and is a scholarship graduate of the American School of Fine Arts in Fontainebleau, France. He is now in camp in Oregon with his wife and three-months-old child. He had just completed designing a much needed defense housing project at Vancouver, Washington.

The second son is an M.D. He served his internship in a New York hospital, is married and has two fine sons. The folks banked on him, because he was the smartest of us three boys. The army took him a month after he opened his office. He is now a lieutenant in the Medical Corps, somewhere in the South.

I am the third son, the dumbest of the lot, but still smart enough to hold down a job as an architectural draftsman. I have just finished building a new home and had lived in it three weeks. My desk was just cleared of work done for the Army Engineers, another stack of 391 defense houses was waiting (a rush job), when the order came to pack up and leave for this resettlement center called "Camp Harmony."

Mary, the only girl in the family, and her year-old son, "Butch," are with our parents—interned in the stables of the Livestock Exposition Buildings in-Portland.

Now that you can picture our thoroughly American background, let me describe our new home.

The resettlement center is actually a penitentiary—armed guards in towers with spotlights and deadly tommy guns, fifteen feet of barbed-wire fences, everyone confined to quarters at nine, lights out at ten o'clock. The guards are ordered to shoot anyone who approaches within twenty feet of the fences. No one is allowed to take the two-block-long hike to the latrines after nine, under any circumstances.

The apartments, as the army calls them, are two-block-long stables, with windows on one side. Floors are shiplaps on two-by-fours laid directly on the mud, which is everywhere. The stalls are about eighteen by twenty-one feet; some contain families of six or seven persons. Partitions are seven feet high, leaving a four-foot opening above. The rooms aren't too bad, almost fit to live in for a short while.

The food and sanitation problems are the worst. We have had absolutely no fresh meat, vegetables or butter since we came here. Mealtime queues extend for blocks; standing in a rainswept line, feet in the mud, waiting for the scant portions of canned wieners and boiled potatoes, hash for breakfast or canned wieners and beans for dinner. Milk only for the kids. Coffee or tea dosed with saltpeter and stale bread are the adults' staples. Dirty, unwiped dishes, greasy silver, a starchy diet, no butter, no milk, bawling kids, mud, wet mud that stinks when it dries, no vegetables—a sad thing for the people who raised them in such abundance. Memories of a crisp head of lettuce with our special olive oil, vinegar, garlic and cheese dressing.

Today one of the surface sewage-disposal pipes broke and the sewage flowed down the streets. Kids play in the water. Shower baths without hot water. Stinking mud and slops everywhere.

Can this be the same America we left a few weeks ago?

As I write, I can remember our little bathroom—light coral walls. My wife painting them, and the spilled paint in her hair. The open towel shelving and the pretty shower curtains which we put up the day before we left. How sanitary and clean we left it for the airlines pilot and his young wife who are now enjoying the fruits of our labor.

It all seems so futile, struggling, trying to live our old lives under this useless, regimented life. The senselessness of all the inactive manpower. Electricians, plumbers, draftsmen, mechanics, carpenters, painters, farmers—every trade—men who are able and willing to do all they can to lick the Axis. Thousands of men and women in these camps, energetic, quick, alert, eager for hard, constructive work, waiting for the army to do something for us, an army that won't give us butter.

I can't take it! I have 391 defense houses to be drawn. I left a fine American home which we built with our own hands. I left a life, highballs with our American friends on week-ends, a carpenter, laundry-truck driver, architect, airlines pilot—good friends, friends who would swear by us. I don't have enough of that Japanese heritage *"ga-man"*—a code of silent suffering and ability to stand pain.

Oddly enough I still have a bit of faith in army promises of good treatment and Mrs. Roosevelt's pledge of a future worthy of good American citizens. I'm banking another $67 of income tax on the future. Sometimes I want to spend the money I have set aside for income tax on a bit of butter or ice cream or something good that I might have smuggled through the gates, but I can't do it when I think that every dollar I can put into "the fight to lick the Japs," the sooner I will be home again. I must forget my stomach.

What really hurts most is the constant reference to us evacuees as "Japs." "Japs" are the guys we are fighting. We're on this side and we want to help.

EXECUTIVE ORDER 9981—ESTABLISHING THE PRESIDENT'S COMMITTEE ON EQUALITY OF TREATMENT AND OPPORTUNITY IN THE ARMED SERVICES

SOURCE *Public Domain.*

INTRODUCTION *Though African Americans had fought in every battle since before the start of the American Revolution, into the Civil War, the Spanish-American War, and both World Wars, they were not considered equal to whites in their military service to the country. The valor of African Americans in World War II was not recognized with the Medal of Honor for actions during the war for 51 years when the first African American was finally so honored. President Harry Truman believed such discrimination among courageous military veterans was not tolerable. In 1948 his order established equal treatment and opportunity in the military and mandated that no one in the military should be discriminated against because of race. He lost the entire southern wing of the Democratic Party when they left the convention and nominated J. Strom Thurmond, then governor of South Carolina, as their candidate for president. Executive Order 9981 ended segregation in the armed forces and created a new working cooperation between the U.S. Department of Justice and the NAACP as the struggle for civil rights moved further into the courts of the nation.*

WHEREAS it is essential that there be maintained in the armed services of the United States the highest standards of democracy, with equality of treatment and opportunity for all those who serve in our country's defense:

NOW, THEREFORE, by virtue of the authority vested in me as President of the United States, by the Constitution and the statutes of the United States, and as Commander in Chief of the armed services, it is hereby ordered as follows:

1. It is hereby declared to be the policy of the President that there shall be equality of treatment and opportunity for all persons in the armed services without regard to race, color, religion or national origin. This policy shall be put into effect as rapidly as possible, having due regard to the time required to effectuate any necessary changes without impairing efficiency or morale.

2. There shall be created in the National Military Establishment an advisory committee to be known as the President's Committee on Equality of Treatment and Opportunity in the Armed Services, which shall be composed of seven members to be designated by the President.

3. The Committee is authorized on behalf of the President to examine into the rules, proc[ed]ures and practices of the armed services in order to determine in what respect such rules, procedures and practices may be altered or improved with a view to carrying out the policy of this order. The Committee shall confer and advise with the Secretary of Defense, the Secretary of the Army, the Secretary of the Navy, and the Secretary of the Air Force, and shall make such recommendations to the President and to said Secretaries as in the judgment of the Committee will effectuate the policy hereof.

4. All executive departments and agencies of the Federal Government are authorized and directed to cooperate with the Committee in its work, and to furnish the Committee such information or the services of such persons as the Committee may require in the performance of its duties.

5. When requested by the Committee to do so, persons in the armed services or in any of the executive departments and agencies of the Federal Government shall testify before the Committee and shall make available for the use of the Committee such documents and other information as the Committee may require.

6. The Committee shall continue to exist until such time as the President shall terminate its existence by Executive order.

UNIVERSAL DECLARATION OF HUMAN RIGHTS, DECEMBER 10, 1948

SOURCE *Universal Declaration of Human Rights (1948): "Universal Declaration of Human Rights," in* General Assembly of the United Nations, *Resolution 217 A (III), December 10, 1948. Copyright © 1948 United Nations. The United Nations is the author of the original material. Reproduced by permission*

INTRODUCTION *In the wake of the atrocities of World War II, many prominent leaders throughout the world saw the need to outline the basic principles of human rights. The United Nations was in its infancy. The reality that six million Jews had died during Adolf*

Hitler's Holocaust was a horror that would never fade. More than one million of them were children not yet teenagers. The rights of these Jewish people were systematically stripped away through careful planning. When all was in place, it led to extermination. Others suffered indignation as well, and the people behind the declaration wanted to ensure that it did not happen again—or if it did, that there would be recourse. Among those who were instrumental in its drafting were Eleanor Roosevelt, widow of the late President Franklin D. Roosevelt; René Cassin of France; Charles Malik of Lebanon; Dr. P.C. Chang of China; and, Director of the United Nations' Human Rights Division, John Humphrey.

PREAMBLE

WHEREAS recognition of the inherent dignity and of the equal and inalienable rights of all members of the human family is the foundation of freedom, justice and peace in the world,

WHEREAS disregard and contempt for human rights have resulted in barbarous acts which have outraged the conscience of mankind, and the advent of a world in which human beings shall enjoy freedom of speech and belief and freedom from fear and want has been proclaimed as the highest aspiration of the common people,

WHEREAS it is essential, if man is not to be compelled to have recourse, as a last resort, to rebellion against tyranny and oppression, that human rights should be protected by the rule of law,

WHEREAS it is essential to promote the development of friendly relations between nations,

WHEREAS the peoples of the United Nations have in the Charter reaffirmed their faith in fundamental human rights, in the dignity and worth of the human person and in the equal rights of men and women and have determined to promote social progress and better standards of life in larger freedom,

WHEREAS Member States have pledged themselves to achieve, in co-operation with the United Nations, the promotion of universal respect for and observance of human rights and fundamental freedoms,

WHEREAS a common understanding of these rights and freedoms is of the greatest importance for the full realization of this pledge,

NOW, THEREFORE,

The General Assembly

Proclaims this Universal Declaration of Human Rights as a common standard of achievement for all peoples and all nations, to the end that every individual and every organ of society, keeping this Declaration constantly in mind, shall strive by teaching and education to promote respect for these rights and freedoms and by progressive measures, national and international, to secure their universal and effective recognition and observance, both among the peoples of Member States themselves and among the peoples of territories under their jurisdiction.

ARTICLE 1.

All human beings are born free and equal in dignity and rights. They are endowed with reason and conscience and should act towards one another in a spirit of brotherhood.

ARTICLE 2.

Everyone is entitled to all the rights and freedoms set forth in this Declaration without distinction of any kind, such as race, color, sex, language, religion, political or other opinion, national or social origin, property, birth or other status.

Furthermore, no distinction shall be made on the basis of the political, jurisdictional or international status of the county or territory to which a person belongs, whether it be independent, trust, non-self-governing or under any other limitation of sovereignty.

ARTICLE 3.

Everyone has the right to life, liberty and security of person.

ARTICLE 4.

No one shall be held in slavery or servitude; slavery and the slave trade shall be prohibited in all their forms.

ARTICLE 5.

No one shall be subjected to torture or to cruel, inhuman or degrading treatment or punishment.

ARTICLE 6.

Everyone has the right to recognition everywhere as a person before the law.

ARTICLE 7.

All are equal before the law and are entitled without any discrimination to equal protection of the law. All are entitled to equal protection against any discrimination in violation of this Declaration and against any incitement to such discrimination.

ARTICLE 8.

Everyone has the right to an effective remedy by the competent national tribunals for acts violating the fundamental rights granted him by the constitution or by law.

ARTICLE 9.

No one shall be subjected to arbitrary arrest, detention, or exile.

ARTICLE 10.

Everyone is entitled in full equality to a fair and public hearing by an independent and impartial tribunal, in the determination of his rights and obligations and of any criminal charge against him.

ARTICLE 11.

1. Everyone charged with a penal offense has the right to be presumed innocent until proved guilty according to law in a public trial at which he has had all the guarantees necessary for his defense.

2. No one shall be held guilty of any penal offense on account of any act or omission which did not constitute a penal offense, under national or international law, at the time when it was committed. Nor shall a heavier penalty be imposed than the one that was applicable at the time the penal offense was committed.

ARTICLE 12.

No one shall be subjected to arbitrary interference with his privacy, family, home or correspondence nor to attacks upon his honor and reputation.

Everyone has the right to the protection of the law against such interference or attacks.

ARTICLE 13.

1. Everyone has the right to freedom of movement and residence within the borders of each state.

2. Everyone has the right to leave any country, including his own, and to return to his country.

ARTICLE 14.

1. Everyone has the right to seek and to enjoy in other countries asylum from persecution.

2. This right may not be invoked in the case of prosecutions genuinely arising from non-political crimes or from acts contrary to the purposes and principles of the United Nations.

ARTICLE 15.

1. Everyone has the right to a nationality.

2. No one shall be arbitrarily deprived of his nationality nor denied the right to change his nationality.

ARTICLE 16.

1. Men and women of full age, without any limitation due to race, nationality or religion, have the right to marry and to found a family. They are entitled to equal rights as to marriage, during marriage and at its dissolution.

2. Marriage shall be entered into only with the free and full consent of the intending spouses.

3. The family is the natural and fundamental group unit of society and is entitled to protection by society and the state.

ARTICLE 17.

1. Everyone has the right to own property alone as well as in association with others.

2. No one shall be arbitrarily deprived of his property.

ARTICLE 18.

Everyone has the right to freedom of thought, conscience and religion; this right includes freedom to change his religion or belief, and freedom, either alone or in community with others and in public or private, to manifest his religion or belief in teaching, practice, worship and observance.

ARTICLE 19.

Everyone has the right to freedom of opinion and expression; this right includes freedom to hold opinions without interference and to seek, receive and impart information and ideas through any media and regardless of frontiers.

ARTICLE 20.

1. Everyone has the right to freedom of peaceful assembly and association.

2. No one may be compelled to belong to an association.

ARTICLE 21.

1. Everyone has the right to take part in the government of his country, directly or through freely chosen representatives.

2. Everyone has the right of equal access to public service in his country.

3. The will of the people shall be the basis of the authority of government; this will shall be expressed in periodic and genuine elections which shall be by universal and equal suffrage and shall be held by secret vote or by equivalent free voting procedures.

ARTICLE 22.

Everyone, as a member of society, has the right to social security and is entitled to realization, through national effort and international cooperation and in accordance with the organization and resources of each state, of the economic, social and cultural rights indispensable for his dignity and the free development of his personality.

ARTICLE 23.

1. Everyone has the right to work, to free choice of employment, to just and favorable conditions of work and to protection against unemployment.

2. Everyone, without any discrimination, has the right to equal pay for equal work.

3. Everyone who works has the right to just and favorable remuneration ensuring for himself and his family an existence worthy of human dignity, and supplemented, if necessary, by other means of social protection.

4. Everyone has the right to form and to join trade unions for the protection of his interests.

ARTICLE 24.

Everyone has the right to rest and leisure, including reasonable limitation of working hours and periodic holidays with pay.

ARTICLE 25.

1. Everyone has the right to a standard of living adequate for the health and well-being of himself and of his family, including food, clothing, housing and medical care and necessary social services, and the right to security in the event of unemployment, sickness, disability, widowhood, old age or other lack of livelihood in circumstances beyond his control.

2. Motherhood and childhood are entitled to special care and assistance. All children, whether born in or out of wedlock, shall enjoy the same social protection.

ARTICLE 26.

1. Everyone has the right to education. Education shall be free, at least in the elementary and fundamental stages. Elementary education shall be compulsory. Technical and professional education shall be made generally available and higher education shall be equally accessible to all on the basis of merit.

2. Education shall be directed to the full development of the human personality and to the strengthening of respect for human rights and fundamental freedoms. It shall promote understanding, tolerance and friendship among all nations, racial or religious groups, and shall further the activities of the United Nations for the maintenance of peace.

3. Parents have a prior right to choose the kind of education that shall be given to their children.

ARTICLE 27.

1. Everyone has the right freely to participate in the cultural life of the community, to enjoy the arts and to share in scientific advancement and its benefits.

2. Everyone has the right to the protection of the moral and material interests resulting from any scientific, literary, or artistic production of which he is the author.

ARTICLE 28.

Everyone is entitled to a social and international order in which the rights and freedoms set forth in this Declaration can be fully realized.

ARTICLE 29.

1. Everyone has duties to the community, in which alone the free and full development of his personality is possible.

2. In the exercise of his rights and freedoms, everyone shall be subject only to such limitations as are determined by law solely for the purpose of securing due recognition and respect for the rights and freedoms of others and of meeting the just requirements of morality, public order and the general welfare in a democratic society.

3. These rights and freedoms may in no case be exercised contrary to the purposes and principles of the United Nations.

ARTICLE 30.

Nothing in this Declaration may be interpreted as implying for any state, group or person any right to engage in any activity or to perform any act aimed at the destruction of any of the rights and freedoms set forth herein.

BROWN V. BOARD OF EDUCATION (EXCERPT)

SOURCE *Public Domain.*

INTRODUCTION *Segregation and discrimination did not end for African Americans with the Thirteenth Amendment to free the slaves. Nor did it end with the Fourteenth or Fifteenth Amendments that guaranteed due process and equal protection, as well as the right to vote despite the color of one's skin. Laws known as "Jim Crow" created a legal segregation that did not provide equality for African Americans, only more ways to keep them subjugated. Schooling was especially unequal as inadequate schools for African Americans were inferior. Many southern states had no college facilities that allowed African Americans to attend at all. In 1954, nearly a century following the Civil War, an African American elementary school student named Linda Brown, living in Topeka, Kansas, would change the direction of American education when she applied to attend the all-white public school that was closer to her home than the African American public school she was expected to attend. When she was denied admission under the auspices of Kansas state law allowing "separate but equal" facilities, she and her parents took the Board of Education to court—with the help of their NAACP attorney and future U.S. Supreme Court Justice, Thurgood Marshall.*

Mr. Chief Justice Warren delivered the opinion of the Court.

These cases come to us from the States of Kansas, South Carolina, Virginia, and Delaware. They are premised on different facts and different local conditions, but a common legal question justifies their consideration together in this consolidated opinion.

In each of the cases, minors of the Negro race, through their legal representatives, seek the aid of the courts in obtaining admission to the public schools of their community on a nonsegregated basis. In each instance, they had been denied admission to schools attended by white children under laws requiring or permitting segregation according to race. This segregation was alleged to deprive the plaintiffs of the equal protection of the laws under the Fourteenth Amendment. In each of the cases other than the Delaware case, a three-judge federal district court denied relief to the plaintiffs on the so-called "separate but equal" doctrine announced by this Court in *Plessy v. Ferguson*. . . .

The plaintiffs contend that segregated public schools are not "equal" and cannot be made "equal," and that hence they are deprived of the equal protection of the laws. Because of the obvious importance of the question presented, the Court took jurisdiction. Argument was heard in the 1952 Term, and reargument was heard this Term on certain questions propounded by the Court.

Reargument was largely devoted to the circumstances surrounding the adoption of the Fourteenth Amendment in 1868. It covered exhaustively consideration of the Amendment in Congress, ratification by the states, then existing practices in racial segregation, and the views of proponents and opponents of the Amendment. This discussion and our own investigation convince us that, although these sources cast some light, it is not enough to resolve the problem with which we are faced. At best, they are inconclusive. The most avid proponents of the post-War Amendments undoubtedly intended them to remove all legal distinctions among "all persons born or naturalized in the United States." Their opponents, just as certainly, were antagonistic to both the letter and the spirit of the Amendments and wished them to have the most limited effect. What others in Congress and the state legislatures had in mind cannot be determined with any degree of certainty.

An additional reason for the inconclusive nature of the Amendment's history, with respect to segregated schools, is the status of public education at that time. In the South, the movement toward free common schools, supported by general taxation, had not yet taken hold. Education of white children was largely in the hands of private groups. Education of Negroes was almost nonexistent, and practically all of the race were illiterate. In fact, any education of Negroes was forbidden by law in some states. Today, in contrast, many Negroes have achieved outstanding success in the arts and sciences as well as in the business and professional world. It is true that public school education at the time of the Amendment had advanced further in the North, but the effect of the Amendment on Northern States was generally ignored in the congressional debates. Even in the North, the conditions of public education did not approximate those existing today. The curriculum was usually rudimentary; ungraded schools were common in rural areas; the school term was but three months a year in many states; and compulsory school attendance was virtually unknown. As a consequence, it is not surprising that there should be so little in the history of the Fourteenth Amendment relating to its intended effect on public education.

In the first cases in this Court construing the Fourteenth Amendment, decided shortly after its adoption, the Court interpreted it as proscribing all state-imposed discriminations against the Negro race. The doctrine of "separate but equal" did not make its appearance in this Court until 1896 in the case of *Plessy v. Ferguson*, supra, involving not education but transportation. American courts have since labored with the doctrine for over half a century. In this Court, there have been six cases involving the "separate but equal" doctrine in the field of public education. In *Cumming v. County Board of Education* . . . and *Gong Lum v. Rice* . . . the validity of the doctrine itself was not challenged. In more recent cases, all on the graduate school level, inequality was found in that specific benefits enjoyed by white students were denied to Negro students of the same educational qualifications. *Missouri ex rel. Gaines v. Canada* . . .; *Sipuel v. Oklahoma* . . .; *Sweatt v. Painter* . . .; *McLaurin v. Oklahoma State Regents*. . . . In none of these cases was it necessary to re-examine the doctrine to grant relief to the Negro plaintiff. And in *Sweatt v. Painter*, supra, the Court expressly reserved decision on the question whether *Plessy v. Ferguson* should be held inapplicable to public education.

In the instant cases, that question is directly presented. Here, unlike *Sweatt v. Painter*, there are findings below that the Negro and white schools involved have been equalized, or are being equalized, with respect to buildings, curricula, qualifications and salaries of teachers, and other "tangible" factors. [In the Kansas case, the court below found substantial equality as to all such factors. In the South Carolina case, the court below found that the defendants were proceeding "promptly and in good faith to comply with the court's decree." In the Virginia case, the court below noted that the equalization program was already "afoot and progressing"; since then, we have been advised, in the Virginia Attorney General's brief on reargument, that the program has now been completed. In the Delaware case, the court below similarly noted that the state's equalization program was well under way. Our decision, therefore, cannot turn on merely a comparison of these tangible factors in the Negro and white schools involved in each of the cases. We must look instead to the effect of segregation itself on public education.

In approaching this problem, we cannot turn the clock back to 1868 when the Amendment was adopted, or even to 1896 when *Plessy v. Ferguson* was written. We must consider public education in the light of its full development and its present place in American life throughout the Nation. Only in this way can it be determined if segregation in public schools deprives these plaintiffs of the equal protection of the laws.

Today, education is perhaps the most important function of state and local governments. Compulsory school attendance laws and the great expenditures for education both demonstrate our recognition of the importance of education to our democratic society. It is required in the performance of our most basic public responsibilities, even service in the armed forces. It is the very foundation of good citizenship. Today it is a principal instrument in awakening the child to cultural values, in preparing him for later professional training, and in helping him to adjust normally to his environment. In these days, it is doubtful that any child may reasonably be expected to succeed in life if he is denied the opportunity of an education. Such an opportunity, where the state has undertaken to provide it, is a right which must be made available to all on equal terms.

We come then to the question presented: Does segregation of children in public schools solely on the basis of race, even though the physical facilities and other "tangible" factors may be equal, deprive the children of the minority group of equal educational opportunities? We believe that it does.

In *Sweatt v. Painter*, supra, in finding that a segregated law school for Negroes could not provide them equal educational opportunities, this Court relied in large part on "those qualities which are incapable of objective measurement but which make for greatness in a law school." In *McLaurin v. Oklahoma State Regents*, supra, the Court, in requiring that a Negro admitted to a white graduate school be treated like all other students, again resorted to intangible considerations: "... his ability to study, to engage in discussions and exchange views with other students, and, in general, to learn his profession." Such considerations apply with added force to children in grade and high schools. To separate them from others of similar age and qualifications solely because of their race generates a feeling of inferiority as to their status in the community that may affect their hearts and minds in a way unlikely ever to be undone. The effect of this separation on their educational opportunities was well stated by a finding in the Kansas case by a court which nevertheless felt compelled to rule against the Negro plaintiffs: Segregation of white and colored children in public schools has a detrimental effect upon the colored children. The impact is greater when it has the sanction of the law; for the policy of separating the races is usually interpreted as denoting the inferiority of the negro group. A sense of inferiority affects the motivation of a child to learn. Segregation with the sanction of law, therefore, has a tendency to [retard] the educational and mental development of negro children and to deprive them of some of the benefits they would receive in a racial[ly] integrated school system. [A similar finding was made in the Delaware case: "I conclude from the testimony that in our Delaware society, State-imposed segregation in education itself results in the Negro children, as a class, receiving educational opportunities which are substantially inferior to those available to white children otherwise similarly situated."]

Whatever may have been the extent of psychological knowledge at the time of *Plessy v. Ferguson*, this finding is amply supported by modern authority. Any language in *Plessy v. Ferguson* contrary to this finding is rejected.

We conclude that in the field of public education the doctrine of "separate but equal" has no place. Separate educational facilities are inherently unequal. Therefore, we hold that the plaintiffs and others similarly situated for whom the actions have been brought are, by reason of the segregation complained of, deprived of the equal protection of the laws guaranteed by the Fourteenth Amendment. This disposition makes unnecessary any discussion whether such segregation also violates the Due Process Clause of the Fourteenth Amendment.

Because these are class actions, because of the wide applicability of this decision, and because of the great variety of local conditions, the formulation of decrees in these cases presents problems of considerable complexity.

On reargument, the consideration of appropriate relief was necessarily subordinated to the primary question—the constitutionality of segregation in public education. We have now announced that such segregation is a denial of the equal protection of the laws. In order that we may have the full assistance of the parties in formulating decrees, the cases will be restored to the docket, and the parties are requested to present further argument on Questions 4 and 5 previously propounded by the Court for the reargument this Term. The Attorney General of the United States is again invited to participate. The Attorneys General of the states requiring or permitting segregation in public education will also be permitted to appear as amici curiae upon request to do so by September 15, 1954, and submission of briefs by October 1, 1954.

It is so ordered.

THE LONG SHADOW OF LITTLE ROCK: A MEMOIR (EXCERPT)

SOURCE *Public Domain.*

INTRODUCTION *Even three years after the sweeping decision of* Brown v. Board of Education, *many people throughout the country were not willing to accept it, least of all in the South. Daisy Bates was an African American woman, born in Arkansas, who in 1952 had become president of the Arkansas branch of the NAACP. Her role as an advocate for the nine students who chose to challenge the system in 1957 and enter the all–white Central High School in Little Rock, Arkansas, gained her a place in history. In this account, she recalls one of those young people, Evelyn Eckford, who had walked into the school alone. Without a phone at home, Eckford had not known that the others were meeting several blocks ahead to walk into school together. Her face and name entered into everyone's home across the United States. How she handled the scary mob and public attention that awaited her that September morning remains a remarkable story.*

Elizabeth, whose dignity and control in the face of jeering mobsters had been filmed by television cameras and recorded in pictures flashed to newspapers over the world, had overnight become a national heroine. During the next few days' newspaper reporters besieged her home, wanting to talk to her. The first day that her parents agreed she might come out of seclusion, she came to my house where the reporters awaited her. Elizabeth was very quiet, speaking only when spoken to. I took her to my bedroom to talk be before I let the reporters see her. I asked how she felt now. Suddenly all her pent-up emotion flared.

"Why am I here?" she said, turning blazing eyes on me. "Why are you so interested in my welfare now? You didn't care enough to notify me of the change of plans—"

I walked over and reached out to her. Before she turned her back on me, I saw tears gathering in her eyes. My heart was breaking for this young girl who stood there trying stifle her sobs. How could I explain that frantic early morning when at three o'clock my mind had gone on strike?

In the ensuing weeks Elizabeth took part in all the activities of the nine—press conferences, attendance at court, studying with professors at nearby Philander Smith College. She was present, that is, but never really a part of things. The hurt had been too deep.

On the two nights she stayed at my home I was awakened by the screams in her sleep, as she relived in her dreams the terrifying mob scenes at Central. The only times Elizabeth showed real excitement were when Thurgood Marshall met the children and explained the meaning of what had happened in court. As he talked, she would listen raptly, a faint smile on her face. It was obvious he was her hero.

Little by little Elizabeth came out of her shell. Up to now she had never talked about what happened to her at Central. Once when we were alone in the downstairs recreation room of my house, I asked her simply, "Elizabeth, do you think you can talk about it now?"

She remained quiet for a long time. Then she began to speak.

"You remember the day before we were to go in, we met Superintendent Blossom at the school board office. He told us what the mob might say and do but he never told us we wouldn't have any protection. He told our parents not to come because he wouldn't be able to protect the children if they did.

"That night I was so excited I couldn't sleep. The next morning I was about the first one up. While I was pressing my black and white dress—I had made it to wear on the first day of school—my little brother turned on the TV set. They started telling about a large crowd gathered at the school. The man on TV said he wondered if we were going to show up that morning. Mother called from the kitchen, where she was fixing breakfast, 'Turn that TV off!' She was so upset and worried. I wanted to comfort her, so I said, 'Mother, don't worry.'

"Dad was walking back and forth, from room to room, with a sad expression. He was chewing on his pipe and he had a cigar in his hand, but he didn't light either one. It would have been funny, only he was so nervous.

"Before I left home Mother called us into the living-room. She said we should have a word of prayer. Then I caught the bus and got off a block from the school. I saw a large crowd of people standing across the street from the soldiers guarding Central. As I walked on, the crowd suddenly got very quiet. Superintendent Blossom had told us to enter by the front door. I looked at all the people and thought, 'Maybe I will be safer if I walk down the block to the front entrance behind the guards.'

"At the corner I tried to pass through the long line of guards around the school so as to enter the grounds behind them. One of the guards pointed across the street. So I pointed in the same direction and asked whether he meant for me to cross the street and walk down. He nodded 'yes.' So, I walked across the street conscious of the crowd that stood there, but they moved away from me.

"For a moment all I could hear was the shuffling of their feet. Then someone shouted, 'Here she comes, get ready!' I moved away from the crowd on the sidewalk and into the street. If the mob came at me I could then cross back over so the guards could protect me.

"The crowd moved in closer and then began to follow me, calling me names. I still wasn't afraid. Just a little bit nervous. Then my knees started to shake all of a sudden and I wondered whether I could make it to the center entrance a block away. It was the longest block I ever walked in my whole life.

"Even so, I still wasn't too scared because all the time I kept thinking that the guards would protect me.

"When I got right in front of the school, I went up to a guard again. But this time he just looked straight ahead and didn't move to let me pass him. I didn't know what to do. Then I looked and saw that the path leading to the front entrance was a little further ahead. So I walked until I was right in front of the path to the front door.

"I stood looking at the school—it looked so big! Just then the guards let some white students go through.

"The crowd was quiet. I guess they were waiting to see what was going to happen. When I was able to steady my knees, I walked up to the guard who had let the white students in. He too didn't move. When I tried to squeeze past him, he raised his bayonet and then the other guards closed in and they raised their bayonets.

"They glared at me with a mean look and I was very frightened and didn't know what to do. I turned around and the crowd came toward me.

"They moved closer and closer. Somebody started yelling, 'Lynch her! Lynch her!'

"I tried to see a friendly face somewhere in the mob—someone who maybe would help. I looked into the face of an old woman and it seemed a kind face, but when I looked at her again, she spat on me.

"They came closer, shouting, 'No nigger bitch is going to get in our school. Get out of here!'

"I turned back to the guards but their faces told me I wouldn't get help from them. Then I looked down the block and saw a bench at the bus stop. I thought, 'If I can only get there I will be safe.' I don't know why the bench seemed a safe place to me, but I started walking toward it. I tried to close my mind to what they were shouting, and kept saying to myself, 'If I can only make it to the bench I will be safe.'

"When I finally got there, I don't think I could have gone another step. I sat down and the mob crowded up and began shouting all over again. Someone hollered, 'Drag her over to this tree! Let's take care of the nigger.' Just then a white man sat down beside me, put his arm around me and patted my shoulder. He raised my chin and said, 'Don't let them see you cry.'

"Then, a white lady—she was very nice—she came over to me on the bench. She spoke to me but I don't remember now what she said. She put me on the bus and sat next to me. She asked me my name and tried to talk to me but I don't think I answered. I can't remember much about the bus ride, but the next thing I remember I was standing in front of the School for the Blind, where Mother works.

"I thought, 'Maybe she isn't here. But she has to be here!' So I ran upstairs, and I think some teachers tried to talk to me, but I kept running until I reached Mother's classroom.

"Mother was standing at the window with her head bowed, but she must have sensed I was there because she turned around. She looked as if she had been crying, and I wanted to tell her I was all right. But I couldn't speak. She put her arms around me and I cried."

THE 1963 INAUGURAL ADDRESS OF GOVERNOR GEORGE C. WALLACE (EXCERPT)

SOURCE *Public Domain.*

INTRODUCTION *As a respected circuit judge in Alabama, George Wallace—with a fairly liberal record on the issue of race relations—entered the 1958 gubernatorial race. Declining to use the staunch segregationist tactics of his opponent who enjoyed the endorsement of the Ku Klux Klan, he was soundly defeated. When he ran again for that seat and was elected in 1962, he was true to his vow never to be defeated that way again. His platform of racial segregation defied federal pressure to integrate public facilities. He was determined that it was a states' right issue. With that stand, he became a national symbol of what the South represented in the minds and hearts of the Southerners who supported him. His inaugural address in January of 1963 further fueled the flames of his notoriety. Many nightly news reports on the problems of the struggle for civil rights included an angry and self-righteous George Wallace, as he defined the opposition for federal civil rights legislation. His stance led him to run for the presidency in 1968 and again in 1972, when an attempted assassination left him paralyzed.*

This is the day of my Inauguration as Governor of the State of Alabama. And on this day I feel a deep obligation to renew my pledges, my covenants with you ... the people of this great state.

General Robert E. Lee said that "duty" is the sublimest word on the English language and I have come, increasingly, to realize what he meant. I SHALL do my duty to you, God helping ... to every man, to every woman ... yes, to every child in this state. I shall fulfill my duty toward honesty and economy in our State government so that no man shall have a part of his livelihood cheated and no child shall have a bit of his future stolen away.

I have said to you that I would eliminate the liquor agents in this state and that the money saved would be returned to our citizens ... I am happy to report to you that I am now filling orders for several hundred one-way tickets and stamped on them are these words ... "for liquor agents ... destination: ... out of Alabama." I am happy to report to you that the big-wheeling cocktail-party boys have gotten the word that their free whiskey and boat rides are over ... that the farmer in the field, the worker in the factory, the businessman in his office, the housewife in her home, have decided that the money can be better spent to help our children's education and our older citizens ... and they have put a man in office to see that it is done. It shall be done. Let me say one more time. ... no more liquor drinking in your governor's mansion.

I shall fulfill my duty in working hard to bring industry into our state, not only by maintaining an honest, sober and free-enterprise climate of government in which industry can have confidence ... but in going out and getting it ... so that our people can have industrial jobs in Alabama and provide a better life for their children.

I shall not forget my duty to our senior citizens ... so that their lives can be lived in dignity and enrichment of the golden years, nor to our sick, both mental and physical ... and they will know we have not forsaken them. I want the farmer to feel confident that in this State government he has a partner who will work with him in raising his income and increasing his markets. And I want the laboring man to know he has a friend who is sincerely striving to better his field of endeavor.

I want to assure every child that this State government is not afraid to invest in their future through education, so that they will not be handicapped on every threshold of their lives.

Today I have stood, where once Jefferson Davis stood, and took an oath to my people. It is very appropriate then that from this Cradle of the Confederacy, this very Heart of the Great Anglo-Saxon Southland, that today we sound the drum for freedom as have our generations of forebears before us done, time and time again through history. Let us rise to the call of freedom-loving blood that is in us and send our answer to the tyranny that clanks its chains upon the South. In the name of the greatest people that have ever trod this earth, I draw the line in the dust and toss the gauntlet before the feet of tyranny ... and I say ... segregation today ... segregation tomorrow ... segregation forever.

The Washington, D.C. school riot report is disgusting and revealing. We will not sacrifice our children to any such type school system—and you can write that down. The federal troops in Mississippi could be better used guarding the safety of the citizens of Washington, D.C., where it is even unsafe to walk or go to a ballgame—and that is the nation's capitol. I was safer in a B-29 bomber over Japan during the war in an air raid, than the people of Washington are walking to the White House neighborhood. A closer example is Atlanta. The city officials fawn for political reasons over school integration and THEN build barricades to stop residential integration—what hypocrisy!

Let us send this message back to Washington by our representatives who are with us today ... that from this day we are standing up, and the heel of tyranny does not fit the neck of an upright man ... that we intend to take the offensive and carry our fight for freedom across the nation, wielding the balance of power we know we possess in the Southland.... that WE, not the insipid bloc of voters of some sections ... will determine in the next election who shall sit in the White House of these United States ... That from this day, from this hour ... from this minute ... we give the word of a race of honor that we will tolerate their boot in our face no longer.... and let those certain judges put *that* in their opium pipes of power and smoke it for what it is worth.

Hear me, Southerners! You sons and daughters who have moved north and west throughout this nation. ...

we call on you from your native soil to join with us in national support and vote ... and we know ... wherever you are ... away from the hearths of the Southland ... that you will respond, for though you may live in the fartherest reaches of this vast country ... your heart has never left Dixieland.

And you native sons and daughters of old New England's rock-ribbed patriotism ... and you sturdy natives of the great Mid-West ... and you descendants of the far West flaming spirit of pioneer freedom ... we invite you to come and be with us ... for you are of the Southern spirit ... and the Southern philosophy ... you are Southerners too and brothers with us in our fight.

CIVIL RIGHTS ACT OF 1964 (EXCERPTS)

SOURCE *Public Domain.*

INTRODUCTION *Quiet acts of civil disobedience in the 1950s gave way to huge—sometimes violent—demonstrations and vocal protest that erupted by the early 1960s mostly throughout the southern United States. African Americans were joined in their struggle by Americans of other races to launch what was to be a final attack on the legalized discrimination that occurred especially in the South in every area from voting rights, to employment, to education, to access to public facilities—everything from restrooms, to lunch counters, to buses. The national nightly news broadcasts carried stories of arrests, boycotts, and even murder of civil rights movement workers. In the summer of 1963, the March on Washington drew thousands of people and culminated in Martin Luther King Jr.'s now famous speech "I Have a Dream." It was in this climate that President John F. Kennedy first initiated the Civil Rights Act that same year. By July 2, 1964 when President Lyndon B. Johnson signed it into law, it contained eleven different titles covering all aspects of what every American could expect as a right. It also served as the mandate from which the Equal Employment Opportunity Commission was created.*

TITLE I—VOTING RIGHTS

Sec. 101. Section 2004 of the Revised Statutes (42 U.S.C. 1971) ... is further amended as follows:. ...

... "No Person acting under color of law shall—"

"(A) In determining whether any individual is qualified under State law or laws to vote in any Federal election, apply any standard, practice, or procedure different from the standards, practices, or procedures applied under such law or laws to other individuals within the same county, parish, or similar political subdivision who have been found by State officials to be qualified to vote;"

"(B) deny the right of any individual to vote in any Federal election because of an error or omission on any record or paper relating to any application, registration, or other act requisite to voting, if such error or omission is not material in determining whether such individual is qualified under State law to vote in such election; or"

"(C) employ any literacy test as a qualification for voting in any Federal election unless (i) such test is administered to each individual and is conducted wholly in writing, and (ii) a certified copy of the test and of the answers given by the individual is furnished to him within twenty-five days of the submission of his request made within the period of time during which records and papers are required to be retained and preserved pursuant to title III of the Civil Rights Act of 1960 (42 U.S.C. 1974–74e; 74 Stat. 88). ..."

Sec. 201. (a) All persons shall be entitled to the full and equal enjoyment of the goods, services, facilities, privileges, advantages, and accommodations of any place of public accommodation, as defined in this section, without discrimination or segregation on the ground of race, color, religion, or national origin.

(b) Each of the following establishments which serves the public is a place of public accommodation within the meaning of this title if its operations affect commerce, or if discrimination or segregation by it is supported by State action:

(1) any inn, hotel, motel, or other establishment which provides lodging to transient guests, other than an establishment located within a building which contains not more than five rooms for rent or hire and which is actually occupied by the proprietor of such establishment as his residence;

(2) any restaurant, cafeteria, lunchroom, lunch counter, soda fountain, or other facility principally engaged in selling food for consumption on the premises, including, but not limited to, any such facility located on the premises of any retail establishment; or any gasoline station;

(3) any motion picture house, theater, concert hall, sports arena, stadium or other place of exhibition or entertainment; and

(4) any establishment (A)(i) which is physically located within the premises of any establishment otherwise covered by this subsection, or (ii) within the premises of which is physically located any such covered establishment, and (B) which holds itself out as serving patrons of such covered establishment.....

(e) The provisions of this title shall not apply to a private club or other establishment not in fact open to the public, except to the extent that the facilities of such establishment are made available to the customers or patrons of an establishment within the scope of subsection (b).

Sec. 206. (a) Whenever the Attorney General has reasonable cause to believe that any person or group of persons is engaged in a pattern or practice of resistance to the full enjoyment of any of the rights secured by this title, and that the pattern or practice is of such a nature and is intended to deny the full exercise of the rights herein described, the Attorney General may bring a civil action in the appropriate district court of the United States.....

TITLE IV—DESEGREGATION OF PUBLIC EDUCATION

Sec. 407. (a) Whenever the Attorney General receives a complaint in writing—

(1) signed by a parent or group of parents to the effect that his or their minor children, as members of a class of persons similarly situated, are being deprived by a school board of the equal protection of the laws, or

(2) signed by an individual, or his parent, to the effect that he has been denied admission to or not permitted to continue in attendance at a public college by reason of race, color, religion, or national origin and the Attorney General believes the complaint is meritorious and certifies that the signer or signers of such complaint are unable, in his judgment, to initiate and maintain appropriate legal proceedings for relief and that the institution of an action will materially further the orderly achievement of desegregation in public education, the Attorney General is authorized, after giving notice of such complaint to the appropriate school board or college authority and after certifying that he is satisfied that such board or authority has had a reasonable time to adjust the conditions alleged in such complaint, to institute for or in the name of the United States a civil action in any appropriate district court of the United States against such parties and for such relief as may be appropriate.....

TITLE VI—NONDISCRIMINATION IN FEDERALLY-ASSISTED PROGRAMS

Sec. 601. No person in the United States shall, on the ground of race, color, or national origin, be excluded from participation in, be denied the benefits of, or be subjected to discrimination under any program or activity receiving Federal financial assistance.. ...

TITLE VII—EQUAL EMPLOYMENT OPPORTUNITY

Sec. 703. (a) It shall be an unlawful employment practice for an employer—

(1) to fail or refuse to hire or to discharge any individual, or otherwise to discriminate against any individual with respect to his compensation, terms, conditions, or privileges of employment, because of such individual's race, color, religion, sex, or national origin; or

(2) to limit, segregate, or classify his employees in any way which would deprive or tend to deprive any individual of employment opportunities or otherwise adversely affect his status as an employee, because of such individual's race, color, religion, sex, or national origin.

(b) It shall be an unlawful employment practice for an employment agency to fail or refuse to refer for employment, or otherwise to discriminate against, any individual because of his race, color, religion, sex, or national origin, or to classify or refer for employment any individual on the basis of his race, color, religion, sex, or national origin.

(c) It shall be an unlawful employment practice for a labor organization—

(1) to exclude or to expel from its membership, or otherwise to discriminate against, any individual because of his race, color, religion, sex, or national origin;

(2) to limit, segregate, or classify its membership, or to classify or fail or refuse to refer for employment any individual, in any way which would deprive or tend to deprive any individual of employment opportunities, or would limit such employment opportunities or otherwise adversely affect his status as an employee or as an applicant for employment, because of such individual's race, color, religion, sex, or national origin; or

(3) to cause or attempt to cause an employer to discriminate against an individual in violation of this section.

(d) It shall be an unlawful employment practice for any employer, labor organization, or joint labor-management committee controlling apprenticeship or other training or retraining, including on-the-job training programs to discriminate against any individual because of his race, color, religion, sex, or national origin in admission to, or employment in, any program established to provide apprenticeship or other training.

(e) Notwithstanding any other provision of this title, (1) it shall not be an unlawful employment practice for an employer to hire and employ employees, for an employment agency to classify, or refer for employment any individual, for a labor organization to classify its membership or to classify or refer for employment any individual, or for an employer, labor organization, or joint labor-management committee controlling apprenticeship or other training or retraining programs to admit or employ any individual in any such program, on the basis of his religion, sex, or national origin in those certain instances where religion, sex, or national origin is a bona fide occupational qualification reasonably necessary to the normal operation of that particular business or enterprise.....

Sec. 705. (1) There is hereby created a Commission to be known as the Equal Employment Opportunity Commission, which shall be composed of five members, not more than three of whom shall be members of the same political party, who shall be appointed by the President by and with the advice and consent of the Senate....

MALCOLM X'S "THE BALLOT OR THE BULLET" SPEECH

SOURCE *Breitman, George (ed.), From* Malcolm X Speaks: Selected Speeches and Statements. *Copyright 1965, 1989 by Betty Shabazz and Pathfinder Press. Reprinted by permission.*

INTRODUCTION *Malcolm X was born Malcolm Little into a hard life that knew little good of white people. His father, Earl Little, became a member of the United Negro Improvement Association (UNIA) and would eventually be identified as a chief in the movement. As a young child Malcolm's family home in Lansing, Michigan was burned down, probably due to backlash against his father's increasing activity in the African American community. When Earl Little was run over by a streetcar, many determined it was no accident—instead, that it was likely a murder by the Black Legion, a hate organization targeting African Americans. Malcolm told his favorite teacher in junior high that he wanted to be a lawyer. He was told that it was an unrealistic goal for someone of his race. He knew violence and crime and spent time in prison, where he converted and became a Muslim with the Nation of Islam. He would eventually change his name to reflect his dissatisfaction with having the name of a man who had once owned his family. This exchange in Cleveland in 1964 occurred just about a year before he was assassinated. He expressed his anger at the oppression he believed white people imposed on his race, explaining that he is not "anti–white" but anti-exploitation. He warned that in the political year of 1964, there was the vote, or the possibility that the country could explode in the violence of that exploitation and oppression. The Civil Rights Act of 1964 was enacted that summer. And cities around the country began to explode in violence for several summers to come.*

Mr. Moderator, Brother Lomax, brothers and sisters, friends and enemies: I just can't believe everyone in here is a friend and I don't want to leave anybody out. The question tonight, as I understand it, is "The Negro Revolt and Where Do We Go From Here?" or "What Next?" In my little humble way of understanding it, it points toward either the ballot or the bullet.

Before we try and explain what is meant by the ballot or the bullet, I would like to clarify something concerning myself. I'm still a Muslim, my religion is still Islam. That's my personal belief. Just as Adam Clayton Powell is a Christian minister who heads the Abyssinian Baptist Church in New York, but at the same time takes part in the political struggles to try and bring about rights to the black people in this country; and Dr. Martin Luther King is a Christian minister down in Atlanta, Georgia, who heads another organization fighting for the civil rights of black people in this country; and Rev. Galamison, I guess you've heard of him, is another Christian minister in New York who has been deeply involved in the school boycotts to eliminate segregated education; well, I myself am a minister, not a Christian minister, but a Muslim minister; and I believe in action on all fronts by whatever means necessary.

Although I'm still a Muslim, I'm not here tonight to discuss my religion. I'm not here to try and change your religion. I'm not here to argue or discuss anything that we differ about, because it's time for us to submerge our differences and realize that it is best for us to first see that we have the same problem, common problem—a problem that will make you catch hell whether you're a Baptist, or a Methodist, or a Muslim, or a nationalist. Whether your're educated or illiterate, whether you live on the boulevard or in the alley, you're going to catch hell just like I am. We're all in the same boat and we all are going to catch the same hell from the same man. He just happens to be a white man. All of us have suffered here, in this country, political oppression at the hands of the white man, economic exploitation at the hands of the white man, and social degradation at the hands of the white man.

Now in speaking like this, it doesn't mean that we're anti-white, but it does mean we're anti-exploitation, we're anti-degradation, we're anti-oppression. And if the white man doesn't want us to be anti-him, let him stop oppressing and exploiting and degrading us. Whether we are Christians or Muslims or nationalists or agnostics or atheists, we must first learn to forget our differences. If we have differences, let us differ in the closet; when we come out in front, let us not have anything to argue about until we get finished arguing with the man. If the late President Kennedy could get together with Khrushchev and exchange some wheat, we certainly have more in common with each other than Kennedy and Khrushchev had with each other.

If we don't do something real soon, I think you'll have to agree that we're going to be forced either to use the ballot or the bullet. It's one or the other in 1964. It isn't that time is running out—time has run out! 1964 threatens to be the most explosive year America has ever witnessed. The most explosive year. Why? It's also a political year. It's the year when all of the white politicians will be back in the so-called Negro community jiving you and me for some votes. The year when all of the white political crooks will be right back in your and my community with their false promises, building up our hopes for a letdown, with their trickery and their treachery, with their false promises which they don't intend to keep. As they nourish these dissatisfactions, it can only lead to one thing, an explosion; and now we have the type of black man on the scene in America today—I'm sorry, Brother Lomax—who just doesn't intend to turn the other cheek any longer.

Don't let anybody tell you anything about the odds are against you. If they draft you, they send you to Korea and make you face 800 million Chinese. If you can be brave over there, you can be brave right here. These odds aren't as great as those odds. And if you fight here, you will at least know what you're fighting for.

I'm not a politician, not even a student of politics; in fact, I'm not a student of much of anything. I'm not a Democrat, I'm not a Republican, and I don't even consider myself an American. If you and I were Americans, there'd be no problem. Those Hunkies that just got off the boat, they're already Americans; Polacks are already Americans; the Italian refugees are already Americans. Everything that came out of Europe, every blue-eyed thing, is already an American. And as long as you and I have been over here, we aren't Americans yet.

Well, I am one who doesn't believe in deluding myself. I'm not going to sit at your table and watch you eat, with nothing on my plate, and call myself a diner. Sitting at the table doesn't make you a diner, unless you eat some of what's on that plate. Being here in America doesn't make you an American. Being born here in America doesn't make you an American. Why, if birth made you American, you wouldn't need any legislation, you wouldn't need any amendments to the Constitution, you wouldn't be faced with civil-rights filibustering in Washington, D.C., right now. They don't have to pass civil-rights legislation to make a Polack an American.

No, I'm not an American. I'm one of the 22 million black people who are the victims of Americanism. One of the 22 million black people who are the victims of democracy, nothing but disguised hypocrisy. So, I'm not standing here speaking to you as an American, or a patriot, or a flag-saluter, or a flag-waver—no, not I. I'm speaking as a victim of this American system. And I see America through the eyes of the victim. I don't see any American dream; I see an American nightmare.

These 22 million victims are waking up. Their eyes are coming open. They're beginning to see what they used to only look at. They're becoming politically mature. They are realizing that there are new political trends from coast to coast. As they see these new political trends, it's possible for them to see that every time there's an election the races are so close that they have to have a recount. They had to recount in Massachusetts to see who was going to be governor, it was so close. It was the same way in Rhode Island, in Minnesota, and in many other parts of the country. And the same with Kennedy and Nixon when they ran for president. It was so close they had to count all over again. Well, what does this mean? It means that when white people are evenly divided, and black people have a bloc of votes of their own, it is left up to them to determine who's going to sit in the White House and who's going to be in the dog house.

It was the black man's vote that put the present administration in Washington, D.C. Your vote, your dumb vote, your ignorant vote, your wasted vote put in an administration in Washington, D.C., that has seen fit to pass every kind of legislation imaginable, saving you until last, then filibustering on top of that. And your and my leaders have the audacity to run around clapping their hands and talk about how much progress we're making. And what a good president we have. If he wasn't good in Texas, he sure can't be good in Washington, D.C. Because Texas is a lynch state. It is in the same breath as Mississippi, no different; only they lynch you in Texas with a Texas accent and lynch you in Mississippi with a Mississippi accent. And these Negro leaders have the audacity to go and have some coffee in the White House with a Texan, a Southern cracker—that's all he is—and then come out and tell you and me that he's going to be better for us because, since he's from the South, he knows how to deal with the Southerners. What kind of logic is that?

So it's time in 1964 to wake up. And when you see them coming up with that kind of conspiracy, let them know your eyes are open. And let them know you got something else that's wide open too. It's got to be the ballot
or the bullet. The ballot or the bullet. If you're afraid to use an expression like that, you should get on out of the country, you should get back in the cotton patch, you should get back in the alley. They get all the Negro vote, and after they get it, the Negro gets nothing in return. All they did when they got to Washington was give a few big Negroes big jobs. Those big Negroes didn't need big jobs, they already had jobs. That's camouflage, that's trickery, that's treachery, window-dressing. I'm not trying to knock out the Democrats for the Republicans, we'll get to them in a minute. But it is true—you put the Democrats first and the Democrats put you last.

I say again, I'm not anti-Democrat, I'm not anti-Republican, I'm not anti-anything. I'm just questioning their sincerity, and some of the strategy that they've been using on our people by promising them promises that they don't intend to keep. When you keep the Democrats in power, you're keeping the Dixiecrats in power. I doubt that my good Brother Lomax will deny that. A vote for a Democrat is a vote for a Dixiecrat. That's why, in 1964, it's time now for you and me to become more politically mature and realize what the ballot is for; what we're supposed to get when we cast a ballot; and that if we don't cast a ballot, it's going to end up in a situation where we're going to have to cast a bullet. It's either a ballot or a bullet.

So, what I'm trying to impress upon you, in essence, is this: You and I in America are faced not with a segregationist conspiracy, we're faced with a government conspiracy. Everyone who's filibustering is a senator—that's the government. Everyone who's finagling in Washington, D.C., is a congressman—that's the government. You don't have anybody putting blocks in your path but people who are a part of the government. The same government that you go abroad to fight for and die for is the government that is in a conspiracy to deprive you of your voting rights, deprive you of your economic opportunities, deprive you of decent housing, deprive you of decent education. You don't need to go to the employer alone, it is the government itself, the government of America, that is responsible for the oppression and exploitation and degradation of black people in this country. And you should drop it in their lap. This government has failed the Negro. This so-called democracy has failed the Negro. And all these white liberals have definitely failed the Negro.

So, where do we go from here? First, we need some friends. We need some new allies. The entire civil-rights struggle needs a new interpretation, a broader interpretation. We need to look at this civil-rights thing from another angle—from the inside as well as from the outside. To those of us whose philosophy is black nationalism, the only way you can get involved in the civil-rights struggle is give it a new interpretation. That old interpretation excluded us. It kept us out. So, we're giving a new interpretation to the civil-rights struggle, an interpretation that will enable us to come into it, take part in it. And these handkerchief-heads who have been dillydallying and pussyfooting and compromising—we don't intend to let them pussyfoot and dillydally and compromise any longer.

How can you thank a man for giving you what's already yours? How then can you thank him for giving you only part of what's already yours? You haven't even made progress, if what's being given to you, you should have had already. That's not progress. And I love my Brother Lomax, the way he pointed out we're right back where we were in 1954. We're not even as far up as we were in 1954. We're behind where we were in 1954. There's more segregation now than there was in 1954. There's more racial animosity, more racial hatred, more racial violence today in 1964, than there was in 1954. Where is the progress?

And now you're facing a situation where the young Negro's coming up. They don't want to hear that "turn-the-other-cheek" stuff, no. In Jacksonville, those were teenagers, they were throwing Molotov cocktails. Negroes have never done that before. But it shows you there's a new deal coming in. There's new thinking coming in. There's new strategy coming in. It'll be Molotov cocktails this month, hand grenades next month, and something else next month. It'll be ballots, or it'll be bullets. It'll be liberty, or it will be death. The only difference about this kind of death—it'll be reciprocal. You know what is meant by "reciprocal"? That's one of Brother Lomax's words, I stole it from him. I don't usually deal with those big words because I don't usually deal with big people. I deal with small people. I find you can get a whole lot of small people and whip hell out of a whole lot of big people. They haven't got anything to lose, and they've got everything to gain. And they'll let you know in a minute: "It takes two to tango; when I go, you go."

I might stop right here to point out one thing. Whenever you're going after something that belongs to you, anyone who's depriving you of the right to have it is a criminal. Understand that. Whenever you are going after something that is yours, you are within your legal rights to lay claim to it. And anyone who puts forth any effort to deprive you of that which is yours, is breaking the law, is a criminal. And this was pointed out by the Supreme Court decision. It outlawed segregation. Which means segregation is against the law. Which means a segregationist is breaking the law. A segregationist is a criminal. You can't label him as anything other than that. And when you demonstrate against segregation, the law is on your side. The Supreme Court is on your side.

Now, who is it that opposes you in carrying out the law? The police department itself. With police dogs and clubs. Whenever you demonstrate against segregation, whether it is segregated education, segregated housing, or anything else, the law is on your side, and anyone who stands in the way is not the law any longer. They are breaking the law, they are not representatives of the law. Any time you demonstrate against segregation and a man has the audacity to put a police dog on you, kill that dog, kill him, I'm telling you, kill that dog. I say it, if they put me in jail tomorrow, kill—that—dog. Then you'll put a stop to it. Now, if these white people in here don't want to see that kind of action, get down and tell the mayor to tell the police department to pull the dogs in. That's all you have to do. If you don't do it, someone else will.

If you don't take this kind of stand, your little children will grow up and look at you and think "shame." If you don't take an uncompromising stand—I don't mean go out and get violent; but at the same time you should never be nonviolent unless you run into some nonviolence. I'm nonviolent with those who are nonviolent with me. But when you drop that violence on me, then you've made me go insane, and I'm not responsible for what I do. And that's the way every Negro should get. Any time you know you're within the law, within your legal rights, within your moral rights, in accord with justice, then die for what you believe in. But don't die alone. Let your dying be reciprocal. This is what is meant by equality. What's good for the goose is good for the gander.

Black people are fed up with the dillydallying, pussyfooting, compromising approach that we've been using toward getting our freedom. We want freedom *now*, but we're not going to get it saying "We Shall Overcome." We've got to fight until we overcome.

Our gospel is black nationalism. We're not trying to threaten the existence of any organization, but we're spreading the gospel of black nationalism. Anywhere there's a church that is also preaching and practicing the gospel of black nationalism, join that church. If the NAACP is preaching and practicing the gospel of black nationalism, join the NAACP. If CORE is spreading and practicing the gospel of black nationalism, join CORE. Join any organization that has a gospel that's for the uplift of the black man. And when you get into it and see them pussyfooting or compromising, pull out of there because that's not black nationalism. We'll find another one.

And in this manner, the organizations will increase in number and in quantity and in quality, and by August, it is then our intention to have a black nationalist convention which will consist of delegates from all over the country who are interested in the political, economic and social philosophy of black nationalism. After these delegates convene, we will hold a seminar, we will hold discussions, we will listen to everyone. We want to hear new ideas and new solutions and new answers. And at that time, if we see fit then to form a black nationalist party, we'll form a black nationalist party. If it's necessary to form a black nationalist army, we'll form a black nationalist army. It'll be the ballot or the bullet. It'll be liberty or it'll be death.

It's time for you and me to stop sitting in this country, letting some cracker senators, Northern crackers and Southern crackers, sit there in Washington, D.C., and come to a conclusion in their mind that you and I are supposed to have civil rights. There's no white man going to tell me anything about *my* rights. Brothers and sisters, always remember, if it doesn't take senators and congressmen and presidential proclamations to give freedom to the white man, it is not necessary for legislation or proclamation or Supreme Court decisions to give freedom to the black man. You let that white man know, if this is a country of freedom, let it be a country of freedom; and if it's not a country of freedom, change it.

If a Negro in 1964 has to sit around and wait for some cracker senator to filibuster when it comes to the rights of black people, why, you and I should hang our heads in shame. You talk about a march on Washington in 1963, you haven't seen anything. There's some more going down in '64. And this time they're not going like they went last year. They're not going singing "We Shall Overcome." They're not going with white friends. They're not going with placards already painted for them. They're not going with round-trip tickets. They're going with one-way tickets.

And if they don't want that non-nonviolent army going down there, tell them to bring the filibuster to a halt. The black nationalists aren't going to wait. Lyndon B. Johnson is the head of the Democratic Party. If he's for civil rights, let him go into the Senate next week and declare himself. Let him go in there right now and declare himself. Let him go in there and denounce the Southern branch of his party. Let him go in there right now and take a moral stand—right now, not later. Tell him, don't wait until election time. If he waits too long, brothers and sisters, he will be responsible for letting a condition develop in this country which will create a climate that will bring seeds up out of the ground with vegetation on the end of them looking like something these people never dreamed of. In 1964, it's the ballot or the bullet. Thank you.

MARTIN LUTHER KING, JR.'S "THE AMERICAN DREAM"

SOURCE *King, Martin Luther, Jr. "The American Dream,"* http://www.stanford.edu/group/King/sermons/65704_The_American_Dream.html. *Copyright 1963 Dr. Martin Luther King Jr., copyright renewed 1991 by Coretta Scott King. Reproduced by arrangement with the Estate of Martin Luther King, Jr., c/o Writers House as agent for the proprietor New York, NY.*

INTRODUCTION *It was a year after the passage of the Civil Rights Act that the Rev. Dr. Martin Luther King, Jr. addressed his congregation in Atlanta. The day was July 4, 1965—the perfect day to talk about rights and equality. On that particular day as he was heading to the airport in Washington, D.C., to fly to Atlanta, his aide, Andrew Young, pointed out that it was an interesting coincidence that they should be passing by the Jefferson Memorial on Independence Day. Dr. King had forgotten that it was the holiday. It was then that he decided he would preach in that spirit of the founding fathers and talk more about what he saw as the ongoing task for African Americans, and a struggle that was not yet ended even if the legal battles had. The Jewish philosopher Martin Buber had just died, and he offered inspiration to Dr. King, too. He reminded people why segregation was wrong—that segregation "substitutes an 'I-It' relationship for the 'I-Thou' relationship and relegates persons to the status of things." King recaptured some of the power of his 1963 "I Have a Dream" speech by repeating his own version of what an "American Dream" should be.*

I planned to use for the textual basis for our thinking together that passage from the prologue of the book of Job where Satan is pictured as asking God, "Does Job serve thee for nought?" And I'd like to ask you to allow me to hold that sermon [*"Why Serve God?"*] in abeyance and preach it the next time I am in the pulpit in order to share with you some other ideas. This morning I was riding to the airport in Washington, D.C., and on the way to the airport the limousine passed by the Jefferson monument, and Reverend Andrew Young, my executive assistant, said to me, "It's quite coincidental that we would be passing by the Jefferson Monument on Independence Day." You can get so busy in life that you forget holidays and other days, and it had slipped my mind altogether that today was the Fourth of July. And I said to him, "It is coincidental and quite significant, and I think when I get to Atlanta and go to my pulpit, I will try to preach a sermon in the spirit of the founding fathers of our nation and in the spirit of the Declaration of Independence." And so this morning I would like to use as a subject from which to preach: "The American Dream." *(Yes, sir)*

It wouldn't take us long to discover the substance of that dream. It is found in those majestic words of the Declaration of Independence, words lifted to cosmic proportions: "We hold these truths to be self-evident, that all men are created equal, that they are endowed by God, Creator, with certain inalienable Rights, that among these are Life, Liberty, and the pursuit of Happiness." This is a dream. It's a great dream.

The first saying we notice in this dream is an amazing universalism. It doesn't say "some men," it says "all men." It doesn't say "all white men," it says "all men," which includes black men. It does not say "all Gentiles," it says "all men," which includes Jews. It doesn't say "all Protestants," it says "all men," which includes Catholics. *(Yes, sir)* It doesn't even say "all theists and believers," it says "all men," which includes humanists and agnostics.

Then that dream goes on to say another thing that ultimately distinguishes our nation and our form of government from any totalitarian system in the world. It says that each of us has certain basic rights that are neither derived from or conferred by the state. In order to discover where they came from, it is necessary to move back behind the dim mist of eternity. They are God-given, gifts from His hands. Never before in the history of the world has a sociopolitical document expressed in such profound, eloquent, and unequivocal language the dignity and the worth of human personality. The American dream reminds us, and we should think about it anew on this Independence Day, that every man is an heir of the legacy of dignity and worth.

Now ever since the founding fathers of our nation dreamed this dream in all of its magnificence—to use a big word that the psychiatrists use—America has been something of a schizophrenic personality, tragically divided against herself. On the one hand we have proudly professed the great principles of democracy, but on the other hand we have sadly practiced the very opposite of those principles.

But now more than ever before, America is challenged to realize its dream, for the shape of the world today does not permit our nation the luxury of an anemic democracy. And the price that America must pay for the continued oppression of the Negro and other minority groups is the price of its own destruction. *(Yes it is)* For the hour is late. And the clock of destiny is ticking out. We must act now before it is too late.

And so it is marvelous and great that we do have a dream, that we have a nation with a dream; and to forever challenge us; to forever give us a sense of urgency; to forever stand in the midst of the "isness" of our terrible injustices; to remind us of the "oughtness" of our noble capacity for justice and love and brotherhood.

This morning I would like to deal with some of the challenges that we face today in our nation as a result of the American dream. First, I want to reiterate the fact that we are challenged more than ever before to respect the dignity and the worth of all human personality. We are challenged to really believe that all men are created equal. And don't misunderstand that. It does not mean that all men are created equal in terms of native endowment, in terms of intellectual capacity—it doesn't mean that. There are certain bright stars in the human firmament in every field. *(Yes, sir)* It doesn't mean that every musician is equal to a Beethoven or Handel, a Verdi or a Mozart. It doesn't mean that every physicist is equal to an Einstein. It does not mean that every literary figure in history is equal to Aeschylus and Euripides, Shakespeare and Chaucer. *(Make it plain)* It does not mean that every philosopher is equal to Plato, Aristotle, Immanuel Kant, and Friedrich Hegel. It doesn't mean that. There are individuals who do excel and rise to the heights of genius in their areas and in their fields. What it does mean is that all men are equal in intrinsic worth. *(Yes)*

You see, the founding fathers were really influenced by the Bible. The whole concept of the imago dei, as it is expressed in Latin, the "image of God," is the idea that all men have something within them that God injected. Not that they have substantial unity with God, but that every man has a capacity to have fellowship with God. And this gives him a uniqueness, it gives him worth, it gives him dignity. And we must never forget this as a nation: there are no gradations in the image of God. Every man from a treble white to a bass black is significant on God's keyboard, precisely because every man is made in the image of God. One day we will learn that. *(Yes)* We will know one day that God made us to live together as brothers and to respect the dignity and worth of every man.

This is why we must fight segregation with all of our nonviolent might. *(Yes, sir; Make it plain)* Segregation is not only inconvenient—that isn't what makes it wrong. Segregation is not only sociologically untenable—that isn't what makes it wrong. Segregation is not only politically and economically unsound—that is not what makes it wrong. Ultimately, segregation is morally wrong and sinful. To use the words of a great Jewish philosopher that died a few days ago, Martin Buber, "It's wrong because it substitutes an 'I-It' relationship for the 'I-Thou' relationship and relegates persons to the status of things." That's it. *(Yes, sir)*. . . .

And I tell you this morning, my friends, the reason we got to solve this problem here in America: Because God somehow called America to do a special job for mankind and the world. *(Yes, sir; Make it plain)* Never before in the history of the world have so many racial groups and so many national backgrounds assembled together in one nation. And somehow if we can't solve the problem in America the world can't solve the problem, because America is the world in miniature and the world is America writ large. And God set us out with all of the opportunities. *(Make it plain)* He set us between two great oceans; *(Yes, sir)* made it possible for us to live with some of the great natural resources of the world. And there he gave us through the minds of our forefathers a great creed: "We hold these truths to be self-evident, that all men *(Yes, sir)* are created equal." . . .

I submit to you when I took off on that plane this morning, I saw men go out there in their overalls. *(Yes, sir, Every time)* I saw them working on things here and there, and saw some more going out there to put the breakfast on there so that we could eat on our way to Atlanta. *(Make it plain)* And I said to myself that these people who constitute the ground crew are just as significant as the pilot, because this plane couldn't move if you didn't have the ground crew. *(Amen)* I submit to you that in Hugh Spaulding or Grady Hospital, (Preach it) the woman or the man who goes in there to sweep the floor is just as significant as the doctor, *(Yes)* because if he doesn't get that dust off the floor germs will begin to circulate. And those same germs can do injury and harm to the human being. I submit to you this morning *(Yes)* that there is dignity in all work *(Have mercy)* when we learn to pay people decent wages. Whoever cooks in your house, whoever sweeps the floor in your house is just as significant as anybody who lives in that house. *(Amen)* And everybody that we call a maid is serving God in a significant way. *(Preach it)* And I love the maids, I love the people who have been ignored, and I want to see them get the kind of wages that they need. And their job is no longer a menial job, *(No, sir)* for you come to see its worth and its dignity.

Are we really taking this thing seriously? "All men are created equal." *(Amen)* And that means that every man who lives in a slum today *(Preach it)* is just as significant as John D., Nelson, or any other Rockefeller. Every man who lives in the slum is just as significant as Henry Ford. All men are created equal, and they are endowed by their Creator with certain inalienable rights, rights that can't be separated from you. [clap] Go down and tell them, *(No)* "You may take my life, but you can't take my right to life. You may take liberty from me, but you can't take my right to liberty. You may take from me the desire, you may take from me the propensity to pursue happiness, but you can't take from me my right to pursue happiness." *(Yes)* "We hold these truths to be self-evident that all men are created equal and endowed by their Creator with certain inalienable Rights and among these are Life, Liberty, and the pursuit of Happiness." *(Yes, sir)* ...

And I would like to say to you this morning what I've tried to say all over this nation, what I believe firmly: that in seeking to make the dream a reality we must use and adopt a proper method. I'm more convinced than ever before that nonviolence is the way. I'm more convinced than ever before that violence is impractical as well as immoral ... We can stand up before our most violent opponent and say: We will match your capacity to inflict suffering by our capacity to endure suffering. We will meet your physical force with soul force. *(Make it plain)* Do to us what you will and we will still love you. We cannot in all good conscience obey your unjust laws, because noncooperation with evil is as much a moral obligation as is cooperation with good and so throw us in jail. *(Make it plain)* We will go in those jails and transform them from dungeons of shame to havens of freedom and human dignity. Send your hooded perpetrators of violence into our communities after midnight hours and drag us out on some wayside road and beat us and leave us half-dead, and as difficult as it is, we will still love you. *(Amen)* Somehow go around the country and use your propaganda agents to make it appear that we are not fit culturally, morally, or otherwise for integration, and we will still love you. *(Yes)* Threaten our children and bomb our homes, and as difficult as it is, we will still love you. *(Yeah)* ...

We have a great dream. *(Great dream)* It started way back in 1776, and God grant that America will be true to her dream.

About two years ago now, I stood with many of you who stood there in person and all of you who were there in spirit before the Lincoln Monument in Washington. *(Yes)* As I came to the end of my speech there, I tried to tell the nation about a dream I had. I must confess to you this morning that since that sweltering August afternoon in 1963, my dream has often turned into a nightmare; (Lord) I've seen it shattered.... I've seen my dream shattered as I've walked the streets of Chicago *(Make it plain)* and seen Negroes, young men and women, with a sense of utter hopelessness because they can't find any jobs. And they see life as a long and desolate corridor with no exit signs. And not only Negroes at this point. I've seen my dream shattered because I've been through Appalachia, and I've seen my white brothers along with Negroes living in poverty. *(Yeah)* And I'm concerned about white poverty as much as I'm concerned about Negro poverty. *(Make it plain)*

So yes, the dream has been shattered, *(Amen)* and I have had my nightmarish experiences, but I tell you this morning once more that I haven't lost the faith. *(No, sir)* I still have a dream *(A dream, Yes, sir)* that one day all of God's children will have food and clothing and material well-being for their bodies, culture and education for their minds, and freedom for their spirits. *(Yes)*

I still have a dream this morning: *(Yes)* one day all of God's black children will be respected like his white children.

I still have a dream this morning *(Yes)* that one day the lion and the lamb will lie down together, and every man will sit under his own vine and fig tree and none shall be afraid.

I still have a dream this morning that one day all men everywhere will recognize that out of one blood God made all men to dwell upon the face of the earth.

I still have a dream this morning *(Yes, sir)* that one day every valley shall be exalted, and every mountain and hill will be made low; the rough places will be made plain, and the crooked places straight; and the glory of the Lord shall be revealed, and all flesh shall see it together.

I still have a dream this morning *(Amen)* that truth will reign supreme and all of God's children will respect the dignity and worth of human personality. And when this day comes the morning stars will sing together *(Yes)* and the sons of God will shout for joy.

"We hold these truths to be self-evident that all men *(All right)* are created equal, that they are endowed by their Creator with certain inalienable Rights, *(Yes, sir)* that among these are Life, Liberty, and the pursuit of Happiness."

We open the doors of the church now. If someone needs to accept Christ, *(Yes, sir)* this is a marvelous opportunity, a great moment to make a decision. And as we sing together, we bid you come at this time by Christian experience, baptism, watch care. But come at this moment, become a part of this great Christian fellowship and accept Christ *(Yes, sir)* as your personal savior.

"BLACK POWER—ITS RELEVANCE TO THE WEST INDIES"

SOURCE *Rodney, Walter. From* The Groundings with My Brothers. *Copyright © 1969. Reprinted by permission of Bogle L'Ouverture Publishers Ltd.*

INTRODUCTION *Walter Rodney was a Guyanese historian who had received his Ph.D. from the School of Oriental and African Studies at the Univeristy of London in 1966, the time of the rise of the political movement of Black Power, not only in the United States but throughout the world. The islands of the West Indies ended the practice of slavery nearly thirty years before the start of the U.S. Civil War; but as with its American counterparts, the legacy of slavery lingered on long after freedom. One hundred years later, just before the start of World War II, the black people of the West Indies revolted. Still under British rule, the living conditions for the poor black people were horrendous. Over twenty years after that, with conditions for black people still suffering, Rodney fueled the flames of unrest with his speeches against white imperialism. After he was expelled, rioting ensued in Kingston and the university closed temporarily. These are some of his words that helped enflame a movement.*

About a fortnight ago I had the opportunity of speaking on Black Power to an audience on this campus. At that time, the consciousness among students as far as the racial question is concerned had been heightened by several incidents on the world scene—notably, the hangings in Rhodesia and the murder of Dr. Martin Luther King. Indeed, it has been heightened to such an extent that some individuals have started to organize a Black Power movement. My presence here attests to my full sympathy with their objectives.

The topic on this occasion is no longer just "Black Power" but "Black Power and You." Black Power can be seen as a movement and an ideology springing from the reality of oppression of black peoples by whites within the imperialist world as a whole. Now we need to be specific in defining the West Indian scene and our own particular roles in the society. You and I have to decide whether we want to think black or to *remain* as a dirty version of white. (I shall indicate the full significance of this later.)

Recently there was a public statement in *Scope* where Black Power was referred to as "Black supremacy." This may have been a genuine error or a deliberate falsification. Black Power is a call to black peoples to throw off white domination and resume the handling of their own destinies. It means that blacks would enjoy power commensurate with their numbers in the world and in particular localities. Whenever an oppressed black man shouts for equality he is called a racist. This was said of Marcus Garvey in his day. Imagine that! We are so inferior that if we demand equality of opportunity and power that is outrageously racist! Black people who speak up for their rights must beware of this device of false accusations. Is it intended to place you on the defensive and if possible embarrass you into silence. How can we be both oppressed and embarrassed? Is it that our major concern is not to hurt the feelings of the oppressor? Black people must now take the offensive—if it is anyone who should suffer embarrassment it is the whites. Did black people roast six million Jews? Who exterminated millions of indigenous inhabitants in the Americas and Australia? Who enslaved countless millions of Africans? The white capitalist cannibal has always fed on the world's black peoples. White capitalist imperialist society is profoundly and unmistakably racist.

The West Indies have always been a part of white capitalist society. We have been the most oppressed section because we were a slave society and the legacy of slavery still rests heavily upon the West Indian black man. I will briefly point to five highlights of our social development: (1) the development of racialism under slavery; (2) emancipation; (3) Indian indentured labour; (4) the year 1865 in Jamaica; (5) the year 1938 in the West Indies.

SLAVERY

As C.L.R. James, Eric Williams and other W.I. scholars have pointed out, slavery in the West Indies started as an economic phenomenon rather than a racial one. But it rapidly became racist as all white labour was withdrawn from the fields, leaving black to be identified with slave labour and white to be linked with property and domination. Out of this situation where blacks had an inferior status in practice, there grew social and scientific theories relating to the supposed inherent inferiority of the black man, who was considered as having been created to bring water and hew wood for the white man. This theory then served to rationalise white exploitation of blacks all over Africa and Asia. The West Indies and the American South share the dubious distinction of being the breeding ground for world racialism. Even the blacks became convinced of their own inferiority, though fortunately we are capable of the most intense expressions when we recognise that we have been duped by the white men. Black power recognises both the reality of the black oppression and self-negation as well as the potential for revolt.

EMANCIPATION

By the end of the 18th century, Britain had got most of what it wanted from black labour in the West Indies. Slavery and the slave trade had made Britain strong and now stood in the way of new developments, so it was time to abandon those systems. The Slave Trade and Slavery were thus ended; but Britain had to consider how to squeeze what little remained in the territories and *how to maintain the local whites in power*. They therefore decided to give the planters £20 million compensation and to guarantee their black labour supplies for the next six years through a system called apprenticeship. In that period, white society consolidated its position to ensure that slave relations should persist in our society. The Rastafari Brethren have always insisted that the black people were promised £20 million at emancipation. In reality, by any normal standards of justice, we black people should have got the £20 million compensation money. We were the ones who had been abused and wronged, hunted in Africa and brutalised on the plantations. In Europe, when serfdom was abolished, the serfs usually inherited the land as compensation and by right. In the West Indies, the exploiters were compensated because they could no longer exploit us in the same way as before. White property was of greater value than black humanity. It still is—white property is of greater value than black humanity in the British West Indies today, especially here in Jamaica.

INDIAN INDENTURED LABOUR

Britain and the white West Indians had to maintain the plantation system in order to keep whites supreme. When Africans started leaving the plantations to set up as independent peasants they threatened the plantation structure and therefore Indians were imported under the indenture arrangements. That was possible because white power controlled most of the world and could move non-white peoples around as they wished. It was from British-controlled India that the indentured labour was obtained. It was the impact of British commercial, military and political policies that was destroying the life and culture of 19th century India and forcing people to flee to other parts of the world to earn bread. Look where Indians fled—to the West Indies! The West Indies is a place black people want to leave, not to come to. One must therefore appreciate the pressure of white power on India which gave rise to migration to the West Indies. Indians were brought here solely in the interest of white society—at the expense of Africans already in the West Indies and often against their own best interests, for Indians perceived indentured labour to be a form of slavery and it was eventually terminated through the pressure of Indian opinion in the homeland. The West Indies has made a unique contribution to the history of suffering in the world, and Indians have provided part of that contribution since indentures were first introduced. This is another aspect of the historical situation which is still with us.

1865

In that year Britain found a way of perpetuating White Power in the West Indies after ruthlessly crushing the revolt of our black brothers led by Paul Bogle. The British Government took away the Constitution of Jamaica and placed the island under the complete control of the Colonial Office, a manoeuvre that was racially motivated. The Jamaican legislature was then largely in the hands of the local whites with a mulatto minority, but if the gradual changes continued the mulattoes would have taken control—and the blacks were next in line. Consequently, the British Government put a stop to the process of the gradual takeover of political power by blacks. When we look at the British Empire in the 19th century, we see a clear difference between white colonies and black colonies. In the white colonies like Canada and Australia the British were giving white people their freedom and self-rule. In the black colonies of the West Indies, Africa and Asia, the British were busy taking away the political freedom of the inhabitants. Actually, on the constitutional level, Britain had already displayed its racialism in the West Indies in the early 19th century when it refused to give mulattoes the power of Government in Trinidad, although they were the majority of free citizens. In 1865 in Jamaica it was not the first nor the last time on which Britain made it clear that its white "kith and kin" would be supported to hold dominion over blacks.

1938

Slavery ended in various islands of the West Indies between 1834 and 1838. Exactly 100 years later (between 1934–38) the black people in the West Indies revolted against the hypocritical freedom of the society. The British were very surprised—they had long forgotten all about the blacks in the British West Indies and they sent a Royal Commission to find out what it was all about. The report of the conditions was so shocking that the British government did not release it until after the war, because they wanted black colonials to fight the white man's battles. By the time the war ended it was clear in the West Indies and throughout Asia and Africa that some concessions would have to be made to black peoples. In general, the problem as seen by white imperialists was to give enough power to certain groups in colonial society to keep the whole society from exploding and to maintain the essentials of the imperialist structure. In the British West Indies, they had to take into account the question of military strategy because we lie under the belly of the world's imperialist giant, the U.S.A. Besides, there was the new and vital mineral bauxite, which had to be protected. The British solution was to pull out wherever possible and leave the imperial government in the hands of the U.S.A., while the local government was given to a white, brown and black petty-bourgeoisie who were culturally the creations of white capitalist society and who therefore support the white imperialist system because they gain personally and because they have been brainwashed into aiding the oppression of black people.

Black Power in the West Indies means three closely related things: (i) the break with imperialism which is historically white racist; (ii) the assumption of power by the black masses in the islands; (iii) the cultural reconstruction of the society in the image of the blacks.

I shall anticipate certain questions on who are the blacks in the West Indies since they are in fact questions which have been posed to me elsewhere. I maintain that it is the white world which has defined who are blacks—if you are not white then you are black. However, it is obvious that the West Indian situation is complicated by factors such as the variety of racial types and racial mixtures and by the process of class formation. We have, therefore, to note not simply what the white world says but also how individuals perceive each other. Nevertheless, we can talk of the mass of the West Indian population as being black—either African or Indian. There seems to have been some doubts on the last point, and some fear that Black Power is aimed against the Indian. This would be a flagrant denial of both the historical experience of the West Indies and the reality of the contemporary scene.

When the Indian was brought to the West Indies, he met the same racial contempt which whites applied to Africans. The Indian, too, was reduced to a single stereotype—the coolie or labourer. He too was a hewer of wood and a bringer of water. I spoke earlier of the revolt of the blacks in the West Indies in 1938. That revolt involved Africans in Jamaica, Africans and Indians in Trinidad and Guyana. The uprisings in Guyana were actually led by Indian sugar workers. Today, some Indians (like some Africans) have joined the white power structure in terms of economic activity and culture; but the underlying reality is that poverty resides among Africans and Indians in the West Indies and that power is denied them. Black Power in the West Indies, therefore, refers primarily to people who are recognisably African or Indian.

The Chinese, on the other hand, are a former labouring group who have now become bastions of white West Indian social structure. The Chinese of the People's Republic of China have long broken with and are fighting against white imperialism, but *our* Chinese have nothing to do with that movement. They are to be identified with Chiang-Kai-Shek and not Chairman Mao Tse-tung. They are to be put in the same bracket as the lackeys of capitalism and imperialism who are to be found in Hong Kong and Taiwan. Whatever the circumstances in which the Chinese came to the West Indies, they soon became (as a group) members of the exploiting class. They will have either to relinquish or be deprived of that function before they can be re-integrated into a West Indian society where the black man walks in dignity.

The same applies to the mulattoes, another group about whom I have been questioned. The West Indian brown man is characterised by ambiguity and ambivalence. He has in the past identified with the black masses when it suited his interests, and at the present time some browns are in the forefront of the movement towards black consciousness; but the vast majority have fallen to the bribes of white imperialism, often outdoing the whites in their hatred and oppression of blacks. Garvey wrote of the Jamaican mulattoes—"I was openly hated and persecuted by some of these coloured men of the island who did not want to be classified as Negroes but as white." Naturally, conscious West Indian blacks like Garvey have in turn expressed their dislike for the browns, but there is nothing in the West Indian experience which suggests that browns are unacceptable when they choose to identify with blacks. The post-1938 developments in fact showed exactly the opposite. It seems to me, therefore, that it is not for the Black Power movement to determine the position of the browns, reds and so-called West Indian whites—the movement can only keep the door open and leave it to those groups to make their choice.

Black Power is not racially intolerant. It is the hope of the black man that he should have power over his own destinies. This is not incompatible with a multiracial society where each individual counts equally. Because the moment that power is equitably distributed among several ethnic groups then the very relevance of making the distinction between groups will be lost. What we must object to is the current image of a multi-racial society living in harmony—that is a myth designed to justify the exploitation suffered by the blackest of our population, at the hands of the lighter-skinned groups. Let us look at the figures for the racial composition of the Jamaican population. Of every 100 Jamaicans,

76.8% are visibly African

0.8% European

1.1% Indian

0.6% Chinese

91% have African blood

0.1% Syrian

14.6% Afro-European

5.4% other mixtures

This is a black society where Africans preponderate. Apart from the mulatto mixture all other groups are numerically insignificant and yet the society seeks to give them equal weight and indeed more weight than the Africans. If we went to Britain we could easily find non-white groups in the above proportions—Africans and West Indians, Indians and Pakistanis, Turks, Arabs and other Easterners—but Britain is not called a multi-racial society. When we go to Britain we don't expect to take over all of the British real estate business, all their cinemas and most of their commerce as the European, Chinese and Syrian have done here. All we ask for there is some work and shelter, and we can't even get that. Black Power must proclaim that Jamaica is a black society—we should fly Garvey's Black Star banner and we will treat all other groups in the society on that understanding—they can have *the basic right of all individuals* but *no privileges to exploit Africans* as has been the pattern during slavery and ever since.

The present government knows that Jamaica is a black man's country. That is why Garvey has been made a national hero, for they are trying to deceive black people into thinking that the government is with them. The government of Jamaica recognises black power—it is afraid of the potential wrath of Jamaica's black and largely African population. It is that same fear which forced them to declare mourning when black men are murdered in Rhodesia, and when Martin Luther King was murdered in the U.S.A. But the black people don't need to be told that Garvey is a national hero—they know that. Nor do they need to be told to mourn when blacks are murdered by White Power, because they mourn every day right here in Jamaica where white power keeps them ignorant, unemployed, ill-clothed and ill-fed. They will stop mourning when things change—and that means a revolution, for the first essential is to break the chains which bind us to white imperialists, and that is a very revolutionary step. Cuba is the only country in the West Indies and in this hemisphere which has broken with white power. That is why Stokely Carmichael can visit Cuba but he can't visit Trinidad or Jamaica. That is why Stokely can call Fidel "one of the blackest men in the Americas" and that is why our leaders in contrast qualify as "white."

Here I'm not just playing with words—I'm extending the definition of Black Power by indicating the nature of its opposite, "White Power," and I'm providing a practical illustration of what Black Power means in one particular West Indian community where it had already occurred. White power is the power of whites over blacks without any participation of the blacks. White power rules the imperialist world as a whole. In Cuba the blacks and mulattoes numbered 1,585,073 out of a population of 5,829,029 in 1953—i.e., about one quarter of the population. Like Jamaica's black people today, they were the poorest and most depressed people on the island. Lighter-skinned Cubans held local power, while real power was in the hands of the U.S. imperialists. Black Cubans fought alongside white Cuban workers and peasants because they were all oppressed. Major Juan Almeida, one of the outstanding leaders of Cuba today, was one of the original guerillas in the Sierra Maestra, and he is black. Black Cubans today enjoy political, economic and social rights and opportunities of exactly the same kind as white Cubans. They too bear arms in the Cuban Militia as an expression of their basic rights. In other words, White Power in Cuba is ended. The majority of the white population naturally predominates numerically in most spheres of activity but they do not hold dominion over blacks without regard to the latter's interests. The blacks have achieved power commensurate with their own numbers by their heroic self-efforts during the days of slavery, in fighting against the Spanish and in fighting against imperialism. Having achieved their rights they can in fact afford to forget the category "black" and think simply as Cuban citizens, as Socialist equals and as men. In Jamaica, where blacks are far greater in numbers and have no whites alongside them as oppressed workers and peasants, it will be the black people who alone can bear the brunt of revolutionary fighting.

Trotsky once wrote that Revolution is the carnival of the masses. When we have that carnival in the West Indies, are people like us here at the university going to join the bacchanal?

Let us have a look at our present position. Most of us who have studied at the U.W.I. are discernibly black, and yet we are undeniably part of the white imperialist system. A few are actively pro-imperialist. They have no confidence in anything that is not white—they talk nonsense about black people being lazy—the same nonsense which was said about the Jamaican black man after emancipation, although he went to Panama and performed the giant task of building the Panama Canal—the same nonsense which is said about W.I. unemployed today, and yet they proceed to England to run the whole transport system. Most of us do not go to quite the same extremes in denigrating ourselves and our black brothers, but we say nothing against the system, and that means that we are acquiescing in the exploitation of our brethren. One of the ways that the situation has persisted especially in recent times is that it has given a few individuals like you and ... [me] ... a vision of personal progress measured in terms of front lawn and the latest model of a huge American car. This has recruited us into their ranks and deprived the black masses of articulate leadership. That is why at the outset I stressed that our choice was to *remain* as part of the white system or to break with it. There is no other alternative.

Black Power in the W.I. must aim at transforming the Black intelligensia into the servants of the black masses. Black Power, within the university and without must aim at overcoming white cultural imperialism. Whites have dominated us both physically and mentally. This fact is brought out in virtually any serious sociological study of the region—the brainwashing process has been so stupendous that it has convinced so many black men of their inferiority. I will simply draw a few illustrations to remind you of this fact which blacks like us at Mona prefer to forget.

The adult black in our West Indian society is fully conditioned to thinking white, because that is the training we are given from childhood. The little black girl plays with a white doll, identifying with it as she combs its flaxen hair. Asked to sketch the figure of a man or woman, the black schoolboy instinctively produces a white man or a white woman. This is not surprising, since until recently the illustrations in our textbooks were all figures of Europeans. The few changes which have taken place have barely scratched the surface of the problem. West Indians of every colour still aspire to European standards of dress and beauty. The language which is used by black people in describing ourselves shows how we despise our African appearance. "Good hair" means European hair, "good nose" means a straight nose, "good complexion" means a light complexion. Everybody recognises how incongruous and ridiculous such terms are, but we continue to use them and to express our support of the assumption that white Europeans have the monopoly of beauty, and that black is the incarnation of ugliness. That is why Black Power advocates find it necessary to assert that BLACK IS BEAUTIFUL.

The most profound revelation of the sickness of our society on the question of race is our respect for all the white symbols of the Christian religion. God the Father is white, God the Son is white, and presumably God the Holy Ghost is white also. The disciples and saints are white, all the Cherubim, Seraphim and angels are white—except Lucifer, of course, who was black, being the embodiment of evil. When one calls upon black people to reject these things, this is not an attack on the teachings of Christ or the ideals of Christianity. What we have to ask is "Why should Christianity come to us all wrapped up in white?" The white race constitute about 20 per cent of the world's population, and yet non-white peoples are supposed to accept that all who inhabit the heavens are white. There are 650 million Chinese, so why shouldn't God and most of the angels be Chinese? The truth is that there is absolutely no reason why different racial groups should not provide themselves with their own religious symbols. A picture of Christ could be red, white or black, depending upon the people who are involved. When Africans adopt the European concept that purity and goodness must be painted white and all that is evil and damned is to be painted black then we are flagrantly self-insulting.

Through the manipulation of this media of education and communication, white people have produced black people who administer the system and perpetuate the white values—"white-hearted black men," as they are called by conscious elements. This is as true of the Indians as it is true of the Africans in our West Indian society. Indeed, the basic explanation of the tragedy of African/Indian confrontation in Guyana and Trinidad is the fact that both groups are held captive by the European way of seeing things. When an African abuses an Indian he repeats all that the white men said about Indian indentured "coolies"; and in turn the Indian has borrowed from the whites the stereotype of the "lazy nigger" to apply to the African beside him. It is as though no black man can see another black man except by looking through a white person. It is time we started seeing through our own eyes. The road to Black Power here in the West Indies and everywhere else must begin with a revaluation of ourselves as blacks and with a redefinition of the world from our own standpoint.

LUSAKA MANIFESTO, 1969

SOURCE *Public Domain.*

INTRODUCTION *The struggle went on for years. On March 21, 1960, in Sharpeville, in the Union of South Africa, police shot into a peaceful demonstration that was held against pass laws for Africans as a part of apartheid regulations. Sixty-nine men, women, and children were killed and about 200 were wounded. Four days later, 29 African and Asian representatives at the United Nations called for an urgent meeting of the Security Council to consider this situation. By the summer, boycotts of South African goods were implemented in countries all over the world, and labor groups refused to service South African cargo ships. Nine years later, in April of 1969, the Fifth Summit Conference of East and Central African States in Lusaka adopted a Manifesto on Southern Africa, and the UN General Assembly—with resolution 2505—welcomed the Lusaka Manifesto on Southern Africa and called it to the attention of nations around the world. This determination of human equality would be one of only many steps in the fight to end apartheid.*

1. When the purpose and the basis of State's international policies are misunderstood, there is introduced into the world a new and unnecessary disharmony. Disagreements, conflicts of interest, or different assessments of human priorities, which already provoke and excess of tension in the world, and disastrously divide mankind at a time when united action is necessary to control modern technology and put it to the service of man. it is for this reason, that discovering world misapprehension of our attitudes and purposes in relation to Southern Africa, we the leaders of East and Central African States meeting at Lusaka, 16th April. 1969, have agreed to issue this Manifesto.

2. By this Manifesto we wish to make clear, beyond all shadow of doubt, our acceptance of the belief that all men are equal, and have equal rights to human dignity and respect, regardless of colour, race, religion, or sex. We believe that all men have the right and the duty to participate, as equal members of the society, in their own government. We do not accept that any individual or group has any right to govern any other group of sane adults, without their consent, and we affirm that only the people of a society, acting together as equals, can determine what is, for them, a good society and a god social, economic, or political organization.

3. On the basis of these beliefs we do not accept that any one group within a society has the right to rule any society without the continuing consent of all the citizens. We recognize that at any one time there will be, within every society, failures in the implementation of these ideals. We recognize that for the sake of human affairs, there may be transitional arrangements while a transformation from group inequalities to individual equality is being effected. but we affirm that without an acceptance of these ideals-without a commitment to these principles of human equality and self-determination-there can be no basis for peace and justice in the world.

4. None of us would claim that within our own States we have achieved the perfect social, economic, and political organization which would ensure a reasonable standard of living for all our people and establish individual security against avoidable hardship or miscarriage of justice. On the contrary, we acknowledge that within our own States the struggle towards human brotherhood and unchallenged human dignity is only the beginning. It is on the basis of our commitment to human equality and human dignity, not on the bases of achieved perfection, that we take our stand of hostility towards the colonialism and racial discrimination which is being practised in Southern Africa. It is on the basis of their commitment to these universal principles that we appeal to other members of the human race for support.

5. If the commitment to these principles existed among the States holding power in Southern Africa, any disagreements we might have about the implementation, or about isolated acts of policy, would be matters affecting only our individual relationships with the States concerned. If these commitments existed, our States would not be justified in the expressed and active hostility towards the regimes of Southern Africa such as we have proclaimed and continue to propagate.

6. The truth is, however, that in Mozambique, Angola, Rhodesia, South-West Africa, and the Republic of South Africa, there is an open and continued denial of the principles of human equality and national self-determination. This is not a matter of failure in the implementation of accepted human principles. The effective Administrations in all these territories are not struggling towards these difficult goals. They are fighting the principles; they are deliberately organizing their societies so as to try to destroy the hold of these principles in the minds of men. It is for this reason that we believe the rest of the world must be interested. For the principle of human equality, and all that flows from it, is either universal or it does not exist. the dignity of all men is destroyed when the manhood of any human being is denied.

7. Our objectives in Southern Africa stem from our principle of human equality. We are not hostile to the Administrations of these States because they are manned and controlled by white people. We are hostile to them because they are systems of minority control which exists as a result of, and in the pursuance of, doctrines of human inequality. What we are working for is the right of self-determination for the people of those territories. We are working for a rule in those countries which is based on the will of all people, and an acceptance of the equality of every citizen.

8. Our stand towards Southern Africa thus involves a rejection of racialism, not a reversal of the existing racial domination. We believe that all the peoples who have made their homes in the countries of Southern Africa are Africans, regardless of the colour of their skins: and we would oppose a racialist majority government which adopted a philosophy of deliberate and permanent discrimination between its citizens on the grounds of racial origin. we are not talking racialism when we reject the colonialism and apartheid policies now operating in those areas; we are demanding an opportunity for all of the people in these States, working together as equal individual citizens to work out for themselves the institutions and systems of government under which they

will, by general consent, live together and work together to build a harmonious society.

9. As an aftermath of the present policies, it is likely that different groups within these societies will be self-conscious and fearful. The initial political and economic organizations may well take account of these fears, and this group self-consciousness. But how this is to be done must be a matter exclusively for the peoples of the country concerned, working together. No other nation will have the right to interfere in such affairs. All that the rest of the world has a right to demand is just what we are now asserting-that the arrangements within any State which wishes to be accepted into the community of nations must be based on acceptance of the principles of human dignity and equality.

10. To talk of the liberation of Africa is to say two things: First, that the peoples in the territories still under colonial rule shall be free to determine for themselves their own institutions of self-government. Secondly, that the individuals in Southern Africa shall be freed from an environment poisoned by the propaganda of racialism, and given an opportunity to be men-not white men, brown men, yellow men, or black men.

11. Thus the liberation of Africa for which we have been struggling does not mean a reversed racialism. Nor is it an aspect of African Imperialism. As far as we are concerned the present boundaries of what will be free and independent African States. There is no question of our seeking or accepting any alterations to our own boundaries at the expense of these future free African nations.

12. On the objective of liberation thus defined, we can neither surrender nor compromise. we have always preferred and we still prefer, to achieve it without physical violence. We would prefer to negotiate rather than destroy, to talk rather than to kill. We do not advocate violence; we advocate an end to the violence against human dignity which is now being perpetrated by the oppressors of Africa. If peaceful progress to emancipation were possible, or if changed circumstances were to make it possible in the future, we would urge our brothers in the resistance movements to use peaceful methods of struggle even at the cost of some compromise on the timing of change. But while peaceful progress is blocked by actions of those at present in power in the States of Southern Africa, we have no choice but to give to the peoples of those territories all the support of which we are capable in their struggle against their oppressors. This is why the signatory states participate in the movement for the liberation of Africa, under the aegis of the Organization of African Unity. However, the obstacle to change is not the same in all the countries of Southern Africa, and it follows therefore, that the possibility of continuing the struggle through peaceful means varies from one country to another.

13. In *Mozambique* and *Angola*, and in so-called *Portuguese Guinea*, the basic problem is not racialism but a pretence that Portugal exists in Africa. Portugal is situated in Europe; the fact is that it is a dictatorship is a matter for the Portuguese to settle. But no decree of the Portuguese dictator, nor legislation passed by any Parliament in Portugal, can make Africa part of Europe. The only thing which could convert a part of Africa into a constituent unit in a union which also includes a European State would be the freely expressed will of the people of that part of Africa. There is no such popular will in the Portuguese colonies. On the contrary, in the absence of any opportunity to negotiate a road to freedom, the peoples of all three territories have taken up arms against the colonial power. They have done this despite the heavy odds against them, and despite the great suffering they know to be involved.

14. Portugal, as a European State, has naturally its own allies in the context of ideological conflict between West and East. However, in our context, the effect of this is that Portugal is enabled to use her resources to pursue the most heinous war and degradation of man in Africa. The present Manifesto must, therefore, lay bare the fact that the inhuman commitment of Portugal in Africa and her ruthless subjugation of the people of Mozambique, Angola and the so-called Portuguese Guinea, is not only irrelevant to the ideological conflict of power-politics, but it is also diametrically opposed to the politics, the philosophies and the doctrines practised by her Allies in the conduct of their own affairs at home. The peoples of Mozambique, Angola, and Portuguese Guinea are not interested in Communism or Capitalism; they are interested in their freedom. They are demanding an acceptance of the principles of independence on the basis of majority rule, and for many years they called for discussions on this issue. Only when their demand for talks was continually ignored did they begin to fight. Even now, if Portugal should change her policy and accept the principle of self-determination, we would urge the Liberation Movements to desist from their armed struggle and to co-operate in the mechanics of a peaceful transfer of power from Portugal to the peoples of the African territories.

15. The fact that many Portuguese citizens have immigrated to these African countries does not affect this issue. Future immigration policy will be a matter for the independent Governments when these are established. In the meantime we would urge the Liberation Movements to reiterate their statements that all those Portuguese people who have made their homes in Mozambique, Angola, or Portuguese Guinea, and who are willing to give their future loyalty to those States will be accepted as citizens. And an independent Mozambique, Angola, or

Portuguese Guinea may choose to be as friendly with Portugal as Brazil is. That would be the free choice of a free people.

16. In *Rhodesia* the situation is different in so far as the metropolitan power has acknowledged the colonial status of the territory. Unfortunately, however, it has failed to take adequate measures to reassert its authority against the minority which has seized power with the declared intention of maintaining white domination. The matter cannot rest there. Rhodesia, like the rest of Africa, must be free, and its independence must be on the basis of majority rule. If the colonial power is unwilling or unable to effect such a transfer of power to the people, then the people themselves will have no alternative but to capture it as and when they can. And Africa has no alternative but to support them. The question which remains in Rhodesia is therefore whether Britain will reassert her authority in Rhodesia and then negotiate the peaceful progress to majority rule before independence. In do far as Britain is willing to make this second commitment, Africa will co-operate in her attempts to reassert her authority. This is the method of progress which we would prefer; it would involve less suffering for all the people of Rhodesia, both black and white. But until there is some firm evidence that Britain accepts the principle of independence on the basis of majority rule and is prepared to take whatever steps are necessary to make it a reality, then Africa has no choice but to support the struggle for the people's freedom by whatever means are open.

17. Just as a settlement of the Rhodesian problem with a minimum of violence is a British responsibility, so a settlement in *South West Africa* with a minimum of violence is a United Nations responsibility. By every canon of international law, and by every precedent, South West Africa should by now have been a sovereign, independent State with a Government based on majority rule. South West Africa was a German colony until 1919, just as Tanganyika, Rwanda and Burundi, Togoland, and Cameroon were German colonies.

It was a matter of European politics that wen the Mandatory System was established after Germany had been defeated, the administration of South West Africa was given to the white minority Government of South Africa, while the other ex-German colonies in Africa were put into the hands of the British, Belgian, or French Governments. After the Second World War every mandated territory except South West Africa was converted into a Trustee Territory and has subsequently gained independence. South Africa, on the other hand, has persistently refused to honour even the international obligation it accepted in 1919, and has increasingly to South West Africa the inhuman doctrines and organization of apartheid.

18. The United Nations General Assembly has ruled against this action and in 1966 terminated the Mandate under which South Africa had a legal basis for its occupation and domination of South West Africa. The General Assembly declared that the territory is now the direct responsibility of the United Nations and set up an *ad hoc* Committee to recommend practical means by which South West Africa would be administered, and the people enabled to exercise self-determination and to achieve independence.

19. Nothing could be clearer than this decision-which no permanent member of the Security Council voted against. Yet, since that time no effective measures have been taken to enforce it. South West Africa remains in the clutches of the most ruthless minority government in Africa. Its people continue to be oppressed and those who advocate even peaceful progress to independence continue to be persecuted. The world has an obligation to use its strength to enforce the decision which all the countries co-operated in making. If they do this there is hope that the change can be effected without great violence. If they fail, then sooner or later the people of South West Africa will take the law into their own hands. The people have been patient beyond belief, but one day their patience will be exhausted. Africa, at least, will be unable to deny their call for help.

20. *The Republic of South Africa* is itself an independent Sovereign State and a member of the United Nations. It is more highly developed and richer than any other nation in Africa. On every legal basis its internal affairs are a matter exclusively for the people of South Africa. Yet the purpose of the law is people and we assert that the actions of the South African Government are such that the rest of the world has a responsibility to take some action in defence of humanity.

21. There is one thing about South African oppression which distinguishes it from other oppressive regimes. The *apartheid* policy adopted by its Government, and supported to a greater or lesser extent by almost all its white citizens, is based on a rejection of man's humanity. A position of privilege or the experience of oppression in the South African society depends on the one thing which it is beyond the power of any man to change. It depends upon a man's colour, his parentage, and his ancestors If you are black you cannot escape this categorization; nor can you escape it if you are white. If you are a black millionaire and a brilliant political scientist, you are still subject to the pass laws and still excluded from political activity. If you are white, even protests against the system and an attempt to reject segregation, will lead you only to the segregation and the comparative comfort of a white jail. beliefs,

abilities, and behavior are all irrelevant to man's status; everything depends on race. Manhood is irrelevant. The whole system of government and society in South Africa is based on the denial of human equality. And the system is maintained by a ruthless denial of the human rights of the majority of the population and thus, inevitably of all.

22. These things are known and are regularly condemned in the Councils of the United Nations and elsewhere. But it appears that to many countries international law takes precedent over humanity; therefore no action follows the words. Yet even if international law is held to exclude active assistance to the South African opponents of apartheid, it does not demand that the comfort and support of human and commercial intercourse should be given to a government which rejects the manhood of most of humanity South Africa should be excluded from the United Nations Agencies, and even from the United Nations itself. It should be ostracized by the world community. It should be isolated from world trade patterns and left to be self-sufficient if it can be. The South African Government cannot be allowed both to reject the very concept of mankind's unity, and to benefit by the strength given through friendly international relations. And certainly Africa cannot acquiesce in the maintenance of the present policies against people of African descent.

23. The signatories of this Manifesto assert that the validity of the principles of human equality and dignity extend to the Republic of South Africa just as they extend to the colonial territories of Southern Africa. Before a basis for peaceful development can be established in this continent, these principles must be acknowledged by every nation, and in every State there must be a deliberate attempt to implement them.

24. We re-affirm our commitment to these principles of human equality and human dignity, and to the doctrines of self-determination and non-racialism. We shall work for their extension within our own nations and throughout the continent of Africa.

DECLARATION OF SANCTIONS AGAINST SOUTH AFRICA BY THE U.S. CONGRESS

SOURCE *Public Domain.*

INTRODUCTION *After years of battle in the U.S. Congress and decades of debate over whether or not the United States should issue sanctions against South Africa for their apartheid policy, in 1986 the fighting was over. African American leaders had been calling for sanctions since the late 1940s when the policies were put into place. The Council on African Affairs began as early as 1946 to organize famine relief campaigns, legal defense funds, sit-ins, and demonstrations at South African embassies, and even petitioned the United Nations. Until 1986 when the United States finally joined in the campaign to end apartheid through these sanctions and up until 1994 when democracy for all people was realized in free elections, many United States citizens petitioned, demonstrated, and pleaded that the government take a stand. African Americans continued to charge that the United States was reluctant because its own policies for so long legalized racism.*

TITLE I — POLICY OF THE UNITED STATES WITH RESPECT TO ENDING APARTHEID

Policy Toward the Government of South Africa

Sec. 101. (a) United States policy toward the Government of South Africa shall be designed to bring about reforms in that system of government that will lead to the establishment of a nonracial democracy.

(b) The United States will work toward this goal by encouraging the Government of South Africa to —

(1) repeal the present state of emergency and respect the principle of equal justice under law for citizens of all races

(2) release Nelson Mandela, Govan Mbeki, Walter Sisulu black trade union leaders, and all political prisoners;

(3) permit the free exercise by South Africans of all races of the right to form political parties, express political opinions, and otherwise participate in the political process;

(4) establish a timetable for the elimination of apartheid laws

(5) negotiate with representatives of all racial groups in South Africa the future political system in South Africa, and

(6) end military and paramilitary activities aimed at neighboring states.

(c) The United States will encourage the actions set forth in subsection (b) through economic, political, and diplomatic measures as set forth in this Act. The United States will adjust its actions toward the Government of South Africa to reflect the progress or lack of progress made by the Government of South Africa in meeting the goal set forth in subsection (a).

Policy Toward the African National Congress, etc.

Sec 102. (a) United States policy toward the African National Congress, the Pan African Congress, and their affiliates shall be designed to bring about a suspension of violence that will lead to the start of negotiations designed to bring about a nonracial and genuine democracy in South Africa.

(b) The United States shall work toward this goal by encouraging the African National Congress and the Pan African Congress, and their affiliates, to —

(1) suspend terrorist activities so that negotiations with the Government of South Africa and other groups representing black South Africans will be possible;

(2) make known their commitment to a free and democratic post-apartheid South Africa —

(3) agree to enter into negotiations with the South African Government and other groups representing black South Africans for the peaceful solution of the problems of South Africa —

(4) reexamine their ties to the South African Communist Party.

(c) The United States will encourage the actions set forth in subsection (b) through political and diplomatic measures. The United States will adjust its actions toward the Government of South Africa not only to reflect progress or lack of progress made by the Government of South Africa in meeting the goal set forth in subsection 101(a) but also to reflect progress or lack of progress made by the ANC and other organizations in meeting the goal set forth in subsection (a) of this section.

Policy Toward the Victims of Apartheid

Sec 103. (a) The United States policy toward the victims of apartheid is to use economic, political, diplomatic, and other effective means to achieve the removal of the root cause of their victimization, which is the apartheid system. In anticipation of the removal of the system of apartheid and as a further means of challenging that system, it is the policy of the United States to assist these victims of apartheid as individuals and through organizations to overcome the handicaps imposed on them by the system of apartheid and to help prepare them for their rightful roles as full participants in the political, social, economic, and intellectual life of their country in the post-apartheid South Africa envisioned by this Act.

(b) The United States will work toward the purposes of subsection (a) by —

(1) providing assistance to South African victims of apartheid without discrimination by race, color, sex, religious belief, or political orientation, to take advantage of educational opportunities in South Africa and in the United States to prepare for leadership positions in a post-apartheid South Africa;

(2) assisting victims of apartheid;

(3) aiding individuals or groups in South Africa whose goals are to aid victims of apartheid or foster nonviolent legal or political challenges to the apartheid laws;

(4) furnishing direct financial assistance to those whose nonviolent activities had led to their arrest or detention by the South African authorities and (B) to the families of those killed by terrorist acts such as "necklacings";

(5) intervening at the highest political levels in South Africa to express the strong desire of the United States to see the development in South Africa of a nonracial democratic society;

(6) supporting the rights of the victims of apartheid through political, economic, or other sanctions in the event the Government of South Africa fails to make progress toward the removal of the apartheid laws and the establishment of such democracy; and

(7) supporting the rights of all Africans to be free of terrorist attacks by setting a time limit after which the United States will pursue diplomatic and political measures against those promoting terrorism and against those countries harboring such groups so as to achieve the objectives of this Act.

Policy Toward Other Countries in South Africa

Sec 104. (a) The United States policy toward the other countries in the Southern African region shall be designed to encourage democratic forms of government, full respect for human rights, an end to cross-border terrorism, political independence, and economic development.

(b) The United States will work toward the purposes of subsection (a) by —

(1) helping to secure the independence of Namibia and the establishment of Namibia as a nonracial democracy in accordance with appropriate United Nations Security Council resolutions;

(2) supporting the removal of all foreign military forces from the region;

(3) encouraging the nations of the region to settle differences through peaceful means;

(4) promoting economic development through bilateral and multilateral economic assistance targeted at increasing opportunities in the productive sectors of national economies, with a particular emphasis on

increasing opportunities for nongovernmental economic activities;

(5) encouraging, and when necessary, strongly demanding, that all countries of the region respect the human rights of their citizens and noncitizens residing in the country, and especially the release of persons persecuted for their political beliefs or detained without trial;

(6) encouraging, and when necessary, strongly demanding that all countries of the region take effective action to end cross-border terrorism; and

(7) providing appropriate assistance, within the limitations of American responsibilities at home and in other regions, to assist regional economic cooperation and the development of interregional transportation and other capital facilities necessary for economic growth.

Policy Toward Frontline States

Sec 105. It is the sense of the Congress that the President should discuss with the governments of the African "frontline" states the effects on them of disruptions in transportation or other economic links through South Africa and of means of reducing those effects.

Sec. 106. (a)(1) United States policy will seek to promote negotiations among representatives of all citizens of South Africa to determine a future political system that would permit all citizens to be full participants in the governance of their country. The United States recognizes that important and legitimate political parties in South Africa include several organizations that have been banned and will work for the unbanning of such organizations in order to permit legitimate political viewpoints to be represented at such negotiations. The United States also recognizes that some of the organizations fighting apartheid have become infiltrated by Communists and that Communists serve on the governing boards of such organizations.

(2) To this end, it is the sense of the Congress that the President, the Secretary of State, or other appropriate high-level United States officials should meet with the leaders of opposition organizations of South Africa, particularly but not limited to those organizations representing the black majority. Furthermore, the President, in concert with the major allies of the United States and other interested parties, should seek to bring together opposition political leaders with leaders of the Government of South Africa for the purpose of negotiations to achieve a transition to the post-apartheid democracy envisioned in this Act.

(b) The United States will encourage the Government of South Africa and all participants to the negotiations to respect the right of all South Africans to form political parties, express political opinions, and otherwise participate in the political process without fear of retribution by either governmental or nongovernmental organizations. It is the sense of the Congress that a suspension of violence is an essential precondition for the holding of negotiations. The United States calls upon all parties to the conflict to agree to a suspension of violence.

(c) The United States will work toward the achievement of agreement to suspend violence and begin negotiations through coordinated actions with the major Western allies and with the governments of the countries in the region.

(d) It is the sense of the Congress that the achievement of an agreement for negotiations could be promoted if the United States and its major allies, such as Great Britain, Canada, France, Italy, Japan, and West Germany, would hold a meeting to develop a fourpoint plan to discuss with the Government of South Africa a proposal for stages of multilateral assistance to South Africa in return for the Government of South Africa implementing —

(1) an end to the state of emergency and the release of the political prisoners, including Nelson Mandela;

(2) the unbanning of the African National Congress, the Pan African Congress, the Black Consciousness Movement, and all other groups willing to suspend terrorism and to participate in negotiations and a democratic process

(3) a revocation of the Group Areas Act and the Population Registration Act and the granting of universal citizenship to all South Africans, including homeland residents; and

(4) the use of the international offices of a third party as an intermediary to bring about negotiations with the object of the establishment of power-sharing with the black majority.

Policy Toward International Cooperation on Measures to End Apartheid

Sec. 107. (a) The Congress finds that —

(1) international cooperation is a prerequisite to an effective anti-apartheid policy and to the suspension of terrorism in South Africa; and

(2) the situation in South Africa constitutes an emergency in international relations and that action is necessary for the protection of the essential security interests of the United States.

(b) Accordingly, the Congress urges the President to seek such cooperation among all individuals, groups, and nations.

Policy Toward Necklacing

Sec. 108. It is the sense of the Congress that the African National Congress should strongly condemn and take effective actions against the execution by fire, commonly known as "necklacing", of any person in any country.

United States Ambassador to Meet with Nelson Mandela Sec. 109. It is the sense of the Senate that the United States Ambassador should promptly make a formal request to the South African Government for the United States Ambassador to meet with Nelson Mandela.

Policy Toward the Recruitment and Training of Black South Africans by United States Employers

Sec. 110. (a) The Congress finds that —

(1) the policy of apartheid is abhorrent and morally repugnant;

(2) the United States believes strongly in the principles of democracy and individual freedoms;

(3) the United States endorses the policy of political participation of all citizens;

(4) a free, open, and vital economy is a primary means for achieving social equality and economic advancement for all citizens; and

(5) the United States is committed to a policy of securing and enhancing human rights and individual dignity throughout the world.

(b) It is the sense of the Congress that United States employers operating in South Africa are obliged both generally to actively oppose the policy and practices of apartheid and specifically to engage in recruitment and training of black and colored South Africans for management responsibilities.

TITLE III — MEASURES BY THE UNITED STATES TO UNDERMINE APARTHEID

Prohibition on the Importation of Krugerrands

Sec. 301. No person, including a bank, may import into the United States any South African krugerrand or any other gold coin minted in South Africa or offered for sale by the Government of South Africa.

Prohibition on the Importation of Military Articles

Sec. 302. No arms, ammunition, or military vehicles produced in South Africa or any manufacturing data for such articles may be imported into the United States. . . .

Prohibition on Computer Exports to South Africa

Sec. 304. (a) No computers, computer software, or goods or technology intended to manufacture or service computers may be exported to or for use by any of the following entities of the Government of South Africa:

(1) The military.

(2) The police.

(3) The prison system.

(4) The national security agencies.

(5) ARMSCOR and its subsidiaries or the weapons research activities of the Council for Scientific and Industrial Research.

(6) The administering authorities for controlling the movements of the victims of apartheid.

(7) Any apartheid enforcing agency.

(8) Any local, regional, or homelands government entity which performs any function of any entity described in paragraphs (1) through (7).

(b)(1) Computers, computer software, and goods or technology intended to service computers may be exported, directly or indirectly, to or for use by an entity of the Government of South Africa other than those set forth in subsection (a) only if a system of end use verification is in effect to ensure that the computers involved will not be used for any function of any entity set forth in subsection (a).

(2) The Secretary of Commerce may prescribe such rules and regulations as may be necessary to carry out this section.

Prohibition on Loans to the Government of South Africa

Sec. 305. (a) No national of the United States may make or approve any loan or other extension of credit, directly or indirectly, to the Government of South Africa or to any corporation, partnership or other organization which is owned or controlled by the Government of South Africa. . . .

Prohibition on Air Transportation with South Africa

Sec. 306. (a) (1) The President shall immediately notify the Government of South Africa of his intention to suspend the rights of any air carrier designated by the Government of South Africa under the Agreement Between the Government of the United States of America and the Government of the Union of South Africa Relating to Air Services Between Their Respective Territories, signed May 23, 1947, to service the routes provided in the Agreement.

(2) Ten days after the date of enactment of this Act, the President shall direct the Secretary of Transportation to revoke the right of any air carrier designated by the Government of South Africa under the Agreement to provide service pursuant to the Agreement.

(3) Ten days after the date of enactment of this Act, the President shall direct the Secretary of Transportation not to permit or otherwise designate any United States air carrier to provide service between the United States and South Africa pursuant to the Agreement. . . .

Prohibitions on Nuclear Trade with South Africa

Sec 307. (a) Notwithstanding any other provision of law—

(1) the Nuclear Regulatory Commission shall not issue any license for the export to South Africa of production or utilization facilities, any source or special nuclear material or sensitive nuclear technology, or any component parts, items, or substances which the Commission has determined, pursuant to section 109b. of the Atomic Energy Act, to be especially relevant from the standpoint of export control because of their significance for nuclear explosive purposes. . . .

Prohibition on Importation of Uranium and Coal from South Africa

Sec. 309. (a) Notwithstanding any other provision of law, no — (1) uranium ore, (2) uranium oxide (3) coal, or (4) textiles produced or manufactured in South Africa may be imported into the United States.

(b) This section shall take effect 90 days after the date of enactment of this Act.

Prohibition on New Investment in South Africa

Sec. 310. (a) No national of the United States may, directly or through another person, make any new investment in South Africa.

(b) The prohibition contained in subsection (a) shall take effect 45 days after the date of enactment of this Act.

(c) The prohibition contained in this section shall not apply to a firm owned by black South Africans.

Termination of Certain Provisions

Sec 311. (a) This title and sections 501(c) and 504(b) shall terminate if the Government of South Africa —

(1) releases all persons persecuted for their political beliefs or detained unduly without trial and Nelson Mandela from prison;

(2) repeals the state of emergency in effect on the date of enactment of this Act and releases all detainees held under such state of emergency;

(3) unbans democratic political parties and permits the free exercise by South Africans of all races of the right to form political parties, express political opinions, and otherwise participate in the political process;

(4) repeals the Group Areas Act and the Population Registration Act and institutes no other measures with the same purposes; and

(5) agrees to enter into good faith negotiations with truly representative members of the black majority without preconditions.

(b) The President may suspend or modify any of the measures required by this title or section 501(c) or section 504(b) thirty days after he determines, and so reports to the Speaker of the House of Representatives and the chairman of the Committee on Foreign Relations of the Senate, that the Government of South Africa has —

(1) taken the action described in paragraph (1) of subsection (a),

(2) taken three of the four actions listed in paragraphs (2) through (5) of subsection (a), and

(3) made substantial progress toward dismantling the system of apartheid and establishing a nonracial democracy, unless the Congress enacts within such 30-day period, in accordance with section 602 of this Act, a joint resolution disapproving the determination of the President under this subsection.

(c) It is the policy of the United States to support the negotiations with the representatives of all communities as envisioned in this Act. If the South African Government agrees to enter into negotiations without preconditions, abandons unprovoked violence against its opponents, commits itself to a free and democratic post-apartheid South Africa under a code of law; and if nonetheless the African National Congress, the Pan African Congress, or their affiliates, or other organizations, refuse to participate; or if the African National Congress, the Pan African Congress or other organizations —

(1) refuse to abandon unprovoked violence during such negotiations; and

(2) refuse to commit themselves to a free and democratic postapartheid South Africa under a code of law, then the United States will support negotiations which do not include these organizations.

Policy Toward Violence or Terrorism

Sec. 312. (a) United States policy toward violence in South Africa shall be designed to bring about an immediate end to such violence and to promote negotiations concluding with a removal of the system of apartheid and the establishment of a non-racial democracy in South Africa.

(b) The United States shall work toward this goal by diplomatic and other measures designed to isolate those who promote terrorist attacks on unarmed civilians or those who provide assistance to individuals or groups promoting such activities.

(c) The Congress declares that the abhorrent practice of "necklacing" and other equally inhumane acts which have been practices in South Africa by blacks against fellow blacks are an affront to all throughout the world who value the rights of individuals to live in an atmosphere free from fear of violent reprisals. . . .

Source: *U.S. Statutes at Large 100 (1986): 1086.*

"THE STATE OF NATIVE AMERICA"

SOURCE *Means, Russell. From "The State of Native America," in* Native American Reader: Stories, Speeches and Poems. *Edited by Jerry D. Blanche. The Denali Press, 1990. Copyright © 1990 by Jerry D. Blanche. Reproduced by permission of the publisher.*

INTRODUCTION *By the time Russell Means, an Oglala Sioux, delivered this address in 1988, he had made a name for himself. When he came to prominence in the late 1960s and early 1970s, he made his goal that of the "reinstitution of pride and self-dignity of the Indian in American." He wanted more for his own tribal people, and all Native Americans, than the stereotypes perpetrated in America for centuries—that of the savage with no culture except that which could be given up for what was thought to be a superior white man's culture. He joined the American Indian Movement, or AIM, founded by activist Clyde Bellecourt and others on the belief that if the federal government were allowed to continue to supervise Native American affairs it would mean the end of their people, and of their culture. For decades the Bureau for Indian Affairs, as the federal agency was known, had less than a sterling record in managing the lives of Native Americans on the reservations. Assimilation was the rule rather than cultural respect of the people who had settled in this country centuries before white men came to explore.*

What I said is, "Hello, my relatives. I am an ally, and I come from Yellow Thunder Camp in our very sacred holy land, the Black Hills."

Back in 1968–70, the state of the American Indian nations in the Americas of the Western Hemisphere was unchanged from 1492. That's in 1968, 1969, and 1970. This is now 1988, and it still remains unchanged from 1492. In 1492 we were considered an "expendable peoples" by Columbus and the governments of Europe, including the Roman Catholic Church. It wasn't until 1897, thirty-two years after the conclusion of the Civil War, that the Catholic Church declared us to be human beings. Until then, the Marine Corps of the Catholic Church, the Jesuits and the Franciscans, considered us to be "beasts of burden." And now they're going to canonize, make into a saint, Father Serra, a slaveowner, a murderer. That is the state of the American Indian nations. The pope is going to canonize an Indian murderer, an Indian slaveowner, Father Serra, who established these missionary outposts for the Marine Corps, I mean the Catholic Church, along the western coast of Mexico and California.

We are an "expendable people." Go down to Brazil and you will see the government forcibly relocating and allowing miners and forestry employees to massively murder Indian people. Go to Paraguay where they still have bounties on the Aiche. Go to Chile, where Pinochet is officially starving the Mapuche to get their remaining lands. Go to Costa Rica, where Weyerhauser is removing Indian people so they can get at their forests. Go to Nicaragua, where the entire government effort has not only relocated but mass murdered, and it continues to this day, the Indian people. Both the left or the right excuse it and would rather deal with dope dealers. Go to Mexico. Go to Alaska. Go to Canada. Come right here to the United States of America, where this government right here today, at this very moment, is relocating and starving to death and completely destroying an Indian nation, the Navajo, in Arizona. Forced relocation, the same thing the Sandinistas are doing.

Welcome to the Americas. Welcome to the Americas, my home, where the dust that you kick up as you walk is made up of the bones of my ancestors. Welcome. For what you have appropriated and for what we have given to you, I will tell you.

Sixty percent of the world's foodstuffs comes from us. Eighty percent of what the average American eats every day comes from us. Non-Indians are continually asking me, "What's some traditional Indian food?" What did you eat today? Did you go to a salad bar? That's all ours."

We domesticated and developed, for instance, over ten thousand species of potatoes. So when the Europeans came over here, what did they take back? One species. So when the blight hit their potato crop, they had nothing to fall back on, and consequently, we got a lot of Kennedys coming over here. When the blight hit one of our potato crops, we had 9,999 to fall back on. And they call me primitive!

Sewage systems we gave to the Europeans. When Cortez and Pizarro and Coronado and all the rest of the conquistadors were over here destroying Indian people and our records, some of the people with them recognized that, hey, these Indians have sewage systems. Let's take it back to Europe and clean up Berlin and

Rome and London and Madrid and Brussels, Paris. And voilà! In less than a generation the amount of disease and the plague that was rampant in Europe dramatically was reduced to less than one percent than what it had been before. Because of the introduction of sewage systems that we gave to the world.

I could go on and on and on. The medicines the advent of pasteurization, named after Louis Pasteur. B.S.! In his own writings he credits the Indians!

Welcome to natural childbirth. The Lamace method. A Frenchman comes over here, studies the Indian way of giving birth, goes back to France, writes it up, and you call it the Lamaze method.

Welcome to the Americas. Welcome. The finest medicines in the world developed here. Developed here! Welcome to the Americas. From quinine to penicillin. Welcome. Codeine.

Welcome to the Americas. But instead of the Europeans, the Asians, the Africans, the Middle Easterners, the Far Easterners, instead of saying "thank you," we are still an "expendable people." Does anyone talk about majority rule in Ecuador or Bolivia or Peru or Panama or the Northwest Territories of Canada or Guatemala? No. You don't hear about majority rule. Because those are Indians, campesinos peasants. Do you see at the family of nations a red person sitting around the table with the family of nations? We are the only color of the human race not allowed to participate in the international community. That's an insult to your own humanity! Think about it! Look around! Your own humanity is being insulted! You live in this modern day and age when an entire people is not even considered to be a part of the international community.

Welcome to the Americas. The states of the American Indian peoples. You blithely continue on in life without an acknowledgement of Colorado or of any of the forty states whose names are derived from the origin of the Indian language. It's amazing how people are not saying "thank you."

[In] 1968 and 1969, 1970, Indians that protested back east were wearing Plains Indians outfits. American Indian people were attending conferences in ties, shined shoes and suits and bouffant hairdos, with pearl earrings on the women. They were afraid to wear beadwork, afraid to wear silver and turquoise. They were embarrassed to announce to the world that they are proud of who they are. I was fortunate to be in the vanguard of a cultural revolution that took place in the late 1960s and 1970s. That cultural revolution enabled our pride and self-dignity to once again become the criteria of what the American Indian nations are all about. It succeeded beyond our wildest plans and expectations, hopes or dreams.

When I sat in Minneapolis with Clyde Belle-court and Dennis Banks in 1969 and we took the American Indian movement into a national and then international organization, I remember when we attended Indian conferences and they wouldn't allow us to speak because we looked "ridiculous" in headbands and beadwork and moccasins and we had a drum with us. Our own people. When Dr. Alfonso Ortiz, a Pueblo Indian from New Mexico, who is a doctor of anthropology at the University of New Mexico, was up in his three-piece suit at the National Indian Education Association, of which I was on the board at the time, he was giving the keynote address at a banquet. The American Indian Movement. We came in. I was sitting up there on the dais with him, and the American Indian Movement came in with all their headbands and all their beadwork and their drum, and we stood, Indian people, at each exit, and wouldn't allow these other Indians in their ties and gowns to leave because they tried to leave. We sang Indian at that conference, the National Indian Education Association, NIEA, which now is somehow wallowing in the left-brain, right-brain arguments. That was the state of the American Indian nations in 1970. The Indian people embarrassed about who they are.

It's changed that cultural revolution. We had to challenge the United States government militarily, and we won again! Again! Because we were right and we're still right.

But understand the state of the American Indian nations. Because we know. You see, at the advent of the opening up of half the world to the rest of the world, we allowed disease and overpopulation of Europe to dramatically decrease, as I said, in the matter of a generation. There were diseases that were rampant and incurable in Europe: the plague, everything. They instituted sewage systems and the population density went from thirty-five per square mile in 1492 down to seven in less than a century because of the opening of the Western Hemisphere and the cleaning up of the environment.

What happened? The disease was contained. The diseases were contained. But have you all learned? What's the disease today that's incurable? AIDS. The revolution comes around again, but this time there is no more Western Hemisphere, no more Indians. Because we already told those moon Indians, "Watch out, they're coming." There's no other place to go.

The message is the same: clean up. You want to cure AIDS? Clean it up. You want to cure all the other diseases, the cancers, every one that pops up every day? Clean up. As Chief Seattle said, "Continue to contaminate your bed and one night you will suffocate in your own waste."

The state of the American Indian nations, that cultural revolution I was talking about of the 1970s. Here's the beauty of that experience: our traditional people gained respect. Our culture gained respect. And we're still struggling. We're now embarking on an economic revolution. The Red Nations of the Western Hemisphere.

But let me tell you something about the state of the American Indian nations. There is Indian activism in virtually every Indian community. Wherever there's more than one Indian, there's activism. That goes whether it's Seattle University, the Navajo, Nicaragua, Argentina, Chile, Alaska, Canada—everywhere we live. And it's infected the world. Because of our cultural revolution the onslaught and attack on indigenous peoples worldwide is now pervasive.

They're getting our own people to call themselves "Native American." They're getting our own people to teach in universities like this about "we come from China." Understand that we do not come from China. That is a racist, a very racist concept that began with Thomas Jefferson, and he only wrote about it in passing, because of our physical characteristics. In fact, the reverse is true. Geologists know it's impossible for us to have migrated from the Western Hemisphere west. Because during the Ice Ages, the ice corridors that were formed along the northwest coasts of the Western Hemisphere made it impossible to migrate from here to the west, or, as the Europeans call it, the Far East. I could never figure that one out. In fact, those same ice corridors made migration from here going west possible. Geologists know this.

Where are the anthropologists around here? Don't they ever visit with geologists? The archaeologists, the official grave robbers of intellectual institutions such as this? Any high school students that have aspirations towards robbing graves, I would suggest that it is one of the most disrespectful professions and dishonorable professions, if you want to call it that, in the world today. There are federal laws protecting grave robbers. What kind of ghouls are archaeologists?

I live at Canyon de Chelly, on the Navajo for aeons. Canyon de Chelly is part of a whole tourist route to go see where Indians used to live. Cliff-dwellers, they're called. The Anasazi people, they're called by "anthros" and "archies." And these peoples, the Diné, the Hopi, all indigenous peoples of that area, the Zuni, the Pueblos, the Apache, those ruins that are in the sides of the cliffs. We never go there. We have respect for that. We have respect. But day in and day out tourists, non-Indian tourists are trampling all over those cliff dwellings. Every day of the year. They call them cliff-dwellers. They want to know what happened. But you know that archaeologists and anthropologists will not consult with Indian people because that would prejudice their findings. So they have come to the conclusions by robbing some of our graves, and this is the most recent, that we were cannibals because these bones were all broken up and in mass graves in a mass area.

Of course, these graves are about six or seven thousand years old. They didn't take into account any earthquakes or a coyote or two hanging around digging up the earth or moles or worms, etc. They didn't even go over to the Hopi and say, "Hey guys, how do you bury your people?" They came to the conclusion we're cannibals. I retorted that if I used the same criteria as anthropologists and archeologists of these learned institutions, I will go to a Christian gravesite, dig up a grave, find a body in a coffin, and say, "Aha! Aha! The white man is saving his dead for future famines! They have found a way to preserve food." That's how ridiculous this grave-robbing has become in the alleged intellectual community. We have our own people believing this. In the same institutions not even protesting it!

I am sick and tired of the state of the American Indian. We had a beautiful cultural revolution, but you know what happens? The government and all institutions are making it even harder for us to know who we are. You see, in this country, the United States of America, the Indian people, we can be anything we want to be. Anything. We can even become archaeologists. But we can't be Indian. It's against the law in this country to be Indian. We can't pray. The last six decisions of the Supreme Court concerning our freedom of religion all denied it. The last Rehnquist decision totally obliterated our right to freedom of religion. In the name of "progress."

We do not have the right to pray in the Black Hills. I know. We are still in court. I have argued. I'm the only non-lawyer ever to argue before a U.S. Court of Appeals. I argued on behalf of the Yellow Thunder Camp against the Black Hills National Forest for their refusal to allow us to pray in the Black Hills according to our ways. But we as Indian people are not allowed, and I'm going to give you a view of what American Indian people are doing to themselves, because we've become our own worst enemy.

Understand this about the U.S. government: they practice and perfect their colonialism on us, here, in the backyard of America, and then export it to the world. If you don't believe it, look at the West Bank, look at South Africa, look at Borneo, look at the Philippines, etc. Then look at yourselves, look in the mirror. What do we think? We cannot, we do not have self-determination. It's called "self-administration," and that's my term. We get to administer someone else's policies.

Do you think Indian people are standing up? No. Do you know who they consider our leaders? The one's who suck off of Uncle Sam. Those are our alleged leaders, who are leaders by permission from the federal government. They're not my leader. Understand colonialism, where you're not allowed a choice of who your leaders are going to be. In fact, it insults your intelligence so much you refuse to participate in the society. Is that why only forty-five percent of Americans vote? Because they refuse opportunity, they refuse choices?

We still have a lot to give to the world. To be independent. We're not allowed to know who our heroes are. Our Indian children, every day, are bombarded with white and black heroes on TV and in school. And that's good, for the white children and the black children, and that didn't come without struggle. But our children, and you think our fancy, educated Indians are doing anything about making sure that their heroes are known to our own children? No. The only heroes they know, and that's because of us, AIM, are the ones from the last century.

What about our heroes from the first decade of this century? Or the second decades? Or the twenties? We had heroes, local and national heroes. And in the thirties, and the forties, and the fifties and the sixties and the seventies and the eighties. Our children don't know the names. In 1950 all the sports media in this country got together and they voted on who was the finest athlete in the first half century. You think they voted Jesse Owens? No! Jim Thorpe. They did it again in 1975.

Who was the finest athlete America produced in the first three-quarters of the twentieth century? Jim Thorpe won again, overwhelmingly so, both times. I go around the Indian nation. I ask Indian teenagers and I ask Indian little kids. Just last week, I asked my daughter, who's in the third grade, "Who's Jim Thorpe?" "I don't know." And yet, one of the high schools on my reservation is called the Thorpes. Nobody on my reservation knows who Jim Thorpe is. None of the children.

I said, "Who's Billy Mills?" He won the 10,000 meters at Tokyo. He's from my reservation. None of the kids know who Billy Mills is. That was just in 1964, for crying out loud.

I say, "Who's the first Indian ever to run for president of the United States?" First I ask, "Who was the first Indian to become vice president of the United States of America?" Charles Curtis. [Curtis served with Herbert Hoover from 1929 until 1933.] Everybody knows that, right? My own kids, other Indian kids don't know that.

I said, "Who's the first Indian ever to run for president of the United States?" I asked my daughter. She didn't know. I said, "It's your dad." [During the 1980s, Means ran for president on two different occasions, once as the Libertarian candidate.]

But you see? I tell my own people: "Quit your complaining. You want to complain to somebody? Look in the mirror. And be a little bit independent."

But Indians and non-Indians: You're penalized today for being independent. If you're not part of the masses, you're penalized. Think about it. In every aspect of your life. Just look at the tax structure if you don't believe.

The state of the American Indian nations. I'm sick and tired of our own people. There's an entire people now in North Carolina who have Indian blood in their veins and want to be federally recognized. To me that's the abomination of what Indian people are. They actually believe that if you're federally recognized by the United States government, that somehow is a positive development. To me it is the most negative.

The Mikasukis, the Seminoles, the ones who defeated the United States of America not once, but twice, the ones that had every Indian killed by the United States of America in that Seminole war, who have never been defeated by the United States government, cost the United States government then a million dollars. This is back in the early 1800s, when a million dollars was a million dollars. Now a million dollars in those terms is about 120 million, OK?

Imagine, in a war where for every death you cause it cost you 120 million dollars. Those Seminoles, the Mikasukis, who still live in the Everglades, back in the 1960s, when Buffalo Tiger was looking for federal recognition and got it, half of his nation refused to be enrolled in the federal government, refused to go along with him. They said, "No, that would legitimize the United States government. The United States government isn't legal."

These primitives, who refuse to be enrolled with their national ID number, refuse to recognize the United States of America, that is who our Indian leaders are. Not somebody funded by the federal government, funded by you all. You're the taxpayers. Funded by you. That's not my leader.

One thing about Indian people, and I just want to give you a small glimpse of who we are. Indian people are not tourists. We have homes that we never leave, and those that do are no longer Indian because they have no more connection.

Understand what that connection is. It's that dust I talked about earlier, that dust that comes from our Mother Earth. And only out of respect can you regain that. The Indian people are fooling themselves, not only in their culture, they've dropped their culture so they can call it a "powwow circuit," and they can dress any way they want to be, to the point where they fight their own people and are dependent on the federal government.

I come from the poorest county in the United States of America, the Pine Ridge Indian Reservation. The poorest county. I moved away from there last year to the home of my wife, a Navajo, Diné. Because that culturally is the way we do things. The man always moves to where the woman is from.

In fact, because we are a matrilineal society, if we had the disrespect enough to take another's last name, it would be the woman's last name, not the man's. Because the male lives a shorter life than the female. So it's a natural sense that the man would go where the woman is from so that because the man, when we leave this earth, then our wife and children are around their relatives and friends. So they'll always be in friendly society, never be alone.

But we have a home. We don't have to look for zen. We don't have to look for Franciscans, you know. We have a way of life. We do not have a religion, we have a way of life. Our way of life is made up of one word: it's called "respect." But it means a lot more. Respect for our relatives' visions. When you understand that everything lives and that everything is sacred and the further you get away from what is natural the less important life becomes.

When you get yourselves locked into the asphalt jungles and there is no life, then even the human being's life is no longer important. My son, who is three years old, we live out on the Diné land in the desert, and I take him to the anthills and I show him and we sit there and we watch the ant people and I tell him about the ant people: "Have respect. Don't walk on their homes." He says, "Well, Reba does it." Reba's our horse. I say, "Reba's part of the earth. We know better."

If you have respect for the ant people then you'll have respect for people in Hiroshima. If you have respect for the ant people then you will have respect for people in Nicaragua or South Africa or anywhere else in the world.

The state of the Indian nation. Do you know the names of these mountains that are so beautiful right here, that you're so proud of you even put them on your license plates? When I moved down to Navajo, my wife didn't take me around. Just every time we traveled around she'd tell me the name of that mountain and that mountain and its history and whose land this is and what family has lived on that land and why.

This is the state of the Indian nations, but we're losing that because our educated Indians who have bought the white man's way will not allow our children to know our own heroes, our contemporary heroes, and what is beautiful and natural and respectful.

The state of the Indian nations. It's important that you know that you cannot break a branch when you're a child because you're breaking the arm of a living being. It's important to understand and be thankful for rain and not curse it because you have to walk in it. And to love the winter, not because you can ski on it, but because it makes you strong as a person, as an individual.

If you know who you are I know who we are because I know the sacred colors. I know that pink stands for medicine. So I ask why? So my elders tell me. You go into the medicinal plants, all that plants that are good for you, inside the bud, not available to the naked eye. It's pink. Poisonous plants do not have that pink. Remember that when you're out there. We don't want to go there. But you tell those Russell people that if they ever come to the United States and have a meeting, maybe we will attend."

Understand the beauty of that. Talk about individual sovereignty, independence. That was the ultimate statement. Here were all these educated Indians in the United States, Canada and the rest of the hemisphere, all the ones with their degrees, all the ones that like this kind of thing, we're hopping, including myself. I wasn't going, but I was all excited about it.

That really sat me down to look at what we are. All of that materialism, all of that ego tripping, didn't mean a thing to these old people. All of these fancy titles after all of these fancy people that were putting on this tribunal. If they ever decide, they'll never have a tribunal over here.

"If those Russell people ever have a meeting over here, then maybe we'll come." I think that is the ultimate statement of sovereignty, individual sovereignty.

The state of the American Indian nations is an exciting state. I see that what goes around comes around. I understand that, because everything that is holy and sacred and good is round. Understand that also. That's part of the male-female balance. The sun is round, the moon is round. Walk up on a hill and you'll see that our sacred grandmother, the Mother Earth, is round. Everything sacred is round. So what goes around comes around.

Our people accomplished a socioeconomic phenomenon in the 1970s, in one decade, in less than fifteen years, not only in the United States of America but in Canada and the rest of the Western Hemisphere.

It's an exciting time to live, and we're fighting, but I'm sick and tired of the educated Indian, because to me they're not educated. They've educated their wisdom out. It's good. I have confidence in people who have education. I have one; my children are getting theirs. I advocate Indians to go on to institutions of higher learning. I hold seminars on it to those that will listen. Drug abuse and alcohol abuse.

But understand that I know what oppression is. I know what sacrifice is. Understand that peoples who come from the barrio, the reservation, the ghetto, we know oppression. So we know how to struggle. We know what sacrifice is. Ask any mother. It's really that simple. Any mother.

So it's an exciting time. And I see it's time now to go to my own people, slap them in the face and hear them say, "Thank you. I needed that."

Because we did it once before, as I told you, at that convention at the NIEA. Understand that we're not through yet.

The sanctity of life is too precious to allow this society to continue to be disrespectful. I have grandchildren, nine grandchildren, and I fought so that my sons and my daughters would have a better way. And I'm not going to allow my sons and daughters to be satisfied so that their sons and daughters get back in the same old rut.

I'm not going to allow these pseudo-Indians who call themselves leaders, who the white man calls leaders. They're an insult to you and to me and to your government to allow these tribal governments to continue.

Understand that you are the next tribal peoples. You're going to be the new Indians of the twenty-first century. You're already feeling the squeeze. Understand. I know the beauty of the male-female balance. I know my creation story, and those that continue to suck off of Uncle Sam are my enemy and the enemy of everyone. It's not just limited to Indians. Maybe to all Native Americans, huh? The state of the Native American.

So I'll leave you with the words of Chief Seattle, and I quote part of his letter and speech to the then-president of the United States of America. He said, "Wave follows wave, and tribe follows tribe. It's the order of nature, and regret is useless. Your time of decay may be distant, but it will surely come. For even the white man's god who walked and talked with him as friend with friend could not escape our common destiny. We may be brothers after all. We shall see."

Thank you.

"GROWING UP IN MISSISSIPPI"

SOURCE *Sue, Sam. From "Growing Up in Mississippi," in* Asian American Experiences in the United States. *Edited by by Joann Faung Jean Lee. McFarland & Company, Inc., 1991.*

INTRODUCTION *The population of small southern towns was—and into the early years of the twenty-first century, continued to be—divided mostly between two races: African Americans and whites. What would it be like if you were of another race, considered a community member only marginally? What if the only other Asian people to date in high school were your cousins? In this essay, Chinese American Sam Sue describes his experiences in such a town in Mississippi. His family's grocery store primarily served the African American community, as did the other Chinese businesses in town. That often created friction among the Asian community and the African American community since business owners were thought to cheat their poor customers. The fact that physical features betrayed race in such a way to make someone undesirable was not made any better when even one's own heritage was lost by such a vast distance from the larger communities. In this case, other Chinese or Asian Americans present in the urban areas of other states were not present there in that small Mississippi. What does it mean when the first time the author even ate in a Chinese restaurant was in the far away city of Cleveland, Ohio?*

"There is this shot in the opening scene of the movie, *Mississippi Burning*, where you see two water fountains. One is broken, and chipped, and water is dripping from it. The other is modern, and shining. A white guy goes up to the nice one, and the black kid goes up to the old one. I remember saying to myself, 'If I was in the scene, where would I drink?'

"As a kid, I remember going to the theatre and not really knowing where I was supposed to sit. Blacks were segregated then. Colored people had to sit upstairs, and white people sat downstairs. I didn't know where I was supposed to sit, so I sat in the white section, and nobody said anything. So I always had to confront those problems growing up. So these experiences were very painful.

"I guess I was always considered marginal with whites and blacks, though I think I got along better with blacks. I really didn't have any childhood friends. I just felt I had nothing in common with them. And I guess I felt there was this invisible barrier. I stayed mostly with my family—I have two older brothers and one older sister.

"I lived in a town called Clarksdale. At the time, there were twenty-five thousand to thirty thousand people there. In the sixties at the height, there were maybe forty to fifty Chinese families in town. Quite a number.

They used to have Chinese parties, and gatherings, and the funny thing about it was they all sort of came from the same village, or district.

"Chinese church was more of a social, rather than a religious event. I always hated the gatherings. I was basically ashamed of being Chinese. I think that's probably true for a lot of Chinese Americans—on the East and West Coasts. Whether they will acknowledge it is something else. But I think there is a lot of self-hatred, induced by society, culture, and circumstance. So I hated to go to these Chinese parties. Besides, it's not like you could date any Chinese girls, because they were all your cousins.

"I was lucky, in that the school I went to was mostly white, because our store was near the center of town, and the school was across the way. But most of the Chinese families lived in black areas so they went to black schools, and the kids got harassed a lot by the blacks. There was a lot of resentment against the Chinese by the blacks, because some of the Chinese families would rip off blacks, because it was part of giving store credit to the black farmers—they got surcharged excessively. Or they might be charged for things they didn't purchase.

"I didn't date at all—not in high school. It was totally unheard of. I remember very painful experiences of asking white girls to see if they were interested or anything, and them mumbling some excuse about being busy that night. But you knew what was going on. My cousin, for instance, had to take his cousin to the senior prom. I didn't think that kind of thing would be a good thing for me, so I didn't go to my senior prom. My reaction at the time to the dating scene was total alienation. I never considered dating a black girl. I don't know if it was racism, but I just felt there was no commonality. Because even though one wasn't accepted as a white at the time, dating a white was seen as going up—that was the thinking then. And I think Chinese women had it harder. I think it was okay for a Chinese man to date a non-Chinese, but not for a Chinese woman to go out with anything but a Chinese. Part of that was that Asian women are presumed to be exotic and submissive, and that's a common theme that runs through the stereotype images.

"Northerners see a Southern accent as a signal that you're a racist, you're stupid, or you're a hick. Regardless of what your real situation is. So I reacted to that by adapting the way I speak. If you talked to my brother, you would definitely know he was from the South. But as for myself, I remember customers telling my dad, "Your son sounds like a Yankee." I think I had a Southern drawl, but it wasn't pronounced. I also mimicked Northern accents because I was so alienated. Maybe I had this deep alienation, even as a kid. I used to read the Times. I'd see this stuff on the television. I grew up on the "Bowery Boys." The television and the radio were my links to civilization. I'd be waiting for eight P.M. to roll around, so that I could reach radio waves from Chicago or even New York. It was like Radio Free Europe for me."

Family: "My role model when I was growing up was my older brother because he was going to college when I was in elementary school. He was bilingual, so he was sort of the link for me between the old and the new country.

"My brother went to Ole Miss (University of Mississippi), and at one point, he was the first Chinese on campus invited to join an all-white fraternity. He was also in the ROTC. Actually it wasn't many years after that that they took away my father's and my oldest brother's citizenship. It was ironic—here he was teaching American government. He was about as American as you can get, and it sort of opened his eyes. Being denaturalized meant he was deportable, so he and my dad had to get waivers, and reapply for citizenship—doing the test again. So they had to be naturalized twice.

"There was a confession period for those who came into the country illegally. Many Chinese confessed, and things were okay. But what bugs me is my dad confessed, and he was nailed to the wall. He came into the U.S. illegally in the 1930s. Later on, he brought my mother and my oldest brother from China. The government took away his citizenship by virtue of him coming here on false papers. He was denaturalized in 1965. That meant what the government gave, it could take away. I mean, Sue is not my real family name. I think it is Jiu."

The Family Store: "Dad said he went to Mississippi because that's where a good number of Chinese from his village had moved to. We, like other Chinese in Mississippi, ran a 'mom and Pop' grocery store. Anything from shotgun shells to fresh meats to corn chop and hog shorts. (Corn chop is feed for chicken, and hog shorts are grain for hogs.)

"My father would open his store about nine thirty in the morning, and close it about ten at night. We would eat after the store closed. We all ran the store, seven days a week. Only on Christmas would he close for half a day. He wouldn't even close the store when my brother got married. I had to run the store. I didn't want to go to Florida for my brother's wedding and let Dad stay home. So I let him go.

"It was a very rural area, and a number of Chinese had done well doing this. I guess economically they fit in to the area because their clientele were mostly black, rural farmers. I guess the black rural farmers couldn't get credit from white storekeepers. I guess that they presumed Chinese store keepers filled a need—providing credit to black farmers who couldn't otherwise get it. I remember for years on end, my father keeping records of people who owed him money. And that's what a lot of other Chinese did too. They filled that function.

"Our store was a social place, people would hang out on Friday, payday. So black customers would be hanging out, drinking beer, and eating sandwiches. It would be packed, with blacks and red necks. It was a place for them to meet.

"My dad didn't have much time to spend with me, so most of the time I would talk to the customers. We would kid around. I'd ask them, "How'd your skin go so black? And they would tell you stories to kid you. "Oh, I rolled down this river bank and got all this mud on me, and couldn't get it off." And I used to believe that stuff, and I thought blacks were really different. A lot of the blacks in our store chewed tobacco, so you'd think their spit was browner than white people's. But on a real gut level, you knew that people were treated different. And it's sort of weird on my parents' level, because on one hand they would make friends with a lot of black people, then on another, they would say racist things about them.

"Back then, the amount of poverty blacks suffered was profound. It doesn't come close to the experience of blacks in urban centers today. You're talking about people who didn't have running water, or who only got it recently. My father used to sell kerosene because people used it to light their lamps. I remember people using Clorox bleach to purify the water. It had chlorine in it, so they would let it sit in the water and kill the germs. Blacks were at the very low end of the scale, and the Chinese were sort of in between. We didn't really fit in. Very rich, aristocratic whites, were at the top end. Chinese really didn't have a place in society. Economically they were better than the blacks, but on a social scale, they didn't amount to very much. I think blacks saw us as Jews. We were in the same position as Jews were in the town. We all sort of played marginal, economic roles. There were quite a few Jews in town. They weren't accepted by blacks or whites either. I don't think whites knew what to make of us.

"Buying a store in California or some other urban center was expensive, whereas buying a store in Mississippi was cheap, so that's why a lot of Chinese families moved there. But you have to remember that there were still racial restrictions. A lot of the Chinese couldn't buy property, or had difficulty buying it. By the time my father paid off the mortgage, the owner said, 'I am not going to convey the title to you.' My understanding was that we had to threaten to sue him to get it."

Housing: "We had to live in the back of our store. It was tenement-like conditions, though we didn't know it at the time. I didn't know how poor we were until I left. Everyone slept in one big room. There was a kitchen in the back. We used to use the place to store goods too, so there would be boxes all around. If you went into the living room, you'd be sitting on a box of laundry detergent. We lived that way until 1970. It was only then that we could consider buying a house. We thought of buying a house in 1966, but it didn't work out. It was a white neighborhood, and the day before closing, we received a telephone call. Someone said, 'If you buy that house, we will burn it.' And we knew it was one of the neighbors calling. One of the Chinese families knew who had called—it was a Pepsi Cola distributor. Many of the Chinese families were so upset about what had happened that they boycotted Pepsi Cola for a long while. We didn't buy the house. The attitude was, if we're not wanted there, we just won't move there. Getting a house in a white neighborhood—it wasn't only impossible—there was no choice. You could either buy a house somewhere, if you could find an owner that would sell it to you, or you could buy property on the outskirts of town and build a house—which is what many Chinese families ended up doing. This way, there were no problems from neighbors because there weren't any neighbors.

"Eventually, my family decided to buy a plot of land and build our home on the outskirts of town near some other Chinese families. We had to get a white man to buy the property and convey the title to us because certain property owners would not sell to Chinese families—and this was as recent as 1970."

Parents: "My father came to the United States in the 1930s from the Hoi Ping district of Canton. Like many Chinese of his generation, he went to California first. He didn't bring my mother. She came later. He worked in a restaurant with several other relatives around the San Francisco area. He said he borrowed money to come over, and the people working in the restaurant, including himself, were working to try to pay off his debt. They also wanted to save enough to go back to Hong Kong or China to get their wives. Eventually he did go back to China for my mother and my oldest brother.

"My dad was sixteen when he came to this country. He learned his English from customers, which would be blacks, or white rednecks. He did not finish school. He just finished the third or fourth grade in China. A friend of mine did a documentary on the Chinese in Mississippi, and she stayed with my dad in his home. She interviewed him, but never used the interview. She said his English was so strange that she would have had to use subtitles with it. He is a Chinese man who can speak English very poorly and does so with a black southern English dialect. It's quite difficult to understand. I can understand him, but it is difficult to communicate with him. And the gap gets even further when you want to get beyond the really simple language. Mom was less able to speak English than the others. One common thread that runs through many Asian lives is that parents spend so much time working for the future of their children, that they don't devote enough time to emotional needs. Either the parents are working and can't be there, or if they are at home, they are so tired they can't devote themselves to the children.

"The thing with Chinese parents is they make you feel like you owe them for the rest of your life—even when they're in the grave. My mother died when I graduated from college in 1977. My father made me feel terrible because he wanted me to work in the store even after I graduated. They had this idea that they were going to pass the store on to me, as stupid as it was. And they knew it was stupid. By the 1970s, the Chinese stores were declining due to mechanization. People used to be cotton pickers and we would sell these leather things for their knees so that when they crouched down they wouldn't have sore knee-caps. But with the advent of such things as cotton-picking machines and large supermarkets, it spelled doom for the Chinese store keepers. Also, kids my age didn't want to stay. Many chose to move to some urban area, such as Atlanta.

"My parents retired in 1978. But two months before the store officially closed, my mom died. It was a double shock for my dad. He not only lost his wife, but also his way of life. He had opened the store at nine AM and closed at ten PM, seven days a week. He did this for thirty years. He never went on trips. He just worked at the store. He felt there was nothing else.

"My dad is still in Mississippi. It's his life. He's been there since the Depression. It is all he knows. We actually tried to move him, but he is so attached to the area—not that he has affection for it, only that he's used to it—he feels it is home. There are still some Chinese there, though most have died, or moved away."

A Monolingual Chinese American: "I didn't learn how to use chopsticks until I left Mississippi. We never used chopsticks at home. I didn't even have any idea of what a Chinese restaurant was until I went to college. My first encounter with a Chinese restaurant was in Cleveland, Ohio. There just weren't any near where I was growing up.

"I can't speak the language, and you feel intimidated by it when you go into restaurants. Like you keep ordering the same dishes because those are the only dishes you can order. You feel that since you are Chinese, you should be able to speak to other people that look like you. Sometimes they have mistaken me for a *juk-kok* [foreign-born Chinese] and started talking to me; I can't understand a word.

"I don't feel Chinese, and I'm not. I identify myself as Asian American. I feel Chinese to some extent, but not necessarily to the extent of knowing much about Chinese culture or tradition. When I was in college, I met these Asian studies majors, and there was a certain amount of resentment in that they could speak the language and know the culture but they didn't know what it was like to be Chinese in a white society. They may have had a superficial understanding of the culture and language, but at the time I sort of felt they were expropriating our culture, and I felt very possessive about Asian women. It's like when I walk outside, I know I will be treated differently. It's not something I like saying. It's not even a political statement. It's just seeing reality. I'm not looking for, or am I supersensitive to, being treated as a Chinese person, or a nonwhite person, but it's there. It's even here in New York.

"One senses it in my profession as an attorney. You're arguing a case before a judge. And the other guy is white, and he's been around. The moment he walks in the office, it's like he says to the judge or the clerk, 'How's so and so?' But when I come in, it's like this stranger walks in—you don't belong here. But when he walks in, it's like family. I feel like I just walked into the wrong club—a place I don't belong.

"I never worked for a large firm. I never had the inclination to do that. It wasn't only a political choice, I really had nothing to talk to them about. There is this sort of Waspish mentality in the profession. I now work in a small Asian law firm. All the jobs I've had since college have been associated with Asian stuff.

"I don't have a burning desire to learn Chinese at this point, though it would be helpful in my work and in certain aspects of my life.

"If I went to China, I would be an American, and that is what I am in that context. So many of my views, as much as I may want to deny it, are American. If I were in a foreign country, I would be homesick. In terms of adopting American culture and values I'm an American. But in terms of feeling there is a difference, then I'm still Asian or Chinese. I feel different. Ask me what I feel different about, and I can't really say. It's not only that people may or may not treat you differently. It's that I am different.

"I left Mississippi in 1973. There was no future for me there. I was so alienated that even if I thought there was something concrete to be done there, I have such bad feelings for the place I wouldn't go back. Being Chinese in Mississippi was definitely a handicap.

NELSON MANDELA'S ADDRESS TO THE PEOPLE OF CAPE TOWN, GRAND PARADE, ON THE OCCASION OF HIS INAUGURATION AS STATE PRESIDENT

SOURCE *Public Domain.*

INTRODUCTION *By 1990 when he was released from his last 26 years in prison, Nelson Mandela had spent most of his adult life fighting against the injustice of apartheid. Born the son of a Tembu Tribe Chief, he was well-educated, having qualified for the practice of law in 1942. He joined the African National Congress (ANC) in 1944. Once the National Party established its sweeping apartheid policies Mandela began resisting them and the government. From 1956 until 1961, when he was finally acquitted, he was on trial for treason. When the ANC was banned in 1960, he presented the case for establishing a military wing within the body. For his actions, Mandela was arrested with other leaders of his resistance and brought to trial in 1963 for plotting to overthrow the government. On June 12, 1964, he was sentenced to life imprisonment along with eight of the other accused. Until 1982, he was housed at Robben Island Prison, off Cape Town; then he was moved to Pollsmoor Prison, on the mainland. Ironically, he became more famous and more respected in prison and gained strength from many supporters throughout the world. When he was released from prison in 1990, he began to work even harder to accomplish his long-held goals. In 1993 he was given the Nobel Peace Prize. And in 1994 he was standing before the world as he was inaugurated as state president.*

Cape Town, 9 May 1994

Mr Master of Ceremonies,

Your Excellencies,

Members of the Diplomatic Corps,

My Fellow South Africans:

Today we are entering a new era for our country and its people. Today we celebrate not the victory of a party, but a victory for all the people of South Africa.

Our country has arrived at a decision. Among all the parties that contested the elections, the overwhelming majority of South Africans have mandated the African National Congress to lead our country into the future. The South Africa we have struggled for, in which all our people, be they African, Coloured, Indian or White, regard themselves as citizens of one nation is at hand.

Perhaps it was history that ordained that it be here, at the Cape of Good Hope that we should lay the foundation stone of our new nation. For it was here at this Cape, over three centuries ago, that there began the fateful convergence of the peoples of Africa, Europe and Asia on these shores.

It was to this peninsula that the patriots, among them many princes and scholars, of Indonesia were dragged in chains. It was on the sandy plains of this peninsula that first battles of the epic wars of resistance were fought.

When we look out across Table Bay, the horizon is dominated by Robben Island, whose infamy as a dungeon built to stifle the spirit of freedom is as old as colonialism in South Africa. For three centuries that island was seen as a place to which outcasts can be banished. The names of those who were incarcerated on Robben Island is a roll call of resistance fighters and democrats spanning over three centuries. If indeed this is a Cape of Good Hope, that hope owes much to the spirit of that legion of fighters and others of their calibre.

We have fought for a democratic constitution since the 1880s. Ours has been a quest for a constitution freely adopted by the people of South Africa, reflecting their wishes and their aspirations. The struggle for democracy has never been a matter pursued by one race, class, religious community or gender among South Africans. In honouring those who fought to see this day arrive, we honour the best sons and daughters of all our people. We can count amongst them Africans, Coloureds, Whites, Indians, Muslims, Christians, Hindus, Jews — all of them united by a common vision of a better life for the people of this country.

It was that vision that inspired us in 1923 when we adopted the first ever Bill of Rights in this country. That same vision spurred us to put forward the African Claims in 1946. It is also the founding principle of the Freedom Charter we adopted as policy in 1955, which in its very first lines, places before South Africa an inclusive basis for citizenship.

In 1980s the African National Congress was still setting the pace, being the first major political formation in South Africa to commit itself firmly to a Bill of Rights, which we published in November 1990. These milestones give concrete expression to what South Africa can become. They speak of a constitutional, democratic, political order in which, regardless of colour, gender, religion, political opinion or sexual orientation, the law will provide for the equal protection of all citizens.

They project a democracy in which the government, whomever that government may be, will be bound by a higher set of rules, embodied in a constitution, and will not be able govern the country as it pleases.

Democracy is based on the majority principle. This is especially true in a country such as ours where the vast majority have been systematically denied their rights. At the same time, democracy also requires that the rights of political and other minorities be safeguarded.

In the political order we have established there will regular, open and free elections, at all levels of government — central, provincial and municipal. There shall also be a social order which respects completely the culture, language and religious rights of all sections of our society and the fundamental rights of the individual.

The task at hand on will not be easy. But you have mandated us to change South Africa from a country in which the majority lived with little hope, to one in which they can live and work with dignity, with a sense of self-esteem and confidence in the future. The cornerstone of building a better life of opportunity, freedom and prosperity is the Reconstruction and Development Programme.

This needs unity of purpose. It needs in action. It requires us all to work together to bring an end to division, an end to suspicion and build a nation united in our diversity.

The people of South Africa have spoken in these elections. They want change! And change is what they will get. Our plan is to create jobs, promote peace and reconciliation, and to guarantee freedom for all South Africans. We will tackle the widespread poverty so pervasive among the majority of our people. By encouraging investors and the democratic state to support job creating projects in which manufacturing will play a central role we will try to change our country from a net exporter of raw materials to one that exports finished products through beneficiation.

The government will devise policies that encourage and reward productive enterprise among the disadvantaged communities — African, Coloured and Indian. By easing credit conditions we can assist them to make inroads into the productive and manufacturing spheres and breakout of the small-scale distribution to which they are presently confined.

To raise our country and its people from the morass of racism and apartheid will require determination and effort. As a government, the ANC will create a legal framework that will assist, rather than impede, the awesome task of reconstruction and development of our battered society.

While we are and shall remain fully committed to the spirit of a government of national unity, we are determined to initiate and bring about the change that our mandate from the people demands.

We place our vision of a new constitutional order for South Africa on the table not as conquerors, prescribing to the conquered. We speak as fellow citizens to heal the wounds of the past with the intent of constructing a new order based on justice for all.

This is the challenge that faces all South Africans today, and it is one to which I am certain we will all rise.

REPORT ON RWANDA FROM AMNESTY INTERNATIONAL

SOURCE *"Rwanda: Mass murder by government supporters and troops in April and May 1994,"* Amnesty International © *1994 Amnesty International. Reproduced by permission.*

INTRODUCTION *The United Nations peacekeeping forces were already in Rwanda in 1993 to help support efforts toward peace that were finally occurring between the Hutu government and the invading guerillas of the Tutsi-led Rwandese Patriotic Front (RPF). These forces were ill-equipped, lacking enough weapons, ammunition, vehicles, and other necessary supplies. It has been reported that one man had attempted to warn the United Nations about a plan to exterminate the Tutsis at a more alarming rate than the Nazis had exterminated the Jews. In the spring of 1994, that warning proved true. Gangs of errant soldiers and kids with machetes organized by the Hutu government began a slaughter that was hard for the world to absorb—almost as it sat back and watched. These forces killed at least 800,000 in 100 days. Amnesty International called for action that would prevent further abuse. For the decade following this horrific event, the United States and the rest of the world's powers could not escape the accusations of neglect.*

Mass murder by government supporters and troops in April and May 1994

1. INTRODUCTION

At the start of April 1994 Rwanda was plunged into the most tragic part of its recorded history yet. By early May 1994 it was estimated that 200,000 people or more, most of them members of the minority Tutsi ethnic group, had been killed in countrywide massacres. More than 300,000 Rwandese have fled to neighbouring countries, most of them to Tanzania, and others to Burundi, Uganda and Zaire. About two million others are reported to be displaced inside the country. Many of those who have fled from their homes are said to be the lucky ones, but a significant proportion have severe injuries. In many cases entire families are reported to have been annihilated. Stories abound of severely traumatized children who are sole survivors of their families.

Virtually all the killers belong to the majority Hutu ethnic group, to which President Juvénal Habyarimana, the head of state whose killing on 6 April 1994 precipitated the massacres, also belonged. Those directing the killings are principally supporters of the former single ruling party, the *Mouvement républicain national pour la démocratie et le développement* (MRND), Republican National Movement for Democracy and Development, particularly members of its youth wing, known locally as *Interahamwe* ("They who attack together"). From the mid-1970s until 1991 Rwanda's Constitution stipulated that all Rwandese citizens were members of the MRND by birth. During the past two years, the MRND has been allied to the *Coalition pour la défense de la république* (CDR), Coalition for the Defence of the Republic, an exclusively Hutu political party. CDR's youth wing, known locally as *Impuzamugambi* ("They who have the same goal"), has orchestrated a violent campaign against any Hutu supporting sharing power with the Tutsi-dominated rebel Rwandese Patriotic Front (RPF), and all Tutsi.

In the months preceding President Habyarimana's death, Amnesty International had received reports that government authorities and the armed forces were supplying military weapons to *Interahamwe* and *Impuzamugambi*. These have subsequently been used in their killing spree. The Presidential Guard is reported to have been in charge of military training of the *Interahamwe* and *Impuzamugambi* to constitute a militia responsible to the armed forces as well as to MRND and CDR officials closely associated with President Habyarimana. The current massacres in Rwanda are being carried out mainly by supporters or sympathizers of MRND and CDR, in conjunction with members of the security forces, particularly those of the Presidential Guard, the Gendarmerie, the regular army and local government police. Most killings are politically-motivated: to destroy the population groups viewed as potential supporters of the RPF and the multi-ethnic parties opposed to the MRND and CDR.

The massacres began soon after President Habyarimana of Rwanda and President Cyprien Ntaryamira of Burundi were killed on 6 April when their plane was brought down by a rocket. The two presidents were returning to Kigali from a regional summit in neighbouring Tanzania to discuss ways to end political crises in Burundi and Rwanda. The massacres are still continuing a month and a half later.

There have been similar waves of massacres, albeit on a much smaller scale, since October 1990 when the RPF launched a war from neighbouring Uganda to overthrow the government. Soon after the war began the MRND government called on its supporters to help government forces fight the enemy — the RPF, locally known as *Inkotanyi*, and its supporters. "The enemy" was used synonymously in government propaganda for the Tutsi ethnic group in general, members of which were attacked solely because they belong to the same ethnic group as most RPF combatants. Hutu identified by President Habyarimana's supporters as being sympathetic to sharing power with Tutsi have also been targeted. Tutsi throughout Rwanda, even in parts where there has been no armed conflict, have been subjected to extreme violence and massacres by government supporters for no obvious reason other than their ethnic origin.

In late October and November 1990 many Tutsi were killed in the northeastern Mutara region where the RPF began its attacks. Surviving Tutsi in the area fled to Uganda. Many Tutsi in other parts of the country were trapped between members of the security forces and Hutu gangs led by local officials. In Kigali mass detentions were carried out at the end of October 1990; most of the more than 7,000 people detained in Kigali were Tutsi.

In October 1990, just after the RPF's first attacks, more than 300 Tutsi were killed in Kibilira district (*commune*), in Rwanda's northwestern prefecture of Gisenyi. Responding to criticism by human rights groups, the government arrested two local government officials accused of masterminding massacres, but released them without trial within a few weeks. Immediately after the RPF briefly occupied the northwestern town of Ruhengeri in January 1991, members of the security forces and Hutu gangs, again with local officials, massacred as many as 1,000 or more Tutsi of the Bagogwe clan in Gisenyi and Ruhengeri prefectures. The clan had taken no particular part in the fighting, but its members were singled out for attack solely because of their ethnic origin. Former President Habyarimana originated from the area, which is dominated by Hutu. Anti-Tutsi propaganda had been particularly fierce there. Central government authorities imposed a news blackout on the region for several months and took no action against those responsible, denying to Amnesty International and others that any killings had occurred.

In March 1992 Hutu in Bugesera region, south of the capital, Kigali, killed as many as 300 Tutsi after the government-owned radio had broadcast what it said was the text of a tract, claiming that the RPF was planning to assassinate prominent Hutu politicians and that it had the support of the *Parti libéral* (PL), Liberal Party. The radio broadcasts reportedly hinted that the Hutu should defend themselves against the enemy and, as on other previous and subsequent occasions, the "enemy" was understood to refer to the Tutsi in general. Following an international out-cry, the government reported that several dozen suspected killers had been arrested. They were soon to be released without any independent investigation to establish responsibility. The only trial reported by the authorities was that of a soldier accused of shooting dead a 55-year-old Italian woman missionary who was helping Tutsi victims at Nyamata Roman Catholic church. The trial appears to have occurred due to foreign pressure and even then the authorities claimed the shooting was accidental. The soldier was sentenced to one-year's imprisonment.

Opponents of talks with the RPF who still dominated the former ruling party and the military stepped up the violence against the Tutsi and members of opposition political parties during the first half of 1993, as there were indications that peace talks between the government and the RPF might produce an agreement. The MRND and CDR rejected any agreement to share power with the RPF, and therefore to share power with the Tutsi. The peace talks began to move forward when, after the MRND formed a government with opposition political parties in 1992, the then Prime Minister and Foreign Minister, both of whom came from parties in opposition to the President, represented the government at the negotiations in the northern Tanzanian town of Arusha. Prime Minister Dismas Nsengiyaremye repeatedly accused President Habyarimana of obstructing the peace talks and condoning political violence. In July 1993 this conflict resulted in the replacement of Dismas Nsengiyaremye by Agathe Uwilingiyimana as Prime Minister. The talks culminated in the signing of a peace agreement on 4 August 1993 and a formal end to the fighting. The Organization of African Unity (OAU) played a significant role in facilitating the talks and drafting of various agreements and sent military observers, the OAU Neutral Military Observer Group (NMOG), to monitor the various cease-fires between the parties to the conflict. Towards the end of 1993, after some months delay, a United Nations (UN) peace-keeping force known as United Nations Assistance Mission in Rwanda (UNAMIR) was deployed to help implement the peace agreement. NMOG was subsequently integrated into UNAMIR. The state-controlled radio and subsequently a privately-owned radio known as *Radio-Télévision Libre des Milles Collines* (RTLM) were used to denounce the peace talks.

The violence continued and the authorities delayed implementing the terms of the peace accord. By the start of 1994 the UN and the international community in general were expressing concern at the government's failure to implement it. The UN Security Council warned that it would withdraw UNAMIR if the stalemate continued. By the beginning of April 1994 it appeared that opponents of the peace accord could not hold out much longer and that the peace accord was going to be implemented. Since President Habyarimana's death on 6 April, blamed on the RPF by government sources, there have been many claims that it was opponents of multi-ethnic power-sharing among the President's own supporters who were behind the killing, as they were the only ones who would benefit from a disruption to the peace process.

After the President's death, the power-sharing arrangement between political parties was set aside and an interim government led by the former speaker of the National Assembly, Théodore Sindikubwabo, was set up. The interim government blamed the killing of President Habyarimana on the RPF and Belgian troops serving with UNAMIR. It evidently had no intention of implementing the peace accord. This and the massacres which started on 7 April led to a resumption of the war between the RPF and government troops. By this time, pro-government militia had been prepared and armed for a "final assault" on the Tutsi. These massacres appear to have been prepared to deprive the RPF of any support. During an operation characteristic of a coup d'etat the Presidential Guard moved quickly to kill the Prime Minister and the President of the *Cour de cassation*, Cassation Court, both of them Hutu, with some semblance of constitutional authority. The new authorities and the military mobilized their supporters against the "enemy" Tutsi and also against Hutu who they suspected of being allies of the RPF — that is to say, critics and opponents of the MNRD and CDR.

The initial killings by the armed forces set the militia killing machine in motion. Government and military authorities appear to have been involved at the highest level in the massacres, with the intention of destroying anyone identified as a supporter or a potential supporter of the RPF; the logic of the authorities' own propaganda was to designate every Tutsi as a potential threat. The subsequent campaign of killings was consequently committed with genocidal intent.

Genocide is a crime against humanity and, whether committed in time of peace or time of war, is a crime under international law (see Chapter 5 below). Genocide is defined in international law(1) not just as killing on a massive scale, but as killing or a number of other acts **committed with intent to destroy**, in whole or in part, a national, ethnic, racial or religious group. The Convention provides for the punishment of those who carry out genocide and also for those who conspire to commit genocide or engage in public incitement to commit genocide, and those who attempt to commit genocide or are accomplices in it. Furthermore the Convention provides for the punishment not only of rulers and public officials who commit genocide, but also of private individuals. Rwanda has been obliged since the country acceded to the Convention in 1975(2) to implement its provisions in law and practice.

The genocidal intent that became apparent through the systematic mass murder of Rwanda's Tutsi was part of a larger picture of political murder. The overall picture was one of a political drive to wipe out all sectors of the population deemed present or future threats to those in power — and one dimension of this threat, the Tutsi, were defined by their ethnicity. The targeting of the Tutsi minority for destruction, as the principal designated enemy, was a major part of this political program of murder. The systematic hunting down and murder of those associated with Rwanda's multi-ethnic opposition parties, Hutu and Tutsi alike, provided a political dimension behind the larger campaign of murder along ethnic lines that has outraged world public opinion.

All of the deliberate and arbitrary killings perpetrated on the authority of Rwanda's armed forces and *de facto* government since 6 April 1994 are gross violations of human rights law. The orchestrated targeting and murder of a huge proportion of the victims along strictly ethnic lines, moreover, requires the international community to meet special obligations under international law above and beyond its permanent commitments to suppress extrajudicial executions and other violations of the right to life.

A first step is to examine the evidence of an intent to commit genocide by the leaders that have dominated Rwanda's government and armed forces since 6 April and the institutions acting on their behalf or at their behest. To this end, the public smearing of the Tutsi minority indiscriminately as "the enemy", evidence that regular and irregular forces were armed and deployed with an explicit mission to destroy the Tutsi population, and the incitement and mass mobilization of the Hutu population by these forces in attacks on the Tutsi minority appear to show such an intent.

2. THE SLAUGHTER OF TUTSI AND THEIR "ACCOMPLICES"

Within hours of the death of President Habyarimana, units of the security forces, MRND and CDR supporters in Kigali and other parts of the country were out on a hunt for Tutsi. Hutu who supported political parties which accept power sharing were also targeted. Within a few days of the start of the killings, massacres were occurring all over the country. The victims were surrounded in their homes and villages. Those who managed to escape from their homes thought the killers would respect churches, but they were tragically wrong. In fact, the confines of church buildings and compounds where many sought refuge appear to have made it impossible for them to escape. Members of the security forces and civilian gangs associated with them followed those fleeing. In most cases when the killers met resistance and could not use traditional weapons, such as clubs and machetes, they first used grenades and then firearms, including automatic weapons. Weakened or dying victims would then be finished off with knives and machetes. Only areas effectively controlled by the RPF appear to have been spared the worst of the carnage.

2.1 Killings of opposition leaders and critics in Kigali

The initial victims in Kigali were Hutu and Tutsi opposition leaders, some of whom were government officials, human rights activists and other prominent Tutsi. These individuals were well-known and their killing appears to have been planned well in advance by the military. There have been persistent, but unconfirmed reports that a list of the victims had already been established by some security force commanders in conjunction with MRND and CDR leaders. The first reported victims were **Prime Minister Agathe Uwilingiyimana**, several other government ministers and the President of the Cassation Court, **Joseph Kavaruganda**. Before she was appointed Prime Minister in mid-1993 Agathe Uwilingiyimana, who was then Minister of Education, had been assaulted by men believed to be members of the security forces. There had also been a grenade attack on the house of Joseph Kavaruganda in 1993. The death of President Habyarimana appears to have provided the killers with a special opportunity to eliminate these officials. The coordinated nature of the attacks and the high profile of the regular army in them suggested considerable planning.

The security forces also launched a hunt for human rights activists who had already been persecuted in previous months and years because of their criticisms of human rights violations. Some of them, such as Monique Mujawamariya and Alphonse Nkubito managed to escape. Alphonse Nkubito, who is also a high-ranking public prosecutor, had survived a grenade attack in November 1993. He had been branded a traitor and supporter of the RPF when in late 1990 he ordered the release of Tutsi detained arbitrarily in the aftermath of the RPF's first attacks. Other human rights activists, such as **Fidèle Kanyabugoyi**, a Tutsi, and **Ignace Ruhatana**, a Hutu, were not able to escape and were killed. Fidèle Kanyabugoyi, a member of a human rights group known as KANYARWANDA, had previously been detained for his human rights activities in 1992 and 1993. He had collected information about the massacre in early 1991 of Bagogwe in northwestern Rwanda. Ignace Ruhatana was among some 30 people tried by the State Security Court in early 1991 on charges of collaboration with the RPF, simply because he had been found with documents critical of President Habyarimana and the government. He was among the few who were acquitted.

Following the first round of killings, soldiers then attacked a Roman Catholic centre in Kigali known as *Centre spirituel christus* and extrajudicially executed about 17 Tutsi, mostly priests and nuns. The killings were not random. European priests and nuns were locked in a dining room while the Tutsi were being killed. Those killed included **Father Chrysologue Mahame**, aged 67 and **Father Patrick Gahizi**, aged 48. The victims appear to have been targeted solely because they were Tutsi, many of them with a prominent social position.

These killings were swiftly followed by a hunt for Tutsi and Hutu who were known to support the politicians who had been killed. Militia set up roadblocks in Kigali and its suburbs. Each individual passing through these roadblocks had to produce an identity card which indicates the ethnic origin of its bearer. Being identified as or mistaken for a Tutsi meant immediate and summary execution. The killers made no attempt to conceal the killings — or hide the bodies after the fact, as witnessed by journalists and other foreign nationals. There was no evidence that either central government or local government authorities or senior army officers opposed the killings by those acting on their authority. Quite the contrary, the evidence suggests the *de facto* authorities and top armed forces leaders had ordered and directed even this early stage of the murder campaign. This conclusion can be drawn in part from the systematic manner in which particular opposition leaders were hunted down and killed, the consistent, coordinated nature of the road-block operations, and the persistent pattern by which Tutsi in general and specific Hutu identified with the opposition were screened out and killed. This suggests orchestration, not mere acquiescence by higher authorities. Evidence of similar coordinated action was to emerge countrywide in the weeks to come. Some Tutsi were trapped and tried to hide within Kigali. Many were quickly found and killed. For example, some Tutsi tried to hide at the stores of the Belgian Red Cross at Gikondo. Soldiers followed them there on 8 April and forced them out. Most were hacked to death while a few were shot dead. Bodies were scattered all around the store, apparently because the victims were killed as they tried to run away from their killers. Another massacre in Gikondo is reported to have taken place at the Methodist church. An unspecified number of Tutsi were reportedly killed there and at least 40 seriously injured.

Wounded civilians tried to seek medical attention at Kigali hospital, but many were killed either before they arrived there or in the hospital itself. For example, soldiers bayoneted to death two men inside the hospital on 11 April. Four days later, seven more patients were killed in the same hospital. The staff at the hospital were powerless to save the victims and the authorities took no action either to prevent further killings or to investigate those which had occurred.

On 17 April more than 100 Tutsi were killed by soldiers and militia at Nyanza, south of Kigali. They had been part of a group of some 2,000 Tutsi who were reportedly intercepted by soldiers and militia as they walked to seek refuge at Amahoro stadium in Kigali where some UNAMIR troops were camped. The attackers hacked some Tutsi with machetes in order to compel them to walk to a place where they would be slaughtered. On reaching Nyanza hill the victims were made to sit down before grenades were hurled at them. A witness saw a pile of at least 100 bodies and said many others were in houses nearby.

2.2 Massacres in northern and eastern Rwanda

Most of the massacres in eastern Rwanda appear to have taken place in the premises of churches where Tutsi and Hutu government opponents had sought refuge. For example, more than 800 people were reportedly killed on 11 April by government supporters and soldiers at Kiziguro Roman Catholic church, Murambi district of Byumba prefecture. Journalists and RPF fighters recovered about 10 survivors from a mass grave near the church. The attackers first forced the Spanish missionaries there to leave, before the killings began. One of the survivors, **Jean Busheija**, said he and some others were forced to carry about 800 bodies into the mass grave. When they had finished carrying the bodies the attackers then turned on them and he threw himself into the grave to escape being hacked to death.

Hundreds more were killed by *Interahamwe* and gendarmes at Rukara Roman Catholic mission in Kibungo prefecture's Rukara district. The missionaries there reportedly asked a local government official to help protect the Tutsi hiding from militia. The official instead decided to cut the water supply to the mission. The missionaries were subsequently forced to leave as the *Interahamwe* and gendarmes attacked, hurling grenades through the windows of the church and finishing off others with guns and machetes. Similar killings of hundreds more were reported at Gahini Protestant church in Rukara district where many bodies were reportedly dumped in a pit latrine.

2.3 Massacres in Cyangugu prefecture

Massacres in Cyangugu prefecture in the southwest have been some of the most horrific and extensive. *Interahamwe* have been able to call on the support of the military when they have met resistance. Many Tutsi fled from their homes early on to escape being killed and took refuge at churches and a stadium in Cyangugu town. Many were killed there. Others were herded into administrative centres where they were systematically killed.

Soon after the killings began, Tutsi fled to Mabirizi Roman Catholic parish in Cyimbogo district. Militia attacked them there, apparently led by a businessman and the recently elected mayor (*Bourgmestre*) of Cyimbogo. The victims resisted and on 9 April the Prefect (governor of Cyangugu prefecture) and Roman Catholic Bishop of Cyangugu visited the area to appeal for an end to the attacks. On 18 April the attackers returned armed with grenades, machine guns and other automatic weapons which they used against the men who were putting up resistance. The attackers also received militia reinforcements from neighbouring Bugarama district. When most of the Tutsi men had been killed or injured, the attackers entered the church compound and killed all males they could lay their hands on, including babies. There were apparently some survivors and the attackers returned two days later. Only just over 300 women and children remained out of the original number of more than 2,000 people who had taken refuge at the church. The Prefect was apparently urged to open the border with neighbouring Zaire to allow potential victims to escape, but he reportedly refused saying that he had received orders to keep it closed. Thousands were also reportedly massacred by militia at Mushaka, Nyamasheke and Nkaka Roman Catholic parishes.

On 14 April three Tutsi Josephite monks in the company of Cyangugu's Roman Catholic bishop, Thaddée Ntihinyirwa, were killed at a roadblock mounted by militia about six kilometres from Nyamasheke parish. The bishop was attempting to evacuate them and several other members of the clergy from the parish. The following day, the militia attacked and killed an unspecified number of Tutsi and Hutu members of the opposition sheltering at the parish.

When the killings began about 5,000 Tutsi and Hutu members of the opposition gathered at Cyangugu stadium where they hoped they would be protected by the authorities from attacks. Amnesty International has received reports that individuals were then regularly picked out by militia and members of the security forces and killed while soldiers at the stadium stood by. On 29 April some tried to escape but militia and local police hurled several grenades at them and opened fire, killing an unspecified number. Those who managed to escape risked being killed as they approached the nearby border with Zaire which the Rwandese authorities had closed. Humanitarian organizations were prevented from visiting the stadium and the Prefect, Emmanuel Bagambiki, failed to facilitate access.

2.4 Massacre at Mukarange parish, Rwamagana district

More than 3,000 people, most of them Tutsi but including Hutu members of opposition political parties, were killed at Mukarange Roman Catholic parish in Kibungo prefecture's Rwamagana district in the east of the country. The victims were first herded into the parish main hall and grenades were hurled at them through windows. An estimated 2,500 were killed there. Some 500 or more tried to run but were mowed down with machine gun fire in the church compound. About 1,000 were reportedly herded towards Lake Muhazi and the attackers continued to shoot them. Only an estimated 50 survived by using banana stems as rafts to cross the lake. A journalist reported that he stopped counting when he reached 3,005 corpses.

2.5 Massacres of hospital patients and orphans in Butare

The programmatic killing campaign has shown no respect for any of the traditional places of special protection or refuge in Rwanda. Churches were the most common traditional places of refuge to be horrifically violated, turned, as in Mukarange parish, into lethally enclosed killing grounds. Hospitals and orphanages followed. The only explanation was that the authorities intended the murder squads to seek out and kill their perceived enemies wherever they were. The sick and the children of the Tutsi were part of the designated enemy.

On 23 April government troops and militia killed about 170 patients and some staff at Butare hospital. The patients were being cared for by doctors of *Médecins sans frontières* (MSF), an international non-governmental humanitarian organization. Shocked by these killings of defenceless patients, MSF decided to leave the hospital. The authorities, who had reportedly given assurances to MSF that there would be no attacks on the hospital, took no action against the attackers or to protect any other potential victims. From the hospital the killers proceeded to a nearby camp for the displaced where they reportedly killed an unknown number of people.

On 1 May people thought to comprise members of the security forces and militia attacked and killed 21 orphans and 13 local Red Cross workers in Butare. The orphans had just been evacuated from Kigali to Butare where it was thought they would be safe. The only plausible explanation for these killings can be the ethnic origin of the victims, reinforcing the impression that the killers acted with genocidal intent. Killings in Butare took place after the Tutsi Prefect of Butare had been replaced in mid-April 1994. He and members of his family were reported to have been subsequently killed.

3. KILLINGS BY THE RPF AND ITS SUPPORTERS

In addition to the massacres by soldiers, militia and others in areas under nominal government control, Amnesty International has also received reports of deliberate and arbitrary killings of government supporters by RPF combatants and by civilians in the areas under RPF control, although not on anything like the same scale. Before April 1994 such killings had occurred in various parts of northern Rwanda. For example, at the start of 1993 there were reports that the RPF killed about 300 Hutu supporters of the government in northwestern Rwanda to avenge massacres of Tutsi. Some Hutu were reportedly shot at that time when they refused to leave their homes and flee to Uganda.

Particularly in the last week, there have been some reports of such killings by RPF combatants since 6 April 1994. In one reported incident in mid-April 1994 an unspecified number of suspected *Interahamwe* were arrested by the RPF and tied in a manner known in Uganda as *kandoya* or "three-piece tying", with the victim's arms tied above the elbow behind the back(3). One of the prisoners called **Kayiranga** was then killed when he was kicked in the chest and head. He reportedly died as he pleaded for mercy. An eye-witness reported that he did not stay to witness the fate of the others. It is likely that this incident was not an isolated one. Hutu fleeing from eastern Rwanda to Tanzania in early May 1994 alleged that they were fleeing from attacks by the RPF. They claimed that some Hutu had been killed and houses burned in their villages.

One RPF commander was reported to have told the press in April 1994 that RPF combatants kill *Interahamwe* when they encounter them. Amnesty International is concerned that such a statement from a senior RPF commander indicates that some prisoners and militia may have been executed by the RPF in violation of basic humanitarian principles.

4. RESPONSIBILITY AND PURPOSE OF THE MASSACRES

Information available to Amnesty International suggests that by early April 1994 the authorities had prepared their supporters both materially and psychologically to carry out the massacres which started on 7 April. Since 1990 the authorities had repeatedly told Rwanda's Hutu population that the RPF was fighting to reinstall a Tutsi monarchy that had been overthrown in 1959 and to seize their (Hutu) land. Political rallies and radio addresses had been used to convey the message that all Tutsi were enemies of the Hutu and supporters of the RPF. Indeed the authorities continually reinforced this interpretation, as virtually no action was ever taken against people who killed or committed other abuses against Tutsi civilians. Many attacks by government supporters were incited, ordered or condoned by the authorities. Each time it only took a radio broadcast calling on government supporters (Hutu) to "take up arms against the enemy" for a massacre of Tutsi to result. Since April 1994 the same pattern has been repeated on a massive scale.

Interahamwe militia were created and armed by leaders of the MRND. Addressing a public rally in Ruhengeri on 15 November 1992 former President Habyarimana denied that *Interahamwe* were involved in violence. He claimed that the militia were being falsely accused by government and judicial authorities who belonged to the opposition. He said that he did not need the army to support him during electoral campaigns, as he and *Interahamwe* were united.

A few days earlier, at a meeting attended by the President in Gisenyi, Léon Mugesera, an official of the MRND, called for the extermination of the Tutsi. He reportedly said that Tutsi should either voluntarily return to what he claimed was their ancestral country of origin, Ethiopia, or be thrown into Rwanda's main river, Nyabarongo, which leads to Lake Victoria and indirectly to the Nile, flowing north(4). He allegedly said that the Tutsi should return to Ethiopia, like Ethiopia's Jewish or Falasha community had returned to Israel.

In December 1990 a journalist known to be close to top government officials published what he called the "Ten commandments" calling for hatred of Tutsi. The commandments urged Hutu to mistrust Tutsi and to have no pity on them, warning that "The Batutsi are thirsty for blood and power and want to impose their hegemony on the Rwandese people by the gun"(5). No action was taken by the authorities in connection with this article, although many other journalists were detained around the same time because they criticized government officials or their policies, without calling for violence.

In addition to killings of Tutsi and opponents of the government which occurred from October 1990 onwards, it was clear by the start of 1994 that MRND and CDR leaders were preparing for a large-scale offensive of some sort. They were arming their supporters and training them in the use of military weapons. In February 1994 UNAMIR officials protested against the existence of training camps and the massive distribution of arms to civilians at a time when the government and the RPF were supposed to be preparing for demobilization of their combatants. In this way, it seems, the ground was prepared for the massacres under the very eyes of representatives of the international community.

The Prime Minister appointed after President Habyarimana's death was reported to have called on government supporters around the country to collect arms from Kigali.

On 30 April the government-controlled radio called on people to take up arms against the enemy all over the country.

Immediately the massacres began, RTLM radio began broadcasting messages calling on the militia to step up fighting the enemy. This radio had continued operating throughout the period since 6 April, broadcasting calls for ethnic hatred and killings; they appear to constitute public incitement to commit genocide when taken in the context of the orgy of killings.

Members of the interim government have neither acknowledged the scope of the mass killing nor called on their supporters to stop attacking defenceless civilians, despite the international outcry. On 28 April the Minister of Foreign Affairs said that only about 10,000 people had been killed, countering estimates that as many as 100,000 had already died in the massacres. He and the Minister of Commerce told journalists that the only way to stop the killings was for the RPF to stop fighting government forces. They appeared to justify massacres of Tutsi on the grounds that the Hutu population was fighting to stop the Tutsi in the RPF from taking power. In mid-May 1994 the leader of *Interahamwe*, Robert Kajuga, told Radio France International that the killings were spontaneous and that the Hutu only fought in self-defence. He added that there was collaboration between *Interahamwe* and the armed forces, and that his militia were helping the army to defend the country.

5. CONCLUSION

Amnesty International is gravely concerned that the Rwandese armed forces and government appear to be responsible for inciting, perpetrating and condoning mass killings, particularly of members of the Tutsi ethnic group. The majority of the victims were killed while unarmed or were trapped in churches and other public places where they hoped they would be protected. The killings went far beyond people suspected of supporting the RPF and targeted any Tutsi of both sexes and all ages. In some cases described above women and girls were spared(6). Statements made by government and other officials since October 1990 were evidently meant to incite Hutu to kill all Tutsi, with apparent genocidal intent. Virtually no one who has incited or perpetrated violence against Tutsi has been brought to justice, mainly because those in positions of responsibility at all levels either supported or condoned these acts. Indeed some Hutu who advocated peaceful and equal co-existence with Tutsi paid with their lives, or those of their relatives. These elements support a conclusion that the killings were planned and orchestrated principally to wipe out the Tutsi ethnic group in Rwanda.

Amnesty International is calling on the relevant bodies of the United Nations to take prompt action to prevent further human rights abuses in Rwanda and also urgently set up a mechanism to investigate and establish whether genocide has been (and is still being) committed in Rwanda and, if so, to identify those authorities who have ordered, incited, encouraged or condoned it. Those identified as responsible for mass killings or genocide should be tried by a competent and impartial court of law. These recommendations are spelled out in more detail in Amnesty International's appeal to the UN entitled, *A call for UN human rights action on Rwanda and Burundi.*

REPORT ON CRIMES AGAINST HUMANITY IN GUATEMALA

SOURCE *"Guatemala Appeal Case: Crimes against humanity remain unpunished in Guatemala,"* Amnesty International, *AI Index: AMR 34/035/2006 (Public) November 17, 2006. Reproduced by permission.*

INTRODUCTION *For 36 years Guatemala was at war—inside itself. During the internal armed conflict, more than 200,000 people had "disappeared" or were killed. Most of the victims—with some reports stating the figure as high as 83 percent—were of Mayan ancestry. The war came to an end in 1996. When the 1998 United Nations–sponsored Commission for Historical Clarification concluded its study, it attributed at least 93 percent of the human rights violations to government forces. Five years after the conflict ended, in May 2001, twenty indigenous communities presented allegations of war crimes and genocide, against General Jose Efrain Rios Montt and others. Because of the problems of the Guatemalan court system, several of the cases had to be taken to Spain to be tried. As a result of obstruction and a lack of cooperation from many of those accused, the endeavor was not always successful.*

On 6 May 2001 twenty-one indigenous communities affiliated with the Association for Justice and Reconciliation (AJR), legally represented by the Center for Human Rights Legal Action (CALDH), presented allegations to the Public Prosecutor's Office against General José Efraín Ríos Montt and others for war crimes, genocide and crimes against humanity committed during Guatemala's internal armed conflict that lasted for 36 years and ended with the signing of the Peace Accords in December 1996.(1)

PROLONGED DELAYS IN THE FIVE-YEAR INVESTIGATION

After the complaint was filed with the Public Prosecutor's Office, a special prosecutor took testimony from approximately 114 eyewitnesses to the massacres (this includes testimonies in the separate case against Lucas García(2) and others). However, the special prosecutor was transferred in December 2004 and a second special prosecutor was appointed in July 2005, but in June 2006 he, too, was transferred. Two months later, yet a third special prosecutor was appointed.(3)

Unfortunately, the office of the attorney general has failed to make progress over the past five years to investigate vigorously the extremely grave allegations. In addition to the repeated changes of special prosecutors and delays in replacing them disrupting the continuity of the investigation, there are a number of other reasons for the slowness of the criminal investigation:

- Apart from testimonies from eyewitnesses, few other lines of investigation have been pursued. Amnesty International understands that no serving or former military officers have been subpoenaed to provide testimony;
- The Defence Ministry refused requests by the Public Prosecutor's Office to hand over military documents due to "state security" and the special prosecutors have not attempted to obtain court orders compelling them to produce the documents during in camera hearings with safeguards for any legitimate security concerns;
- There have been numerous dilatory appeals by General Efraín Ríos Montt and the others on procedural questions;
- Some courts lack independence from the political branches of government and can be susceptible to political pressure. There is no effective system to strengthen their independence and protect those judges and lawyers who are threatened.(4)

THE CRIMINAL INVESTIGATION IN SPAIN AND THE EXTRADITION REQUEST

Given the stagnation of the case in the Guatemalan judicial system, the lack of political will of the government in supporting measures to end impunity for past human rights violations, in 1999 the Nobel Peace Prize-winner Rigoberta Menchú filed cases of genocide, torture and murder in Spanish courts.

The Spanish National Court (*Audiencia Nacional*) took jurisdiction of the case in 2006, after Spain's Constitutional Court (*Tribunal Constitucional*) ruled in 2005 that Spanish courts can exercise universal jurisdiction over crimes under international law committed during Guatemala's internal armed conflict.

National Court Judge Santiago Pedraz carried out a fact-finding trip to Guatemala in June 2006 but was forced to return empty-handed due the "obstructionism" and lack of cooperation of those accused of atrocities and of the Guatemalan judicial system.

However, despite these obstructions, on 7 July 2006 Judge Santiago Pedraz charged several former Guatemalan military officers, including Ríos Montt, with genocide, torture, and other crimes against humanity, and issued international arrest warrants for their involvement in atrocities committed under their command responsibility.

According to international law, no state has a better claim than any other to initiate an investigation and, if there is sufficient admissible evidence, a prosecution for crimes committed against the entire international community. Indeed, in certain cases, any state may exercise such jurisdiction even if the territorial state has commenced an investigation or even a prosecution or has reached a final judgment. It is crucial that investigations on human rights violations and prosecution of those responsible are not hampered by political consideration. Amnesty International is calling on the Guatemalan authorities to comply with Guatemala's obligations under international law by ensuring the judicial process initiated on 6 May 2001 in Guatemala against General Efraín Ríos Montt and others for crimes against humanity is carried out in a prompt, impartial and effective manner while also supporting the legal process initiated by judge Santiago Pedraz in the Spanish Courts. If it does not carry out such an investigation in accordance with international standards, then it should promptly extradite the accused to Spain.

Background information

In 1998 the UN-sponsored Commission for Historical Clarification (a 'Truth Commission') concluded that over 200,000 people had 'disappeared' or were killed during the internal armed conflict which ended in 1996. Of the victims it could document and identify, 83 percent were of Mayan origin. Some 93 percent of human rights violations were attributed to government forces.(5) General José Efraín Ríos Montt headed the Government of Guatemala from March 1982 to August 1983, which corresponds to one of the highest peaks in human rights violations of the 36-year internal armed conflict. These included killings, rape, torture, enforced disappearances and genocide perpetrated against the indigenous population.

"DARFUR: A 'PLAN B' TO STOP GENOCIDE?"

SOURCE *Justin Raimondo, "What About Darfur? The Case Against Intervention," www.antiwar.com, May 1, 2006. Reproduced by permission.*

INTRODUCTION *The conflict in Darfur, the Sudan, began in 2003 when one rebel group claimed that Khartoum was neglecting the region and favoring the Arabs over the black African natives. Ongoing tension has long existed between the nomadic Arabs who wanted to maintain their grazing rights and the farmers from Fur, Massaleet, and Zagawa. Two main rebel groups, the Sudan Liveration Army (SLA) and the Justice and Equality Movement (JEM) attempted peace talks, but ethnic divisions continued to create problems. A military group known as Janjaweed was accused of trying to "cleanse" vast areas of the black population and claims of genocide have been made, though the United Nations has indicated that no blatant acts of genocide have occurred—even though the deaths have been staggering at no fewer than 200,000 people, according to what little can be determined. In a country whose landscape is often harsh and unforgiving, it has been a war that created refugees in camps where people have been able to find little peace. In testimony before the Senate Foreign Relations Committee, in April 2007, Andrew S. Natsios, the President's Special Envoy to Sudan discussed the conflict and possible solutions.*

Andrew S. Natsios, President's Special Envoy to Sudan

Testimony Before the Senate Foreign Relations Committee

Washington, DC

April 11, 2007

Thank you, Mr. Chairman and Members of the Committee. I appreciate the opportunity to be here with you today to discuss how the United States (U.S.), together with the United Nations (UN) and our international partners, is addressing the crisis in Darfur.

A great deal has happened since I last gave testimony — some of it frustrating, some of it hopeful — but what has not changed is the Administration's firm commitment to ending the violence and responding to the immeasurable suffering of the people of Darfur. The only U.S. interest in Darfur is a peaceful end to the crisis. Our goals are to provide life-saving humanitarian assistance to the millions of people who have been affected by violence; to promote a negotiated, political settlement to the conflict within the framework of the Darfur Peace Agreement; to support the deployment of a robust African Union (AU)/UN hybrid international peacekeeping force; and to ensure the successful implementation of the Comprehensive Peace Agreement (CPA). We have no military or economic interests in Darfur and we oppose any effort by any group to separate Darfur from Sudan. While we have a relationship with the Sudanese government on counter-terrorism issues, this relationship has not prevented us from elevating humanitarian and human rights concerns to a pre-eminent position in our policy toward Sudan. As a country and as a government we are appalled by the atrocities that have occurred in Darfur including those in 2003 and 2004 when some of the worst violence occurred, and the United States has made solving conflict in this region a priority.

This is the third war in Darfur in just over twenty years, but it is by far the most destructive in terms of lives lost and people displaced. The current war is not a 'simple' conflict between Arab and African tribes, but a much more complex dispute fueled by drought and desertification, disputes over land rights, competition between nomadic herders and farmers, and longstanding marginalization of Darfur by the Government in Khartoum. The Sudanese government's disastrous decision to arm, direct, and pay Northern Arab tribes, now called the Janjaweed, as their proxies in the war against Darfur's rebels led to genocide and resulted in the deaths of hundreds of thousands of innocent civilians and the destruction of their villages and livelihoods.

Since then, the security situation on the ground has continued to evolve and has become increasingly chaotic. The Government of Sudan (GOS) is using the same strategies against Darfur that Sadiq al-Mahdi first developed and used against the south in the 1980s. By manipulating pre-existing tribal divisions, creating militias drawn from the youngest and most disenfranchised members of Arab tribes, forcing people from their homes, and separating them from their traditional leaders, the government has created a lawless environment where banditry and violence are on the increase as rebel groups and tribal structures fragment and begin to fight amongst themselves. We are now seeing more examples of Arab on Arab violence in Darfur, localized tribal conflicts, and looting, extortion, and hijacking by rebel groups. In January and February of this year, 80,000 people have been forced from their homes and into camps because of violence. In addition, regional political agendas are being played out in Darfur and violence and refugees are spilling across borders into Chad and the Central African Republic.

Against this backdrop, however, there are some small signs of hope and progress. Credible reports from Darfur indicate that there has been a slow, steady decrease in civilian casualties since January 2007 and direct fighting between the Sudan Armed Forces (SAF) and non-signatory rebel groups has virtually ceased in the past months. When I visited Sudan in October and again in December 2006, a broad range of GOS officials appeared to believe that they could solve their 'Darfur problem' through military means. This policy has proven to be a disaster as government troops have taken a beating at the hands of rebels and as they have lost weapons and equipment to rebel forces. I have stressed to Khartoum and the rebels that a military solution is not possible, as have our allies. Several regional powers have also begun to play a positive role. Most notably, in late February 2007 Libya brokered an agreement between Chad and Sudan to reduce hostility along their common border. Unfortunately, this appears to have unraveled in recent days and we note with great concern the recent attacks inside Chad against civilians in the villages of Tiero and Morena and escalating violence along the border.

However, these types of constructive efforts are welcome and we encourage Libya and other regional powers to work closely with the UN and AU on these initiatives.

Perhaps most heartening, groups inside Darfur are beginning to push back against the terrible violence they have seen over the past four years. The Nazir of the Southern Rizegat, the leader of an Arab tribe in South Darfur, has remained neutral over the course of the conflict despite attempts to draw him in. In other parts of Darfur, there are indications that Arab and African tribes are trying to rebuild cooperation, with a few scattered reports of groups returning looted livestock to the original owners and beginning to meet and trade in traditional markets.

We will continue to watch the security situation very closely. If the government and rebel groups continue to exercise restraint between now and the end of the rainy season, there will have been a full 20 weeks of relative quiet, enough time to restart political negotiations. If, however, either side breaks the fragile calm that appears to be holding between government and rebel forces inside Darfur — directly or through their proxies — we will take this as a clear signal that the parties to the conflict are not serious about the peace process and will respond in the strongest possible terms.

The current security environment has had an extremely negative impact on humanitarian operations in Darfur and eastern Chad. The U.S. Government's (USG) first and most urgent priority is to ensure the continued delivery of life-saving humanitarian assistance to the two and a half million internally displaced persons (IDPs) and refugees living in camps in Darfur and eastern Chad. While civilian deaths may have declined in recent months, people are still being forced from their homes and nearly 80,000 new IDPs have flowed into camps in January and February of this year. The U.S. has called upon all actors in Darfur — including the government, the Arab militias, the rebel signatories and the non-signatories — to cease all interference in the delivery of humanitarian aid. Representatives from NGOs have told me that there are now so many rebel groups in Darfur, it has become virtually impossible to negotiate deals for safe passage of workers and supplies. The number of security incidents against humanitarian agencies has increased, with more than a dozen local Sudanese staff killed, one expatriate woman sexually assaulted, and approximately 120 vehicles hijacked over the course of 2006. Much of this violence, particularly the theft of vehicles and supplies, has been perpetrated by rebels who seem more intent on stealing and looting than representing the people of Darfur. In my trips to the region I have met repeatedly with rebel leaders and have insisted that this type of activity cease immediately. While none of the rebels took responsibility for incidents, this message was clearly heard and we have seen a slight decrease in vehicle hijackings over the past few months, although the number remains unacceptably high.

Relief efforts are also being slowed by bureaucratic obstacles and continual harassment by the Government of Sudan. Visas and travel permits are routinely delayed or denied and humanitarian goods languish in customs for months. This seriously undermines the ability of aid workers to deliver needed supplies and services to civilians in the camps. We have pressed the government continually on this point, stressing that they should facilitate — not block — the delivery of humanitarian relief. During my recent trip to Sudan in March, I met with President Bashir and insisted that his government lift burdensome bureaucratic restrictions on relief workers. He gave his verbal assurance that this would happen and U.S. pressure, together with that of other donors, led to a breakthrough agreement signed March 28 between the Government of Sudan and United Nations that should significantly improve humanitarian access. If the agreement is implemented as written, it will signal the Sudanese government's intention to improve the humanitarian environment for aid agencies.

I should mention that despite difficult and dangerous conditions, humanitarian workers have done a remarkable job of providing life-saving assistance to two and a half million IDPs and refugees in Darfur and eastern Chad. This is currently the largest humanitarian relief operation in the world and the U.S. is the single largest donor of humanitarian assistance. We have contributed more than $2.6 billion in assistance to Sudan and eastern Chad in FY 2005 and FY 2006 and have provided more than 72% of all humanitarian assistance to Sudan. USAID is sending 40,000 metric tons of food aid to Darfur every month and the U.S. provided 50% of the appeal by the UN World

Food Program in 2006. In addition to food, the U.S is providing shelter, water, sanitation, health, and hygiene programs for those in need. We are also working to protect vulnerable populations such as women and children by improving physical safety and providing immediate services to victims of violence. Given the extremely rugged conditions in Darfur, this assistance is saving lives every day and we need to recognize the tremendous work the humanitarian community is doing.

The only way to achieve long term progress in Darfur is to promote a political settlement among all the parties to the conflict within the framework of the Darfur Peace Agreement, and this is where we are now focusing our attention. We strongly support a leadership role for the United Nations and African Union and stand ready to support the important work of Special Envoys Jan Eliasson and Dr. Salim Ahmed Salim. We believe that the UN and the AU can play a critical role in keeping the attention of the international community focused on a negotiated settlement and can help channel disparate initiatives into a coordinated peace process. This will help minimize duplication and confusion and will guard against 'forum shopping' by parties to the conflict. Again, these are issues that I raised in my most recent visit to Sudan in March and I received expressions of support for negotiations — without preconditions — from the Government of Sudan, including President Bashir. It remains to be seen whether the GOS will make good on these statements, but there appears to be a growing consensus among key members of the ruling coalition that a peace agreement with non-signatory rebel groups may be the only way out of the current crisis.

As the central basis for negotiations, the U.S. supports the Darfur Peace Agreement (DPA) signed by the GOS and the faction of the Sudan Liberation Movement headed by Minni Minawi (SLM/MM) on May 5, 2006. Despite some limitations, the DPA is a good agreement that outlines ways to address the root causes of the conflict, creates space for the delivery of humanitarian aid, and gives international forces a robust mandate to protect civilians and humanitarian workers. In further negotiations among non-signatories and the GOS, we support adding amendments, annexes, or clarifications to the DPA. What we do not support is starting from scratch and spending another year negotiating a new agreement that will likely be worse for the rebel movements and the people of Darfur. We have made this point to all parties involved.

We recognize, however, that implementation of the DPA has been slow and this has made rebel groups reluctant to join the political process. We have called repeatedly on the government to implement key portions of the agreement, including disarmament of Arab militias and empowerment of the Transitional Darfur Regional Authority. One of our most important tasks is to bolster the position of Minni Minawi, the sole rebel signatory to the DPA, in order to show that embracing peace yields dividends. He has been marginalized by the government on key decisions related to Darfur and the package of reintegration assistance promised to his troops under the DPA has materialized very slowly, if at all. Most recently, a violent and deadly March 24 attack by the GOS on a house run by SLM/MM in Khartoum and the fatal ambush of a senior commander in Darfur, only serves to raise questions about the seriousness of the GOS commitment to a negotiated peace. Non-signatory factions might ask why they should sign the Darfur Peace Agreement if the GOS continues to brutalize parties to the agreement.

The number of rebel groups now operating in Darfur also complicates a negotiated settlement. As I mentioned earlier, the GOS has played a major role in splintering opposition movements into factions and has attempted to buy off one group at a time rather than pursuing a broader peace through transparent negotiation with all parties. This tactic of divide and conquer creates inequality, dissatisfaction and mistrust among rebel factions, delaying or preventing the creation of a unified political position. Surrounding countries have also exacerbated divisions by providing support for rebel groups in pursuit of their own geopolitical agendas. As a result, we now confront a confusing array of rebel factions, the number of which fluctuates up to as many as fifteen at any given time. Rebel leaders frequently appear more focused on their own ambitions than on the well-being of people in Darfur. No peace agreement would have been possible in Southern Sudan had there been multiple rebel factions each with a different political agenda.

In January I met with rebel leaders to gain their perspective and to deliver a strong message from the U.S. government that they need to unify politically and support humanitarian operations. I stressed that while the people of the United States are appalled by the atrocities committed against the people of Darfur, the rebels should not translate that into support for their political movements, many of which are personality based and the goals of which are obscure. I have urged them to renounce the violent overthrow of the government of Sudan, which some have been publicly advocating, and which is an impediment to peace negotiations. I urged them to be flexible and practical about their demands in any upcoming negotiations; they will not get everything they ask for.

We have begun to see a number of good, new initiatives that feed into broader UN and AU efforts to negotiate a political settlement. One particularly promising initiative that the U.S. strongly supports is the process being led by First Vice President Salva Kiir, who is also the President of Southern Sudan. With the blessing of Khartoum, Vice President Kiir has consulted with Darfur's tribal leaders, community groups, and non-signatory rebel leaders in order to find a workable solution to the Darfur crisis. The Sudan People's Liberation Movement (SPLM) can play an important role in advising the Darfur non-signatory groups since they have the experience and credibility that comes from successfully negotiating the Comprehensive Peace Agreement with Khartoum.

Recently, international attention has focused on the need for an enhanced peacekeeping capacity in Darfur. The African Union peacekeepers have done, and continue to do, an admirable job under extremely difficult conditions, but a more robust force is needed. African Union troops have come under increasing attack, with the most recent incident resulting in the death of five Senegalese peacekeepers in Northern Darfur. Two Nigerian peacekeepers were killed earlier in March. Missions that were once carried out as a matter of course, for example protection details for women leaving IDP and refugee camps in search of firewood, have now been halted and the threat of increased rapes and attacks is very real. The USG has provided over $350 million in support to the approximately 7,700 strong AMIS force since FY04. This includes construction and operation of 34 base camps, maintenance of vehicles and communications equipment, pre-deployment equipment and training, and strategic airlift. However, the AU has reached the limit of its capabilities, and a robust force with the command and control of the UN is desperately needed in order to function effectively and minimize the risk of atrocities in the future. The AU itself has called for a transition of the African Union Mission in Sudan (AMIS) to a United Nations operation.

Transition of the current African Union Mission in Sudan to a more robust hybrid AU/UN peacekeeping operation remains a policy priority for the United States. UN Security Council Resolution (UNSCR) 1706 of 31 August 2006 has a robust mandate, including the protection of civilians, and remains the touchstone for the U.S. position on peacekeeping in Darfur. In November 2006, the UN and AU convened a high level meeting in Addis Ababa where key players, including the Government of Sudan and the five permanent members of the UN Security Council, agreed to a three-phase plan that would culminate in a hybrid AU/UN peacekeeping force of 20,000 troops and police under UN command and control.

This plan was reconfirmed at an AU Peace and Security Council meeting in Abuja and by a UN Security Council Presidential Statement (PRST). Sudan has repeatedly told us over the past months that they agree to the Addis framework; and the PRST was done at their specific behest. However, in a March 6 letter that President Bashir sent to UN Secretary General Ban Ki-Moon, he essentially rejected the Addis Agreement's Phase II Heavy Support Package, effectively also scuttling the third phase or hybrid force. Furthermore, he stated: "Command and control after provision of the support packages is the responsibility of the African Union, with the necessary support from the United Nations." UN command and control of the hybrid operation was agreed to by all parties in Addis, including Sudan, as an essential component of any force. This is not negotiable.

We are very concerned with President Bashir's letter rejecting major portions of the heavy support package. We are hopeful that an April 9 meeting in Addis Ababa signals that the GOS is willing to reconsider its position. We trust that the GOS will honor its commitments and move swiftly to implement all remaining phases of this agreement, including a vigorous joint AU/UN peacekeeping force under UN command and control. The U.S. government strongly opposes any efforts by the Sudanese government or others to renegotiate, once again, the agreement reached in Addis Ababa on November 16, 2006. The failure to implement the Addis framework is not acceptable and will soon be met, as we have long stated, with a more confrontational approach.

I would like to add a word about international pressure on Khartoum. In January, I made a visit to China where I had positive meetings with several key officials, including State Councilor Tang Jiaxuan and Assistant Foreign Ministers Cui Tiankai and Zhai Jun. The Chinese have been largely supportive of our efforts to resolve the Darfur situation through peaceful means and have been publicly encouraging Khartoum to allow the AU/UN hybrid force as agreed to in Addis. We confirmed with them our position that our interests in Darfur are solely humanitarian and we have no economic or military interests behind our policies. We also made it clear that we are not pursuing regime change in Sudan unless the people vote for a new government in free and fair elections agreed to under the Comprehensive Peace Agreement framework. China's Ambassador to the UN Wang Guangya played a vital and constructive role in helping to broker the Addis compromise. During his recent visit to Khartoum, Chinese President Hu Jintao encouraged Bashir to show flexibility and allow the AU/UN hybrid force to be deployed. While we welcome and encourage China's efforts to apply diplomatic pressure on the Government of Sudan, we look to Beijing to join with the international community in applying more forceful measures, should Khartoum remain intransigent. China's substantial economic investment in Sudan gives it considerable potential leverage, and we have made clear to Beijing that the international community will expect China to be part of the solution.

Similarly we are pleased with the emergence of broad international support for the humanitarian needs of people in Darfur. Many countries in Africa and around the world have echoed UNSCR 1706 and called publicly for Khartoum to admit UN peacekeepers and abandon its futile effort to impose a solution by force. During my October trip, I also made a stop in Egypt where I met with the Egyptian Foreign Minister Abul Gheit and Secretary General of the Arab League, Amr Moussa. Mr. Moussa and the Arab league have recently played a much more active role in urging the Sudanese government to take a more constructive approach to the Darfur crisis.

Despite all this, the regime in Khartoum continues to find the weapons it needs for conflict, to find markets for its products, and to find investors. So while I have conveyed a real appreciation here today for many international efforts to push Sudan in the right direction, I also want to be quite clear: the world needs to do more. Congress, individual activists, and the huge array of committed non-governmental organizations can and should continue to shine a spotlight on Khartoum's enablers.

While our primary topic today is Darfur, the crisis there must be seen in the context of our overall policy goals in Sudan; ensuring the implementation of the Comprehensive Peace Agreement and supporting the democratic transformation of Sudan through free and fair elections in 2009. Unless there is progress on these two broader goals, there is little chance that we will be able to find a lasting solution to the crisis in Darfur. The international community needs to recognize the fact that southern Sudan is at a cross roads. The CPA has created a fragile peace between the north and the south after two decades of conflict during which more than 2.4 million people died and four million were displaced. However, over the next year, several important steps must be taken to ensure that the CPA succeeds. Armed militias still threaten the security of southern Sudan. These groups must be demobilized or integrated into the SAF or the SPLA, and the withdrawal of the Sudanese Armed Forces from all areas of the south must stay on schedule. The southern economy is finally growing, but north-south boundary disputes, including the lack of implementation of the Abyei Border Commission's decision, and a lack of transparency in oil contracts keep the south from getting its full share of oil revenues. The pilot census must proceed in order to lay the foundation for elections in 2009, and legislative reforms — including the election law — must be passed. Without international action to energize implementation of the CPA, the most likely outcome will be two Sudans, not John Garang's vision of a united "New Sudan".

Should the CPA collapse it is likely that security issues will be the cause. At ceremonies to celebrate the CPA's second anniversary on January 9th, Salva Kiir, the first Vice President of the Government of National Unity and the President of the Government of southern Sudan, accused the Sudan Armed Forces (SAF) of deliberately violating the security provisions in the CPA. South of Juba and along the border between northern and southern Sudan, other armed groups associated with the central government remain a serious and destabilizing problem in the South. In Malakal, a state capital on the Nile, such tension led to combat in early December 2006; only the aggressive and timely intervention of United Nations Mission in Sudan (UNMIS) troops prevented the violence from spreading. I visited Malakal just after the incident to show the support of the U.S. government for the UN's efforts to stabilize the situation.

It is my belief that one of the most important efforts we are undertaking in southern Sudan is to support the transformation of the Sudan People's Liberation Army (SPLA) into a smaller, more professional military force. This will offset outside efforts to destabilize the GOSS through militias or other armed groups. The discipline and competence afforded by modern, professionally trained troops and officers will prove a stabilizing factor in Southern Sudan. At the same time, the UN, U.S. and other partners need to press forward with reform of the police and criminal justice sector so that local conflict does not escalate, thus requiring an SPLA response. Reform of the security sector in Sudan is proceeding, although more slowly than we would like. According to UNMIS, the UN Mission in Southern Sudan, SAF redeployment from southern Sudan is verified at 68 percent but further progress is hindered by delays in other security related requirements, such as the formation of units composed equally of SAF and SPLA troops known as Joint Integrated Units (JIUs). SPLA redeployment from the transitional areas along the north/south border is mostly complete but is being held up due to a delay in the formation of the Joint Integrated Units. CPA security provisions need to be implemented now or conflict is likely to erupt in several areas around oil rich Abyei and near Juba. Joint Integrated Units have been assigned locations in the main towns but are without proper training or support. Contrary to the provisions of the CPA, companies in these battalions remain in separate units for both housing and training. The SPLA is gradually downsizing into a professional army, but still needs proper training, facilities and administration for the downsized force. The U.S. plans to financially and materially support this important process of providing strategic training and mentoring to the SPLA at key levels. This assistance will not include any weapons or weapons systems and is specifically provided for under the CPA.

Economic issues divide the north and south. The Sudanese economy is growing at a rate of 12% per year. Their Gross Domestic Product will double in the next six years if current growth rates are maintained, after having already doubled over the last five years through a combination of growth and currency appreciation. Wealth is concentrated in greater Khartoum (in the Arab triangle between Dongola, El Obeid, and Kasala) while other regions of the country remain impoverished and neglected. Under the CPA, the Government of National Unity is required to begin making sizeable increases in the budgets and revenues in 2007 to impoverished provinces throughout the country. These provinces have yet to see the benefits of oil revenues. The Parliament has approved these expanded provincial budgets, however the money has not yet been sent to the provinces by the Ministry of Finance.

The U.S. is a major partner for aid, but not for trade. Unilateral economic sanctions are a central element in the U.S. economic policy toward Sudan. As a result, the United States has negligible trade with Sudan and minimal investment in the country. At the same time, Sudan has built stronger economic ties with China, India Malaysia and Gulf Arab states and substantial trade continues with Japan and Europe. The Darfur Peace and Accountability Act (DPAA) and the President's Executive Order 13412 modified the U.S. comprehensive sanctions regime against Sudan under Executive Order 13067 by easing many restrictions with respect to the Government of Southern Sudan, and certain other geographic areas, though Sudan, and specifically the Government of Sudan, is still subject to significant sanctions under U.S. law.

On the surface, Sudan's political reform has moved forward. The National Congress Party (NCP) and the Sudan People's Liberation Movement (SPLM) formed the Government of National Unity (GNU), organized the parliament and distributed positions at senior levels of government as they had agreed in the CPA (though civil service reform is still outstanding). The SPLM established the Government of Southern Sudan in Juba, with a limited number of positions for its NCP partners, and likewise set up the ten state governments in the south. The new government in Juba is still a weak institution in its infancy, especially in such areas as service delivery, financial management and human resource development. In recent months, however, I am happy to note that President Salva Kiir has taken steps to confront the issue of corruption in his government. In the past weeks he took decisive action to counter corruption among GOSS officials with alleged involvement in mismanagement of resources, which we believe was a needed step in improving the management of the GOSS.

Below the surface, there has been little political transformation. Whether in Khartoum or in Juba, military officers are in charge. The NCP uses the instruments of state power, particularly the security services, to limit the scope for opposition parties and to manipulate the public agenda. It would be seriously challenged in a genuinely free and fair election. The SPLM, which has broad popular support in southern Sudan, has made impressive first steps to establish itself in the north but has never faced elections itself.

There remains a major risk that elections will not be held on time. The CPA specifies that before elections, a census will be conducted throughout Sudan, but arrangements for the census are falling behind schedule. If the elections are to be held as scheduled, the census must be expedited.

Despite these serious shortcomings, there has been some progress under the CPA. Peace is holding in the south for the first time in twenty-four years. The GOS has transferred over $1 billion in oil revenues to the new GOSS. Designed by both the north and the south, the new Sudanese Pound has been introduced as the new common currency. A new government has been created in the south, commerce is thriving, the economy is growing, displaced people are returning to their ancestral homes and farms, and 75% of the 40,000 militias (most created by the GOS during the war) have been demobilized or merged into either the northern or southern armies. There is no famine in southern Sudan. We should not underestimate these achievements or the benefits of peace and increased economic growth for the average southern family. These are not insignificant achievements, but these achievements are fragile and at risk because of a failure to carry out all of the provisions of the CPA.

Overall, the situation has more cause for alarm than for reassurance. U.S. policy intended the CPA to be a turning point for Sudan's transformation from an authoritarian state to a more just and democratic state that can be a partner for stability and security in a dangerous part of the world. Sudan is now at the halfway mark between signature of the peace accord and its first major turning point, national elections. The Assessment and Evaluation Commission (AEC), set up to monitor CPA implementation, has only a muffled voice because both the NCP and SPLM must agree to any of its decisions. The ruling National Congress Party, which has been alarmed by this trend, has done little to create the atmosphere for Southerners to want to remain in Sudan: the continuing conflict in Darfur and the tactics used by the central government there only confirm Southern fears that nothing has really changed in Khartoum. The CPA needs renewed, high level international political attention. Along these lines, the United States strongly supports the proposal being considered for an East African summit through the regional Inter-Governmental Authority on Development (IGAD) to re-assemble the heads of state in the region involved in supporting the initial CPA agreement, to review progress to date and define steps needed to accelerate implementation.

These are our objectives: to provide life-saving humanitarian assistance to the millions of people who have been displaced from their homes and affected by violence in Darfur; to promote a negotiated, political settlement to the conflict that is agreed to by all parties within the framework of the Darfur Peace Agreement; to support the deployment of an AU/UN hybrid international peacekeeping force to protect civilians and ensure continued humanitarian access; and to ensure the successful implementation of the CPA. However, if we find the Sudanese government is obstructing progress on these objectives, the United States government will change its policy and will pursue more coercive measures. The burden is on the Sudanese government to show the world that it can meet and implement the commitments it has already made.

Thank you, Mr. Chairman and Members of the Committee for your time and interest in this important matter.

Index

Boldface *page numbers refer to the main entry on the subject. Italic page numbers refer to illustrations. Tables and figures are specifically denoted with an italic t or an italic f respectively.*

D

F

I

J

K

M

O

P

Q

S

T

U

V

W